OAK LAWN PUBLIC LIBRARY
3 1186 00637 3237

S0-AFN-289

THE ENCYCLOPEDIA OF

AMERICAN PRISONS

THE ENCYCLOPEDIA OF AMERICAN PRISONS

Carl Sifakis

Facts On File, Inc.

The Encyclopedia of American Prisons

For information contact:

Facts On File, Inc.
132 West 31st Street
New York NY 10001

Library of Congress Cataloging-in-Publication Data

Sifakis, Carl.
The encyclopedia of American prisons / Carl Sifakis.
p. cm.
Includes bibliographical references and index.
ISBN 0-8160-4511-9
1. Prisons—United States—Encyclopedias. 2. Prisoners—United States—Biography—Dictionaries.
3. Correctional personnel—United States—Biography—Dictionaries. I. Title.
HV9471.S54 2002
365.973—dc21 2002022675

Facts On File books are available at special discounts when purchased in bulk quantities for businesses, associations, institutions, or sales promotions. Please call our Special Sales Department in New York at (212) 967-8800 or (800) 322-8755.

You can find Facts On File on the World Wide Web at http://www.factsonfile.com

Text and cover design by Cathy Rincon

Printed in the United States of America

VB FOF 10 9 8 7 6 5 4 3 2 1

This book is printed on acid-free paper.

For Maria-Luise and Edi

Contents

Introduction

In this volume there is the steady determination to describe the staffers who oversee prisons as *guards*. However, most keepers resent being referred to as *guards*. They are, they point out, more correctly to be called *corrections officers*. The use of the term *guard* tends to be disrespectful to the officers who contain many who are considered the nation's most violent offenders. Not long ago, New York governor George Pataki came under criticism for referring to the rank and file as *prison guards* rather than *corrections officers*. The governor was hardly being deliberately disrespectful; rather, he was using standard terminology used by virtually all elements of the print and broadcast media. The public also overwhelmingly refers to these officers as *guards*.

Is the observation of any real import in a study of the prison system in America, or is it simply a nagging image problem that guards face? The answer goes beyond the guards themselves to the hierarchy in charge of the prison systems. These professionals almost always are members of various "Departments of Corrections." Since the last three decades or so of the 20th century—years of enormous growth of prison systems in almost every jurisdiction—the password seems to be *corrections*. An accuracy or a contradiction in terms? Forbidding prisons have been erected in what could be regarded as a geometrical phenomenon, but they bear such titles as *correctional centers* or even *reformatories*. Today, the reality is that such terms no longer have any genuine differences. A house of corrections or a correctional center or a reformatory or a grim state prison have much more in common than they have separating them. Some facilities may be more "advanced" because of technological developments that allow for more efficient confinement methods, such as televised supervision of inmates, but through the course of almost two centuries, probably the most laudable improvement of the prison cell has been the installation of toilets in place of the "bucket brigade."

This does not mean that there were no attempts to improve prisons, but it is equally the truth that our early prisons could only be accurately described as "hellholes." They were frequently the sites of universal riots, debauchery, corruption, and cruelty. The first great advance of the prison system in America was the Pennsylvania or Quaker system of the 1820s. It was regarded as a shining breakthrough in penology. The Pennsylvania system's Eastern Penitentiary was completed in 1829 to fulfill the Quaker ideal of prisoner isolation. The cells were windowless, measuring about 8 by 12 feet, and the inmate had his own "exercising yard," surrounded by a 20-foot brick wall. The walls between the cells were thick and virtually soundproof so that an inmate never saw another inmate, only a few guards, chaplains, and an occasional pious person who was permitted entrance to pray and offer spiritual advice. Prisoners never left their cells for more than one hour for exercise. Needless to say, a great number of prisoners went insane under the Pennsylvania system. There is no need to consider rival systems here, such as the Auburn system, which many found at least slightly less restrictive (although it produced the brutal Capt. Elam Lynds, who throughout the decades has come to be regarded as the worst prison warden in America), that being fully developed in the following text, especially in the entry JAILS AND PRISONS.

Here it is sufficient to point out the bottom-line progress made by American prisons since the isolation ideas of the Pennsylvania system. Today, the most significant development has been the emergence of the "supermax" and other maximum-security prisons, based largely on the Quaker ideals of almost complete isolation. Today, prisoners in supermax facilities are kept in their cells about 23 hours a day with only an hour of exercise in a completely separated exercise yard. The insanity rate among inmates is generally believed to be as high or higher than in Eastern's heyday. In almost 200 years, American penology has never really improved on the concept of isolation to *contain* prisoners. Simply put, it means putting them away and then *guarding* them.

Of course, there have been many fits and starts in efforts to *correct* prisoners. For whatever reasons, political or public attitudes or interference, they generally had only brief periods of success.

Easily, the greatest of these was the reformatory movement born in 1870 at a conference called in Cincinnati by the National Prison Congress. It was hosted by Ohio Gov. Rutherford B. Hayes, a future president of the United States who enthusiastically embraced the reformatory concept. "It may seem to be in advance of the present day," he told the conferees, "but it is, as we believe, but anticipating an event not far distant, especially in cases of repeated convictions, under proper restrictions, be made to depend on the reformation and established good character of the convict." The congress adopted a progressive stand in its Declaration of Principles that announced that the "supreme aim of prison discipline is the reformation of criminals, not the infliction of vindictive suffering." It proposed important sanitary improvements, the professionalization of staff, and, above all, the importance of education, and it insisted that a prisoner's will must be won over rather than destroyed.

Despite all its promise, the reformation movement, important observers later found, was proven to be a failure. Its shining light, Zebulon R. Brockway, who became known as the father of the reformatory, would eventually be banished for misdeeds, including abuse of prisoners in his care and faking of his results. Overall, the reformatory died for many reasons, including being saddled by pseudoscientific tenets and other false beliefs that made many offenders mostly permanent prisoners of the state and subjected many to castration or sterilization.

With the fall of the original reformatory movement and other ill-fated movements, all that really remained for enlightened prison reforms were such former prisoner reformers as Ed Morrell, who became a national hero after being freed from long imprisonment and became known, with perhaps only slight exaggeration, as the most tortured prisoner in U.S. history. He started an important reform movement when he was freed and attracted huge audiences at popular or political investigative forums around the country. Among the great reform wardens were two from Sing Sing, Thomas Mott Osborne and after him Lewis E. Lawes; perhaps the most important of all was James V. Bennett, director of the U.S. Bureau of Prisons from 1937 to 1964. Bennett raised the federal prison system from the depths of chaos and malfeasance to the pinnacle of respect, to be emulated by other more progressive state systems. On his retirement, however, Bennett's massive rehabilitative programs were whittled away by successors. For years after his retirement, Bennett maintained an office in the bureau's Washington headquarters where he had some visits from VIPs. One account states, "Ex-prisoners who found themselves down on their luck were still welcome to come by Bennett's office for advice and, if need be, a little cash drawn from royalties on his writings (or, in later years, straight from his own pocket)."

Today the Bureau of Prisons is not known for any major rehabilitative programs. Instead, under Bennett's successors, the emphasis has been in building more prisons and especially increasing the number of supermax prisons to contain "the worst of the worst."

By the 1970s and 1980s, the lock-'em-up forces had become dominant in the prison field. They oppose all parole, probation, and rehabilitation as a waste of taxpayer money. They invariably quote from a celebrated study by Robert Martinson, recognized as one of the most influential voices of prison treatment of offenders. His research reached the conclusion after years of study that no programs of rehabilitation have ever been successful, or as he termed it, "nothing works," which became the motto of the hard-liners. His findings gave great impetus to the hard-line approach.

But in the 1970s Martinson started to amend his views. He started to align himself with other scholars who insisted that a number of rehabilitation programs do work at least some of the time if used on the right prison inmates. According to his colleagues, Martinson was in the process of formulating his follow-up research that indicated that "something works" after all, but he died in 1979 before he could speak definitively. As a result his fellow researchers were shattered, and hard-liners kept right on citing Martinson's nothing works motto.

It is obvious that the hard-liner movement gained considerable strength from the 1970s onward, but it would also be misleading to give the impression that the rehabilitation movement ever enjoyed vast popularity. The public, one social observer noted, as moviegoers readily accept the idea of brutality as the way of life in prison and often even root for the "bad guys," but surveys of these same audiences show they do believe that prisons should be tough and convicts not "coddled." In real life, the convicts are once again the bad guys.

Actually, it is very difficult to differentiate between so-called humanitarian or "coddling" phases and those of the hard-line approach. In point of fact, the hard-line approach is almost always in vogue, perhaps with some differences of degree. The 1980s and 1990s were especially pronounced in the tough prison viewpoint. Hard-liners demanded the end of parole, of probation, of early release and the construction of more and more prisons, regardless of cost (although many such proponents often were not around when such financing was required). Yet, experts have started to discern a new swing of the pendulum in the early 2000s. In 2001 the *New York Times* front-paged a long story under the banner of "Inmate Rehabilitation Returns as Prison Goal."

Despite stands that a few years earlier could mean dismissal or at least one's being buried in unproductive duties, corrections officials, parole agents, and the like are speaking out more forcefully now for rehabilitation as a vital goal. In Missouri, the director of the state Department of Corrections summed up the new approach: "People ask, 'How much time is enough?' But they should ask, 'How do you want them when they come out?'" because 97 percent of inmates are eventually going to be released.

In a sense, the new approach has been dictated by numbers as the criminal justice system wrestles with its most serious problem—the high and growing rates at which released inmates are being shipped back to prison. Long before the very hard-line approach peaked in the 1980s and 1990s, *corrections* had lost its meaning, and rehabilitation was discredited and largely abandoned in many state prison systems. Todd Clear, a professor at John Jay College in New York, declared, "With the huge expansion of prisons starting in the 1980s, most prison systems gave up believing they had any responsibility for changing offenders or what happened after offenders were released." This view was undoubtedly reinforced by the "nothing works" attitude that became prevalent for a time in academic research. "The objective," said Professor Clear, "became that prisons should be just for punishment and politicians competed to see who could make prisons more unpleasant, taking away things like television and education classes."

In the forefront of the new rehabilitation drive are the states of Missouri and Oregon, with others like Washington, Ohio, Wisconsin, and Texas offering programs, although at least at first somewhat less comprehensive. Texas now requires every inmate to do a full day's work with mandatory schooling for inmates with less than a seventh-grade education, which for inmates is a very high standard. Still, in that state many of the work programs are the old-style prison jobs like stamping out license plates. But this, officials say, does at least instill the work ethic. Prisoners who refuse to work or take mandatory educational class can lose their right to watch television or make purchases in the canteen.

In Oregon, rehabilitation programs are much more advanced. Inmates are tested to identify educational, social, or mental barriers the individual may face. Ironically, the impetus for the Oregon effort stemmed from a 1994 referendum approved by the voters requiring prisoners to work 40 hours a week as most taxpayers on the outside have to do at the very least. Oregon officials took this to mean that they had to work to provide the types of jobs that would be meaningful after an inmate was released.

Oregon's lead in this matter at the beginning of the 21st century was well illustrated by inmate Todd Ragsdale doing 10 years for assault. Ragsdale was placed in an advanced computer class, constructing customized computers for state agencies. By the time he "walks," there is general agreement that he will be fully qualified for an outside job that pays more than $50,000 a year. Other inmate students experience comprehensive training for telemarketing and for using computers to map water and tax districts from aerial photographs. The telemarketing work has inmates answer questions for the Department of Motor Vehicles and the secretary of state's office, saving the cost of state employees. The job potential for such inmates was considered high, certainly when measured against producing license plates.

The demand by Oregon prisoners for placement in coveted work and training assignments has given the state a bonus in prison discipline. Because a disciplinary report against an inmate may result in his being eliminated from the program, there was a drop of 60 percent in such major reports, including violence or attempted escape, from 1995 to 2001. Recidivism among returning parolees sent to Oregon prisons in 2000 dropped from 47 percent to 25 percent. Even some members from the hard-line camp accept the wonders of Oregon's advanced job-training methods. The head of Crime Victims United of Oregon applauded the program, saying, "The thing people need to know is that most of these folks are to come out again. So we think it's smart policy to try to change them while they're locked up, so that when they return to society there will be fewer victims on the street."

Polls in the new century show a growing public acceptance of using nonimprisonment methods to deal with many offenders. This is even true in the treatment of many drug abusers: Larger numbers of citizens favor that program over the filling of prisons with nonviolent users.

Some experts insist that the swing to rehabilitation is on a rapid increase and that the real test of such programs will come during the next several decades.

The swing toward rehabilitation cannot be said to be complete, obviously, but by mid-2002 two Supreme Court decisions indicated a strong swing away from the death penalty in two important categories. The first is that of the mentally retarded, which divided the High Court into two factions: the conservative and the more liberal (plus two of the usually more conservative members). By a 6-3 vote the Court declared that a "national consensus" rejected the execution of the mentally retarded as being excessive and inappropriate. As of June 2002, 18 of the 38 states that have a death penalty now prohibit such executions. In his majority opinion, Justice John Paul Stevens said this marked a "dramatic shift in the state legislative landscape," in a period when anticrime legislation remained extremely unpopular, "powerful evidence that today our society views mentally retarded offenders as categorically less culpable than the average criminal."

The 2002 decision was the first major break in Court opinion since 1989 when, while striking down a specific death sentence, it ruled that "executing mentally retarded people is not categorically prohibited by the Eighth Amendment." In 1979 only two death penalty states barred the execution of the retarded, and in the decision of that year the controlling opinion, written by Justice Sandra Day O'Connor, held: "While a national consensus against the execution of the mentally retarded may someday emerge reflecting the 'evolving standards of decency that mark the progress of a maturing society,' there is insufficient evidence of such a consensus today."

There followed a deluge of states banning executions of the retarded. In 2001 the Supreme Court had decided to revisit the subject and planned to do so in *McCarver v. North Carolina*, but then North Carolina made the case moot by joining the ranks of states opposed to such executions. The Court then substituted *Atkins v. Virginia* instead. Before that there were numerous cases that made an impression on public opinion and probably did much to force court reconsideration. One of the most prominent was the January 1992 execution of Ricky Ray Rector, who had killed a policeman. It was this case in which Arkansas governor Bill Clinton, then a presidential candidate, gained considerable notoriety and criticism from a number of his most ardent supporters. Clinton broke off his campaign efforts to return to Arkansas to oversee the Rector execution and, some later charged, to demonstrate his credentials as a law-and-order candidate.

Rector was clearly brain-damaged and had even undergone a lobotomy. Those who observed him in the hours before his execution believed that he was mentally retarded. The *Washington Post* reported that, just hours before he died, Rector "carefully put aside the slice of pecan pie that came with his last meal. Rector always liked to eat his dessert right before bedtime, and he apparently expected to return to his cell for his pie after he had received the fatal injection ordered by Arkansas Gov. Bill Clinton." No one could say he bore a grudge against Clinton. He told his lawyer he intended to vote for him for president in the November election.

After the Rector execution, more and more states moved to the anti-execution side in the matter of the mentally retarded, so much so that in 2002 Justice O'Connor herself switched and indicated a new national consensus had emerged. The three dissenters in the case, Rehnquist, Scalia, and Thomas, insisted that while there was something to be said for popular abolition of the death penalty, there was nothing to be said for incremental abolition by the Supreme Court. Their argument also boiled down to a consideration of numbers. Justice Scalia pointed out that only 18 states out of 38 with the death penalty—or 47 percent—had opted for abolition. The majority pointed out that left out of this equation were all the states which barred the death penalty in toto, the District of Columbia, and the federal government. Justice Stevens argued that it was important to consider more than the numbers, but the direction of change as well. Adding to Stevens's argument was that even most of the states that allowed executing the retarded simply were not carrying out such penalties.

Justice Scalia observed that the states that had altered their position had done so recently and might well opt later to go back to executing the retarded. Observers disagreed and pointed out that even the Atkins case had come close to being found moot. The Virginia State Senate had voted to abolish capital punishment for the retarded, and the House decided to delay its action until the Supreme Court rendered its decision. That decision seemed likely to continue the trend that Justice Stevens had pointed to. And while the minority dismissed polls, all show a strong opinion against executing the retarded. Joshua Marquis, an Oregon district attorney and supporter of the death penalty, made an exception of the retarded: "Rational prosecutors who support the death penalty do not want Lenny from *Of Mice and Men* executed." He was referring to the retarded character in John Steinbeck's novel. (For more on this subject see MENTALLY RETARDED AND CAPITAL PUNISHMENT; and RECTOR, RICKY RAY.)

Just four days after the Supreme Court's barring the execution of mentally retarded condemned persons, the High Court issued another ruling that, at least to some, appeared to offer new evidence that the justices were moving inexorably closer to eventually striking down capital punishment as well. However, that conclusion was still to be considered a "stretch." What the court did in its new 7-2 finding in *Ring v. Arizona* was invalidate the death penalty laws in five states: Arizona, Colorado, Idaho, Montana, and Nebraska. It also put the practices of four other states—Alabama, Delaware, Florida, and Indiana—in question. Almost certainly there would have to be changes in federal law concerning the use of aggravating factors which could induce a death penalty, even though there was no charge of those factors in the indictment.

The High Court found that juries rather than judges had to decide whether a convicted murderer should get the death penalty. Reformers have long argued for that, especially in certain states in which the public hails the idea of "hanging 'em high." In the first five states, the juries announce their verdict and judges can find for the existence of "aggravating factors" in the crime. On that basis, they alone can determine who gets the death penalty and who does not. In the other four states, the jury can present an advisory verdict on life or death, but the judge can overrule that opinion and impose the death penalty.

From the critics' point of view, this practice is flawed for reasons not specifically dealt with by the *Ring* decision; that is, that so many judges are elected officials and so are conditioned to make their decision on life-and-death matters by how they will fare in reelection campaigns. In Alabama it was found that judges went against jury findings about 25 percent of the time. This is a political climate most judges would prefer not to face. But in Alabama, as an example, William Bowen Jr., the former presiding judge of the Alabama Court of

Criminal Appeals, says this leads to a heightening of the pressure to impose the death penalty. Judge Bowen stated, "Judicial politics have gotten so dirty in this state that your opponent in an election simply has to say that you're soft on crime because you haven't imposed the death penalty enough. People run for reelection on that basis, because the popular opinion in the state is 'Let's hang 'em.'"

Reversals that remove the judge's role in not following a jury's recommendation are not as sweeping as the one banning executions of the mentally retarded, yet still, reformers say, chip away at the concept of the death penalty. If major change in court attitudes on capital punishment occurs, the eroding of the judge's power to set his or her own standard will be relatively minor compared to mounting evidence of DNA findings freeing condemned prisoners on death row.

Taken as a whole, attacks on the death penalty, critics say, weaken various parts until the structure falls. And renewed emphasis on rehabilitation adds to the mix as well. It might be overly optimistic for reformers to believe all their reforms will move at a rapid pace, but at the same time the glacial record of the status quo is changing, much to the dismay of the hang 'em high proponents.

Entries A to Z

Abbott, Burton W. (1928–1957) victim of controversial execution

Burton W. Abbott was convicted and sentenced to death for the kidnap-murder of 14-year-old Stephanie Bryan in 1955 after a sensational trial. In a sense, his 1957 execution was to prove even more sensational.

The case against Abbott had been circumstantially strong, but the prosecution had difficulty establishing a direct link between the suspect and the victim. Scientific examinations at the time (pre-DNA) showed that hairs and fibers found in Abbott's car matched those from the girl's head and clothing. Still, the doubts had been strong enough to cause the jury to deliberate seven days before finding Abbott guilty.

Sentenced to the gas chamber, Abbott launched appeal after appeal to ward off the carrying out of the sentence. Each was turned down, but he won many stays, some only hours before his scheduled execution.

On March 14, 1957, his last appeal failed; he was taken to the gas chamber at San Quentin. At 11:15 A.M., the tiny gas pellets were exploded beneath Abbott's chair. Just then, the telephone "hot line" buzzed from Gov. Goodwin Knight's office to Warden Harry Teets. "Hold the execution," a governor's assistant ordered, only to be informed that it was too late—the gas had been released. The governor had ordered a stay for one hour for a reason that was never officially explained, but, of course, the matter was moot. At 11:25, Abbott was dead. While some in the media dubbed it the "Oops Execution," in its more lasting memory it has often been cited by forces opposed to capital punishment, not because of the merits of the claim of innocence, but as stark evidence that once the state takes away a person's life, it cannot restore that life.

Abu-Jamal, Mumia (1954–) long-term condemned man

By 2001, the battle to save one of the most controversial black prisoners under sentence of death in the country was fast approaching the two-decade point. He was Mumia Abu-Jamal, who has become a prolific writer and opposer of the death penalty. His case was undoubtedly the most frustrating to prison officials and others, one of whom has been quoted as bemoaning the fact that "Jamal just doesn't want to die." Abu-Jamal's supporters have campaigned unceasingly to keep it that way.

Although Abu-Jamal, who had never previously been convicted of any crime, was convicted for killing a cop, his supporters have insisted that he is not guilty. At age 15, Abu-Jamal was a member of the Black Panther Party and minister of information for the Philadelphia chapter. When the party fell apart, Abu-Jamal turned to broadcasting and at age 25, he was regarded as one of the top figures in Philadelphia radio and interviewed many

Mumia Abu-Jamal, convicted of killing Philadelphia police officer Daniel Faulkner in 1981, leaves a Philadelphia court in 1995. (AP/Wide World Photos)

luminaries. He won a Peabody Award for his coverage of the pope's visit, was president of the Philadelphia Association of Black Journalists, and was dubbed by *Philadelphia* magazine as "one to watch."

Abu-Jamal never compromised on his beliefs, and the *Philadelphia Inquirer* called him "an eloquent activist not afraid to raise his voice." That, however, caused him to lose jobs at black stations and forced him to drive a cab to support his family. Supporters charged that he was consistently subjected to police harassment, including, they said, a cocked finger and "bang, bang" from a smirking cop.

This set the stage for the deadly events of December 9, 1981, when Officer Daniel Faulkner stopped a Volkswagen driven by Abu-Jamal's brother and a dispute followed. The brother hit the officer, who began to beat him with a 17-inch flashlight. Abu-Jamal jumped out of his nearby cab, armed with a .38. Shots were fired. Abu-Jamal was hit, and the officer died. The question was: Who had shot the officer? Several witnesses saw another shooter flee the scene. Jamal's weapon, located nearby, was found empty, save for five shell casings. What surprised many was the fact that the police said they did not smell Abu-Jamal's gun barrel to see if the gun had been fired.

Police relied heavily on the eyewitness account offered by Robert Chobert, a cabbie, who said he saw Abu-Jamal stand over the officer, fire shots into him, and then run away. However, this was contradicted by the police themselves, who said that Abu-Jamal, himself shot, had not run away. Two other supposed witnesses told stories with contradictions in them. Cabbie Chobert could be said to be a very sympathetic witness for the police because he was at the time on probation, was driving that night with a suspended license, and may have hoped to avoid being charged.

None of this helped Abu-Jamal in court. He was brought before Judge Albert F. Sabo, a jurist dubbed by the *Inquirer* as a "defendant's nightmare." Another judge once described Sabo's courtroom as a "vacation for prosecutors" because of his bias toward convictions. Writing in *New York Newsday,* Terry Bisson called the murder trial "a policeman's dream." When Abu-Jamal was denied the chance to represent himself he was defended by an attorney who was later labeled incompetent.

Since his conviction, Abu-Jamal's supporters have campaigned for a new trial before an unbiased judge. Attorney Leonard Weinglass filed a motion to have Judge Sabo removed because he could not provide even the "appearance of fairness."

Journalist Bisson said:

> *Mumia's Black Panther history was waved like a bloody flag: Had he said, 'All power to the people?' Yes, he admitted he had said that. . . . Thus with Judge Sabo's help, an award-winning radical journalist with no criminal record was portrayed as a police assassin lying in wait since age 15. After Mumia's conviction, Sabo instructed the jury: 'You are not being asked to kill anybody,' since the defendant will get 'appeal after appeal*

after appeal.' Such instruction, grounds for reversal since Caldwell v. Mississippi, *was allowed in Mumia's case.*

As the years passed, Abu-Jamal's status as a cult figure was dismissed by others as being the only radical-chic cause to survive into the 1990s. Among those rallying to his cause were the likes of Norman Mailer, Cornell West, Ed Asner, Whoopi Goldberg, Susan Sarandon, and Oliver Stone. Others, not to be considered liberal "bleeding hearts," included Sterwart Taylor Jr. of the *National Journal,* who agreed to the call for a new trial, describing Abu-Jamal's trial "grotesquely unfair." The *Yale Law Review* published one of Abu-Jamal's articles. National Public Radio's *All Things Considered* scheduled a series on the condemned man's commentaries but then canceled it following protests from the Fraternal Order of Police. When Abu-Jamal's book, *Live From Death Row,* appeared, it was greeted by a boycott, and a skywriter circled the Boston offices of the publisher with a trailer proclaiming "Addison-Wesley Supports Cop Killers." In the anti–Abu-Jamal campaign, journalist Bisson reported that "Officer Faulkner's widow had gone on TV claiming Mumia smiled at her when her husband's bloody shirt was shown—even though the record shows that Mumia wasn't in the courtroom that day." (In fact, during his trial, he was kept in a holding cell and read about his own trial in the newspapers.)

The controversy raged on. In 1999, Evergreen State College in Washington State featured Abu-Jamal as a speaker at its commencement. Abu-Jamal was heard from the Pennsylvania death row. Of course, proexecution forces were outraged.

Efforts were made to mute Abu-Jamal. He was now assigned to the State Correctional Institute in Waynesburg, Pennsylvania, a new supermaximum security prison designed to eliminate human contact. The Pennsylvania Department of Correction banned journalists access to the entire state prison population, which came to be known to prisoners as the Mumia Rule. Just before the ban went into effect, two radio interview personalities visited Abu-Jamal. Even though the recording session would be held without physical contact, the female engineer was required to strip and pass through a metal detector. Abu-Jamal was subjected to a full cavity search and remained handcuffed and at times shackled to the waist. This was done even though the interview was conducted in a noncontact visiting cubicle and the visitors were separated from Abu-Jamal by a thick wall of plexiglass.

Still although there was a frustrated sentiment voiced that "Jamal just doesn't want to die," the fact appeared clear that the case, by the turn of the century, would go on in what now appeared to be the joining of a new debate on the death penalty. In December 2001, a federal judge overturned Abu-Jamal's death sentence.

AIDS rampant in prisons

It may be a lowball guess that tens of thousands of prisoners are infected with the human immunodeficiency virus (HIV) that causes AIDS. This makes prisons one of the most dangerous incubators of the epidemic. New York State estimated in 2001 that it had 9,000 HIV-infected inmates statewide, more than 1 percent of all HIV-infected Americans.

Recent accurate estimates of the prisoners with AIDS are much harder to accrue. In 1994, a National Institute of Justice survey showed that AIDS was close to six times more prevalent among prison inmates than in the general population. It is agreed that the rate has risen since then. However, there are no recent studies on the subject as corrections officials lower an iron curtain on researchers being allowed to study the extent of illegal behavior in their institutions.

Still, there is no doubt the figure is very high. One study in Tennessee found that 28 percent of inmates reported injecting drugs behind bars. Because needles are rare behind prison walls, it is extremely common that they have to be shared, which certainly accelerates the spread of the disease. Other reasons for the AIDS explosion behind bars is that consensual homosexuality is common, and so also is forcible sex. FBI figures have indicated that 9 to 20 percent of federal inmates had been raped, which indicates that, because of the criminal population mix, the rate is higher in state prisons. Prisoners have high rates of drug use, simply do not practice safe sex or use clean needles, and have sex and drug partners with high rates of infection of their own.

By comparison to the rest of the industrialized world, prisons in the United States do relatively little to cut the risks of infection. As the *New York Times* has put it, "Most prisons ignore the risks." The states do far less than is done in Europe, Australia, and New Zealand, where the use of condoms, and bleach and clean needles has been approved. In this country, only Mississippi and Vermont offer inmates condoms. So do four urban jail systems—New York, Philadelphia, Washington, D.C., and San Francisco. Even fewer offer bleach. The states often cite as a reason not to distribute condoms that they can be used for drug smuggling. This excuse is offered by the state of New York, even though condoms provided for conjugal visits have caused no problems. Institutions that do distribute condoms to all prisons likewise state that condoms are not misused. The fact is that most prison officials around the country do not employ such tactics because it would be seen as an acknowledgment of illegal activities that they supposedly are expected to eradicate. Many prison systems in more conservative or religious areas fear that they would lay themselves open to encouraging sex and drug use. Many of these systems are subject to budget oversight from powerful influences pushing their own social agendas.

By and large, many jurisdictions try to control their HIV problem by testing inmates to find those who are HIV infected. There is debate as to whether testing should be forced or done on a voluntary basis. Then there is the question of what to do with the information, which is normally confidential, but the idea of maintaining confidentiality in such a closed environment is a utopian goal. Guards and other prison employees are frequently put in an environment where the potential for violence is great and the exposure to blood is frequent. If guards shy away from certain prisoners, inmates gauge the situation quickly. Some prisons have sought to isolate HIV-infected inmates, but this results in aggressive resistance by these prisoners, behavior in line with those in the outside world. Such inmates insist that the procedure is based on ignorance and prejudice, punishes them for being ill, and cuts them off from most prison programs. As a result, most institutions segregate inmates only in their living areas and allow them access to other activities.

Prison officials have to wrestle with the problem of the cost of treatment. The result is often a shortsighted policy of treating AIDS patients but not the HIV infected. Although drugs such as AZT have proved effective in delaying the onset of AIDS in some HIV patients, the cost is too high to provide medication to patients before they have full-blown AIDS—thus guaranteeing a steady flow of new critical cases.

There is a solid consensus on the need to supply more AIDS education and care, but approaches that stress solely "safe sex" are considered by critics to be ineffective. In any event, programs are underfinanced and inadequate almost everywhere. New York State points out that the cost of fighting AIDS has gone from $40 million to $70 million a year recently. But a 1999 report by the New York State AIDS Advisory Council stated that programs remain inadequate: Prison doctors and nurses lack sufficient training to deal with AIDS, and health care and access to new medical facts about the disease vary greatly from prison to prison. The advisory council pointed out the need for preparing prisoners for release. Education about AIDS only works if it resonates with prisoners, and programs must be linked with health care on the outside so that patients on antiretroviral drugs can continue their treatment.

In some cases, within prisons, hospice care in an isolated section for dying prisoners is provided where they can self-administer pain-relieving drugs, but in most cases the great majority of prisoners go back to society. High-risk patients may have received medical care and AIDS education, but they will not obtain the same after release. In effect, say critics, they are simply flushed out of the prison.

Alabama a growing death-penalty state

Depending on one's viewpoint, the state of Alabama, by the dawn of the new century, had become one of the finest law-and-order jurisdictions in the nation or one that could be disparaged as a "hang 'em all" state. What is certain is that Alabama can lay claim to the fastest-growing death row in the country with the largest number of condemned persons per capita, save for Nevada. Although Texas has long been considered the most death-penalty-prone state, Alabama's condemned inmates per capita is twice that of Texas with 188 persons slated to die.

A major explanation for this record—but hardly the only one—is the fact that although Alabama law permits juries to recommend whether a person found guilty of a capital crime should be executed or sentenced to life imprisonment, state judges routinely overturn the more lenient punishment. Roughly one-fourth of death-row inmates as of mid-June 2001 were there following a judge's imposition of the death penalty contrary to jurors' findings. No other state comes anywhere close to such a record.

Critics blame the situation on a political climate that elected judges face in the state. William Bowen Jr., the former presiding judge of the Alabama Court of Criminal Appeals, said most judges would prefer not to have such reversal power since it heightened the pressure to impose the death penalty. Judge Bowen was quoted by the *New York Times* as saying, "Judicial politics have gotten so dirty in this state that your opponent in an election simply has to say that you're soft on crime because you haven't imposed the death penalty enough. People run for re-election on that basis, because the popular opinion in the state is 'Let's hang 'em.'"

The state's death-penalty practice, fueled admittedly by public opinion, is nevertheless contrary to what was happening in other parts of the country, with some states suspending or considering suspension of executions, reviewing the practice of executing mentally retarded prisoners, and taking into consideration the disparities of who is put to death. Alabama by contrast has held firm on such matters, providing no guarantee of a lawyer after the first direct appeal, a policy in common only with Georgia.

Ever since *Gideon v. Wainwright,* the U.S. Supreme Court's 1963 decision, every defendant has the right to a lawyer for trial and a direct appeal. Alabama complies with that right and pays for lawyers for poor people, as does every other state. However, although not required by law, every death-penalty state save Alabama and Georgia guarantees legal representation to condemned prisoners should they lose their initial appeal.

As a result, a 2001 count put 30 prisoners on death row in Alabama with no lawyers to pursue further appeals. Critics said that it was only a matter of time until Alabama puts to death someone who has not had the full protection of the legal system. In two recent cases, the federal courts intervened to stop executions in instances in which they found a risk of wrongful execution when the prisoners were unaware of legal deadlines and could not prepare their own appeals. The appeals were granted only after volunteer lawyers from out of state filed emergency petitions. In Alabama, a nonprofit organization represents prisoners, but Bryan Stevenson of the Equal Justice Initiative of Alabama insists, "We don't provide the resources to give people a full defense. The system puts prisoners in the position of investigating new facts and present claims of legal error, which is a little tough when you're on death row."

In death-penalty jurisdictions other than Alabama and Georgia defenders can ask a state court judge for a review or ask a federal judge to grant a writ of habeas corpus, a legal judgment that says the condemned person is held in custody in violation of the Constitution. Usually, in such a case, the state officials are directed to grant a new trial or a sentence hearing. Prisoners can offer new DNA evidence and alibi witnesses who were never heard in the original trial. After the facts indicated that such petitioners were granted decisions that overturned death sentences, the Congress voted in 1996 to restrict matters to just one habeas-corpus petition and set the filing time to one year after conviction or the discovery of new evidence.

Under Alabama law, such petitions filed in state courts are limited to two years, and if a prisoner cannot find a lawyer to file the case, the habeas right will expire. Alabama does allow $1,000 to lawyers to work on such appeals, but the sum does not do much to cover the costs of growing complex litigation. In Georgia, about $700,000 a year is appropriated for a nonprofit center that employs six lawyers to prepare appeals, but in Alabama, Stevenson's center receives no state funds and relies solely on private donations. Alabama consistently has opposed reviews after the first appeal. Attorney General Bill Pryor said of second appeals: "These appeals are crucial only for Monday-morning quarterbacks who try to second-guess things and create issues that were probably not real in the first place. It's an abuse of the habeas corpus process to retry the case after it's already been tried and appealed."

One case in which the writ of habeas corpus was granted was that of Christopher Barbour, who was convicted of the stabbing murder of a 40-year-old woman. Barbour, 31, confessed to the crime but later insisted his confession had been coerced. Three lawyers began to handle his appeals but dropped out for several reasons, and the case was dormant for more than two years, as the appeal times expired and the state set his execution date. However, Barbour finally won a stay in federal court after the NAACP Legal Defense and Educational Fund filed for a stay. The judge ruled that even though the times for appeals had passed, Barbour's new claims of innocence merited a hearing, particularly relating to new DNA evidence. Under Alabama law, the DNA evidence could not be presented.

Attorney General Pryor said that the stay granted two days before the slated execution was proof that inmates could obtain counsel. "They can get some of the best lawyers in the country to represent them, much better than the people of Alabama could afford if we were paying for it."

Because of the situation in Alabama, the Legal Aid Society has set up a project to recruit out-of-state lawyers to represent Alabama prisoners, but its advocates say that they never know from case to case if a lawyer can be found for a prisoner whose execution is near. Furthermore, a survey in 2001 showed that many major law firms are restricting the number of pro bono cases on which their lawyers can work because of the high costs to the firms.

Thus, the bottom line in death row appeals in Alabama increasingly comes down to money, with the state insisting that it cannot absorb the costs that are routinely accepted in other states.

Meanwhile, death row continues to enlarge with more condemned persons, including many who have had the penalty imposed by elected judges over a jury verdict of life.

Alcatraz Prison

As the French philosopher Blaise Pascal noted, whenever civilized nations occupy an island, they turn it either into a prison or a fortress. John Godwin, a leading historian of Alcatraz, noted that Pascal was right on both counts, as Americans converted the island into both a fortress and a prison. In 1853, Congress, apparently worried that San Francisco could someday be attacked from the ocean, voted $500,000 for the city's harbor defenses, and Alcatraz Island became the site of the first U.S. fortification on the Pacific coast. Certainly Alcatraz in San Francisco Bay would have given any enemy a very hard time, but no enemy ever showed up, and Fort Alcatraz never fired a shot in anger. The U.S. government thereafter used Alcatraz for other purposes, as a prison for a number of suspicious people, everyone from army offenders to Confederate rebels to hostile Indians to German civilian internees and conscientious objectors, Spanish prisoners of war, and those suspected of radicalism. For a time, much of the island served as a medical convalescent center for troops returned from Cuba.

Above all, it was a white elephant, never fully utilized, and later suffered from the indignity of not being "escape proof." Admittedly, that was not due to great prisoner breakouts that challenged the tides, but rather with forged papers made in the army prisoner compound that indicated that four prisoners had been issued a pardon. It turned out that no pardons had been issued, and by that time the four should have been long gone. They were not; three of them started to celebrate as soon as they reached the mainland and, blind drunk and boasting of their exploit, were arrested by a military patrol. The fourth man did escape and was never heard from again.

It would be an exaggeration to say that this incident soured the government on the value of Alcatraz as a place of military imprisonment. The U.S. Army, in due course, was glad to give up its claim there when the Department of Justice decided they needed to have a secure site for a prison because criminals imprisoned in the early 1930s just wouldn't stay put. John Dillinger engineered the breakout of 10 of his prison buddies from Indiana State Prison. Four months later, they returned the favor, busting him out of Lima City Jail. Harvey Bailey and Wilber Underhill escaped Lansing Prison, taking the warden along as hostage. Tom Holden and Frank Keating escaped from Leavenworth, and Baby Face Nelson from Wheaton. The escape try that really inflamed the public was an unsuccessful one in which a carload of gangsters tried to liberate Frank Nash in Kansas City. They killed four officers and wounded two

Alcatraz Prison in San Francisco Bay (Author's collection)

others, but they also killed the man they were trying to free.

This was the situation that caused U.S. Attorney General Homer Cummings to look for a prison that would be capable of holding the public enemies. Alcatraz fit the bill in many respects, and, even better, it afforded another subtle value as yachts and other pleasure craft played around the Rock, mocking the prisoners who would be there. Cummings saw this as another form of punishment of the worst prisoners who could be confined there.

The new federal prison on Alcatraz opened on January 1, 1934, under the wardenship of James A. Johnston. Although the warden had previously earned the reputation as a "penal reformer," he would rule "the Rock" with an iron hand.

Hardened criminals were shipped in large batches from other prisons, the schedules of the trains carrying them kept top secret. The first batch, the so-called Atlanta Boys Convoy, captured the public's imagination, conjuring up wild stories of huge gangster armies plotting to attack the convoy with guns, bombs, flamethrowers, and even airplanes to spring dozens of deadly criminals. However, the first mass prisoner transfer and those following went without any hitches. By the end of the year, the prison, now dubbed America's Devil Island, housed more than 250 of the most dangerous federal prisoners in the country. The city of San Francisco, which had fought the establishment of a superprison on Alcatraz, now found it a prime tourist attraction; picture postcards of Alcatraz—invariably inscribed, "Having wonderful time; wish you were here"—were mailed from the city.

The prisoners, however, wished that they were almost anywhere else. Johnston followed the principle of "maximum security and minimum privileges." There were rules, rules, rules that turned the place into a living but silent hell. A rule of silence, which had to be abandoned after a few years as unworkable, meant that the prisoners were not allowed to speak to each other either in the cell house or the mess hall. A single whispered word could bring a guard's gas stick down on a prisoner, and the punishment could be much worse; he might be marched to "the hole" to be kept on a diet of bread and water for however long it pleased the warden and the guards.

In the regular cell blocks, a convict was locked up in his cell for 14 hours a day every day, without exception. Lockup was at 5:30 P.M., lights out at 9:30 P.M., and morning inspection at 6:30 A.M. There was no "trusty" system and so no way a convict could win special privileges. Although good behavior won no favors, bad behavior was punished with water hosing, gas-stick beatings, special handcuffs that tightened with every movement, a strait jacket that left a man numb with cramps for hours, the hole, a bread-and-water diet, and, worst of all, the loss of "good time," by which all federal prisoners could have 10 days deducted from their sentence for every 30 days without an infraction. But the harsh treatment proved too much for the prisoners and too difficult for the guards to enforce, even with an incredible ratio of one guard for every three prisoners. Within four years, the rule of silence began to be modified, and some other regulations were eased as well.

Incredibly, despite the prison's security and physical isolation, there were numerous attempts to escape from Alcatraz, but none were successful. In 1937, two convicts, Ralph Roe and Teddy Cole, left the workshop area during a heavy fog, climbed a Cyclone fence 10 feet high, and then jumped from a bluff 30 feet into the water. They were never seen again, but there is little doubt that they were washed to sea. The tide ran very fast that day and the nearest land was a mile and a quarter away through 40° water. The fact that the two men, habitual criminals, were never arrested again makes it almost certain that they died. Probably the closest anyone came to a successful escape occurred during a 1946 rebellion plotted by a bank robber named Bernie Coy. During the 48 hours of the rebellion, five men died and 15 more were wounded, many seriously, before battle-trained U.S. Marines stormed ashore and put an end to the affair. Escape attempts proved especially vicious on Alcatraz because convicts with so little hope for release or quarter were much more likely to kill guards during a break.

Many more prisoners sought to escape prison by suicide, and several succeeded. Those who failed faced long stays in the hole after being released from the prison hospital. Others escaped the reality of Alcatraz by going insane. It remains a moot point whether Al Capone, who arrived there in 1934 from Atlanta Penitentiary, where he had been serving an 11-year sentence for tax evasion, won parole in 1939 because of the advance state of his syphilitic condition or because he too had gone stir crazy like so many others. Taken to his Florida mansion, he kept casting for "big ones" in the lavish swimming pool.

Alcatraz in the 1930s housed not only the truly notorious and dangerous prisoners, but also many put there for vindictive reasons, such as Robert Stroud—the Birdman of Alcatraz—who along with Rufus "Whitey" Franklin was one of the most ill-treated prisoners in the federal penal system. The inmate roster including the tough gangsters who truly belonged, such as Dock Barker, and those who did not, such as Machine Gun Kelly, who had never even fired his weapon at anyone. There were also such nontroublesome convicts such as former public enemy Alvin "Creepy" Karpis.

Through the years, there were many calls for the closing of Alcatraz, some in the name of economy because it cost twice as much to house a prisoner on Alcatraz as in any other federal prison. Senator William Langer even charged that the government could board inmates "in the Waldorf Astoria cheaper."

By the 1950s, Alcatraz had lost its reputation as an escape-proof institution and had become known simply as a place to confine prisoners deemed to be deserving of harsher treatment.

By the time "the Rock" was finally phased out as a federal prison in 1963, it was a crumbling mess and prisoners could easily dig away at its walls with a dull spoon.

See also: ALCATRAZ PRISON REBELLION; ALCATRAZ PUSH-UPS; ATLANTA BOYS CONVOY; JOHNSTON, JAMES A.; RULE OF SILENCE; STROUD, ROBERT FRANKLIN.

Alcatraz Prison rebellion U.S. Marines needed

It is possible to overstate the 1946 attempted *escape* from Alcatraz as a *rebellion* when actually it was the former, albeit a very brilliant one. Part of the plot was to turn loose a number of prisoners to confuse the authorities so that the real plot could unwind in the confusion. The escape ran into hitches, and the melee then turned bloody as U.S. Marines invaded Alcatraz Island in a skirmish that took 48 hours to run its course, leaving five dead, 15 others wounded, many seriously, and two convicts later sentenced to die in the new California gas chamber. To quell the uprising, trained sharpshooters were flown in from other prisons, and battle-trained U.S. Marines stormed the prison under the command of Gen. Joseph "Vinegar Joe" Stillwell and Frank Merill, of the famed Merill's Marauders.

The brain behind the plot was one of the least likely of suspects, 46-year-old Bernie Coy, who still had another 16 years to serve for bank robbery. The prison administration thought of Coy as just a Kentucky hillbilly bandit, but Coy had learned much in Alcatraz, including its physical setup. He discovered a critical weakness in the Alcatraz security system, while he was working as a cellhouse orderly and figured that he could overpower the tier guard. Then he could release a few confederates and work his way up to a gun gallery, a floor-to-ceiling cage of bars behind which was housed the one man with all the weapons in the entire building. Basically, this armed guard never left the cage except to inspect D Block, the isolation section.

One May 2, according to plan, Coy was waiting for the guard when he left the cage. He attacked, and a brutal battle took place before the convict finally knocked him out. Coy grabbed up a number of weapons and a large supply of ammunition and brought in his fellow plotters. Moving swiftly, they captured all nine guards in the building and locked them in two cells. They then released most of the other prisoners and let them arm themselves—but Coy and his men headed swiftly for the corridor door and locked it after them so that the other prisoners could not follow; the confusion was overwhelming.

The plotters planned to use hostages to cross the prison yard, seize the prison launch, and speed across the bay before an alarm would even be sounded. On the mainland, they would hop into waiting cars, supplied by friends of Joseph Paul "Dutch" Cretzer, bank robber, murderer, and former Public Enemy No. 4. Besides Cretzer, others among the escapers were Sam Shockley, a mental defective and a close buddy of Cretzer; Marvin Hubbard, an Alabama gunman and close buddy of Coy; Miran Edgar "Buddy" Thompson, a robber, murderer, and jailbreak artist who previously had escaped from eight prisons; and Clarence Carnes, a 19-year-old Choctaw Indian doing 99 years for kidnapping a farmer across a state line after breaking out of a prison where he was doing time for murder.

The plot fell apart because a prison guard, in violation of orders, had neglected to return one corridor key to its place on a keyboard. The escapers desperately tried to force the lock with other keys but only succeeded in jamming it. The timetable for a fast escape had failed; the prison launch left the island. Coy was not ready to give up, however. Leaving Cretzer in charge of the hostages, Coy with Hubbard went off to communicate with Warden James A. Johnston over the prison phone system. Coy had warned Cretzer not to harm any of the guards because they were vital to a desperate optional plan he had devised. Under this alternative, Coy figured to use the guard-hostages to enter the staff living compound where the guards' families, including some 30 young girls, lived. With these hostages, Coy figured, the authorities would be forced to let them off the island.

Back with the hostages, Cretzer was not buying that idea. He realized that as soon as the convicts headed in the direction of the family area, the guards on the walls would open fire, killing the escapers and their guard hostages as well. The guards simply would not let the cons take their families. Actually, Cretzer wanted to kill all the guards; he had killed one guard in a gunfight, and the prison authorities already had the body, facts that he did not tell Coy. Cretzer had nothing to lose, and if all the guards were murdered, he might avoid being accused of doing the actual shooting; perhaps the blame would fall on Coy.

At the same time, the moronic Schockley and the cunning Thompson kept egging Cretzer to kill them all in another example of there being no honor among murderers. Thompson had the same motivation as Cretzer, in fact all the more so. If all the guards were dead, Thompson realized, there would be nobody alive among the prison employees who could tie him into the escape plot. Thompson figured that he might get away with it. Only Carnes, who was close to Coy and Hubbard, opposed killing the guards. Suddenly, Cretzer cut loose in murderous fury. He blazed away with shot after shot at the guards in the two cells. All of them went down. Thompson ordered Carnes to enter the cells to see if any of the guards were still alive. Carnes went into the cells at gunpoint and saw that most of the guards were alive, but Carnes said that all the guards were dead. Actually, only one was dead, five were badly wounded, and the remaining three hadn't been hit at all but were feigning death.

Meanwhile Coy returned from his talk with Warden Johnston—who predictably stalled for time—and was shocked to see the apparent slaughter of all the guards. Without the hostages, Coy knew, the entire escape was doomed. Furiously, he sought Cretzer—who wasn't there: He had vanished into the milling chaos of the rioting prisoners. In blood rage, Coy and Hubbard searched for Cretzer. Now they had to avoid guards moving into attacking positions, while they stalked Cretzer, who, at the same time, was in the same mode, avoiding the guards and looking to kill Coy and Hubbard before they got him. The main plot was finished, and now the subplots became paramount.

Meanwhile, news of the mass break attempt and wild rumors spread throughout San Francisco. Thousands swarmed to the waterfront to watch as 80 U.S. Marines stormed ashore in full combat dress and guard sharpshooters slipped into the prison. They found the hostages, including one already dead, and brought them out. The seriously wounded guards had compresses over their wounds—an anonymous inmate had treated them, undoubtedly saving the lives of three or possibly four of them, and then slipped away, never to be identified.

Additional sharpshooters moved in. Holes were cut in the roof of the building, and grenades were tossed inside, forcing most of the rioting prisoners to retreat to their own cells. But the remaining trio, Coy, Hubbard, and Cretzer, still stalked one another while successfully evading the grenade blasts. The duel descended into the darkened utility corridors—concrete trenches below the cell blocks where plumbing and electric wires were buried. The pursuing guards heaved gas grenades through the ventilator shafts, but the trio could not be dislodged, instead returning fire on the guards stalking them.

The convict trio failed to find each other until almost the end. Cretzer by then had been wounded by bomb shrapnel and Coy by gunfire. According to Clark Howard's *Six Against the Rock,* the most definitive study of the escape attempt, Cretzer, not the guards, killed Coy. Cretzer finally spotted his prey, leaped out of the shadows, and shot him in the face, neck, and shoulders. Cretzer tried then to get Hubbard but was forced to flee as guards closed in. Hubbard managed to drag Coy off into a dark tunnel and remained with him until he died.

In the meantime, guards cornered Cretzer and killed him with grenades and gunfire. By this time, the great escape attempt was in its 42nd hour. Hubbard continued to elude pursuers for several more hours, but finally four guards closed in on him and loosed a barrage of gunfire. Hubbard took two killing rifle shots, one in the left eye, the other in the left temple. The escape effort was over after 48 hours.

The investigation that followed, much to the bitterness of the authorities, focused not so much on the deadly violence as upon the brutal conditions in the prison. It was discovered that one prisoner, Whitey Franklin, who had attempted escape in 1938 with two others, had received an added life sentence for killing a guard and had spent every day since then, more than seven years, in the hole.

It was almost an anticlimax when the three survivors among the plotters were brought to trial. Carnes got life to go along with his 99 years. Thompson and the obviously insane Shockley were sentenced to death, the first inmates to be sent to San Quentin's new gas chamber. As they left the courtroom, Shockley winked at reporters and said confidently, "They'll never gas me. I'm crazy."

On December 3, 1948, the pair was executed.

See also: JOHNSTON, JAMES A.

Alcatraz push-ups prison currency

In its day Alcatraz deserved its reputation as the harshest federal prison. But there were what seemed to be some "perks" as well, rather out of place with the concept of tough incarceration for the toughest convicts. Prisoners soon recognized Alcatraz as the best prison for "eats and smokes." On the matter of food, federal guidelines called for a minimum of 2,000 calories, but Alcatraz served up meals that ran to 3,100 to 3,600 calories per day. When Mrs. Homer Cummings, the wife of the attorney general, visited Alcatraz in the mid-1930s and partook of the standard convict dinner—soup, Beefaroni, beans, cabbage, onions, chili pods, hot biscuits, ice cream, iced tea and coffee—she exclaimed: "Why, this is more than we eat at home!" It was estimated the average "guest" on the "Rock" put on 15 to 20 pounds during his term, and some 40 pounds or more.

Along with this rather lavish menu, Alcatraz had a liberal smoking program. Each prisoner was issued three packs of cigarettes a week, and when that supply was used up, he could get all the loose tobacco he wanted from free dispensers to roll his own. This worked out well for the prison administration because cigarettes lost the currency value and bribing power they enjoyed in other prisons.

The upshot of this, ironically, produced a genuine health benefit. A curious practice of paying debts had to be devised by the inmates to cover gambling or barter activities. Such debts could be wiped out by doing so many push-ups, thus allowing inmates to have some "action" and offering something of an antidote for their overfeeding.

Alternates to Violence Project (AVP) prisoner-inspired program

Although it is common to regard prisons as hotbeds of violence, many prisons, in fact, do not receive much attention until a riot or scandal occurs—and no attention if such events do not occur. One of the most successful programs with this result is Alternates to Violence Project (AVP), which had been developing in New York State since 1975. The program was inspired by a number of lifers with little or no chance of winning their own freedom.

Such lifers, known as inmate trainers, go through basic and advanced workshops and run the program, explaining to other prisoners the causes of violence, how violence can escalate, and how to dampen potentially violent confrontations.

The success of AVP is attested to by those taught by the inmate trainers. One, Lowell Thomas, doing 20 years to life, declares, "I grew up in a violent neighborhood." He found violence "was how you solved all conflict. Through AVP, my attitude has changed dramatically."

The AVP trainers themselves truly believe in their message. One says, "It's the only program that is really working to provide rehabilitation for inmates." Another AVP trainer, George Lombardo, is a top booster of the program. "Jails tend to build hatred. AVP is the only program aimed at reducing violence that works. This program will get people out and help them to stay there."

The vital nature of the program is the fact that almost all violent persons eventually are released from prison. It is how well they learn to curb their own violence that will determine how safe citizens will eventually be.

Amnesty International (AI) worldwide reformer group

Before 1960, prisoners in many countries had no ability to protest violations of their human rights. That changed in 1961 when Peter Berenson, a London lawyer published an ad in the *London Observer* in which he launched an "Appeal for Amnesty" from which Amnesty International was born. What triggered Berenson's outrage was reading an account of two Portuguese students imprisoned for raising a toast to freedom—in a nation that had next to none of that at the time.

Since that time, Amnesty International has been involved in great struggles for human freedom involving political prisoners and protecting the rights of human-rights protesters all over the world. It campaigns against capital punishment and for the freeing of all prisoners of conscience and fair trials for all prisoners. It has protested all forms of torture and brutality against prisoners.

In 1974 its first director, Irish human-rights advocate Sean MacBride, was awarded the Nobel Peace Prize. As long as the group's emphasis was on rights violations around the world, official thought in Washington, D.C., was not discomforted, but as more investigations focused on the United States, such opinion changed. AI has focused on specific conditions in various institutions. One report in 2000 in Connecticut cited complaints in the state's only prison for women that male guards routinely did pat-down searches of inmates and that the guards also were present when the inmates undressed or showered. A spokesperson for the prison system said that it was unaware of any recent claims of sexual abuse but would investigate. It was generally assumed that such abuses would not take place any longer. As part of its campaign against capital punishment, AI condemned the executions of juveniles or those convicted of crimes committed when they were juveniles. A report that it issued in 1996 stated that "since 1990, only four countries worldwide are reported to have executed juvenile offenders: one was executed in Saudi Arabia, and one in Pakistan, in 1992; one in Yemen in 1993; and six in the United States." The group held that nine juvenile offenders had been executed in the United States since 1985 and that "over 35 remain under sentence of death."

AI labeled a number of prison inmates meeting its definition of "political prisoners," one being Martin Sostre, a fighter for both prisoner and Muslim rights whom a court judged had been subjected to racial brutality and punishment.

The group, of course, has been in the forefront of the movement to halt the new chain gangs that sprang up in the 1990s, calling for the federal government to investigate chain gangs as possibly being in violation of international treatment of prisoners. It specifically pointed out that the use of leg chains was clearly outlawed under the United Nations Standard Minimum Rules for the Treatment of Prisoners. It declared: "This is the first time in recent history that the practice of shackling inmates together in chain gangs had been sanctioned by a U.S. state, and is clearly a retrograde step in human rights." Under assault from attacks from Amnesty International and other human-rights groups, attempts to establish chain gangs had peaked by the new century. Many of the ruder aspects of the chain system were abolished, and some states moving toward adoption of the system generally pulled back. AI has received credit in some circles for swaying public opinion even in some southern states. In Mississippi, the reelection campaign of Lt. Gov. Eddie Briggs was stalled and eventually lost, polls indicated, when for several weeks he geared his support of chain gangs as the main issue of his campaign.

AI frequently did the "spade work" in many prison scandals that, besides exposing poor conditions there, aided in saving a convicted murderer from death. One case was Joey Giarratano, who was on death row in Virginia's Mecklenburg Prison, convicted of murdering a woman and her daughter, although it became obvious that he confessed to facts of which he had no free-thinking knowledge. From a mindless twerp on death row, he went on to become one of the most accomplished inmates in Virginia's history, a student of Joseph Campbell, the philosophy of Soren Kierkegaard, and the writings of theologian Dietrich Bonhoeffer, a prisoner of conscience who died during the Nazi regime. Giarrantano won the support of Amnesty International, the Southern Coalition on Jails and Prisons, and conservative columnist James Kilpatrick. He was interviewed by Caroline Kennedy and filmed by *First Tuesday,* the European equivalent of *60 Minutes.* He published several articles on constitutional law and became known as one of the nation's best constitutional litigators; as such, he carried out a successful landmark case that guaranteed legal representation to death row inmates through the length of their appeals, not merely through the first round. He became one of the few Virginia prisoners to win conditional clemency in that state. His sentence was changed to life imprisonment in 1991 because of doubts about his guilt. He could have been granted a new trial; however, the state attorney general's office held to the rule that new evidence had to be submitted within 21 days of the original conviction and declined to do so. Giarrantano was still imprisoned into the 21st century.

AI has found it not always easy to make its point in the United States. In 1994, the organization called on the United States set up a "Commission on Capital Punishment" to measure the value of the death penalty to decide if it should be ended. In connection, Amnesty International called on President Bill Clinton for a moratorium on executions until the commission could make its report. Clinton made no response.

Angel of Sing Sing (Kathryn Lawes)

warden's wife

No fiction writer would dare invent the career of Kathryn Lawes, the so-called Angel of Sing Sing, and hope to pass off the tearjerking story of her death as likely or believable. But it did happen.

Kathryn was the wife of Sing Sing Warden Lewis E. Lawes and mistress of the grim prison on the Hudson for 17 years. She was known to the prisoners as a kind, understanding woman who wrote letters for them, helped their families, and cared for them in the prison hospital. So legendary were her good deeds that she was considered an angel of mercy.

In 1937, at the age of 52, Kathryn Lawes was killed in a car crash, an event that stunned the prison inmates. Their anguish was genuine when they learned that her funeral would take place in a church outside the prison walls. A committee of prisoners protested to Warden Lawes and insisted the convicts had a right to pay their last respects.

Lawes decided to gamble on his men, an act that today would be regarded as clear, even criminal, folly. Lawes had in the past allowed many prisoners to go home on emergency visits without escorts, a practice that had left him open possibly to career-ruinous criticism if anything had gone wrong. Now Lawes was taking a far greater risk.

The night before the funeral, the south gate of Sing Sing swung open and out trudged a silent procession of murderers, swindlers, thieves of all kinds, marching out of the prison to the warden's house, a quarter of a mile away. There were no guns trained on them, and not a single guard accompanied them; yet not one man strayed from line nor looked for the chance to escape. When the men entered the house, they silently passed the bier, many uttering a short word of prayer, and then walked outside, reformed their ranks, and marched silently back to their prison.

Angolite, The prisoners' journal at Louisiana's Angola prison

Generally regarded as one of the two or three most important prisoner publications in the country, *The Angolite* is known for frequently "shaking up" the corrections hierarchy with its reports from what is generally regarded as perhaps the harshest prison in the South. The journal operates under court-ordered protections and, under its longtime editor Wilbert Rideau, has effected numerous penal reforms and publicized the plight of prisoners confined to the Louisiana State Penitentiary at Angola. Some led to groundbreaking court decisions on prisoner's rights. Many articles from the journal have been reprinted or used as source material by the general press.

Excerpts from *The Angolite* were published by Times Books, and segments were narrated on National Public Radio. The book has become required reading in many criminal-justice courses. In an era in which "no-coddling" codes dominated prison procedures, *The Angolite* has published numerous studies contrary to the finding of the "get tough" doctrine, which demands that prisoners do hard time because there is no way they can be reformed anyway. Typical was a story in 1996 on studies that received little or no attention in the general media:

> *Two studies, one from Tennessee and the other from Iowa, show that parole does work. Despite all obstacles, the overwhelming majority of parolees do reintegrate into the community and sin no more.*
>
> *For two years the Tennessee Sentencing Commission and the state's Bureau of Investigation tracked 3,793 prisoners released between July 1, 1989, and June 30, 1991. Most were parolees. Within two years of release, 24.7 percent were returned to prison for committing a new crime, 14.5 percent were reimprisoned for violating parole or probation rules, 14.3 percent were rearrested but not returned to prison and nearly half of them, 46.5 percent, were not even arrested. . . .*
>
> *In Iowa, for two years the parole board followed 1,039 parolees released between October 1, 1990, and April 1, 1991. Within two years of release, 324 parolees were reimprisoned for a "failure rate" of 31 percent. This means 69 percent succeeded in society and stayed out of prison.*

The editorial positions taken by *The Angolite* did not necessarily endear the publication with corrections officials, just as Rideau himself was hardly an unbounded joy for Warden Burl Cain. The warden took some very restrictive steps for a time at least against the publication. He shut off the phone line the writers had always used to gather information from outside sources, and he ordered the staff to earn money no longer for articles they wrote for outside publications, again a privilege long granted to the journalists. Because the warden was at the time involved with the author of a prospective book about his administration, it was generally felt that he was out to remind the staff who was in charge of Angola and whose virtue was not to be questioned in conversations with the author. The book, *God of the Rodeo,* was a critical success as was the later reputation of *The Angolite* as well. It remains still an important voice of dissent on penal matters.

See also: RIDEAU, WILBERT.

asbestos removal and similar health hazards for prisoners

At the Eastern Oregon Correction Institution in the 1990s, officials had a large problem on their hands when a state fire marshal ordered the removal of asbestos hanging off pipes as an imminent health hazard. Fortunately, officials had the perfect workers to do the job, prison inmates who were ordered to do the work peeling off and bagging the asbestos. The institution saw no reason to supply any real protective clothing for the inmates or, for that matter, for their guards. The prisoners spent some 45 hours removing the asbestos in prison khakis and cotton work gloves.

The prisoners and their supervisors suffered pain in their lungs, coughed up black fluid, and later experienced other health problems. One prisoner tried to get the prison administration to listen to complaints and filed a grievance asking to be taken off the work duty or to be provided with proper protection. After a number of complaints, the prison turned the work over to a professional asbestos removal firm, which removed more than 1,100 pounds from the prison attics.

About a year previous to this situation, an asbestos assessment report had resulted in prison officials being notified that the asbestos presence in the prison attics posed considerable risks to inmates and employees of the institution. In 1995, the U.S. Ninth Circuit of Appeals ruled that prison authorities had been deliberately indifferent to the dangers of asbestos both on inmates and on staff. It found that under such conditions, even a relatively short prison term could end up being a lingering death sentence.

There have long been charges that when work-release programs are utilized, the dangers of nonprotection of prison labor leaves inmates subject to extreme abusive situations. Prisoners from the Franklin County Workhouse made what to them probably appeared a very attractive rate of $5.00 an hour to separate meal from the ash stream at a trash-burning Shaneway power plant in Columbus, Ohio. Unfortunately the prisoners had to do the work with their bare hands, minus any protective clothing or equipment. The prisoners worked directly in the stream of toxic ash two times those allowed by OSHA Standards, while cadmium levels were at five times, lead at 138 times, and dioxin at levels 770 times the ambient air in the community. All the work-release prisoners in the ash stream developed symptoms indicating dioxin exposure. The workhouse utilized prisoners for at least one and a half years and perhaps as long as four years, clearly increasing their exposure, certainly calling for more prudent use of prisoners and for shorter periods, if nothing else.

With a bit of tongue in cheek, the prisoner-run *Prison Legal News* opined, "Nonviolent offenders serving short sentences of 6 month or less in county and city jails are a perfect marginal transient population for deadly work." Under such "happier" circumstances, the inmates would be possibly long-gone before complications appeared.

Atlanta Boys Convoy mass shipment of convicts

Following its opening as a federal prison in January 1934, the former military prison on Alcatraz Island in San Francisco Bay began to receive prisoners from other prisons. The operative phrase at the time was *a super cage to hold super criminals.* The basic criteria concentrated on prison troublemakers and those most likely to attempt to escape.

Populating Alcatraz quickly was quite a logistical problem, and it was decided to ship these dangerous convicts en masse in convoys from each institution. The first of these, known as the Atlanta Boys Convoy, caused a tremendous amount of excitement and a good deal of fear around the country. On August 14, 1934, 53 hardened criminals were taken from their cells in Atlanta Penitentiary, chained hand and foot, and loaded into a train composed of special steel coaches with barred windows and wire-meshed doors. This was a time when hysteria about gangsters was at its zenith.

Ideally, the plan was to keep the operation quiet, but this proved impossible; when the public learned of the plan to move "the Atlanta boys," there were wild rumors, fed by the press, of huge underworld armies mobilizing armored cars, flamethrowers, machine guns, and even aircraft to set the convicts free. The federal government took measures that were appropriate for a military operation in hostile territory. The prisoners were chained to their chairs and denied toilet privileges other than on a carefully worked-out schedule. The train's route was not revealed but the unexplained closing of certain rail stations along the way fueled public speculation, even though some of the closings apparently were part of a disinformation program on the course of the train.

Meanwhile at Alcatraz, Warden James A. Johnston was kept fully advised and tracked the train's progress day and night on a large wall map. Approaching Oakland, the train was shifted away from the main rail terminal to a little-used but easier to guard one at Tiburon. The train cars were run straight onto a ferry barge and escorted to the Rock by the Coast Guard.

The prisoners were in dreadful shape following their ordeal, having been chained in close quarters where they could hardly move and certainly could not sleep. All were coated with sweat and grime, most suffering swollen feet from their irons, and many barely able to walk.

Their terrible journey was over, but their ordeal in the most restrictive federal prison in history was just beginning. When all were finally deposited in their cells, Warden Johnston wired Attorney General Homer Cummings: "FIFTY THREE CRATES OF FURNITURE FROM ATLANTA RECEIVED IN GOOD CONDITION—INSTALLED—NO BREAKAGE."

See also: ALCATRAZ PRISON.

Attica Prison Riot worst prison insurrection in American history

The Attica prison riot in September 1971 was probably a child of its time, when the nation was wracked by political tumult. A little more than a year earlier, a nervous Ohio National Guard opened fire on students at an antiwar riot at Kent State University, killing four; just two weeks before the Attica uprising, a California tower guard shot Black Panther George Jackson to death in a much-disputed incident; a week later, Attica prisoners called a hunger strike in honor of Jackson; only 13 men ate breakfast, and only seven ate lunch.

The scene was set for Attica to explode. The spark was minor and was based on misunderstandings. On September 8, an Attica guard mistakenly thought two inmates had been fighting. Later that evening, the two prisoners were taken from their cells for punishment. A rumor, not any more true than the fight that never happened, spread throughout the cellblock that they had been beaten. It had all been somewhat silly, but the most violent prison riot was ready to begin the following morning at the prison located 40 miles east of Buffalo, New York.

The riot, a most tragic and most controversial one, was finally smashed by a massive assault of 1,500 heavily armed sheriff's deputies, state troopers, and prison guards, during which 28 prisoners and nine guards being held hostage were killed. State officials claimed at first that the guards had their throats slashed by the convicts and that one of them had been emasculated.

The riot started when about 1,000 prisoners among the inmate population of 2,254 seized a portion of the prison compounded in the process of taking more than 30 guards and civilian workers captive. The convicts issued a written statement with five demands, including higher wages and greater political and religious freedom, along with the declaration, "The incident that has erupted here at Attica is not a result of the dastardly bushwacking of the two prisoners Sept. 8, 1971, but of the unmitigated oppression wrought by the racist administration network of the prison, throughout the year."

The convicts also demanded total amnesty and no reprisals for the riot. Negotiations took place between the inmates and Russell G. Oswald, the state commissioner of corrections. Most of the deliberations were handled through the liaison of an "observers committee," consisting of representatives of government, several newspapers, the radical Young Lords and Black Muslims, and other social and professional groups.

While police and correctional officers attempted to resecure Attica Correctional Facility, dead and wounded inmates lay on catwalks following the September 13, 1971, prison riot. (Author's collection)

Oswald accepted most of the prisoners' demands but refused to fire Attica superintendent Vincent Mancusi and turned down total amnesty. Gov. Nelson Rockefeller also refused the amnesty demand and requests of the observers committee that he come to Attica and personally join in the negotiations.

Early on the morning of September 13, Oswald read an ultimatum that listed his concessions and demanded the release of the hostages. The prisoners answered by displaying a number of hostages with knives to their throats. The bloody but successful assault followed. During the 24 hours after the assault, state officials made much of the convicts' violence and the sadistic murders of the hostages during the attack. Then came the official autopsies, which showed that none of the dead hostages had had their throats cut and none had been mutilated. All had been shot. In further contradiction of the state version, it was found that prisoners had been in possession of no guns. All the hostages had been killed in the crossfire of the police attackers.

Angered state officials summoned other medical examiners to check the findings of the Monroe County medical examiner, Dr. John F. Edland, who reported that state troopers had stood over him while he performed the autopsies, evidently to guard against any cover-up of the supposed throat-slashing evidence. Commissioner Oswald, who previously had told reporters that "atrocities were committed on the hostages," could not believe Dr. Edland's findings. According to one newspaper, "He suggested that some sinister force—conceivably—motivated Dr. Edland to heap blame and shame on the authorities who decided to storm the prison." The other medical examiners who were called in were also subjected to close observation but concurred in Dr. Edland's findings.

After long public hearings, a congressional subcommittee issued a report in June 1973 that criticized the methods used by prison officials and the police and condemned the brutality and inadequate medical treatment given wounded convicts after the attack. Previously, a nine-member citizens fact-finding committee, chaired by Robert B. McKay, dean of New York University Law School, had filed a final report that condemned Rockefeller's failure to go to Attica as well as the chaotic nature of the attack. The committee declared the riot was a spontaneous uprising that stemmed from legitimate grievances.

The autopsies' findings, as well as later reports, stunned the small village where the prison stood and most of the guards lived. Hatred toward the prisoners shifted to angry disbelief and in many cases to vitriolic accusations that the authorities had recklessly risked lives by ordering the retaking of the prison.

Several indictments followed, and on December 30, 1976, succeeding Gov. Hugh L. Carey pardoned seven former Attica inmates and commuted the sentence of an eighth in a move to "close the book" on the bloody uprising. He also declared that no disciplinary action would be taken against 120 law officers who had participated in the attack.

The closing of the book was not complete, however. In 1977, the first of a series of lawsuits was filed on behalf of a number of guards who were taken hostages and of the relatives of the hostages who were killed. They contended that law-enforcement officials used excessive force in retaking the prison and asked $20 million in damages. The trial was delayed a full year after appellate courts ruled that the state had to produce the "debriefing" statements made by the guards and troopers shortly after the riot. Another delay, of about a year, followed when appeals were filed by 19 guards and troopers who had been cited for contempt by the trial judge after they took the Fifth Amendment on questions concerning the retaking of the prison.

Eventually, these claims were settled, but dragging on were the claims of inmates that they had been horribly abused not only in the retaking of the prison but in the aftermath. The inmates contended that what followed was an orgy of reprisals carried out by prison guards and law-enforcement officers, many charges later being substantiated. Prisoners were forced to crawl naked over broken glass, and one inmate had a screwdriver shoved repeatedly into his rectum. Possibly the worst-abused inmate was Frank B. Smith, who was assaulted, burned, and subjected to threats of castration and death. In 2000, Smith, then 66 and working in Queens, New York, as a paralegal, dedicated to prisoners' rights cases, proclaimed victory in the fight to win a settlement for suffering endured by the prisoners.

Although the offered settlement of $8 million for the prisoners and $4 million for their lawyers was well below what the ex-prisoners had sought, it won approval by the prisoners, who otherwise would see the case dragged out for many more years. By 2000, an estimated 400 of the inmates were already dead, but about 400 others were to share in the awards, determined on an individual basis by a federal judge. The awards varied widely but were estimated to average out to $20,000 per individual. Most of the prisoners were believed to feel that more important than the money award was the fact that the settlement held the government accountable for its action.

The immediate effect on Governor Rockefeller did in no way stunt his actions. While he continued to implement some of the previously agreed-upon reforms, he also pushed through strict drug laws. One effect of these laws was to make the state's prison population soar. During the next 25 years, it grew by 560 percent.

Auburn, New York, civilian prison riot

an uprising not likely to be repeated

It was undoubtedly the strangest prison riot in America, and one hardly likely to be repeated in more recent times. It took place in Auburn, New York, in the spring of 1821 when that notorious prison fell under control of a new warden, or technically an "agent and keeper." Capt. Elam Lynds later won the "honor" of being regarded as the worst warden ever to run an American prison.

Under Lynds, discipline at the prison was tightened severely and was governed by the "cat," a whip made of strands of cowhide about 15 inches long. Every keeper was issued such a whip; Lynds himself carried a long bullwhip. Lynds ordered the guards to use their cats liberally and harshly, and when they did not do so with enough enthusiasm, Lynds frequently took matters to his own whip.

Word spread to the outside Auburn community of the vicious punishments Lynds meted out, and despite the fact that the inmates were obvious malefactors, popular resentment built against Lynds, the citizenry seeing him as a slur against the community's good name. One day in the spring of 1821, Lynds ordered three convicts to be whipped, but three guards, as angered as much as others about Lynds's methods, all in succession refused to carry out his orders. Lynds summarily fired them on the spot. Finally, Lynds brought in a blacksmith, Jonathan Thompson, who worked in the town and had him flog the prisoners.

When Thompson left the prison that evening, he was surrounded by a group of vigilantes who had heard about what had happened. The mob ripped off Thompson's clothes, covered his entire body with hot tar, and paraded him around the prison on a rail. It cannot be reported that Lynds attempted to interfere. The chief vigilante, Lewis Warren, trotted alongside the blacksmith, plucked feathers from a shrieking hen, and stuck them in the tar.

Unfortunately for the protesters, the prisoners heard about what was happening, revolted, and set numerous workshops ablaze. Lynds suppressed the revolt and emerged in a stronger position, now that his methods were necessary to control the convicts. Warren and three others were arrested and convicted of rioting. Warren paid a fine of $80, a considerable sum in the period, and the others went to jail for two months.

Lynds went right back to his harsh ways, and in the succeeding months, numerous prisoners died, many having gone insane. Some died of "consumption," and some by suicide. One convict leapt out of his cell over the fourth-floor gallery and landed on the stone pavement. Another slashed his veins with a piece of tin and bled to death. Another convict bashed his head against the cell wall until he destroyed one of his eyes.

Gov. Joseph C. Yates visited the prison and was so horrified by what he found that he pardoned some of the survivors instantly. Again though, supporters of strict security rallied to Lynds's support; he remained on duty and went on to other scandals. Finally, however, it all became too much, and Lynds was transferred out. It was not a bright day for American penology when he was charged with building a new state prison to be called Sing Sing. He did so solely with convict labor and his bullwhip, and he proceeded to greater infamy.

See also: LYNDS, ELAM.

Augustus, John (1785–1859) "Father of Probation"

In 1841, John Augustus, a Boston shoemaker, initiated the practice of probation. He appeared in court and requested that the judge give him several weeks to reform a lawbreaker instead of sending him to jail. Augustus was granted his request, and after some weeks, the shoemaker satisfied the judge that the offender had genuinely reformed.

On this volunteer basis, Augustus continued his reform efforts, convincing the Boston courts of the principle of friendly supervision in the community. He frequently paid the fines of many persons who had been jailed and then worked on their rehabilitation.

As Sheldon Glueck put it: "His method was to bail out the offender after conviction, to utilize this favor as an entering wedge to the convict's confidence and friendship, and through such evidence of friendliness as helping the offender to obtain a job and aiding his family in various ways, to drive a wedge home. When the defendant was later brought into court for sentence, Augustus would report on his progress toward reformation, and the judge would usually fine the convict one cent and costs, instead of committing him to an institution."

See also: PROBATION.

authority and surrogate rape

victimizing prison inmates by staff

Most prison inmates insist that rape offenses committed by staff members are far more common than outsiders tend to believe. It is very easy for guards to commit inmate rape; they are greatly aided by the fact that they have access to prisoner records that indicate if a prisoner has an outside family or friends to whom the prisoner might complain. With no outside aid, most inmate complaints against guards go unheeded. Generally, the prison authorities will do little to the guard if he simply denies all and insists that the prisoner is trying to frame him because he is a strict disciplinarian. It is also most difficult to determine if instead the inmate is using sex as a way to obtain special privileges.

A variation of such authority rape is what is known as surrogate rape, in which a staff member "sets up" a prisoner for rape by some inmate sexual predator, with a promise of immunity from punishment and some special privileges. As Victor Hassine, a noted prisoner writer, states in *Life Without Parole: Living in Prison Today,* "Surrogate rapes are seldom documented in prisons because of staff conspiracies of silence. The victims of surrogate rape are often convicted for particularly repulsive crimes, such as child molesters, or inmates who have filed official grievances or law suits against staff members."

B

Bailey, Harvey (1889–1963) gangster and "King of the Golden Age of Prison Breaks"
He was in his day regarded as one of the great bankrobbers of the 1920s and 1930s with an amazing career of masterful jobs, but he would gain greater fame as a master criminal whom no prison could hold, earning the title of "King of the Golden Age of Prison Breaks." His early career, until he was close to 30, was spent as a confidence operator who, even though caught several times, usually talked his way free from arrest or from lockup by one ruse or another. There was some suspicion that he did not just rely on a golden tongue, but also utilized bribes as part of his pattern. Amazingly, guards appeared to have turned him loose on his promise that he had a big caper in the works and would share the proceeds with a cooperative jail guard.

One of his major jobs was the robbery of the U.S. Denver Mint for a half-million dollars in untraceable bills in 1922 with Jim Ripley and others. Even though he was identified, Bailey stayed out of the law's way by reverting to a quiet, unassuming citizen living off the proceeds of his crimes. In 1931, he and Eddie Bentz, another master criminal, knocked off the Lincoln National Bank and Trust Company in Lincoln, Nebraska; at that time, this was the largest bank robbery committed in the country with loot coming to more than $1 million in cash and securities.

Bailey later joined up with some other gangsters and knocked over a bank in Fort Scott, Kansas. However, he was later apprehended and sent to the Kansas State Penitentiary. The full method of escape he masterminded there has never been revealed, but again Bailey's smooth tongue probably played a major role in the escape, along with such hard cases as Wilbur Underhill, Bob Brady, Eddie Davis, and Jim Clark. Most of the escapees, Oklahoma bandits, headed for the protection of the Cookson Hills, but Bailey opted to go off on his own, figuring that the search for them would center there.

On his own Bailey exchanged some shots with a pursuing posse and was badly wounded in the leg. Bailey made it to the notorious Shannon Ranch in Texas, a regular hideout for criminals on the run, waiting for things to cool down to act on his plan to reach Mexico. Bailey picked an unfortunate time to try the ranch because it was also being used for holding Charles F. Urschel, one of the most famous kidnap victims of the era. Bailey was not involved in that crime, but, still incapacitated, he was captured by raiding FBI agents looking for the kidnappers, including George "Machine Gun" Kelly, Kathryn Kelly, and Albert Bates, who had by that time fled.

Bailey was clapped in a 10th-floor cell in the modern Dallas County jail from which the local newspaper assured his readers that Bailey, despite his reputation, could not escape, headlining its account:

SEVEN BARRED DOORS OR GRILLS FACE GANGSTERS IF THEY TRY TO SPRING BAILEY FROM JAIL

It was true, the press had to admit, that a few other prisoners had gotten away before, but that was "through trickery." Officers were "keeping a close watch on Bailey to avoid any such turn of events."

It took Bailey all of two weeks to convince one of his jailers, Deputy Sheriff Thomas L. Manion, to smuggle in some saws for him to use on the prison bars. Bailey assured Manion that he had not been involved in the kidnapping, which was reassuring to the officer, and then he offered to share the take on his next few bank jobs with the errant Manion, which appeared to have been even more reassuring.

The saw provided was not as hard as it might have been. Bailey frequently tired at the chore, so the deputy took his place at the bars. When the saw developed a tendency to stick, the deputy raced out to a hardware store and bought a can of oil to make the sawing easier.

By the early morning of September 4, 1933, Labor Day, Bailey had almost completed cutting through three bars. Manion brought in a Stillson wrench, and shortly after 7 A.M., Bailey wiggled his bulky frame through the opening. Using a gun provided by the dim-witted Manion, Bailey took keys from another jailer and walked down to the sixth floor, overpowered a guard, the elevator operator, and two other jailers, and rode down to the main floor. There, he accosted Deputy Sheriff Nick Tresp and forced him at gunpoint to escort him to the garage across the street, where Bailey took the first car he saw and drove off with Tresp as his prisoner. A posse of some 100 vehicles was formed in nearby cities, and after a wild chase, Bailey was captured in Ardmore, Oklahoma. When Tresp found himself being handcuffed to Bailey, he protested, "I'm a jailer."

Handcuffed and manacled, Bailey was returned to Dallas under a heavy guard. One asked him, "What did you think you would prove, Harve?"

Bailey was tired and probably knew this would be his last escape. "Well," he snapped, "I got out, didn't I?"

Bailey refused to testify against the Urschel kidnappers and was sent to Leavenworth to serve a life sentence. He was paroled at age 73 in ill health in 1962 and died the following year.

Bennett, James V. (1894–1978) longtime early director of U.S. Bureau of Prisons

More than any other individual, James V. Bennett was responsible for the creation of the U.S. Bureau of Prisons. During his reign from 1937 to 1964, he introduced major penal reforms. In 1919, Bennett, the son of an Episcopal minister, went to work in Washington, D.C., for the U.S. Bureau of Efficiency, a now-defunct agency charged with seeking ways to improve the performance of the federal bureaucracy. By 1923, having graduated with a law degree from George Washington University, Bennett was assigned to assist a congressional committee investigating the federal penal system, then regarded, logically, to be in shambles.

Bennett started to check seven federal prisons and later had the figure increased to 19, both federal and state institutions. He returned from a nationwide tour, sickened, later writing: "With prisons, men are routinely strung up by the thumbs, handcuffed to high bars, kept for weeks in solitary confinement on bread and water, are whipped, paddled, and spanked, spread-eagled in the hot sun, locked up in sweatboxes, confined in tiny spaces where they can neither lie nor sit nor stand."

The federal institutions, to say nothing of the state prisons, were hard to get a handle on because each facility was run more or less independently by a warden appointed by the attorney general. As was common in many other government agencies, such appointees tended to be political hacks with little or no knowledge of how to run a prison. Bennett reported the federal prisons as being "vast, idle houses filled with a horde of despairing, discouraged, disgruntled men, milling aimlessly about in overcrowded yards."

It was Bennett's report to Congress that triggered the formation of the Bureau of Prisons under the Justice Department. The first head of the bureau was Sanford Bates, the head of the Massachusetts prison system and a highly regarded reformer. Bennett was named Bates's chief assistant and succeeded to the top post six years later when Bates moved on to another position.

Bennett immediately launched a gung-ho approach to what he considered to be the "gut issue" of prison reform. He later recalled, "I made it plain to all the wardens that there was to be no lashing, no use of the strap, no handcuffing men to the bars, no improper solitary confinement." It was to prove to be a traumatic experience for both prisoners and guards alike.

It worked, and the previously maligned federal system became the most progressive and respected correctional system in the nation, with considerable pressure exerted on at least some state systems as well. Bennett maintained a policy of rehabilitation and insisted that bureau employees treat inmates as individuals entitled to human dignity. The federal system launched programs for psychiatric counseling and medical care. (Before that federal prison hospitals were referred to by convicts as "butcher shops.")

Bennett received money from Congress for educational and vocational classes and put prisoners to work by creating programs that allowed them to earn money for themselves and their families. Under Bennett, separate prisons were built for mentally ill inmates, for drug addicts, and for offenders under the age of 22. Bennett played a key role in the establishment of the Juvenile Delinquency Act of 1938, and he set up the first of the nation's halfway house programs to aid inmates in their reintegration into society.

Bennett's main preoccupation, however, was the idea of rehabilitating his convicts. He felt that he came up with the proper formula for what he regarded as a sure cure for crime. It was referred to as the medical model of rehabilitation, not to be confused with the decades-earlier medical model theory of crime that spawned such outrageous applications as the pseudoscientific theory of eugenics, with its bizarre ideas of social control including sterilization.

Bennett, by contrast, felt that when a criminal committed a crime, he was "sick" but could be "cured" if properly diagnosed and treated. By the late 1950s, criminologists claimed that crime was caused by offenders who had lived in a bad environment and had little education, few job skills, and a low self-image. Convicts in the late 1950s and 1960s underwent programs to determine by

James V. Bennett, longtime director of the U.S. Bureau of Prisons (Federal Bureau of Prisons)

tests what their failings were and then were treated with the proper methods in each case. There would be intensive periods of education, vocational training, and psychotherapy that had to be completed before an inmate could be considered cured. By the time Bennett retired in 1964, he considered that he had put penology on a true course. His first successor continued his program until he had to retire on account of bad health. In the meantime, public opinion had become exasperated with the crime rates and demanded tougher treatment of criminals. The later heads of the bureau accordingly steadily junked Bennett's program, claiming that its recidivist rate was not that much different from other methods. Many argued, however, that Bennett's program had not had a proper tryout, and some wondered how many "recidivists" actually had done no more than be returned to prison for technical violations of their paroles, drinking, associating with bad characters, and so on. However, the point was moot: Rehabilitation was supplanted by a new approach—expansion. More and more prisons were built, and inmates were incarcerated for longer periods.

Bennett continued his program for penal reform until his death in 1978, after having served in retirement as vice chairman of the American Bar Association's Select Committee on Criminal Law and as an official delegate to the United Nations Conference on Crime and Corrections. Bennett never apologized for his commitment to the cause of penal reform.

Berkowitz, David (1953–) Son of Sam; killer incarcerated less stringently

In comparison to notorious serial killer Charles Manson, David Berkowitz, the Son of Sam murderer, is not held behind bars under as stringent a set of conditions, perhaps in recognition that he is less of a danger to himself and others than Manson is. Berkowitz held New York City in a grip of terror from July 1976 to August 1977. In all, he fired a total of 31 bullets into 13 young women and men, killing six and severely wounding seven in eight separate attacks. Generally, the victims were young women or couples parked in cars at night. Eventually, during the manhunt for him, Berkowitz picked up the nickname Son of Sam, which he got after writing letters to newspapers and signing them Son of Sam. Sam, the killer wrote, was the person really responsible for the crimes because he kept ordering him, the Son of Sam, to do his bidding. Next, the Son of Sam started to write that various "demons" were responsible for the state of terror. Son of Sam's first victims were brunettes, so thousands of women became blondes. But he then killed a blonde. His victims had long hair, so women with long hair cut their hair short. Then Son of Sam shot women with short hair. Parents of teenage daughters refused to let them out at night.

David Berkowitz, known as Son of Sam, is seen during an interview at Attica prison in New York on February 22, 1979. Berkowitz said he killed six persons and wounded seven because of an "unknown urge to kill." (AP/Wide World Photos)

On August 10, 1977, 11 days after he killed his last victim, 20-year-old Stacy Moskowitz of Brooklyn, and blinded her escort, Robert Violante, Son of Sam was captured. He was identified as 24-year-old Berkowitz, a mailman and former city auxiliary policeman, who was caught after a number of minute clues were tracked to him.

He pleaded guilty and three state justices, from counties other than where the crimes were committed, each followed one another to the bench; each sentenced him to terms of 25 years to life, the maximum allowed by law at the time. All the justices said that they wished they could have passed harsher sentences and made some of the sentences consecutive, but under the law, the sentences had to be merged in a cumulative penalty not exceeding 30 years, which meant the 25-year-old murderer had to be released in 2008, when he would be 54.

Meanwhile, Berkowitz was involved in a number of imbroglios, the major one being a book and a movie to be made about him. There was all kind of talk about the profits to be derived from such enterprises, about how much the Son of Sam would get, and about how much would go to the surviving victims and the families of the dead.

When Berkowitz became aware of the dealings, he said he would not cooperate "in any way" with the book or the movie. He said, "Maybe after some disturbed person sees the movie, he too will go out and kill some people, and then someone will make a movie about him, then another and another."

In any event, Berkowitz was not going to receive any share of any future proceeds. The state legislature passed the "Son of Sam Law," which prohibits a criminal from profiting financially from his crimes.

Berkowitz is currently serving his sentence in the maximum-security prison in Sullivan County. He is known as a shy prisoner who spends much of his time assisting troubled inmates. He helps clean them up and reads them their mail. He told an interviewer, "God gives me strength." He speaks of his cell as his "humble abode." His cell contains some religious books, newspapers, and loads of sneakers, seemingly a passion of his. He has through the years barely altered his appearance, except for a mustache, at least from time to time, and has developed a bit of a paunch. Otherwise, he maintains the fairly innocuous look he had at the time of his arrest. Besides having a date certain for his mandated release, Berkowitz has been eligible for parole since 1992, but it has never been granted.

Beto, George (1916–1991) "last" of the hard-nosed prison disciplinarians

It might be less than accurate to call George Beto the last of the tough, hard-nosed prison disciplinarians, but it is clear that in the latter part of the 20th century, Beto belonged with the legendary wardens who ruled their domains with virtually unchecked authority, using force to maintain institutional order—men like Elam Lynds, Zebulon Brockway, and Joseph Ragen. Beto's misfortune was to operate in an era when society had become less tolerant of violence and what is acceptable physical force.

An ordained Lutheran minister with a doctorate in education, Beto first worked in corrections in the 1950s on the Illinois Board of Parole. In that period, he was greatly influenced by Joseph Ragen, the tough superintendent of the Stateville and Joliet prisons. He then moved on to Texas to become president of Concordia College and served on the Texas Board of Corrections in 1962. In his 10-year rule there, Beto instituted the hard-nosed style of his model, Ragen.

For a considerable period, Texas prisons under Beto were considered to be efficient and safe for their inmates, but that belief was shattered by a federal class action lawsuit, *Ruiz v. Estelle*. W. J. Estelle was Beto's protégé and his successor as director of the Department of Corrections. The court found that the Beto system, especially in its building tender system, permitted the most brutal convicts to run the cell blocks and led to violence and forcible rape of other prisoners, very often younger first-time offenders. The courts also found that the Beto-Estelle system violated inmates' constitutional rights and ordered it dismantled. Despite this, Beto had—and continues to have even after his death in 1991—strong support in Texas and elsewhere for his concept that prisoner obedience, hard labor, and literacy training was the only way to run a successful prison.

See also: BUILDING TENDER SYSTEM.

Billington, John (?–1630) America's first death-penalty victim

John Billington was a member of the original *Mayflower* voyagers who landed at Plymouth Rock in 1620. He was to become America's first murderer (at least of a white man killing another white) and consequently the first to pay the supreme penalty for his crime.

Even before the Pilgrims first landed, Capt. Miles Standish had more than enough of Billington aboard ship. Billington was a foul-mouthed brawler from the slums of London, and at one time Standish had been forced to make an example of him by having his feet and neck tied together. That did nothing to alter Billington's behavior; he became the terror of the Plymouth colony, having confrontations with a number of other Pilgrims.

Usually, Billington was able to impose his will on others, but that was not the case when it came to John Newcomen, a neighbor, who was disdainful of Billington's threats. One day, in 1630, Newcomen went into the woods to hunt, and Billington ambushed him from behind a rock with a blunderbuss. It was obvious that Billington had carried out the deed, and he was seized by other colonists and, according to colony rules, was subjected to a fast trial and just as swift an execution. The Pilgrims were convinced that fast justice caused others to reconsider their own acts.

Ironically, many Americans today proudly trace their ancestry back to the *Mayflower* and Billington, the American colonies' first murderer, again within the scope of white-on-white crime.

Birdman of Alcatraz See STROUD, ROBERT FRANKLIN.

Birdmen of Sing Sing convicts as pet lovers

The title of this entry is a misnomer of sorts. Probably other prisons readily could be listed instead of Sing Sing. One can refer to Sing Sing because of a 2000 book *Newjack* by Ted Conover, who wanted to do a book about Sing Sing and their guards but was denied permission by authorities. A resourceful journalist, he then applied for a job as a guard, was unwittingly accepted, and "served a one-year sentence" in the prison to come up with an insightful work of great value to the public and those in the field of corrections as well.

He hardly had to probe far to catch glimpses of good in wallows of evil. He found that probably even more than people in the outside world, inmates appreciate pets and that many prisoners brought back food from their mess hall to feed to the birds who accessed the prison through small openings in outer windows that were not accessible from the inside. Tiny sparrows feasted regularly on the breadcrumbs that prisoners stuffed in the chain-link fence along the gallery so that they could watch the birds feed. Some inmates high up in the tiers studied birds in nests and anxiously observed the care newborn babies need to survive. Another prisoner took care of a baby owl that had fallen from a nest. Without the inmate's ministrations, the owl would have perished, but instead it thrived and would sit on its guardian's hand.

There was a time when larger pets were allowed in prisons. Charles Dickens visited Eastern Penitentiary in 1842 and observed a convict who kept rabbits in his cell. Eastern prisoners were kept isolated almost constantly, and the rabbits were obviously an important comfort to that inmate. Dickens watched the prisoner being let out in the sunlight for a short time, looking haggard and pale and clutching a white rabbit to his breast. Dickens felt the man's manner resembled that of a rabbit.

In the 1930s, Warden Lewis E. Lawes banned prisoners in Sing Sing from tending rabbits; this caused quite an uproar. Perhaps the warden did so because of the pungent odors that permeated the prison or for health reasons. Other animals could not be successfully banned, and to this day there are colonies of wild cats living inside and outside the outer walls. They take the sun and congregate near buildings where they know inmates will toss out food for them.

A spider makes an excellent pet in the cells of some inmates. The creatures do not have to extend themselves much more than building their webs. The inmates keep them content by catching roaches to feed them; the inmate cannot leave, the roaches don't, and the spiders won't as long as their food is catered to them. As one prisoner said, "My cell has much less roaches."

Few birds are ever mistreated by prisoners, but one such instance occurred in Conover's presence. When he was leaving the mess hall after breakfast, he saw a sparrow perched on a trash can with food in its mouth to feed its wide-mouthed offspring. Just then, an inmate porter used his broom to chase the parent one way and to shoo the baby another. Conover demanded to know why the porter had done so.

The inmate snarled, "I want her to know she can't save it." Conover wondered, "Was this part of a conversation he'd been having with himself about his own life? Make mother admit the truth?"

"Blood In, Blood Out" prison gang rules

The rule in a number of prison gangs, started by the Aryan Brotherhood, a vicious white gang, is "blood in, blood out," meaning that the only way an inmate could join was by killing someone and that the only way he could get out was death.

Since the prison race riots of the early 1970s, many prison gangs of all colors have frequently demanded such a standard. The same credo soon spread outside of prisons and was adopted by street gangs as well.

However, gangs outside of prison never adhered to such a policy as a general rule. There is a misconception that blood in, blood out applies to Mafia crime families. Despite the general belief fired by some sensationalist writers, that was never true in the Mafia. One could buy his way into a crime family by being a "producer" or a big moneymaker. Many major mafiosi have been able to retire with the fruits of their illegal activities and walk away from the mob, a classic example being big shot Frank Costello. Sometimes, of course, Mafia men were required to leave their rackets' future income to their crime families as the price of retirement. Such a price is highly popular with mafiosi because it means more gravy for those left behind.

Basically, blood in, blood out is enforced solely within prisons and by young gang members on the outside who are prime candidates for going behind bars.

Blue Code rule of silence on guards informing on one another

Although there has been considerable public description of the alleged code of silence among the police about informing on one another—the so-called Blue Wall of Silence—it is said by some observers that it hardly matches what is referred to as the "Blue Code" among prison guards.

There are many reasons, they say, why the blue code can be rigidly enforced, chief among them being that prisons operate under a microscope so that much of all activities is noted. When there is suspicion that an inquiry is being made into allegations of guard misconduct, it is hardly possible to be kept a secret. Whenever a guard is summoned to make a statement, other guards at their posts in the prison control center know about it and record the time span of the interview. If it was short and sweet, the guards could assume the guard had denied any knowledge of any misconduct; if, however, a guard had taken part in a long session, that seemingly would indicate that the guard was doing some "snitching."

An added ingredient of the Blue Code was that such a suspect guard would be subjected to severe retribution, his message box and locker would be decorated with snitch graffiti, and he would receive middle-of-the-night obscene telephone calls. If the guard then complained to the prison administration, that would merely confirm that he was a violator of the blue code.

boot camps a less-than-sparkling record

Boot camps are one type of punishment—aimed at youths—that does not arouse strong opposition from the public. Much of the public regard boot camps as the equivalent of military training and have the idea that the armed forces have an excellent ability to make "men." Boot camps have a long history in U.S. penology, going back to the reformatory ideas of Zebulon Brockway, who promoted programs that combined education, athletic events, military drills and regulation, and religious instruction. The first of the modern boot camps opened in Georgia in 1983. Also known as shock incarceration, it combines military training with the traditional rehabilitation philosophy and was intended for the first-time, nonviolent offender.

In their first three years, boot camps were considered a brilliant success, with only 20 percent of those sent to boot camps said to be returning to a life of crime. Other states proceeded to jump on the bandwagon.

Boot camps called for offenders to spend a short time in a program involving physical training, hard labor, and very strict rules. Boot camps were supposed to scare young offenders away from future unlawful endeavors. At many boot camps, the offender's head was shaved and personal possessions were locked up. The wearing of a uniform was required, and cigarette smoking was forbidden. Offenders arose at about 5 A.M. and started off with rigorous physical training. The inmates had to clean their barracks usually twice a day, were forbidden to speak without permission, and especially were not permitted to complain about the rules or their work assignments.

By 1995, boot camps were regarded as the most promising idea in the battle against juvenile crime. Dubbed the Leadership Challenge with Maryland in the lead, it called for sending teenage criminals to boot camps under what was called "a cost-effective intermediate punishment." Prison wardens backed the idea which, after all, did cut down the number of offenders sent to their institutions. The guiding force behind the program was

Lt. Gov. Kathleen Kennedy Townsend, who previously had been an assistant attorney general in the Clinton administration.

Under the Townsend leadership and the example of Georgia, several states embraced the Maryland program. Unfortunately, the results proved to be more than just disappointing, according to a national survey of the boot-camp idea. The recidivism rate ranged from 64 to 75 percent. Georgia's previous low rate shot up as well.

If asked, the men who ran *genuine* boot camps could have predicted that the juvenile programs would not work out as adherents had expected. "The key reason we are successful," noted Sgt. Maj. Ford Kinsey, who supervised drill instructors at the U.S. Marine Corps' recruitment base at Parris Island, South Carolina, "is that we have a clientele down here that chose to be here on their own. They are not here because a judge said you should go here. Our population comes with a lot more positive attitudes." He explained that when "a kid graduates from Parris Island, he is just beginning a four- or five-year enlistment in the Marine Corps. It is not like they spend 11 months here and we just throw them out onto the streets."

Aside from the startlingly high recidivist rates, the boot camps were plagued by scandals of routine and brutal beatings of inmates by guards. In Maryland, Gov. Parris N. Glendening and Lieutenant Governor Townsend suspended the state's camps and fired the top five juvenile justice officials. Soured by similar results, officials in Colorado, North Dakota, and Arizona dropped their programs, and others scaled back in their efforts amid predictions that they too would fold eventually. In Georgia, a Justice Department investigation concluded that the state's "paramilitary boot camp model is not only ineffective, but harmful."

A number of experts regarded the boot-camp experiments as nothing more than cynical political maneuvers. Dr. David M. Altschuler of the Institute for Policy Studies at Johns Hopkins University described them as "just another knee-jerk reaction, a way to get tough with juveniles that resonated with the public and became a political answer." Gerald Wells, a senior associate at the Koch Institute, declared, "People thought boot camps shaped up a lot of servicemen during three wars. But just because you place someone in a highly structured environment with discipline does not mean once they get home and out of that, they will be model citizens."

Perhaps the major problem with boot camps was the budget issue. Get-tough ideas resonate with the public, but when it came to the extra expense involved in follow-up, the money was not there. Besides, with a drop in the juvenile crime rate since 1994, along with the country's overall drop in the juvenile population, it became even harder to interest voters to pay for individualized rehabilitation. All the public wanted was a "magic bullet" that would make young criminals vanish.

As a result, the 27,000 young people who were sent to boot camps each year were largely sent to prison instead. Gerald Wells warned that as bad as boot camps proved to be, "once you start incarcerating kids, you have lost. But unfortunately, that is where we seem headed."

Brennan's Opinion dissent on the electric chair

Throughout the history of capital punishment in the United States, the courts have never been able to reach the opinion that the electric chair constituted "cruel and unusual punishment." In recent decades, Supreme Court Justice William Brennan was one member of the High Court who stood against the use of the electric chair.

In an opinion he wrote:

> *Witnesses routinely report that, when the switch is thrown, the condemned prisoner cringes, leaps and fights the straps with amazing strength. The hands turn red, then white, and the cords of the neck stand out like steel bands. The prisoner's limbs, fingers, toes and face are severely contorted. The force of the electrical current is so powerful that the prisoner's eyeballs sometimes pop out and rest on his cheeks. The prisoner often defecates, urinates and vomits blood and drool. The body turns bright red as its temperature rises, and the prisoner's flesh swells and his skin stretches to the point of breaking. Sometimes the prisoner catches on fire, particularly if he perspires excessively. Witnesses hear a loud and sustained sound like bacon frying and the sickly sweet smell of burning flesh permeates the chamber. This smell of frying human flesh in the immediate neighborhood of the chair is sometimes bad*

enough to nauseate the press representatives who are present.

Brennan's description was hardly complete. After death, the demeaning task of the execution team continues. Guards have to leave the body untouched for 30 minutes to an hour after the victim has been pronounced dead.

One case where the result lay somewhere between the usual and the gruesome was the 1985 electrocution of Morris Mason in North Carolina. The guards let him cool for some 30 minutes, and exhaust fans were used to draw off the odor of seared flesh. The death squad stuffed their nostrils with Vaseline, and some wore surgical masks. The dead man's joints had fused so that it was necessary for the guards to break his arms, legs, and back to get the body to lie flat on the gurney. The sound was described similar to the cracking of crab shells.

That awesome task completed, the dead man was wheeled off for an autopsy, a mandatory requirement being that the cause of death had to be officially determined.

Despite all the many mishaps to occur in electrocution, the Supreme Court into the 21st century never determined, unlike Brennan, that the electric chair represented cruel or unusual punishment. (However, it should be noted that Florida, one of the more execution-prone states, finally eliminated the use of "Old Sparky" in favor of death by injection, it having become clear to the legislature that the public had increasingly become disenchanted with the method.)

Brockway, Zebulon R. (1827–1920) celebrated figure in penology

If one had to pick the most important figure in U.S. penology, many would choose Zebulon R. Brockway, although by the end of his career he was considerably tarnished. In 1848, at the age of 21, Brockway was a clerk in Wethersfield Prison in Connecticut. After holding various positions in prison administration in New York State, Brockway became superintendent of the Detroit House of Correction in 1861, where he pioneered ideas on rehabilitation through education, trade training, and good behavior programs that allowed inmates to complete their sentences quickly.

Brockway left Detroit when he was unable to get an indeterminate-sentence bill through Michigan's legislature. However, New York had a more reform-minded legislature which had passed a comprehensive indeterminate-sentence bill. In 1876 the Elmira State Reformatory for young men ages 16 to 30 opened; Brockway was recruited to be its superintendent. For the next 25 years, Brockway made Elmira a world-famous institution with visitors from other continents coming to study its methods. Brockway instituted the first formal parole system, as well as a program for rewarding prisoners with promotions to better "grades" with more privileges. Under this method of operation, Brockway claimed a very high rate in rehabilitating his prisoners.

Actually Brockway was far less successful in managing Elmira. He was investigated more than once by the New York State Board of Charities on charges of using excessive and cruel punishments. Brockway was finally ousted for the brutal flogging of prisoners, for feeding them with inferior foods, for mental cruelty, and for failing to try to prevent the spread of diseases.

Despite this, Brockway continued to be—and still is—celebrated as one of the great humanitarians in American penal reform. He wrote of his experiences in *Fifty Years of Prison Service.*

See also: ELMIRA REFORMATORY.

bucket brigade primitive prison toilet practice

There are still jurisdictions where the so-called bucket brigade remains in use, although no longer in major institutions, except in rare situations. The bucket brigade was still in vogue in Sing Sing, San Quentin, and Joliet in the 1950s. In *Life Plus 99 Years,* Nathan Leopold reflected on the practice in Joliet as inmates made the daily run from their cells with a bucket of excrement: "As each man approached he removed the cover of his bucket, dipped it in the trough, sloshed it around several times, and then flung the contents into an enormous cesspool at the right. A 12-foot square held the stinking excrement of almost 2,000 men."

Leopold regarded the bucket brigade as epitomizing the prison life that he endured. "The very fact that the schedule called for coming directly from the disgusting chore of emptying one's excrement to breakfast, with no chance of washing one's hands, seemed to be deliberately contrived to humiliate the convict and to make his lot as uncomfortable as possible."

building tender system (BT) prison management system now prohibited by the courts

Made extremely popular in Texas by George Beto and his protégé-successor as director of the Texas Department of Corrections, W. J. Estelle, the building tender system (BT) utilized tough, violent-prone inmates who were appointed by prison officials to "tend" other prisoners. One of the main appeals of the method was that it saved on the cost of hiring more guards to do the same work. The "BTs" very efficiently kept the inmates terrorized into submission. Despite official denials, the system gave the most hardened criminals the license to rape and beat other prisoners in their cell blocks.

A federal class-action suit found that "inmates sleep with the knowledge that they may be molested or assaulted by their fellows at any time. . . . It is impossible for a written opinion to convey the pernicious conditions and the pain and degradation which ordinary inmates suffer within prison walls—the gruesome experiences of youthful first offenders forcibly raped; the cruel and justifiable fears of inmates, wondering when they will be called upon to defend [*sic*] the next violent assault."

Despite an impassioned defense by the Beto-Estelle forces, the BT system was ordered banned by the court, which appointed a monitor to see there was compliance with the decision.

See also: BETO, GEORGE.

"Burger King beefs" point of convict anger

On the surface, the concept of "Burger King beefs" would appear to the public to be of minor import, but to prisoners it is a bone of real contention. The problem or the scam, as far as inmates are concerned, involves, for example, a prisoner removed from prison for a short time who is going to federal court to testify at a legal proceeding. The rules call for such prisoners to be fed during regular mealtimes during traveling. In a typical case—so far as inmates are concerned—the prisoner is informed by his escort that instead of being fed en route, he will be rushed back to his institution and be fed there. However, when the inmate arrives back at prison he is confronted with the situation that mealtime has passed and he is, in effect, told, "Tough."

It is, say inmates, a case in which the escorts, at this time federal marshals, simply pocket the money and let the prisoner go hungry back in prison. If the facts are accurate, the matter is penny-ante but not to the prisoner. To a man who has been confined for a number of years, it is a big deal. One sympathetic guard at Leavenworth is quoted by Pete Earley in *The Hot House* as saying, "To you and me, eating at Burger King isn't a big deal . . . but to a guy who's been locked up ten or fifteen years, it's a real treat. It makes them feel like they are still part of the outside world." Of the alleged skimming by federal marshals this guard said, "It's not right, and I want inmates to know I don't play that game."

Burns, Robert Elliott (1890–1965) escapee who ended the chain gang

Probably no escaped prisoner did more to bring about penal reform than did Robert Elliott Burns, a multiple escapee from Georgia's notorious chain gang who fired up America's conscience with his writings about the cruel system.

An unemployed World War I veteran in his late 20s, Burns teamed up with two strangers to burglarize a grocery store for $5.80. For this offense, Burns was sentenced to six to 10 years on the Georgia chain gang. In 1922 Burns made a dramatic escape from the chain gang and made his way to Chicago where, by 1930, he had risen to a high post on a magazine. That year, Georgia authorities finally found Burns and sought his return to that state. Burns voluntarily returned to Georgia after being promised by officials that he would get a pardon.

Instead Burns was returned to the chain gang.

Burns by then enjoyed considerable notoriety, but that was nothing compared to that earned by an act that no other prisoner had ever done: He escaped from the chain gang for a second time. He assumed a new life in New Jersey and began to write articles for magazines about his personal story and exposing chain-gang conditions. The articles were enlarged into a book, *I Am a Fugitive from a Georgia Chain Gang* and actor Paul Muni starred in a movie as Burns. The book and movie evoked a national and international reaction of sympathy and outrage.

The outrage by Georgia officials was of a contrary sort, and Burns was once more located. Georgia demanded his extradition. New Jersey Governor A. Harry Moore held a special hearing in the Senate Chamber of the State House in Trenton. Noted defense attorney Clarence Darrow presented Burns's case, which soon turned into a "trial" of Georgia's penal system. Typical was the description of the "sweat box," a barrel with iron staves on top in which "insolent" inmates were kept, often with near-fatal results. It was revealed that prison cages built for 18 men actually housed 34 convicts. Backed up by support by several other governors, Governor Moore rejected the extradition request, and Burns remained a free man inside New Jersey.

Nevertheless, Georgia did not cease its efforts to recapture its most-publicized and embarrassing fugitive. In 1941, Governor Eugene Talmadge renewed a request to win custody of Burns, citing improvements made in the penal system. The claim was disputed by penal reformers who said the changes were in name only, not in fact.

In 1945, Governor Ellis Arnall scrapped the chain-gang system and invited Burns to return to Georgia. He did and the governor immediately commuted his sentence to time served. A free man at last, Burns returned to his New Jersey home and continued in his support of penal reform movements until his death in 1965.

C

California Coalition for Women Prisoners

The California Coalition for Women Prisoners started in 1995 to seek reforms in the human- and civil-rights treatment of female prisoners in the state, with membership including community figures, female prisoners current and previous, and prisoners' families. The main focus at first was to seek a lawsuit filed by prisoners at the California Institution for Women and the Central California Women's Facility to obtain better medical care. Today, it has expanded its activities into raising public consciousness about conditions for incarcerated women and to press for reforms. Among its top efforts is seeking the release of women dying of AIDS and other terminal illnesses, as well as pressing for protection of female prisoners from sexual assault and abuse by keepers and other prisoners. It also campaigns for justice for battered women. Community members spend considerable time maintaining contacts with coalition members in prison. (Address: 100 McAllister Street, San Francisco, California 94102; Telephone: [415] 255-7036)

capital punishment death-row appeals

It is standard litany that there is great abuse by condemned prisoners to stretch out their lives by filing appeal after appeal to postpone their executions. However, prisoners' rights groups insist the delays are state mandated with rules that cannot be obeyed in any timely fashion. It is true that before a person can be executed, there is a not-insignificant string of state and federal appeals, and when a prisoner fights the death sentence, the appeals process can take many years.

One reason is a lack of lawyers who are capable of representing condemned persons and who have received the necessary training. In California, lawyers must have at least four years of criminal defense experience. They have to attend special classes on appellate work and must have carried through on seven appeals cases. The result is that many lawyers have no interest in the work.

Additionally, death-row appeals require long hours, a lack of prestige, and overall low pay. Furthermore, the success rate is not high. Most lawyers doing such work say it is very frustrating to spend a huge amount of time on an appeal for a defendant who has been convicted of a grievous murder or murders about which public opinion is inflamed. Almost inevitably, such appeals are tossed out by strict higher courts.

As a result, many death-row inmates never even succeed in obtaining a lawyer. In Pennsylvania, about half of 196 death-row inmates had no lawyers.

Also, as the appeal process creeps along, public outrage, inflamed by the press, grows. In California, the appeals transcripts must be certified for accuracy by the murder trial judge. Because transcripts can run several hundred pages, even a thousand pages or more, it has to be painstakingly reviewed for errors by not only the judge but also the court reporters, court clerk, and trial attorneys. The delays in a long transcript review can add years to a case, and the condemned man's lawyer generally is denounced for delaying a resolution.

Typical of such delays is the case of Dean Phillip Carter, a serial killer who was sentenced to death in 1989 for murders he had committed five years previously. Two years later, in 1991, he drew a second death penalty for the rape-murder of a woman near San Diego. It was three and a half years before Carter obtained an appeals attorney. Seven years after his first death sentence, Carter had not even filed his appeal because the trial record was still being certified. The *Los Angeles Times* headlined its story: "An Even Longer Wait on Death Row."

The extent of state-mandated delays is such that from 1978, when the death penalty was restored in California, to April 1996—almost 18 years—only three condemned persons had been put to death.

See also: EXECUTION METHODS.

Capone, Al (1899–1947) abused prisoner

At the height of his power, Al Capone was sentenced to a year in prison on a gun charge in 1929; it was a piece of cake for him. The helpful warden of Pennsylvania's Eastern Penitentiary, Herbert B. Smith, saw to it that his prestigious "guest" had all the required creature comforts. "Big Al" had a large one-man cell, which he furnished with rugs, pictures, a desk, a bookshelf, a dresser, lamps, and a $500 radio console—top of the line for the era. Other prisoners received visitors only on Sundays, but Capone enjoyed such privileges seven days a week. Capone had to struggle along without a telephone in his cell, so he made do with the one in the warden's office, with required privacy, whenever he desired.

Capone's imprisonment was in line with his exalted station. Later on, when Capone was sent to prison big time for tax evasion and an 11-year sentence, he went first to Atlanta Penitentiary and in 1934 to forbidding Alcatraz, the federal prison in San Francisco Bay newly opened to hold the worst of the nation's criminals.

Something happened on Capone's shift to Alcatraz: he became a very unhappy prison camper. He could pay for favors, but he received very little. Simply put, Capone was not king of the bay. The convicts of Alcatraz had their own social order. Capone did not rank high, learning the facts of Alcatraz life when he had to line up with other convicts at the barber shop for his haircut.

It never occurred to Capone that he did not belong at the head of the line. He cut ahead of James Lucas, a tough Texas bank robber doing 30 years. Lucas knew who Capone was but was less than impressed. "Hey, lard ass," he snarled, "get back at the end of the line."

Capone turned and gave Lucas a withering look that would have chilled many a mobster on the outside. "You know who I am, punk?" Capone asked.

Lucas turned red with anger, snatched the scissors from the inmate barber, and jammed the point to Capone's neck. "Yeah, I know who you are, greaseball," he said. "And if you don't get back to the end of the line, I'm going to know who you *were*."

The stunned Capone moved to the back of the line and never again tried to pull rank in Alcatraz. That did not, however, protect him from further hostility. Because he had backed down, Capone had less prestige than ever. When the convicts staged a protest after a prisoner died after the warden had denied him medical treatment, believing he was malingering, Capone ignored the protest. He stayed on his prison job in the laundry and was denounced by other prisoners as "rat" and "scab." For his protection, Capone was allowed to remain in his cell until the work strike was crushed.

When he returned to work, an unknown convict threw a sash weight at his head. Capone was shoved aside by another convict, train robber Roy Gardner, so that the weight merely struck his arm and opened a deep gash. After that, Capone was transferred to new chores mopping up the bathhouse, where Capone picked up the disparaging nickname of "the wop with the mop."

One day, his arch nemesis, Lucas, sneaked up behind him in the shower room and stabbed him in the back. Capone had to be hospitalized for a

Al Capone (Author's collection)

week, and Lucas went to the hole (solitary confinement). There were other attacks on Capone, but friendly convicts, attracted by Capone's payment of money on the outside, protected him. Among the plots from which Capone was saved was one to spike his breakfast coffee with lye. On another occasion, Capone was on his way to the dentist when a convict jumped him from behind and tried to strangle him. Capone fought free and knocked down his attacker.

Such reports reached the press, which informed eager readers how far the "King of the Chicago Gangsters" had fallen. Capone's wife accused the prison administration of deliberately doing nothing to protect her husband. She petitioned the attorney general to have Capone transferred to another prison. She was turned down, and the persecution of "the wop with the mop" continued.

Later in his confinement, Capone started to slip in and out of lucidity, something prisoners recognized as the first signs of an inmate going "stir crazy." Capone's condition was obviously further complicated by an advanced stage of syphilis, picked up in his mob whorehouse days. Whatever the case, most convicts, including many of the hardcase types who had hated Capone, eased up on him. It was the custom among Alcatraz inmates to extend sympathy to any convict going stir crazy; because the rate of such an affliction was estimated to affect perhaps 60 percent of the inmates, most convicts understood that it could happen to them.

In January 1939 it was clear to officials that Capone could no longer take the rigors of the Rock, and he was transferred to the Federal Correctional Institution on Terminal Island near Los Angeles. In November, he was released from custody, destined to become increasingly less coherent during the remaining eight years of his life. When he was released to his Florida mansion, Chicago reporters asked his longtime faithful aide, Jake "Greasy Thumb" Guzik, if Capone was returning to control of the mob. Guzik replied, "Al is nutty as a fruitcake."

The sentiment was most sympathetic, actually, and the mob saw to it that Capone could live in the style they thought he deserved, even though he might be unaware of it.

"carrots and sticks" amenities method for controlling inmates

There is one school of thought that says prisons should be used to rehabilitate convicts, and another school that says they should punish them. Then there is a third school of thought, which says a prison's main duty is neither to rehabilitate nor to punish convicts, but to contain or control them. Some of these corrections officials are among the most hard-nosed in any prison system; yet, frequently, they find themselves labeled as "coddlers" of criminals. It is a charge that rankles many tough corrections people who use the "carrot-and-stick" method of running their prisons.

One such official, speaking anonymously, attacks these so-called experts who find coddlers all over the place as "being as bad—no, make that worse—than fuzzy-minded reformers. All they can say if there's any kind of program that inmates like, it must be bad and shows we are 'soft on crime.'" To them, the principles of the carrot and stick is the finest way, the safest way to run a prison loaded with tough cons always ready to explode.

Prisons in every section of the country have faced the rhetoric that they are running a weak system, full of fun for felons who should be having none of that. Fanned by political oversight—or undersight as some corrections people claim—the public in the last two decades of the 20th century have grown to resent pictures of convicts playing handball, shooting hoops, or lifting weights. Writing in the *Hartford Courant*, Dana Tofig found that

> *Wardens and correction officials say that weight rooms, basketball hoops, televisions, radios and other pleasantries accomplish two very important tasks inside a prison. They are a powerful management tool, and they occupy a prisoner's time.*
>
> *However, much of the public is fed up with crime, and pictures of basketball hoops and fully stocked libraries in prisons only make them more disgusted. Politicians, in recent years, have tapped into that frustration and called for the elimination of such amenities. In Connecticut, changes have been made, but they have been tempered by the reality that recreation and education serve an important purpose.*
>
> *It's rhetoric vs. reality in the get-tough-on-crime '90s.*

More and more people even in get-tough states like Texas are starting to support what is called carrots and sticks. "The people who are in charge of running prisons have a much more practical view of the importance of amenities than outsiders, especially politicians," says Timothy Flanagan, dean of the College of Criminal Justice at Sam Houston State University in Texas.

In Connecticut, the prison system as a whole represents carrots and sticks. Prisoners are shuttled around among prisons and among security levels. Cybulski Correctional Institution in Somers County is the carrot where most prisoners want to go. "It's still prison," Tofig notes, "but there are plenty of activities that help pass the days, or years, and sometimes help the prisoners straighten themselves out."

Among the institution's offerings are bumper pool and Ping-Pong tables in the dorms, a weight room, a basketball court, televisions and radios on almost every bunk, a library, and other recreational and educational offerings.

But within the system there are also stick facilities, such as Walker Special Management Unit in Suffield, where recreation for its higher-security prisoners is a walk around a cage. An even tougher stick is located at Northern Correctional in Somers, the most secure prison in the state. There, recreation for the inmates is limited to shuffling in circles around an open-air concrete pen in shackles.

One of the sticks used on prisoners at Cybulski is to transfer to a tougher prison as punishment for infractions. The carrot is amenities; the stick is the loss of amenities.

A 1996 survey by Sam Houston University of more than 800 wardens, superintendents, and commissioners about the usefulness of various amenities showed overwhelming approval for recreation, television, and educational programs inside the prison. The majority backed the presence of weightlifting, intramural sports, hobby and crafts programs, and the like. Less than 25 percent felt VCRs, radios, televisions, and musical instruments should be eliminated or reduced.

Dean Flanagan observes, "Amenities provide incentives for inmates to stay out of trouble. We do need to consider what it's like to work in these institutions."

At Cybulski, errant prisoners find themselves under real heat when they are caught in an infraction. Their hope is not to be transferred. If they aren't, they are determined not to go wrong again but instead to "chill down."

"carrying baby" ball-and-chain punishment

It is a common scene in modern-day cartoons, the convict wearing a ball and chain. The custom does not have the humorous connotation in its sordid history. Many institutions and jurisdictions have made use of such contraptions. When the first federal penitentiary at Leavenworth, Kansas, was being built at the end of the 19th century, the ball and chain was used, some said excessively, on inmates from the army stockade at Fort Leavenworth. All that was required was a show of disobedience, and the prisoner had to "carry the baby," a 25-pound ball on a chain. To walk, the prisoner had to carry the ball about, often for many months, until the authorities were satisfied.

The local press carried considerable stories about the harsh conditions, especially "baby," at the prison under construction. These conditions were said to have caused many fledgling guards to quit.

Although the specific ball and chain has largely disappeared, it is generally acknowledged that present-day heavy leg irons are almost as good as "baby."

cell door courtesy mark of respect

Most prison inmates follow a set procedure when appearing at the cell door of another inmate. Even if the door is open, the visiting inmate is expected to pause outside the cell, knock, and await an invitation to enter. This is regarded as a mark of respect between prisoners, an attitude they do not experience when dealing with guards.

However, the practice is not entirely one involving good manners. At best, a failure to knock before entering can indicate the lack of esteem in which the inhabitant is held or that the entering convict is a leader or a higher-up in the prisoners' pecking order. More importantly, especially if more than one intruder enters, it indicates that they intend to do psychological or even physical harm, perhaps even of the killing kind. Some convicts react quickly to such a real or imaginary threat and fight back, often employing a hidden homemade weapon. Such a prisoner will face certain retribution by the keepers, but most inmates agree, "he done the right thing."

cell extraction often criticized as "excessive force"

Probably nothing upsets prisoners in maximum-security prisons more than the method of "cell extraction" that they claim is shown in its various forms on television to indicate they are all wild dogs and getting the treatment of which the treat-'em-tough majority in the population approves. That was one of the major criticisms made by Human Rights Watch, a highly respected international human-rights organization. In respect to the two supermaximum-security prisons in Indiana, Human Rights Watch cited "cruel, inhuman and degrading treatment." The group said that the Indiana Department of Corrections had violated "the International Covenant on Political and Civil Rights and the UN Standard Minimum Rules for the Treatment of Prisoners" as well as the ban on "cruel and unusual" punishment under the Eighth Amendment to the U.S. Constitution.

As far as cell extraction is concerned, whenever a prisoner leaves his assigned cell, he is handcuffed behind his back with a lead strap, more or less a "dog leash," held by a guard. Before the cell door is opened, the prisoner is required to cooperate in this by putting his hands through a slot for handcuffing. For trips outside the immediate area near the cell, the inmates were also shackled at the legs. One convict offers this explanation of why inmates are so indignant about this method of removing a prisoner from a cell. He claims that it goes far beyond simple indignity: "When guards only see you in a cage or at the end of a chain, they just can't relate to you as a person." Undoubtedly this is further inflamed by race because the guards are overwhelmingly white and African Americans are a significant proportion of the inmate population. Recently (presumably in response to much criticism of the method as "overkill"), reforms now allow movement of some inmates without handcuffing.

What hasn't changed was the actual cell extractions in many supermaxes where Human Rights Watch discerned "that the use of force was rampant in the early years of both Indiana facilities, and although there has been some moderation of the method, it appeared to outsiders that the forceful cell extractions still amounted to excess brutality." The method was carried out by "at least five correctional officers wearing body armor, helmets with visors, neck supports, and heavy leather gloves." What bothered Human Rights Watch was that, although such an extreme measure could be justified on some occasions, it appeared to be the only option, whereas in the past, it was the method that seemed to be the option of first choice with as many as eight extractions a day occurring in one of the facilities.

(It may be noted that "suiting up" can be a rigorous job for guards, and in retaliation for what some maximum-security inmates considered excessive cell extractions, prisoners in a Wisconsin maximum-security facility covered their cell windows so that guards had to suit up to enter, check on them, and remove the covers. As one inmate later reported, "Five hours and 26 'cell extractions' later . . . guards were tired and mad. They put in a lot of work that day.")

In other cases, men are stripped down on the beds to immobilize them in what is called "four-point restraints." There are specific guidelines on how this is to be accomplished, especially when inmates are suicidal or pose an imminent threat. But while there has been somewhat of an improvement here after the previous warden left his post in mid-1995, the charge remains that the method is used to excess and that Mace, tear gas, and beatings are also used, reflecting back to the previous warden who "encouraged and condoned the unnecessary use of physical force" and "pursued the vision of total control with a single-minded and lawless intensity: beating prisoners into submission on the slightest pretext or provocation."

Certainly, television reports on various supermax prisons seem to have difficulty avoiding graphic depictions of the cell extraction in action, which some observers judge to be almost celebratory in tone.

cell thieves

It is hardly unexpected that theft among inmates is a hallmark of virtually every prison; the population composition makes this inevitable. However, the level of theft can be regarded as the measure of the prison administration's control. Petty theft is to be expected, but when it is out of control, prison gangs operate with virtual impunity, sweeping through cell blocks, ignoring guards, and taking whatever they want from disorganized inmates. The bigger, more prosperous, and powerful these gangs become, the more the guards are reluctant to act, and, it has been charged, the more they tend to turn their backs on any criminal activity. Institutions can claim that they are unable to prevent such depredations because virtually all victims refuse to make a formal complaint. This, too, is to be expected because prisoners so victimized will be labeled by the thieves—and for that matter all other prisoners—as "snitches." A convict who snitches against cell thieves will snitch against others.

Under prison codes, the victim becomes the villain.

As a rule, a number of prisons let inmates settle such matters among themselves provided no major violence results. Some prisoners are tough enough to avoid having to deal with cell thieves. They have generally done this by punishing any convict trying to rob them. Prison gangs see such prisoners fight back and, considering all the potential victims around, they generally decide to leave likely tough victims alone. As for the less fortunate inmates, generally the administration frequently does little for them. It appears that some guards do not intervene because they feel that thefts and intrusions in cells are nothing more than justified punishment for incarcerated inmates.

Other prisons are a bit more "helpful," and holes may be drilled in the cell-door tracks so that they can be locked from outside with a padlock, even when the master lever is opened. In such institutions, the commissary may sell padlocks that can fit in the hole. (The padlocks may from time to time be cut by the keepers because allowing them to be used amounts to a confession that the administration cannot control security in its facility. Others live with that admission.)

Of course, prison gangs cannot really be stopped by padlocks. The gangs simply wait until an inmate is alone in his cell, and then the gang of thieves rush in when he is asleep or using the toilet. Unless the prisoner knows how to be prepared for such an attack, he can be overwhelmed quickly. One way is for a prisoner to just happen to have in his cell a wooden floor brush made of heavy oak that can easily kayo an invader or two. This is not a contraband weapon but merely a misplaced piece of prison equipment that the guards, when spotting it, will simply confiscate to be returned to the sergeant.

Prisoners have had to come up with other means of defense that does not stick out as contraband, and once again that can mean the heavy padlock. Many prisons allow the sale of heavy-duty combination locks so that the inmate can secure some of his possessions inside the cell. Instead, the inmate puts the heavy lock in a sock and wields it as a blackjack, a far more potent weapon than the "shanks" (homemade knives) with which intruders arm themselves. A lock in a sock is a perfect defense weapon and is not subject to being seized in a shakedown.

Tough nonvictims advertise their prowess with this defensive weapon and generally are safe from victimization. They do so by such methods as rigging up an empty milk carton that is tied by a small towel between some of the bars. This is accessible from the outside so that the inmates may toss in stuff when they are outside their cell and do not wish to bother to reenter it. Of course, that means that anyone might grab whatever is inside the milk carton. As a consequence, nothing of any real value is placed in there, except things the prisoner or prisoners, if they are double-celled, don't mind losing.

Under such circumstances, if someone does grab something and the cell occupant knows it and, more importantly, if other inmates know he knows it, action must be taken. The inmate is permitted time to set up the offender for retribution in a way that does not, in turn, set the "victim" up for punishment by guards. Rendering such retribution merely enhances the cell owner's toughness and is once again a warning to more-violent gang thieves that he would not make a good target.

Chappleau, Joseph Ernst (1850–1911) first man sentenced to die in the electric chair

Joseph Chappleau should have been the first man to die in that new-fangled instrument of death, the electric chair. Instead he was spared that fate and went on to become perhaps the most popular prisoner in New York State at the turn of the last century. The celebrated warden of Sing Sing, Lewis E. Lawes, later credited Chappleau with doing more than any other man to mold his philosophy of modern penology.

A New York farmer, Chappleau had murdered a neighbor named Tabor allegedly over some poisoned cows, and he was sentenced to be the first man to die in the electric chair in 1889. There were powerful forces seeking to get the procedure underway, and Chappleau was regarded as the first convenient candidate for the new punishment. Unfortunately or fortunately, as the case might have been, the chair was not completed in time for Chappleau's slated execution date, and he won commutation of his sentence to life imprisonment. (Actually, there may have been some consideration given to the theory that a more deserving killer had come along in the case of an ax-murderer named Willie Kemmler.)

The sparing of Chappleau did not meet with much opposition even in his home community because there was a general belief that the real motive for the murder was that there had been an affair between Tabor and Chappleau's wife. Once Chappleau was spared the death penalty, he became an inmate uniquely popular with both guards and other convicts at Clinton Prison. He was more simply regarded as an unfortunate man who had been trapped by fate.

Lewis Lawes himself was a rookie guard in 1905 at Clinton when Chappleau saved his life during a prison yard melee. Even though he could have been regarded as a traitor to the rioters, he was not condemned by them because he was regarded as a "straight guy" acting the way he had because it was the right thing to do.

Lawes himself came to cite Chappleau as a murderer who was not likely to commit another murder and possibly the best argument against capital punishment, a fate Chappleau had escaped for purely technical reasons.

Chappleau died in the prison hospital in 1911 at the age of 61. Guards and prisoners alike were glad, feeling that he had finally won release from the burdens of his life.

CHIPS—Children of Incarcerated Parents Program

CHIPS—Children of Incarcerated Parents Program—is administered by the Center for Community Alternatives, a private, nonprofit agency. A support group for the children of imprisoned parents, CHIPS focuses on students with disciplinary problems and a penchant for violence. It seeks to help children and parents preserve or restore family bonds, especially when those ties have been broken by imprisonment. It seeks to make the public aware of the effects that imprisoning parents can have on children, to increase school attendance, and to cut school suspensions by decreasing disciplinary infractions. It prepares educational materials for caregivers and community agencies.

Support groups of five to 10 children meet weekly and cover subjects such as self-esteem and shame, isolation, how to make positive choices, setting goals, self-reliance, and substance abuse. The children are taken on visits to correctional facilities and introduced to legal matters such as parole and release. The children are exposed to monitoring on job training and employment possibilities. (Address: 115 East Jefferson Street, Syracuse, New York 13202; Telephone: [315] 422-5638)

Clemency and Commutation actions short of pardon

Although clemency and commutation sometimes are cited as pardons, they are not. Clemency has a long standing throughout history. Many rulers have used clemency as forgiveness for a convicted person's crimes, but it did not necessarily mean the person would be pardoned, whereby he would get back all rights and property taken from him. In a number of countries in this century, whole blocks of clemencies have been granted to a large number of people at the same time. This happens, for instance, when a new government comes to power in a country and could mean that foreigners barred from coming into a country for past offenses would be forgiven and thus could return. This has happened in a number of cases to foreign students.

Clemency was quite a frequent act in the 19th and early 20th century in the United States when it was common for governors to issue general clemencies that turned loose a large number of prisoners. There were of course charges at times that such acts had the odor of bribery clinging to them; in other cases, some chief executives found it necessary to open the state's prisons for new offenders. There have been remarkable situations in which pardoned individuals, guilty of very serious crimes, including murder, never left their prisons but instead got jobs as guards.

Before the era of life-without-parole, most persons, even those serving life, could expect to win clemency after being in prison for a large number of years. In the case of the death sentence, a governor could commute the sentence, which would not necessarily free the person but would allow him or her to seek parole, as would be the case for lifers, and the like.

In many states, although a governor might have the right to grant clemency, the prisoner is required to win approval of both the pardon board and the governor. The parole board in such cases reviews the prisoner's record to decide if it should recommend that the governor grant clemency. Often, only a simple majority is required. When the prisoner is doing life, the clemency is called a commutation, and the sentence is cut. This is what convicts refer to as a "time cut." However, a recommendation for a commutation does not necessarily have an immediate effect. Once the paperwork on the case is complete, it is sent to the governor's office for his or her signature. This may be done in a matter of days, or, as has happened, the recommendation may lie around for years. When the commutation goes into effect, the record for good behavior might result in a "cut to time served" and, thus, immediate release.

After the assassination attempt on President Harry Truman by Puerto Rican nationalists, one of the gunmen, a badly wounded Oscar Collazo, was sentenced to death for the murder of White House sentry Leslie Coffelt during the attack. Collazo's partner in assassination, Griselio Torresola, had been shot dead in the assault. In due course, Truman commuted Collazo's death sentence to life imprisonment. In September 1979, President Jimmy Carter, "for humane reasons," commuted the life sentence to time served; four days later, Collazo was released, and he returned to Puerto Rico. There were some recriminations about the commutation, that it was done for political reasons—which it probably was—but in a rather short time, the objections were forgotten.

Even when hard-and-fast rules were in place, commutations have gone through. Such was the case in the murder of famous "Scarsdale Diet" doctor Herman Tarnower by Jean Harris, a cultured woman and headmistress of an exclusive school for girls. The pair had an affair lasting some 14 years, but the doctor was straying quite a bit. When she shot Tarnower to death in the bedroom of his lavish home, Harris was quickly apprehended, and said it had been an accident. Hardly anyone believed that, and even her strongest female supporters saw the case as one in which the victim "had done her wrong." The crime occurred at the time of heightened female expectations and demands for social equality with men. In cases of this sort, men seldom drew as harsh a sentence as Harris did—a mandatory 15 years to life. Under New York State law, "mandatory" meant Harris had to serve at least 15 years.

An attempt by Harris supporters to win her clemency failed, and she was due to remain in prison until 1996. She became active in prison reform and wrote a book about her prison experiences. She started to experience heart problems in 1993 and at the age of 69 had her sentence commuted by Gov. Mario Cuomo, after serving slightly less than 12 years of her minimum 15-year term.

In 1998 possible clemency for a convicted murder became an international cause célèbre. When Paraguayan Angel Francisco Breard was arrested in Virginia on a capital charge, Virginia authorities failed to inform him that he had a right to confer with Paraguayan consular officials, as required by the Vienna convention. Breard's later claims were rejected by U.S. courts, and he then turned to the International Court of Justice, where a unanimous bench, including a U.S. judge, ordered that the United States "take all measures at its disposal" to stop Virginia from carrying out the execution. Secretary of State Madeleine Albright urged that the execution be halted, warning it would "limit our ability to insure that Americans are protected when living or traveling abroad."

Gov. James Gilmore remained unmoved, declaring that the international court had no authority to interfere with Virginia's criminal justice system. Breard was executed.

A different commutation result took place in Missouri in 1999 when Darrell Mease was convicted after he admitted to killing a 19-year-old paraplegic and the victim's grandparents. Mease made no convincing case of legal or rehabilitative grounds to avert the death penalty. However, Pope John Paul II appealed to Gov. Mel Carnahan to show mercy to the condemned man. Carnahan, himself a believer in the death penalty, nevertheless commuted the death sentence to life without parole. The governor made it clear that his act was solely a tribute to the pope and did not mean he had changed his mind about the death penalty or about Mease's guilt. Shortly thereafter, Carnahan was locked in a tight race with John Ashcroft, who was up for reelection to the U.S. Senate, and it remained to be determined whether his commutation would help or hurt him. Carnahan died in a plane crash shortly before the November 2000 election, but it was too late for his name to be removed from the ballot. He defeated Ashcroft, and Carnahan's widow was named to fill the position.

It could be argued that in both of these recent cases, the governors bowed to political imperatives in reaching their decisions, but their right to do it could not be disputed, and whether or not the convicts deserved mercy was irrelevant. The decision was to be made within each chief executive's prerogative.

As long as there are prisoners serving very long or life sentences, not of the "without-parole" stipulation, clemency and commutations of sentences will continue. There are many who feel that releasing older inmates is less threatening to society. Marilyn Tower Oliver in *Prisons: Today's Debate* offers some reasons offered by many for commutations for aging inmates: "Keeping them in prison takes up room that could be better used to house younger criminals who are a danger to others. Aging prisoners also cost the state more money because they have more serious health problems. They are also more likely to be victimized and injured by younger inmates."

Clinton-Auburn 1929 prison riots

In 1929, a series of bloody disturbances hit New York State prisons. On July 22, Clinton at Dannemora, the "Siberia of New York," blew up as the 1,600 inmates started a mass protest about overcrowding. It quickly escalated into a full riot, and the police and the national guard moved in and killed three prisoners. Six days later, Auburn Prison blew up as well. Actually, this was part of a well-organized escape plot. A trusty threw acid in a guard's face at the prison arsenal and passed out weapons to prisoners who streamed out of their cells. The four ringleaders planned to create confusion, which would allow them to escape. Some inmates went on a rampage and destroyed part of the prison, including six shops. Meanwhile, the four masterminds seized guards as shields and made it over the wall. They commandeered passing cars for a getaway but were finally cornered and seized. Meanwhile, the uprising ended when the convicts inside the prison were driven into cell blocks by machine gun, rifles, and tear gas. Two convicts were killed and three guards, a fireman, and 12 convicts were wounded.

Retribution for the uprising was quick and sweeping, although it was later estimated that only 80 prisoners had been involved. All prisoners were returned to their cells, and all privileges were halted.

Despite close surveillance, a new disturbance occurred on December 11 when some inmates acquired guns that were secreted and not found in the previous escape try. After a violent struggle, during which the principal keeper was killed, the warden and several guards were taken hostage. The cons threatened to kill their captives unless the gates were opened.

The inmates were informed they would be allowed out, but as they moved through the guard room, they were ambushed by state police using gunfire and tear gas. The hostages were freed, and the control of the prison was once more asserted. Eight inmates had been killed, and several prisoners and employees had been injured.

A great show was made about New York asserting increasing toughness, and in time that was the case. Auburn was largely rebuilt, and reforms in the prison were quietly introduced. Of course, Clinton and Auburn still remained a menace, but the danger level did drop. E. R. Cass of the American Prison Association said, "It seems we have to have bloodshed and millions of dollars' worth of damage before we ever improve things."

Coal Creek Rebellion uprising against leased convict use

During the 19th century, constant protests against the use of the leased-convict system charged the practice to be detrimental not only to labor but manufacturers as well. Most states gave short shrift to such complaints because the lease system filled state coffers. It reached, said some historians, the proportions of an addiction on the part of the politicians.

The dispute reached a climax in the 1870s when competitors of the Tennessee Coal, Iron and Railroad Company charged that the firm's use of leased convict labor gave it an unfair advantage. Nothing was done to stop the practice, thanks to the company's alliance with state lawmakers.

In 1891, the emboldened company decided to lock out all union workers when they would not sign what was called a "yellow-dog" contract, which would bar them from union membership. The company replaced the barred workers with leased convicts. This led to the explosive Coal Creek Rebellion. Rampaging miners invaded the lease confinement areas and released 400 prisoners, loading them on trains that went to the state capitol. Tennessee Coal fought back by filling the work camps with new leased convicts.

The miners not only freed those prisoners as well, but also proceeded to burn the prison stockades to the ground. As a result, goaded by public opinion, Tennessee finally got rid of the convict lease system. During the next several years, states started to place restrictions on the use of prison labor by private enterprises or to stop the practice entirely. It was not until the New Deal period that laws came about that put the nail in the coffin on leased labors. The war against leased-convict labor took decades and held up into the latter part of the 20th century, when the use of prisoners for private labor started up again with a vengeance.

Coffin, Rhoda M. (1826–1909) prison reformer

Born in 1826, Rhoda M. Coffin, a Quaker, and her husband Charles became leaders in the prison reform movement. As an exponent of separate prisons for women, Rhoda Coffin was instrumental in the founding of the first all-female prison, the Indiana Reformatory Institution for Women and Girls, in Indianapolis in 1873. Previously the Coffins had investigated the Indiana State Prison at Jeffersonville and were appalled to find that women prisoners had sexual contacts with male prisoners and were at times whipped into sexual submission by male guards.

Rhoda Coffin worked tirelessly to have women prisoners transferred to a separate institution and won public support. The Indiana Reformatory for Women was established with the first entirely female staff, completely independent of the male hierarchy of the state penal system.

Cohen, Mickey (1913–1976) mobster maltreated in prison

What happens to high-profile criminals who go to prison? In the case of well "connected" mobsters of the Mafia stripe, the results are not too unpleasant because there is a large contingent in some facilities that gives all of them a protective base. It may well be true, as some observers note, that the federal government concentrates mafiosi in a few prisons so as to keep them free of harassment from tough cons. If this procedure was not followed, there could, these observers say, be considerably more violence occurring within the prison system and probably without, too: The mobs arrange for vengeance to be taken on the relatives of inmates who attempt to abuse mobsters not used to being on the victim end of violence.

Other high-profilers face more serious problems, a prime example being West Coast mob king Mickey Cohen. A power in the lucrative gambling racket in California, Cohen was nevertheless on the outs with the Mafia. Cohen, an underling of Bugsy Siegel, took control of the rackets after Siegel was murdered and was not about to let the East Coast syndicate in. As a result, Cohen was targeted for several murder attempts but survived them all.

What he could not survive was legal onslaughts by federal prosecutors, and he was sent to jail. After a shorter prison stint, he drew a second sentence in 1961, this one for 15 years for tax violations. In prison, Cohen did not enjoy the mystique offered to Mafia types but was an easy target for other violent cons. He was subjected to a number of attacks by cons and, to hear him tell it, much abuse from guards. Then in 1963 Cohen was sitting in a prison TV room in Atlanta Penitentiary when another convict hit him over the head with a lead pipe. Cohen was in a coma for two weeks. The once-flamboyant gangster was partially paralyzed and, according to the prison grapevine, was no longer in possession of all his faculties. He was later transferred to the federal facility at Springfield, Missouri.

The fact was that Cohen became to the outside world virtually a nonperson. With so little known of him, some sloppy Robert Kennedy assassination theorists decided he was still around in Los Angeles, allegedly controlling a couple of major racetracks and, while there, coming into contact with a young horse walker named Sirhan Sirhan. According to this bizarre and inaccurate theory, Cohen took Sirhan under his wing and eventually directed him to assassinate Robert Kennedy.

West Coast mobster Mickey Cohen is shown here at a 1950 trial at which he testified. (AP/Wide World Photos)

Actually, nonperson Cohen was still in prison, not fully mobile and more concerned with—according to his later autobiography—resisting the homosexual advances from a prison guard. By 1969, when Kennedy was killed by Sirhan, Cohen was at least getting around with a walker.

In 1972, Cohen, still in need of a cane and no longer any sort of power in the underworld, limped out of prison, a very embittered ex-convict. In 1974 he started to gain attention for prison reform, outlining many of the abuses he had suffered and observed done to others. Then Cohen announced he was in touch with certain parties who knew the whereabouts of kidnap victim

Patricia Hearst, something on which he failed to deliver, which weakened his prison abuse campaign. His autobiography appeared in 1975, and Cohen died in 1976.

See also: CAPONE, AL.

Colonial punishment a patchwork system

Degrees of punishment in Colonial America varied greatly from one jurisdiction to another. By and large, the harshest colonies were New York and the South, with the latter usually the most stern. Theft in New York was punishable by multiple restitution and whipping, but in many southern colonies, the death penalty was often imposed when the sum involved was more than 12 pence. In New England and the Quaker settlements of West Jersey and Pennsylvania, a thief or burglar might receive a lesser penalty, at least in a manner of speaking, in the form of branding.

Overall, the punishment for crime tended to be less severe in the colonies from which most colonists had come. In New England and the Quaker settlements in Pennsylvania and West Jersey, punishments tended to be less harsh, with the main thrust coming in the form of humiliation. Mary Mandame, in 1639, supposedly the first female sex offender in Plymouth, was required to wear a badge of shame on her left sleeve. Had she not done so, she would have been branded in the face with a hot iron. In Mary's case, and in virtually all others, the mere threat of such punishment brought compliance.

In New England, vagrancy brought punishment in the stocks, while the scold could expect the ducking stool. There was a serious penalty for murder and "witchcraft"—hanging. Burglars faced branding.

In many New England settlements, a man could commit the following offenses—lying eight times, swearing four times, beating his wife twice, or criticizing a court once—and face a fine the equivalent of $10.

Of course, many times the first punishment in New England did not end the matter. A mere flogging or confinement in the stocks in the Massachusetts Bay Colony in the early 18th century constituted the initial punishment. Offenders were required to wear on their arm or bosom for a year or for many years a large letter cut from scarlet cloth. The letter identified the crime being punished, such as A for adultery, B for blasphemy, D for drunkenness, I for incest, P for poisoning, R for rape, and T for thievery. However, it was soon decided that this punishment was too inhumane, and it was dropped.

Whipping, almost anyplace, often went to excess so that the convicted person often was left crippled for life. In New England, an attempt was made to prevent this abuse by limiting the lashes to 39, as called for under Mosaic law. Contrary to common belief, no one, not even a witch, was burned at the stake in New England. New York and the South did engage in burning and quartering. In the great Negro Plot of 1741 in New York, many blacks were put to the stake. Quartering was apparently reserved for blacks, save for charges of treason. In Maryland, a black who killed an overseer first had a hand cut off, then was hanged, and finally was quartered.

It was said that perhaps the sternest punishments of all were meted out in Virginia. A slave who ran away might have an ear nailed to the pillory and then cut off. Criticism of the authorities could result in the offender's being pilloried with a placard, losing both ears, doing a year's service for the colony, or having his or her ears nailed to the pillory. Virginia probably decreed castration of blacks more than any other colony, even though this meant the loss for the owner of gaining more slaves through breeding.

See also: PILLORY.

Colorado State Prison riot

One of America's bloodiest riots took place in 1929 in the Colorado State Prison at Cañon City. It revolved around an escape plot involving five desperate convicts, who had managed to have two revolvers and ammunition smuggled in to them. The five provoked a riot in the dining room, overpowering the guards, and then releasing all the inmates of cell block 3. The five then used their guards as hostages and demanded that the warden permit them to escape through the gates. The warden refused to comply.

The cons then shot a guard and threw his body into the yard. They repeated their demands but received no response. Then, over the next 17 hours, the inmates were overpowered by tear gas, machine guns, and dynamite. Six more guards had been murdered, and 12 inmates were wounded. The five convict ringleaders had committed suicide.

Colson, Charles W. (1931–) founder of ministry for prisoners

During his politically active period, Charles W. Colson was special counsel to President Richard Nixon. In his own way, Colson represented the "conscience" of the pre-Watergate White House as typified by his statement that he would walk over his own grandmother to help Nixon. That seemed to be the byword for all the close associates of the president. It was a philosophy that sent many of Nixon's inner circle to prison for various Watergate-related offenses—including Colson.

In prison, Colson appeared to make the most determined transformation of character as he became convinced that a ministry for men and women in prison was vital. After he was released, Colson founded in 1976 a nonprofit, volunteer-based organization called Prison Fellowship Ministries to minister to prisoners, ex-prisoners, victims, and their families and to promote biblical standards of justice to the criminal justice system. Under Colson's lead, a broad array of volunteers with a wide variety of backgrounds and denominations formed and participated in numerous in-prison and community ministries. There is considerable evidence, probably best described as anecdotal, that indicates that the work of the ministries may be having some rehabilitative impact on released prison inmates, or for that

Charles Colson, right, chairman of Prison Fellowship Ministries, greets inmates at the Winfield Correctional Facility in Winfield, Kansas. (AP/Wide World Photos)

matter on inmates while they are behind bars. Many inmates report being aided by the Colson program by working while incarcerated, including aiding their families and their victims with some of the earnings, which admittedly are not great. As one such inmate told Colson, "I can either lie here on my prison bunk and cost the taxpayers about $16,000 a year, or I can be out here doing something productive, paying back society." Thus, the Colson approach in part can reflect former Chief Justice Warren Burger's framing of the debate on released prisoners: "Do we want prisoners to return to society as predators or as producers?"

community service penalties in lieu of jail time
Community service is a concept that has grown considerably since it was first introduced in California in the mid-1960s. There, municipal court judges worked out a pattern of sentencing certain traffic offenders to doing certain unpaid labors. Today, community service is utilized in every state in the union. Offenders now do a myriad of chores for governmental or private nonprofit agencies, painting buildings, maintaining parks, removing trash from roadsides, and renovating nursing homes and schools.

A recent estimate by the Bureau of Justice Statistics estimates that at least 6 percent of all felons nationally are now ordered to do community services, which may be combined with other sanctions. The state of Washington is the most ambitious in using the concept with about one-third of felons doing community services.

Service is an option for misdemeanor offenders who would otherwise be put behind bars. The Center for Alternative Sentencing and Employment Services (CASES) runs a program under which thousands of convicts since 1979 have done 70 hours of supervised community service. The program last ran up a completion rate of 65 percent. Offenders who do not complete the program are resentenced after CASES makes a report.

Community service readily can include shorter prison terms than usual followed by a stretch of community service. This has many virtues, relieving cell occupancy and still allowing some supervision after the confinement period.

"comparative proportionality," theory of
seeking like sentences
The theory of "comparative proportionality" has been tested for use in capital-punishment cases; many convicts insist that it should be applied more readily in all types of sentences. Indeed, a trigger of many prison riots is the anger exhibited by inmates who have a real or a perceived feeling that the punishment for serious crimes is excessive in some cases and light in others, even though the charges are very similar.

The standard case cited in capital-punishment cases is that of Robert Alton Harris, who killed two young boys following a bank holdup. He was sentenced to death but appealed on the basis that he could only be executed if other criminals who have committed similar crimes also drew the death penalty. The California courts rejected Harris's claim that without a review of like sentences, his constitutional rights were being violated. A U.S. district court agreed with the state courts, but then the U.S. Court of Appeals for the Ninth District vacated the death sentence because the failure to examine such a death sentence proportionally violated the Constitution.

However, the U.S. Supreme Court reversed that finding with only William Brennan and Thurgood Marshall dissenting. The 7-2 majority under Byron White found that comparative proportionality was not a "constitutionally required element of the capital sentencing system." Harris died in the gas chamber in April 1992, the first person executed since the restoration of the death penalty in California.

But the alleged disproportionate method of sentencing in other felony cases remains a thorn in the administration of the prison system as inmates continue to rage about the alleged uneveness of what they regard as their own harsher treatment.

compartmentalization of offenders
screening them to keep them out of prison
Compartmentalization of offenders may be the wave of the future insofar as freeing up space in prison for more serious criminals. Advocates insist many offenders have treatable conditions that in many cases can see great improvement in the proper environment. That environment does not include placing them amid other criminals in

repressive situations. A low-grade drug addict is not going to be "cured" in a high-security facility because drugs are readily available behind bars, the only requirement being the ability to pay for supplies. To do this, the offender must engage in other criminal activities to come up with the money. That may involve robbing other prisoners, turning to prostitution, stretching their outside family's resources, or even pressuring them to risk arrest themselves by smuggling in drugs.

Prisoners with alcohol addiction problems, gambling addicts, and even some minor sex offenders would benefit themselves (and of course society in general) by being segregated in separate groupings in specialized treatment centers staffed by trained counselors. Drug addicts, for instance, can be treated with substitute drugs to lower their need for the real thing. By being confined at all times, they can still function in a better atmosphere than that offered by prisons or release to the streets.

Some recent examples of offenders sentenced to such treatments would include former great baseball player Darryl Strawberry and actor Robert Downey Jr. In July 2001, Downey received what was described as "yet another second chance." Under a plea agreement in yet another drug case, he was sentenced to one year in a rehabilitation program rather than jail, after he pleaded no contest. The judge warned that Downey could face up to four years in prison if he violated the terms of the agreement. Downey lost his role in the TV series *Ally McBeal*. Strawberry, for his part, later was convicted of more infractions, and in 2002 he was sentenced to three years in prison. "Halfway houses" handle some such cases, but frequently, such houses are placed in communities where neighborhood groups are opposed to their presence.

Another objection sometimes made is that the success rate of such treatment seldom reaches anything approaching 100 percent; indeed, having drug addicts who manage to stay drug free for a short term thereafter would have to be considered a smashing success at a 12 or 13 percent rate. When a high-profile offender fails at immediate reformation the first, the second, or even the third try, compartmentalization suffers a black eye. But many in the corrections field see it as a valuable asset in the entire scheme of imprisonment methods. Some state prison systems see a value in the method if it frees up cell space that can be better utilized, cut the need for building expensive facilities, or, in some cases, permit a state to free prison space that can be rented out to the federal government for some of its excess populations.

condom use in prisons underused protection method

With the ravages of AIDS growing enormously in prisons, some observers find it bizarre and outrageous how little use is made of condoms to help in the fight against the awesome disease. As of 2001, only two states, Mississippi and Vermont, offered condoms to inmates. A handful of urban jail systems do the same, among them New York, San Francisco, Washington, and Philadelphia.

Most institutions simply ignore the utilization of condoms. For some, the rationale offered is that they can be used in drug smuggling, but of course because drugs are smuggled into prisons, it is not difficult to ship in condoms with them. Thus, even though condoms are available in the New York City area, they are banned in the rest of the state. Despite these bans, the state does give condoms to inmates for conjugal visits. It is clear that most jurisdictions refuse to make condoms available out of fear that the system could be accused of encouraging sex, either consensual or in forcible rape. (For the same reason, most jurisdictions not only will not supply needles for injecting drugs or, for that matter, bleach for use to clean dirty needles.)

Critics insist that such penal systems ignore reality rather than face acknowledgment of illegal activities. In a sense, this is understandable because correction facilities are subject to legislative controls in the formulation of their budgets, and many such bodies have too many hardliners or religious adherents who oppose the use of condoms.

As a result, condom use is down in prisons, AIDS is up, and virtually all victims of HIV and full-blown AIDS can end up simply being released into the outside world.

See also: AIDS.

"Convict Airlines" federal marshal's prison run

More or less a regular airline that follows a cross-country route that can change from day to day, depending where its cargo has to be dropped off or picked up, the flight of usually a 727 jetliner makes stops near various federal prisons or occasionally a state institution as a matter of accommodation. The cargo consists of prisoners being sent to one federal prison or another. To prison guards and inmates alike, it is called Convict Airlines.

When, for instance, the jet touches down at Kansas City International Airport, a marshal reads off the names of prisoners who are to be sent on to Leavenworth Penitentiary. As each prisoner is called, he is checked to make sure he has neither slipped out of the chains on his ankles nor managed to unlock his handcuffs. The prisoners are ushered onto a bus. It is a long, tedious, careful procedure, somewhat akin to an escorted tour so that nobody is lost. Once the bus has been loaded, a three-armed guard contingent oversees the cargo. One guard is positioned in a metal cage at the rear of the bus with a pump shotgun on his lap; another, armed with a shotgun, is at the front of the bus, outside a wire-mesh screen that holds the shackled prisoners; the third guard drives the bus and is armed with a pistol. A van takes up its position in front of the bus and leads it from the airstrip to the prison. The van's main mission is to prevent any interference from any source with the bus route.

As the bus reaches the prison, the cargo is efficiently unloaded, and the transfer is now complete. In the meantime, the 727, loaded with fresh, new cargo, took off for its next stop at another facility. Although Hollywood loves to fantasize about escapes from Convict Airlines, that has never happened.

costs—execution vs. life imprisonment

Ask the average person during the last three or four decades of the popular view of harsh treatment of prisoners, and there will be general agreement that the costs of keeping convicts imprisoned for life is too expensive when compared to the costs of executing the more heinous among them. They bridle at paying an estimated $20,000 or more annually to keep a lifer for the rest of his or her years. On this dollars-and-cents basis, it would, they say, be much cheaper to execute murderers. And what about those prisoners convicted of capital crimes who end up in supermaximum-security prisons with costs running as much as $50,000 a year?

This is not a position that holds water. As the late Supreme Court Justice Thurgood Marshall said in an opinion, "When all is said and done, there can be no doubt that it costs more to execute a man than to keep him in prison for life."

Admittedly, experts do have difficulty pinpointing the exact costs between the two alternatives, but there is little doubt the cost of executions runs somewhere between one-and-a-half and five times the cost of keeping an inmate confined for life.

Serious study of the problem has produced only limited literature. Certainly, the most intensive research was done by Margot Carey, whose basic findings were reported in the summer 1985 edition of the University of California at Davis Law Review. In her study, she attributes part of the costs to what she describes as "super due process," not necessarily in a pejorative sense. According to Carey, because of constitutional requirements "litigation can follow. Appeals in most cases are allowed at various stages, and not only through an initial appeal. Even when condemned persons cannot get full cooperation from a state entity, outside reform groups can take up the defense and this too saddles the prosecution with additional costs. This has and will continue to force recalcitrant states to do more to enhance the justice process." With DNA evidence becoming more prevalent and convictions in death sentences thrown out, the costs still may rise as some prosecutors decline to accept such findings and launch attempts for a reversal. In those cases, the death-row drama can continue longer still. Some reformers insist that some such appeals are no more than the effort to protect the prosecuting office's good name. In a recent case, a prosecutor continued to fight the DNA evidence, preferring to go along with the evidence offered by two jailhouse informers, often regarded as the most questionable sort of witnesses—such persons sometimes give false testimony in an effort to manipulate the system, knowing that if they cooperate, the authorities will go easier on them even without an explicit promise or deal. Frequently, according to reformers, the state may seek to appeal legal clearance of condemned men for the basic desire to avoid lawsuits and damages.

Figures in 1999 indicated that in Texas, it costs $53.98 a day to house and feed each death-row inmate. This does not include all the various costs listed above. As one authority has stated, if society wants to execute persons who deserve the sentence of death, it must do so "regardless of cost."

"Cowboys, The" accused brutal federal prison guards
In late 2000, the federal prison authorities faced what has been apparently the worst guard scandal to hit the system. The locale was in the Administrative Maximum Facility in Florence, Colorado, sometimes popularly referred to as the Alcatraz of the Rockies or Super Max. The facility has been attacked by reformers as being based on a brutal concept of near total isolation of prisoners, but a virtue from the federal authorities' view was that guards had less need for much direct contact with inmates.

Yet, despite this, there was the alleged appearance of what has been described as a rogue group of guards known as "The Cowboys." Among the charges made against five of the group and two others was that they choked handcuffed prisoners, mixed human waste into their food, and threatened other guards with a warning that if they informed the authorities of such acts, the Cowboys might not come to their assistance if they were attacked by prisoners.

The indictment against the seven guards stated that one inmate was choked until his eyes bulged and that a guard who objected to the abuses was specifically warned that members of the Cowboys might not come to his aid if he was later attacked by an inmate. In total, the indictment listed 52 incidents carried out against at least 20 inmates. Reports of the alleged depredations against the inmates first surfaced in July 1999 when a defecting Cowboy testified that among the infractions that led to Cowboy punishment of prisoners included one for such minor acts as kicking a door.

At the time of the indictment, six of the seven corrections officers still were in the federal prison system. Critics of the supermaximum prison are less concerned with prosecution in the case than they are with laying blame on the federal prison officials. They insist that using such terms as the prison being "the worst of the worst" aids in setting a mindset among guards that totally dehumanizes inmates and seems to permit no-holds-barred treatment of them.

Contamination of prisoners' food by guards is a standard complaint made by prison inmates. They clearly suspect that they are frequently given food that contains not only feces but insects and rodent parts as well. Again, for inmates in some institutions, this is a given, and according to prisoners, it causes them to adopt a form of defiance. In *Life Without Parole,* inmate-author Victor Hassine puts the situation and the result in a Pennsylvania prison: "If you throw a prisoner in a dark cave, he'll learn how to see. If you feed him rats, he'll still eat. In fact, if you give him enough rats, he'll get fat. You can try feeding him cockroaches to punish him more, but he'll eventually get fat on those too. As inmates sometimes boast, 'What doesn't kill me only makes me stronger.'" And Hassine adds: "Once you start down the road toward ruthless punishments, there's no turning back."

It would appear that keepers seem to take some inspiration from public sentiment for tough treatment of prisoners as well.

"cracked on" sexual approaches
It is not true that most prisoners end up being subjected to sexual rape. Prisoner predators constantly search out new sexual conquests among newcomers, or "fish," probing to see if they will be a victim. The law of the prison is that the likely victim is the weak fish who does not know how to repulse an advance or to figure out that he is being "cracked on," that is, being judged for a sexual victim role.

Prison author Victor Hassine quotes a prisoner who said, "Every convict's been 'cracked on' (sexually propositioned), whether he knows it or not. And any man who says otherwise is either lying or he just don't know what time it is." Hassine himself tells of being cracked on the very first day he entered Pennsylvania's Holmesburg County Prison. He entered wearing his street clothes, which were drenched in sweat and added to his fear and terror. In a holding room, a huge powerfully built man weighing at least 250 pounds asked his clothes sizes. When he disappeared, the guard supervisor in the room ordered him to strip.

The bulky prisoner returned with a bundle of clothes and hovered over Hassine, whom he hurriedly dressed as the supervisor left the room. The man informed Hassine what a rough place the prison was and that if he requested him as a cellmate, he would look after him and keep him safe.

Hassine was prudent enough to refuse the offer—forcefully. "At the time," Hassine recalled, in his celebrated book, *Life Without Parole,* "I thought Sherman was simply trying to bully me and extort money. It didn't occur to me until later that he was pressuring me for sex. I've since learned that many sexual approaches in prison do not involve threats or violence.

"I sometimes shudder to think what may have happened to me if I had been so intimidated that I accepted Sherman's offer for protection. I was strong enough to pass this test of weakness, along with others that I've endured in prison. For inmates who fail these tests, prison becomes one long ordeal after another in a never-ending nightmare. Because over 90 percent of these victims will be released back into the community, the nightmare of prison rape inevitably haunts us all."

Cyclops notorious Leavenworth pimp

Perhaps the most frightful long-term ogre of the federal penitentiary at Leavenworth, Kansas, "Cyclops" was well known to incoming prisoners, who heard on the grapevine what could happen if they fell into his clutches. Deadly and cold-blooded, Cyclops was a convicted murderer from Washington, D.C. Sporting a glass eye, he controlled a major portion of the pimp trade in the institution.

Cyclops's specialty did not involve handling homosexuals but rather "fuck boys," an argot for a young inmate who is not a homosexual but is turned into a prostitute in prison. There was no way a young inmate could avoid Cyclops short of killing him, something no one has done. For most the terror is so complete that they submit to his orders. A fuller account of Cyclops and his ilk is discussed in *The Hot House* by Pete Earley, who was given unlimited access to Leavenworth by the Federal Bureau of Prisons.

D

Daniels, Murl (1924–1949) parolee on a murder spree

Mass murderer Murl Daniels became the center of controversies in the late 1940s in the aftermath of his actions after parole. Together with another parolee, Daniels committed a series of senseless murders in Ohio in 1948, making him the main quarry in what came to be labeled the "greatest manhunt in Ohio history." Daniels and his partner, John Coulter West, had done time together at the Mansfield Reformatory, where, Daniels later said, they formed a compact to "take care" of one or more of the guards who had mistreated them. Daniels was doing 1-to-25 [years] for a stickup, and West, a feeble-minded man, was doing 1-to-7 for stealing tires off a truck.

Some critics of the U.S. justice and penal systems have said that Daniels never should have been paroled, while others declared that the state had been negligent in permitting an inmate such as West to mingle with a dangerous psychopath like Daniels.

When the pair were paroled, they teamed up to commit stickups all around the Midwest, committing a number of murders along with their robberies. Then they remembered their compact to kill their former guards, especially one named Willis Harris. They headed for Mansfield but could not locate Harris. They decided to get Harris's address from his superior, John Elmer Niebel, who ran the reformatory farm. They broke into the Niebel house about midnight and decided they had to hold him and his wife and daughter until after they had killed Harris.

They took the trio to a cornfield outside of town and ordered them to take off their clothes to make it more difficult for them to give an alarm if they worked loose from their bindings. Suddenly, the criminals realized they had neglected to bring any rope with them. So they shot all three to death and headed for Cleveland. When they were identified as the killers, an intensive manhunt followed. Daniels and West raced around the state, killing a farmer to steal his car and later a truck driver for his truck.

They came close to making it out of the state with the truck, a haulaway carrying new Studebaker cars. Police waved them through a number of roadblocks until a sheriff realized the truck was heading back to the auto plant rather than away from it. The pair was ordered to stop, and West opened fire, hitting a trooper before he himself was killed. Daniels meekly surrendered.

Daniels had no illusions that he would be able to avoid the electric chair and defiantly explained why they had wanted to kill Harris. Daniels told police, "I wanted to take this Harris out. I'd like to took him out, I'd like to fought him, and I'd like to have fought him with bare fists. I'd like to have beat him down to a pulp and I'd like to have stumped his face right in the ground, just give him a beating he would never forget. . . . A fellow what would pick on somebody when he's in jail, he's not much of a man. . . . When you're in a place like that, pulling time, it's hard, it's hard as hell to do. When you've got somebody over you and they're riding you all the time, like he did, everything you do is wrong, and he's hollering at you from daylight to dark and gives you all the rotten jobs, and things like that, it really makes it tough on you, see, when a guy's riding you on top of all this environment."

For its part, the reformatory had a different line. Harris and Superintendent Glattke flatly denied that Harris even knew either Daniels or West. The records showed that the pair had been assigned to the hog farm, while Harris was in charge of the horse barn. As far as that dispute was concerned, journalist John Bartlow Martin observed in *Break Down the Walls:* "People familiar with the reformatory point out, however, that overseers like Harris, in charge of a single department of the farm, sometimes 'borrow' inmates from one another without altering the official records. (Superintendent Glattke denies this is common.)"

Murl Daniels died in the electric chair on January 3, 1949.

Davis, Angela (1944–) political activist charged in prison escape plot

In 1972, Angela Davis was charged with kidnapping, murder, and conspiracy in connection with the highly publicized shoot-out at the Marin County Courthouse in San Rafael, California, in August 1970. Few political figures have been so enmeshed in a criminal case including prison escapes than the young black activist, a former acting assistant professor of philosophy at the University of California at Los Angeles.

However, before she was brought to trial, Davis fled and ended up on the FBI's list of the 10 most wanted fugitives.

Davis was born in Birmingham, Alabama, and took part in a number of civil-rights demonstrations with her mother when she was about 12. She graduated from Brandeis University, did postgraduate work in West Germany, and then enrolled in the University of California at San Diego in 1967, studying under Marxist philosopher Herbert Marcuse. As she became more radicalized in her beliefs, she took part in the activities of a number of militant black organizations including the Black Panthers. She also joined the Communist Party in 1968. The following year, she accepted an offer to teach four courses in philosophy at UCLA. Within a matter of months, she was fired after her membership in the Communist Party was revealed by an informer converted by the FBI. A court order returned her to her courses, which, by 1969–70, were described as among the most popular on campus. Obviously fearing some outside reaction to Davis, the school administration monitored her classes and described them as "excellent." However, the Board of Regents, of which Governor Ronald Reagan was a member, would not reappoint her.

The regents were most upset about Davis's speeches in support of the Soledad Brothers, a group of black prisoners who had formed a Marxist revolutionary group at Soledad Prison. Three of the Brothers—George Jackson, Fleeta Drumgo, and John Cluchette—were charged with murdering a white guard shortly after three other blacks involved in a fistfight had been shot dead by a tower guard. The local district attorney had labeled the killings justifiable homicide.

The Soledad Brothers' Defense Committee was formed to support the three prisoners, with Davis playing a principal role. She carried on a clandestine correspondence with George Jackson before she'd even met him. Finally, the charges against the trio were dismissed, but other ramifications in the case occurred.

Davis had received a number of threats against her life and legally obtained several guns for the defense of Soledad House, her base during the trio's trial. On August 7, 1970, Jackson's teenage brother Jonathan, Davis's constant companion during this time, took the guns Davis had bought and entered the Marin County Courthouse, where James McClain, a San Quentin inmate, was being tried for a prison stabbing. The younger Jackson sought to free McClain and two other inmates who were brought there to testify for the defense and, with them, to take white hostages who could be held as ransom for the release of the Soledad Brothers. Jackson passed guns to the three convicts and supervised the taking of five hostages

Black militant activist Angela Davis is seen in the offices of the New York Committee to Free Angela Davis on Fifth Avenue in New York City on April 3, 1973. (AP/Wide World Photos)

from the courthouse, among them Judge Harold Haley and D.A. Gary Thomas. In the parking lot, a gun battle broke out and Judge Haley, Jackson, and the two inmates were killed. Thomas was gravely wounded but survived, although permanently paralyzed.

Because the guns could be traced to Davis, she was indicted on murder, kidnapping, and conspiracy charges and became the object of a nationwide hunt. The FBI finally captured her in a New York City motel, and she was extradited back to California. Held without bail and declaring herself to be a black political prisoner, Davis said, "Prisoners—especially Blacks, Chicanos, and Puerto Ricans—are increasingly advancing the proposition that they are *political* prisoners. They contend they are largely the victims of an oppressive politico-economic order, swiftly becoming conscious of the causes underlying their victimization." (These generally are the sentiments that have radicalized many prisoners, giving wardens many problems with which to cope.)

Davis was held without bail. A worldwide Free Angela movement sprang up, and she was finally granted $102,000 bail. Her trial began on February 28, 1972, after a number of procedural delays.

Legal experts later were to comment that the prosecution's case was astonishingly weak. It was based largely on the premise that Davis's "passion for George Jackson"—who in the meantime had been killed the previous August while allegedly attempting to escape from prison—had led her to plot the courthouse kidnappings. The defense insisted there was no evidence at all linking Davis to the kidnapping or to the planning of it.

On June 4, 1972, a jury of 11 whites and one Mexican American took only 13 hours to clear Davis on all counts.

Davis, Katharine Bement (1860–1935) reformer penologist

Katharine Bement Davis was one of the most important penologists of the early 20th century, her work greatly advancing reforms in women's prisons. She suffered, as did most reformers of that period, in her belief in the principle of eugenics, which held that criminals commit crimes because of inferior "germ plasm," or genes, and, therefore, the best way to prevent more crimes was to prevent them from reproducing by keeping them behind bars or other means. Thus, sterilization gained in practice in a number of prisons.

In 1901, Davis at 41 became head of the new women's reformatory in New York State at Bedford Hills. There, research was carried out that seemed to justify the theory of eugenics that confining the "feeble-minded" for life under open-ended or indefinite sentences was the way to reduce time. A tireless promoter of the theory, Davis received huge research grants from wealthy individuals. In 1913, Davis left Bedford Hills, considered a great success, and took other corrections posts in New York City.

By 1925, however, the eugenics movement was on the wane as experts concluded that its germplasm theories were no more than pseudoscience. By the time Davis died in 1935, eugenics as a theory of crime control had been totally dismissed. However, Davis continued to hold respect for her innovative early efforts in penology and the search for a medical model for treatment of criminals. Because she also hired female researchers, she is regarded as one who opened the way for the nation's first women social scientists.

See also: EUGENICS; ROCKEFELLER, JOHN D., JR.

D.C. Blacks large ethnic prisoner group

Although it might be thought that the Aryan Brotherhood would constitute the most feared prison inmate group, the fact is that the so-called D.C. Blacks probably are deserving of that "accolade." Black inmates from Washington, D.C., are regarded by guards to be the most difficult to control. Many are in the federal prison system simply because there is a lack of sufficient confinement space in the nation's capital. Reflecting the population count in D.C., they are virtually all blacks. In some federal prisons, D.C. Blacks are the largest single ethnic group from any single city and, indeed, can make up as much as 10 percent of the overall prison population.

Well schooled in the use of violence, they are "locker-knockers," thieves who ransack the personal lockers of other prisoners, a crime that offers inmates no redress. More seriously, they are notorious for seeking out new inmates for sex, with all that entails—use of the victims bodies for limitless sex, farming them out for prostitution purposes, or selling the victims to the highest bidder.

Dead Man Walking critically acclaimed film

Some experts, such as Nicole Hahn Rafter and Debra L. Stanley, have admitted that a few decades ago, the film *Dead Man Walking,* as a Hollywood product, would hardly have been "considered suitable for serious students of the American prison. Yet it closely follows actual events in the life of a real person, Sister Helen Prejean, who befriended a rapist-killer on death row at the Louisiana State Penitentiary. Although the film fictionalizes actual events, it does not prettify them, and it offers an accurate, close-up view of death row to which most viewers would not otherwise have access."

By contrast no serious student would hold *The Shawshank Redemption,* based on a novel by Stephen King, while entertaining, as much of an accurate picture of prison life.

Dead Man Walking: An Eyewitness Account of the Death Penalty in the United States by Prejean, a Catholic nun, appeared in 1994 and was made into a Hollywood film in 1996 in which she is played by Susan Sarandon. Sister Helen became a spiritual adviser to death-row prisoners. She was involved in the prison system after brutal killer Matthew Poncelet (played by Sean Penn) wrote her a letter asking her to be his spiritual adviser. Sister Helen travels to the Angola prison to meet him on death row. At first, Poncelet insists he is innocent, that the rape-murder was the work of his partner in the crime. He claims that they had been drinking and drugging that night. There are numerous intense conversations between the pair as Sister Helen seeks to have the prisoner achieve some serenity as he accepts responsibility for his crime. As part of her new ministry, Sister Helen visits with the victims' parents to aid them in dealing with their anger and to invite their forgiveness.

On a personal level, the nun is a fervent foe of the death penalty, but in her work she herself has been forced to confront both sides of the issue. Very few films have ever struck such emotional highs, and it is left for each member of the audience to determine his or her own feelings about murder and the death penalty.

death penalty and George W. Bush called "World Champion Executioner"

"He is the world champion executioner." Those were the words for President-elect George W. Bush by Robert Badinter, the former French justice minister who ended capital punishment in France in 1981. "He is a horrible symbol of your mania for the death penalty."

There is little doubt that riding the wave of the popularity of the death penalty aided Bush in gaining and holding control of the Texas governorship. However, political observers did not see the position as any particular boon to Bush in his narrow electoral college win and loss of the popular vote in his battle with Al Gore in the 2000 presidential election. It certainly did not help him in his world status among the major Western industrial countries, all of whom now oppose the death penalty.

"What we know about the new president," said Claudia Roth, a member of the German Parliament, "is just two things. He is the son of President Bush, and he has sent 150 people to their death in Texas, including the mentally ill."

There was a view expressed that such opposition to Bush might actually over time be a plus for him in future political campaigns. However, there was also a growing recognition that the thrust of the Judeo-Christian beliefs, which now oppose the death penalty, has achieved unanimity in the Western democratic world, save for the United States (and Israel, where the penalty is still permitted for Holocaust war criminals, which time will eventually remove as an exception).

Political observers in Europe see the new U.S. president facing political fire for his identification with what is now regarded as a barbaric custom. Today, in the rest of the democratic world, capital punishment has been elevated to an abuse the equal of torture and genocide, all three of which have been banned by the European Convention on Human Rights. In 2000, concern about executions in the United States is of limited interest, but in Europe the coverage has become greater. Students stage noisy campus rallies denouncing Texas, and European politicians make regular journeys to the United States to meet with death-row inmates.

Chris Stalker of the British branch of Amnesty International said, "From a campaigning perspective, it's useful to have the most identifiable villain in the White House." He added, President Bush would "have a lot of trouble on this when he comes here" in the form of demonstrations.

Privately, German politicians worry that if the public in Europe goes into the streets on any Bush visit, they would be forced to raise the issue with the U.S. president. The impact, they worry, would gravely cripple cooperation between the United States and Europe.

Near inauguration time, a Bush spokesman insisted that Bush looked forward to working with European leaders despite the disagreement on capital punishment. He said, "Governor Bush believes that capital punishment ultimately saves lives and reduces crime." However, casting Bush's position that he "was sworn to uphold the laws of the state of Texas and he took his responsibility very seriously" does not play well in Europe, where people are simply "baffled" by the Bush position, which they feel runs counter to the United States's reputation of defending human rights around the world.

Former French justice minister Badinter notes, "I am regularly asked to speak about this at European universities. I wish you could see how perplexed they are, that the U.S. permits this barbarous deed."

In response to the drumbeat of criticism that precedes specific executions, especially those involving youthful or mentally deficient defendants, U.S. diplomats hand out an explanation about executions that are clearly defensive in tone. "The death penalty is an emotional and controversial subject. Public opinion polls have shown that 66 percent of the American public opinion support the death penalty. On the other hand, some major American organizations, such as the American Bar Association and the Texas Catholic Bishops, have called for a moratorium on its use on humanitarian and human rights grounds."

The deterrence argument falls on deaf ears. According to Owen Williams, a British death-penalty foe, there is no justification for the deterrence claim: "There are more homicides in Texas than in Britain. So where's the deterrent effect? And there is no social value in state-sponsored murder."

European attitudes on the U.S. death penalty may well harden as more and more cases of DNA findings free death-row inmates, and there is considerable skepticism to the claim made by Bush that Texas, the most prolific of the execution states by far, somehow makes no errors.

There is considerable speculation that Bush will curtail any visits to Europe for fear of the anti-U.S. demonstrations that would be equal to those against President Nixon in parts of the world. Thus, observers argue, the death penalty could eventually kill off the role of the United States as the moral and practical leader of the free world.

death penalty in southern states greater than elsewhere but with huge variations from one to another

It is well known that southern states are far more prone to exercise the death penalty than their northern neighbors. During the first 15 years after the U.S. Supreme Court reinstated the death penalty, 89 percent of the 140 executions carried out were in southern states, not surprisingly where the support for the death penalty is the strongest. But even in the South, the number of executions varies.

In a 1996 study, authors Richard E. Nisbett and Dov Cohen point to the discarded institution of slavery as the root of the death penalty and the way it was carried out in various states. They say that capital punishment, like slavery itself, is a system that "legitimized violence for the purpose of discipline, control and punishment" and, as such, was to be practiced much more readily than in nonslave states nationwide and in the South itself. According to the researchers, "It is possible that the practical demands on southerners of forcibly maintaining a slave and caste system created the institutions, procedures and actors capable of carrying out real violence." They contrast the situation between Virginia and North Carolina: The former was a state of large tobacco and cotton plantations that required slave labor, and North Carolina, while it also had plantations, nevertheless primarily raised tobacco in relatively small holdings, worked by the farmers and their families rather than slaves.

Under those circumstances, North Carolina's penchant for capital punishment was lessened compared to its neighbor to the north. This was not to say that North Carolina was not tough on crime and murder, but its courts were far more likely to allow hearings on new evidence, which, of course, resulted in a slower execution rate. Virginia courts, especially its supreme court, hardly ever granted retrials, even when there was an overwhelming view by outsiders that new evidence seemed more convincing. Virginia was viewed as determined to hold the line on established procedure and, it was charged, refused to admit court error because that might lessen public confidence in the quality of justice in the state.

As a result, many defense lawyers insist appeals for retrials are virtually always doomed to failure even if the cases would enjoy far better prospects in other state jurisdictions.

Death Row guide book to execution in the United States

This annual compendium of the condemned in the United States not surprisingly meets with a certain uneasiness for a number of readers and reviewers. The *New York Times Magazine* dubs it "GRIM READER," as it contains a roster of each person on death row and, at the same time, has a "Who

Was Who" section. The publication is *Death Row: The Encyclopedia of Capital Punishment.* There have been nine editions since 1989. It prides itself, in the words of the publisher, with supplying "bits of trivia and humor" that make it "fun to read without compromising its high standards." Clearly it is not in the vein of *Dead Man Walking.*

The current editor-publisher is Bonnie Bobit, who clearly brings strong opinions to her creation, noting, "I am tired of living in a country that allows killers to walk freely on the streets where 25,000 Americans are murdered each year. And, I am sickened when I learn that another 'first-offense' rapist or murderer is allowed to plea bargain to a lesser crime for a 10-year chip, which converts to a 'Get Out of Jail Free' card upon maturity in four-and-a-half-years."

Bobit has, according to the book's promotional material, earned a reputation as a "death row historian and as one of the country's leading authorities on capital punishment," and that to aid in her creation, she has "conducted original research, sometimes officiating victim and inmate mediations, and interviewed some of the nation's most dangerous criminals in our toughest prisons."

Reviewers are quite prepared to regard *Death Row* as a symbol of the development of U.S. culture. In the words of one, "Talk about your captive audience. *Death Row* is an annual book to end all annuals," and in a country with very fixed attitudes about the death penalty, Peter Bowes for BBC Radio One calls it "America's hottest new book, features all the States' death row inmates—mug shots and their spine chilling stories of murder and mayhem. It's the ultimate coffee table guide to the men and women heading for the execution chamber."

death row murder See PRISONIZATION.

Debs, Eugene V. (1855–1926) running for president from a prison cell

"Debs! Debs! Debs!" Eugene Debs was generally regarded as the greatest, most eloquent labor leader in U.S. history. In 1893, he had formed the first industrywide union, the American Railway Union, and became an eloquent spokesman for the labor movement. Whenever he appeared, crowds of immigrant railroaders cried his name over and over in adulation.

Eugene V. Debs (AP/Wide World Photos)

It was the type of reaction Debs received all his life. After doing time in Atlanta Penitentiary for opposing World War I as a pacifist and socialist, he was released in 1921. In what may have been the most amazing incident in that hard-as-nails prison, Warden J. E. Dyche allowed all 2,300 prisoners out of their cells to bid a final farewell to the stooped 65-year-old man. Walking out of the prison gate, there was a rousing ovation—and shouts of "Debs! Debs! Debs!" from the prison. Debs turned, tears coursing down his cheeks, and raised his hat and cane in a heartfelt goodbye.

Gene Debs was the most remarkable prisoner in U.S. history. Many hardened convicts, with not a shred of social consciousness, nevertheless regarded Debs as one of their own. That became evident after he had been arrested after making an antiwar speech in 1918, condemning the World War. Convicted under the Espionage Law, he was sentenced to 10 years. Debs told the judge: "Your honor, years ago I recognized my kinship with all living beings, and I made up my mind that I was not one bit better than the meanest of earth. I said then, I say now, that while there is a lower class, I am in it; while there is a criminal element, I am of it; while there is a soul in prison. I am not free."

When Debs was sent to Moundsville Prison in West Virginia, convicts, having heard of his statements in court, greeted him as a hero. Even the warden treated him with warm respect. Within two months, officials in Washington were so upset that they transferred Debs to the much tougher and meaner Atlanta Penitentiary. Once again, Debs was treated with the highest respect. As convict #9653, he shared a cell with five other prisoners, toward all of whom as well as others he showed perfect respect. Although he was a heavy smoker, Debs gave up his entire tobacco ration so that his fellow inmates had more. Cellmates and visitors all commented that he was a true martyr and likened him to another man in spirit and manner, Jesus Christ.

The longer he stayed behind bars, the more popular Debs became. Debs had run four times as Socialist candidate for president and saw no reason not to do so again in 1920 from behind bars. He was permitted to monitor the vote tallies on the phone in the warden's office. He received a remarkable 919,000 votes.

Well before the election, the White House had been besieged with petitions for clemency or pardon, but President Woodrow Wilson told members of his staff that he regarded Debs as a traitor and that he would never win a pardon from him. He never did. But incoming President Warren G. Harding did pardon Debs in 1921—with the proviso that he never run for president again. That was not much of a restriction because his prison term had weakened Debs terribly. The pardon had not dampened his views at all. He said, "It is the government that should ask me for a pardon."

After leaving the prison, Debs was squired to the White House for a visit with Harding and then returned home to Terre Haute, Indiana, for a rally before a huge and cheering crowd—"Debs! Debs! Debs!"

In failing health because of his imprisonment, Debs died in 1926, drawing eulogies from a wide political spectrum. The Socialist Party went into steady decline after his death, but Debs is still celebrated in activist circles and, it might be noted, among prison inmates as well.

Debs would have enjoyed the tribute paid to him in 1993 by Ray Luc Levasseur, a convict now doing 45 years in connection with bombing U.S. military contractors, the South African consulate, and General Electric offices, activities of which Debs would never have approved.

Levasseur wrote: "Remember Eugene Debs: He was one of the first socialists I ever read, before I moved on to the hardcore. I used to quote him in letters—'where there is a lower class I am of it, where there is a criminal element, I am in it, while there is a soul in prison, I am not free.' I don't know if he wrote this before or after his stint in Atlanta, but it always impressed me. Enough so I named a cat after him."

debtors, punishment of

In the Colonial period until the first decade of the 19th century, the most common crime in America was debt. More than 75,000 debtors a year went to prison for the offense. The practice of imprisoning debtors was an English custom readily imported into the colonies, and it also became common that such persons could be sold into service for periods of time to pay off debts. The amount of money owed by debtors had little to do with the jail sentence they served. A survey in one Pennsylvania penitentiary in 1829, after a number of reforms had already gone into effect, showed that almost 100 inmates were doing time for owing amounts of less than $1.

Still, it cannot be said that punishment of debtors came close to the level that had been the practice in England, where a bankrupt who sought to conceal some of his assets could be executed.

Many prominent Americans ran afoul of debtor laws. Alexander Macomb, a leading figure in a massive land fraud, went bankrupt and was imprisoned for debt. William Duer lost an apparent $2.5 million in speculations, setting off a financial panic, and was forced into jail by his creditors. John Pintard, secretary of New York's first insurance company and assistant commissary of prisoners in New York during the Revolution, was imprisoned. So was General Light Horse Harry Lee.

The most prominent person caught in the debtor net was Robert Morris, the "Financier of the American Revolution" and the richest man in the country. Not all observers give Morris quite that much credit. Nathan Miller in *The Founding Finaglers* offers up a contrary view that "The Revolution financed Robert Morris not the other way around." In any event, just a decade after the Revolution, Morris was drowning in personal debts. When some of his creditors would not forgive his indebtedness, he was lodged in the Walnut Street jail. His sons put up high rent so that after a while he was given a private room. Morris's family supplied him with considerable comforts, including a writing desk, books, maps, a copying press, a bed, furniture, and a looking glass. Morris was allowed to walk abroad at times and Morris's wife and daughter often visited him. In 1798, George Washington was in Philadelphia recruiting an army for a possible war against France, and he dropped in to see his old comrade and they dined in the Morris prison room.

Morris was fortunate to have served only roughly three and a half years, being released in 1801 under a new law regulating bankruptcy. Generally speaking, imprisonment for debt began to be eliminated during the early years of the 19th century following a backlash against the practice. By 1800, strong reform movements were active, and some state legislatures passed poor debtor and insolvency laws that provided liberal "prison limits" for debtors posting bonds that sometimes extended throughout an entire country. Yet, despite these improvements debtors still languished in prison.

It became clear to reformers that the only true cure was the absolute and total ban on jailing debtors, and laws were passed that totally banned imprisonment of debtors, or at least restricting the rules under which imprisonment was sought. In 1821, Kentucky became the first state to act, followed by New York a decade later. North Carolina, South Carolina, and Florida were the last to act, constitutionally forbidding imprisonment for simple debt in 1868.

"deep sixing" modern-day torture of prisoners

It may work slightly differently in various facilities, but the custom of "deep sixing" is best described by the methods employed at California's Corcoran Prison in the 1990s and apparently for many years earlier, with death a touch-and-go matter.

Roscoe Pondexter, a former six-feet-seven-inch player for the Boston Celtics professional basketball team, apparently found a greater appreciation for his skills as a brutal guard or "fish cop" at Corcoran. Pondexter turned state's evidence against other guards and described for the court his duties strangling inmates while his cohorts busied themselves crushing and yanking the victim's testicles. Pondexter was quoted in the *Los Angeles Times* as saying, "We called it Deep Six. It's like taking a dive underwater and not coming up. You give the prisoner only enough air to hear your message. . . . It wasn't in the manual. It wasn't part of the official training. It was grandfathered to me by my sergeant and the sergeant before him."

"As the body count mounted," as one account put it, "even Corcoran Warden George Smith had to acknowledge the barbarism." The warden had long denied any misbehavior on the part of his guards. He told the *Times:* "I'll admit that some of my staff have gone crazy."

Dennison, Stephen (1909–) "oversentenced" prisoner

One of the most bizarre "oversentencing" imprisonments—the term later given to the case—was that of Stephen Dennison, who was sent to a New York reformatory at age 16 for stealing a box of candy. Suffering brutal treatment in the institution, Dennison became regarded as a rebellious troublemaker. Transferred to state prison, and because of continuous minor infractions, he had years and years added to his sentence. Incredibly Dennison ended up doing 34 years for the crime of stealing a box of candy. Found "buried alive" in an underground solitary cell, he was finally released in 1959.

Dennison sued the state for compensation and after a seven-year struggle, the New York Court of Claims granted him $115,000. The court declared, "No amount of money could compensate Dennison for the injuries he suffered and the scars he bears." Dennison's award worked out to slightly more than $3,000 for each year he spent behind bars.

Dickens, Charles (1812–1870) studying prisons in the United States

In his *American Notes* (1842) English novelist Charles Dickens relates his study of the U.S. prison system. Like many other foreign visitors and religious figures, he was at first taken with the perfect order that seemed to pervade Pennsylvania's Eastern Prison, where prisoners were kept in isolated cells with no contact with others. As he walked the institution's awesome and quiet passages, Dickens was overwhelmed by the almost deathly silence, hearing only the occasional taps of a shoemaker's hammer by an inmate at work in his small cell or the hardly audible sounds of a weaver's shuttle.

Dickens talked to many of the prisoners and soon was overwhelmed by their loneliness. Dickens happened upon an inmate who apparently was allowed to keep rabbits in his cell. When the prisoner was allowed to leave his cell to talk to Dickens in sunlight, the author was struck by how pale and wan the man appeared. The prisoner was holding and stroking a white rabbit at his breast. To Dickens, the inmate's manner seemed to resemble that of a rabbit.

It was apparent to Dickens that his initial favorable reaction to Eastern was misplaced and that a strict and hopeless form of 24-hour-a-day solitary confinement was wrong and cruel. Dickens concluded that "this slow and daily tampering with the mysteries of the brain, to be immeasurably worse than any torture of the body, and because its ghastly signs and tokens are not so palpable to the eye and sense of touch as scars upon the flesh; because its wounds are not upon the surface, and it exhorts few cries that human ears can hear; therefore I the more denounce it, as a secret punishment which slumbering humanity is not roused up to stay."

Dickens was undoubtedly ill pleased by the results of his determination to right more of the inhumaneness he had found. Perhaps he was most disappointed that some of the horrors would later be passed over. He was particularly upset by an inmate who, in his 11th year in bitter isolation, had descended to the practice of peeling the skin from his fingers. Not much would change, and certainly not for the better, over the next century and half. A Harvard Medical School professor, Dr. Stuart Grassian, studied the effect of 23-hours-a-day confinement in the new "supermax" prisons and reported that some U.S. prisoners now were "even descending to the horror of eating parts of their own bodies."

Dillinger, John (1903–1934) sentencing scandal

Few experts on crime would deny that it was an unfair sentence at the age of 21 that started John Dillinger on the road to becoming Public Enemy No. 1. In 1924, Dillinger and an older man, Ed Singleton, attempted to hold up a grocer on a darkened street. Dillinger was armed with a .32 revolver in one hand and a bolt wrapped in a handkerchief in the other. Dillinger hit the grocer on the head with the bolt and when the grocer fought back, the gun went off but caused no damage. Singleton fled the scene, leaving Dillinger with an empty getaway car. In short order, both culprits were caught.

Dillinger was the first to be brought to court. He was assured by the local prosecutor that because he was a first offender, he would be treated lightly if he pleaded guilty. Dillinger did so and was shocked when he was sentenced to 10 to 20 years. Dillinger's partner in the crime, 10 years older, was brought before a different judge and drew a far shorter sentence and was freed in two years. Dillinger ended up doing nine years and came out of prison very embittered.

Back in his hometown of Mooresville, Indiana, he was quiet and amiable. Most people in town were sympathetic to Dillinger, believing that Singleton had masterminded the crime. Many wondered if Dillinger would avenge himself on Singleton, who, rumor had it, had built a special place in his house to hide from Dillinger and always carried a knife.

Dillinger had no time for such trivial pursuits; he was moving into big-time crime with advice given by more hardened criminals behind bars and the names of those to contact to engage in robberies to raise money to finance a breakout from prison by his closest pals. The Public Enemy legend was about to begin.

Gangster John Dillinger, center, strikes a pose. Dillinger is pictured awaiting trial for the murder of a police officer during an East Chicago bank robbery. (AP/Wide World Photos)

As Wayne Coy, a state official, said in 1934: "There does not seem to me to be any escape from the fact that the State of Indiana made John Dillinger what he is today. . . . Instead of reforming the prisoner, the penal institutions provided him with an education in crime."

divorce and inmates at nearly maximum levels
Surveys find that 85 percent of married men who go into prison end up being divorced by the time they leave, and that among the balance, some 50 percent will see their marriages collapse in the first year. There are many reasons for the high divorce rate while a man is a prisoner. Alienation is great as the spouses, generally both parties, become suspicious of the other. The prisoner feels it is inevitable that the wife is cheating on him. There is also the belief held by some inmates that prison guards are "hitting up" their wives after visiting hours. This is strictly forbidden, but it has happened. Additionally suspicions fester whenever the wife misses a visiting day. The fact that most prisons tend to be in more isolated areas makes it difficult and expensive for regular visits; above all, the wife feels the strain on the family budget because of this, and, with time, the resentment grows, enhancing the attitude that the prisoner has deserted her by going to prison.

Other pressures build up as the outside spouse becomes more aware of the extent of homosexual or lesbian activities that are rampant in most prisons. One convict has been quoted, "When a guy starts getting letters from his wife that ask, 'Are you being true to me?'—that's the whole ball game."

According to religious groups working with prisoners, the few marriages that manage to survive usually involve the inmate working in his incarceration, and no matter how small the pay is, it has a salutary effect if he is able to send some money home. "My monthly check indicated to us that I was still a participating member of the family."

The catch is that prison work at reasonable levels is extremely low paying and is subject to cancellation and interruption if the prison goes on lockdown (prisoners being restricted to the cells because of some general crackdown). Some wives see this cut of their stipend as the result of some squandering of money by the inmate for anything as innocuous as buying some candy bars to drugs.

It is clear, however, that when the strains are resisted by both spouses, the marriage can survive, and aid can be given to the released inmate in a family relationship that manages to cope. Unfortunately, such outcomes are quite rare.

Dix, Dorothea Lynde (1802–1887) prison reformer

In 1841 Dorothea Dix, a consumptive 39-year-old teacher, went to the East Cambridge, Massachusetts, House of Correction to teach Sunday school; she was shocked at what she found. In one cell there were two women, barely clothed and shivering. It was March, and jailers had tossed them into the otherwise empty cell without mattresses, furniture, or even a bucket for waste. At the time, temperatures in the area frequently fell below zero; yet, jailers saw no need to give the women blankets or clothing. In that period, it was a fairly common belief that the insane were immune to cold and pain, something not true of a dog or cat.

At first, Dix concentrated on the conditions of the mentally ill, but by the nature of her campaign, she addressed the matter of the treatment of all prisoners so that she eventually won the sobriquet of "angel of mercy" of prison reform.

It was not easy for Dix to begin her crusade: She had no political allies, did not come from an influential family, and, as a woman, was forbidden to address the Cambridge Court where such complaints had to be heard. She had to rely on a written plea, which she did. She also determined that she had to gain support of important community leaders. She begged two of the state's notables, educator Samuel Gridley and legislator Charles Sumner, to visit the prison. What they found enlisted them wholeheartedly in what became a far-ranging campaign.

As Dix traveled the country, wanted or not, she found that Massachusetts had neither the worst prison system nor the worst treatment for the insane or mentally ill. She uncovered cases of prisoners being tied to chairs, doused with ice water, leeched, beaten, and starved. It was not physically easy for Dix to do. She was extremely fragile, and she was traveling alone under dangerous conditions, but she pressed on. In her home state alone, she traveled more than 8,000 miles by steamboat, barge, carriage, and stagecoach to visit every jail, asylum, and hospital. She found a prisoner kept in a cage for 17 years and another chained to a fence for almost two decades, suffering gangrene that caused both his feet to be amputated. The reforms that followed in Massachusetts changed the prison landscape in the state. It hardly made the state's prisons places of joy, but the improvement was highly visible and won Dix many accolades.

Dix proved a terror in the rest of the country. When she found cruel treatment, she reported the administrators who were responsible to the authorities, to the courts, and to the newspapers, leading one observer to comment, "To have Miss Dix . . . find anything neglected or amiss, was considerably worse than an earthquake." In her wake, Dix always left reform and sweeping improvements.

Dix took a hiatus from her prison reform work when she was appointed superintendent of women nurses for the North during the Civil War. Immediately after the war, she resumed her prison reform campaign. Much in demand around the world, Dix traveled to Europe and visited many countries from England to Turkey, pushing her crusade to improve the lot of prisoners and especially of the mentally ill, who were flung behind bars as worthless criminals. In every country she visited, her initiative and perseverance produced much-needed reforms. She died in Trenton, New

Jersey, on July 17, 1887, at the age of 85, active to the end, stopping confinement horrors wherever she found them.

double celling overcrowding scandal

> *I know about the gray food. The four men in a cell. The odor of excrement that is overpowering on certain tiers. I know that every month there are areas where the gang control becomes so complete that the guards refuse to walk through for days.*
>
> —Scott Turow, *Presumed Innocent*

The practice is known to prison administrators as "double celling"—putting more than one inmate in a single cell to accommodate surplus. It is estimated that possibly as many as 60 percent of all federal and state prisoners share their cells with other inmates. Offhand, this may not seem to the casual observer to be a terrible imposition and that two prisoners per cell could be rather reasonable. In actual fact, many corrections officials will privately concede that double celling does more to guarantee that prisoners eventually returned to the outside world will become "better," more brutal criminals.

Double celling permits the most horrendous practices to occur in what objectively must be regarded as standard institutional policy. The courts have intervened in only the most egregious examples of double celling. In a famous Texas legal case, *Ruiz v. Estelle,* the federal court record states:

> *In March of 1977, a young inmate at the Clements unit was confined to a cell already occupied by two older inmates. For the following weeks, his predatory cellmates tortured and preyed upon the youth. A summary of some of the abuses they inflicted on him were as follows: . . . While bound with towels, he was forced to commit unnatural sex acts and endure blows from fists and a candy can. Still later, burning matches and a lighted cigarette were placed on his unprotected skin. Brandishing a broken glass, the predators threatened to kill him if he informed on them. . . . When he finally succeeded in reporting his pitiable situation to an officer and was rescued, it was discovered that he had sustained multiple bruises, contusions, multiple second degree burns, a swollen left ankle, and scalp lacerations. . . .*

However, even when such brutality does not result, the evils of double celling are nothing short of dehumanizing. The average cell consists of an open, unscreened toilet bowl (often minus the seat) so that fitted into a space next to the double beds one prisoner is frequently lying in the bed only inches from where his cellmate is defecating. As a former inmate puts it, "double celling guarantees guys will come out double the criminals than when they went in."

If prisons are viewed as crime factories, it can be argued that double celling is the key ingredient that perpetuates the system.

What has been called a moderate view of the problem has been offered by Sue Titus Reid in *Crime and Criminology:* "Double celling of inmates has been and should be looked at in the context in which it occurs. The Supreme Court approved double celling in *Rhodes v. Chapman,* involving a relatively new prison in Ohio. But the Court emphasized that in that prison, inmates were frequently out of their cells; the cells were reasonably large, well heated and ventilated, many with windows that could be opened, and noise and odors were not a problem. The Supreme Court has also upheld the double celling of jail inmates, but this does not mean that in some circumstances, where inmates are brutalizing one another, where space is inadequate, and where other problems are created by overcrowding, the Court would approve double celling."

Reformers who are opposed to double celling today insist that the practice is all the more troubling because of the explosive growth of illness caused by sexually transmitted diseases, including HIV and AIDS.

drowning torture a new wrinkle

"Water cures" of all sorts were long used in prisons against inmates, with the result that many died. These generally involved pouring torrents of freezing water on a person who had been suitably restrained, generally in a wooden barrel. However, as these methods came under constant attacks from reform and religious groups in the 19th century, brutal keepers switched to a more tame, or at least more exquisite, method. In this practice, the victim was still restrained and suffered a new form of water torture. The use of icy water was not needed (with all the evidence it might leave), and water was again poured over the prisoner, but now he had a wooden hopper placed around his neck. The water could be poured in just above his mouth and nose, so he suffered the agonies of near-drowning over and over again.

It was not until later in that century that this crowning cruelty seemed to be banned in most jurisdictions.

But all drowning torture techniques did not cease. Another form was discovered to be in use in California's Corcoran Prison, regarded by reformers to be one of the state's worst penitentiaries. Corrections officers were described as "deep-sixing" inmates whom they felt to be deserving of brutal punishments. According to whistle-blower testimony, while several guards busied themselves crushing an inmate's testicles as he lay in a vat of water, the deep sixer would, as one described it, go about strangling the inmate "like taking a dive underwater and not coming up. You give the prisoner only enough air to hear your message."

See also: "DEEP SIXING."

drug courts recent promising effort in rehabilitation

By the turn of the century, the concept of special drug courts seemed to have been an idea on the move. During the 1990s, there was growing frustration on many sides of the jamming of minor drug offenders into overcrowded prisons that obviously would be better served with more space and discipline for violent criminals. But the problem was actually more than who should be sent to prison; the problem with so many drug cases is that they were clogging the court systems as well.

A case in point was Dade County, Florida, where the saying was, in 1991, that minor drug violators were hanging from the rafters in the area's jails and prisons. Roughly two-thirds of the 9,000-plus drug arrests were for possession, not for manufacturing or dealing. Finally, a local Judge Herbert M. Klein stepped down from the bench for a year to attempt to solve the dilemma. One of the first conclusions he reached was there was a need to do more than attempt to find a way for prisons and jails to accommodate the flood of offenders. He determined that the key was on the demand side, to reduce the numbers seeking drugs.

The result was what became known as Miami's "Drug Court," backed by Judge Klein and others but most importantly included the then state attorney for Dade and future U.S. attorney general, Janet Reno. The official name was the Diversion and Treatment Program.

Basically, the program, aimed at users but not sellers and at those with no record of violent crime, gave the chance to enter into a structured program of long-term treatment rather than incarceration. If the offender successfully completed the program—which included a year or more of a combination of detoxification, counseling, education, vocational courses, fellowship meetings, acupuncture, urine tests, and regular court appearances to monitor his or her progress—he or she, could have the original charge dismissed and the record sealed.

Moneywise, the cost of the entire program for a single offender was estimated to equal the cost of incarcerating him or her for nine days. Far more important than the money saved was the fact that in most cases it would be the first and last brush with the law with most participants. The usual repeater rate for such offenders was about 60 percent. For Drug Court graduates, it was about 11 percent. After a few years, that rate did more than double to about 20 to 23 percent for graduates to be rearrested, but this was caused by the expansion of the program to cover many hard-core criminals. But that rate was still phenomenal when compared to what happened to the average criminal.

During the first few years, the same program in Boston did not have a single participant retrogress, but no one expected that it could hold there. It proved to be a resounding success.

In Dade County's drug court, Judge Stanley Goldstein, who presided there from day one, was not sure that it would work or that there could be any way to straighten out crack users. He was quoted in the ABA journal as thinking, "There was no way we were going to get people off crack cocaine. I saw people who had come out of the sewers so addicted to cocaine they would sell their firstborn." But after seeing people returning from treatment, he said, "They were starting to come back to me clean, wearing decent clothes, with a job and clean urine drops. I was more shocked than anyone. We had taken in trash and turned out human beings." Within the first few years, more than 25 jurisdictions around the country had picked up the drug-court idea, and it continued to grow thereafter.

In *The Tough-on-Crime Myth,* Peter T. Elikann, J.D., the author, finds the rearrest rates as inspiring. "It's very tough, much cheaper than jail, and then gives them the education, and job training to get to work and get on the tax rolls. It's exciting and operates as living testimony against the viewpoint that would spend a fortune to 'lock-'em-up' for a long period of time with hardened violent criminals and then released them unskilled and unequipped so that they might prey on the public. That's the logic of rehabilitation."

Drug Treatment Alternative to Prison (DTAP)

The Drug Treatment Alternative to Prison program (DTAP) represented the first attempt at a prosecution-run program in the nation to shift prison-bound felony drug offenders to residential drug treatment. DTAP concentrates on drug-addicted individuals, arrested for felony drug offenses, who have prior convictions only for nonviolent felonies. DTAP is a long-term 15- to 24-month residential therapeutic program as an alternate to prosecution and incarceration. If the offender completes his or her program successfully, criminal charges are dismissed. They are then provided with assistance to locate housing and jobs. If the offender fails to complete the program, he or she is returned to court and prosecuted on the original charges. (Address: Brooklyn Municipal Building, 210 Joralemon Street, Room 407, Brooklyn, N.Y., 11201; Telephone: [718] 250-2231.)

drunks, confinement of arrests of one-third of all persons

Easily, something in excess of 1 million persons are arrested annually in the United States for public drunkenness. As a result, somewhere between 25 to 40 percent of people in jail today are there for public inebriation. Even in those states where public intoxication has been decriminalized, arrests are simply made for disturbing the peace, loitering, or disorderly conduct. The costs of arresting, booking, jailing, and trying public inebriates are in the hundreds of millions annually; in one year during which a count was made, the figure was put at $300 million.

Such arrests and confinement represent a major drain on the scanty resources available to financially pressed and very overcrowded jails. Arrestees are put in cells that cost anywhere from $25,000 to $60,000 to build and another $7,000 to $26,000 or so annually to maintain. Many inebriates have been arrested hundreds of times on the main charge or various offshoots. The great majority are in vital need of rehabilitation and health services. A study has indicated that 85 percent of those who commit suicide in jail were intoxicated at the time, and more than 50 percent of these kill themselves during the first 12 hours of confinement.

A study of 3,000 inebriates in New York State showed that 20 percent had bone fractures; 50 percent had wounds, burns, or cuts; 20 percent had hallucinations; 20 percent suffered from severe brain damage; 20 percent had severe gastrointestinal bleeding; 25 percent had indications of seizure disorder; and 15 percent had cardiopulmonary problems—these singly or in combinations.

It is hardly surprising that the National Coalition for Jail Reform can issue a report saying, "The Public Inebriate: Jail Is Not the Answer." Because society is much more interested in filling up jails and prisons in general, there is very little money left over for treating inebriates. Thus they are dumped into the same jail institutions and weigh down the efforts and money being extended to deal with the crime problem—clearly a counterproductive situation.

Dry Tortugas 19th-century federal hellhole prison

Dozens of 19th-century state prisons deserved to be called "hellholes." The federal government, too, had one of that type that towered over any others in its domain: Fort Jefferson, situated on a Florida coral reef in the Dry Tortugas. Built in 1846, its name was a total misnomer, and as a fort, it was useless. The waters around it turned out to be too shallow for enemy ships ever to sail within cannon shot.

An embarrassed U.S. government finally gave up on its military use, and it was converted into a prison, unofficially known as Dry Tortugas Prison. Nature cooperated in making it a hellhole. Although it was torturously hot, plagued by swarms of mosquitoes, and riddled with yellow fever, at the time, no connection was made between the illness and the annoying insects. The prison was hit with periodic epidemics during which men often died faster than they could be buried.

Everyone suffered there—the prisoners, the guards, the soldiers still stationed there, the officials. The guards were exceptionally brutal to the prisoners, a behavior probably, in part, attributed to their own sufferings.

It was no secret that the government decided to reserve Dry Tortugas for their worst prisoners, those deserving of "special treatment." One such prisoner was Dr. Samuel Mudd, a Maryland physician who set the leg of John Wilkes Booth during the latter's flight from Washington after shooting Abraham Lincoln. Although Mudd had no connection with the assassination, as was proven years later, the hysteria of the day led to his conviction in the conspiracy. He was sentenced to life and sent to Dry Tortugas, where he was subjected to endless torture by the guards. Under orders from superiors, the guards kept Mudd chained to the floor of his cell and abused him regularly.

A particularly deadly outbreak of yellow fever in 1867 truly ravished the prison. Michael O'Laughlin, another of the convicted Lincoln assassination conspirators, died, and all the army surgeons perished as well. Dr. Mudd surprised officials by offering to treat the prisoners, soldiers, and guards through the epidemic. He did so, even though he contracted the disease himself. After the epidemic ended, grateful administrators did not return Mudd to his chains.

Because of his humanitarian efforts and a four-year campaign by his wife, Dr. Mudd was released from his life sentence in 1869 and returned to Maryland. Because of the publicity about conditions in the Dry Tortugas hellhole, the prison was abandoned in the early 1870s. In 1934, the prison became a national monument.

Throughout the 20th century, efforts were made to obtain a complete pardon for Dr. Mudd, whose claims of complete innocence had long before been totally accepted. In 1979, President Jimmy Carter notified Dr. Richard Mudd, grandson of Dr. Mudd, that he firmly agreed that his grandfather had been unjustly convicted. The president regretted that the military commission's guilty verdict was not one that could be set aside by presidential action.

Duffy, Clinton T. (1898–1982) rehabilitation warden of San Quentin

Cut of the same cloth as Warden Lewis E. Lawes of Sing Sing, Clinton Duffy was in the mid-20th century regarded as one of the leading prison-warden reformers of the era. He was outspoken in his views that rehabilitation rather than punishment for criminals was the correct and only successful prison philosophy. California turned to him in desperation in 1949 to reform San Quentin Prison after its long history of chaos, scandal, and collapse. Through the 1930s and 1940s especially, San Quentin was regarded as one of the worst penal institutions in the entire nation. It had built on its previously unsavory past as the site of numerous riots, hunger strikes, and escape attempts, all problems readily ascribed to gross mismanagement and an inability to do anything other than "contain" the inmates, with alarming ineffectiveness.

In 1949, California fired the warden and the entire San Quentin board. Named as a temporary warden for 30 days, Duffy became at the time the youngest warden ever of a major prison in the United States.

Duffy had grown up in the very shadow of San Quentin, the son of a prison guard at the maximum-security prison. He started at San Quentin as a clerk, and studying the prison from the inside, he became convinced that the facility was doomed to becoming a monument of social decay unless basic American ideals could be instituted to provide certain worthy criminals a second chance.

Duffy had already formulated many of his plans in his mind and thus could move swiftly. He ended the practice of corporal punishment, in which San Quentin had for decades been a leading practitioner. In place of such punishment,

Duffy set in place a system of privileges and revocation of privileges—the inmates were said to have certain privileges but could lose them for misbehavior. He also allowed the establishment of a prison radio station and instituted a night school for inmates. At the time, most California prison administrators were firm believers in the "Auburn system" in use in most prisons for well more than a century and for a firm punitive approach. These elements criticized Duffy as soft and warned that the inmates would grab control of the prison in the face of such weakness. But the success of Duffy's methods soon transformed him from a "30-day wonder" to a warden with a 12-year tenure. Contrary to his critics' warnings, no prisoners escaped or even attempted to escape. San Quentin was no longer a no-man's land, and Duffy thought nothing of walking alone through any part of the prison with no worry about his personal well being.

It was a striking example of how a very bad prison had the potential for humaneness if rationally managed.

After Duffy left his position, he continued to have a major influence on penal matters, especially on the death penalty. Duffy as much as any one person led to the abolishment of hanging as an execution method in California (as well as in other states).

Duffy did not grant the hanging proponents' argument that most such executions could be very clean jobs. In his capacity at San Quentin, he witnessed 60 hangings and described most of them as "dirty" jobs in which the victim's suffering lasted much longer than a few minutes of thrashing. Duffy described a dirty hanging as one in which the condemned man would strangle to death slowly, a vile process that could take as long as a quarter-hour. The dying inmate's wheezing would be extremely loud and indescribable, except to someone who has heard the hysterical squealing of a dying pig. The victim might even bob up and down on the rope like a yo-yo as he or she fought for air. Sometimes the inmate's legs, even when bound together, would whip far out in search of a perch. It might become necessary for a guard to seize the victim's legs and hold them steady so that the violent churnings did not break the rope, a development that might sicken the witnesses. When death would finally come, it might be difficult to determine for whom the agony had been worse, the condemned or the witnesses.

Sometimes, the killing was even messier. A poorly placed knot occasionally gouged out a chunk of the face and head, and witnesses saw this gory mess drop to the floor.

Eventually hanging was replaced by the gas chamber as the proscribed method of execution, and that did not please Duffy. To the rest of his days, he viewed executions as a demeaning process for all, including the state.

Dwight, Louis (?–1854) prison reformer

Louis Dwight first intended to join the ministry, but an accident damaged his lungs and he was forced to do something other than sermonizing. He toured the countryside distributing Bibles to prison inmates and was appalled at the conditions he found. He discovered that convicted criminals and the most innocent of persons were treated with horrific callousness.

He visited the District of Columbia jail and found three women and three mulatto brothers and their sister, ranging from age 4 to 12 lying in filth on the floor, with no bedding, and unable to wash themselves. Two white women were wrapped in blankets, but the rest were not so lucky. Ironically, the children were confined, in an act of Christian charity, to keep them from falling into the hands of slave traders. Their white father was dead, and his wife—the children's mother—was unable to care for them. Their father's last will gave the children their freedom, but his executor moved to sell them to clear his debts. The local marshal committed the children to prison to keep them from bondage. After that, the children's plight was ignored. The girl was ill and lay surrounded by her brothers. Dwight was unable to do anything about their plight but determined to immerse himself in prison reform and in the battles of the philosophies behind competing correction theories. In his early 20s, Dwight became an ardent opponent of the so-called Pennsylvania system, most notably as practiced at the Eastern State Penitentiary in Philadelphia. Inmates were held in separate cells and allowed no group activities from the day they arrived until they were released. The problem was, Dwight pointed out, that such a system led to high rates of insanity.

Dwight came out in support of the Auburn system used in that New York prison. Prisoners were separated in their cells, but they congregated during the day in factorylike workshops with total silence required at those times. At the age of 32, Dwight headed the Boston Prison Discipline Society in 1825 and was in the forefront in battles about the two prison systems. Indeed, Dwight deserved credit for carrying much of the campaign for Auburn, and whenever he heard of a new prison planned in any state, he packed up his graphs and charts and headed to influence the adoption of a prison system.

Dwight can be credited with having carried the case of the Auburn system to eventual triumph. What he had going for him was the not insignificant fact that the Auburn system was cheaper: The cells could be smaller because the convicts were not housed there 24 hours a day, and cheaper construction was possible because cells could be built upward more easily than in the Pennsylvania system. Undoubtedly, the cheaper costs influenced many jurisdictions.

It might be a slight overstatement to dub Dwight as the "father of the rule of silence," but that silence won support from many quarters. Many regarded Auburn as a shining example of what could be accomplished by proper discipline and design. Visitors who witnessed the operation of the dining hall in which 635 inmates were served were astonished how little noise and confusion occurred. One clergyman wrote, "The whole establishment, from the gate to the sewer, is a specimen of neatness. The unremitted industry, the entire subordination and subdued feelings of the convicts, have probably no parallel among an equal number of criminals." Dwight himself considered it a "noble institution" and "worthy of the world's imitation."

Although in time the silence rule would lose adherents, Dwight's works aided that system to continue well into the 20th century. Dwight was so committed to the virtues of silence that he advocated that it be adopted in schools as well as prisons. He worked tirelessly for his beliefs until his death in 1854.

E

electric chair execution method on its last legs
There was considerable tension in 1979 when John Spenkelink, a 30-year-old murderer, was slated to become the first person in 15 years to die in Florida's electric chair after the Supreme Court reapproved the death penalty. What if "Old Sparky," as the chair was affectionately known, at least in some circles, was not up to snuff after such a long layoff?

As it turned out, there was no cause for worry on the mechanical operation of Old Sparky. It worked like a charm. The same, however, could not be said for its operators. The death house guards had a dreadful time coercing Spenkelink to cooperate. A Venetian blind was dropped over the window through which witnesses were expected to watch Spenkelink being brought in and strapped in the chair. Instead, Spenkelink put up a strenuous fight for his life even before appearing in the execution chamber.

As a result, when the blind was finally opened, the doomed man was already strapped down with a gag in his mouth. It was not something that should have happened under death-house ritual. Death-house guards are supposed to know how to handle a condemned man and to coax him into being cooperative. However, the guards themselves were out of practice, and Spenkelink's action had been so ferocious that it was deemed best to spare the witnesses such distraction; after all, the electrocution itself was to be the show.

As already noted, that part of the operation went without fault. After that, however, Old Sparky's performance failed to win many more plaudits, and, as will be noted later, the electric chair eventually went to the scrap heap itself.

Well more than 1,000 men and women have gone to the "hot seat" since it was adopted in 1890, with many ghoulish and macabre attached incidents. In 1926, in Florida, a condemned man named Jim Williams sat in the chair waiting for death when an argument broke out between Warden John S. Blitch and Sheriff R. J. Hancock, each of whom argued that it was up to the other to throw the switch. After 20 minutes, poor Williams collapsed. He was carried back to his cell, and the dispute was transferred to the courts. Eventually, the decision was that the sheriff had to do the chore, but by that time the Board of Pardons decided that Williams had suffered more than a death sentence already, so the death sentence was commuted to life imprisonment.

During World War II, two convicted murderers were under death sentence when the state switched to electrocution from hanging. The War Production Board decreed, however, that the materials required for the chair could be better used against the country's military enemies and would not grant a Priority. No chair, no executions.

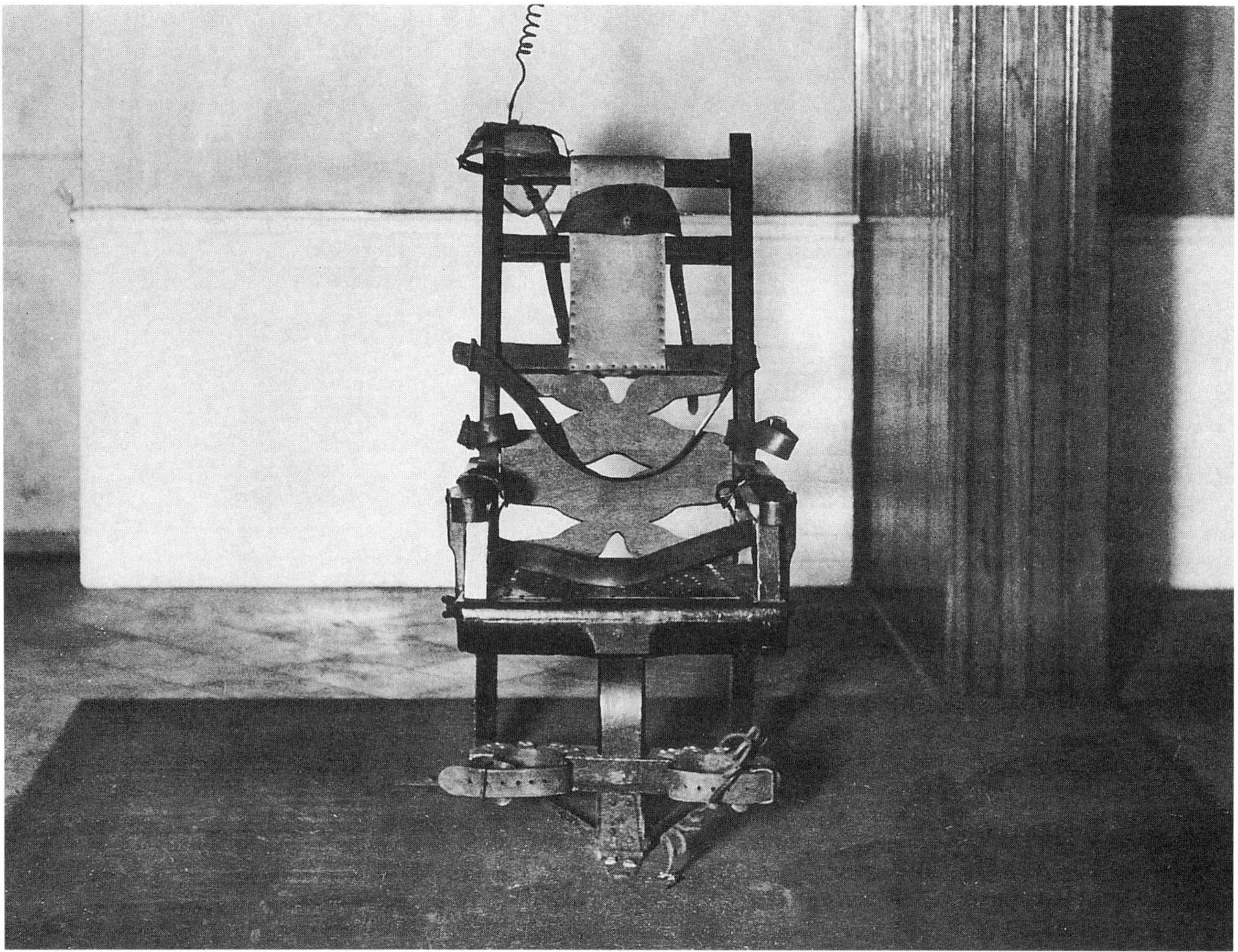

Early electric chair. The older versions worked as well or as badly as the later models. (Author's collection)

The usual electric chair has two legs in back and a heavier single leg in front, all bolted to the floor to keep the chair itself from "dancing" when the power is initiated. Extrawide arms are fitted with straps to hold the arms of the condemned rigid; other straps go around his chest and abdomen. The wiring around the chair is covered with rubber matting.

Actually, the chair is a simple contraption, as indicated by the fact that some southern states have brought mobile or portable chairs into the courtroom where the sentence had been pronounced. It turns out that worry about the chair dancing may have been eliminated if some simple procedures were followed.

In Mississippi, the chair was carted around in a van with its own generators and controls. A power line led from the truck's generator into the packed courtroom. When a newsman once asked Sen. Theodore G. Bilbo if the practice was any different from lynching, he responded, "Ah, this is pretty tame compared to a lynching."

A good execution involves a three-minute drill, with the prisoner strapped into the chair quickly. Inexperienced guards practice with the straps in advance to avoid fumbling delays. This so-called humane character of electrocution is not actually aimed at the victim, but to spare the feelings of the witnesses. A tight mask placed over the prisoner's face is intended to hide the facial distortions when the "juice" is turned on. The mask must be especially tightened around the eyes to keep them from popping out from their sockets.

There are two popular myths about the execution chamber that almost never happen: No time is permitted for long good-byes or last statements, although a famous gangster of the 1930s did manage to call out, "Give my love to mother"; also, the lights never dim in the rest of the prison because the chair is always powered by a separate source. Hollywood prefers the light-dimming routine because it allows the scriptwriter the chance to stage a prisoner protest or to achieve special dramatic effect.

Once the executioner is sure that everyone is clear of the chair, a switch is thrown, and the raging current pitches the victim against the bindings with terrible force. His or her hair stands up, and his or her flesh turns beet red. The executioner tries to time it so that the switch is flipped when the prisoner's lungs are empty or there will be a gurgling noise as air is forced from the lungs by the shock of the current. The first jolt, executioners have learned by trial and error, should be 2,000 volts or slightly more, after which it is cut back to 1,000 volts to prevent what witnesses might take as unseemly burning of the body. Once again, emphasis is on preventing the witnesses from suffering an undue dismay.

At this stage, the victim may very well pass waste. The tradition of a last hearty meal for the condemned is not what the executioner ordered. Almost certainly, mouth foam will seep out from under the hood. Often, the electrical jolt may be repeated to make sure the victim is dead. When Arthur Lee Grimes was executed in Alabama in 1954, the doctor found his heart still beating. The doctor stepped back and waited for it to stop, but instead of expiring, Grimes started to shudder violently and thrash against the straps. He started to regain consciousness, gasping and sucking for air. It took seven full minutes of juice in six massive jolts in all to guarantee that Grimes was truly dead.

If proponents of electrocution are embarrassed by the Grimes execution, they were even more so after the first electrocution in 1890 of William Kemmler, an illiterate Buffalo, New York, huckster who took an ax to his mistress, Tillie Ziegler.

In the 1880s, a New York State legislative commission was established to decide if hanging should be abolished. After viewing a number of hangings, including that of a woman who slowly strangled to death, the members were determined to eliminate the use of the noose. It is doubtful that the committee would have come up with the idea of the electric chair but for a monumental battle building up over business profits.

On death row, Kemmler became a minor pawn in a gigantic economic battle between two industrial greats, Thomas Edison and George Westinghouse, fighting for control of the budding electric-power industry. Edison developed the first electric power system through the use of low-tension direct current (DC). Westinghouse then devised his alternating current (AC) system, which was much superior because it was easier and less costly to install. Edison sought to discourage the use of AC by pointing out its death-dealing potential. It was all he could do because he was dealing with an opposing product that was far superior. Edison decided to send a young engineer named Harold P. Brown around the country to astonish people by electrocuting stray dogs and cats—and even horses. When Brown took his show to Albany, the special commission wondered if he could kill an orangutan. Brown obliged. The unlucky orangutan caught fire, but that did not worry the commission for coming up with the idea for an electric chair. After all, a human being wasn't covered with hair and so was not likely to catch fire. The unit voted for an electric chair using AC.

Westinghouse was appalled, realizing the use of his system for executions was not great public relations and could hurt acceptance of the system by the public. He hired top legal talent, including Bourke Cochran, then regarded the leading lawyer in the country, and spent much more than $100,000 in a losing effort to save Kemmler from the chair. (Since that time, pro-Westinghouse supporters have denied that Westinghouse was involved in the Kemmler defense, but most observers have not taken that claim very seriously.)

While Cochran appealed the case for Kemmler to the Supreme Court, seeking a ruling that the punishment would be unconstitutional, Edward F. Davis, the electrician at Auburn Prison, started to build the chair in the institution's woodworking shop. Although authorities tried to keep the work a secret, newspapers presented diagrams that closely resembled what the real chair looked like. The papers also hastened to inform their apprehensive readers that the contraption "was not at all uncomfortable to sit in."

After the High Court ruled against Kemmler, his execution went forward on August 6, 1890. As one observer later put it, "His manner indicated a state of subdued elation, as if he were gratified at being the central figure of the occasion."

But the execution was horribly botched. A first jolt of 17 seconds failed to kill him and shocked doctors watched Kemmler's breast heave and his heart resume beating. Panic ensued in the execution chamber, and finally the current was turned on again for another 70 seconds at 1,300 volts. Some of the witnesses fainted, and another retched and bolted from the room. Finally, William Kemmler was dead. Unfortunately, the flesh on Kemmler's back was badly burned, and his muscles were carbonized. When his body was autopsied, a witness described his flesh as well-cooked beef. Quite naturally, newspapers reported Kemmler had been "ROASTED ALIVE!" The *Buffalo Express* predicted in an editorial that "Kemmler will be the last man executed in such a manner." It was not a very accurate prediction.

Despite worldwide protests of the tortures involved in the new extermination method, the electric chair was here to stay. In time, executioners learned to perfect the technique—at least to some extent. They watched the condemned man's hands. When they turned pink, other parts of the body, nearer to the source of the electrical charge, are far darker and closer to being burned. Unfortunately, in later years "overburning" still occurred.

Sadly, the public seemed to find something fascinating about botched jobs; thus, when the first electrocutions of four murderers took place at Sing Sing in 1891, the roads in Ossining near the prison were jammed with tourists and sightseers hoping to be present when something went wrong. However, the chair worked four times without a problem. Then in 1903, three brothers were executed, and one of them, Fred Van Wormer, started to move in the autopsy room. A rush call brought executioner Robert P. Elliott back to the prison. By the time he arrived, Van Wormer had expired, but it was decided to be prudent and the dead man was hauled back to the chair and given another 1,700 volts.

There were often intriguing suggestions of survival after death. When murderer Ruth Snyder was executed along with her lover Judd Gray for the murder of her husband, her lawyer sought a court order to prevent the performance of an autopsy on her body, a legal requirement to determine the cause of death. The lawyer planned to revive her with adrenalin. The plan never went through when the court rejected the move. A number of condemned persons have swallowed all types of metal objects under the belief that somehow this would cause the electric chair to "short." In the 1950s, a prisoner named Donald Snyder entered his Sing Sing death cell weighing 150 pounds and soon started to eat and eat and eat. Snyder had come up with the bizarre idea of being too fat to fit into the chair. Weightwise, he performed wonders, eventually raising his bulk to more than 300 pounds. When they asked him what he wanted for the traditional last meal, he replied enthusiastically, "Pork chops, eggs and plenty of 'em!" He spent his last few hours speculating with a guard on how the newspapers would go wild when it turned out that he couldn't be executed.

A New York City tabloid wrote finis to the plot: "The hot seat fitted him as though it had been made to order."

Despite all the contrary evidence that indicated botched executions, burnings, gasping for air, and continuing heartbeats, there are those who insist that electrocution is immediate and painless. They could cite the case of Harry Roberts, a New York killer who informed the prison doctor as he was strapped into the chair: "Doc, my last act is going to be for science. We'll see how fast this juice really works. The moment I feel it, I'll wiggle this finger." It did not wiggle.

A more-or-less authoritative source, depending on one's viewpoint, would be Dr. Harold W. Kipp, who, as chief medical officer of Sing Sing, attended more that 200 executions. Dr. Kipp said: "The effect of electricity is instantaneous brain death. What observers see are muscle contractions, not agony."

As not all medical authorities agreed with this enthusiasm for electrocution, the hunt went on for a more humane method of killing. They apparently found it in the gas chamber, and during the 1920s and 1930s, it was touted as truly superior to electrocution and hanging.

By the late 1990s, only four states still required death by electrocution—Florida, Alabama, Georgia, and Nebraska. Two others, Kentucky and

Tennessee, switched to offering condemned men a choice of execution, electrocution or lethal injection.

In recent years, protests against the electric chair centered mainly on Florida, where the chair continued to produce botched efforts from time to time. In a 1967 incident, flames and smoke arose from Pedro Medina's head when the electric current was turned on. The cause was attributed to the sponges in the chair's headpiece. Although an autopsy report insisted that Medina had died instantly and suffered no pain from the fire, a one-year moratorium was ordered on executions. By a 4-3 vote, the Florida Supreme Court ruled that electric-chair executions, even in the Medina case, did not violate the ban on cruel and unusual punishment. (It was the same finding the courts made in hanging cases, when there was slow strangulation or even having their heads ripped off when the body was dropped.)

In the 1990s, flames shot out of masks, and the smell of burned flesh filled the witness rooms in more Florida executions. Similar malfunctions had occurred in other states. The next botched-up killing involved Allen Lee Davis, whose blood seeped through his shirt and the buckle holes of the chest strap. Bloody photographs of Davis were posted on the Internet and were to be studied in a U.S. Supreme Court review to determine if electrocution was a violation of the Constitution. It was said that there was an excellent chance the High Court would rule against electrocutions after so many viewers had seen what had happened.

These horrid examples of a malfunctioning chair led to further claims that the state of Florida was incapable of carrying out executions competently and that the Supreme Court was set to review the state's record. The Jeb Bush administration at first sought to give condemned men the right to choose between the electric chair and lethal injection, but by that time, the state legislature had decided that Florida had suffered enough in the controversy, and the senate voted unanimously and the house by 102 to 5 to get rid of the chair once and for all.

electric shock punishment instead of prison controversial alternative

Although the idea had not gotten that far, there was an effort during the last two decades to restore corporal punishment rather than imprisonment as a method of punishment for offenders. It soon became apparent that it was not likely that old-fashioned methods such as the whipping post would fly for long because, inevitably, there would be cases of resultant permanent physical damage.

In the 1980s, the idea of the use of electric shock as a feasible method of corporal punishment came to the fore. In 1983, Graeme Newman, a leading authority on punishment, expounded the view in his book, *Just and Painful: A Case for the Corporal Punishment of Criminals,* calling for the use of electric shock as a general punishment. According to Newman, the technique inflicts punishment only where it belongs—on the offender rather than on his family, who, of course, suffers immensely when he goes to prison.

Under Newman's thesis, all offenders would receive the same penalty for the same crime, and no added penalty would be applied because of previous crimes. Thus, says Newman, this would make the punishment fit the crime, not the criminal, as the punishment would work on the offender's body, not on his mind.

As an added fillip, Newman offers such benefits as sparing the public the expense of incarceration as well as the costs of families being forced onto welfare.

Quite obviously, opponents of the idea cite a number of objections, not the least of which is that the use of electric shock in unauthorized ways that would promote brutality and torture, ranging from such "mild" uses as cattle prods that were used on civil-rights protesters to the more vicious ones like the infamous "Tucker telephone." The latter came to public exposure during the probes of the conditions at Arkansas's Cummings and Tucker prison farms in the late 1960s. While all sorts of charges were made and perhaps only partially verified, the investigation established the existence of a particularly awesome torture device used in the institutions. It consisted of a telephone, a heavy-duty battery, and the necessary wiring. An inmate would be stripped, and one end of the wire would be fastened to his ankle or wrist and the other end to his penis. The electric shocks sent through his body caused awesome agony until he lost consciousness. Although such devices were known to be used against dissidents in a number of Latin American countries, the only official authority known to use them as a matter of routine was SAVAK, the Iranian secret police before the overthrow of the shah.

Civil libertarians have argued that the availability of electric-shock techniques in prisons would lead quickly to routine overuse. In the last two decades, the punishment failed to attract too many proponents, even in an era when the public has demanded sterner treatment of law violators.

electronic monitoring (EM) arguments on its value

Electronic monitoring (EM) all started in 1979 when a judge in New Mexico noted a comic strip in which Kingpin, the underworld archenemy of superhero Spiderman, took advantage over Spiderman by slipping him an electronic bracelet. The judge contacted a number of computer companies asking them to replicate the comic-strip plot in some fashion. In 1985, a former Honeywell executive came up with a device that soon matured into a successful industry.

First-time offenders and nonviolent criminals are sometimes given an electronic home-monitoring device in the form of an ankle bracelet that monitors the convicted person's whereabouts and keeps him or her out of prison for the entire sentence length. There have been a number of success stories reported. As a part of some probation terms, the ankle bracelet cuts down on the number of in-person checks on the defendant. The monitor sends signals that will indicate when contact is broken. If the offender leaves without authorization, the signal is broken and he or she is considered to be a violator. Not following any of the rules on probation can put the violator behind bars.

A telephone is used to link the bracelet into a computer so that if the offender strays too far, generally about 150 feet, a message is sent to the police. On the other hand, the monitors can be adjusted so that a prisoner can go to work; the monitor can also be programmed to distinguish between traveling to work and attempting to escape and even to detect the use of drugs or alcohol. In one setup, a parole board keeps tabs on parolees with EM. A computer memorized the sound of the parolee naming 22 different states. The parolee is called at various hours and is requested to state a new combination of eight of these states. If the computer does not recognize the voice answering, the parole board is notified.

EM manufacturers eagerly offer success stories, but critics find the claims less than convincing. Writing in *Justice Quarterly*, published by the Academy of Criminal Justice Sciences, researchers Ronald Corbett and Gary T. Marx claim that growing acceptance of EM is based on a persistence of various "technofallacies" that are false beliefs of technological solutions for social problems. They say law-enforcement agencies are receptive to EM despite evidence of its failings, which include breakdowns caused by environmental conditions and by computer, power, and telephone failures. Corbett, deputy commissioner of the Massachusetts Department of Probation, and Marx, a sociology professor at the University of Colorado, say that it is wrong to have EM embraced automatically simply because it is a new technology.

They warn that the corrections field is rife with the acceptance of fads and panaceas and that new technology is inherently attractive to an industrial society. "Technical innovation becomes synonymous with progress. To be opposed to new technologies is to be a heretic, to be old-fashioned, backwards, resistant to change, regressive, out of step. . . . Agency administrators become fond of the new and the original as a matter of careerism and survival. Fast-track reputations are more likely to be built on introducing new programs than on maintaining the old; few professionals want to be regarded as caretakers. Invitations to speak at conferences, media coverage, job offers, and, most significantly, the availability of grant money depend on the implementation of novel approaches."

There is mounting evidence that EM program enthusiasm runs high even when the data may call them into question. A three-county random test of EM programs in California showed that 35 percent of convicts involved had a technical violation, and 35 percent had an arrest after six months. Probation with EM was found to produce rearrest rates identical to those of offenders kept under regular supervision. An Indianapolis study found no significant differences between EM and human monitoring; the study indicated that nearly 44 percent of all participants "sneaked out" on the monitoring. A Georgia report led to a research finding that EM was a failure and that it even seemed to exacerbate recidivism rates. According to another study in Arizona that concentrated on cost effectiveness, "the evidence suggests that EM did not reduce and might very well increase overall correctional costs due to net widening."

Independent of the Corbett-Marx report, the *Los Angeles Times* reported that a review sponsored by the U.S. Department of Justice on EM devices concluded they did not save money, free jail beds, or deter crime. A three-year study of EM in Oklahoma found that the devices were useful only in a narrow segment of defendants and prisons and even there showed no meaningful impact. Tracking cuffs or not, neither type of defendants was more likely to turn up for appearances in court, nor did the device seem to affect recidivism rates.

A major criticism of EM by some experts claims that even though the technology makes the control of offenders easier, at the same time, as one of these critic says, it "may make more difficult the part of the job that involves motivation of offenders and gaining their cooperation." In prison, inmates have much time to work on escape plans precisely because they have so much time, but the opportunities are far greater for offenders on EM because they are generally free of officials snooping on what they are doing. EM practitioners are focused on controlling offenders so that treatment becomes at most an "add-on," leading to the observation, "Under these conditions, there is likely to be little if any real treatment provided."

There is an abundance of technical failures in such systems. Of course, because the systems operations are governed by enthusiastic vendors and program entrepreneurs, there is a great opportunity not to acknowledge any weaknesses. A study in Florida indicated that EM was found to have "technology [which] has proven both reliable and unreliable," working or breaking down under certain conditions, and because the technology is applied and interpreted by humans, there is "the possibility for errors and corruption."

Technical failures are many and varied, including in earlier methods the chance that the wearer received a shock while bathing. Transmissions can be blocked or distorted by lightning, closeness to an FM radio station, the metal in mylar wallpaper and trailer walls as well as some house construction materials, or from water in a water bed. Poor telephone lines may issue signals that cannot be read accurately. Telephone, power, and computer failures may give off a false violation signal or the reverse. Voice verifications may not work in many areas.

Above all, there is the problem of private contractors having less accountability than those in the public sector, and, as with any system with flaws, offenders are constantly probing for ways to beat it. The question remains, what has Spiderman wrought?

Elmira Reformatory 19th century's new idea for penal institutions

In 1870, a gathering of prison officials met in Cincinnati, Ohio, to plan the reform of U.S. penitentiaries. One fundamental belief they stated was that prisoners, especially younger ones, need special attention with vocational education. A leader at the meeting was Zebulon R. Brockway, superintendent of the Detroit House of Correction.

In 1876 reform-minded New York State opened its Elmira Reformatory with Brockway in charge. Intended for young men from 16 to 30, it soon was the most innovative facility of its type.

Brockway pushed through programs for prisoner classification, education, and vocational training, indeterminate sentencing, and parole. In many ways, Elmira served as a model for both reform schools and penitentiaries. It sported such things as a school, a library, a glee club, a gymnasium, and an athletic field. The inmates published their own newspaper and got moral instruction from the scriptures. When they were not working, inmates wore military-style uniforms, carried toy swords and rifles (a style to be followed in many reform schools), and drilled to an inmate fife and bugle corps.

The most important aspect of the reformatory's program was the indeterminate sentence so that inmates could shorten their terms by good behavior. However, by the end of Brockway's quarter-century reign, problems were showing up in Elmira and in other institutions following its example. The indeterminate sentence had holes in its execution. Inmates learned to beat the system by doing those activities that would meet parole boards' inclination to release them. It also became apparent that the policy would only be as good as those who administered it. The indeterminate sentence sometime became an awesome and arbitrary weapon. Prisoners were sometimes locked up based on the whim or hostility of guards and wardens rather than on objective criteria. Many prisoners had no way of knowing how long they could be incarcerated, a fearful feeling.

Adding to the woes of Elmira was Brockway's fall from grace, despite his worldwide reputation. Investigations showed that Brockway's rehabilitation record was less than he claimed and that brutality was far too common. He had prisoners whipped or starved and served contaminated food, causing some inmates to break down. When this happened, he transferred them to prisons for the insane. He was finally forced to retire under the pressing investigations.

Nevertheless, Brockway still made important improvements overall that continued to this day. Separating young prisoners from older, hardened criminals is still the norm, although under attack by advocates of tougher prison treatments for young and old. Women prisoners now are generally housed separately from men. It can be said that Brockway bore a good deal of the credit for the development of the concept that all prisoners should not be treated alike and for the need for minimum-, medium-, and maximum-security prisons.

See also: BROCKWAY, ZEBULON R.

"embarrassment punishments" mild carryover from branding days and public humiliation

For many years, such punishments as branding or using the stocks were used both to punish offenders physically and to humiliate them considerably. That concept, at least in the latter situation, is used much more than the public realizes by the courts to embarrass nonviolent offenders. Drunk drivers are at times sentenced to watch autopsies being performed. The same is also being done in some jurisdictions against teenage drug dealers involved in small-time sales. In other cases, minor drug dealers may be ordered to work with AIDS patients.

Some criminals are offered the choice of going to jail or taking out a newspaper ad carrying an apology for what they have done. Occasionally, a slumlord may be ordered to live in one of his heatless and/or rat- and vermin-infested buildings. It is felt this particular punishment extracts an added measure of embarrassment at a landlord's country club or church.

An additional argument for such embarrassment punishments is that they save the heavy costs of imprisoning such offenders. However, the custom draws a fair amount of criticism because, in practice, such punishments generally go to the wealthier members of society. Civil libertarians note that the poor or the holders of unpopular religious or political beliefs are seldom accorded such creative sentences. In addition, the hard-line side protests that the judge should follow the laws as called for by lawmakers and the punishment for specific crimes.

Supporters of the practice point to the fact of the high cost of building a prison cell and that a person who is not a real danger to the public is better left on the outside where he or she can be working and paying taxes rather than doing jail time for which the public must pay. It is also felt that putting minor criminals in prison hardly reduces crime because so few felony offenders, by contrast, actually go to prison. In the case of drug and stolen-car rings, their confinement hardly cripples such operations because their leaders simply recruit new and willing replacements so that little more than revolving-door justice occurs. Would it not be better if offenders could work and, in the process, repay the victim and the community; receive drug, alcohol, and mental health counseling; do community service; or stay in school? Jail time, they argue, is also a "school" where minor offenders learn how to become better criminals than before.

employment needs of released prisoners

There are two main needs for newly released prisoners: sufficient "gate money" and employment.

The need for cash is pressing. The released convict needs clothing, first of all. Most prisons require incoming prisoners to send their clothes home upon incarceration. At the time of release, when many inmates have no family left or interested in them, they must be given replacements for their clothing. This is coupled to some extent with gate money, a grant when the inmate leaves. (Some prisons will only give such funds if the inmate hadn't acquired a savings account from work duties during imprisonment.) Many prisons give very small amounts, out of which the ex-inmate must pay for transportation, food, clothing, shelter, and other expenses until he or she receives a paycheck.

A job itself is vital, a matter demonstrated by a study reported by Sue Titus Reid, J.D., Ph.D., in *Crime and Criminology* in a job placement program in Seattle: "The data indicated that those who were employed full time had an 87 percent chance of successfully completing their parole, compared with only 55 percent for those who were employed half time, and 27 percent for those who worked only occasionally."

There are many types of programs available to aid ex-offenders in obtaining employment. One of the most successful is offered by the Alston Wilkes Society, the nation's largest private, nonprofit organization offering services to present and former inmates and their families. Many of the inmates move from institutions to an Alston Wilkes home, where they are required to obtain a job within three weeks, make rent payments, and save 20 percent of their income. There are classes given in filling out job applications and in role-playing interview sessions. Needy clients receive donations of clothing and tools.

Unfortunately, assessment and evaluation of community-based programs have failed to determine which of such employment services are the most effective. This is because of the vast variation in the types of services offered; also, while most programs claim that the majority of their clients are successfully placed in jobs and that clients also have a lower rate of recidivism than comparison groups, the outcomes are often inconsistent. The methodological adequacy of most evaluations remains open to question.

escaped murderers' recidivist rates

According to recent records, murderers who escape from prisons tend to repeat acts of murder while on the loose at a 6 percent rate. Although this tends to surprise some observers as being quite low, it must be remembered that escaped murderers generally enjoy freedom for a relatively short time before being recaptured. By and large, while on the run, most try not to engage in any homicidal acts because police searches inevitably seize on such crimes to pinpoint where the escapees have gone.

eugenics crime-prevention theory or pseudoscience?

Perhaps the dominant penology theory in the United States from 1870 to about 1925 was that of eugenics, which held that what was necessary to control crime was open-ended or indefinite sentences. According to eugenicists, most criminals committed crimes because they possessed inferior "germ plasm" or genes. Thus, under the theory, the best way to control such criminals was to keep them from reproducing by confining them forever or at least through their child-producing years. (Some prisons went further and engaged in sterilization.)

Soon, additional research seemed to indicate that many prisoners were "feeble minded" and therefore inferior through heredity. These incarcerants, too, had to be prevented from breeding. Today, we generally do not confine the feeble minded, but we have most readily executed them for capital crimes.

One of the leaders of the eugenics movement and its prison application was Katharine Bement Davis, head of the women's Bedford Hills reformatory in New York State. A huge amount of research was carried out there because of Davis's ability to recruit wealthy individuals to fund such operations. A leading representative of the wealthy backers was John D. Rockefeller, who not only provided money but actually became part-owner of the state institution, a remarkable situation certainly by present-day standards.

By 1925, the eugenics theory was being dismissed as little more than pseudoscience, and its ideas virtually disappeared by 1935, although some of its premises, such as the indefinite sentences, remain in some crime-control models but without the germ-plasm beliefs.

See also: DAVIS, KATHARINE BEMENT; ROCKEFELLER, JOHN D., JR.

Further reading: *Creating Born Criminals* by Nicole Hahn Rafter.

Evans, Wilbert Lee (1946–1990) "death-row hero"

There was no stranger drama of a condemned man on death row than that involving Wilbert

Evans. Before his slated execution, the *Richmond Times-Dispatch* dubbed Evans a hero, and guards catered to him. He was treated like royalty with morning coffee and the morning paper brought to him by guards. While the other condemned prisoners sweltered in the summer heat, Evans could have shaved ice on request and conversed with guards like old buddies. Evans could enjoy relaxing in the day room for much of the day, away from the confining cells on death row.

Clearly, the prison betting line was that Evans, a vicious murderer, would not be executed.

As irrational as it seemed, Evans's treatment was extremely logical. He had been one of the 12 original plotters in the great death-row escape of May 31, 1984, from Mecklenburg Correctional Center, the commonwealth of Virginia's pride as an escape-proof prison, the first time in U.S. history for such an operation from death row. With incredible cunning, six inmates pulled off the amazing caper; six others, including Evans, opted out at the last minute, most of them because they decided that they had a better chance at a new trial and exoneration in their cases. Actually, that may have been true for one or two, but several dropped out more likely in fear that the escape plan would not work and the would-be escapees would be killed.

Still, those remaining behind had their hearts and sentiment with the escapees and aided them in the preliminary preparations before the actual breakout, for example, holding guards taken prisoner by various subterfuges and stripping them of their uniforms for the escapees to don. (This entry hereafter is concerned only with the case of inmate Evans. The full story of the breakout by the Mecklenburg Six is told in a separate entry.)

One of Evans's duties was to hold the guard-hostages as well as a female nurse who was also taken. When a couple of the death rowers sought to have the nurse strip down as well and be tied up, Evans resisted the idea, both he and the woman realizing that rape at the very least was sure to follow. Evans prevented that from happening, saying, "There won't be no killing and there won't be no raping. You gettin' what you wanted. Now get outta here and leave this poor woman alone."

Some of the men in the escape wanted to kill a guard or two to demonstrate how stern they intended to be with any pursuers, but the remaining inmates, and especially Evans, were not going to let that happen. Later, prosecutors would disparage Evans's acts, calling them calculated to gain him a better clemency argument, but several of the hostages credited Evans and another, Willie Turner, with saving their lives. The nurse, Ethel Barksdale, insisted in her case Evans had saved her from probable death.

After the breakout, the remaining inmates in the plot went into lockdown, but soon Evans was released on the pleas of the guard-hostages and Nurse Barksdale.

In due course, over a period of days all the escapees, either singularly or in pairs, were recaptured after their act, which electrified the nation as the lead item for days on both national television and the front pages in newspapers around the country and elsewhere.

Evans made no bones that he felt he deserved a reward for what he'd done. "I'll get a commutation for this," he said later. "I'm Wilbert Evans. I kept people from getting killed."

In the time that followed, the state went about the business of executing every escapee when his date with death was due, as well as those who had remained behind. Then there was the special case of Evans. No matter what those on the outside thought, many on the inside paid homage to Evans.

As the final date for his execution arrived on October 17, 1990, Evans still expected to be spared. Prison guards and officials as well as Nurse Barksdale wrote affidavits imploring the governor for clemency.

However, as Virginia newspapermen Joe Jackson and William F. Burke Jr. wrote in *Dead Run* about the great mass escape: "Evans' timing was as bad as could be. L. Douglas Wilder, the state's first black governor and Chuck Robb's successor, had once been an opponent of the death penalty. Yet he campaigned for office as a supporter of executions and now was running for the presidency. He had reason to believe he would be Willie Horton-ized if he spared a black cop killer. In addition, the national campaign to save Giarratano—'Joey G.,' another of the original plotters who did not take part in it—whose execution was scheduled soon after Evans's, made it politically difficult for Wilder to grant two clemencies back to back. Giarratano's defenders included Amnesty International and columnist James J. Kilpatrick. Evans had his lawyers and family."

In the early evening of October 17, the U.S. Supreme Court turned down Evans's appeal without comment. Only Thurgood Marshall dissented, denouncing the execution as "dead wrong."

It was, to say the least, unusual for the death squad who had the duty of carrying out the penalty: They knew their fellow guards were still begging for it to be stopped. Four of the guards who had been held as hostages insisted to investigators—and the governor possessed a letter from Sergeant E. B. Harris—that the condemned man had "saved some of the officers from harm and almost certain death" and, following the escape, "has shown me and the majority of the staff nothing but respect." In addition, the warden who had been brought in after the escape pointed out that commuting Evans's sentence to life might in the future cause other prisoners to follow his example "in the eventuality of a riot or serious hostage situation."

At 10:52 P.M., Wilder concluded his study of the arguments and rendered his decision: Evans was to die.

Six minutes later, Evans was dead.

See also: MECKLENBURG SIX.

The hanging of Black Jack Ketchum, who was decapitated in the process (Author's collection)

execution methods the favorite five

There have been five main methods of executions in the United States, all having their periods of vogue; four of them lost their popularity either because of their cruelty or because of "complications" in their operations. (There were a few other methods, mostly imported from Europe earlier in our history, such as crushing by weights, drawing and quartering, and burning at the stake, the latter two virtually employed only against blacks. These were abandoned obviously because their extensive uses would invite serious criticisms in a changing world.)

The methods are best discussed in their general usage and popularity.

HANGING

Today, hanging has been used in only two states since the restoration of the death penalty in 1976, Washington and Delaware. At one time, the method was almost universal in every state in the Union. Hanging in older times was always considered a lowly form of punishment, frequently a death reserved for cowards. The Bible, in Deuteronomy 22–23, says, "And if a man have committed a sin worthy of death; and thou hang him on a tree; his body shall not remain all night upon the tree; but thou shalt in any wise bury him that day; (for he that is hanged *is* accursed of God;) that thy land be not defiled, which the LORD thy God giveth thee for an inheritance."

In time hanging was judged unworthy of important personages; beheading was considered more proper. The main argument against hanging is that it is far more cruel and painful than other methods; on the other hand, proponents of hanging always argued that its very repulsiveness makes it more of a deterrent. Had that been the case, hanging would have eliminated murder and other capital crimes centuries ago.

Years of refinement have gone into the technique in an effort to achieve what is called a "clean" hanging. When that occurs, which according to experts happens only in a minority of the cases, the following should take place:

First of all, there is no longer the embarrassment of the rope slipping from the crossbeam because it is now attached to a chain suspended from the gallows crossbeam. The noose is adjusted so that the knot is positioned extremely tightly behind the victim's left ear, and a black hood is placed over the head so that witnesses will be spared the condemned's final grimaces. In some cases, the hangman does not spring the trapdoor himself; his job is limited to fixing the knot, binding the legs together to prevent disconcerting kicking, and centering the doomed correctly over the trapdoor. Then the hangman gives a signal, and three people on the platform each cut a string, only one of which springs the trapdoor. When this occurs, the knot ideally will strike behind the left ear, instantly knocking the doomed unconscious. If things work to perfection, just the right number of small bones of the cervical vertebrae in the neck are broken so that the head is not ripped off. The bones should then collapse on the spinal cord, cutting off oxygen to the brain and paralyzing the rest of the body. Rapid brain death follows. That makes for the ideal clean hanging, but it doesn't happen all that often.

Still, there is a less-clean job that satisfied most hanging fans. In such cases, the victim's thrashing at the end of the rope lasts for only a few minutes. Wheezing can be heard but does not reach the fever pitch of the really botched job. The stench, however, is quite troublesome because the victim often urinates, defecates, and ejaculates at the same time. The resultant odors, mixed with an overwhelming one of perspiration, is somewhat sickening for many viewers, especially as human waste runs down the victim's legs and drops to the floor. Finally, after a relatively short few minutes, the violent shudders subside and the rope stops dancing. There is one final jerk, just a bit of twitching and then quiet.

So much for the relatively good hangings. Former San Quentin warden Clinton Duffy, who witnessed 60 hangings, described most hangings of being of the less than clean sort. In a "dirty" hanging, the condemned will strangle to death slowly, a vile process that can take as long as a quarter of an hour. The wheezing is extremely loud and indescribable, except to someone who has heard the hysterical squealing of a dying pig. The victim may even bob up and down like a yo-yo, fighting for air. Sometimes the legs, even when bound together, whip far out in search of a perch; it may become necessary for a guard to seize the legs and hold them steady so that their violent churnings do not break the rope, a development that might upset the witnesses. When death finally comes, it may be difficult to determine for whom the agony was worse—the condemned or the witnesses.

Of course, sometimes things become even messier. A poorly placed knot occasionally gouges out a chunk of the face and head, and witnesses see this gory mess drop to the floor. When the noted outlaw "Black Jack" Ketchum was hanged in New Mexico in 1901, he shouted out as the hood went over his face, "Let 'er go!" The rope did so, decapitating Ketchum as he hurtled into space. It cannot be said that society did not learn something from the incident and the admonishment was made that witnesses should not seat themselves in the front row, as in the Ketchum hanging those witnesses were splattered with blood.

A similar disquieting situation occurred in the 1930s in West Virginia when a wife murderer named Frank Myer was hanged. He was a very bad hanging candidate, being heavyset with a short neck and what were described as "soft bones." When the trapdoor opened, Myer's body plummeted to the concrete floor and was followed by a second thud as his head landed nearby. Several of the witnesses retched as the head rolled a few feet in their direction, and later some of the witnesses said that they would never attend a hanging again.

The sheer messiness of hangings finally led to the abandonment of the method in most states, which either opted for the electric chair or the gas chamber. One state, Utah, has not been able to sever its sentimental attachment to hanging, but it at least has offered the condemned a choice of either the noose or the firing squad. Hanging lost that popularity contest and has not been practiced in decades.

SHOOTING

For decades condemned men in Utah opted for the firing squad over hanging, two of the most illustrious examples being labor hero Joe Hill, almost certainly executed for a crime he did not commit, and Gary Gilmore, the first man executed after the Supreme Court reimposed the death penalty. It can be argued that in some respects death by firing squad is the most "humane" method of all. The condemned man is strapped down in a chair against an oval-shaped canvas-covered wall. A doctor locates the heart precisely and pins a cloth target directly over it. Unless the victim objects, he is hooded.

Just 20 feet away in a canvas enclosure, five sharpshooters are armed with .30-caliber rifles loaded with a single cartridge. However, one rifle has a blank so that each marksman can later rationalize that he did not do the killing. The shooters place their weapons through slits in the canvas, and all fire in unison when the order is given. Four bullets thump into the heart, making death virtually instantaneous and probably painless. With such a fine method of killing, it may be surprising that more jurisdictions haven't switched to death by shooting instead of going the other way. There are good reasons for this. One is the fact that the execution is bloody, and society does not wish to see the resultant mess to remind it that a human being has been slaughtered. Even more important is the situation in which some of the marksmen turn "chicken" or "cheat." If a marksman wants to make sure he does not fire the fatal bullet, he will aim "off-heart" and therefore can satisfy himself that the victim died long before his shot could have taken any effect. In 1951, the height of official embarrassment resulted when all four marksmen hit the victim, Elisio J. Mares, on the right side of the chest so that he bled slowly to death. Because of such "inefficiencies," it is obvious that death by firing squad will not stage a comeback in the art of executing people.

ELECTRIC CHAIR

The electric chair as an instrument of death was born out of necessity. In the 1880s, demands were sweeping the nation in outrage against the number of botched hanging executions, and the anti–capital-punishment lobby was pushing hard for the elimination of the death penalty. The answer came in what was the new technology of the day: We will simply electrocute people. Since that time, more than 1,000 men and women have gone to what popularly is called the hot seat, and no matter that the electric chair produced far more bizarre and ghoulish incidents than other methods because of quirks in the law. In Florida, in 1926, a condemned man named Jim Williams was in the chair waiting for death when an argument broke out between Warden John S. Blitch and Sheriff R.J. Hancock, each of whom insisted it was the other's duty to throw the switch. The argument went on for 20 minutes until poor Williams collapsed. He was carried back to his cell while the dispute was sent to the courts. Eventually, a ruling was made that the sheriff was required to do the job, but the Board of Pardons decided that Williams had done enough penance and commuted his death sentence to life imprisonment.

During World War II two convicted murderers, Clifford Haas and Paul Sewell, beat the death sentence when one state switched to electrocution from hanging. The War Production Board said the materials required for the chair could be better used fighting the Japanese and the Nazis and refused to grant a priority. No chair, no killing.

The usual electric chair has two legs in back and a heavier single leg in front, all bolted to the floor. The extrawide arms are fitted with straps to hold the victim's arms rigid; other straps go around the chest and abdomen. The wiring around the chair is covered with rubber matting.

Actually, the electric chair is a rather simple contraption, as indicated by the fact that some southern states have used portable or mobile chairs. In Mississippi, it was carried around in a van with its own generators and controls so that it could be brought into the courtroom where the defendant was convicted. A power line led from the the truck's generator into the packed courtroom. When a newsman once told Sen. Theodore Bilbo that the practice was little different than lynching, he responded, "Ah, this is pretty tame compared to a lynching."

Ideally, an electrocution is a three-minute drill, with the prisoner strapped into the chair quickly. Inexperienced guards practice with the straps in advance to avoid fumbling delays. The so-called humane character of electrocution is probably best measured by what the witnesses are spared rather than what happens to the condemned person. A tight mask is placed over the prisoner's face to hide the facial contortions when the "juice" is turned on. The mask is especially tight around the eyes, hopefully to keep them from popping out of their sockets.

Two popular myths about the execution chamber almost never happen: There are no long goodbyes or last statements, although a famous gangster of the 1930s did manage, "Give my love to mother," and the lights never dim in the rest of the prison because the chair is powered by its own source. Hollywood prefers the light-dimming routine because it gives a scriptwriter an opportunity to stage a prisoner protest or to achieve special dramatic effect.

Once the executioner is sure that everyone is clear of the chair, a switch is thrown, and the raging current pitches the victim against the binds with terrific force. His or her hair stands up, and his or her flesh turns to the color of beets. If the executioner fails to flip the switch when the prisoner's lungs are empty, there will be a "gurgling" noise as air is forced from the lungs by the shock of the current. The first jolt, executioners have learned by trial and error, should be 2,000 volts or slightly more, after which it is cut back to 1,000 volts to prevent what witnesses might take as unseemly burning of the body.

At this stage, the victim may pass waste. The tradition of a last hearty meal for the condemned is truly a tribulation for the executioner. Almost certainly, mouth foam will seep out from under the hood. Often, the electrical jolt may be repeated to make sure the victim is dead, a worthwhile precaution. When Arthur Lee Grimes was executed in Alabama in 1954, the doctor found his heart still beating. He stepped back and waited for it to stop, but instead of expiring, Grimes started to shudder violently and thrash against the straps. He started to come back to consciousness, gasping and sucking in air. It took seven full minutes of juice, six massive jolts in all, to end his life.

Proponents of the electric chair found such lapses as the Grimes execution lamentable, just as they did the world's first electrocution, that of William Kemmler in New York in 1890.

In the 1880s, a commission was established to determine if hanging should be abolished. After viewing a number of hangings, including that of a woman who slowly strangled to death, the findings were not surprising. But it is doubtful, had it not been for a monumental technological battle over business profits being waged by Thomas A. Edison and George Westinghouse for domination of the then-budding electric-power industry, that the idea of an electric chair would not have occurred. Edison had developed the first electric power system in 1882 by the use of low-tension, direct current (DC). Westinghouse brought out his alternating current (AC) system two years later. AC utilized light, easily installed wires compared to the expensive heavy-wire installation required for DC. Faced with an opposing product that was clearly superior, Edison decided that his best hope lay in disparaging AC in the public's eye, and he dispatched a young engineer, Harold P. Brown, to stage shows around the country to demonstrate that system's death-dealing potential. Brown shocked folks by electrocuting stray dogs and cats and even horses. When he took his show to Albany, the special commission wondered if he could kill an orangutan. He could and did. The unfortunate orangutan even caught fire, but that did not upset the commission from then coming up with the concept of an electric chair. A human being wasn't covered with hair and so was not likely to catch fire. The electric chair was born.

Kemmler's execution was not a happy affair. A first jolt did not kill him, and shocked doctors watched Kemmler's breast heave and his heart resume beating. Panic engulfed the execution chamber, and finally the current was turned on again for a full 70 seconds at 1,300 volts. Some of the witnesses fainted, and another retched and bolted from the room. At last, William Kemmler was dead.

Unfortunately, the flesh on Kemmler's back was badly burned, and his muscles were carbonized. When his body was autopsied, a witness described the flesh as well-cooked beef. Despite worldwide protests of the tortures involved in the new extermination method, the electric chair was there to stay. In time, executioners learned to watch the condemned person's hands. When they turn pink, other parts of the body, nearer the source of the electric charge, are much darker and closer to burned. "Overburning" remained a problem in later years.

The public tended to find fascination in botched-up jobs, and when the first electrocutions of four murderers took place at Sing Sing in 1891, the roads from Ossining to the prison were jammed with sightseers and tourists hoping for something to go awry. But the chair worked without a hitch four times. However, in 1903, disaster struck at Clinton Prison when one of three brothers executed, Fred Van Wormer, started to move in the autopsy room. The executioner, Robert P. Elliott, was summoned back to the prison. By the time he arrived, Van Wormer had expired, but there was unanimous opinion that no chances should be taken. The dead man was jammed back into the chair and given another 1,700 volts.

Survival after death in the electric chair has always been an intriguing idea. When Ruth Synder was executed along with her lover Judd Gray for the murder of her husband, her lawyer sought a court order to prevent any autopsy, a legal requirement to determine the cause of death. The lawyer planned to have her revived with adrenalin. The try was never made as the courts rejected the move. A number of condemned persons have swallowed all types of metal objects under the belief that somehow this would cause the electric chair to "short." In the 1950s a prisoner, Donald Snyder, entered his Sing Sing death cell weighing 150 pounds and soon started to eat and eat and eat. He had the novel idea of being too fat to fit into the chair. Weightwise, he did remarkably, eventually tipping the scales at more than 300 pounds. His request for the traditional last meal was, "Pork chops, eggs and plenty of 'em!" He spent his last few hours speculating with a guard how the newspapers would go wild when it turned out that he couldn't be executed.

A New York tabloid wrote finis to Synder's bizarre effort: "The hot seat fitted him as though it had been made to order."

Contrary to all the evidence of botched execution, burnings, gasping for air, and continuing heartbeats, there are many experts who insist electrocution is immediate and painless. They can perhaps take comfort in the case of Harry Roberts, a New York slayer who informed the prison doctor as he was strapped into the chair: "Doc, my last act is going to be for science. We'll see how fast this juice really works. The moment I feel it, I'll wiggle this finger." It never wiggled.

Dr. Harold W. Kipp, who, as chief medical officer of Sing Sing, attended more than 200 executions, insisted: "The effect of electricity is instantaneous brain death. What observers see are muscle contractions, not agony."

None of this offers any concern to other terrible consequences of executions and their effect on the execution-room guards after death has occurred. Seldom are such matters discussed, possibly for its ill effect on popular opinion. Often, guards are left with the demeaning post-execution procedures. They at times have to leave the body untouched from 30 minutes to an hour after the pronouncement of death. Exhaust fans are used to draw off the odor of microwaved flesh. The death squad stuff their nostrils with Vaseline and even wear surgical masks. The deceased's joints fuse so that it is necessary for the guards to break arms, legs, and back to get the body to lie flat on the gurney. The sound has been likened to the cracking of eggshells; in the case of convicted atom spy Ethel Rosenberg in 1953, her limbs were described as having been "frozen in place."

In recent years, protests against the electric chair centered mainly on Florida, which had a fairly regular record of botched jobs. In a 1967 incident, flames and smoke arose from Pedro Medina's head as the current went on. The cause was said to have been the sponges in the headpiece. A one-year moratorium was imposed after that, and an autopsy report insisted that Medina had died instantly without suffering any pain from the fire. The Florida Supreme Court ruled by 4-3 vote that electric-chair executions did not violate the ban on cruel and unusual punishment. (Around the country courts have been singularly unable to find much in the way of cruel and unusual punishments, even when hanging victims ended up having their heads ripped off when the body was dropped or when the result was slow strangulation.)

Then in 1990 and 1997, flames shot out of masks of the inmates, and the smell of burned flesh filled the witness room. There were similar malfunctions in other states. The next botch-up involved Allen Lee Davis, whose blood seeped through his shirt and the buckle holes of the chest strap. Bloody photographs were posted on the Internet and were to be considered in the U.S.

Supreme Court to determine if electrocution violated the Constitution.

All these events of a malfunctioning chair weighed heavily on the state of Florida, added to claims that Florida was just incapable of carrying out executions competently; the U.S. Supreme Court was set to review the state's electric-chair practices. The Jeb Bush administration at first sought to give the condemned the right to choose between the electric chair and lethal injection, but by then, the state legislature had quite enough of the controversy and voted unanimously in the senate and by 102-5 in the house to get rid of the chair. Late in the century, the trend was toward lethal injection. Before that, back in the 1920s and 1930s, the gas chamber had been gaining ground as being truly superior to electrocution and hanging.

GAS CHAMBER

In the 1920s, reformers were sure they had come up with the idea of a humane execution method. It was the gas chamber, which was introduced in Nevada in 1924. Later, the reformers would change their mind about that, but at the time the execution of a murderer named Gee Jon was considered a great success, and a Carson City news account bragged that Nevada had moved "one step further from the savage state."

After Nevada, the gas chamber was adopted by eight other states—Arizona, Colorado, Maryland, Mississippi, Missouri, North Carolina, Wyoming, and California. The California gas chamber was the most prominent for its wide use. Built in 1938, it has been the site of many high-profile executions, including those of Barbara Graham, Caryl Chessman, and Burton W. Abbott, whose gassing in 1957 was particularly embarrassing. Abbott's execution was almost stayed by an order of Gov. Goodwin Knight. When the phone call came from the governor's office, the gas pellets had already been dropped behind his chair so the execution proceeded.

The gas chamber is designed with two chairs so that two executions can take place at the same time. (Double executions almost certainly guarantee newspapers good quotes. When kidnapper and murderer Bonnie Heady died in the Missouri gas chamber along with her partner, Carl Austin Hall, she asked guards not to strap in her man too tightly. "You got plenty of room, honey?" Heady asked. Hall replied, "Yes, Mama." Thus satisfied, the woman smiled and sat back to breath the deadly fumes.) Under the chairs are shallow pans into which tubes from a small vestibule are fed a mixture of water and sulfuric acid. A lever is pulled, and bags with 16 1-ounce cyanide pellets are dropped into the mixture. Fumes rise swiftly, and the victim dies quickly—once in a while. Some reporters who have covered various types of executions regard the gas chamber as the most vile and inhumane of all.

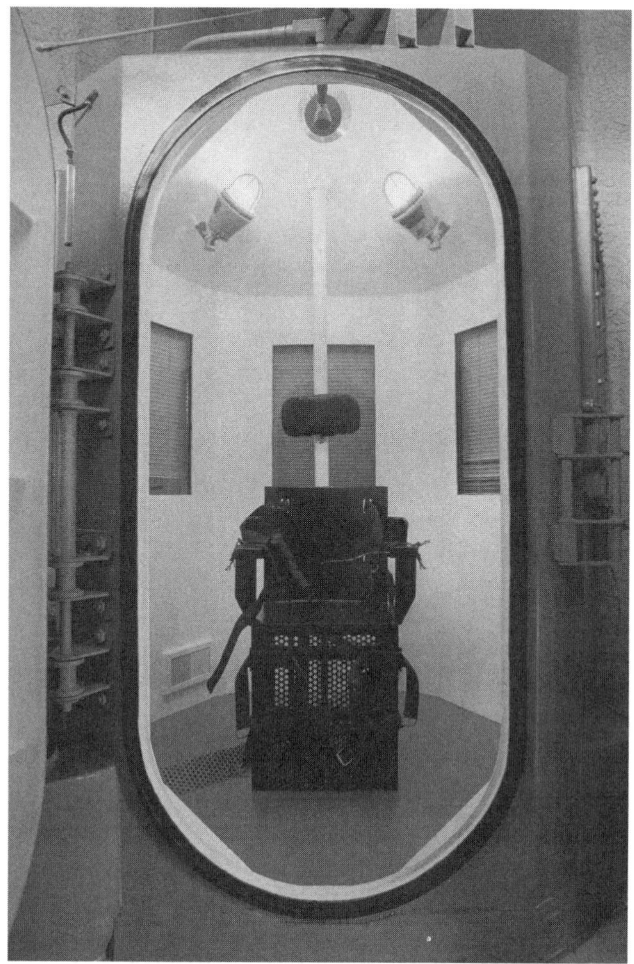

View of the gas chamber used for executions inside "Death House" at the Florence prison complex in Florence, Arizona (AFP/CORBIS)

Essentially, the victim strangles to death without the courtesy of a rope. He is forced to do it to himself as he battles for oxygen that is no longer there, except in a "frozen" state that is useless to the body. The condemned person is often told that as soon as he or she smells an odor resembling rotten eggs, he or she should count to 10 and then take several deep breaths. This, the victim is told, will cause him or her to pass out quickly and die without pain. That generally is not what happens. Human instinct, the body's instinct, is to live. The victim will gasp and wheeze, struggling for air, mouth opening and closing like a beached fish. Often, there are screams or sobs. Choking, the doomed person thrashes about, pulling on the bonds. Occasionally, it is reported, a victim will break an arm free, usually in the process severing the skin, so that blood may spurt over the windows through which the witnesses are watching.

Asphyxiation comes slowly. The thrashing victim's face turns purple and the eyes bulge. He or she drools and a swollen tongue hangs out. Still, death has not occurred. The death process takes eight or nine minutes. The record, although statistics are not definitive on the matter, appears to be 11 minutes in a North Carolina execution.

Caryl Chessman's ordeal of dying in 1960 may not have been the most unusual but it received greater media coverage than most executions. He tried to make his dying easier by inhaling quickly and deeply as he could. By prearrangement with a newsman witness, Chessman was to signal if the pain became agony. Shortly after his ordeal began, Chessman looked toward the reporter and nodded his head vigorously, the signal that the dying process was indeed agonizing. Finally, his head slumped to his chest and his tongue popped out.

A woman reporter described what happened next:

> *I thought he must be dead but no, there was another agonizing period during which he choked on the gas. And again. And then again. There was a long period, another deep gasp. At the fourth such straining, Chessman's head lolled in a half circle, coming forward so that he faced downward with his chin almost touching his chest. This must be the end. But the dying went on.*
>
> *A deep gasp, then his head came up for an instant, dropped forward again. After two or three deep breaths, which seemed something like sobs, a trembling set up throughout his body. Along the line of his broad shoulders, down the arms to his fingers, I could see the tremor run. Then I saw his pale face grow suddenly paler, though I had not thought that it could be after his 12 years in prison. A little saliva came from his lips, spotted the white shirt that a condemned man wears for his last appearance. Even more color drained from his face and the furrows in his head smoothed out a little. And I knew he was dead. . . .*

There seemed to be considerable sentiment among the witnesses to the Chessman execution that death in the gas chambers was not really as painless a process as it was billed. None of the methods of executions in this country have met that criterion, and the search for the perfect method of killing continued.

LETHAL INJECTION

The newest method of capital punishment in the United States is death by lethal injection. Lethal injection had been considered as an execution method as long ago as the 1880s. In 1886, a special commission in New York State considered the idea of injection to replace hanging but decided to go with the new idea of electrocution as being the most humane method. No other country has gone to lethal-injection executions. In 1953, the Royal Commission Inquiry on Capital Punishment assembled by King George dropped lethal injection as a substitute for the noose. Back in the United States, things changed in 1982 when the first lethal-injection execution took place in Texas. It was, of course, offered as the most humane method around, but critics said that its main appeal was that it was a less troublesome method for the state to employ. In the beginning, states that wished for the injection style had considerable time to formulate their procedures, which would become known to the inhabitants of various death rows sardonically as "the ultimate high." Under procedures established in Oklahoma in 1977, death is to occur by the continuous injection of "an ultrashort-acting barbiturate in combination with a chemical paralytic agent." Death would be almost instantaneous, with the condemned person simply falling asleep and expiring, and death officially would be attributable to coronary arrest. The same year, Texas joined Oklahoma, and Idaho and New Mexico followed later, with many other states having similar plans under consideration. Because of the long processes of appeals, there was considerable time to work out

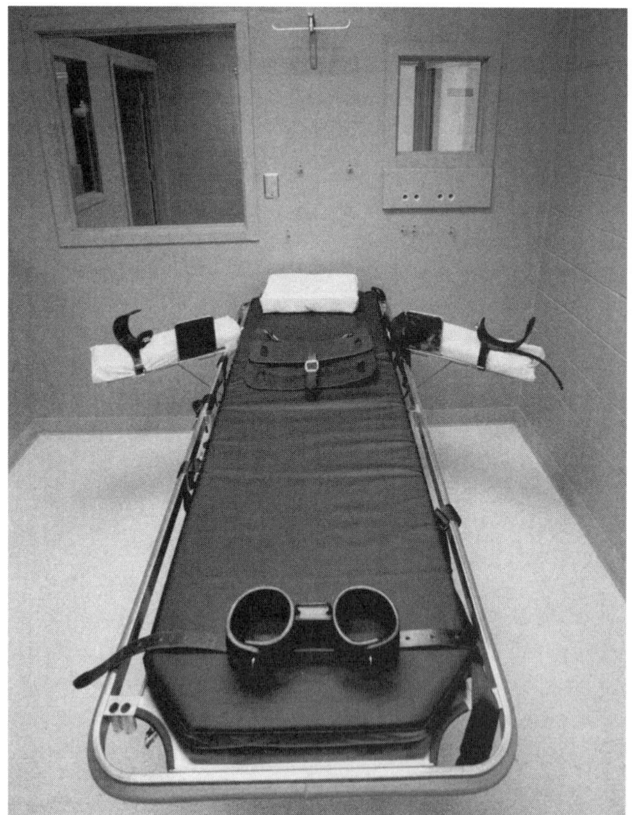

The execution chamber at Oregon State Penitentiary, shown here in Salem, Oregon, has been used to put condemned prisoners to death by lethal injection. (AP/Wide World Photos)

the exact procedures that would be followed for the some 200 persons under death sentences by mid-1981.

Oklahoma's plans were typical. There would be no more "last mile" walks through the basement to the electric chair. Instead, there was what condemned men called the "last ride." The doomed would be strapped onto a stretcher and transported, head propped up, to the third floor of the administration building to be executed there in view of about 30 persons. Among them would be six news reporters and five persons chosen by the condemned. The executioner would be one of three unidentified medical technicians, who would stand behind a panel through which a tube would be passed and connected to the condemned person's arm or leg. The three technicians would inject a dark fluid into the tube, but none would know which of them was injecting the lethal substance.

In essence, this would be similar in approach to the firing-squad technique of supplying one marksman with a blank. The argument has been made that execution by injection is more humane than any other method of legal killing, but it must be noted that as society becomes more "humane," the anonymity of the procedure increases to a point where the actual killing is done by only one person in three.

The American Medical Association passed a resolution in 1980 labeling participation in such executions by doctors as unethical. By 1982, the first injection execution was carried out in Texas, and, not surprisingly, it proved to be a botched affair. Prison employees had considerable difficulty in trying to pierce with a large needle the badly scarred veins of the condemned man, and blood splattered all over the sheets. Among those witnessing the fouled-up attempt was the prison doctor. For a first-time effort, it was not, however, as bungled as the first electrocution, that of Willie Kemmler.

As of 1999, 24 states had carried out death by lethal injection, some offering prisoners alternate methods of executions still carried out in their jurisdiction—electric chair, hanging, gas chamber, or shooting. In 1980, when some of the more rabid advocates of capital punishment, including some in Congress, proposed that the exacting of the death penalty be shown on television, many opponents of capital punishment were appalled. Other opponents could not see why, saying that a steady diet of executions on television would eventually lead to public revulsion to capital punishment. They pointed out that it was not student demonstrations or the draft-card burners who stopped the Vietnam War; rather, it was television. Through the constant showing on the evening news of the blood and violence occurring in a senseless conflict, the U.S. public became sickened. The same thing would happen, they said, after a dozen or so execution spectaculars were viewed on the home screen.

Lethal injection indeed might well be one of the less-appreciated methods of injection when exposed to public gaze. One that might well disturb the public would be the inordinate time needed to carry out the execution. Executioners have been rather poor at finding a vein to be used for the injection. In Virginia, in 1996, 22 minutes were needed to find a suitable vein in the arms or legs of Richard Townes Jr. before one was finally located in the top of his right foot. In 1990, the South Carolina execution of Michael Eugene Elkins required 40 minutes to locate a usable vein in his neck. Both these men were longtime drug users, as are many on death row, and they had apparently had access to injectionable drugs during their years in their death cells—a not uncommon situation—and had continued to abuse their veins. It was probably true that they could have helped guide their executioners to a good vein but apparently enjoyed the few extra minutes of life afforded to them, which might prove troubling to a television audience.

An added problem is that the style in many injection executions calls for the doomed person to be placed on the gurney, arms outstretched and legs together straight ahead. Some witnesses have noted the resemblance of the position with that of a crucifixion, a situation that would be particularly upsetting to many religious persons.

Admittedly, this is more a matter of form than substance and might well have some "show-stopping" qualities. However, social observers see something more at work, continuing a long trend in executions whereby one method of execution after another is hailed as a great "humane" advance and then falls aside as unacceptable. Will lethal injection meet the same fate? If so, it may indicate, as the death penalty progresses, that fault will continue to be found with every method so that eventually, in a period of reform, capital punishment will once again tumble from favor. These social observers claim to see the beginnings of that in the slow but apparent lessening of public favor for executions and a shift toward life sentences. This is gaining favor as continuing evidence of DNA findings results in freedom for many apparently incorrectly doomed persons. In that sense the method of execution becomes of lesser import than the matter of the death penalty per se.

executions, public

By 1936, the feeling in the United States was that public executions, brought from the Old World to the New World, were a shameful practice, and there was no doubt that the last public execution, that of Rainey Bethea, a 22-year-old black man, in Owensboro, Kentucky, that year stands out as one of the most shameful. Rainey had killed a 70-year-old white woman, and public opinion was at fever pitch. The county sheriff, Florence Thompson, decided to stage the execution in an open field so that thousands of witnesses could watch. It was a decision that guaranteed mob behavior among the crowd. By the night before the execution, the town was flooded with visitors from all over the country. There was drunken revelry that was marked by calls for a mass lynching of blacks. Somehow, that violence did not occur, but only some six blacks remained in town, the rest of the blacks having fled for safety.

On the morning of Bethea's hanging, 20,000 revelers gathered at the site of the execution. Each time the hangman tested the scaffold and it snapped open, the crowd responded with appreciative cheers. By that time, the sheriff, now fearful that the crowd might get out of hand, decided to speed up the execution, and at 5:12 A.M. Rainey reached the scaffold in the eerie dawn.

When the bolt snapped, a joyous roar swept over the field, and the crowd surged forward. Souvenir hunters almost immediately attacked the dangling, still-warm body, stripping off pieces of the dead man's clothing and, in some instances, using knives to carve out souvenir-sized hunks of flesh. Doctors had a hard time to work through

A public hanging for which the public paid well for seats. Of course the scene depicted was generally more romantic than the real life (or death) actuality. (Author's collection)

the melee to certify Bethea's death. They cried out that his heart was still beating. The spectators groaned and pulled back. It was not until 5:45 that death was finally pronounced. There was now no stopping the trophy hunters from going on the attack, and a great scuffle took place for the death hood.

The first execution in this country took place in 1630, more than three centuries earlier, and it too was a public affair. The doomed man was John Billington, one of the original pilgrims from the *Mayflower.* The charge was murder and the Pilgrims, as much as others of that day, considered public executions as a powerful warning to others to stay away from wrongdoing.

Throughout the decades, such public executions were little more than circuses, drawing proportionally a far greater audience than 20th-century sporting events. It was customary in the Old West to reserve many hangings for the weekend so that as many folks as possible could enjoy the festivities. When a hatchet murderer named John Johnson was hanged in 1824 in New York City at 13th Street and Second Avenue, there were 50,000 spectators on hand.

Albert Hicks (Author's collection)

Probably the most spectacular hanging in New York was that of killer Albert E. Hicks on July 13, 1860, on Bedloe's Island, the future home of the Statue of Liberty. There was limited space on the island, but many, many thousands more were accommodated by the mass of ships—everything from small craft to large excursion vessels—that choked the waters around the island. Hawkers in rowboats did a water-office business, weaving in and out of craft peddling their wares. Almost everyone turned a bit of money because of Hicksie, as he was called. He was one of the great villains of the day, and jailers in the Tombs charged admission to the public who wished to see the blackguard shackled to the floor of his cell. An added few cents entitled a visitor to exchange a few words with the murderer.

Even the great showman, Phineas T. Barnum, whose American Museum enjoyed great popularity, wanted a piece of the action. Barnum dickered with Hicks about obtaining a plaster cast of his head and bust to display in the museum. After considerable back and forth, with Hicks knowing he was in the carriage seat, the deal was closed for the sum of $25 and two boxes of nickel cigars. Upon completion of the cast, Barnum brought Hicks a new suit in exchange for his old one, which would grace a display dummy. Before leaving the Tombs, Hicks would complain to the warden that Barnum had cheated him, that the new suit was shoddy and inferior to his old one.

Even when Hicks left the Tombs for his execution, he still complained about Barnum's suit, which did not fit properly, but he was told by the warden that there was not enough time for alterations.

Hicks was ushered from the jail to the mainland dock by a fife-and-drum corps and a procession of carriages full of dignitaries. Thousands along the route cheered Hicksie, and he cheerfully waved back. Following in the procession were carriages full of dignitaries, who did not seem to receive nearly as much applause. The hanging itself was described by one historian as being a high old time.

After the money-making potentials revealed by the Hicks execution, it became common for many communities and many sheriffs to ban public executions, which allowed too many freeloaders in without payment. Instead, executions were done under private circumstances so that officials could run a ghoulish sort of black market with invitations going at a hefty price. The practice of many public executions continued, however, well into the 20th century when the disgraceful execution of Bethea Rainey spelled finis to the custom.

See also: BILLINGTON, JOHN.

ex-felons ever-growing problem and menace

Although the public receives great comfort to see more security in a growth of prisons to house increasing numbers of convicted offenders (although picking up the tab is often a matter of some controversy), some experts are now focusing on what they see as the true growing menace of a future explosive crime wave. They warn that we cannot build our way out of a crime plague. Michael J. Mahoney, executive director of the John Howard Association in Chicago, a private prison and criminal-justice watchdog agency, warns, "High walls, barbed wire, and armed guards give people a certain sense of security, but it's largely illusory. Very few dangerous criminals are locked up at any one time."

Are longer sentences the answer—or are they as well an illusory solution? Does the idea that keeping a convicted person off the streets longer mean that he or she cannot commit other crimes in that time and is therefore a plus? According to William Rentschler, publisher of the Rentschler Report, what long prison sentences accomplish is actually to "turn a minor street miscreant into a hardened lifetime professional. It is time to seek an end to the misguided self-defeating, enormously costly reliance on prison and reject their continued existence, except as the punishment of last resort, to be reserved for violent, dangerous, and chronic offenders."

If that doesn't happen and we hold to the opinion-poll determinations that (1) prisons can't rehabilitate and anyway that they should punish and (2) the answer is to "throw away the key," critics ask "Can the latter really be done?" The fact is that prisoners *must* be released and that the real problem we are creating, say these reformers, is the birth of a massive army of ex-felons. Since 1985, the prison population in the United States, not counting the more than half-million people in jails at any given time, has compounded at a rate of about 6 or 7 percent a year. Despite truth-in-sentencing laws, which mandate that many prisoners serve 85 percent of their sentence before being eligible for parole—very popular with the public—the figures show, during the last decade, that on average more than 40 percent of inmates are released in any year. In 1985, 463,284 inmates were released. Writing in *The Atlantic Monthly* in June 1999 Sasha Abramsky used these figures to assume that the statistical relationships remain constant and came up with "a worst-case scenario" that "some 600,000 will be released in 2000, some 887,000 in 2005, and about 1.2 million in 2010."

When factoring in "lower release rates because of three-strike laws and truth in sentencing, and even taking into account estimates that 60 percent of prisoners have been in prison before, there will still be somewhere around 3.5 million first-time releases between now and 2010, and America by then will still be releasing from half-million to a million people each year."

In what other observers consider an understatement, Abramsky observes, "That is an awful lot of potential rage coming out of prison to haunt our future."

It is difficult to describe this army of ex-felons as anything other than a time bomb of horrendous implications on future crime. The prisons in the United States are bulked up with terrible overcrowding, a certain implication for prison violence and more violence later. Less than 10 percent of prisoners are sentenced to life, which means that 90 percent will be released, and they come out of an era in which job training and certainly schooling is regarded by many as "coddling prisoners." Thus, these releasees will have not acquired any meaningful job skills or will have lost them in prison, and they are therefore predictably the least interesting to employers, which in turn means that they will saddle their communities with terrible economic problems. Currently (in 1999), among black men aged 25 to 34 with less than a high school education, the unemployment rate stood at 50 percent. If prison and jail inmates are added, that figure climbs to well more than 60 percent.

Street counselors dealing with ex-felons know how common the threat is when one says, "Society has turned its back on me, and I will do more than that. Prison taught me what real rage is, and I'll use it."

Meanwhile the tide of ex-felons keeps growing and will grow unless or until a genuine solution to the problem is found. Throwing away the key is the answer—if it can ever be thrown far enough.

Farnham, Eliza (1815–1864) warden of first separate penal institution for women

Before 1839, New York's female prisoners were housed for many years in squalid conditions in the attic room of Auburn State Penitentiary. Finally, in 1839, Mount Pleasant Prison opened in Ossining, New York, near Sing Sing. It was the first separate penal institution for women in the nation.

The first chief matron, or warden, was Eliza Farnham, a 28-year-old Quaker, a firm advocate of rehabilitation as well as a believer in firmness and kindness. Like many other penologists of the era, she erred in her support of the erroneous principles of phrenology. Ironically though, her beliefs nonetheless advanced the so-called medical model of criminology, which recognized that some offenders were sick and in need of cures.

Unlike other prisons of the day, and especially Sing Sing, she broke with the rule of silence that was imposed on male prisoners, allowing 30 minutes of quiet conversation each day. This alone was enough to earn the disdain of Farnham by the rigid administration in Sing Sing. She followed the principle of trying to fill her prisoners' "medical needs" and developed the earliest forms of incentives for good behavior. She also established the first prison nursery in the country.

What finally led to Farnham's downfall was allowing inmates to receive educational benefits and permitting them to read in their cells. This induced the ire of Sing Sing's chaplain, who found novel reading to be the work of the devil. Under continual attacks, Farnham finally was forced to resign in 1847, a victim of Sing Sing harassment by an administration that feared that the Farnham method might be forced on the male prison. Today, Farnham is recognized as an advocate of prisoner treatment far ahead of her time.

Fathers Behind Bars group seeking to promote visitation by families of male inmates

Fathers Behind Bars is a group run by prisoners for prisoners with the goal of assisting male inmates to continue or reestablish contact with their families and enhance family unity. The organization (P.O. Box 86; Niles, Michigan 49120; phone [616] 884-5715) helps in setting up institutional parent groups for imprisoned fathers, teaching basic parenting skills, and preparing inmates for their role of fatherhood.

Ferris, Danny (?–?) jailhouse entrepreneur

Just because offenders are imprisoned, even for life, does not mean that they must give up hustling. This is more simply done by crooked operations in house, so to speak, and victimizing other inmates. However, Danny Ferris saw a bigger world outside and was determined to get a piece of that tempting pie. When his operations were uncovered in the early 1990s, the media dubbed it accurately as the "national jailhouse shopping network."

The in-prison con game operated out of Miami's Dade County jail, where there was a legal requirement that inmates were to be provided with access to telephones. The scam was the brainchild of Ferris, a con man convicted of murder, who for four years made local calls and 1-800 calls free of charge. The telephone proved a better weapon than a gun for Ferris, who simply ordered all sorts of merchandise over it and stole an estimated $2 million—and Ferris did it all on credit! He had accomplices on the outside who provided him with hundreds of credit card numbers (recovered from hotel dumpsters and the like), and Ferris in turn used the numbers to order from catalogs by telephone. He had the goods sent overnight to drops used by his accomplices who then sold the goods and split the profits with the convict. Expensive items rolled in—such as Rolex watches, video cam-recorders, gourmet gift baskets, and even champagne. A particular favorite was gold and silver coins that lost little in value except the sales commissions involved.

Although he made a fortune, Ferris was never greedy, later telling interviewers, "I split right half with everybody. I mean, I never took more than half. I got robbed a lot, but, again, you kind of take it on the chin. You know what I mean? It was like you said, 'Heck, it was all free.'"

In time—some said an inordinately long time—Ferris was exposed. Then the jail officials learned that they could not legally deprive him of his phone rights, but they did cripple his illegal business—they thought—by raiding his cell and confiscating hundreds of credit card numbers.

Ferris did manage to hold out a single number and turned right around to order a newspaper ad and telephone answering service. The advertisement ran in *USA Today* and offered, "Cosmetics package, $89.95 value for only $19.95. All major credit cards accepted. Please call Regina Donovan Cosmetics." Of course, Ferris would never do anything as fraudulent as not supplying the cosmetics and keeping any money. He was not interested in the money. What he wanted was a fresh batch of credit card numbers.

Eventually Ferris was caught again. He took it rather philosophically, or defiantly, reportedly saying, "What are you gonna do? Give me the electric chair." What he got was five years added to his original sentence, which was life imprisonment. However, Ferris was not out of the woods. He ended up being transferred to a tougher Florida state prison, where much more stringent rules were applied to telephone calls.

Meanwhile back at Dade County jail, other inmates started working Ferris's scam. It was as though they did not understand anything like proprietary rights. One inmate, probably to Ferris's dismay, even was put in Danny's old cell and set up business. After the CBS television show *60 Minutes* featured the whole rip-off, jail officials removed the in-cell telephones and made prisoners make their calls in open corridors and the like. The jailhouse shopping network then went bankrupt. One prisoner was reported to have shaken his head, saying, "Danny would have found a way." In the new era of contraband cell phones in prison, he probably could have.

finger wave body search

A routine search technique of prisoners, male and female, is to have them bend over and spread their cheeks. However, prisoners consider this nothing more than an exercise in humiliation because such a visual search will reveal nothing about the inmate other than that he or she might have hemorrhoids.

What must be done instead, but usually only occurs when there are real reasons for suspicion, is what inmates call a finger wave. This requires a guard to carry out a digital examination to determine if the inmate is hiding contraband such as drugs, hacksaws, keys, and the like inside a metal cigar tube—in the inmate vernacular, a "butt plug"—far up the rectum.

Despite these facts, most prisons still conduct the common visual check.

firing squad See EXECUTION METHODS.

"fish" inmate newcomers ripe for prison predators

Often, the most frightening time for newcomers to a prison occurs on their arrival when they are referred to as "fish." Sometimes, the fish arrive in a barred van, and other inmates gather nearby, whistling and offering sexual invitations. Any young-looking arrivals know what to expect, although they are kept away from older prisoners until they are processed and issued clothes. They are then sent to the "fish tier," where they can be viewed by old-timers looking for a sexual partner or a potential victim to be robbed and exploited in other ways.

Most fish gravitate to a tough con who can offer them protection from others if they take on the role of a sexual punk, one who does all chores for a mentor, such as doing laundry, as well as providing sex on demand.

Most prisons insist that they combat such sexual exploitation, but their records clearly leave much to be desired.

flogging early punishment in America

Because prison systems did not come into being until the 1770s, the whipping post was pretty much the punishment of choice for lawbreakers. Of course, the more heinous criminals were dispatched by hanging. Initially, floggings were done with knotted rawhide in a "knout." However, these whips were later replaced by several bounds of leather rawhide, referred to as the cat o' nine tails.

Even after the appearances of prisons, flogging hardly decreased in use. Imprisonment was not regarded as sufficient punishment for crime, so flogging drew few protests. The practice was generally a brutal affair that left the victim permanently scarred and quite often crippled.

The Quakers led the first efforts to eliminate flogging, and after the Revolutionary War, they and other reformers made headway by denouncing the whipping post as an "English" device.

Still, the custom died slowly, especially on the frontier where there was a need for quick justice. Miners' courts meted out far more flogging penalties than hangings, often because the punishment could be meted out on the spot, whereas a malefactor facing death usually was given time to "make peace with your Maker," which necessitated the condemned man to live through the night, get a square meal of sorts, and so on. As a result, miners eager to return to their claims in hopes of striking it rich opted for the good old whipping post. In that sense, floggings saved many a malefactor from the noose.

In the 20th century, floggings virtually disappeared although Maryland reinstituted the penalty at the judge's discretion for wife beatings in 1933 after some three-odd decades. Delaware continued flogging for use prior to incarceration for a number of offenses. Flogging also continued in vogue in some prisons as a punishment for convicts, but even here, they were largely abolished thanks to modern ideas of penology. Still a few institutions in the South admitted its use, and others are believed to practice it secretly.

Folsom Prison's "back alley" "torture as a fine art"

It may be an arguable claim, but by the early decades of the 20th century, California's Folsom Prison was regarded as the most brutal prison in the country, with its torture chambers located in its "back alley." This was a section that was boarded off from the rest of the cell houses. It was here that Ed Morrell, a former convict who would later be regarded as the most important prison reformer of the era, found that torture was carried out as a "fine art." He said, "In there the groans and moans of the victims were lost in empty air."

Here were dreaded dungeons where the whip, the notorious lime cell, and the derrick, among other barbarities, were used on inmates.

Although the derrick was used in various forms, it was nowhere utilized more freely than at Folsom. According to one account as many as 10 inmates per day went to the derrick, not all for offenses committed in the prison but because of previous transgressions—robbery and the like carried out against the Southern Pacific (SP) Railroad. At the time, Folsom was regarded as the SP's prison: The warden and many of the guards were former railroad detectives said to be charged with breaking resistance to the Southern Pacific and its aggressive efforts to take over rights of way.

Sentences on the derrick might be for as much as 50 hours, but the maximum length a person could stand it was about five hours; the longest sentence had the punishment meted out over 10 days.

Located in the lower level of the back alley, the derrick was a block and tackle suspended from a balcony over the convict's head. The inmate's arms would be yanked backward and his wrists secured with handcuffs. Then a guard would pull a rope attached to the handcuffs so that the prisoner was drawn upward. With the victim's heels off the floor, the attendant would give the rope a sharp jerk and tie it fast to a cleat on the side of the wall. The weight of the prisoner's body would force the handcuffs to bite into his wrists as he swung limply from the block and tackle. Then the guard would release an inch or so of slack so that the prisoner could steady his position, the tips of his shoes barely resting on the flagstone of the dungeon. Prisoners who had suffered on the derrick said later that with the initial pain they were overcome by a sense of reeling drunkenness, followed by the return of pain that steadily increased to an excruciating level.

A prisoner's ordeal on the derrick might continue for two hours in the morning and then resume for two hours in the afternoon. Once sentenced to the derrick, a prisoner could have the punishment interrupted or suspended only for medical reasons. A common ailment caused by the punishment was bleeding from a prisoner's kidneys. The prison doctor (called the croaker by prisoners) would be summoned when a prisoner's shoes were soggy with blood. This might gain a prisoner a three-day respite in the prison hospital, but he would then be returned to the dungeon to complete his punishment. Even those prisoners who suffered relatively mild torture on the derrick fell limply to the floor when released and crawled on hands and knees back into the dark shelter of their cells, moaning piteously from their bruises.

The derrick remained in use (as did that of the lime cell) until 1911, when an outraged legislature outlawed all forms of corporal punishment at places of detention. However, it was believed some limited forms of derrick punishment continued thereafter for a number of years.

See also: LIME CELL; MORRELL, ED.

Fortune Society aiding ex-convicts

Probably the most well-known ex-convict rehabilitation organization in the United States, the Fortune Society, founded in 1967, has at its heart a one-to-one counseling program, ex-offender to ex-offender, that uses tutoring programs to raise education levels and encourage development of careers. Since that time, thousands of new persons have come to the Fortune Society's New York offices for help, among them much more than 100 teenagers a year, mostly with arrest and conviction records.

The organization resulted from an instance of life inspired by art, in this case a 1967 Off-Broadway play, *Fortune and Men's Eyes,* written by ex-convict John Herbert. The producer, David Rothenberg, set up a weekly forum that permitted audiences to learn about prison life and problems. Ex-convicts in the forum began to understand how little the "square world" knew about the prison experience. Members of the audience soon were inviting ex-convict panels to speak to their church or school groups.

The society operated out of Rothenberg's office for more than a dozen years but then opened offices on Park Avenue South with a full-time staff of 18 ex-cons and nine others, plus hundreds of volunteers. Since that time, the society has successfully found jobs for 300 or more ex-offenders a year. The society, with its one-to-one style, does not claim to have a magical formula for crime prevention and reduction but rather shares those experiences that have worked in practice. Many other programs and localities have utilized many of the Fortune Society's strategies.

Today, Joanne Page, the current director in New York, is recognized as a top expert on the subject of the release-from-prison trauma undergone by many ex-convicts.

See also: RELEASE-FROM-PRISON TRAUMA.

Frank, Leo (1884–1915) lynched prisoner

The murder of 14-year-old Mary Phagan became a cause célèbre in the South in 1913 and that of her alleged murderer, Leo Frank, a cause célèbre in the North. Frank was a 29-year-old Atlanta businessman, a Brooklyn-born Jew, president of the National Pencil Co. and president of the Atlanta chapter of B'nai B'rith. Mary was found strangled and beaten to death in the pencil factory's basement, and Frank was accused of her rape-murder, with considerable testimony by a semiliterate black, James Conley, employed at the factory.

In an anti-Semitic atmosphere, Frank was convicted of murder and sentenced to death. However, strong evidence of a police frame-up and witness statements by others unearthed by the famed private detective William J. Burns strongly implicated Conley as the actual killer, but public attitude still held to the conviction of Frank. Ironically, this was probably the first murder case in the South in which the word of a black was taken over that of a white man. Going against this firestorm of public opinion, Gov. John M. Slaton, in an act of political suicide, commuted Frank's death sentence in June 1915.

There was much jubilation in the North with the press proclaiming, "The reign of terror in Georgia is over."

It was not.

On August 17, 25 members of a secret vigilante group, the Knights of Mary Phagan, entered the Milledgeville Prison Farm and, without any resistance of the guards, dragged Frank away with them. Frank was taken on a ghastly 175-mile ride to Marietta, Mary's hometown, and lynched before a howling gloating mob. The lynchers then proudly posed around the hanging corpse. The verdict of history was clearly that Leo Frank was innocent. From a penal viewpoint, it was probably the first time in Georgia history that a lynching victim was taken from a state penal institution as distinguished from a jail before trial. The overwhelming independent judgment was this could not have been done without the cooperation, or at least the clear neglect, of the prison authorities and guards.

"frivolous" prisoner lawsuits frequent target of official complaints

Long a bone of contention by corrections and law officials is the number of lawsuits filed by prisoners with grievances that are said to clog up the court system. Others, including some judges, tend to see such efforts as attempts to disparage any claims of prisoners' rights so that serious claims will go unheard.

Especially targeted are lawsuits brought by prisoners acting in their own right or with the aid of "jailhouse lawyers," frequently because the inmates are too poor to afford an attorney to press their case. Undoubtedly, and all sides agree, there are numerous actions brought with little or no merit. But most judges recognize that an innocent inmate must have access to the courts. Chief judge of the Second Circuit Court of Appeals Jon O. Newman has put it, inmates serving their prison sentences "retain their legal rights. Most fundamentally, the right not to be victims of abuse, as many of them are, and the right to minimum standards of sanitation and habitation, and ancillary rights to practice their religion and main access to the courts."

Judge Newman stated, "The prisoners have their important legal rights, but unless a lawyer steps forward to assert their rights, there can be no vindication."

Not surprisingly, opponents cite "frivolous" lawsuits and the need to curtail them. In that regard, Judge Newman's attention was drawn to a letter written to the *New York Times* by four state attorneys general supporting action to curtail prisoner litigation and the need for effective representation of prisoners. The letter was printed by the newspaper at face value with the contention by the writing officials that the three cases cited were "typical" of suits brought by prisoners: "Typical of such suits is the case where an inmate sued, claiming cruel and unusual punishment because he received one jar of chunky and one jar of creamy peanut butter after ordering two jars of chunky from the prison canteen. Or the inmate who sued because there were no salad bars or brunches on weekends or holidays. Or the case where a prisoner is suing New York because his prison towels are white instead of his preferred beige."

Judge Newman in turn wondered about the characterization of these suits "because, though I have seen many prisoner suits that lacked merit, it has not been my experience in 23 years as a federal judge that what the attorneys general described was at all 'typical' of prisoner litigation."

The judge obtained copies of the complaints in the three cases. His findings were part of a commencement speech he made to the graduating class of Brooklyn Law School in April 1996. According to Judge Newman:

In the peanut butter case, the prisoner did order two jars of peanut butter from the canteen and one was the wrong kind. But he did not sue

because he received the wrong product. He sued because, after the correctional officer quite willingly took back the wrong product and assured him that the item he had ordered would be sent the next day, the authorities transferred the prisoner that night to another prison, and his account remained charged $2.50 for the item that he ordered but never received. Maybe $2.50 doesn't seem like much money, but out of a prisoner's commissary account, it is not a trivial loss, and it was for loss of those funds that the prisoner sued.

As for the beige and white towels, the suit was not brought just because of a color preference. The core of the prisoner's claim was that the prison confiscated the towels and a jacket that the prisoner's family had sent him, and disciplined him with loss of privileges. In the case, the prisoner stated, the confiscation, "cause[d] a burden on my family who work hard and had to make sacrifices to buy me the items mention[ed] in this claim."

Lastly, the salad bar claim allegation turns out to be a minor aspect of a 27-page complaint alleging major deficiencies including overcrowding, lack of proper ventilation, lack of sufficient food, confinement of prisoners with contagious diseases and food contamination by rodents. The inmate's reference to the food was to point out that basic nutritional needs are not being met. The claim mentioned that the salad bar was available to corrections officers and to prisoners in other state prisons. It is hardly a suit about lack of a salad bar.

Judge Newman concluded, "I do not mention these cases and the letter of the four attorneys general to pass judgment on their merits, but to remind you that while there are many frivolous claims, those in responsible positions ought not to ridicule all prisoner lawsuits by perpetuating myths about them."

In a fairly erudite response to public dissemination of so-called Top Ten Frivolous Suits, the inmate-published *Prison Legal News* (*PLN*) printed its own "Top Ten Non-Frivolous Prisoner Lawsuits."

One was a finding that a 150-year-old prison in Massachusetts violated inmates' Eighth Amendment rights with massive vermin infestation, fire hazards, and cells with no toilets in which prisoners were locked at night. The use of chemical toilets, a federal court found, resulted in huge health and sanitation hazards, which it said, " . . . the unsanitary conditions that attend the use of toilets in the cells and emptying of them in the slop sink area call to mind the much that 'boils up and pours over' in the gloomy second river of hell, the Styx, described by Dante." *PLN* noted, "This isn't Dante, it's the United States in 1995!"

In a case brought before a federal court in the District of Columbia, prison officials were found liable for systematic abuses of women prisoners in a D.C. prison. Among the findings were insults, sexual harassment, sodomy, rape, assaults, and other matters. In addition, the physical conditions of the facility were dilapidated and a health hazard, and medical care was woefully inadequate. The court also found that women prisoners were discriminated against by gender in regard to programs available to similarly situated male prisoners.

A federal court in California found a massive pattern of abuse at the Pelican Bay state "supermax" prison, citing the fatal shooting of unarmed prisoners to break up minor scuffles, nonexistent medical and mental health care, placing naked prisoners in phone booth–sized wire mesh cages outside in low temperatures, and hog-tying prisoners to their toilets for up to 12 hours as punishment for making noise. The court specifically cited one case in which guards stripped a prisoner and put him in a tub of 160-degree water. Above all, the court found that the brutality was known to have occurred and was condoned by high-ranking California prison officials. The matter came before the court by litigation filed by the inmates, and the court later appointed counsel.

In yet another case, a Denver, Colorado, jury took on the case of former prisoner Arthur Nieto, who claimed damages for deliberate indifference to his serious medical problems. Nieto was held at the Delta Correctional Facility when he developed a cold and sinusitis. This developed into a sinus infection and then spread to his brain. The medical staff ignored his worsening condition, and by the time he was finally taken to a hospital, he had a 105-degree temperature and, according to his lawyer, "his eye had bulged out of the socket and was discharging green pus." He was finally subjected to a number of surgeries and hospitalizations but ended up with permanent brain damage that paralyzed his left side and left him with "major cognitive deficiencies." The jury awarded Nieto $1.8 million in damages but then reduced the figure to $1.44 million because he had failed to take medication even though his attorney noted that "he was too disoriented to do that."

PLN took these sample cases from a 12-month period in which they were reported in their columns and called them part of "a small sampling" of literally hundreds of reports the publication had covered from August 1995 to July 1966.

PLN reported, "These are the cases not mentioned by the Attorney Generals or the DOC's [Department of Corrections] when they talk about prisoner litigation."

G

Gas Chamber See EXECUTION METHODS.

"gassing" "bombing" attacks on guards

In prison lore, the introduction of the San Quentin gas chamber in California led to a counterattack by death-row inmates in the form of cellmade "gas bombs." The ingredients were usually collections of urine and feces, a brew used by inmates in many prisons such as San Quentin. The appearance of gas bombs in the death house was a relatively new practice, and the concoctions were expertly prepared. The urine and feces were stored for a long period of time and were used with precision when finally loosed in a guard's face.

Normally, death row was not the scene of many such offenses against guards because in the past there was always the strong hope for clemency, reversal of sentences, and at least long delays in the carrying out of executions. Some experts say the growing use of gassings on death row was perhaps the start of growing resistance in general to the authorities by San Quentin condemned men. By 2000, San Quentin's death row was generally acknowledged as being the most violent in the nation, and gassings were very common occurrences. One condemned man told his lawyer, "What are they going to do to me? Shoot me?"

See also: SAN QUENTIN DEATH ROW.

"Get Tough With Convicts" States a growth field in Corrections

There is no doubt that a major portion of the U.S. public favors tougher treatment with convicts. They also favor putting more people in prison. And as the number of prisoners increases, more people in turn demand that prison life become tougher. As a result, many prison administrators have banned programs and facilities that they are known to actually favor—television privileges, weight-lifting equipment, computers, and the like. Congress has stopped Pell grants, which helped inmates pay for college courses. In New York, Gov. George Pataki eliminated the Sing Sing Correctional program of state tuition assistance. In Illinois, vocational and college classes in three of its correctional institutions were discontinued.

The reintroduction of chain gangs in a number of states is generally regarded by penal experts as a reflex action by authorities to make prisons less comfortable for inmates and more comfortable for politicians who feel that the practice has become very popular with the public. "Photo ops" for public officials are enormous even if the work done by the chain gangs is less efficient and safe even if the prisoners have the leg shackles but are not attached to one another. Alabama was the first state to bring the chain gang back in 1995 and was followed closely by Arizona, Florida, and Iowa. At least six other states—Indiana, Missouri, Oklahoma, California, Washington, and Wisconsin—put legislation in the works. Alabama later drew back somewhat by eliminating the need to have the men shackled together, which increased the danger of inmate violence or the possibility of traffic accidents when the prisoners worked along highways.

A determined effort to make South Carolina more acceptable to the public's majority desire for more toughness eliminated televisions and air conditioning from cells, banned intramural sports, and ordered the elimination of beards and long hair. This led to an uprising in one facility by Muslim and Rastafarian inmates on religious grounds. At least 10 states—California, Texas, Ohio, North Carolina, New York, Florida, Louisiana, Arizona, Mississippi, and Wisconsin—cut back on prisoner access to recreational activities. The Security Act of 1995 was aimed at keeping federal prisoners from participating in activities that could increase their fighting ability or strength.

Inmates, prisoner-rights groups, and many prison administrators regard such cutbacks as extremely shortsighted. Many institutions already don't follow safety or minimal health standards, a situation that can only become worse. Anything that cuts down on facility ventilation, they note, greatly increases the spread of tuberculosis among inmates who, after they are released, may cause the spread of the highly contagious disease in the general population.

Perhaps the most alarming of all cuts, according to these groups, is the reduction of educational opportunities for convicts, something that more than half the states have done. Survey after survey shows that inmates who pick up an education behind bars are less likely to commit new crimes when they are released.

A study by Anne Piehl, an assistant professor at the John F. Kennedy School of Government at Harvard, showed that male prisoners in Wisconsin who enrolled in high school classes were 10 percent less likely to be rearrested four years after release than convicts who took no such classes.

A reduction of 10 percent of the prison population would, according to the study, save the United States $29 billion a year.

Gideon v. Wainwright See RIGHT TO COUNSEL.

good-time credits reduction of prisoners' sentences based on good behavior

Good-time credits for convicts were established almost as soon as the states started to build prisons in the early 1800s. The idea was that prisoners could earn a reduction of sentence if they behave in prison. In some jurisdictions, this might result in one day off for every five days served; however, the average good-time law allows the deduction of one month off for the first year of good behavior, two months for the second, and so on until the sixth year, when a prisoner can earn six months off his sentence for every year of good behavior.

Some reformers have objected to such an arrangement because the formula is of more aid to a long-term offender than to a short-termer, who is more likely to be a first offender and more likely to be a better rehabilitation risk. When a prisoner has been sentenced by a judge to a definite term, good time is subtracted from that figure. If the sentence is "indeterminate"—that is, say five to ten years—the time is taken off the minimum term. Many convicts cynically regard the use of good time more as a benefit for the prison administration maintaining order and obtaining more labor from them. What can be rather explosive and has caused a number of riots is the subtraction of good time when a convict violates rules. Law-and-order proponents also find the law unjust when inmates can go free in less than half their maximum sentence.

The first good-time law was enacted in New York in 1817. It applied only to first-time prisoners with sentences of less than five years. Such inmates could have their term reduced by one-fourth. In a sense, this would have reduced the complaints of those favoring longer terms for prisoners. However, there seems to be no record of the law ever being applied. After New York, some states including Connecticut, Tennessee, and Ohio passed similar laws, but they appear to have been used very sparsely.

It was after the Civil War that good-time statutes really caught on, following the example of the "Irish system," whereby a convict could win freedom by earning a certain number of "marks," or credits. Within three years of the end of the Civil War, states passed such laws, and today they are the norm. Some states allow for these reductions in sentences to be enhanced by "industrial good time." This may be in the form of shop work, instead of seeking training programs that develop skills and trades, and especially developing the attitudes that will or could be of far more value upon release into society. Some industrial good time is gained for volunteering to take part in medical experiments. However, usually these credits only apply to the convict's first parole hearing rather than the sentence itself. If the inmate loses in the first parole try—usually the case—such credits go down the drain. Of course, when this is the result, most convicts feel that they have been "conned" by the system.

A problem that frequently arises is that convicts take their good-time benefits as a right. This is especially a problem when a new inmate is immediately credited with what would be maximum time off and then loses some of the credits whenever he or she violates prison rules. Convicts tend to see this as something given with one hand and then taken back by the other. As stated previously, this has become a major cause in a number of prison riots.

In the past, it has been very difficult for prisoners to persuade the courts to consider the way prison officials reach decisions on applying discipline, especially when there is some loss of liberty to the inmate. Finally, the U.S. Supreme Court ruled in *Wolfe v. McDonnell* in 1974 that a prisoner who loses good-time credits without any sort of hearing was entitled to some of sort of due process. The High Court set conditions that included a 24-hour written notice of the charges and a hearing before a discipline committee. The Court also granted permission for the presentation of some evidence and to call witnesses, provided that institutional control was not endangered. The disciplinary committee was then required to provide its decision and explain the reasoning behind it.

This was not all prisoners' advocates wanted, however. The Court refused the inmate the right to cross-examine witnesses or to have a lawyer present, although it was sometimes permissible to have a staff member or another prisoner to assist the inmate. The overall effect was to grant prisoners a certain amount of rights in such disciplinary proceedings—in short, some due process but not the full amount allowed to a defendant at a criminal trial.

See also: PRERELEASE PROGRAMS.

groupies of death row sometimes viewed as the "ultimate turn-on"

There is an axiom about the women who flock in spirit to condemned men. It is that the more vicious or shocking the crime for which they were convicted, the more women will be attracted to the men. In recent years, the most striking example of "murder groupies" was the young women who became known as "Ted groupies" and were a public phenomenon during the trial of serial killer Ted Bundy. They were seated in the first row behind the defense table and giggled for joy whenever their beau ideal turned toward them and flashed a handsome smile. The fact that they knew he was accused of killing young women much like themselves apparently offered special delight.

The groupies of death row are unique among crime groupies. Many women are attracted to convicts doing time, and many others can be classified as murder groupies who form psychological attachments to convicts sentenced to life with or without parole. There are many psychological theories offered about their behavior, but the most vivid of all are those offered by women who focus on men facing almost certain execution. Many men on death row seem to be bewildered themselves by the women's attraction to them. No letters sent to prisoners are more pornographic than those for condemned men. Many of the letter writers include Polaroid shots of the woman in every imaginable naked pose with apt descriptions of the sex acts she would like to perform with the condemned man.

Linwood Briley, the leader of the infamous mass escape of six condemned men from the Mecklenburg (Virginia) Correctional Center's death row in 1983, the only mass escape from death row in any U.S. prison, was deluged with offers of pornographic admiration both before his escape and after his later recapture. It was something that left him amazed, to say the least. A typical admirer sent Linwood scores of letters and naked photographs and promised him sex in every manner imaginable, describing the facts as the heaven that awaited him when he won his freedom. Linwood shared some of the communications with a death-row buddy who joked with him that the young female would be "waiting a long time for salvation."

Linwood kept up his communications with the female, apparently among others, a very common pattern among condemned men. While it cannot be said that much scholarly research has studied the phenomenon of death-row groupies, a work by Sheila Isenberg, *Women Who Love Men Who Kill,* found that virtually all such females come from abusive or loveless backgrounds. From the women's perspective, the relationships that develop are most rewarding, the men responding with a stream of letters and numerous collect calls.

According to Isenberg, the "forced chastity" between the couples added to the "romance" for the relationship. Others see the women attracted by the controlled nature of the relationship, something generally new to the women, but others see the sex as a new form of control, one in the hands of the women, always with the promise of uninhibited intimacy if and when the killer got free, a goal always stated. The condemned man himself adds to the romance by promising to be a one-groupie man. He may not keep that promise, but both parties achieve rewards they need. The woman has a relationship that she controls, probably for the first time in her life. The men gain a helpmate, one who fights for a retrial or release for him and buoys him up with total belief in his innocence. If there is an element of deliberate or self-induced delusion involved here, it is not to be unexpected. Within the concepts of the state putting people to death on a very selective basis, it is from the doomed men's perspective just one more insanity in the web in which they find themselves.

guards, prison

The saying goes, with apologies to Gilbert and Sullivan, that "a prison guard's lot is not a happy one." A leader of the New York State guards' union has been quoted that guards have a higher divorce rate, heart disease, and alcohol addiction than any other state civil servants—and the shortest life spans. Prison is clearly just about the most stressful place there is—both for the inmates and their keepers.

The fears guards have, of course, are headed by the convicts. They live in constant jeopardy facing the inmates, not merely from violence, but also from the possibility of contracting AIDS or tuberculosis. When Ted Conover started working on his 2000 book *Newjack* about guards' life at Sing Sing, he found that a corrections officer had recently infected his family with prison-contracted TB and another one had succumbed to a resistant strain. Surprisingly to Conover, he found that a sense of shame infected a number of guards. One union rep named Kingsley from an upstate prison was described as admitting "that probably 90 percent of the officers he knew would tell strangers they met that they worked not in a prison but at something else—say carpentry—because the job carried such a stigma." The guard rep described prison work as being all about waiting—the prisoners waiting for their sentences to end and the corrections officers for their time to retire. As the rep put it, for the guards, it was "a life sentence in eight-hour shifts."

Most guards clearly feel unappreciated by their superiors and especially by the politicians and by the public in general.

Back in the 1950s or so, esteem for prison guards was probably the lowest since the terrible conditions of the 1800s. The image of brutal guards as depicted in Hollywood films met general acceptance by the public. A leading investigative reporter of the day, John Bartlow Martin, who delved into many notorious prison riots of the period for leading popular publications—an endeavor that would enjoy little such interest in most popular magazines today—concluded that much was wrong with guards of that time.

In a best-selling book, *Break Down the Walls,* Martin pointed out the special difficulties at prisons during periods of full employment when guards drew very little pay compared to others, making ideal recruitment most difficult. But the problem went much deeper than low salaries. "Who wants to be a prison guard?" Martin asked. "A few, a very few, men become guards in a missionary spirit. A few take the job because it gives them a license to use a club. (A criminologist at a large northern penitentiary once knew a guard who reached sexual orgasm while witnessing an electrocution.)"

Martin focused on the vast majority in between the missionary and the sadist, men who simply needed to make a living, who stumbled on to this sort of employment, and who wanted a steady job and the security of government work. "Most of them have worked previously as farmers, truck-drivers, or common laborers. Some are not sadists but nonetheless enjoy their power over other human beings; they may belong to the lower middle class, their houses may be shoddy, their wives may nag at them and their children disobey them, they may be forever falling behind in their installment-plan payments—but when they get to work each morning hundreds of men tip their caps and call them 'sir,' and at any moment they can put a man in The Hole if they don't like his looks."

Back then—and probably equally true today—most prison guards suffer from low morale. They frequently have two enemies, as do most inmates—although not the same ones. Prisoners look upon their keepers as their enemie
remaining foes are other i
in the latter c
The g
course,
today—
under s
than wh
pensions
they can l
ity by a w
the old d
Joseph Rag
guards. Dr
Ragen's dis
could be ve
searched as h
a number of l
and two cans o
"The stuff he w
but he had to c
Guards will start
ing barbitals in t
carrying money; a
the big job." That i

Ragen could, in
guards, exhibit a de
The warden strictly ... than
necessary with inmat ... certainly with their families. Once he caught a guard in a hotel with the wife of a prisoner. Ragen recalled the situation with a touch of frustration and yet satisfaction. "I didn't get a chance to fire him—he went home, told his wife about it, and shot himself."

Another common foe for many guards is some of their counterparts. Some observers report considerable friction between old-school COs (corrections officers) and newer recruits, and there are many instances of racism between guards that suddenly explode into view. After a series of such explosions at Martin Correctional Institution (MCI), in Florida in 1995, the *Palm Beach Post* headlined one story in a series as "Racial Tensions Growing at MCI: A Probe Details Racist Mail and Slurs Directed at Black Officers." The series of articles detailed a long-standing tradition of harassing, threatening, humiliating, and intimidating of blacks by their white co-workers.

Such harassments are endemic in many prisons, and they are hardly limited to black guards. In one California prison, a Jewish guard was handcuffed to a fence by fellow COs, who later were found to be neo-Nazis. A white guard paraded around with a swastika carved in the wooden stock of his rifle; another showed off his Ku Klux Klan membership card. A black guard in California suffered harassment by white co-workers and had his new truck vandalized until finally he was forced to request a transfer out of his highly prized supervisory post.

Of course, such guard-on-guard racism pales to significance compared to what many label the
cist brutality common in many prisons by
rds on inmates. Often singled out as among the
e brutal is Corcoran State Prison in California,
ch has been described as a leader in so-called
ator fights in which rogue COs stage and
r on battles between inmates of rival ethnici-
d gangs, many of whom seek to fight to the
Maximum-security Corcoran was in the
ited in a number of other brutality scan-
1995, eight guards and officers were fired
reatment of 36 black prisoners transferred
ison from Calipatria State Prison, some of
ere charged with assaulting guards. In
the prisoners were said to have threat-
e over Corcoran when they got there.

urned out that a Calipatria lieutenant had called ahead to inform a Corcoran associate warden that the stories about the 36 prisoners was nothing but unfounded rumors. However, the rumors were passed on to the guards, but the officer did not bother to report the denials coming out of Calipatria.

About 30 officers turned out to greet the incoming shackled prisoners, who were seized one by one from the bus, some by their testicles, and choked, punched, and thrown to the ground. One prisoner's ribs were broken, and another's head was smashed into a window, breaking it. Another had a towel stuffed down his throat, and another's face was banged into a concrete wall. Prisoners were taken indoors for more punishments.

The associate warden was cited in his termination notice as "validating" the action taken against the arriving prisoners as appropriate "disciplinary action" and failing to investigate the injuries reported by the new arrivals. He also authorized $1,000 worth of overtime for guards who met the bus. Although eight firings were made, the men all filed for administrative appeals, and five had their punishments reduced to suspensions for a period of time; a lieutenant and sergeants among them were demoted to correctional officers. The discharge of the assistant warden and a captain was not changed.

Of the case, the warden later said that officials "do not tolerate our staff abusing inmates—we never have and we never will." And he added, "We are not a bunch of knuckle-dragging thugs."

Two years later, a "deep-sixing" scandal broke at the prison. The custom, in place for many years, was revealed by one regarded as about the worst of the prison's COs, Roscoe Pondexter, a bruising former bench-warmer from the Boston Celtics, who turned state's evidence. He was a "fish cop" whose duty, as one account put it, was "strangling inmates underwater while other guards crushed and yanked the victims' testicles." The fish cop explained, "It's like taking a dive underwater and not coming up. You give the prisoner only enough air to hear your message. . . ."

After this scandal, the warden had a new observation to make about his guards: "I'll admit that some of my staff have gone crazy."

The fact remained that in a number of prisons, organized groups of guards operate as violent racists. In Corcoran, the bus greeters were known as "sharks," or sometimes more facetiously as the "welcome wagon." Many of the sharks were said to come in on their days off if a busload was due. At the California Institution for Men at Chino, another group called itself SPONGE, an acronym for "Society for the Prevention of Niggers Getting Everything." Then there was the less overt outfit called the "European American Officers Association." In 2000, the new supermax federal prison at Florence, Colorado, was plagued by a renegade group of guards called "The Cowboys." Often aimed at inmates of color, a number of Cowboys were accused of choking handcuffed inmates, mixing waste into food, and then discouraging whistle blowers among the guards and nursing staff by warning that if they were attacked by inmates, they might not have any assistance.

Naturally, brutality among prisoners is much larger in scope and, of course, in population. This behavior pattern of criminals becomes a license to those elements of guards who take the job, as Martin put it, to use clubs. All guards learn to live with the constant threat of violence. Various guards react in varying ways. Guards who are less prone to brutality actually do in many cases express contempt, at least privately, for brutal types. Kelsey Kauffman, a former Connecticut police officer, in her book *Prison Officers and Their World* (1988), interviewed guards who described some of their fellow officers as thriving on violence and basically being no different morally than the inmates. Some were described as doing their thing as a way to gain prestige. One prison guard at Bridgewater in Massachusetts described his violent co-workers as "banana heads. They look for trouble."

Yet, guards in the vast middle actually will carry out violence as well, many feeling that, at times, brutal treatment appeared to be a deterrent. Some are simply carried away by events. Brutality incidents are rarely carried out in a one-on-one manner. Such situations become all the more dangerous for the inmate who is put at a numerical disadvantage and at the same time stirs up group psychology. Kauffman quoted an interviewee who explained, "Once one guy throws the first blow, they like all get their courage up and say, 'Okay, it's accepted. Let's do a number on him.'"

There are some brutal guards who operate only with a few chosen others who, they know, will never inform on them, but, actually, the code of silence will keep guards in the vast middle quiet because they may have genuine fears for survival, especially if failure to conform to the silence code puts them in an isolated position that could result in their deaths.

America's number-one brutal warden, Elam Lynds, who was Sing Sing's first warden, felt that he had to treat his guards almost as badly as he did the prisoners and thus make them behave in his own image. It worked for Lynds, and although his influence today is virtually repudiated, there are those who say the prison system remains a trap for two sorts of people, the inmates and too many of their keepers.

See also: "COWBOYS, THE"; "DEEP SIXING"; LYNDS, ELAM; RAPE IN PRISON.

guards' dictionary

To themselves, the average prison guard and others are the masters of the place, with the right to do virtually what they please. This of course would be denied by prison administrations. The guards themselves generally become angry with even being called *guards* by outsiders, despite its obvious generic usage, *hacks* by the inmates. They refer to themselves as *correctional officers*. However, they do accept the convicts' descriptions of some of them as *supercops*. The term is used pejoratively by prisoners to refer to guards whom they feel needlessly harass them. The guards accept the term as describing a strong guard, one not likely to fall for inmates' tricks.

Other terms used by prisoners have a different meaning for guards as well. Guards and inmates use the term *snitch* to refer to a prisoner who informs on others, but the guards are much more venomous when they use the term against other guards who are suspected of informing on brutal behavior or other infractions by some of their fellows. Brutality in the form of beating of prisoners is likewise generally denied by guards and their superiors, but guards do have a justifying term for such acts that allegedly never happen—*thump therapy.*

Just as the use of the word *guard* rankles them, they insist on calling all prisoners *inmates,* which prisoners resent because the feel they are being insulted by use of a term better used in a mental ward. Other prison employees likewise resent the use of the guards' description of them as *weak sisters*. Actually, there are more other staff employees than guards, many of whom receive higher pay. Among the staffers are psychologists, ministers, hospital employees, maintenance people, supervisors of special prison operations, as well as secretaries, teachers, counselors, and administrators in charge of special prison activities, and food stewards who supervise inmate cooks.

To the guards, these are all weak sisters because they have no authority to oversee them or to run the cell blocks, and many of these are viewed as weak because their jobs require them to help inmates.

As the guards would have it, they are the men of strength who prevent a prison from collapsing.

"guard wars" convict traps for guards

They've started to call it *guard wars*—the tricks prisoners use to hurt or humiliate their keepers. The standard method is "sliming," filling a cup with urine and feces, letting it curdle, and then tossing the contents in a guard's face and eyes, causing pain to the eyes and more painful humiliation in general.

Many guards have learned the hard way when carrying out a cell search not to put a hand or finger where they can't see what can happen. Instead, a small screwdriver should be used to run along the metal tip above a cell door. There might be a booby trap there. Inmates are fond of taping razor blades along the edge of a door frame in hope that a guard might run his fingers along the edge. Because finding narcotics is a big plus for guards, some carelessly make a sad mistake when finding a small packet of white powder by deciding to taste it. It will turn out to be caustic toilet-boil cleaner.

Some of the more technically adept inmates have even hooked up homemade listening devices in a room used by guards to overhear when a search is planned and to discover other important intelligence.

See also: "GASSING"; "SLIMING."

Gurule, Martin F. (1979–1998) mass death-row escape planner

Probably the nearest thing to a successful mass escape from death row after that from Virginia's death row in 1984 by the Mecklenburg Six was the attempted breakout by seven condemned men from Texas's Huntsville Prison complex on Thanksgiving Night 1998. Martin Gurule was said to have been the leader. It fell short of the would-be escapees' hopes when a guard spotted the seven jumping from a roof inside the institution. Under fire from the guard, six of the men dropped to the ground; only Gurule kept going.

Gurule avoided a rain of bullets and cleared two razor-wire-topped perimeter fences. A massive hunt for Gurule by hundreds of law officers, tracking dogs, trucks, and helicopters followed in more than 17,000 swamp areas infested with water moccasins. After a week, it appeared that Gurule may have made good his escape.

However, on December 3, two off-duty prison employees found his body while fishing less than a mile from the prison. It appeared Gurule had been dead from the time of the breakout.

See also: MECKLENBURG SIX.

...se stop for many convicts ...n which a number of ...ontrolled atmosphere. ...ion by some neighborhood groups ... to having such places located in their community and the removal of such houses on occasion, halfway houses receive growing advocacy from corrections professionals as a helpful method of returning offenders back to society. In other cases, some offenders are sentenced directly to live in a halfway house rather than going to prison.

Although most halfway houses and similar residential centers are not locked, there is very tight supervision. Residents can leave to go to school or to work, but they have to be checked in and out. On staff changes or at night, head counts are made to account for all residents. Alcohol and drugs are not permitted, nor are tools that can be used as weapons. Many halfway houses are compartmentalized, focusing on specialized groups of offenders, such as those with alcohol or drug problems, gambling addicts, and sex offenders, and they are staffed with trained counselors. Some inmates with good-behavior records in prison are released to halfway houses to attend school or to hold jobs in a more natural environment, but they have to follow rules that increase their readjustment to the outside world. In some special facilities, women with preschool children are permitted to have their children with them, and day care is provided so that school or jobs can be scheduled.

Obviously, halfway houses concentrate on treating causes of an inmate's problem rather than continuing to punish him or her.

Such homes are not popular with the majority of the general public, who opt for imprisonment rather than what some regard as "coddling" of criminals. Sometimes, the uproar can be explosive. In New Jersey in January 2001, the state supreme court ordered the parole of a man who, along with a confederate, killed two police officers in brutal fashion in 1963. The man, Thomas Trantino, at one time sentenced to death for the crime and later having the punishment reduced to life, was eligible for parole since 1979. Police groups, families of the victims, and politicians strove successfully nine times to thwart his bids for freedom. In 2001, the state's highest court by a 4-1 vote ordered him transferred to a halfway house within 30 days, saying his release after 37 years was probably long overdue. At age 62, Trantino had spent more time behind bars than any other current inmate in New Jersey.

The ruling took note of the anger and public pressure that had surrounded the case, declaring: "Portions of this record can be read to suggest that under the law Trantino was eligible for transfer to a halfway house and subsequent release several years ago, but that public pressure prevented that from occurring. No matter how great the pressure, agencies of government cannot ignore the law in special cases. At its core, this case is more about the rule of law than it is about Thomas Trantino."

Trantino, by the court's ruling, would have to stay in the halfway house for one year to demonstrate his ability to reenter society successfully. One argument used against Trantino's release was that he had failed to take responsibility for the murders and often said that he was too drunk on the night of the shootings to remember what happened. One of the conditions of his halfway house term required that Trantino demonstrate that he could remain sober and law abiding during the trial 12 months. If he were to violate any of the rules, he could be returned to prison.

In New York State, halfway houses are operated by private companies contracted by the state. The houses range in size from 10 beds to 500 beds. Nonviolent offenders live under conditions that govern when and where they can come and go, whom they may visit, and who can visit them, as well as when and whether they can hold a job. The inmates must account for 100 percent of their time and whereabouts. Violent offenders like Trantino enjoy fewer privileges. Nonviolent offenders eventually can earn the right to visit family members whose homes have been inspected by corrections officials. They can visit a church, a store, or a movie theater, as long as the house staff knows exactly where they are going and they check in before, during, and after their visits. Violent offenders earn such visits only if they are with a staffer.

Halfway houses have from time to time been caught in the web of such controversial cases as Trantino's, and many supporters wish that the operations of such prerelease centers would be as free of controversy as possible. Others, however, insist that the enormous sums required to continue building prisons at the rate of the recent few decades may modify taxpayer objections to halfway houses, which clearly appears to be an idea that has come and promises to grow. In New York, halfway houses can contain some 3,000 offenders; without such facilities, prison overcrowding would become even more acute. The trend is clearly for more halfway houses rather than fewer.

hanging once the almost universal execution method in the United States

Today, only a handful of states allow for execution by hanging, and often the condemned person can pick a different option. In Utah, for instance, most condemned prisoners, offered a choice will opt for the firing squad over hanging. There is a valid explanation for this because hanging proved to be the most "dirty" method with easily the most botched executions of any kind.

For a long time, the very messiness of hangings seemed to meet with some approval by the public, which seemed to turn out in the hopes that something would go wrong. Some devoted hanging experts also applauded the frequent painful and cruel attempts at hanging as a deterrent factor for other lawbreakers. (Because hanging, in all its repulsiveness, went back in history for many centuries, one might have expected that, by the 20th century, murder and other capital offenses might have been deterred out of existence.)

There was always a ritual that, through practice and refinement, was supposed to make hangings cleaner. The clean technique—which experts estimated occurred less than half of the time—developed a number of improvements. First of all, the embarrassment of the rope slipping from the crossbeam of the gallows is avoided by having the rope attached to a chain suspended from the crossbeam.

The hangman's duty is to adjust the knot so that it is positioned extremely tightly behind the left ear. (It was always helpful when the hangman had not built up his nerve by excessive drinking, which could cloud his performance.) A hood is then placed over the victim's head so that witnesses do not have to see the final grimaces. In some jurisdictions, the hangman does not spring the trapdoor himself; he fixes the knot and binds the legs together to prevent kicking and positions the doomed person correctly over the trapdoor so that the victim drops without hitting an obstruction.

The hangman then signals that all is ready so that three people in a little booth on the platform can each cut a string, only one of which springs the trapdoor. With the drop, the knot ideally will strike behind the left ear instantly, bringing on unconsciousness. When all goes properly, just the right number of small bones in the cervical vertebrae in the neck are broken so that the head is not ripped off. The bones should then collapse on the spinal cord, cutting off oxygen to the brain and paralyzing the rest of the body. Rapid brain death ensues.

Result: A very clean hanging.

Other jobs were much less clean but still regarded as satisfactory. That happened when the victim's final thrashing lasted only a few minutes. Considerable wheezing might occur but not to the extent of a really dirty job. There was, of course, other unpleasantness involved, for example, the stench of the victim urinating, defecating, or ejaculating—or all three at the same time. Other odors, such as that of overwhelming perspiration, added to the sickening scene, especially when topped by human waste running down the deceased's legs and dropping to the floor. Ensuing violent shudders might last only a few minutes, and then the rope would stop dancing. After one final jerk, there would be just a bit of twitching and then quiet.

So much for clean or relatively clean hangings, again usually a minority of the cases involved. Former San Quentin warden Clinton Duffy witnessed some 60 hangings. Following is a paraphrase of Duffy's description of the more common dirty hangings:

"The hideous process of the hanging of a doomed man goes on for a quarter of an hour, with strangulation doing very slowly. His wheezing is extremely loud and best described as the hysterical squealing of a dying pig. Sometimes the victim may even bob up and down on the rope like a yo-yo as he struggles for air. Even his bound legs whip far out as though seeking a perch. Sometimes a guard must grab the legs and hold them steady so that his violent churnings do not break the rope. Now is the time that many witnesses become most sickened. With death, it is difficult to tell whose suffering was worse, that of the doomed man or the witnesses."

A truly messy job involved that of the notorious outlaw "Black Jack" Ketchum, a noted rival of Butch Cassidy for leadership of numerous gangs. Ketchum's capture was a sensation, and newspapers from coast to coast covered his trial, including even the *New York Times*. It was considered sufficient that Ketchum could be convicted of "attempted train robbery" because that offense called for the death penalty.

Ketchum was able to watch through his cell window as the scaffold for his execution was built. "Very good, boys," he yelled to the workmen as they completed their task, "but why don't you tear down the stockade so the boys can see a man hang who never killed anyone."

On the day of his execution on April 26, 1901, the doomed man "leaped" up the gallow steps, the *Times* correspondent reported. Ketchum helped in adjusting the noose around his neck and announced cheerfully, "I'll be in Hell before you start breakfast." After the black cap was placed over his head, Ketchum called out, "Let 'er go."

The trap was sprung, but the weights had been amateurishly adjusted, and Ketchum's head was torn from his shoulders. Later, some writers could not resist embellishing the victim's last words to "Let her rip."

Oddly, the ghoulish revision was most pleasing to reformers. For the first time, the public received front-page coverage of the abomination of hanging, and more and more people came to conclude that technique could be quite troubling. The swing of public opinion needed several more decades to fester in opposition, and the dirty hangings continued. In West Virginia in the 1930s, a wife murderer named Frank Myer was hanged even though the hangman himself undoubtedly regarded him as poor hanging material. Myer was heavyset with a short neck and what was described as "soft bones." When the trapdoor was released, Myer's body crashed to the concrete floor, followed by a sickening second thud as his head landed nearby and proceeded to roll toward the witnesses, several of whom could not contain their violent reactions. In interviews after the execution, several insisted that they would never again attend a hanging.

One after another, states abandoned hanging, and even those that continued to permit it generally offered the condemned another option, that of shooting or the electric chair.

When the Supreme Court reimposed the death penalty, the first execution occurred in Utah, where Gary Gilmore was offered the choice of the noose or the firing squad; he opted for shooting. Clearly, hanging would never return to its good or bad old days.

Harris, Ambrose See PRISONIZATION.

Haviland, John (1792–1852) designer of Eastern Penitentiary at Cherry Hill, Pennsylvania

In 1820, a group of Pennsylvania Quakers hired a young British architect named John Haviland to design a new prison that would adhere to the Quaker concept that solitary confinement around the clock would eventually lead prisoners to achieve introspection and repentance. The prisoners put in such a prison would be free of "contamination" from other prisoners.

The prison that Haviland designed at Cherry Hill consisted of individual cells 11 feet 9 inches long, 7 feet 6 inches wide, and 16 feet high. That is somewhat larger than the space allotted in some maximum-security prisons today, but the inmates at Cherry Hill also worked in their cells, doing such chores as metalworking, spinning, and shoemaking, with no escape 24 hours a day from the foul and unwholesome air that always filled the cells.

Haviland's design did allow prisoners out for an hour a day to exercise, but this was in an individual walled yard adjoining the cell. Inmates were allowed to see or communicate with no one. The prison design was in the form of a giant wagon wheel that radiated out from a central hub. The cells had two doors, one of lattice and the other solid, both kept closed. The inmates were put in their cells and remained there, alone with work and the Bible. Religious services were held but did not impair the isolation of the prisoners. A minister would stand at the end of a long corridor, and the solid doors were opened, but the inmates still could not see the minister or any other prisoner. A black curtain was drawn over the lattice door, and the inmates could only sit on a tiny stool and listen to the minister's words.

Haviland's design drew hundreds of visitors from around the world to study the system. Many, especially the more fervently religious, found the prison inspiring. Others attacked it viciously, including Charles Dickens, who found Cherry Hill inhumane. Critics pointed out that the total silence at the prison was a myth. An inmate being taught a trade had to have an instructor, which was not exactly solitude, and others had to come out of their cells in groups to perform prison maintenance work, which also was not solitude. Also, critics were correct that prisoners held in the strictest isolation will nonetheless, with much ingenuity and fortitude, find ways to communicate with one another, using tapped out messages or other methods. It was further charged that even if solitary could be enforced, far less regenerations would occur compared to cases of madness.

While the Cherry Hill or Pennsylvania system was started, New York came up with a rival system; the so-called Auburn system appeared in New York at its main prison. Here, the inmates were allowed out of their cells by day to work together in shops, but they were also forbidden to talk to one another. They marched to their work posts in lockstep, with downcast gazes. In Auburn, the cells were only 3 feet wide, 7 feet long, and 7 feet high—about one-eighth the size of the Cherry Hill cells. The cells rose five tiers high. They were inside cells, built back to back and positioned in the center of a cellhouse shell. If anything, the New York system was more cruel, with the staff employing floggings and other brutalities with the approval of superiors.

Yet, in the end, the New York system was bound to win out. The Pennsylvania method required too much space, and the idea of having inmates work in the cells was contrary to the burgeoning industrial revolution. Still, Haviland's design remained very popular in many penal systems, although with some modifications. It remained the model in later systems such as the federal penitentiary at Leavenworth, Kansas, and the state facility at Trenton, New Jersey, among others. Haviland's designs were even more widely utilized in the rest of the world and can be seen in Asia, Africa, and much of Europe. Belgium actually dismantled its entire penal system and rebuilt it to Haviland's standards.

In the United States, Haviland designs are slowly disappearing, mainly as older prisons start to crumble, to be replaced by more "enlightened" designs. However, in some cases where new prisons are built near these older ones with a view to being a total replacement, it is often the case that the older prisons are kept in use, inefficient as they might be. The need for additional cell space keeps them from being dismantled (or in some cases being turned into museums). The lesson, say some observers, is that we can always find a way to preserve even bad prisons.

Hell's Angels behind bars power of the cycle gangs

By and large, the most powerful gangs behind bars tend to be black, such as the D.C. Blacks, who were very powerful and violent on the outside and went to prison in such numbers that they automatically became dominant in several prisons. White gangs by contrast tend to be much smaller but can play a role in in-prison rackets such as gambling and drug trafficking. However, when they become too big or rich, they are almost certain to be challenged by the black gangs.

An exception are the Hell's Angels and other cycle gangs who tend to enjoy a measure of respect by inmates, even those committed to cornering racket sources. The involvement of cycle gangs on the outside has often been emphasized by the fact that drug traffickers, including Mafia crime families, often use cycle gangs when shipping drugs cross-country. Cycle gangs have been used as escorts, particularly for shipments going from Florida and Georgia north to Philadelphia, where many of the supplies are divided and shipped to New York and other states and from where the rest are forwarded to Montreal.

The fact that the divisions took place in the Philadelphia area has not been lost on black traffickers within the large Graterford Penitentiary near that city. It is known to them that drugs that reach them come from the Philly supply chain. As a result, the Hell's Angels and others have been able to entrench themselves in the prison. It is recognized that their power extends far beyond their numbers. These cyclists have strong connections with large gangs on the outside and have the ability to apply pressure and indeed violence on the outside that can impact badly on black gang inmates.

As drug dealers in prison the Hell's Angels and their ilk extend their moneymaking ability because of their business orientation and discipline. The cycle gangs are generally not interfered with by other gangs and are looked on by them as a source of supplies.

hepatitis C in prisons more threatening than HIV or TB?

It is very difficult to measure the amount of infection present in adult prisons. The HIV-positive infection rate in federal and state institutions runs just slightly more than the 2 percent level. TB is harder to calculate because not that many federal/state systems and city/county systems issue reports on TB.

This may mean that the larger menace may be hepatitis C, which is known to infect a significant proportion of all inmates. There are some experts who have estimated that 40 percent of the inmate population may be infected with hepatitis C. This is a deadly, infectious disease that attacks the liver after lying dormant for many years. There is no sure cure for the disease, which is spread through contact with contaminated blood and spreads like wildfire behind bars where intravenous drug users are among the most common carriers.

Because almost all prisoners eventually are freed from prison, it is certain that many of them will bring the disease with them to the outside world.

hole, Pennsylvania's worst

It may be a fruitless endeavor to find the worst solitary units within the U.S. prison system in the 20th century. Certainly, however, Pennsylvania would rank high on the list, some of its solitary units aptly described as four-by-four-by-fours. The figures describe, shockingly, the full dimensions of a punishment cell in *feet*. Thus, a prisoner confined in the hole would be unable to stand up or lie down fully. His choice of sleeping position ranged between sitting or fetal. The prisoner was fed two slices of bread and water in the morning and the same ration in the afternoon. Only every third day did he receive a full meal.

The four-by-four-by-fours were finally abolished in the mid-1950s when the governor brought in a new commissioner of corrections to bring about reforms because the prisons in the state were clearly reaching the boiling point and the threat of riots was rising. Three meals a day were ordered for prisoners in the punishment cells, they were given exercise time outside their cells, and corporal punishment was prohibited.

The changes caused a growing resentment by many guards who felt that unruly prisoners were not being sufficiently punished. Perhaps what caused the greatest backlash was a requirement that hole inmates were entitled to have a light in their cells. Keeping men in permanent or near-permanent darkness had always been seen as a must by prison hard-liners, but now the rules were changing on that as well. Prison employees found a way to fight back, by in effect proclaiming, "Okay, if they need light we'll give them light!" In what is believed to have been the first use of a new punishment technique, solitary cells were equipped with 24-hour lighting that never went out. Getting to sleep and then staying asleep became a new ordeal for prisoners. One state prison went as far as building a cell out of transparent plexiglass in a "glass cage," as it was called, which guaranteed a truly unyielding source of light.

While some reforms were affected, resistance to them kept the state's prisons in such an outrageous condition that finally, in the 1970s, a court-ordered consent degree had to be issued that did improve matters, especially in the hole.

However, even then certain reforms remained hard to institute. A limit was put on the time for which a prisoner could be consigned to the hole, generally a maximum of 180 days. Guards got around that restriction by how they wrote up misconduct reports. The general method had been to list all infractions in a single report, but now the guards listed each infraction separately—struggling with restraints, cursing a guard, and so on. As a result, troublemakers could still go to the hole for years at a time.

The end result of this was that solitary cells were filled to capacity. Soon, the state was forced to go to double-celling, and solitary just wasn't solitary anymore. The headaches went much further for prison administrations as continuing violence in the general populations caused many prisoners to ask for protective custody. These prisoners ironically had to be stashed away in cells with the same restrictions placed on troublesome inmates. In the end, punishments for misbehaving prisoners had to be cut back because there was no room for all of them. Through the years since then, conditions in Graterford, the state's top-security prison, continued in a state of flux, with anger still shown by inmates and by their keepers as well.

Hole, the prison isolation punishment

"The Hole," is, and in a number of cases, remains a gruesome isolation punishment for "incorrigible inmates." Let us look at the way the Hole was operated for many years at Leavenworth federal prison. Inmates were flung into a dark, windowless cell that was bare of any furnishings. A hole in the floor functioned as a latrine. If a prisoner did not become more cooperative, rations would be cut so that one barely could stay alive. Again, under the federal system, considered less brutal than those in other jurisdictions, not all prisoners went into windowless cells, but the cells took on the name of *the Hole*. Actually, solitary confinement was the punishment, but at Leavenworth additional horrors took place because so many convicts were sent to the Hole that two to as many as five prisoners were confined in what was supposed to be a single-inmate cell.

Any Hole prisoner who continued to be a problem was put into a "side-pocket" cell away from all other prisoners and virtually completely isolated. There was a bed bolted to the wall, a toilet, and a sink. As further punishment if a prisoner still remained aggressive, guards were permitted to "spread-eagle" an inmate on the bunk in what was called a "four-point position," with each limb chained to a corner.

Eventually, reforms in the federal system made conditions less odious, triggered in part by publicity about the treatment accorded to Robert Franklin Stroud, later known as the "Birdman of Alcatraz," who spent 26 years in the Leavenworth Hole.

Despite some improvements in most prisons, few among the public ever comprehended the full horrors of the Hole, and it was only in recent years that the courts started to take up the question of the constitutionality of such cells. Judges started to reject steadily the claims of prison officials that such cells are a necessary part of institutional discipline.

The strip cell at California's Soledad Prison was shut down by court order. Each such cell measured 8 feet 4 inches by 6 feet, with rear and side walls and the floor made of solid concrete. One prisoner, cited in a court case, spent his first eight days totally naked, sleeping on the floor with only a stiff canvas mat that "could not be folded to cover the inmate." The only other accommodation was a toilet that was flushed by a guard outside the cell, once in the morning and once at night. The cell was without light or heat and was never

An officer makes his rounds in the solitary confinement maximum security unit at the Albert C. Wagner Youth Correctional Facility in New Jersey. The solitary cell consists of a toilet, an outlet, a desk top, a bed, a sink, and a metal stool. (AP/Wide World Photos)

cleaned so that the floors and walls were "covered with the bodily wastes of previous inhabitants."

A federal court found solitary confinement cells at New York's Dannemora Prison little different, although the cells did have sinks ("encrusted with slime, dirt, and human excremental residue"). The court also found that prisoners were kept nude for days while the windows just across from the cell were left wide open during the night—even in subfreezing temperatures.

Leonard Orland, a University of Connecticut professor of law, developed a program in which his students were sent to prison for a weekend as part of their class work. He himself once spent 24 hours in the Hole of a Connecticut institution. It was nothing more than a windowless 4-by-8-foot steel box, with a single light bulb and a small peephole controlled from outside. He was not, however, alone in the cell. There were three cockroaches in the sink. In his book *Prisons: Houses of Darkness,* Orland described his experience as being confined in a "very small stalled elevator." He observed: "Its effect on me was devastating: I was terrified; I hallucinated; I was cold (I was nude and the temperature was in the low 60s). When the time came for my disciplinary hearing, I was prepared to say or do anything not to return to the hole. And yet I could not have experienced a tenth of the desperation of those men from whom the situation is a genuine one."

Horton, Willie See "WILLIE HORTONIZATION" OF CRIMINAL JUSTICE POLICY.

House of Refuge **first—and unsuccessful—effort for better treatment of errant juveniles**

The House of Refuge opened its doors in 1825 in New York City. It was one of the earliest institutional facilities for children and was funded by private donations. The House of Refuge was born out of the work by the Society for the Prevention of Pauperism, which was one of the first groups to call attention to "those unfortunate children from 10 to 18 years of age, who from neglect of parents, from idleness and misfortune have . . . contravened some penal statute without reflecting on the consequences, and for hasty violations, been doomed to the penitentiary by the condemnation of the law."

The House of Refuge thus started on a high moral plane. It admitted two types of children: those convicted of a crime and sentenced to incarceration, and those who were not convicted but were destitute or neglected and who were in imminent danger of becoming delinquent.

This was the first time that children and adults were jailed separately. However, how much differently the children fared in the House of Refuge could be open to debate. Superintendent Joseph Curtis was a very hard taskmaster and devised a system of rewards and deprivations, probably the latter being the more readily employed. Discipline was imposed, and infractions were put to a trial by a jury composed of peers, with Curtis as judge. Thus, Curtis could weigh the actions of the peer jury to see that the proper justice was rendered. Solitary confinement, reduction in food allowances, the silent treatment, and whippings were very common. If the children were deemed to have committed a serious offense, they were clapped in irons.

Boys and girls were required to work, the boys making various goods that could be sold and the girls doing domestic service. All moneys earned were given to the house for upkeep. Children could be apprenticed and released to the custody of masters. All inmates were subject to recall if further character building appeared needed.

In their treatment of children, the house was considered the authority of first importance, superseding a parent. If a parent or parents objected, they were almost always unsuccessful at winning back their children. Houses of refuge started up following the New York model in Philadelphia and Boston. The Boston House of Reformation was state supported, and corporal punishment was prohibited. In the private-funded Philadelphia House, each child had his or her own small cell, lighted and ventilated and with a bed and a shelf.

Black children were not accepted in these houses initially, but in 1834, the New York house started working up plans for the "coloured section" of its institution. One official, Nathaniel C. Hart, declared there was an extreme need for facilities for blacks. He described the great increase in the growth of poverty-stricken black children in the cities, blaming this on the policies in southern states that forbade free blacks to "reside among them."

New immigrants were also subject to discrimination. People who arrived destitute might automatically be labeled criminals or "paupers"—which in the view of the day amounted to the same thing—and see their children incarcerated as a matter of course. By 1829, 58 percent of the refuge-house inmates were from the immigrant population. In that sense, it may be said the houses of refuge, whatever their first intent, aided in the patterns of discrimination that had become common in society. Under those circumstances the houses of refuge did not meet their mission in full, and many children, many of nonimmigrant status, remained in prison. In the late 1820s, the Boston Prison Discipline Society reported some shocking statistics on the number of persons under 21 who were committed to adult prisons. In Vermont and Virginia (Richmond), the figures were 1 to 7; in New Hampshire and Maine, 1 to 5; and in Connecticut, 1 to 3. The report added that many of the children were under 12 years of age. This problem continued for years afterward: During 1845, 97 children between the ages of six and 16 were sent to the House of Corrections in Massachusetts. The houses of refuge continued also with their own standards of operations, which meant that they remained harsh institutions, but in that, they merely reflected the general practices of the day.

Clearly, the problems of juvenile delinquency and detention were not to be solved by the houses of refuge, and further efforts and reforms would be needed.

See also: JUVENILE DELINQUENCY; SHIP SCHOOLS.

Hudson v. McMillian See THOMAS, CLARENCE.

humming bird brutal prison torture

It was by many accounts the most horrendous torture ever practiced in any U.S. prison and led to bloody riots at the Oregon State Prison at Salem. "The humming bird" belied its innocent-sounding name and involved placing a prisoner, chained hand and foot, in a steel bathtub filled with water. The prisoner was then rubbed down with a sponge attached to an electric battery. A striking description of torture's agonizing effects was the following: "Two or three minutes and the victim is ready for the grave or the mad house."

During World War I, bloody riots took place at Oregon State, in large measure aimed at eliminating the humming bird as a vile instrument of torture. The riots failed in the short run, and the leaders of the uprising themselves were subjected to the humming bird. However, the resultant publicity apparently was so devastating that its use in Oregon prisons was discontinued shortly thereafter.

imprisonment alternatives new efforts and their drawbacks

In an effort to reduce the size of prison populations, some new methods are being tried in some jurisdictions. Writing in *California Prisoner,* Corey Pearson details two of the latest:

1. Requiring offenders to apologize for their crimes in an advertisement in the local paper. The apologies indicate the history of prior criminal activity and an explanation of his or her most recent crime. Then follows an apology for the act. The criminal must pay for the ad, which almost always has been utilized by repeat offenders who choose to place such an apology to avoid going to prison. The prosecution may be attracted to the idea because it costs the state nothing.

2. Making use of advocates to work with the offender at least 30 hours a week. (This can be regarded as the equivalent used in alcohol rehabilitation.) The advocate is available whenever the offender is tempted and can be provided by a volunteer or paid support system. Says Pearson, "The fundamental concern is that the programs demonstrate both care and supervision for the individual. However, because these programs focus on the individual needs, they do not replicate easily."

Pearson notes that the main problem involved is that the alternatives have not really been tried for "the population that would otherwise be in prison." In short, they are middle-class programs, for persons who are generally capable of avoiding the criminal justice system trap and abyss again. Thus, the average jail or prison inmate is cynical of such efforts. Pearson cites the saying, "Money talks and bullshit walks," which is "used by blacks, Hispanics and the poor within the jails of America. Thus, those with money will be heard, and either go free or go into a select alternative program. Those without money and/or resources walk, generally in one direction—towards incarceration in one of the already overcrowded and dismal prisons."

Pearson observes dual systems, "with prison for lower class prisoners, and alternatives for those who rarely go to prison, society is doing nothing for most prisoners."

Such alternative programs are utilized more in Europe and might succeed better in the United States if there is admission that the system needs to change. Some experts say this requires a change in the attitude that prison is the best and only alternative that is of any use.

See also: "SPLITTING TIME."

incapacitation theory "just get criminals off the streets"

On the face of it, there seems to be little to quarrel about. The theory of incapacitation of criminals means keeping them behind bars; the standard public view is that while they are there, they can inflict no further crimes on society. The theory and the highly popular strikes laws are what the public wants, but these are coming under increasing criticism by many experts who feel that the incapacitation theory leads to minimal results, save in criminals who are still in their violence-prone years or in a select few types of crimes.

The great impetus in recent years that pushed the incapacitation program was a RAND corporation study of prisoners in three states, which indicated that the offenders averaged 187 crimes per year. This led to the contention that if you imprisoned 1,000 people, you would prevent 187,000 crimes, and under those findings, it was clear that there would be considerable savings to the public treasuries and society at large if this was done. Obviously, if the 187 quota stood up and was used on enough offenders, crime per se would soon be wiped out. The trouble was that while the mean number was 187, the median number was 10 to 15 crimes, and the most serious flaw, according to Marc Mauer of the Sentencing Project, is assuming that those who commit so many crimes are likely to be imprisoned, rather than the relatively minor offender. A study of prison populations indicates that this is hardly the case.

Says Mauer: "There is no reason to believe that there exists an endless pool of non-incarcerated offenders who are committing 187 crimes a year. Instead, expanding prison capacity will result in an increased commitment of marginal offenders, not repeat offenders who are already being incarcerated."

The real knock on incapacitation as it is often practiced is that the replacement factor in crime is completely ignored. In the case of drug offenders and many kinds of gangs, the imprisonment of a few offenders only leads to the replacement with new members, eager to enter the rackets. As criminologist Alfred Blumstein says, "Incapacitation removes crimes from the street only if crime leaves the street with the offender."

This does not mean that many reformers are opposed to incapacitation of serious violent criminals whom society has a right to see put away. Many violent crimes are committed by a small number of sociopaths, and in such cases, confinement is clearly a plus. Criminals such as sex offenders, armed robbers, and burglars are not replaced immediately. As one legislator puts it, "Incarcerating a sex offender does not create a job vacancy to be filled by another sex offender."

A cynical interpretation of the actual facts by Peter T. Elikann in *The Tough-On-Crime Myth* states: "Fortunately for the violent criminals, so much prison space is being reserved for drug offenders and nonviolent lawbreakers that there's little room left for the violent ones." Elikann further raises the point, obvious to many in law enforcement, that at least half of all violent crimes are committed by teenagers, but most prisoners are in their twenties. "So you're often imprisoning them at the end of their life in crime anyway and not providing the public with any further measure of safety."

Many prosecutors freely admit that by age 29, the violent crime activities of most offenders have dropped tremendously, but any enlightened treatment of the imprisonment system runs into strong opposition of the "lock-'em-all-up" supporters who are quick to attack any release of any offender who then commits another crime, even those sentenced under various strike laws that are totally nonviolent. While there is growing demand by the public that young criminals who engage in school shootings be locked up, there are obvious indications that heavy sentences for most young violent criminals are not supported, say many reformers, when they could be imposed outside certain ethical boundaries.

international rates of incarceration no match for the United States

Although at the turn of the 21st century the largest portion of the U.S. population probably believes that the U.S. justice system is too given to "softie" treatment and coddling of those in prison, as opposed to most other countries, the facts do not support the contention. In 1979, the National Council on Crime and Delinquency issued a report on "International Rates of Imprisonment" that showed that the United States was in third place for incarcerating its people. Only South Africa and the former Soviet Union ranked higher. That turned around by the 1990s as the United States easily outdistanced South Africa and the newly constituted Russian Federation to stand as the world's top jailer.

To use figures from the 1990s, because they are complete for all countries, the United States slapped 565 per 100,000 persons behind bars. In other countries, the imprisonment rates were not climbing and indeed were actually declining. In the rest of the industrialized world, this country incarcerates as much as eight times as many of its own as do other countries. The rates elsewhere roughly for the comparable period were:

- United Kingdom, 93 per 100,000.
- Italy, 80 per 100,000.
- Japan, 36 per 100,000.
- Netherlands, 69 per 100,000.

Even the steadily industrializing Philippines was at a rate of only 30 per 100,000.

The declining rate of imprisonments could not be attributed to leftist or liberal governmental action. In the early 1990s, the Conservative governments of British prime ministers Margaret Thatcher and John Major pushed through a new Criminal Justice Act with the stated goal of "a significant reduction in the number of offenders in custody." The goal was to cut the British prison population by 35 to 50 percent, and the act called for greater use of community-based punishments to achieve that goal. Thatcher's reasoning was that prisons do not cut crime and cost too much. Adopting a similar policy of alternate punishments took the prison population down to 34,398, compared to 56,870 three decades earlier.

Even South Africa near the end of its apartheid era had embarked on an effort to cut the number of its prisoners, declaring the ineffectiveness of a prison-only crime-fighting campaign. The nation's Department of Correctional Services stated: "Rehabilitation can best be achieved within the community where the prisoner is to lead his life in the future. Bearing economic realities in mind, the increasing demand (for prison cells) does not appear to be viable or affordable."

Some other smaller countries do have more sophisticated penal problems. Denmark, for instance, finds that a sure way to make a criminal a repeater is to subject the prisoner to harsh experiences behind bars, and a strong effort is made to assure that a prisoner is not stripped of all dignity. This does not make the offender happy to be in prison. The most important punishment is that the offender is deprived of liberty, and once this is done, the Danes can pay much more attention to rehabilitation. In Norway, authorities are so petrified of the dangers of overcrowding that lawbreakers often have to wait their turn before being incarcerated for their punishment. Of course, it can be argued that such practices may be possible in small, relatively homogeneous societies and are not applicable in major portions of large countries like the United States that have a major crime problem.

However, even a country like Mexico, with its reputation for brutal prisons, has in recent years made enormous changes. In *The Tough-On-Crime Myth,* Peter T. Elikann is enthused about the new penal attitudes there.

> *Near Tijuana is La Mesa Penitentiary, where prisoners were given permission to save the prison money by building their own housing, establishing nearly seventy businesses that they run themselves and are open to commerce, and being allowed to bring their loved ones there to live with them. Their warden, Jorge Duarte Castillo, who died in 1995, thought this was important because not only does it help to maintain the family, but it also reduces the occurrence of violence. The inmates understand that if they cause trouble, their families will be taken away. Almost every prisoner participates in educational programs there from high school to vocational skills such as auto mechanics and electronics. Duarte said he had allowed all this, including alcohol rehabilitation, because he knew that eventually almost everyone will go back into society and he wanted them to be fully prepared to reenter society and thrive.*

Again, it cannot be said that specific programs can in toto be applied to the United States, but the fact is that experts agree that the get-tough attitudes of the public, to which more correctional systems cater, clearly limits the development of numerous pilot programs that might prove valuable. Instead, a state such as California places well more than 600 people behind bars for every 100,000 people who live there, outstripping every country on Earth. Yet, there has been no significant effect on the crime rate; even when the national crime rate has fallen a bit, California has never been described as leading the pack.

"iron gag" early-19th-century prison punishment

The early American prisons, such as Pennsylvania's Eastern Penitentiary, were determined to enforce silence and to punish any misbehavior by inmates. They resorted to extreme measures to deal with violators of established discipline. In 1833, much of an investigating committee's efforts to curb inhumane treatment of prisoners cited especially the use of the "iron gag" for enforcing silence. It was described by the committee as "a rough iron instrument resembling the stiff bit of a blind bridle, having an iron palet in the center, about an inch square, and chains at each end to pass around the neck and fasten behind."

Investigating specifically the suspicious death of convict Matthew Maccumsey, the committee reported:

This instrument was placed in the prisoner's mouth, the iron palet over the tongue, the bit forced as far as possible, the chains brought round the jaws to the back of the neck; the end of one chain was passed through the ring in the end of the other chain drawn tight to the "fourth link" and fastened with a lock; his hands were then forced into the leather gloves in which were iron staples, and from thence round the chains of the gag between his neck and the chains; the straps were drawn tight, the hands forced up toward the head, and the pressure consequently acting on the chains which press on the jaws and jugular vein, producing excruciating pain, and a hazardous suffusion of blood to the head.

The report concluded that in Maccumsey's case, the device was "so forcibly fastened that his blood collected and suffused up into his brain and he suddenly died under the treatment." The disuse of the iron gag must have been most troubling to prison officials because the attachment of the instrument had the salutary effect of countering another perceived vile behavior, that of masturbation. At least officials still had recourse to the straitjacket for that, of course, even though it, too, came in for a matter of criticism for overuse.

Jackson, George (1941–1971) Soledad Brother

Although he died by gunfire in San Quentin prison in 1971, George Jackson remains a mythic figure to black prisoners throughout the prison system for his overall radical resistance to prison authority and for his searing political letters that were published in book form as *Soledad Brother: The Prison Letters of George Jackson*. The book won him worldwide acclaim as well as rave reviews from the likes of Jean Genet and Jean-Paul Sartre.

Jackson had his first run-in with the law in Chicago in 1955 when he was 14. Later, his family moved to Los Angeles, where he followed the rule of the streets and moved up to petty theft and then burglary and robbery. When he was convicted at age 18 for robbing a gas station of $70, he was given an indeterminate sentence that could run anywhere from one year upward. Judged to be an incorrigible prisoner, he was still there more than a decade later.

In the meantime, Jackson became a revolutionary, as his letters increasingly showed by their call for battles against racial injustice. Despite seven years during which he was in solitary confinement, he kept himself intellectually sharp by constant reading. He followed Leninist-Maoist lines and advocated violent revolution. He proved to be a powerful leader of black prisoners and was revered by radical youths. He felt that the U.S. prison system existed to immobilize black men. He wrote:

> *Blackmen born in the U.S. and fortunate enough to live past the age of eighteen are conditioned to accept the inevitability of prison. For most of us, it simply looms as the next phase in a sequence of humiliations. Being born a slave in a captive society and never experiencing any objective basis for expectation had the effect of preparing me for the progressively traumatic misfortunes that lead so many blackmen to the prison gate. I was prepared for prison. It required only minor psychic adjustments.*

Jackson was transferred to Soledad Prison, where he took part in and led political study groups. In 1969, Soledad was a cauldron of racial tension, and violence exploded when three black inmates were shot to death by a white guard. Some days later, a white guard was beaten to death, and Jackson and two others were charged with murder, facing the death penalty. The trio became known as the Soledad Brothers and drew enormous attention, both nationally and internationally.

Jackson was transferred to San Quentin to await a murder trial. The appearance of *Soledad Brother* converted the trio into heroes of the black revolution.

Jackson did not live to stand trial, being shot to death August 21, 1971, during what was described by authorities as an escape attempt. Besides the 30-

year-old Jackson, a number of guards and convicts were killed. Jackson was said to have hidden a handgun in his hair. It was a story that few black inmates or his outside supporters believed, many feeling that the charge against Jackson had been trumped up. Further providing ammunition for the Jackson supporters was the fact that the remaining two Brothers were acquitted.

See also: DAVIS, ANGELA.

Further reading: *The Road to Hell* by Paul Liberatore.

jails and prisons an overview

One of the first prized institutions brought by settlers to the New World was the jail, a place where lawbreakers could be held while awaiting their fate at trial and their subsequent punishment. In the early colonial period, about 150 offenses called for the death penalty. If that was not always carried out, it was because many persons were deemed more valuable in servitude. For these, the immediate punishment was the same as for those facing penalties for lesser crimes—branding, whipping, maiming, and public humiliation.

The jail was basically not a place where offenders were held for long periods of punishment. For that, a newer institution was required, a purely American idea—the state prison or penitentiary. This invention would prove to have a profound effect on correctional policy in this and many other countries.

Jails recede far back in dark and brutal history when, in the words of one historian, they appeared "in the form of murky dungeons, abysmal pits, unscalable precipices, strong poles or trees, and suspended cages in which hapless prisoners were kept." Later, old jails were less than escape

Ancient small-town prison (Author's collection)

proof, and those charged with keeping them received extra compensation for shackling prisoners. Offenders were not segregated by any rational system so that some had as much to fear from their fellow prisoners as from their keepers. The conditions in jails a few hundred years ago were abominations: The food was poor, and there was no treatment for any medical conditions. The idea of rehabilitation was beyond comprehension to the keepers. The new Americans prided themselves on their jails as being rather humane and a replacement for harsh corporal punishment; in time, prisoners may have had difficulty figuring which was worse. Things had not improved much in the 1920s when a leading federal prison inspector who had toured some 1,500 jails found many of them in wretched shape, so much so that many prisoners said they would gladly serve a year in prison than a half-year in a city or county jail.

Most jails, inspector John Fulling Fishman said, were unbelievably filthy institutions where, with few exceptions, there was "no segregation of the unconvicted from the convicted, the well from the diseased, the youngest and most impressionable from the most degraded and hardened. Usually swarming with bedbugs, roaches, lice, and other vermin." Fishman added, the jail "supports in complete idleness thousands of able-bodied men and women, and generally affords ample time and opportunity to assure inmates a complete course in every kind of viciousness and crime" and " . . . the worst elements of the raw material in the criminal world are brought forth blended and turned out in absolute perfection."

A few years later, in 1931, the National Commission on Law Observance and Enforcement called the U.S. jail the "most notorious correctional institution in the world." What happened during the next half-century? Virtually nothing in the way of improvement. The media in the 1980s was replete with descriptions of the U.S. jail as "the worst blight in American corrections" and where "anyone not a criminal when he goes in, will be one when he comes out."

One of the main faults with the typical jail, say critics, is that it is financed and run on a local basis, which guarantees the administration will have to hop to the whims of local politics. Many are run by the local sheriff, usually an elected official. Few have exhibited interest in regularly inspecting the jails or improving them, which, of course, requires the expenditure of public moneys. In recent years, some states have taken control of their jails, but in most jails, the standards remain low and rehabilitation programs are nearly invisible. Jail staffing is seldom good. The hallmark is low pay and very little job training. Of course, there is little supervision of the situations in which inmates find themselves; there is also little protection from homosexual attacks. The small staffs guarantee the number of suicides, the predominant cause of death in jails that usually occurs on the very first day of incarceration.

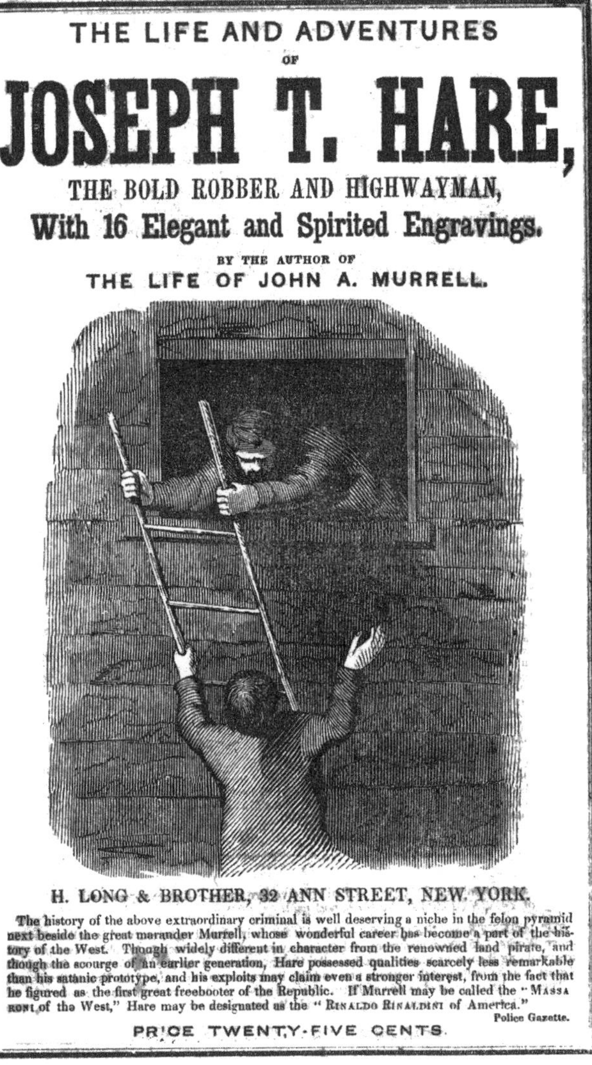
THE LIFE AND ADVENTURES
OF
JOSEPH T. HARE,
THE BOLD ROBBER AND HIGHWAYMAN,
With 16 Elegant and Spirited Engravings.
BY THE AUTHOR OF
THE LIFE OF JOHN A. MURRELL.

H. LONG & BROTHER, 32 ANN STREET, NEW YORK.

The history of the above extraordinary criminal is well deserving a niche in the felon pyramid next beside the great marander Murrell, whose wonderful career has become a part of the history of the West. Though widely different in character from the renowned land pirate, and though the scourge of an earlier generation, Hare possessed qualities scarcely less remarkable than his satanic prototype, and his exploits may claim even a stronger interest, from the fact that he figured as the first great freebooter of the Republic. If Murrell may be called the "MASSARONI of the West," Hare may be designated as the "RINALDO RINALDINI of America."

Police Gazette.

PRICE TWENTY-FIVE CENTS.

As shown here, escapes were easily pulled off in early days. (Author's collection)

Some important jail facts as offered by the National Coalition for Jail Reform include the fact that

- 80 percent of those held while awaiting trial are there solely because they are unable to raise bail funds.
- 600,000 mentally ill persons go through jail systems each year.
- 500,000 young people under age 18 are put in adult jails and lockups each year.
- the adult suicide rate in jail is 16 times greater than the general public's.
- 70 percent of inmates incarcerated in jails have committed nonviolent crimes.
- more than one-third of jails are more than a half-century old.
- 77 percent of jails have no medical facilities.
- in 81 percent of all jails, inmates are held in an area of less than 60 square feet each—about the size of two mattresses.
- at least 10 percent of jails are under court order, and many have litigation pending against them for overcrowding, lack of treatment facilities, and other problems.

Certainly the early history of U.S. prisons did not represent any improvement of the jails of their day. The first state prison was the notorious Newgate, established at Simsbury, Connecticut, in 1773. It was an abandoned copper mine in which prisoners were chained together to live and work some 50 feet beneath the earth. Many of the prisoners were Tories who were incarcerated there during the Revolution. The first prison riot at Newgate occurred in 1776 when prisoners set fire to a massive wooden door in an attempt to reach a drainage channel that led to freedom. The riot was an awesome failure: Smoke filled the mine, choking a number of prisoners to death and disabling the rest.

Newgate certainly set the pattern for hellhole prisons in this country. Almost immediately, prison reformers appeared, but it is debatable whether their early efforts to achieve humane treatment of those imprisoned benefited or harmed prisoners. The first reform of prison practices was attempted in 1790 at Philadelphia's Walnut Street Jail, which was renovated through the efforts of a group of Quakers called the Philadelphia Society to Alleviate the Miseries of Public Prisons, an organization that exists to this day as the Philadelphia Prison Society. A 19th-century historical account describes the unreformed Walnut Street Jail in its early days as a scene of "universal riot and debauchery . . . with no separation of those accused but yet untried, not even those confined for debt only, from convicts sentenced for the foulest crimes . . . no separation of . . . age or sex, by day or night." In short, it was a happy hunting ground for villains.

After the jail was remodeled in 1790, the sexes were for the first time housed separately in large, clean rooms. Debtors were segregated from other prisoners, and children were removed from the jail entirely. Hardened offenders were placed in solitary confinement in a "penitentiary house," and prisoners were given work and religious instruction. Within a short time, however, the Walnut Street Jail became overcrowded, and a new institution had to be built.

About this time, two new prisons were built that were soon to function as the models for what became the Pennsylvania and Auburn prison systems. Eastern Penitentiary was built to further the Quaker idea of prisoner isolation. Prisoners were confined in windowless cells about 8 by 12 feet with running water and toilet facilities. Each prisoner had his own "exercising yard," about 8 by 20 feet, surrounded by a high brick wall. The walls between the cells were thick and virtually soundproof so that an inmate never saw another inmate, only a few guards, chaplains, and an occasional pious person who came by to pray and offer spiritual advice. Needless to say, great numbers of prisoners went insane under the Pennsylvania system, but that did not stop it from becoming popular both elsewhere in the country and around the world.

Also in 1829, a rival system, which eventually gained wider acceptance, was launched with the building of a new prison in Auburn, New York. The trouble with the Pennsylvania system, said the New York prison experts, was that the convicts spent too much time praying and working alone and thus could not "pay for their keep" through convict labor. At Auburn, the prisoners worked together by day fulfilling convict-labor contracts, but in all other aspects the isolation of the Pennsylvania system was maintained.

Silence remained the rule even when inmates worked together in the shops. The prisoners marched in lockstep, their gaze always downward. In Warden Elam Lynds, the system had a devoted champion. He felt that the purpose of the system was to break the prisoners' spirits. He personally flogged prisoners and urged his guards to treat the inmates with contempt and brutality. A typical and sometimes lethal punishment instituted by Lynds was the water cure. A prisoner's neck was fastened in an iron yoke, and then a stream of icy water was poured on the inmate's head. In a variation of this, the prisoner was shackled naked to a wall and a high-pressure water hose was turned full blast on the inmate's back. The convict was plastered to the wall by the force of the water, and the pain was excruciating. Most happily, in Lynds's view, the torture left no marks.

The Auburn system spread quickly in use throughout the country because it was far more economical to operate than the Pennsylvania system. In Auburn, the cells were reduced in size to only 7 feet high, 7 feet long, and 3 1/2 feet wide. As the Auburn system spread, the methods of repression were refined: The striped uniform was introduced in Sing Sing (where Lynds moved as its first warden), and the floggings, the sweatbox, the straitjacket, the iron yoke, the thumbscrew, and the stretcher became widespread. The latter device had a number of variations. A convict could be handcuffed to the upper bars of the cell so that his toes barely touched the floor, and the inmate was usually left in that condition the entire day. Or inmates had their ankles chained to the floor and their wrists tied to a rope that passed through a pulley attached to the ceiling. When the rope was pulled, the prisoners were stretched taut. Some prisons built sweatboxes into the cell door, actually a double door, into which a prisoner could be placed in a space so small that it allowed no mobility. In other prisons, this type of sweatbox was not considered nearly stern enough. It would be, after all, more effective if the sweatboxes were placed near a fireplace so that the suffering could be intensified.

The Auburn system was clearly based on cruelty and repression, with the rationale that such treatment would reform the prisoners. Although the theory proved a failure, some of Auburn's practices have been adopted in varying degrees by more modern prisons.

In the post–Civil War period, however, penologists, dissatisfied with both major prison systems, did begin to experiment with new ideas. In 1870, mainly through the efforts of such penologists as Enoch Cobbs Wines and others who formed the American Prison Association, the reformatory system came into being. Through their efforts, the Elmira Reformatory in New York opened in 1876. Although the reformatory idea was intended for all ages, at Elmira, it was limited to prisoners between the ages of 16 and 30. The guiding principle of the Elmira system was reformation rather the expiation of guilt, and it was hailed by many as the greatest advance in penology since the substitution of the prison for the medieval method of maiming and/or execution.

Incoming prisoners at Elmira were automatically placed in the second of three grades. If and when they showed improvement, they were moved up to the first grade and, upon continued improvement, won parole. If they turned out to be troublemakers, they were dropped to the third grade and were faced with the prospect of having to work their way back up. Many of the prisoners were sentenced to indeterminate terms so that they could be afforded the full benefit of the reformatory concept. By the end of the century, 11 states had adopted the reformatory concept, but by 1910 the innovation had all but collapsed. Most guards and even wardens proved incapable of administering a complex grading program, and in the majority of systems, the advancement of inmates was based on favoritism or the ability not to rock the boat rather then their progress in achieving a full-scale reformation. Under such conditions, many reformatory graduates went out and committed new crimes.

It is not unusual for a number of prisons to retain the name of *reformatory*, but they are merely part of the general prison system. Despite the claims of penologists, there have been little genuine advances in prisons since the introduction of the reformatory. Currently, prisons are essentially divided in three major classifications: maximum security, medium security, and minimum security. Because of reform wardens like Thomas Mott Osborne and Lewis E. Lawes, both of Sing Sing, who had an impact on penological theories, much of the blatant cruelty and squalor of the 19th-century prisons has been markedly reduced. Still, extremely punitive concepts have persisted, as indicated in the 1930s by the establishment of Alcatraz as a "superprison" for the worst federal prisoners, an American Devil's Island. According to some estimates, almost 60 percent of the inmates went "stir crazy" there. Alcatraz undoubtedly left its mark not only on many of the prisoners but on many of the guards as well. The prison soon lost its original purpose as a place of confinement for escapers and other troublemakers and became a place to lodge inmates who simply were deemed deserving of harsher treatment, such as Al Capone and, later on, Morton Sobel of the Rosenberg spy case. By 1963, Alcatraz was abandoned, having proven an unqualified failure. Some critics ascribe the same deficiencies that showed up in Alcatraz with the more recent "supermaximum" prisons that have sprung up in use not only by the federal government but within many state systems as well. What these detractors cite as a major flaw is the fact that even among inmates of the supermaxes, most will have to be released. This is often not appreciated by the public, who are furnished with information involving a small segment of supercriminals who never will be released.

Thus, there is a body of critics who see the entire U.S. prison system as a failure and as facing long-term collapse. Overall, critics have charged that prisons have failed to reform criminals or even to act as a deterrent to crime. Moreover, prisons are generally conceded to be schools for crime, especially for younger convicts who are certain to be freed. They have learned the "better" ways of criminal activities, and indeed those who have suffered sexual abuse behind bars in large measure later practice the same aggression on others, both on newcomers entering the prisons and in their activities on the outside. Their rationale is that "I've paid my dues, and I have a right to get some satisfaction by treating others the way I was treated."

And there is no way to keep them all behind bars.

For every 4,500 inmates who are released, nearly 5,000 new prisoners have to be accommodated. Prisons cannot realistically be used as places of confinement and retribution. Even with the building of additional prisons, inevitably the shortage of space must win out just as a pyramid scheme eventually collapses. As of the end of 2001, U.S. prisons and jails held 2.1 million inmates. The growth has been persistent with a few fits and starts for slight slowing from time to time, perhaps caused by the activities of the courts ordering declines of the prison populations in many jurisdictions. Back in 1985 the total for all prisoners was less than 800,000.

Without rehabilitation programs, the problem of prison riots would increase manifold. Such riots became commonplace in the 20th century, evidenced especially in three great waves —1929–32, 1950–56, and 1968–73—of prison rebellion. The most tragic riot, although most observers do not credit it with being an actual riot, occurred at the Ohio State Penitentiary in Columbus on April 21, 1930. More than 300 prisoners died in a fire that, prison officials claimed, was started by inmates. More likely, an electrical failure caused the fire, which the prison guards were ill trained to handle, being obsessed with the idea that it was a riot intended to produce a mass breakout. Certainly, there was reason enough for a riot because the prison was jammed with 4,300 inmates in accommodations designed for 1,500.

The worst riot in the 1950s occurred at the overcrowded Southern Michigan State Prison at Jackson. Guards were seized as hostages, and inmates roamed the prison, setting fires and smashing windows. The damage toll—in 1950 dollars—was put at $2.5 million.

The worst two-year span of prison riots occurred in 1970–71. Among the major disturbances were the following:

- January 1970: Soledad Prison, Salinas, California. Three black convicts and a white guard killed during a race riot among prisoners.
- July 1970: Holmesburg Prison, Philadelphia, Pennsylvania. Eighty-four prisoners and 29 guards injured in a riot with pronounced racial overtones.
- October 1970: Tombs prison, New York, New York. Convicts held 26 hostages to protest overcrowded conditions.
- November 1970: Cummins Unit prison farm, Grady, Arkansas. About 500 convicts rioted

to demand separate facilities for whites and blacks.

- August 1971: San Quentin, California. Three inmates, including George Jackson, and three guards killed in what was described as an escape effort.
- September 1971: Attica Prison, Attica, New York. Thirty-two prisoners and 11 guards being held hostage killed by prison guards and state police rescuers in the aftermath of a four-day protest over prison conditions.

Various studies indicate that there are many causes for prison riots, some of the main ones being inconsistent sentencing and parole policies; prisoner-perceived unfair sentencing; pent-up anger; racial tensions; public and official indifference to conditions; idleness; lack of rehabilitative programs; and most recently, the activity of radical and revolutionary groups in the inmate population that regard all convicts as political prisoners. But probably the main cause fueling riots is the matter of overcrowding. When a prisoner is assigned to a cell no larger than a small bathroom (with the bunk taking the place of a bathtub), that is frequently an overcrowding of one. However, as the prison's population soars, desperate wardens add another inmate into that same space and, incredibly, in some cases a third and even a fourth inmate; the situation then quickly becomes incendiary.

Still in recent decades, prison riots have lessened (despite some brutal exceptions), and there is some dispute over the reason for this. Officials like to claim that they have gotten a better handle on the problem and have installed correctional safeguards. However, a more common explanation not acknowledged by officials is the growing intervention of the courts in correcting many abuses, even appointing court monitors to make sure the courts' edicts are followed by officials. However, as the treat-'em-tough attitude remains dominant in public opinion, prison populations will grow. Yet, with prison expansion, despite all the claims by hard-liners that financing will be forthcoming, it probably will not.

The money is there one way or another to build new prisons but not the optimum or even of the type corrections might want. Communities faced with the loss of farming or industrial jobs have gotten into bidding wars to build new prisons, floating their own bond issues if necessary. One community did so and then found that no prisoners came. For a time, hard-pressed citizens were forced to bankroll the interest on the bonds. Finally, the community arranged to bring in some prisoners from other states and house them for a fee. However, this was less than a crowning success as the outside jurisdictions found themselves under court stricture to improve the prisons of this type. Some pulled their prisoners out and others insisted on costly improvements, which saddled the community with more costs than had been anticipated. But the prison bubble has continued to expand. Sayre, Oklahoma, a town of 4,114, built a 1,440-inmate, 270-employee prison and persuaded the Corrections Corporation of America to house its privately contracted prisoners there. The city manager enthused: "In my mind there's no more recession-proof form of economic development. Nothing's going to stop crime."

From 1992 to 2001, 245 prisons sprouted in 212 of the nation's rural counties, many in Great Plains towns of Colorado, Oklahoma, and Texas, areas that had been stripped of family farms and upended by the collapse of the oil boom of the 1980s. These prisons have not been free of economic problems, although employment obviously has been up. Unfortunately, some businesses had their woes. A Texaco station 100 yards from the prison, the closest business, saw sales go up, but there were more bad checks, mostly from the prison guards. The problem is the wage scale at these new institutions, which pay from $17,000 to $19,000 a year. In Sayre, 70 percent of all guards quit within a year, some for better-paying jobs in the recovering oil fields. Sooner or later, some observers say, towns like Sayre will find they will have prisons where the guards want and get higher pay, especially through unionization, even in areas where unions previously had little traction.

The dynamic of prison-guard pay is best illustrated in California, where wages spiraled. The most dramatic period of increases occurred from 1980 to 1996. In 1980 the average salary of prison guards in the state was $14,400 annually. By 1996, the average had soared to $44,000 and with benefits, well more than $50,000. This was at the time $10,000 more than the average teacher's salary. California is regarded as a strong law-and-order state, where three-strikes-and-life was born. Parenthetically, the guards' union collected about $8 million a year in dues and expended twice as much in political contributions as did the California teachers union, which is 10 times greater in size. It has been charged that "friends of prison guards" receive inordinate political contributions from the guards' union. At $44,000 in annual salary, California prison guards received 58 percent more than guards in other states. It is generally assumed that prison guards will exercise their growing power to emulate California. Even as the prison population grows more slowly or even levels off, state costs in support services will obviously continue to go upward, and prison construction still will increase because of the staggering problem of overcrowding. Other services will suffer. As James Alan Fox, a professor of criminal justice at Northeastern University, put it: "We're a long way from the point where crime is not a major political issue. The political agenda is still heavily weighted towards punishment, and many states are much more willing to spend money on prison construction than on new schools."

There are few political figures who will stand firm on holding down the cost of vital support services and wages in prisons. To do otherwise is to risk the wrath of hard-liners. Instead, they will be more likely to curtail prison programs to help or even control the inmate population. If not, once again there will be the charge that they are soft on convicts. The further drop-off in rehabilitative programs more than likely inevitably will relight the flames of prison rioting.

Yet, in the last half of 2000, there was actually a drop of 0.5 percent in state prisons populations, breaking a string of increases since 1972. The drop was attributed to a drop in crime going back to 1992, new attitudes in offering more drug offenders treatment rather than locking them up, and finally a greater willingness by parole officers to help parolees instead of sending them back to prison for minor infractions.

"Jefferson's Penitentiary" early plan for a new type of prison

It has come down to us as "Jefferson's Penitentiary," although it did not come to fruition as such. During the Revolution, Thomas Jefferson took an active role in what could be regarded as prison reform of its time.

Jefferson recommended the abolition of the death penalty for all but treason and murder, with penal slavery as the substitute. Jefferson personally drew up prison designs following the plans of the Frenchman P.G. Bugniet. Jefferson meticulously followed up on all details. Concerning the building material, he noted, "It has been suggested to me that fine gravel mixed in the mortar prevents the prisoners from cutting themselves out, as that will destroy their tool."

Jefferson's penitentiary rested on acceptance of the penal code he had developed, but it was deemed too lenient, and it was not even proposed until late 1786, when it still fell one vote short of acceptance.

In 1806, with Jefferson in the White House, Virginia finally approved plans for construction of a new penitentiary capable of imprisoning about 200 inmates at hard labor. Architect Benjamin Latrobe relied heavily on Jefferson's sketches.

Jena, Louisiana, juvenile prison troubled for-profit facility

It turned out to be virtually a flashback to 19th-century prisons for children, and it ended up with the Wackenhut Corrections Corporation, the second-largest private-for-profit company in the country, announcing that it was giving up a contract to run a juvenile prison at Jena in central Louisiana. It turned out to be a disaster for all concerned, the inmates, the company, and the state.

The surrender by the company followed the disclosure of numerous abuses after a court case was tried and the Justice Department found that, among other things, the young inmates were physically abused and deprived of adequate food and warm clothing.

In early April 2000, the Louisiana Department of Public Safety and Corrections took over the prison after a state investigation found that part of a videotape that apparently showed abuse by a guard was missing. Judge Mark Doherty had been holding hearings on the prison and denounced Wackenhut for failing to give the inmates enough food and warm clothing, and he heard evidence of abuse by guards.

The jurist was so enraged by the evidence that he released 11 boys he had sentenced because of conditions at Jena. "This isn't a victory for me, but for the kids and for justice."

At this point, Wackenhut threw in the towel for a juvenile facility at Jena. The company insisted that it had made "extensive improvements" at the site, but that suits filed over conditions at Jena forced the company to abandon its contract.

See also: PRIVATE PRISONS.

Johnston, James A. (1876–1958) Alcatraz warden
If Alcatraz Prison was to prove to be controversial, the same could be said of James A. Johnston, the institution's first and long-term warden. Alcatraz, in all of its repressive measures, most of which had to be toned down in time, could be said to have been the mirror image of all Johnston, a veteran penologist, believed—or at least came to believe and practice.

Actually, Alcatraz may have altered Johnston almost as much as it did a number of its inmates.

When Johnston was named in 1934 by the U.S. Department of Justice to be the first warden of a new maximum-security, minimum-privilege federal prison on Alcatraz Island in San Francisco Bay, many old prison hands were surprised. He did not seem to be the right man for the job. Previously, he had served as warden of both Folsom and San Quentin prisons, California's toughest, but he had a reputation as a reformer.

James A. Johnston, former warden of Alcatraz (Federal Bureau of Prisons)

From the beginning, Alcatraz was Johnston's creation; he personally designed the cell blocks and composed the most restrictive regulations ever used in a federal prison in the United States. Johnston was referred to in the popular press as being "tough but kindly." The convicts had a different view, however, calling him Saltwater Johnston because they considered him as bitter as salt water.

The rules that Johnston laid down were so severe that they are credited with having driven any number of convicts "stir crazy." For the first four years, a rigid "rule of silence" prohibited the convicts from speaking a word in the cell blocks, in the mess hall, or at work. A single word uttered without permission meant instant punishment, often in solitary confinement for a period that could run into several months. It was an abrupt, astounding change for a warden who, in a dozen years, had reformed San Quentin in more ways than had been accomplished in the previous 50. There, he had introduced individual treatment of convicts, established honor camps, abolished corporal punishment, and did away with the ugly striped prison uniform. At Alcatraz, the Hole became a standard punishment. In the cramped space, a convict slept on concrete and received only water and four slices of bread a day. Solitary was a little better because the prisoner had a bunk and one regular meal a day.

During the so-called Alcatraz Prison Rebellion of 1946, really just an escape attempt by six convicts, Johnston proposed an all-out attack on the cell blocks by armed guards and grenade-throwing U.S. Marines. When his superior in Washington, Bureau of Prisons head James Bennett, said that he was worried about "what public reaction will be if a large number of innocent inmates are unnecessarily killed," Johnston responded stiffly, "Mr. Director, there are no *innocent* inmates in here."

The investigation following the 1946 rebellion revealed that one prisoner had been held in total isolation for more than seven years. Johnston bristled when asked how much longer the man would remain there and said, "As long as necessary for discipline." The warden insisted that the FBI agents preparing a murder case against three members of the six-man escape group interview them in the dungeon. He only relented when the officers explained that any statement they got from the prisoners under those circumstances might well not be admitted in court.

There is little doubt that Johnston was personally brave. Even in periods of unrest—and Alcatraz was almost constantly beset by strikes, sit-ins, and riots—Johnston always entered the dining hall alone and unarmed; of course, machine-gun toting guards patrolled the catwalk outside. He would taste the soup and then take his position by the door, exposing his back to the convicts marching out. During a strike in September 1937, a young convict known to be mentally deficient attacked the 61-year-old warden, battering his face in, knocking out several teeth, and stomping on his chest before guards could tear him away. It was a week before Johnston was able to get out of bed. His assailant went to the Hole for a long stay. As a lifer, he faced death if convicted of attacking a prison officer, but the warden never brought charges.

Johnston retired as warden in 1948, a man who had believed in rehabilitation but who had during 14 years molded a prison incapable of rehabilitating anyone. Summing up his tenure, he said: "Atlanta and Leavenworth had sent me their worst. I had done my best with them." Johnston died at the age of 82, having outlived many a younger con who had sworn to celebrate on the day the warden died.

See also: ALCATRAZ PRISON: ALCATRAZ PRISON REBELLION; ATLANTA BOYS CONVOY; RULE OF SILENCE.

Jon, Gee (?–1924) first gas-chamber victim

When Gee Jon was slated to be the first condemned man to die in the gas chamber in Carson City, Nevada, in 1924, efforts were made by reformers to make his a humane execution. A bill was pushed through to have the condemned men put to death by poison gas, which would be piped into the cell. The plan was for the execution to take place while the prisoner was asleep with no prior notice given. Reformers felt this would spare condemned men going through the macabre preparations for the execution as well as having to await a preestablished time of execution.

However, this was an idea that could not be put into practice. Prison officials found they could not figure out how to carry out such an execution without having the gas spread and kill off a number of other prisoners.

Thus officials had to construct an airtight chamber, and Jon required all the horrific preparations the reformers hoped to spare him. He was escorted into the execution chamber with a stethoscope attached to his chest. He was strapped into a chair under which cyanide pellets tied in a gauze sack hung on a hook. The chamber was cleared and the execution proceeded with a lever pulled, allowing the pellets to drop into a pan filled with a mixture of water and sulfuric acid.

Within seconds, deadly fumes started to rise, and in a short time, the condemned man's heartbeat stopped. A Carson City reporter found much to praise in the operation and assured readers that Nevada had moved "one step further from the savage state."

Jordan v. Fitzharris **rewriting the standards on solitary confinement**

It had long been the custom of the federal courts not even to consider brutality charges arising from the administering of solitary confinement. This represented the "hands-off" doctrine under which the courts regarded it generally beyond their duty to rule on the way prisons carried out their policies.

Then, in 1966, a California inmate named Jordan at Soledad sued on the basis that his solitary confinement represented "cruel and unusual punishment." Charged with only a minor disciplinary infraction, Jordan said he was kept for 12 days in a tiny strip cell totally naked with no light, ventilation, or body covering. He had to sleep on a bare concrete floor with no ability to clean himself, and he was forced to eat in the filth and stench of his own body wastes and vomit.

Officials at Soledad were said to be totally astonished when a federal district judge decided to hold a hearing to determine the accuracy of Jordan's claims. Never before in California had a federal judge intruded in the practices of the state's penal institution on such charges.

The judge heard testimony that confirmed the charges and ruled, "when, as it appears in this case at bar, the responsible prison authorities in the use of the strip cells have abandoned elemental concepts of decency by permitting conditions to prevail of a shocking and debased nature, then the court must intervene . . . to restore the primal rules of a civilized community in accord with the mandate of the Constitution of the United States."

A permanent injunction was issued on the conditions of solitary confinement, and the judge advised the prison administration to follow the disciplinary procedures offered by the American Correctional Association.

A few months later, the U.S. Court of Appeals for the Second Circuit further denuded the "hands-off" doctrine in a New York case on conditions very similar to the Jordan case. Prisons were put on notice in that decision that they could not allow subhuman conditions that "could only serve to destroy completely the spirit and undermine the sanity of the prisoner. The Eighth Amendment forbids treatment so foul, so inhuman and so violative of basic concepts of decency."

It should be noted that since *Jordan* and later rulings of that sort, the judiciary has been frequently attacked by "treat-'em-tough" advocates who object to interference by the courts in what they more or less regard as the duties of prison authorities.

Jukes **alleged family of criminals**

No criminal study in the 19th century more electrified penologists than that made by Richard L. Dugdale. It set the tone for penal punishment for many years—until it was dismissed as nonsense. Dugdale, a civic-minded New York merchant, was a volunteer inspector for the prestigious Prison Association of New York, and in the 1870s, he published his study—*The Jukes: A Study in Crime, Pauperism, Disease and Heredity.*

Dugdale began his research in upstate Ulster County and found four males and two females in jail under four family names who seemed to be blood relatives. He looked into their family history for an explanation of their apparent disproportionate activities in crime. Using official records from prisons, courts, and other sources, he satisfied himself that he had traced a family's roots back to the mid-1700s to a colonial frontiersman and tavern keeper whom he called Max. Max was descended from early Dutch settlers. Tracking the clan through five generations, Dugdale found

"540 blood relatives," starting with Max's two sons. He also turned up 169 others related by marriage or cohabitation. The sons of Max married two illegitimate sisters, identified by Dugdale as harlots. He identified one of these sisters as "Margaret, mother of criminals" and described her as "the progenitor of the distinctly criminal line of the family."

Before Dugdale was finished with the Jukes, he had indicted some 200 as criminals from murderers to thieves. The clan could boast no fewer than 50 prostitutes and close to 300 pauperized adults and wards of the state. The rest, he concluded, were a depraved, debased, foul, and diseased lot. He claimed to work out that the public treasury was looted for prison costs, public assistance, and the like totaling a then-astounded figure of $1.3 million.

Penologists and others rallied around the concept of the Jukes and determined that heredity was clearly responsible for such a tidal wave of feebleminded individuals and that they and their current ilk of what today are called mental retards had to be locked up and the keys thrown away.

By the beginning of the 20th century, Dugdale's methodology came under attack by researchers in what had to be regarded as strong recrimination of those who had embraced the pseudoscience of the study. The prison reformer and warden Thomas Mott Osborne concluded that Dugdale had operated under the assumption that every criminal he discovered must have been a Juke and that every Juke was probably a criminal. Osborne marveled at Dugdale's ability to trace family bloodlines among the illegitimately born. Among the supposed Juke criminals whom Dugdale exposed was "a reputed sheep-stealer"; "a petty thief but never convicted"; a man "supposed to have attempted rape"; and an "unpunished and cautious thief." Then there was a very offensive lad about whom it was "impossible to get any reliable information, but it is evident he was a leader in crime."

In addition to Osborne, other sociologists went after the Juke thesis, and rapidly it started to fall into disrepute. However, in 1916, Arthur H. Estabrook seized the Juke mantle and claimed that since the 1870s, the Jukes had indeed continued to spawn yet more criminals and unworthies. Estabrook allowed that there were a lot of good "Jukes" for, happily, the Jukes had started to marry beyond the breed. He insisted that the theory of hereditary criminality and immorality was still alive and well. However, today both Dugdale and Estabrook have little support because of their failure to give any weight to the influence of cultural and environmental factors in the development of criminal behavior.

juvenile capital punishment a long American history

> *The USA carries out more executions of juvenile offenders (people sentenced to death for a crime they committed when they were under the age of 18) than almost any other country in the world.*
>
> —Amnesty International

If anything, there has been an erosion of resistance by much of the public to the concept of executing juveniles. This became more pronounced in the school shootings of children by children in the late 1990s, which resulted in a growing demand of harsher punishment of children—such as life sentences and even the death penalty. There had been in more recent decades the supposed (and erroneous) belief that youngsters of various ages should be treated less harshly or that there be minimum age restrictions in severe punishments.

If we look back in history, it has been an old American custom to do quite the opposite. Death-penalty historians have determined that from 1624 to 1986, some 281 persons under the age of 18, generally considered juveniles, were put to death in what is now the United States. The standards for executions of juveniles were derived from English law. It has long been presumed that the Mother Country far outdistanced its colony in the practice. That may not have been true. The United Kingdom did indeed long sanction the death penalty for teens and preteens for such varied crimes as murder, rape, theft, and pickpocketing, but accounts of many such death sentences being pronounced were not necessarily an indication they were carried out. Richard Streib noted in 1995:

> *Research at Old Bailey revealed that although more than one hundred youths had been sentenced to death from 1801 to 1836, none had*

been executed. While some cases do exist, it appears settled that execution of youths was never at any time common in England.

The first well-documented execution of a juvenile took place in Roxbury, Massachusetts, in 1642. Thomas Graunger went to the scaffold for having sodomized a cow and a horse. The all-male jury sentenced him according to the Old Testament law described in Leviticus 20:15.

From the 1890s through the 1920s, the executions of juveniles numbered from 20 to 27 per decade, or about 1.6 percent to 2.3 percent of all executions. In the 1930s—when the number of executions rose greatly—the number of juvenile executions followed that general pickup to a figure of 41. Then when public support for capital punishment waned and was outlawed for a number of years (after executions had about stopped on their own), executions of the young dropped off. As more recent public support for both capital punishment for adults and an equally fervent demand for executions of juveniles grew, it became apparent that more of the young will face that grim fate.

Two decisions by the U.S. Supreme Court in 1988 and 1989 prevented the executions of juveniles under the age of 16.

By contrast, in 1945, black 15-year-old Willy Francis committed murder and went to the electric chair in Louisiana not once but twice. His first electrocution failed when the chair functioned improperly and did not kill him. He went back to his cell, and a legal contest ensued as to whether a second try the following year was cruel and unusual punishment. The Supreme Court decided that the unsuccessful execution was only cruel because of an accident and that it "did not make the subsequent execution any more cruel in a constitutional sense than any other execution." In 1947, Francis, then 17, went to the chair a second and fatal time. The matter of his being 15 at the time of the crime was simply not a deciding factor.

By a recent count, several states provide no minimum age for execution but do require that age be a factor in sentencing. Among them are Arizona, Arkansas, Colorado, Florida, Maryland, Mississippi, New Mexico, Pennsylvania, South Carolina, Washington, and Wyoming. Three other states—Delaware, Oklahoma, and South Dakota—have no minimum age for executions, and age is not a factor in sentencing.

States at that moment with a specific age for executions of children are:

18 years: California, Connecticut, Illinois, Nebraska, Ohio, Tennessee

17 years: Georgia, New Hampshire, Texas

16 years: Montana, Nevada

15 years: Louisiana, Virginia

14 years: Alabama, Idaho, Kentucky, Missouri, New Jersey, North Carolina, Utah

10 years: Indiana

Because of changing attitudes toward the death penalty, some alterations to the above listings may occur. Depending on the states, the procedures are still subject to judicial appeal and may or may not include any minimum-age standards.

juvenile delinquency

One of the most perplexing problems for the penal system is how to handle juvenile delinquents. They were not a problem in early colonial days when, more or less, every offender was a criminal, period. Until the Revolution, settlers in this land lived under English common law, which held that juvenile offenders from the age of seven were accountable for their acts and could face the same penalties imposed on adults for various offenses. Although a judge had discretion to determine the culpability of children seven to 24 years of age, when they were brought before fire-and-brimstone jurists, many youths suffered harsh sentences, including numerous executions of children as young as eight for such offenses as burning a barn with "malice, revenge, craft and cunning." A famous case was that of 12-year-old Hannah Ocuish, hanged for the killing of a six-year-old child. A contemporary account, which in tone applauded the execution, declared, "She said very little and appeared greatly afraid, and seemed to want somebody to help her." Protests that she was too young to die enjoyed very little public support.

Overall, however, the punishment of juveniles was much more lenient in the colonies than in England. Corporal punishment and incarceration were gradually replacing the hangman's rope, especially in the post–Revolutionary War period.

Strange boys were chased out of early towns as likely criminals. (Author's collection)

In 1825, the House of Refuge was founded in New York by private donations. It admitted children who were convicted of crimes and those so destitute or neglected that they were in imminent danger of becoming delinquent. This marked the first time that children and adults were jailed separately.

By today's standards, the House of Refuge was a harsh institution, but in that, it merely reflected the general practices of the time. Children were often put in irons, whipped, placed in solitary confinement, forced to survive on a reduced food supply, and subjected to an enforced routine of silence. The institution had the right to act as a parent for neglected or criminal children, and parents who objected seldom were able to win the release of their offspring. Houses of refuge were set up in Boston and Philadelphia, and both instituted reforms on the treatment of juveniles. Boston banned corporal punishment, and Philadelphia housed each child in an individual cell. By 1834, the New York house took the radical step of accepting black children. In 1856 the first girls' reformatory, the Massachusetts Industrial School for Girls, opened.

The 1860s saw the start of an ill-fated experiment, "ship schools," where young offenders were sent to sea on special vessels. Disciplinary problems, heavy operating costs, and protest from adult seamen that they might lose jobs dealt the ship schools a quick death. In the 1870s and 1880s, what became known as the child-saving movement began under the leadership of a number of women's clubs. Through these efforts, separate courts for juveniles were established in 1899 in Illinois, Rhode Island, and the city of Denver, Colorado.

The first federal effort to combat juvenile delinquency came with the establishment of the Children's Bureau in 1912. Under federal encouragement, many states and large cities opened special reformatories for juveniles. These institutions did not solve the juvenile delinquency problem or clarify how juveniles could be rehabilitated through confinement. To this day, brutality, homosexuality, and rioting remain ever-present problems.

Following the approaches to aiding troubled juveniles expounded by John Dewey, Karen Horney, Carl Rogers, Erich Fromm, and others, an era of get-tough approaches to juvenile delinquency took over in the 1970s. This public attitude was bolstered by such horrors as New York City's "laugh killing" in July 1978, the senseless slaying of a 16-year-old seminary student by a 13-year-old boy, a tragedy that some experts said would have a greater impact on the United States's attitude toward juvenile crime as any offense ever would. The killing took place in front of Teachers College at Columbia University when the 13-year-old and a 15-year-old companion approached the seminary student, Hugh McEvoy, and a friend, Peter Mahar, 15, who were sitting on a railing. According to later testimony, the 13-year-old boy asked McEvoy, "What are you laughing at?"

With that, the 13-year-old, who had a record of 10 arrests, nine within the previous 18 months, shot McEvoy. It turned out that the killer could only be tried in family court and receive a maximum sentence of 18 months in a "secure facility," with the option that his sentence could be renewed. After some 18 months, the 13-year-old automatically would be able to receive home passes and furloughs. The subsequent uproar over the laugh killing brought speedy passage of what became known as Carey's law, named for Gov. Hugh Carey, which allowed juveniles to be tried for murder like adults and be sentenced to life in prison. It was predicted that the laugh-killing law would spread throughout the country—and it did.

The case can be made that juvenile criminals are actually being more harshly treated than adult criminals.

One case that appeared to confirm this opinion was reflected in the U.S. Supreme Court *Gault* decision. Gerard Gault, a 15-year-old Arizonan, was on probation for a minor property offense. During that time, he and a friend made a crank call to a neighbor in which they made obscene comments. Gault was ordered to be sent to a training school until he reached 21. An adult facing the same charge would have been fined $50 or given a two-month sentence. The High Court ruled that Gault's constitutional rights had been violated: He had never gotten a notice of the charges nor had he been advised by a lawyer, and he was not able to question witnesses. However, many other court decisions have gone against youths mainly because it was ruled so under the concept of *parens patriae,* which gives the state the right to promote the welfare of juveniles, in effect, acting as their parents.

Despite all the hubbub for punishing youths as adults, many judges resist the pressure, feeling that once a juvenile is put in an adult prison, he is lost. The repeat rate of such juveniles is much higher than that of juveniles who are treated otherwise. A survey in Minnesota showed that more than 90 percent of juvenile offenders who did time in the state's most restrictive facilities chalked up adult records before they turned 23, and more than 70 percent went to prison. Among male offenders sent to reform schools, the rearrest rate within two years was between 53 and 77 percent. Among those who insist that adult prisons don't work for juveniles are probably the majority of prison wardens, who have also learned that such juveniles are the hardest to control and do not adapt to the restrictions that most adult prisoners more or less accept.

It is very difficult to make long-term studies of juvenile delinquency because of the absence of reliable statistics concerning juvenile crime in the 19th century or even the first three decades of the 20th century until the appearance of the FBI's *Uniform Crime Reports.* Even the use of these reports is not that helpful and can cause misleading conclusions about a "juvenile crime wave" based on an increase in juvenile arrests. Certain types of crimes, both violent and nonviolent, are typically juvenile offenses and explode upward when a crop of baby-boom youths hits the crime-prone ages.

The newest stage of such a development was predicted for 2005–10.

See also: BOOT CAMPS; HOUSE OF REFUGE; JUVENILE RIGHTS MOVEMENT; SHIP SCHOOLS.

juvenile rights movement fairer treatment in court

Until about 1960, juveniles charged with crimes and facing incarceration had received very little support from the courts for what juvenile-rights advocates considered fairer treatment. Court decisions had long established that the doctrine of *parens patriae* gave the state the right to involve itself in children's lives in a way that was different from the treatment of adult offenders. It amounted to the idea that the state knows best and that even the parents' rights counted for less than what the authorities held.

A case that turned this around was that of Gerald Gault, a 15-year-old who was on probation for committing a minor property crime in Arizona. While on probation, he and a friend stupidly made a crank call to a neighbor and used some obscene remarks. When they were arrested, the court sentenced Gault to be incarcerated in a training school until the age of 21. Juvenile-rights advocates complained bitterly that an adult who had done the same thing probably would have been fined approximately $50 or, at most, be sentenced to a brief incarceration.

The U.S. Supreme Court ruled in favor of the juvenile in 1967, finding that his constitutional rights had been violated. Gault had not received a notice of the charges and had not been advised by an attorney. The Court also found that Gault had not been helped by the juvenile court but harmed by it and that the procedure used had clearly violated his due process rights under the 14th Amendment.

What the High Court ruled was that juveniles had four basic rights in any hearing that could lead to their incarceration: right to notice; right to legal counsel; right to question witnesses; and protection against self-incrimination. However, in another decision, *McKeiver v. Pennsylvania,* the Court denied the right to jury trial in juvenile court.

In another major decision, *Schall v. Martin,* the Court decided concerning 14-year-old Gregory Martin, who had been arrested and charged with robbery, assault, and possession of a weapon. Martin and two others were accused of hitting a boy over the head with a loaded weapon and stealing a jacket. Martin was held before trial because the juvenile court believed that there was a serious risk, if released, of his committing another crime. Martin's lawyer argued that holding him before trial was punishing him before he was found guilty. The Supreme Court returned to *parens patriae* and said that holding Martin was constitutional because it protected both the juvenile and society and that the government had an interest in promoting the welfare of juveniles.

Another decision of interest to juvenile-rights activists was *Harris v. Caledine* in 1977, in which the West Virginia supreme court of appeals ruled that the right of young Gilbert Harris was violated. He had been guilty of being absent from a school without permission. He was then placed in a secure facility with other juveniles who were guilty of far more serious crimes. The court found that this violated West Virginia's due process clauses of the state constitution. They found it was cruel and unusual punishment as well.

The fact remains that many juveniles are incarcerated for what are called status offenses rather than delinquency offenses. The latter are crimes against people or property or are drug offenses. Status offenses, such as young Harris's charge, are violations that would not be considered crimes if committed by an adult—such as drinking, violated curfews, truancy, running away from home, or being out of the control of parents. Under the West Virginia decision, such status violators could no longer be incarcerated with juveniles who have committed more serious offenses. However, if status offenders break valid court orders or have run away after being placed in a residential environment by court order, they can be put in a secure prison. In the last quarter-century, however, the number of status offenders in secure prisons has fallen enormously.

juvenile suicide and murder in adult prisons

Much has been made in recent years of the number of children under the age of 18 who are executed. In a nine-year period in the 1990s, seven juveniles (when they committed their capital offense) went to their deaths. Some may find this lamentable or worse, but the case can be made that they are merely the tip of the iceberg. In point of fact, many, many more juveniles were in actuality sentenced to death during that same period and died just as tragically and horribly. In one year alone, 45 children met their death while confined with adult offenders for crimes deemed worthy of incarceration with the most violent and deadly prisoners.

These children died at the hands of others and some by their own hand. Children who are sent to adult confinement are prime candidates for murder and suicide. In Texas, a teenage boy was sent to an adult prison where he was repeatedly beaten and raped by adult inmates. He wrote home to his father that he could no longer tolerate the abuse. He hanged himself in his cell.

As such tragedies become more and more common, it might be some comfort if the justice system was at least "discriminate" in how youths are handled. But it is not always the case, bringing into question the justice system's ability to handle the assignment in an equitable sense. Reformers cite the case of an Idaho youth of 17 who was put behind bars in terrifying circumstances for not paying $73 in traffic fines. In quick order, he was tortured and murdered by adult prisoners.

State laws do little to prevent such tragedies. Such juvenile offenders fall victim to the "tough on crime" syndrome that cannot stop with lifelong sentences for some adult offenders. Inevitably, say some reformers, attitudes toward juvenile crime must harden as well. Says the American Civil Liberties Union, "Every day, more and more prosecutors are moving young offenders into the adult court system without any regard to the child's age or circumstance."

State statutes do little to stop the trend. In Massachusetts, a 14-year-old can be prosecuted as adult and be incarcerated in adult prisons. In Oregon, the minimum age is 12, and in Wisconsin it is 10. Reformers denounce the trend of tough treatment of juveniles as breaking down a century-old system of protecting children from contact with adult prisoners.

In a recent case, a mentally disabled 15-year-old stole $2 from a classmate for food. He was charged as an adult on counts of extortion and strong-arm robbery. The punishment could be a sentence of 30 years to life. Leaving aside whether or not such incidents are unknown to many or most school students, there remains the question of what will happen to such youthful offenders when they are released in 10, 20, 30 years. As Barry Glick, a former New York State corrections official and chairman of the American Correctional Association's task force on youthful offenders, notes, "People forget that even though they've done some heinous, violent crimes, they are still adolescents. If you are exposing them to models who are criminals, what are they learning? They're streetwise kids who are learning to be better criminals." It has been shown that children are more likely to be abused physically and sexually in adult prisons and are more likely to continue committing crimes after their release. They, of course, come out of confinement far more antisocial than those who are left in the juvenile system where there is a much greater emphasis on treatment and education. How much of this exists in the adult prisons? In some, the answer is none.

The move to punish youthful offenders harshly as adults, ignoring the consequences, followed a steep rise of the juvenile murder rate in the late 1980s into the early 1990s with the result that teenage prisoners came to be regarded as morally culpable and responsible as adults. As of mid-2001, 45 states had passed or amended legislation to send not only violent offenders into the adult system but also teenagers convicted of burglary and drug offenses. By the latest figures available from the U.S. Justice Department, 7,000 juveniles were incarcerated in adult jails or prisons.

Another line of criticism made by reformers is that three-quarters of such juveniles are children of color, a percentage far greater than that of adult criminals of color, despite the fact that most juvenile crimes are committed by whites. When such former juveniles leave the system, assuming survivability, they bear a felony record so that their future in the outside world is vastly constricted, especially because new technological advances make it much more difficult to hide one's past. Their most likely alternative: more crimes.

Prior to that, juvenile offenders cause enormous problems for the adult penal system, even aside from their victimization. Correction officials acknowledge they are now saddled with a juvenile delinquency of their own. Some of the young prisoners are difficult to control and endanger the older inmates in some cases. Prison systems that isolate the juveniles from the adult population are often doing it for their own self-defense. The problem is that in many systems, the lack of finances forces the prisons to come up with mere jury-rigged responses. Merely keeping them isolated in separate wings of a facility seldom is very effective. The teenagers often still have close encounters with adults at meals, in the library, and in recreation periods.

Several states are moving to improve their systems. In Florida, in May 2001, the legislature passed a measure that required offenders under 18 in adult prison to be housed in special units. In Texas's adult prison in Brazoria, juveniles are isolated in a unit and are in school half of the time; the rest of the time is spent in counseling and treatment. Diana Coates, who heads the Texas Department of Criminal Justice program for juveniles who have been sentenced as adults, finds that the system must cope with new challenges. These are prisoners who talk a lot—and keep outgrowing their shoes. In a few systems, the age separation of adults and children extends to 21. Some observers see in these situations that the fissures in a policy of treating juveniles as adults creates many new problems and consequences.

Perhaps the state doing the most to cope is Pennsylvania with, in 2001, a 500-bed prison at Pine Grove for such teenagers. The $71 million facility concentrates on treatment and education, and it has found it helpful to give teenage inmates a fourth meal in the evening. This is a sandwich and fruit during the week and pizza, cheeseburgers, or a hot sandwich on the weekends. This was inspired by a national survey asking juvenile offenders what they considered the most important prison incentive.

Pine Grove Warden Barry Johnson said to the *New York Times,* "Everyone thought they would say parole or prerelease. They said pizza."

Warden Johnson added: "It shows that they are adolescents. They live very much for the minute—which makes them very dangerous inmates. They're not like adult inmates, who will listen to orders of a correctional officer." That means that the juvenile offenders can be a real threat to adult inmates. "We have found," the warden said, "that the adults are as much afraid of the kids as the kids are of the adults. The kids can gain a tremendous reputation if they can take out an adult inmate."

Some see such developments as merely the competition and rule of the streets. But within the confined borders of a prison establishment, the rules and motivations simply become more intensified. The actions of adult sexual predators intensify, too, as they pursue gang rape as the more prudent and successful modus operandi.

The brutal cycle of sexual victim and predator (whoever that may be) continues in its various forms. Without doubt the situation becomes reinforced in those facilities where the prison administration holds to the get-tough approach; whenever one is committed as an adult, he is to be treated as one with indifference, whether above or below the cut-off age.

This has led some veteran corrections officers to turn whistle blower. One wrote to a newspaper columnist, as reported by Christian Parenti in *Lockdown America:* "There are prison administrators who use inmate gangs to help manage the prison. Sex and human bodies become the coin of the realm. Is inmate 'X' writing letters to the editor of the local newspaper and filing lawsuits? Or perhaps he threw urine or feces on an employee? 'Well, Joe, you and Willie and Hank work him over, but be sure you don't break any bones and send him to the hospital. If you do a good job, I'll see that you get the blondest boy in the next shipment.'"

See also: RAPE IN PRISON.

Kemmler, William See EXECUTION METHODS.

Keyes, Asa (1877–1934) imprisoned corrupt district attorney

In the early 20th century, Asa Keyes was acknowledged to be one of the most prolific district attorneys in the nation. In 25 years in that Los Angeles position, Keyes sent no fewer than 5,000 offenders to San Quentin. Then there were those he didn't send away, taking huge bribes to see that things went light for them. As a result, Keyes himself was convicted and sent to that very forbidden prison where he had consigned thousands.

Obviously, Keyes did not become very popular among San Quentin convicts, who were, in fact, clearly considered likely to kill him if they got the opportunity. Officials decided the only safe place to keep Keyes out of harm's way was in the prison's death row.

There, Keyes renewed an acquaintanceship with Herbert Emerson Wilson, the era's "king of the safecrackers." Wilson also was in protective custody on death row. After his conviction, Wilson had informed on many underworld confederates to win a reduced sentence. Wilson had been convicted of murder but before trial had prudently paid Keyes $50,000 to "go light" on him. Wilson got only life imprisonment instead of hanging. With that sentence and with his deals on convictions of others, Wilson could look forward to eventual release.

Wilson worked on his memoirs with Keyes's help on the first draft. Once, Keyes suggested that the book should end with some note that "Crime Doesn't Pay." Wilson didn't agree, saying, "I've told the readers that you're here and I'm here, and that we're going to be in here for a long time. . . . If a reader is so damn stupid he can't figure it out for himself that crime doesn't pay, after reading all the facts of my story, then nothing I can add could ever hope to enlighten him."

Keyes's own sentiments of his own life in San Quentin are most enlightening in his amended attitude toward prisons. In 1931 he told the *San Francisco Chronicle:*

> *The mass resentment and hatred of 4000 men which seems as tangible as the prison walls, the monotony of endless days without hope, the association with the dregs of humanity, all combine to turn the average prisoner into a worse man instead of a better one.*
>
> *I don't know what to suggest in place of prisons. . . . It is a thing far more terrible than most people realize.*

Released in 1931, three years before his death, Keyes found a job based on his background as a car salesman.

"kill on sight" battle cry of the Aryan Brotherhood
Of all the criminal gangs in prison, the Aryan Brotherhood is recognized as the most ruthless and savage white gang. The gang was born in San Quentin around 1970 and earned its reputation the hard way, through brutal attacks and murders of other gangs. Outright racists, the Aryan Brotherhood (AB) set out to establish its power by attacking enemy black and Hispanic gang members. But its really awesome power was established when it issued its infamous "kill on sight" orders so that its members were required to come out each morning as soon as the cell doors were opened and attack black inmates whether or not they were members of a gang.

During the so-called prison race wars that lasted until 1975, the AB proved to be the most merciless in the prison and continued to be a power after an uneasy truce was achieved. The AB remained feared killers as they took over key prison rackets as drug smuggling, extortion, and gambling and took on contract murders for other gangs.

It was not considered wise for any other gangs to attack an AB member. Such an act could trigger another kill-on-sight bloodbath by the Aryan Brotherhood.

"knuckle voice" restricted communication method used by prisoners
The "knuckle voice" was not an invention of American convicts but rather was developed by a nihilist doctor of the inner circle, during his imprisonment in the St. Peter and Paul fortress in St. Petersburg. He taught the system to other Russian prisoners so that it became commonly used in that country. The code, based on a pattern called the Siberian Square, was used by prisoners to rap out messages to each other.

It was laid out as follows:

	1	2	3	4	5	6
1	A	B	C	D	E	
2	F	G	H	I	J	
3	K	L	M	N	O	
4	P	Q	R	S	T	
5	U	V	W	X	Y	Z

There were five spaces each way, making (A): one, space, one—or two short taps; (B) one, space, two—or one short tap followed by two short taps, and so on for the other three letters of the first line of five, each of which started with one short rap, being the first group. (F) started the second line and was two, space, one—or two short taps followed by one. (J) was two, space, five, or two short taps followed by five. (Y) was the fifth letter in the fifth line being five, space, five and (Z) being the letter in the odd square became five, space, six.

Ed Morrell, an American prisoner in San Quentin under sentence of life in solitary in the dungeon, once had the system shown to him by an escaped convict from Russia. Morrell, who would become one of the most amazing and later celebrated prisoners in the United States, never had dreamed that he would have any use for the system, but now he did. He was confined in the dungeon with the only other prisoner in San Quentin who was doomed for life and placed in solitary, Jake Oppenheimer, the so-called Tiger of the Prison Cage. The Tiger had been there much longer than Morrell and was dying to communicate in some fashion, but they were 13 cells apart. Morrell sought to teach him the system, but because neither had paper or pencil, Morrell tapped out the code endlessly; the Tiger, however, could not comprehend the meaning. Finally, after nine months, communication was made and the pair had a measure of human contact.

It was years before the guards figure out that the pair was communicating rather than having simply gone crazy, a more normal result of such incarceration. When Morrell was later released from solitary confinement—the first of several moves that would finally result in his freedom—and returned to the general prison population, he taught the code to other inmates so that none ever again could be left in total isolation if there was anyone else like him. The system quickly spread virtually to every prison in the country, just at it is practiced all around the world.

See also: MORRELL, ED.

Kogut, William (1880–1930) "self-executioner"
In the annals of San Quentin lore, William Kogut, death-row convict #1651, was in a sense an

insignificant killer, his crime little remembered, but he was far more infamous for the last victim he was to claim. That act was to alter the way death rows around the nation have operated ever since.

When Kogut, a very belligerent condemned man, entered San Quentin in 1930 sentenced to be hanged for the lethal stabbing of a woman, he sneered he would never be executed, that he would choose his own way of dying. The sentencing judge heard that same boast and did not dismiss the threat but specifically warned the prison authorities to keep from Kogut all weapons or tools, no matter how unlikely, that would facilitate a suicide attempt. Death-row guards therefore kept an especially close watch on Kogut, as though his survival to face death in the prescribed manner was a form of deadly contest. Kogut seemed rather cool in his actions, his only diversion being playing solitaire with one of the two decks of cards he was permitted to keep in his cell.

Then in the early morning hours of October 10, 1930, not long before his slated execution, the prison was ripped by a terrific explosion. Guards rushed to Kogut's death-row cell and discovered him lying in a pool of blood, his face little more than a blob.

It took the coroner and a group of chemists several days to determine how Kogut had managed to kill himself. The only activity the guards could describe Kogut of having engaged in was his constant preoccupation with playing solitaire, hardly an unusual pastime on death row. What Kogut was doing was busily scraping all the red spots on the cards—the diamonds and hearts—with his thumbnail. He then soaked the residue with water in his tin cup, producing a moist pulp. He then poured it into a hollow knob from his cot and plugged up the knob with a second knob. Kogut now had what he wanted, a potential deadly bomb. The bits of playing cards were made of cellulose and nitrate, and when mixed with a solvent formed pyroxylin, an explosive that could be set off by heat. Kogut had fashioned a homemade pipe bomb.

Then he did what he had to do to fulfill his boast. He put his bomb in his tin cup and placed it on the small heater in his cell. He laid his head on the cup and waited for the inevitable explosion that cheated the hangman.

Kogut's suicide trick was never again duplicated in San Quentin or, in fact, any other death row. Condemned prisoners still are permitted playing cards, but the decks are routinely collected and checked.

L

La Tuna, Texas, Federal Correctional Institution "stool-pigeon haven"

It can be called "stool-pigeon *haven*"—not *heaven.* The La Tuna Federal Correctional Institution has housed some of the most notorious—and valuable—informers in recent decades. Perhaps the most famed trio of all would be underworld snitches Joe Valachi, Vinnie Teresa, and Jimmy "the Weasel" Fratianno, but there were many others.

Twenty-one miles outside El Paso, Texas, La Tuna looks much like a Spanish adobe church. It is not a "hellhole" but it is hot, dry, and miserable. And it is not a "country club" either; in fact, if the government wanted its informers better kept and in better physical security, many other institutions would do better.

Yet, most informer detainees found La Tuna probably less wanting than any other place. What the informers soon learned was that the guards there were probably the most reliable in the federal prison system. Virtually all the guards, they determined, were of Mexican descent. Vinnie Teresa, the snitch whose testimony destroyed much of the New England Mafia, was, at first, very leery of them. He figured that because they came from impoverished backgrounds, they would not know how to say no if mobsters dangled large sums of money before them. If that happened, Teresa knew he would be a dead man.

Instead, Teresa discovered, the guards were friendly, understanding, and, most impressive, not on the take.

Joe Valachi, the star informer for Senator John L. McClellan and the Senate Permanent Investigations Subcommittee, was equally apprehensive when shipped to La Tuna. Indeed, when Teresa shipped in later, Valachi was sure he was a hit man who was commissioned by the mob to kill him. Valachi's time had been etched by similar worries. He had killed one federal prisoner in Atlanta whom he thought had been assigned to murder him. Now, Teresa was haunted by renewed fears. Finally, the pair had a "sit-down," and after a probing discussion, each decided neither was out to "whack" the other.

Not that both did not suspect possible mob treachery: When a small plane circled overhead while the pair were taking the sun on a patio reserved for trusties or honored prisoners, Valachi was outspoken that the craft was a Cosa Nostra plane with a hit man ready to blast the two of them. The FBI investigated the mysterious flight and later informed guards they should fire some shots if it ever flew over too low thereafter. The plane never reappeared.

Teresa and Valachi became close friends, which proved very important to Valachi because he never received any visitors. His wife and family had forsaken him, a situation about which he said, "I don't blame them."

Joseph Valachi, former Cosa Nostra mobster, is shown October 1, 1963, as he tells a U.S. Senate rackets subcommittee the inner workings of the crime organization. Sentenced to life at La Tuna Correctional Institution in El Paso, Texas, he feared that there he would be assassinated on mob orders. (AP/Wide World Photos)

Valachi long harbored some illusions that someday he would be allowed to go free, and he turned bitter when that never came to pass. However, he had killed a federal prisoner, and there was no way the government could ever turn him loose. Also, Valachi was a dying man, suffering from cancer. When Valachi was on his deathbed, Teresa was permitted access to him to help nurse and care for him.

Later, Jimmy Fratianno occupied the "Valachi suite" at La Tuna, and it was here that most of the interviews for his biography, *The Last Mafioso* by Ovid Demaris, were conducted.

La Tuna is now a byword in the criminal world, a symbol of the fact that the federal government can protect informers, that as a stool-pigeon haven it is completely safe—although perhaps not the country club that white-collar stock-market or Watergate offenders occupied.

Lawes, Kathryn See ANGEL OF SING SING.

Lawes, Lewis Edward (1883–1947) Sing Sing warden

He became a storied cult figure in his day. But in more recent years, with concepts in penology having shifted toward the "treat-'em-rough" school, Warden Lewis E. Lawes would be viewed as a "bleeding-heart" corrections type. Nevertheless, in his 21 years in charge of Sing Sing Prison in Ossining, New York, he was a committed voice for the philosophy that prisons should try to rehabilitate prisoners.

The son of a prison guard, Lawes took up the same profession at 22, but unlike the old-time guards (and most of the new ones), he viewed and studied penology as a science and soon bounded up the system, building a reputation as a realistic reformer. In 1915, at 32, he became superintendent of the New York City Reformatory and then was tapped by Gov. Alfred E. Smith for the difficult, perhaps thankless position of warden of Sing Sing.

Lawes in quick order accomplished perhaps the most difficult task in penology, gaining the respect of both the guards and the inmates. One of the first goals he achieved was reducing greatly the incidence of corporal punishment. Lawes once said:

> *It became quickly apparent to me that under conditions as they were, the prison warden, to be effective, would have to constitute himself not as an instrument of punishment but a firm, frank friend in need. He would have to stretch humanitarianism to the limits of the law, with a stiff punch always in reserve. I have been charged, since my incumbency, with being too kind. I wish I could plead guilty to the accusation, but my sense of duty will not permit it. My job is to hold my men and, as far as possible, to win them over to sane, social thinking. And I judge the effectiveness of that job not so much by obedience to rule,*

for rules can be enforced, but by the humor of the general prison population.

Lawes established a system for inmate self-government that for him had a very definite meaning—the government of self. Under Lawes, the prisoners' Mutual Welfare League was charged with regulating the leisure hours of the inmates, subject only to approval. However, unlike methods used in other prisons, the prisoners enjoyed no power over other prisoners, which Lawes regarded as a certain way to create friction. Machinery was established whereby an inmate with a pressing problem could see him.

Lawes was frequently willing to gamble on his prisoners, often allowing them leave to visit home for a funeral or to go to the bedside of a dying relative. They were honor bound to return, and they did. Lawes often loaned money to prisoners being discharged, and almost always they would return it, some coming to the prison gate years later with the money. Lawes could thus dedicate one of his books "to those tens of thousands of my former wards who have justified my faith in human nature."

Although Lawes was forced to carry out his official duties to preside over many executions, he was a bitter foe of capital punishment and toured the country campaigning to abolish it. He opposed the death penalty because of the infrequency and the inequity of its application and often the martyrdom it could provide to a convicted murderer. He felt that all these problems weakened the entire structure of social control and actually encouraged the desperate criminal toward the extreme penalty. "He knows," Lawes declared, "that his gamble with the death penalty is safer than with a long term in prison for a lesser offense."

Lawes retired in 1941, having held the post longer than any other warden. His predecessor had only lasted six weeks.

See also: ANGEL OF SING SING.

Leopold and Loeb thrill murderers

Two of the most notorious "lifers" in prison were 18-year-old Richard "Dickie" Loeb and 19-year-old Nathan Leopold, both from very wealthy Chicago families. Considering themselves intellectually superior to others, they decided to stage a killing merely to demonstrate to themselves their supposed brilliance. They picked as their victim another wealthy child, 14-year-old Bobby Franks. As wise as they thought they were, Loeb and Leopold were caught rather easily.

Loeb soon confessed and then Leopold. The trial that followed exhibited strong hostility to both murderers, which was compounded by the defendants' smirks and antics that further inflamed public opinion. Despite this, that courtroom magician, the great Clarence Darrow, managed to get the pair off with a life sentence rather than the hangman's noose.

As prisoners, the two murderers continued to draw considerable attention. News exposés reported that the pair enjoyed favored treatment in prison. Unlike many other convicts at Joliet, each was put in separate cells, crammed with books, desks, and filing cabinets. They were permitted to eat in the officer's lounge away from other inmates and had their meals cooked to order. They were permitted to visit each other's cell and were allowed their own garden.

Richard Loeb, left, and Nathan Leopold, right, at their trial in 1924 (Author's collection)

Nathan Leopold in July 1957, shortly before he won parole. (Author's collection)

Over the years, Loeb's homosexuality turned more aggressive, and he was known for relentlessly pursuing other inmates. In 1936, he was killed in a homosexual brawl. By comparison, Leopold made considerable adjustment in his behavior. However, his appeals for parole were rejected three times. At his fourth appeal, poet Carl Sandburg pleaded for him, saying he would be willing to allow Leopold to live in his home. In March 1958, Leopold won his parole.

He said, "I am a broken old man. I want a chance to find redemption for myself and to help others." He published his memoirs, *Life Plus 99 Years,* and went to Puerto Rico to work among the poor as a $10-a-month hospital technician. Three years later, he married a widow. He died of a heart ailment in 1971.

See also: WORLD WAR II AND PRISON INMATES.

lethal injection See EXECUTION METHODS.

lime cell prison torture

One of the most hellish tortures ever used in U.S. prisons was the so-called lime cell, which remained quite popular in a number of institutions well into the 20th century. A prisoner would be led to a cell where the white coating of lime ran some 3 inches thick. A guard would sprinkle the cell with a hose, resulting in a white mist from the exploding chloride of lime filling the cell, and then the prisoner would be shoved inside.

A graphic description of what ensued was offered by Ed Morrell, a convict, later pardoned, who became a national hero and leading spokesman for prison reform and the elimination of the practice of torture in penal institutions in many parts of the country:

> *I clutched my burning throat with both hands, then reeled and fell to the floor. That only brought me closer to the volcano of fiery death. Struggling frantically I scratched at the jutting stones of the dungeon trying to pull myself to my feet.*
>
> *I then staggered, groping blindly until I hit the door. I pounded upon it with my bare hands.*
>
> *Cramping pains tore at my bowels. My breath grew hot. It had the intensity of molten lead. My fingers, hands, and arms finally became number, and paralyzing shocks stunned my brain. Had I been offered a draught of deadly poison in that awful agony I would have drunk it with gratitude—anything to escape further torture in that lethal chamber of Hell.*

During his ordeal, Morrell hallucinated that his head was down and his feet up and that he was starting to whirl and was shot off into space. When the door was opened, a guard reached in with a long hook and dragged out his limp body. A hose's cooling waters stifled the burning fumes and slowly brought him back to life.

> *The whole gruesome deed hardly consumed six minutes in actual time, but I had been dead for ages. Two guards laid hold of my legs and dragged me back to the cell where I had spent the night.*
>
> *What I suffered for the next ten days beggars description. The delicate mucous membrane of*

my mouth and throat was seared and burnt. My eyebrows and eyelashes were gone. I could not speak above a whisper. Physically I was a wreck.

Despite official denials, the lime cell remained a favored form of punishment until recent years. Certainly, Hollywood was fond of depicting it in a number of films. Finally, nationwide prison reform supposedly ended the inhuman practice. Yet, reports seem to indicate it is still practiced in isolated instances.

See also: FOLSOM PRISON'S "BACK ALLEY"; MORRELL, ED.

Further reading: *The 25th Man* by Ed Morrell.

Lobaugh, Ralph ex-prisoner with release-from-prison trauma

An ex-prisoner who received considerable media attention, Ralph Lobaugh was released from an Indiana prison in 1977 after 30 years and having fought vigorously the last 14 to win his freedom. He ended up being cited by many observers as the classic case of an ex-prisoner suffering release from prison trauma.

It turned out that freedom was more than he could take. After only two months, he found he could not cope with the outside world and decided to return to prison, quoted as saying he "just wanted to live in a cell again and be with his old friends."

See also: RELEASE-FROM-PRISON TRAUMA.

lockups lowest level of confinement facility

A lockup can be regarded as the lowest level of confinement of offenders or of those who will not be charged with any crime and is generally operated by police in police stations or headquarters. Some may occupy a separate section of a jail building. Designed to be at most a temporary holding facility with arrestees usually to be held no more than 48 hours, not counting weekends and holidays, lockups are also used to dry out inebriated people and to hold youths until their families can be notified or a different sort of placement arranged. Unfortunately, quite a few people end up stuck in the cracks. One individual who had no knowledge of police routines was held in a lockup for many months. He was quoted as explaining that "I figured I was found guilty and was serving a sentence, but nobody told me what it was."

It is impossible to categorize lockups nationwide. There has never been a national survey of lockups and, thus, no overall information dealing with their conditions, size, and population. Lockups are frequently used as a dumping ground for individuals with whom society cannot deal, such as the homeless. Because newspaper accounts of deaths in lockups are very prevalent, it is obvious that the rate is very high. Because support groups for the lockup population are at best spotty, the practices in lockups can be described as neglected more than any other sort of confinement.

Lombroso, Cesare (1836–1909) popularizer of the "born-criminal" concept

The most prominent criminologist worldwide in the 19th century, with widespread acceptance of his beliefs in the United States, Cesare Lombroso of Italy dominated much of prison practices with his classification of criminals as "degenerate" and "atavistic." The latter was the concept that criminality was a biological throwback to an earlier stage of evolution and savage humanity. In short, he embraced the concept of the "born criminal," that criminality was a product of heredity.

Lombroso engaged in prodigious research in measuring thousands of convicts, living and dead (using some techniques that, according to some later researchers, bordered on medieval witch-hunting methods in their zeal). In this fashion, he came up with a number of criteria that established the "criminal type." By the late 1870s, he had catalogued how authorities and the courts might be alerted to what Lombroso saw as suspicious traits. Some of these were:

an asymmetrical face

an excessive jaw

eye defects

a receding forehead

a peculiar palate

scant beard

wooly hair

long hair

fleshy or swollen lips

long arms
darker skin
abnormal dentition
twisted nose
precocious wrinkles
inversion of sex organs
lack of moral sense
vanity
cruelty
frequent gambling
using criminal argot
cynicism

Lombroso developed various categories of criminals, the worst of the lot being the "insane criminal" and the "epileptic criminal." The insane criminal was one who was mentally deficient and therefore a born criminal, with primitive behavior that made the person prone to criminal activity. The epileptic criminal turned to crime because of epilepsy. Lombroso offered up the "occasional criminal," which was subdivided in two categories. The "criminaloid" had strong criminal tendencies but the nature of a chameleon who could be influenced by his adaptation to his surroundings—criminal when the situation was ripe but otherwise apparently normal. Then within the group there was also the "pseudo criminal" who involuntarily committed petty crimes but could be socially correct in other aspects.

Lombroso developed an evolutionary scale, with, of course, noncriminal men ranking highest. The criminaloid was accorded the position just below noncriminal. Then there were criminal man and then noncriminal women. Criminal women were the last category with Lombrosian physical traits that resembled those of the criminal man. To Lombroso, all "primitive" women were prostitutes. Thus, Lombroso came to the conclusion as quoted by Stephen Jay Gould in *The Mismeasure of Man:* "We are governed by silent laws which never cease to operate and which rule society with more authority than the laws inscribed on our statute books." (Incidentally, Lombroso did allow normal moral women to escape primitive women–prostitutes characterization. He could recognize a prostitute by her skull, nose, arms, thighs, and facial wrinkles, and he offered a simple way to spot the normal moral woman: She could be identified by her "passivity, docility and apathy towards sex.")

Lombroso's doctrines had an immediate impact in the United States in the study of the social sciences and fed right into the new study of criminology, which was then in the process of being accepted as a part of sociology in some colleges and universities. Lombrosian thought loosed researchers of all stripes to put prison inmates under special observation. Experiments broke out in any number of prison facilities, where researchers were welcomed in the full support of the administrations.

A prison chaplain in San Quentin, August Drahms, published a massive Lombrosian study that worked down the prison inmates to three major categories. There was, said Drahms, first the instinctive criminal who simply was predisposed to commit crimes. Then there was the habitual criminal for whom Drahms noticed some ideas beyond the born criminal of the first group; Drahms allowed they could somewhat derive inspiration more from their environment than from "parental fountains." Finally, there was the single offender who committed an isolated crime that was out of character and situational in nature. Not that the chaplain had any brief for any of them. They were all criminals and therefore morally, physically, and mentally inferior. What Drahms's study allowed was a sort of Orwellian principle that some convicts were morally, physically, and mentally inferior to others.

Another study of some note was conducted by Rufus Bernard von Kleinsmid, who studied 5,600 inmates and concluded that "these men are physically inferior to the average young man not in prison and presumably normal." Other researchers produced like presumptions. Most of these studies, reported Richard Milner in *The Encyclopedia of Evolution,* for decades "were taken very seriously by university professors, government policymakers, and police departments." Naturally, prison administrators were readily informed of what their charges were truly like.

Lombrosian principles were to have enormous influence on many subjects and mostly on the new belief of eugenics, but the principles of Lombrosian thought carried within them many problems and oversimplifications that would make it the butt of parody, whether intended or not. In his celebrated 1899 classic book, *The Theory of the Leisure Class,* sociologist and economist Thorstein Veblen applied the slogan of the "survival of the fittest" to U.S. free enterprise. Men like Carnegie and Rockefeller, according to Veblen, had no claims of being themselves naturally selected as business leaders and the like. Veblen leaned on Lombroso to label them as atavistic throwbacks themselves and not the "fittest" members of the human species. Veblen lumped them right along with lower-class thieves and murderers whom Lombroso had studied. Veblen saw the powerful industrialists as criminals with "predatory aptitudes and propensities carried over . . . from the barbarian past of the race . . . with the substitution of fraud and . . . administrative ability" for naked violence. They were, for Veblen, throwbacks to plundering barbarian tribes and a lingering hindrance to social progress.

Veblen's work hardly destroyed Lombrosian thought, but the sheer weight of its controversial theories proved to be too much, and it went into a lingering decline, as did eugenics, which Lombroso had helped father. By the mid-1920s both were practically forgotten.

Lowell, Josephine Shaw prison reformer

Although she was symbolically tarred by her association with the eugenics theory and influenced greatly by the very unscientific study by Richard Dugdale of the so-called Jukes family (from which she, like many other welfare-minded experts, determined that heredity rather than environment was responsible for poverty and crime), Josephine Shaw Lowell nevertheless is regarded today as a leading reformer on the imprisonment of women.

The sister of Robert Gould Shaw, who gained fame for leading and dying with a black regiment for the North in the Civil War, she was also widowed by the death of her husband in the same conflict. Lowell continued her support for the war by helping in the direction of the Women's Central Association of Relief for the Army and Navy.

Named the first female commissioner of the New York State Board of Charities, Lowell insisted on what she called "scientific philanthropy," with aid determined by sociological studies rather than simple alms giving. In time, she came to hold that feeble-mindedness, now called mental retardation, à la Dugdale and eugenics, caused crime, and she blamed promiscuous and feeble-minded women for its spread. Her solution: Encourage law-abiding persons to produce more children and prevent poor, feeble-minded women from having that ability by keeping them in custody through their childbearing years.

Yet, Lowell's reputation still comes through to us as a genuine reformer in her campaigns to take women prisoners out of male institutions and put them in separate women's prisons with an all-female custodian force. She was the founder of the women's reformatory prison at Bedford Hills, New York. Lowell died in 1905 before the eugenics movement went into its permanent decline. Ironically, one of Lowell's successors as the head of Bedford Hills, Dr. Jean Weidensall, joined with other researchers, such as Dr. Edith Spaulding and William Healy, who pioneered the new science of criminal diagnosis to dismiss the idea of criminality being an inherited trait but rather caused by a variety of physical, social, and mental causes, interrelated and interactive.

Lynds, Elam (1784–1855) first warden and "Whip of Sing Sing"

He would be commonly referred to in the press of the 19th and 20th centuries as the "Whip of Sing Sing" for the brutal fashion in which he built Sing Sing using only convict labor. He did it with the whip and the exercise of monstrous force, but the charge was readily dismissed because the entire prison was built with no expenditure of public funds. It was an accomplishment that delighted the political powers in Albany.

He was known in his day—an era when enlightened treatment of convicts was hardly celebrated—as the wickedest warden in America. He remains so into the present time. A full century after Lynds's reign as warden, another warden of Sing Sing, Thomas Mott Osborne, wrote, "We are just now getting rid of the Lynds' influence." Another warden, Lewis E. Lawes, added, "Bit by bit, one reform at a time, the memory of Captain Lynds is being scrubbed out of the stones of Sing Sing."

What can only be described as the atrocities Lynds committed so exercised the village of Sing Sing in the 1820s that the citizenry changed the village's name to Ossining.

Many of Lynds's innovations became standard for decades to come in many prisons. It was Lynds who originated the first striped uniforms for convicts, prisoners marching in lockstep or close marching, and prisoners passing each other with downcast eyes so that they never came face to face with one another. Lynds also prohibited inmates from talking either in or out of their cells and had them do hard labor from dawn to dusk. Above all, he whipped prisoners and ordered his guards to do the same. "Whip 'em till they drop," he ordered his guards until he won his nickname of the Whip of Sing Sing.

Lynds had fought with valor in the War of 1812, rising to the rank of captain, and after the conflict he obtained the position of principal keeper at the new state prison in Auburn, New York, where his stern administration won him many admirers. When the warden of Auburn died, Lynds succeeded him in 1821 at the age of 37. Thus began what is now regarded as the darkest period in penal history as the prison became known as the harshest in the nation, which did, however, make him the darling of prison discipline societies and their allies in the legislature.

Lynds gave the disciplinarians all they could hope for, talking the legislature into letting him choose 80 prisoners to be held in solitary confinement in the first of 550 individual cells being constructed at the prison. The inmates were to be held there until the completion of their terms. If any ever broke their silence, they tasted Lynds's whip. During the first two years of Lynds's treatment, only two of the 80 who were not lucky enough to go free survived. The rest either died, committed suicide, or went hopelessly insane. With a record like that, Lynds was ordered to extend the system as more cells were completed. (These cell blocks were the ones after which all others around the world would be patterned.)

For six days of the week, the inmates were out of the cells from dawn to dusk doing hard labor, and then they went back to their unlit, unheated, and unsanitary cells for the long silent night. On the seventh day, the prisoners remained locked up the entire 24 hours. The Rev. Louis Dwight, head of the Boston Prison Discipline Society, was lavish in his descriptions of Lynds's concept of labor, beatings, and silence:

> *The whole establishment, from the gate to the sewer, is a specimen of neatness. The unremitted industry, the entire subordination and subdued feeling of the convicts, has probably no parallel among an equal number of criminals. In their solitary cells they spend the night, with no other book than the Bible, and at sunrise they proceed in military order, under the eye of the turnkeys, in solid columns, with the lock march, to their workshops; thence in the same order, at the hour of breakfast, to the common jail, where they partake of their wholesome and frugal meal in silence. Not even a whisper is heard through the whole dining area. The convicts are seated in single file, at narrow tables, with their backs towards the center, so that there can be no interchange of signs. If one has more food than he wants, he raises his right hand, and the waiter changes it. When they have done eating, at the ringing of a little bell, of the softest sound, they rise from the table, form the solid columns, and return under the eye of their turnkeys to the work-shops. . . .*
>
> *At the close of the day, a little before sunset, the work is all laid aside as one and the convicts return in military order to the solitary cells; where they partake of their frugal meal, which they are permitted to take from the kitchen, where it was furnished for them, as they returned from the shops. After supper, they can, if they choose, read the Scriptures undisturbed, and then reflect in silence on the errors of their lives. They must not disturb their fellows by even a whisper. . . . The men attend to their business from the rising to the setting sun, and spend the night in solitude."*

Such glowing testimonials were not universal. Lynds's whippings became a scandal, so much so that the Auburn residents staged an almost unheard-of riot against the prison for being too rough on inmates. In one case, Lynds ordered guards to whip three prisoners and three guards in a row refused to comply. Lynds fired them on the spot and brought in a village blacksmith to carry out the penalty. When the blacksmith left the prison, a mob of townsmen—they preferred the title of *vigilantes*—fell on him and tarred and feathered him very roughly. Lynds wisely remained within the prison.

Nothing would stop his whippings. One time, he flogged a prisoner 500 times. He lashed prisoners having fits and those who were insane, and there was no telling how many went insane under his ministrations. The huge increase in insanity, and suicides plagued Lynds as prison reform associations began to spring up and all railed against his oppressive tactics. Particularly outrageous was a case in which a guard, on Lynds's orders, entered the cell of a female prisoner, one of 100 kept in the segregated south wing of the prison, and whipped her severely. Within a month the woman died, and when her body was shipped to a medical college, it was determined that her death had not been from natural causes. In the flood of protests, even Lynds's devotees could not save his position, but they were able to put him in charge of the building of a new prison at Sing Sing on the Hudson River, which Lynds pledged to construct free of any cost to the state.

The site was chosen because it could be reached by boat and because a large quantity of marble rock and good building stone was available and not too difficult to quarry. Lynds arrived in the spring of 1825 with 100 chosen prisoners from Auburn. They were issued striped uniforms, the first of that time ever used. Lynds wanted such uniforms because they would stand out against the background of trees, making it obvious when a prisoner attempted to escape.

Under Lynds's lash, it took only three years for the workforce to complete the prison, building individual cells for themselves and for 400 other convicts and a chapel room for 900 more. It was an amazing accomplishment especially because the convicts had labored without a retaining wall and yet none had escaped. Their labors were harsh. When the prisoners could work less during the winter months because of less daylight, Lynds cut their food rations, reasoning that they did not need to have the same level of nourishment. He did not bother to inform his superiors in Albany of this and sold the surplus food to outside merchants. Lynds continued this practice throughout his reign. That rather than his $1,000 annual salary would make him a very rich man.

Aside from such light-fingered activities, Sing Sing was built without cost. The prisoners quarried stone for their own cells; at the same time, they also cut beautiful slabs of light gray stone, almost like granite, for sale to state and local communities in New York as well as New England, the income from which lined Lynds's pockets. State legislative inspectors were so pleased by the lack of cost to build the prison that no one bothered about additional tons of stone always stacked by the river bank for shipment to private builders at bargain prices.

Once the prison was completed, grateful authorities gave him a free hand in running it, ignoring the final judgment of his Auburn record. Lynds offered a three-word instruction for his guards: "Punish! Punish! Punish!"

Lynds said, "I don't believe in reformation of an adult criminal. He's a coward, a willful lawbreaker whose spirit must be broken by the lash. Why is it one guard, armed with a whip, can control twenty convicts? They are afraid of him. I'll teach them to fear my guards. And all of them, guards included, to fear me. This is the only way to conduct a prison." Lynds was described as personally meeting every new batch of prisoners shipped up from New York City. He would scan the commitment papers to find the new arrival with the worst record, pull him out of line, and have him strapped to the whipping post. Lynds would give him 10 lashes.

His most prized victims were prisoners who had assaulted a prison guard before being sent up. He would single out a man like that for special and regular punishment. One man who managed to free himself from Lynds's torment was working at the rock quarry and refused to run when some explosives were set off.

Even though he inspired acts of that sort, Lynds always sought to establish himself as a man without fear. He constantly would parade in the midst of inmates who truly hated him.

One example of Lynds's lack of fear is reported by two French writers, G. de Beaumont and A. de Tocqueville, in their famous book, *On the Penitentiary System of the United States,* published in 1833. Lynds learned that a prison barber was threatening to kill him if he ever got a chance to put a razor to his throat. The warden summoned the barber to give him a shave. By the time the near-hysterical barber finished his chore, he was a nervous wreck. Lynds laughed at him. "I know you threatened to kill me, but I knew you wouldn't. Unarmed, I'm stronger than you are with a weapon. Now get out."

If Lynds was a terror to the prisoners by day, he was far worse by night. The French writers described the Lynds technique as he would prowl on tiptoes through the silent galleries of the prison at night, his whip in hand, listening for violators of the no-whispering rule:

> *It was a tomb of living dead. . . . We could not realize that in this building were 950 human beings. We felt we were traversing catacombs. A faint glow from a lantern held by an inspector on the upper galleries moved slowly back and forth in the ghostly darkness. As it passed each narrow cell door we saw, in our imagination, the gateway to a sepulcher instead. . . . The watchman wore woolen moccasins over his shoes on the gallery floor. There was not a sound.*

Not a sound until some unfortunate cried out in anguish when his cell door was thrown open and the terrible whip cracked. Not even prisoners guilty only of talking in their sleep were exempt from the rawhide punishment.

The truly telling blow against Lynds was made by Col. Levi S. Barr, an ex-army officer and lawyer under a three-year sentence. When it was proved that Barr had been falsely accused and was cleared of any crime, he was a powerful spokesman against Lynds, the first that Lynds had ever faced. It had to be understood that under the law at the time, no prison inmate could testify in a legal proceeding.

"In my three years of confinement," Barr informed the state legislature, "I ate no butter, cheese, milk, sugar, no turnips, beets, carrots, parsnips or vegetables of any kind save potatoes, no soups or strengthening drinks. . . . I have gladly eaten the roots of shrubs and trees that I dug from the ground in which I labored. . . . I saw no exception among individuals around me. . . . There were some who told me they ate the clay they worked in. . . . It at least filled their stomachs."

Now a deluge of exposures erupted about Lynds. It was found that contractors who supplied the food for the inmates always billed the prison for a certain quality of meat but supplied a much cheaper grade. Lynds insisted on half the difference in value as his kickback. It was also revealed that the garbage swill from the convicts' food that was sold to pig farmers proved inferior. The problem was solved by dumping half of the prisoners' rations directly into the garbage so that it would be good enough for pigs. The inmates simply were given less to eat themselves.

An inspector of prisons, John W. Edmonds, brought forth additional charges. There was evidence that some prisoners enjoyed double food rations if they had the money to pay the warden. Edmonds also said that Lynds had covered up the fact that several prisoners had escaped from Sing Sing. In that fashion, Lynds kept his supposed good works intact and on the side still drew supplies and rations for the missing men.

In 1845, Lynds was forced to resign. It cannot be said this was because of his inhumane treatment of convicts. He had crossed the line owing to financial and other forms of malfeasance. Lynds lived another 10 years in comfortable retirement, buying a fashionable home and making a number of profitable business investments, all presumably on his $1,000-a-year salary.

It can be said that Elam Lynds died in personal disgrace, but his penal beliefs and practices lived on after him. Many would say these excesses have yet to be totally eradicated.

See also: AUBURN, N.Y., CIVILIAN PRISON RIOT.

"Mafia Manor" Lewisburg, Pennsylvania, Federal Penitentiary

Whatever may be said about the more cushy prisons of olden days, especially for organized crime figures, there can be no doubt that in recent decades the federal prison of choice for mafiosi has been the Lewisburg Federal Penitentiary, tucked in amidst the dark hills and abandoned coal mines of central Pennsylvania. The institution's proximity to New York and New Jersey, the heartland of more than half of the Mafia membership in the United States, and the scores of wise guys sent there earned it the name *Mafia Manor,* a sobriquet not to be totally discarded. It was not an exaggeration to say that mob men confined there found it as close to a home-away-from-home as a prison could be.

Certainly, the mob men knew how to make their lives the most bearable as any prison inmate could have it. Because they almost never are involved in disputes—because of the fear they inspired in other inmates—they never have to resort to any force that would bring them into collision with prison officials.

By the 1960s, Lewisburg held hundreds of Mafia or Mafia-connected inmates, all intent on having a rather jolly confinement. They had protection from black prison gangs, a generous supply of candy and cigarettes—both much in demand during confinement—and less than onerous work assignments. In one case, a wise guy's entire daily chore was turning on the prisonwide radio each morning.

Especially well accommodated over recent years were the likes of John Gotti, Paul Vario, the notorious Johnny Dio, Joe Pine (a Connecticut crime boss), Carmine Galante, and Henry Hill (of *Wiseguys* fame). All these men were assigned to an honor dorm in a separate three-story building, which Hill described as looking more like a Holiday Inn than a prison. There were four inmates to a room with comfortable beds and private baths. The place had an unlimited supply of wine and liquor, contraband kept in bath oil or aftershave jars. Contrary to the rules, these guests cooked in their rooms. Most rooms had a stove, pots and pans, and silverware. Hill related, "We had glasses and an ice-water cooler where we kept the fresh meats and cheeses. When there was an inspection, we stored the stuff in the false ceiling."

Some of the residents in Mafia Manor ate in the regular mess hall no more than a half-dozen times or so throughout their entire terms. During his confinement, Carmine Galante, an underboss and killer under Joe Bonanno and a convicted narcotics mastermind, roamed the prison with immunity, fearless even of the toughest black leaders. Whenever he approached a pay phone with a long line of inmates waiting to use it, he would bull his way to the head of the line and yell, "Get off the fucking phone, nigger!" It would not have been tolerated from any other white prisoner.

After Galante's release, he made a strong effort to take over most of the actions of all five crime families in New York. Instead, he was murdered. There was, it was said, great joy in Lewisburg.

However, it was said the bribery of guards continued as usual. Certainly, there were guards who were not on the take, but they would, said Hill, never inform on those who were.

See also: MAFIA WARNING; MAFIOSI BEHIND BARS.

Mafia warning alleged threats by mafiosi against guards

It may or may not be apocryphal, but it is not hard to find prison guards who truly believe that it happens. The standard story is that a Mafia convict becomes annoyed with a guard and seemingly just gives him a hard look. However, a little later, one way or another, the guard is furnished with a photograph of his wife and children. A mafioso will let the guard know either in words or nothing more than a smile that it was very easy for the mob to obtain such a photograph. The message could not or need not be any clearer than that. Essentially, the mob is informing the guards of what most inmates already know: Its reach is boundless either "on the street or in the can."

Because a far more common problem is guards being "on the take"—the preferred way the mob prefers to handle matters—there are cynics who feel that such guards try to spin phony stories around the so-called Mafia warning. In any event, there is little doubt that many guards tend to accept the idea as a real possibility.

Mafiosi behind bars always kings of the hill

They are kings of the prison—some say any prison. They are the mob guys, the mafiosi doing time, said to be the easiest time possible. A recent description of Mafia convicts serving their sentences in Leavenworth, known as one of the toughest federal prisons, noted that the wise guys are very recognizable dressed in immaculate style, prison issue to be sure but brand new, white shorts and cotton shorts pressed to perfection. They puffed on the finest cigars available from the commissary. They wore gold chains around their necks—with no worry that some predatory cons might try to seize them. For years in Leavenworth the late Anthony "Tony Ducks" Corallo, the godfather of the Lucchese crime family in New York, exercised the word of a law in the prison. The boys laughed when he expected them to laugh and agreed somberly when that was required.

Tony Ducks never caused any trouble, at least outwardly, instead acting like a perfect gentleman. Most wise guys do because it increases the possibility of parole.

The fact is that in some prisons in past years, mob guys ran the prison the way they wished. It was Mafia tradition.

Most Chicago journalists probably agreed that the Valley Gang leaders, Frankie Lake and Terry Druggan, allies of the Capone mob, served probably the most comfortable prison stretch until their "ordeal" was discovered.

They had been sentenced to one-year imprisonment in the Cook County Jail, but the politicians known to be enjoying the monetary benefits of watching over the pair were determined that they suffer no inconvenience. One powerful political boss, Morris Eller, told Sheriff Peter Hoffman, "Treat the boys right." The imprisoned pair were said to have also distributed $20,000 in bribes to Warden Wesley Westbrook and other officials in the institution. As a result, the boys enjoyed a unique imprisonment, even by corrupt Chicago standards.

When a newspaper reporter went to the jail to interview the pair, he was informed, "Mr. Druggan is not in today." The reporter then asked about Frankie Lake. The response: "Mr. Lake also had an appointment downtown. They'll be back after dinner."

A newspaper exposé then revealed that the Valley Gang chieftains simply did as they pleased. Druggan's chauffeur-driven limousine picked them up so that he could spend most of his evenings with his wife in their plush Gold Coast apartment. Lake generally headed for his mistress's home. The boys dined in the best Loop restaurants, went to nightclubs and theaters, shopped, played golf, and—if worried about their health—could visit their own doctor or dentist.

For taking part in this miscarriage of justice, Sheriff Hoffman was fined and given a month in jail. Warden Westbrook drew a four-month sentence.

It cannot be said that the mob learned a lesson from this affair. When Capone himself was sent to Pennsylvania's Eastern Penitentiary on a gun charge, Warden Herbert supplied him with many comforts. He had a large one-man cell, which he furnished with pictures, rugs, a desk, a bookshelf, a dresser, lamps, and a $500 radio console—tops for that period. Other prisoners got visitors once a week, but "Big Al" enjoyed such privileges every day of the week. Capone was inconvenienced by not having a phone in his cell, but he could stroll into the warden's office and shoo the warden out if he needed privacy.

Mob boss "Lucky" Luciano had considerable benefits when incarcerated in New York's Clinton State Prison, with his private cell sporting curtains over the cell door and an electric stove. He doted over a pet canary, and his prison uniform sported a silk shirt and highly polished shoes. Paid inmate guards saw to it that Lucky was not troubled by unwanted visitors among the inmates, but when he was so inclined he could dispense advice and orders and even grant special favors.

Mob big shots had the ability to get all the favors they wished in state institutions; even some federal prisons could offer reasonable comforts for wise guys. Probably the most accommodating of these for many years was Lewisburg Federal Penitentiary, which earned the identity of "Mafia Manor."

See also: "MAFIA MANOR"; MAFIA WARNING.

Mahan, Edna (1900–1968) women's reformatory superintendent

Today, the former women's reformatory at Clinton, New Jersey, is named the Edna Mahan Correctional Facility for Women in recognition of one the most innovative and respected prison administrators in the United States in the 20th century. Unlike administrators at many other women's facilities who lost much of their rehabilitative thrust, Mahan stuck to her beliefs through her 40-year career at Clinton. She remained in the forefront of those who continued to advocate and develop methods that encouraged prisons to maintain their independence and take responsibility for their own lives. Born in 1900, Mahan earned a degree in education and gravitated to postgraduate work in juvenile research. In this field, she was greatly influenced by Dr. Miriam Van Waters, the superintendent of the Los Angeles Juvenile Hall.

Van Waters became superintendent of the Framingham, Massachusetts, women's reformatory in 1923 and, a year later, brought in Mahan, who had moved up in juvenile positions in California to a research project at Harvard Law School. Impressing a number of leaders in corrections there, Mahan was offered the post as head of Clinton Farms in New Jersey. It marked the beginning of four decades there for Mahan, who fought unceasingly for humane treatment of the female inmates. Mahan was soon recognized nationwide as the head of one of the most progressive facilities for women prisoners.

A pioneer in the concept of an open institution, Clinton Farms shifted to low levels of security, with iron bars removed from the windows. Many housing units in the "cottage" design were utilized so that observers found it more in appearance to a college campus than a prison. Inmate self-government was established in the institution, and the inmates were permitted to elect representatives to help manage the facility. A system was created to promote self-discipline, inmate supervision, and mentoring. Inmates were offered programs to promote positive behavior and rehabilitation. Within the cottages, inmates were encouraged to exercise responsibility for the behavior of all the residents.

In many parts of the country, there were no programs in place for inmate mothers to care for their children. A nursery cottage for infants born at the institution existed for a number of years, but because of overcrowding, the nursery later was located in the hospital.

Mahan instituted the first halfway house of women in New Jersey; eight inmates at a time could be accommodated there. Mahan also fought hard to win equal pay and opportunities for women in corrections administration.

Universally respected by corrections people and inmates, Mahan died in 1968. In her memory, Clinton Farms was renamed the Edna Mahan Correctional Facility for Women.

Manson, Charles (1934–) today's most guarded prisoner

Generally speaking, the most outrageous serial killers often are isolated behind bars for their own protection (and perhaps to protect prison guards from the prisoner). Probably the best example of that is Charles Manson, who spends virtually all his time in a 13-by-7-feet cell in the highest-security wing of the state prison at Corcoran, Califor-

Cult leader Charles Manson leaving the Los Angeles courtroom of his murder trial in 1969 (AP/Wide World Photos)

nia. The San Joaquin farmland is far from the Los Angeles neighborhoods where his "family" went on a murderous rampage in 1969 that left seven brutally killed, including actress Sharon Tate, who was eight months pregnant.

Manson's cell has no bars, which are considered too risky, and he contacts guards and other staffers through tiny holes. Manson is a pariah among even others in the high-risk wing, and he has no contact with any of them. He has "walk-alone" status, exercising alone, and is permitted an occasional visitor, with, at recent count, 11 on his approved list.

Virtually all of his waking cell time is spent watching TV or working on model animals. He enjoys making what one staffer calls "righteous" animal models, although one of a lifelike coiled snake was confiscated.

Manson's original death sentence was commuted to life after the U.S. Supreme Court banned the death penalty for a period of time. Technically, Manson is free to apply for parole and has done so on some occasions. He was turned down, and given the way he is guarded in prison, it is most unlikely that he would ever be paroled, probably to protect society from him and vice versa.

See also: BERKOWITZ, DAVID.

Marion Penitentiary highly regimented federal facility

Although the "Super Max" federal prison in Florence, Colorado, constructed in the 1990s, now is the nation's top maximum-security facility, Marion Penitentiary in Illinois, which held the mantle previously, is still viewed by reformers as the worst of that type. Amnesty International has categorized it as inhumane. While Super Max holds the most violent federal inmates, Marion has the more high-profile offenders.

On the roster are such criminals as "Nicky" Scarfo, the homicidal former "godfather" of the Philadelphia crime family; Jimmy Coonan, the equally homicidal ex-head of the Westies, New York's Irish mob with ties to the Mafia; and many others of organized crime's most prolific killers. Other offender types incarcerated at Marion include John Walker, the navy man who sold classified information to the former Soviet Union; Edwin Wilson, a government employee who sold weapons to Gadhafi's Libya and conspired to kill eight witnesses who could expose his crimes; and Jonathan Jay Pollard, who spied for the Israelis. It could be debated whether these prisoners were at Marion because they constituted a continuing menace to the nation and society or because they were considered to be deserving of greater punishment.

In the case of another high profiler, Mafia crime-family leader John Gotti, the answer was most certainly both. Confined in maximum security since his imprisonment in 1992, Gotti could be said to have been in total isolation, with only a few visits from family members and his attorneys.

Kept in an 8-by-7-feet underground cell for 22 to 23 hours a day, he knew many of the other closely confined inmates such as Scarfo and Coonan, as well as many other mob inmates, but he never saw them in prison. With reports of cancer ailments, Gotti was assigned no work, no communal recreation. His food was delivered through a slot in the cell door. His cell consisted of no more than a single cot, a basin, a toilet, and a black-and-white TV. It was said he did not even get a chair on which to sit. To avoid spending all his time prone on his cot, Gotti folded his mattress into an L shape, which he propped against the wall to simulate a chair. He was described as spending his time exercising by doing about 1,000 push-ups daily. When allowed to shower, Gotti faced transfer shackled in chains inside a movable cage.

Mob boss John Gotti sits in New York Supreme Court in Manhattan, January 1990, charged with involvements in the shooting of a union official. (AP/Wide World Photos)

For a time, it was said that even though kept in such rigid confinement, Gotti still maintained some control on Mafia affairs by issuing orders to his son, John Jr., or his brother, but with his son also imprisoned, it was thought his grasp on power definitely weakened and that Gotti was regressing, at least to the extent of being overwhelmed with depression and feeling sorrow for himself. This was seen in the conversations he had with family visitors, claiming there was nothing he could do, that he had simply played with the cards dealt him throughout his life of crime.

Although most lifers sent to Marion are kept there only for 30 months and then transferred to a regular maximum-security prison, Gotti was not moved until he needed treatment for his cancer in a federal prison hospital. The legal scuttlebutt is that his attorneys were fearful of making an issue of the matter out of worry that Gotti would simply be sent to the even-more-confining Florence Super Max. There was also some speculation that if he were shifted to any lesser facility, Gotti would face physical attacks from convicts seeking to achieve a "rep." There is also some thought that authorities kept Gotti in Marion hoping that the strenuous conditions might finally cause him to break and inform on his own mob to gain some sort of leniency. A more common view is that officials wanted him as a valuable object lesson to other mafiosi of what could happen to them if they refused to cooperate. Gotti died of cancer in June 2002.

Martinson, Robert (1927–1979) sociologist author of "nothing works" theory

No researcher had more impact on correctional treatment in the 1970s than Robert Martinson with his proclamation that "nothing works" in programs to rehabilitate criminals. Coming as they did with the rise of a get-tough wave in the handling of prisoners, Martinson's findings were seized on the right to push the idea of sterner punishment of criminals. Ironically, Martinson was beginning to recant his views by his death in 1979 but was ignored, and his findings have long been used as a firm blow against the theory of rehabilitation.

After teaching in California, Martinson shifted to the City College of New York as the head of the department of sociology and director of the Center for Knowledge in Criminal Justice Planning. Based on a number of evaluations of rehabilitation programs through the 1960s, Martinson and some of his CCNY colleagues concluded that "with few and isolated exceptions, the rehabilitative efforts that have been reported so far have had no appreciable impact on recidivism."

In 1974, Martinson published in the journal *Public Interest* one of the most controversial research reports in the history of U.S. corrections, "What Works? Questions and Answers about Prison Reform." Martinson's conclusions provided ammunition to prison critics of all stripes, many of whom picked up on his theme that nothing worked and reinforced their view that crime reflected fundamental flaws in human nature or individual personalities and bolstered their calls for deterrence, retribution, and incapacitation. Ironically, those of liberal persuasion also supported some of Martinson's findings that indeterminate sentencing often produced unfairness and longer terms for black prisoners than white prisoners. At first, other researchers supported Martinson's findings, and Martinson received much of the credit or blame for capitalizing on the mood in the country to scrap a whole system of civil drug treatment in favor of a punitively oriented series of drug laws, the toughest in the nation.

Within a few years, other scholars began to insist that a number of rehabilitation programs work some of the time with some inmates. According to Nicole Hahn Rafter, chair of the Division on Women and Crime of the American Society of Criminality, in her work, *Prisons in America,* written with Professor L. Stanley, "By 1979 Martinson himself had moderated his original conclusions, but he remained famous for the original report that seemed to say, 'Nothing works.' Martinson died before he could complete his follow-up research and speak definitively about the success of rehabilitation programs."

Still, in debates about correctional policy the phrase *nothing works* is often heard.

Mathie, Michael (1968–) maximum-security millionaire

Perhaps the most favored prisoner in the U.S. penal system is Michael Mathie, an inmate in New York's maximum security Elmira Correctional Facility. He can be said to be doing his time (10 to 30 years for manslaughter) standing on his head, being the favorite of both inmates and guards. He has become known to all as "our resident millionaire" because of his ability to play Wall Street. In 1999, Mathie earned a gross income of $899,969, virtually all from capital gains.

As his profits mounted in the three years before that and since (minus undoubtedly some downward movement in the market correction of 2001), he became a favorite of inmates with access to some money to invest and to guards seeking advice in investing their retirement portfolios. Given his success, everyone listens.

Mathie's accomplishments, undoubtedly one of the odder success stories of the new U.S. fascination with playing the market, cannot be said to have started out as the American dream. He was charged when he was 21 in 1989, along with three other men, in the killing of a man; Mathie's version was that the four of them were convinced that the victim had been abusing the daughter of one of them. The victim died in a vicious manner.

Lodged in the Suffolk County jail, Mathie said he was raped numerous times by the chief of internal security, and in 1996, he won a $750,000 settlement in a federal civil suit. The judge trying the case ruled that the evidence against the jail official was "overwhelming" and "an outrageous abuse of power and authority." Mathie since then insisted that he had pleaded guilty to manslaughter and conspiracy to escape the rapes to which he was being subjected. No criminal charges were brought against the jail officer because the district attorney's office said that there was insufficient evidence to prosecute. In the end, Mathie's award was reduced to a half-million dollars, and he used $75,000 of that to trade stocks.

There was no legal impediment to Mathie to do so even though there was a prohibition on convicts having computers or running a business from behind bars, but none of the transactions take place in Elmira. He calls his father, a retired postal police officer, collect from a pay telephone, sometimes as often as 10 times a day, and his father then places trades on the Internet. The phone bills run from $500 to $1,200 a month. He has no legal problems because inmates have a First Amendment right to discuss anything they want on a phone so long as it is legal.

His trading day starts at 4 A.M., when he watches news of the European markets on ABC and PBS. There is no cable TV, but Mathie seems to get by with other sources. Each day, he receives tons of financial publications including *The Wall Street Journal* and *Investor's Business Daily,* as well as *Value Line Investment Survey* and *Barron's.* For a time, corrections officers who had to deliver his mail complained about the volume, but with the stock tips he handed out, the complaints dropped off.

He has made some astonishing investments (if being in a stock two and a half hours can be called an investment), during which time he once bought a Chinese stock at $18 and sold it 150 minutes later at $70 for a profit of $150,000. Not that he has not taken his lumps: In the market drop of August 1998, he watched his market value drop $750,000. Much of his largesse has gone to his family—a $145,000 home for his father and some other relatives, a Lincoln and a Suburban for each of his two sisters, as well as all sorts of home improvements to all. He has also done much for others, posting a $25,000 reward for information that obtains a conviction of the killer of Steven Maida, a family friend's son. He has donated money to the Catholic Church to fund presents and the like for inmates in juvenile detention. He has given money to other prisoners who needed it for such purposes as funding their appeals, including $2,000 to an inmate to pay for DNA testing that he hoped would clear him of his murder conviction.

Mathie talks of starting a nonprofit organization to help young people when he is released. In 2000, Mathie was denied parole. Since 2001, he pulled back on his stock trading as many professional Wall Street gurus had done, but he remains certain that the market will turn in coming months and even predicts the NASDAQ will hit 6,500 by the end of 2002 which during the year seemed unlikely. If it did not and Mathie continues to be denied parole, the inside prison joke is he will really have the time to hold his investments for the long term.

Maury County, Tennessee, jail fire death of the innocents

One of the most tragic jail fires in U.S. history was that of the Maury County, Tennessee, jail in Columbia. Not only did a number of inmates perish, but so did many of their relatives who were trapped during visiting hours. In all, the death toll came to 42.

The fire was started by a juvenile prisoner on June 27, 1977, during visiting hours. Most of the victims succumbed to the inhalation of cyanide and carbon monoxide gases that were produced by the burning of plastic padding in the young arsonist's cell and then were transmitted rapidly throughout the institution through the ventilation system. As the deadly gases poured from air ducts into the inmates' cells, the visitors panicked and raced through the cell block, screaming in fear.

When a deputy who was carrying keys to the cell block realized what was happening, he hurried to unlock the bars but he was bowled over in the stampede and the keys were lost. There was a duplicate set of keys hanging in the jailer's office, but by that time no one had the presence of mind to locate them. By the time the cell doors were battered open, 42 persons had fallen victim to the deadly fumes, almost all of them prisoners or visitors. In some cases, entire families were wiped out; one inmate, for instance, died along with his parents, his wife, and his sister. Ironically, many of the inmates had only been charged with crimes and had not even been convicted.

McVeigh, Timothy (1968–2001) reaction of other prisoners at the prison when the Oklahoma City bomber was executed

There is little reason in this work to retell the career and crimes of Timothy McVeigh, who took the lives of 169 men, women, and children in the devastating bombing of the Alfred P. Murrah Federal Building in Oklahoma City on April 19, 1995. It rather reflects on the inside drama that occurs at the place of execution by inmates of the federal penitentiary at Terre Haute, Indiana, in June 2001.

The inside drama could be described as practically nothing.

If the guards were actually certain that the inmates would riot when the execution was being carried out and planned for that eventuality—it was reported by a visitor to a relative that prisoners thought this was the case—it didn't happen. It

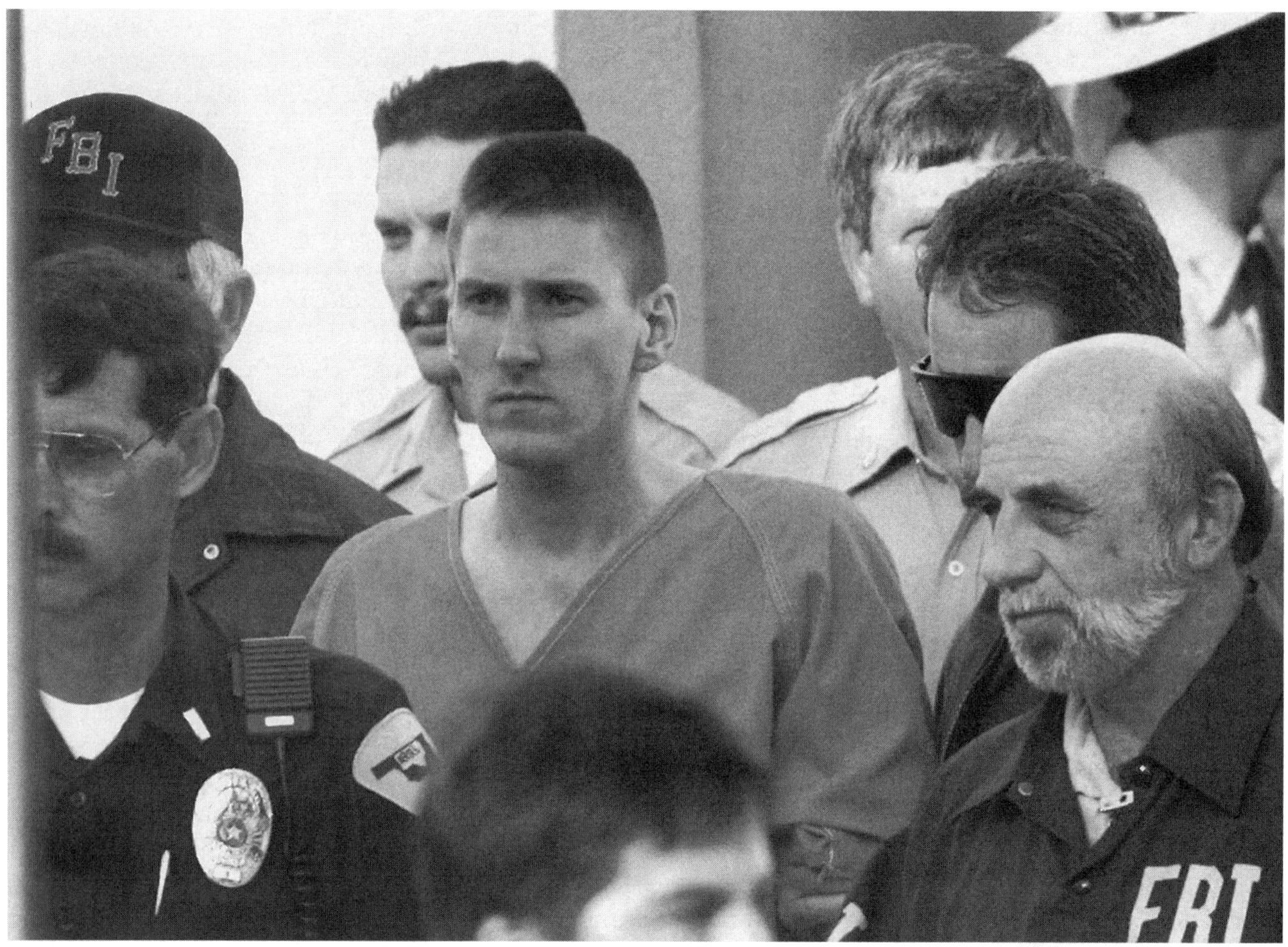

Timothy McVeigh is escorted from the Noble County Courthouse in Perry, Oklahoma, on April 21, 1995. McVeigh, later convicted of the Oklahoma City bombing, watched television, napped, and paced about his cell in the last few hours before his execution by lethal injection. (AP/Wide World Photos)

was treated by some prisoners as more of a lark rather than an upset that one of their own was being put to death.

Amanda Coyne, a freelance writer, wrote in the *New York Times* rather dispiritedly that the inmates had no interest in telling "the world that murder—no matter who the culprit—is wrong. Shouldn't they be the ones to talk about how killing for killing simply begets more killing?"

Instead, Coyne's brother-in-law, doing time on a drug charge, was perhaps typical of most inmates, describing the impending execution as "kind of just another thing, Amanda." The brother-in-law added about McVeigh, "But get this. On his last commissary, he ordered nine cappuccinos. Now there's a run on them. Some of the guys are planning a toast on Monday morning. And under his choice of ice-cream flavors, he wrote down 'executioner's special.'"

Coyne quoted her brother-in-law, "It's the guards who are all keyed up. They think we're going to riot. They think that someone's going to create a scene for all those cameras out there."

The brother-in-law added ("with a hint of embarrassment," Coyne reported), "Hell, in here, most people are just worried about their yard time." And another inmate listening to the conversation in the visitor's room added, "There will be trouble, though, if we don't get to watch the NBA [basketball] playoffs."

Thus, outside of a bit of wiseacre defiance about a planned toast, there was no reaction, and the execution went on a few days later without a hitch.

This, however, appears to be more and more atypical, considering inmate reactions at executions. On San Quentin's death row, there has been a surge of violence with the injury of a number of guards. Similarly, other condemned men have vowed to struggle all the way to the last moment before being executed in the electric chair or by injection. In some cases, unlike the idea of old-style Hollywood movies, death row is not the solemn, mournful area during, somewhat before, or as the execution process starts. Prisoners have been known to scream and curse at executioners, guards, witnesses, and others as they proceed to the death house, seen or unseen.

"You're next, you m———! Hope you like it!" they scream. They save up feces and urine bombs to stink up the entire cell block, leaving the area a smoke- and gas-filled no-man's land filled with a stench that rivals, some said, a botched, burning electric-chair execution.

One of the most spectacular protests and/or riot-escapes took place in North Carolina on April 18, 1985. Being executed was James "JB" Briley, one of the six members of the famous breakout from the supposedly escape-proof death row at Mecklenburg penitentiary. Both before the escape and after he and the others were captured and returned, JB was feared and hated by virtually all the other condemned men. JB was clearly, as he demonstrated in the killings that sent him to death row originally, a brutal, pathological killer. Still, the convicts took JB's cause and staged their riot. Officials and guards had expected trouble but had far more than they had anticipated. Just before 8:00 that morning, a group of inmates jumped four guards in the recreation yard in a plan to take hostages and prevent the execution and perhaps even effect a mass escape. More guards rushed in—foolishly—with their nightsticks, but they, too, were easily outnumbered as more inmates descended on the melee, brandishing shanks—homemade knives. The guards were forced to stand back-to-back as the cons circled them, ducking inside the nightsticks and slashing at them. Before enough reinforcements could arrive to save their buddies, nine of them were injured, six seriously.

North Carolina was determined that the uprising would not prevent JB from being put to death at the proscribed time. He died at 11:07 P.M.

Why had prisoners rallied to JB but not to McVeigh? There is little doubt that at least, in part, it was the nature of his mass murders. Many prisoners could better comprehend one-to-one murders, no matter how vicious, but the slaughter of innocent children, especially, was more than that with which they could cope. That provoked a great indifference, even if the first federal execution in decades should have been regarded by them as the ultimate threat. On the outside, one man-on-the-street interviewee had pronounced himself "unalterably opposed" to the death penalty but that he felt somewhat "queasy" about protesting McVeigh's execution.

There may have been a certain apathy among the prisoners about McVeigh—along with some satisfaction at being a part of history. However, there was also perhaps a certain amount of indifference. Prisoners, in their own way, like many in society at large, are indifferent to anything but their own interests. Thus, yard time and, more importantly, NBA playoff games were more vital in their interests. Executing the worst criminal in U.S. history was of historical note—but there would be hell to pay if anyone deprived them of the basketball playoffs.

Mecklenburg Six participants in the only mass escape from death row

It was a fantasy reserved for fictioneers—the mass escape of killers from a U.S. prison's death row. When it happened, it was an electrifying development that sent shock waves not only through the state of Virginia, but all through the nation and, indeed, foreign countries as well. The resultant media attention turned out to be probably as troubling to corrections officials in the state as the escape itself, exposing an incredible overconfidence and incompetence among prison officials and guards. Blended in with the horror of the event was the inescapable brilliance of the caper itself, which took months in the planning and involved, amazingly, condemned men who managed to scout out weaknesses in the institution's operations. In his introduction to *Dead Run,* the definitive account of the mass escape by multi-Pulitzer Prize nominees–newsmen Joe Jackson and William F. Burke Jr., author William Styron makes no bones about the nature of the escapees and their comrades on death row who aided them in their remarkable act. Author Styron calls them authentic monsters who committed horrendous crimes but that "the slick connivance and stratagem of the escape itself" makes it "hard not to admire the desperate skill of these men, pulling off such an unprecedented caper."

The acknowledged leader of the escape was a vicious murderer, Linwood Briley, who was aided by his even more brutal and violent brother, James B. "JB" Briley. Others were Earl "Goldie" Clanton, Willie Leroy Jones, Derick "Baylock" Peterson, and Lem Tuggle. Many other death rowers aided but did not take part in the plot, including six who were to be part of the escape but dropped out, partly in friction with the basic plan. The "punk" lovers of the Briley brothers were clearly too fearful to go along but loyally rejoiced when the escape was successful. Some death rowers who declined to go along did so because they were sure the plotters would run afoul of guards at some stage of the effort and end up being shot dead—in retrospect, an overestimation of the guards' vigilance. When they learned that the plotters had made good their escape, many of the condemned men cursed themselves for not having gone along.

Key to the escape was that the Briley brothers controlled death row, far more than the guards themselves. The Brileys ran all sorts of rackets—from prison booze to drugs—which could not have been possible without the cooperation of many guards, a number of whom smuggled for the brothers. Linwood, with the aid of another condemned man, actually grew huge marijuana plants in a cell. Odors from the booze and marijuana failed to rouse the curiosity of the guards, nor did the naked bulb placed in position to nurture the plants. The guards' later reaction was mere shrugs: If the place was run like a madhouse, it was still more quiet than the average madhouse.

Corruption of some guards appeared to have been vital to the escape plan. Death row was subjected to a number of searches, and JB needed to have his "shank" protected. He had hidden it in a washroom and was fearful that it would be found before he could try to retrieve it. Incredibly, he convinced a cooperative guard to get it for him and hide it in another place where he would have access to it. Shanks were not generally part of any plan to escape, so probably the guard assumed that JB had other uses for it.

Originally, there were 12 doomed men in on the escape, but as the time of the caper drew near, six dropped out, some having no faith in the plot and others thinking that they had a shot of winning an appeal, probably representing considerably more vain hope than anything else; winning appeals were hard to come by in Virginia. The remaining six had to worry about being betrayed, either by one among the dropouts or by other inmates of death row who had not been included in the escape: There was, they knew, little honor among the doomed. But the plot held, and some who did not go still played their roles in supporting the escape.

Late in the evening of May 31, 1984, Earl Clanton, roaming free without attracting attention, slipped into the guards' washroom and remained hidden until JB gave him a signal. Then he slammed into the control room and released the pod where his confederates were. The control guard, then facing Clanton and two others, could do nothing but surrender. According to a prearranged plan, they soon held about a dozen surprised guards plus two female nurses. Two of the escapees wanted to pause to rape one of the women, but discipline held that such tactics would delay critical matters. The six donned uniforms stripped from their prisoners and made it to the front entrance. A guard with a shank to his throat was forced to call up, "Bring a van around to the sally port gate. Hurry now, we have a situation here."

It worked, and the six escapees looking like guards were able to drive off. Not a shot was fired at them.

If the breakout had gone as smooth as silk, the aftermath proved much more common in the experience of escapees. Their plans after that were nebulous; all they could expect to do was to breath some free air for a time, while the state, the FBI, and others launched an all-out manhunt, roadblocks blanketing the state. The first two, Clanton and Peterson, lasted only 19 hours. They had stripped off their outfits for a sweatsuit or a T-shirt and sweatpants. Hungry, they bought some wine and cheese and hid out in a laundromat. Then Peterson tried to call his mom. The FBI traced phone calls to that number, and the pair was cornered still in the laundromat, partaking of wine and cheese. Faced with a huge posse, the pair gave up without a struggle.

The four remaining escapees were still together but then split up. They had stolen a pickup truck. Because the first two had been picked up so quickly, pursuers thought the others were in the same area, but they had moved. The Brileys gave Jones and Tuggle $25 that had been taken from the hostages—and kept $800 for themselves. With so little money, Jones and Tuggle stayed loose and they moved up into New England, selling some tools in the truck. Finally, needing more money, Tuggle took the truck and went off looking for some loot, telling Jones that he'd be back for him. Whether he intended to return or not was of no consequence. He entered a gift shop in Woodford, Vermont, and robbed the woman owner of $100. The frightened woman was not so rattled that she didn't take down the vehicle's number. A short time later, he was boxed in by a number of police cars. Tuggle gave up, and Jones was on his own. He continued toward the Canadian border, only 10 miles away.

He broke into a house and called his mother to say that he was going to Canada. They both cried, his mother urging him to surrender. They would kill him if he went back, he said; they would never forgive him for what he'd done. His mother agreed but said that he would be running all his life. She told him that people never forgive but God does. Willie Jones surrendered, and although God forgave him, Virginia still executed him. The state would execute all six in due course.

The Brileys lasted a while longer. They were supposedly spotted all over the East, and when Tuggle and Jones were caught, additional sightings came from Canada. They were, before their capture, to become subjects of popular culture: "The Ballad of the Briley Brothers" played on radio as the manhunt dragged on. Meanwhile the Brileys found work of sorts in North Philadelphia in a struggling garage—for no pay but for some food and a place to sleep. They had enough money for that for a while. So the Brileys had dumped Tuggle and Jones in North Philadelphia and had never left. The FBI searched the area continually, and finally six cars and a large white van closed in on the garage. Twenty officers jumped out, and others appeared on rooftops. The Brileys were taken away in handcuffs. The last of the Mecklenburg Six were recaptured. The brothers had been free for 19 days. Four months later, as Linwood's execution loomed, he told an interviewer, "I had my nineteen days. They couldn't take that away."

Three weeks later, the escape retribution began. The warden and the chief of security were suspended for a time and then transferred. A state report blamed the escape on mistakes committed by the guards, while ruling out institutional problems such as poor and inadequate staffing, poor training, and low morale. Some employees resigned, including the chief nurse and two assistants who said they had written the governor a year earlier to warn about the prison's dangerous conditions. They had never received a reply. Then five officers-hostages were fired, including two control-booth guards. After warning prison officials that they would also be fired if the chaos continued, the head of the Department of Corrections himself then resigned. His replacement went a year later as did his superior, the state secretary of public safety. The final ravages of the Mecklenburg Six were to cause the state bureaucracy to devour its own.

Men Against Sexism

See "TOUGH FAGS."

mentally ill inmates and ex-inmates

a growing problem

In 1859 the New York State Asylum for Insane Convicts opened in connection with the Auburn State Prison. It was the first separate unit for mentally impaired convicts and represented a growing awareness around the country that prisoners need to be confined in separate units, according to their needs.

This was an important development because mental illness, then as now, was a critical problem in prisons; the rate of mental illness there is much higher than in the outside population. Obviously another positive move was the establishment of institutions in the general population for sufferers of mental illness and mental retardation, as well as of senility.

Such a system stayed in place for about a century, although certainly not perfectly for those being held for criminal activity. Throughout the latter part of the 19th century and well into the 20th century, doctors and lay persons argued as to whether mentally disabled prisoners should be treated as "mad" or "bad"—in short whether they were mental patients or criminals.

That matter became more or less moot as the political climate changed in the 1970s when, in many states, mental institutions were regarded by some political figures as suspiciously "socialistic." There followed rapid moves by states to "deinstitutionalize" their mental hospitals as well as homes for the mentally retarded. As a result, many patients were flushed out into the community, many to become derelicts. Others soon wound up in prisons.

This was to become a major problem for prisons, with all sorts of ramifications. One problem, involves inmates serving long sentences and who developed Alzheimer's disease in their later years. Far greater are the cases of prisoners who entered prison in relatively healthy shape but who gave way to the stress of prison conditions, a malady inmates refer to as going "stir crazy." Prisoners who are brought in with mental-health difficulties take far longer to adapt to prison life, and some never do. Those with severe mental disabilities have difficulty following rules, and some turn violent and may well be subject to unpredictable outbursts.

Imprisonment of the mentally ill in correctional facilities is a tremendous financial burden for prisons, and resort is made to frequent administration of drugs to control such inmates; however, experts are sharply divided over how much of these drugs should be prescribed. An important added cost is the fact that the mentally ill often become the catalysts in many prison riots and behave in violently erratic ways. In many riots, too, one of the demands by riot leaders is the removal of the "crazies" and "howlers" from the prison population.

Some court decisions have laid out rules to prevent the deliberate indifference by prison authorities to an inmate's mental disabilities. However, many prisoners fall through gaping holes, and upon completion of their sentences, some releasees are still as bad as they have been in recent years. They are simply flushed out to society. Some jurisdictions have a somewhat better record in handling the newly released. New York State, for instance, at least gives inmates a supply of their medications on release. In pending court matters in 2000, it was indicated that New York City does not do this and resisted in court being required to do so. In a state judge's stinging rebuke that the city insisted it would take to appeal, the city administration was ordered to arrange for continuing health care for the mentally afflicted.

How immense was this problem is indicated by the fact that 25,000 inmates in Rikers Island are treated for mental illness while doing their time, and this did not include other city facilities. The city simply contended that inmates at Rikers have no legal right to the kind of prerelease planning required for mental patients under state law.

It remained obvious that the same attitude could be found around the country. Reformers contend that not only do prisons create worse criminals than they are sent, but also that they release more mental cases than originally supplied them.

mentally retarded and capital punishment

slowly grinding to a halt?

In 2001, the latest move up to then to prevent the execution of the mentally retarded took a step forward when the North Carolina state senate by a vote of 47 to 1 passed legislation to bar the execution of the mentally retarded. The governor announced that he would sign the bill. Under the terms of the new measure, a person is regarded to be mentally retarded if his IQ is below 70 and he has significant difficulty in performing basic functions of life, including communicating, taking care of himself, living at home, or working as was the case with a man named McCarver. This continued a recent trend, although one marked by fits and starts. Unlike recent measures passed elsewhere, the North Carolina statute had what some reformers called the "good grace" to make the measure retroactive.

The history of the execution of the perceived or actual mentally ill or retarded has been littered with disputes. To cite just a few: Jerome Bowden was found guilty of the murder of a woman in Georgia during a robbery in 1976. He was finally executed in 1986. The day before his execution Bowden's IQ was about 65, which is generally considered retarded. However, state psychologists did not feel that such a score meant that he was unable to consider right from wrong, and so he went to the chair. A notorious case was that of an Arkansas condemned man, Ricky Ray Rector, who had killed a policeman. Rector was brain damaged, having had a lobotomy. Presidential candidate Bill Clinton left the New Hampshire campaign trail to hasten back to his duties as Arkansas governor to preside over Rector's lethal-injection death (and, say many, to demonstrate his claim as a law-and-order candidate). Rector was so far out of it that in his last meal he left aside his slice of pecan pie to eat later, after, he thought, receiving his lethal injection and returning to his cell for dessert. No one could say that Rector was vindictive toward Governor Clinton. He told his lawyer that he intended to vote for him for president in the November election.

In its resolution entitled "Safeguards Guaranteeing Protection of the Rights of Those Facing the Death Penalty," the United Nations Economic and Social Council endorsed a stand toward the eliminating of the death penalty for persons suffering from mental retardation or extremely limited mental competence, whether at the stage of sentence or execution.

In the aftermath of the Bowden case, Georgia banned the execution of those found "guilty but mentally retarded." In the next few years, others followed, including Kansas and Colorado. After that, there was the deluge of the first half of 2001, following North Carolina's mentally retarded strictures. During the first half of 2001 Connecticut, Arizona, Florida, and Missouri enacted laws to prohibit the execution of someone who is retarded. It seemed to be a case of rapidly growing momentum, and although it might be denied in some quarters, there seemed to be a growing recognition that something had to be done about foreign opinion. That was exhibited in an unusual amicus curiae (friend of the court) brief from a group of nine distinguished U.S. diplomats. They found the practice of executing the mentally retarded to be a "cruel and uncivilized practice" and, probably more important from their normal focus, they argued that the practice diminishes the moral authority of the United States and makes it easier for authoritarian countries to avoid criticism of their human rights record.

The brief noted: "The degree to which this issue has strained our diplomatic relations can be measured by the extent to which important bilateral meetings with our closest allies are now consumed with answering diplomatic demarches challenging these practices. The persistence of this practice has caused our allies and adversaries alike to challenge our claim of moral leadership in international human rights."

The nine diplomats were now all retired, but many left the foreign service only recently, and their views reportedly represented a view widely held by people still in the service who are not free to speak out. Among the diplomats so speaking out in the McCarver case, Thomas R. Pickering, the informal dean of the U.S. diplomatic service and one who had held more ambassadorial posts than anyone in U.S. diplomatic history, said it was the right thing to do. It was clear from the brief that he and the others prepared that the practices "increase U.S. diplomatic isolation and impair other United States foreign policy interests."

According to the *New York Times,* although the brief was limited to the matter of executing the retarded, they and many at the State Department and embassies around the world really oppose the death penalty in toto. Another signer of the brief, Felix G. Rohatyn, who was ambassador to Paris from 1997 to 2000, said in an interview following the filing of the brief: "For practically the full four years I was in Paris, there was not a single speech I made where the first or second question was not: 'How can you people do this? Why do you execute minors? Why are there so many minorities on death row?'" Rohatyn added that his experience in France led him to rethink his support for the death penalty and that he now favored a moratorium.

Less than a week before the brief, in the McCarver case, Johnny Paul Penry, facing execution for the rape-murder of a Texas woman, received his decision from the U.S. Supreme Court. Previous trial testimony from a psychologist stated that Penry had the mental capacity of a six year old. Despite this Penry was convicted and lost all his appeals through the appeals process in Texas as well as the U.S district court and the U.S. Court of Appeals. The U.S. Supreme Court justices concurred in part and dissented in part in a decision that struck down the death sentence but it held that "executing mentally retarded people convicted of capital offenses is not categorically prohibited by the Eighth Amendment." Some considered the 1989 decision unusual to say the least but found it possible that it would have more significance in the future—as Justice Sandra Day O'Connor added: "While a national consensus against execution of the mentally retarded may someday emerge reflecting the 'evolving standards of decency that mark the progress of a maturing society,' there is insufficient evidence of such a consensus today."

By a dozen years later, the "score" could be said to have changed considerably: By late 2001, of the 38 states with the death penalty, 18 plus the District of Columbia and the federal government had now barred the death penalty for a person who was mentally retarded at the time of the crime.

Certainly, by late in his governorship, George W. Bush still represented a majority view when he voiced his opposition to a legislative effort to exempt the mentally retarded from the Texas execution law, saying, "I like the law the way it is right now." However, the new national consensus was clearly edging closer, but in the meantime, the mentally impaired in states declining to eliminate such death penalties still face the specter of death, which they may or may not even understand. Reformers stand sure that time is in their favor, but many executions can still go forward until the "evolving standards of decency that mark the progress of a maturing society" is reached—or not.

See also: RECTOR, RICKY RAY.

Merrick, Dick, and Jebb Sharp beating the noose

Botched executions were not a rarity in the Old West, but none ever achieved the dark humor involved after two badmen, Dick Merrick and Jebb Sharp, were convicted in 1864 for robbing and killing a horse trader named John Bascum. Lodged in jail in Jackson County, Missouri, the pair awaited the carrying out of the sentence of death by hanging the next morning.

The pair were the only inmates of the jail until late in the evening when a couple of drunks were brought in to sleep it off. Then the following morning, Merrick and Sharp were brought out by guards and duly hanged. They had been offered the opportunity to express a few words, but they seemed so stupefied by fear that they were unable to talk.

After the hanging, Sheriff Clifford Stewart returned to the jail and was stunned to see Merrick and Sharp still awaiting their fate. Slowly the truth dawned. The hanging victims were the two drunks who had been sleeping off their inebriation. They had not yet come to and did not comprehend what was happening.

Embarrassed jailers rushed the information to the sentencing judge, who came up with a ruling that would have pleased any condemned pair ever, a form of Old West logic that defied description. The judge ruled that because Merrick and Sharp had not been hanged at the prescribed time, they had to be released.

Needless to say, the pair took this as an urgent moment to "raise dust," and they disappeared into history, never heard of again.

But the affair became a cause for jocularity in Jackson County, and it became known as "pulling a Dick Merrick."

"Monsieur New York" acclaimed hangman

The most acclaimed hangman of the 19th century was "Monsieur New York," the state's official hangman, whose real identity was never revealed and apparently added great mystique to his "grand works," as they were heralded by an admiring if sensational press in the early 1850s. Monsieur New York came out of the Washington Market where he had labored as a butcher's assistant. But he had higher aspirations, hoping to emulate the celebrated Jack Ketch, Great Britain's high executioner, whose works and press he studied eagerly.

He became a hangman only because an opening developed in New York City when the previous hangman abruptly quit because his identity was so well known that he was cheered or hissed on the street and that children asked if they could hang around with him. Monsieur New York volunteered to a murder execution, and the authorities, dubious but also desperate, gave him a lethal tryout. It turned out that he did a masterful job—"beautiful" the authorities called it—and he was hired. They also decided to keep his identity secret. Some newspapers thought *Monsieur New York* was a bit pretentious and gave him a more prosaic nickname, *George*. By any name, he was a great craftsman, and New York enjoyed a golden age in hanging as the new man dispatched the condemned with a minimum of disconcerting suffering, prolonged strangling, or that most embarrassing mishap, unwarranted decapitation.

Now Monsieur New York's fame spread, and he was sought after by communities in many parts of the country. He charged $100 per execution plus all expenses, which could include a carpenter's fee for building the proper gallows and the cost of a sound rope. An added benefit to the communities is that it kept those troublesome antihanging reformers at bay by giving them little about which to complain. Newspapers in areas where he popped in for a lethal quickie assured their readers that "his daily visits to the slaughterhouse had made him familiar with the use of the windlass to the perfection of an application for the humane accommodation of the law-breaking community." During the Civil War, the army also availed itself of Monsieur New York's unsurpassed abilities, having him dispatch from time to time high-ranking malefactors both Union and Confederate.

Then tragedy almost struck when the brilliant hangman suddenly refused to do any hangings for the current sheriff of New York City. As a result, the *Police Gazette* angrily denounced a substitute so that "the departure of John Real was sadly bungled." The sheriff promptly placated his star executioner, who then returned to duty.

For a time, neighborly jealousy caused New Jersey to ignore the famed hangman for a local lad. To add insult to injury, New Jersey did provide Monsieur New York with an invitation to the hanging of one Bridget O'Brien for the murder of her mistress. All Monsieur New York had to do was view the gallows and declare to newsmen, "Boys, that Jerseyman will make a mess of the job."

Seeing disaster looming, he was overtaken by anger when he saw how the Jersey hangman was handling the rope. "What are you trying to do," he cried out. "Then," one account of the event reported, "unable to restrain himself, the scientific strangler pushed his way through the crowd and saw to it that Bridget was sent out of this vale of tears in as laudable style as conditions would permit and the hand of an artist could assure."

In the 1880s, Monsieur New York's last decade of service, a newspaper revealed that he lived with his family in a house around 125th Street and the East River and that he was a member of the Methodist church. Famed crime historian Herbert Asbury reported that this intelligence fueled much speculation about his identity, and many a family man in the area, determined to clear himself of suspicion, made it a point to be seen on the street in the neighborhood whenever an execution was taking place downtown. The identity of Monsieur New York to the end remained a tantalizing mystery.

Mooney, Tom (1892–1942) labor martyr and political prisoner

Labor organizer Tom Mooney was a prison and labor martyr for more than two decades, a man who split public opinion in violently opposite camps. On July 22, 1916, during a Preparedness Day parade in San Francisco, a bomb exploded on the sidewalk, killing outright or wounding mortally 10 persons and injuring 40 others. Among those charged with the bombing were two labor organizers, Mooney and Warren K. Billings.

Following the Preparedness Day parade massacre, the case against Mooney and Billings was very weak, but both, in a period of anti-Red sentiment, were found guilty, Billings sentenced to life imprisonment and Mooney sentenced to be hanged. Revelations in 1918 that much of the evidence against Mooney had been perjured and that other evidence was highly questionable eventually caused even the trial judge to join in the long fight to clear him. President Woodrow Wilson prevailed on Gov. William Stephens to delay the execution, and the governor eventually commuted Mooney's sentence to life. Labor unions and other organizations kept up the battle to free Mooney, but one governor after another declined to grant him a rehearing or a pardon, and Mooney remained in San Quentin.

Despite the strong conservative cast of the state, it was remarkable how many supporters flocked to Mooney's banners, many not even being inhibited by the support he received from the Commu-

A public demonstration protests the imprisonment of Tom Mooney. (Author's collection)

nist Party and other radicals. Perhaps the most striking fact was that the various San Quentin wardens could hardly have been classified as anti-Mooney, and they considered him a model prisoner. One warden, Frank J. Smith, could not wait to leave his position to call him innocent and joined in the movement to free Mooney. "Knowing him to be innocent," Smith said, "I placed Mooney in the position of steward of the officers' and guards' mess, a position formerly held by a free man. He rendered better service than the civilian before him. . . . He has been the victim of a terrible mistake." Other wardens faced some headaches for the treatment of Mooney, but they all held firm in sanctioning his privileged status.

The numbers of Mooney's supporters grew. Among those who visited Mooney besides his wife and mother, were Eugene Debs, who called on him shortly after his own pardon, Norman Thomas, Lincoln Steffens, Upton Sinclair, Theodore Dreiser, William Z. Foster, Sinclair Lewis, and Mayor Jimmy Walker of New York. Other prominent supporters were George Bernard Shaw, Stephen Vincent Benet, Edna Ferber, Will Irwin, Carl Sandburg, James Cagney, Boris Karloff, Edward G. Robinson, and William Randolph Hearst.

Sherwood Anderson declared: "He should be turned loose. They should quit it. There should be a limit, even to our inhuman cruelty."

Time after time, however, governors refused to agree to a pardon for Mooney. It was apparent that nothing would happen until a liberal governor was elected, something that the electorate seemed to conclude in 1938. By that time, Gallup polls found that most Californians and an overwhelming majority of Americans favored a pardon. In January 1939, the state's newly elected liberal governor, Culbert L. Olson, set in motion what he had clearly intended to do. Mooney was ordered sent from the prison to the state assembly's chamber for a highly publicized review of his case. Before a live radio audience, Mooney was freed by the governor after having served 22 and one-half years, and the following day, thousands turned out to welcome him back to San Francisco with a giant victory procession that moved up Market Street along the very route of the 1916 Preparedness Day parade.

Upon his release, Mooney observed that he probably had been more valuable to the labor movement behind bars than he could have been if he had stayed out of prison.

There was now little more for Mooney to do. He was very healthy when he entered prison, but years of hard confinement and constant scrutiny under a public microscope sapped his health. He suffered from bleeding ulcers, for which he required hospitalization several times. He also had nervous problems, including fits of depression, hardly unlikely for a man who had been incarcerated wrongly. His health problems enveloped him following his freedom, and three years later, he was dead in 1942. He was 59 years old. Billings, released some months later than Mooney under a commutation by the governor, died in 1972 at the age of 79.

Further reading: *The Mooney Case* by Richard H. Frost (Stanford, Calif.: Stanford University Press, 1968).

mop-handle punishment alleged brutal treatment of prisoners

In 1997, New York City and indeed the rest of the nation was shocked at the treatment of an arrestee by police. Abner Louima, a Haitian immigrant prisoner, was brutalized in a police-station bathroom by a white police officer who rammed a stick up his rectum, inflicting severe internal injuries that required three operations. The attack inflamed racial tensions in the city, and the officer, Justin A. Volpe, was sentenced to 30 years; another officer who looked on drew a long term as well.

Public opinion was appalled by the case and assumed it to have been a rare occurrence. However, there was a different opinion on that behind prison bars among practiced prisoners. Although police work on the outside was more likely to attract attention eventually, the same obviously could not be said in penal institutions, where punishments more likely are carried out more rigidly and not subjected generally to meaningful oversight.

Writing in *Prison Legal News,* a publication with wide distribution throughout the country, cofounder and coeditor Paul Wright conjured up what prisoners did not view as an uncommon scene—prison guards taking a number and standing in line outside a mop closet, awaiting their turn at a prisoner hog-tied, naked on the floor. It was said that some of the guards also sported blood stains and bits of teeth and bone embedded in their jack-boots.

The mop-closet treatment was regarded by prisoners as one of several tactics used by guards saying, "It's time you learned a lesson, boy."

Morrell, Ed (1869–1946) tortured convict and hero prison reformer

It is safe to say that in recent decades Ed Morrell, perhaps the most tortured prisoner in the history of U.S. penology, would not have won the acclaim he received in his heyday, the early part of the 20th century. He became a national hero after surviving the worst punishments possible at the hands of the prison hirelings of some of the most outrageous robber barons of the day. He endured constant inflictions of pain and became known as the Dungeon Man of San Quentin. When he was finally released, governors and the reform-minded sobbed openly, and Jack London etched his sufferings in *The Star Rover.* He addressed to tumultuous applause the legislatures of both California and Pennsylvania and became the only ex-convict ever to be called to Congress to advise of inmate prison matters.

Morrell had been the youngest member of a gang known as the California Outlaws, which made war in the 1880s on the land-grabbing Southern Pacific Railroad, the most hated business enterprise in California.

Pennsylvania-born Morrell came to California in 1891 when he was 20 years old. He found injustices in the area little different from those he had witnessed in his own anthracite region of Pennsylvania, where the Mollie Maguires, a secret labor society, came into existence. The beautiful San Joaquin Valley appeared to offer a new life, but he soon discovered, as in his native state, that law and order were on the side of money and might. Life in the valley was a bitter experience. Land agents working for the railroad were swindling the settlers with the help of the law. Anything perpetrated by the gunmen on the railroad, popularly called the Octopus, was deemed to be legal, including such atrocities as the Slaughter of Mussel Slough, in which seven settlers had been murdered. Railroad undercover agents spied among the settlers to weed out any troublemakers, who were dealt with brutally. Under the circumstances, it was inevitable that an organization like the California Outlaws would spring up in the valley. They existed solely to steal from the Southern Pacific, robbing its express car but never victimizing passengers or stealing the mail.

Railroad agents tried bribes and threats to area residents to betray the Outlaws. In a countermeasure, the gang planted 20-year-old Morrell as their own spy in the employ of the notorious Big Bill Smith. In time, the gang dwindled down to 25 men, 24 regular Outlaws headed by Chris Evans and the Sontag brothers, George and John, plus Morrell. When Evans was finally captured, a plot was formulated to have the badly wounded Outlaw leader killed while attempting to escape. Smith assigned Morrell a key part in the plot. Instead, Morrell pulled off a real escape for Evans and went along with him, carrying or half-dragging Evans through the valley and surrounding hills for weeks while being pursued by hundreds of railroad agents, Pinkertons, and Wells Fargo men.

The pair was sheltered by one hill family after another, but finally they were betrayed by a huge reward offer. Both were captured, and Evans drew a life sentence. Morrell was sentenced to hard labor in Folsom Prison. Folsom at the time was known as the private lockup of the Southern Pacific. The warden was a former railroad detective, as were many of the guards. Some time later, it was discovered that the warden was still carried on the railroad's payroll despite his state position.

Folsom was a mankiller with a blood-curdling history. Many of the convicts who were not strong enough to endure the brutal labor conditions and tortures were known to have charged the armed guards deliberately or even to have hurled themselves into the turbulent waters of the American River to at least enjoy a more merciful death.

Sent to the rock pile under the sweltering sun and supervised by guards, Morrell was disciplined for imaginary infractions. Then he committed the cardinal error of stepping out of line in formation, a minor infraction at best, and he was given 50 hours on the derrick. Few inmates ever drew 50 hours; the more general treatment called for 10 hours spread over two or three days. But Morrell had clearly been marked for special treatment.

The derrick was a block-and-tackle arrangement whereby a man was suspended with his arms bound behind his back and the tips of his shoes barely resting on the dungeon floor. The pain was excruciating and frequently resulted in bleeding from the kidneys, which was why the usual punishment was limited to five hours a day in two equal periods. On one occasion, Morrell needed 13 days because his kidneys bled so badly that his keepers dared not make him go the five hours per day.

After the derrick, Morrell received one punishment after another, and he was informed by the warden that his ordeal would continue without respite until he revealed the identities of the California Outlaws still at large. On one occasion, the Outlaws successfully bribed a guard to look the other way so that Morrell could escape. However, another guard learned of the plan. The warden decided to let Morrell try to get away and stationed guards outside the prison walls to gun him down. Morrell never came out. He was saved by the warden's wife, known as the Angel of the Prison, who sent word to Morrell through another convict. Morrell had to endure more tortures because he would not reveal the escape plan or say who had warned him.

He was given several doses of the lime cell, a fiendish torture chamber lined with a coating of lime. A guard would hose down the walls, and a white mist from the exploding chloride of lime would envelope the cell. The prisoner would be tossed inside, would immediately feel as though his throat was on fire, and actually would think that his breath was aflame. Morrell was once subjected to the lime cell for 10 consecutive days, and his eyelashes and eyebrows were completely burned away. His nose, throat, and mouth were so seared that his voice dropped to a faint whisper.

Through all his ordeals, Morrell's spirit never wavered, and he even organized other escape attempts and riots. Finally, he was transferred to San Quentin—where once again he was deemed worthy of special treatment. On his arrival he was given 20 days in solitary for "looking at" a guard. When he came out, the same guard made another complaint against him, and he was sent back for 30 more days.

Morrell regularly drew the penalty of the "San Quentin overcoat," which resembled a supertight full-length straitjacket. The overcoat was a coffin-shaped piece of coarse, heavy canvas with brass eyelets along the sides and two inside pockets for the hands. First, Morrell would be wrapped in a blanket, not to ease the pain but rather to avoid leaving too many marks and bruises in case he died and also to make the overcoat fit more tightly. Then the garment was fitted around him and laced tightly.

After enduring this punishment, Morrell was framed on a charge of having a gun smuggled in to him for an escape. He was ordered to solitary confinement in San Quentin's dungeon for the rest of his life. There was only one other prisoner undergoing the same treatment there, Jake Oppenheimer, who was known as the Tiger of the Prison Cage. The two had never seen each other and were separated by 13 cells, but they eventually learned to communicate using a form of "knuckle talk," with various knocks on a steel wall indicating different letters. It was the first use of such a method of communication in an American prison and has since been adopted in almost every prison in the world.

In 1903 San Quentin's most brutal and villainous warden, disgraced by numerous scandals, was forced to resign. The next warden learned from the captain of the yard, John C. Edgar, that Morrell had been framed on the gun charge and made an investigation. As a result, Morrell, famed as the Dungeon Man, was returned to the general population. In 1906, Edgar took over as warden and worked unceasingly for Morrell's release. Edgar did not live to see the fruition of his efforts, but two years later, the acting governor, Lt. Gov. Warren Porter, personally came to San Quentin to present a pardon to Morrell.

The San Quentin Morrell left was far different from the San Quentin he had entered. The new warden, John E. Hoyle, was the first of the state's progressive penologists, and his administration marked a new era in the treatment of prisoners, one made possible by the U.S. public's embrace of Morrell as a genuine hero. Now for the first time, there was genuine interest in the administration of prisons and for humane treatment for inmates. (It was not of course an opinion that would remain in force for very long.)

Morrell was acclaimed wherever he went. He lectured before overflow crowds on prison reform, especially on the abolition of corporal punishment; organized the American crusade to promote changes in the administrations nationwide; and was applauded universally by legislators, often with tears in their eyes, when he addressed their bodies. Jack London's *The Star Rover* and Morrell's own autobiography brought more fame to the man on whom so much evil had been expended. Much of the torture methods to which he had been subjected were at least in large measure ended. Morrell died in 1946 at the age of 75, not living to witness the return to a more stern treatment of prisoners and the argument about whether offenders were sent to prison as punishment or for punishment.

See also: "KNUCKLE VOICE"; LIME CELL; OVERCOAT.

Mothers Inside Loving Kids (MILK) helping women maintain contact with their children

Perhaps the best and most understanding of any program within female prisons to aid women inmates to stay in touch with their children is offered by the Virginia Correctional Center for Women. It is Mothers Inside Loving Kids, or MILK. For four days annually, all-day contact visits are allowed between mother inmates and their children. Support-group discussions are held regularly to discuss ways in which incarcerated mothers can maintain an influence on their children's lives. Prominent speakers discuss matters of child development, discipline, and how a mother can maintain contacts with a child's school. The mothers are also advised on child protective services.

Before an inmate can enter the program, she must complete a parenting course run by the prison. Barred generally from taking part are women whose crime involved in some way being harmful to a child, as well as prisoners who have run up a number of prison infractions. The MILK members pay $1 monthly dues and raise the funds necessary to stage the family visits.

"muling" trick to send messages during lockdown
The purpose of a lockdown is to confine prisoners in their cells so that no communications with other inmates are possible during a period of potential crisis, such as a suspected jailbreak plot or punishment. However, officials at times are deluding themselves if they think that a lockdown cannot be broken and messages cannot be sent between prisoners, sometimes with an impressive measure of sophistication. One such method is known as muling, which can be utilized through the toilets in cells on tiers directly above and below one another.

Each inmate places his pillow over the open toilet and sits and rises up quickly a few times. A vacuum is created and the waters "flushed" down the tiers. Only a small amount of water remains in the bottom of each toilet and can readily be swabbed dry. The "reception" through the toilet pipes is said to be far clearer than that through a telephone. The prisoners "hang up" by simply flushing their toilets—after first setting the time for their next communication.

Boston Strangler Albert DeSalvo is seen here during a visitor dance with senior citizens at Walpole State Prison, where he was later murdered. (Author's collection)

murders in prison way of death behind bars
Robert Lee Carroll, a felon being held in the Sumter County Jail in the ever-overcrowded Alabama corrections system, was watching some basketball in 1989 when fellow inmate William "Sunshine" Sanders accidentally hit him with the ball, causing Carroll to spill a glass of water. The pair exchanged a few words, and Carroll, feeling that he had been "dissed," went back to his cell and got hold of a wire shank. He returned and proceeded to stab Sanders to death. It landed Carroll on Alabama's death row.

Murders in prison are very much a way of death. The motives can be great or trivial, as in this case. Murders and violence are so common in prison because the characters are so bad and the environment so envelopes them.

In recent years, compared to the "good old days" remembered by lifelong prisoners during which brutality and murders were not as prevalent as in later times, violence has escalated to such an extent that inmates themselves characterize their world as being one dominated by the law of the jungle.

Violence, says lifer Victor Hassine, "becomes a form of escape for many inmates. In creating and maintaining a predatory environment, these men were able to focus all their attention on fighting one another. The more hostile the environment, the more they saw themselves as victims and less responsible for their own actions." Convicts, according to Hassine, in recent years developed an "obsession with violence" that would prove "as destructive as any narcotic addiction."

Many major prisons have what has been designated a "meat-wagon crew," a special unit set up by the medical staff to handle emergencies in the prison blocks. The unit consists generally of a staff medical nurse, an inmate who wheels a gurney, and another with medical equipment and oxygen. In short, it was a sort of ambulance charged with getting the wounded back to emergency care. Actually, the meat wagon is more often a coroner's wagon, removing not the hurt but the dead. Many such corpses were overdose victims, but others were victims of bloodthirsty violence.

See also: PRISONIZATION.

Murton, Tom (1928–1990) Arkansas reform warden Thanks to the 1980 Robert Redford movie, *Brubaker,* Tom Murton, on whom the character Brubaker was based, became the best-known prison warden in recent decades. He was also to be perhaps the most hated by much of the corrections establishment. In 1967 Arkansas's Tucker Prison Farm was rocked by scandal when Gov. Winthrop Rockefeller, carrying on an investigation by outgoing Gov. Orval Faubus, fired Superintendent Pink Booher and three wardens, J.L. Markburn, Bob Hensley, and H.H. Chadick, in the midst of an investigation of the state's prison system. However, the governor denied that the firings were in any way connected with the death of a 50-year-old inmate of peritonitis. Arkansas's Assistant Attorney General Eugene B. Hale issued a report describing the prison as the site of "torture, brutality and extortion and gross wrongdoing." There were reports that Tucker inmates who testified to investigators were later beaten by "goon squads" of prisoners.

An Arkansas State Police report chimed in with many accounts of abuse.

Two of these were:

- LL-33 said he was stripped of all clothes. The warden then stuck needles under his fingernails and toenails. His penis and testicles were pulled with wire pliers, and he was kicked in the groin. Two other inmates then ground cigarettes into his stomach and legs, and one of them stuck him in the ribs with a knife. The coup de grace came from an inmate who squeezed his knuckles with a pair of nutcrackers.
- LL-53 came to Tucker in October 1964 and was told that unless he became the punk of a rider, he would be whipped. He refused. Two days later, the rider ran his horse over him, knocking him to the ground. The rider then dismounted and beat him with the rubber hose and stomped him until one tooth was knocked out. He received this type of treatment for two or three weeks and was finally sent to the hospital, where the inmate doctor told him he could not stay unless he paid $20. He had only $10 and was allowed to stay one day.

Gov. Rockefeller brought in an outsider to institute reforms to the system. He was Murton, a 37-year-old former justice professor and head of a U.S. stockade in Alaska. Rockefeller clearly gave him carte blanche—for a time. Murton's first official act was to abolish flogging and torture. When the warden of the larger Cummins Unit prison farm, the companion prison to Tucker, heard that Murton had banned corporal punishment, he came to Murton and demanded that it be restored because his prisoners now wanted the same thing. Murton turned him down.

Other Murton reforms shook up the system. He moved death-row inmates out of isolation and converted the death house to a hospital. He brought in a nonprofit blood bank and fired the local physician who was making between $130,000 to $150,000 a year to do the job. Inmates started earning $7 instead of $3 for giving blood, with the rest of the profits going to the prison's medical fund.

A short time later, the Cummins warden resigned, and Murton took over both institutions. He extended his reforms to Cummins and especially continued a plan to eliminate the prisons' trusty system. The trusties effectively ran the system. The Arkansas prison system, generally regarded as the worst in the country, operated on very little money, with a staff ratio of 1 to 65 compared to the national average of 1 to 7. Prison authorities therefore relied on trusties and "riders"—mounted inmates who guarded convicts in the fields. Prisoners were required to work up to 14 hours a day, six days a week, in the fields for no compensation at all. The squeeze was always on the inmates to provide better foods and the like for their superiors. Corruption was the Tucker-Cummins way, and violent deaths were common.

How common would shortly shock the nation. Murton soon discovered that nearly 200 prisoners were listed as escapees. According to inmates, the prison grounds might contain more than 100 bodies and that the dead men had antagonized previous wardens. Murton ordered grounds to be dug up. Two hundred escapees never being found was a remarkable statistic because, normally, most escapees failed to stay out of the law's clutches for very long. Evidently, Arkansas flowered with master escapers.

Murton had an escapee problem of his own: Prisoners took off in droves. During his first month there were three escapees, in the second eight, and in the third six. Most were trusties; then, in a 10-day period, 25 trusties took off. The gun-toting trusties had run the prison and had the best accommodations and choice food while the bulk of the inmates received scraps. The trusties had the right to shoot anyone they wished, and if they claimed the man was trying to escape, they could be rewarded with early release themselves. Now that it was becoming apparent that Murton was going to break up Arkansas's corrupt trusty system, the boys failed to see the virtues of imprisonment and took off. Virtually all were picked up quickly, unlike the previous missing 200.

Within a short period of time, the hunt of the prison grounds centered on a large mule pasture. Murton was quoted in the *New York Times* as now saying he suspected that some 213 missing men had been murdered and buried in unmarked graves. The nation's and indeed the world's media converged on Cummins. With television cameras grinding, digging commenced, and soon three bodies were exhumed in unmarked graves.

Scott Christianson wrote in *With Liberty For Some:* "Cummins inmates cheered. State officials panicked.

"Arkansas editorial writers fumed that Murton was disgracing the state. . . . Two months later, Governor Rockefeller fired him. Corrections officials throughout the country continued to criticize Murton for his methods, even as many acknowledged that some convicts probably had been murdered at Cummins."

What of any more possible bodies? Murton was gone, and nobody was doing any more snooping.

Murton did not have to wait a decade for vindication in *Brubaker.* His reform efforts led to a federal court decision that conditions at Cummins Farm violated the Eighth Amendment prohibition against cruel and unusual punishment.

Nevertheless, despite many efforts, Murton was unable to find another post in corrections, leading him, hardly illogically, to conclude that he was being blacklisted. He became a criminal justice professor at the University of Minnesota, continuing to write about the Arkansas scandal. He retired to raise poultry in Oklahoma and to continue his writing on prison reform until his death in 1990.

mutilation punishment of criminals

Although in no way did mutilation to punish criminals in the United States ever reach the volume as practiced in Europe, it still was quite prevalent, especially in New England and the South. For contempt of court or perjury, the punishment in these areas could be losing part of an ear or having one's tongue pierced with a hot iron. Slander in Virginia called for a convicted person to have one's tongue bored through with an awl, while criticizing the Colonial authorities included losing both ears or, for lesser offenders, having one's ears nailed to a pillory. Post-Revolution runaway slaves often received the latter penalty because the paramount concern was that the punishment did not cause the slaveowner to lose equity, yet still to mete out considerable pain to the errant slave.

If a slave was convicted of attempting to rape a white woman, castration was the mode of punishment, so here again the slave was still left pretty much intact, assuming he survived the ordeal.

Once a criminal was committed to prison, the mutilations often remained at the discretion of the keepers. Early in the 20th century, a veteran prison official, J.C. Powell, wrote *American Siberia* and described prison camps in Florida where keepers hung prisoners by their thumbs and let them writhe in agony. When death did not result, Powell said, the prisoners' thumbs were deformed and stretched so that "they resembled the paws of certain apes."

mutilations by inmates "acts in self-defense"

In addition to mutilations as punishment for crimes and by keepers for real or alleged infractions, many mutilations have been carried out by prisoners themselves as acts of "self-defense" to escape brutal punishment. Late in the 19th century, New York's Sing Sing prison inflicted many punishments that were later to be denounced as too cruel. One of these was the "paddle," used in the institution for what could be described as relatively minor offenses, a 3-feet-long heavy leather paddle that was used to inflict up to 315 lashes, as they were called. The blows were administered by the principal keeper or specially assigned "sluggers" on complaint from contractors or foremen that the prisoners were not working hard enough or were failing to meet their quotas on finished goods.

Unable to avoid the punishment, many prisoners risked mutilations to themselves by hurling themselves from the upper galleries, seeking broken legs, which would delay the paddling. Of course, not all inmates got away with that tack, many being less fortunate and ending up with broken necks, a sure death sentence.

Many self-mutilations are brought about because the inmates know nothing else to do or have lost their sense of reason. One case involved a troubled prisoner who was allowed to have access to a razor for shaving and slowly and deliberately over time started to slash ever deeper in his throat area. He was deprived of the razor and placed in special confinement until he was deemed to be a menace to himself no longer. After that, he immediately resumed slashing at his throat. (The record does not seem to indicate the final results of his self-mutilations.)

Perhaps the most startling example of convict self-mutilations occurred in 1951 in Louisiana's notorious Angola Prison when 37 white inmates severed their achilles tendons with razor blades. They hoped that this would finally win their way out of beatings administered to them in work lines or in the work camps. The news of the mass mutilations were to be kept secret, but when words of the acts leaked out, the local and national press swarmed in, and the news became front-page copy throughout the world.

Louisiana Governor Earl Long tried to make this into a money-saving operation for the taxpayers, declaring "Angola will be on a paying basis before I leave office." It turned out that the public did not share his indifference to convict life. (It was suggested in some quarters that the matter would have been more trifling to some if the inmates had been black.)

Long was obliged to agree to investigations and recommendations that hard-liners never thought would come to pass. Eventually, great reforms took place, and some press quarters celebrated the "new Angola." Clearly, no such mass self-mutilations have occurred since, as more and more reforms in all parts of the country have taken hold.

names of prisons not necessarily descriptive
One should not place any strong significance in the names of any prisons, that is, whether they are called prisons, penitentiaries, reformatories, penal institutions, or correctional facilities. In broad measure, it may be said that whatever names they are called actually represented the prevailing attitudes toward punishment when the prisons were built or that they may reflect a change in name to meet current popularity. Thus, penitentiaries originally were intended to invoke the idea of penitence, which is not what such institutions can fairly be described as doing today. Similarly, reformatories were intended to reform, a record today facing subjective interpretations. In the era that carried over into the 21st century, *reform* may be described as a dirty word in the public's view; thus, no new facilities tend to be given that name. Today most prisons are called correctional facilities because, apparently, they are intended to "correct"—a neutral term that can be said to meet with approval of much of the public, a sort of description that is in the eye and the perception of the viewer.

Prison inmates are not involved in such semantics. They know what a prison is—"the joint."

National Prison Hospice Association (NPHA)
With the growing number of prisoners serving life or life without parole, the work of the National Prison Hospice Association (P.O. Box 3769, Boulder, Colorado 80306-0941) has greatly increased. The organization promotes hospice care for terminally ill inmates and those faced with dying in prison. It helps to devise support and aid in developing patient-care procedures and management programs for corrections professionals.

The NPHA is vital for the transmission of information between prisons and hospices on programs as they develop. The organization's aim is to achieve "a comfort-oriented unit that allows seriously ill patients to die with dignity and humanity and with as little pain as possible in an environment where they have mental and spiritual support."

National Rifle Association (NRA) anti-coddling stance
The NRA is one of the most outspoken critics of what it regards as coddling and overspending on prison inmates. It offers unique guidelines for the operations of prisons and in what may be regarded as a novel criterion, claiming that the U.S.'s penal inmates enjoy a standard of living three times that of the poverty line. In an article in the *American Journal,* its official publication, it denounces "Luxuries in prison . . . [which] have raised the cost of imprisonment so that it's now nearly three times the poverty level." The NRA puts the cost of keeping a prisoner at $23,000,

while the "honest person is considered to have an acceptable standard of living if he gets by on $8,000 a year, the federal poverty line."

Putting on a spin that concurs with its own agenda, the NRA holds that this "anathema to justice threatens our Second Amendment rights by aiding and abetting those who use the 'prisons are too expensive' excuse to take away our firearms civil rights under the guise of crime-fighting."

The NRA draft of a Crime Doesn't Pay Prisons Act would establish a minimum standard for prison conditions that states could not fall below but could rise above. Thus, a prison administrator who chooses to permit certain "perks" to reward good behavior could do so. Because the NRA has generally attacked tennis, basketball, and handball courts, it is obvious that they would fall, especially under any $8,000 a year standard of living.

According to the NRA's *American Guardian,* "convicted murderers, rapists and robbers [would not] continue to be better off than many honest men, women, and children. After all, preferential treatment of prisoners over the poor is unheard of in all the world, except America. Doesn't that make it 'cruel and unusual'?"

New Mexico prison riot inmates killing inmates

It easily was the bloodiest prison riot in U.S. penal history in terms of inmates slaughtering other inmates. It started in the early morning of February 2, 1980, when a convict mob broke into the prison's control center, unleashing years of pent-up venom. A number of guards were taken as hostages, but none were ever hurt during the ensuing 36 hours of the murderous nightmare. Thirty-three prisoners who were not spared were largely inmates who were being held in protective segregation.

Informers, or "snitches," guilty or not, were horribly and savagely murdered. Some were burned to death with blowtorches, hacked to pieces, decapitated, and castrated. In addition to the 33 murdered, hundreds of others were raped, beaten, tortured, or terrorized. Some observers later depicted the carnage that was found by rescuers who moved in as the equal of that found by Allied troops when they liberated the Nazi death camps at the end of World War II.

Although the rampaging convicts had numerous complaints against the institution, all hostages were found to be alive. After 36 hours, the prison, which had been the subject of much physical destruction, was retaken without a shot having to be fired. As for the underlying causes for the riot, there was, of course, the usual suspects—overcrowding, rotten food, lax security, and corrupt officials. Later, a Justice Department study found the penitentiary to have been ignored for years and one of the harshest, most punitive prison environments in the nation. It is now recognized by officials that the institution was rife with nepotism, totally untrained personnel, corruption, filth, uncomfortable and unsanitary living conditions, fire hazards, and sexual abuse. Mentally disturbed inmates were kept in plaster body casts with holes only available for urination and defecation. *Corrections Magazine* observed, "At Attica, the disturbance was tightly controlled by a small group of powerful inmates. But in New Mexico, the inmates, leaderless and uncontrolled, went berserk."

As a result, the hate-maddened convicts focused on one main "beef"—common to all prisons but heated to a fiery frenzy in New Mexico—the use of snitches by the administration. Some years earlier, the penitentiary instituted an aggressive informer system with rewards offered to inmates who were willing to inform on others. The impact on the convicts in general was that of bitter rage and, in the atmosphere of fear thus created, led one prisoner to complain, "Hell, you can't trust your best friend anymore." Prison officials were so dependent on gaining informants that almost everyone in any sort of official capacity took part in the aggressive program. In *The Devil's Butcher Shop: The New Mexico Prison Uprising,* considered by many experts as perhaps the best book written about any prison riot and certainly the best on the New Mexico events, the author reports on a prison minister who told an inmate, "My son, God wants you to be a snitch."

Such information came to be considered only a sidebar by the general public in their judgment of the inmates. As Nicole Hahn Rafter and Debra L. Stanley note in *Prisons In America,* "Whereas television coverage of Attica tended to arouse public sympathy with the inmates as well as the hostages, scenes of carnage and mutilation at Santa Fe alienated the public from the inmates' cause." In *With Liberty For Some,* Scott Christianson declares, "The riot confirmed an image of prisoners that more and more Americans had been conditioned to hold: prisoners were animals. Wild, dangerous, vicious animals."

See also: SNITCHES.

"nigger stick" tactic for stay-awake punishment

That the prison officer's club is the nigger stick rather clearly indicates against which types of prison inmates it is primarily used. Of special use in solitary confinement, a prisoner is in a cell where a light is kept burning 24 hours a day, "making it," said one court, "all but impossible for him to sleep." A judge explained how the "all but" could be eliminated: "If he did doze off, it was not for long, as a guard came by every half-hour and ran a 'nigger stick' noisily across the bars."

Some jurisdictions have altered their rules and regulations in the face of court orders, but it would be foolish to believe that the nigger stick has gone the way of the dodo bird or that who gets most of the treatment has changed.

no-hostage federal rule escape-prevention regulation

Since 1931, the Federal Bureau of Prisons has followed the rule that under no circumstances were guards to open a gate for would-be escapees because they were holding a hostage.

The last time such a thing took place was in December 1931 when seven inmates appeared at the front gate at Leavenworth Penitentiary brandishing several revolvers that had been smuggled into the prison for them. They threatened to kill the guard, Oscar Dempsey, unless he opened the front gate, at the time controlled by a guard outside the walls.

"Go ahead and shoot!" Dempsey responded. "I'm an old man, so it don't matter."

Desperately, the prisoners seized Warden Thomas B. White, who happened to be inside the compound and threatened to kill him. Guard Dempsey then opened the front gate. Commandeering a car, the convicts took off with White as hostage. The escapees were cornered in a farmhouse a few hours later, and in the ensuing gunfight, three convicts were killed; the rest eventually surrendered but not until they shot Warden White.

White survived and in time returned to his post. Immediately after the incident, the bureau issued orders for all its prisons that forbade guards from ever opening a gate for anyone holding a hostage, regardless of his or her identity. The rule has never been violated.

nonprison residential programs and intermediate sanctions growing nonincarceration systems

Residential programs that put offenders in structured environments, including halfway houses, are growing in use around the country. They are intended to allow offenders to leave to go to work or for such approved activities as drug treatment. In such states as Minnesota and Wisconsin, residential models provide support for residents who have to make restitution payments to victims, as well as child support out of their income from community work.

One of the most heralded plans is the Griffin Diversion Center, operating since the early 1970s in its Georgia community. Directions stress work, education, and community. The residents are required to work eight hours a day, maintain the center, perform additional community services on the weekends, attend classes or counseling during evening hours, and submit to regular drug testing. They take part in clothing and food drives and have never faced any resistance from neighbors.

One reason for this is that the public is starting to understand that a growing prison population is placing a huge burden on taxpayers. They are willing to look for solutions, provided that the seriously guilty do full time. There are a number of offenders for whom the public would accept the idea of "intermediate sanctions," which effectively means lesser punishments that still offer an effective method of penalty. This cuts the cost of building and operating prisons, as well as both the human cost of the offender's lost potential and the destabilized families left behind for the welfare system. In addition, the public acknowledges that intermediate sanctions cut prison overcrowding that produces riots. Riots frequently result in millions of dollars in damages that the public treasury has to replace.

The answer clearly involves incarceration for criminals who endanger the community and penalties short of full prison for nonviolent offenders. Happily, the idea is catching on, despite the still-inflamed attitudes about prison in general.

O

Ohio State Penitentiary fire worst in U.S. penal history

In 1930, the Ohio State Penitentiary was a tragedy waiting to happen, being one of the most overcrowded institutions in the country, originally designed for 1,500 inmates but jammed with 4,300. In addition, the prison could be described as a "sieve" because of the number of escape attempts that took place there. As a result, the administration and the guards were extremely edgy.

Realizing that the situation had to be improved, state authorities ordered an expansion of the facility, and in the ensuing construction work, some easing of conditions took place. However, the work left many of the cell blocks filled with scaffolding and littered with piles of wood scraps and tar paper.

On April 21, 1930, at about 5:30 P.M., the inmates had just returned from their evening meal when suddenly flames erupted from the construction rubble and flashed up the scaffolding. Within a matter of seconds, the top two tiers of the six-tier cell block were enveloped in fire and smoke.

The action of the guards was later described as inaction. Reporter John Bartlow Martin described the guards as automatons, who at first saw their duty as simple: They had to keep prisoners locked up. As Martin put it, "They simply could not bring themselves to unlock the cells and let the

The charred ruins of the cell block after a fire in the Ohio State Penitentiary in Columbus, Ohio, are shown on April 22, 1930. More than 300 inmates were killed in the fire. (AP/Wide World Photos)

Prisoners work to clear away debris after a fire at the Ohio State Penitentiary on April 22, 1930. (AP/Wide World Photos)

inmates escape the flames." The first reaction by the warden and the guards was one of suspicion that the fire had been started as part of a planned breakout.

As a result 320 inmates died hideously. Ironically, Warden Preston Thomas's first call for aid did not go to the fire department but to the National Guard, whose assistance he asked to contain the prisoners. Indeed, the first fire alarm actually was sounded by a passerby *outside* the prison walls. There is no telling how many inmates would have roasted to death in their metal cages, save for that act.

By the time the fire had reached horrendous proportions and the warden finally ordered the cell doors opened, it was too late for many of the victims. The intense heat warped the locks and the keys would not work. As the roof started to crumble on the caged men, one inmate found himself freed from his cell, so he seized a sledge hammer and saved an estimated 136 men, but hundreds of others literally roasted alive in the cell "ovens."

In the prison yard, guardsmen with bayonets drawn broke the freed and now surly inmates into small groups so that they could more readily be watched. Meanwhile, a new panic developed outside the prison walls as those prisoners' relatives living in the Columbus area attempted to storm the prison to save the trapped men. Soldiers had to be sent to all entrances to prevent people from *breaking into* the prison.

As obsessed as the prison administration was with possible escapes, only one inmate fled, doing so by changing into civilian clothes and calmly parading through the mob of soldiers, police, guards, and onlookers to stroll away calmly. Three and a half hours after the blaze started, it was brought under control.

The controversy over the handling of the disaster continued for many months. Public groups demanded the ouster of Warden Thomas. As disaster expert James Cornell later observed, "They had some good reasons. Every possible fire regulation had been ignored, no fire drills had been held, the guard staff had received no emergency training, and almost every official had demonstrated gross incompetency. Yet no action was taken against the prison authorities. The warden maintained the fire was deliberate; more likely, it resulted from an electrical short circuit."

"One Strike Rape Bill" ever more harsher prison punishments

The crescendo of "three strikes and two strikes and you're out" laws could be said to have reached its climax when California added a new provision on sex crimes with its "One Strike Rape Bill," which passed into law in 1994. Under existing sentencing laws, a single rape involving a weapon resulting in conviction required an eight-year sentence. In practice, this meant that a prisoner would probably be released in five years or so.

As outrage built and stronger sentences were demanded, Republican state senator Marian Bergeson offered up a new revision that would have required that virtually all sex offenders be sentenced to life in prison without the possibility of parole. The proposal immediately drew critical fire from those who found that the punishment was so harsh that it could cause rapists to kill their victims to prevent identification.

The final version was watered down to some extent so that the penalty for rapes involving torture, kidnapping, or burglary with intent to commit rape was set at 25 years to life. Lesser sex offenses were set at 15 years to life. The sex offender who drew the old eight-year sentence (which meant about five years) would now have to do almost 12 years and then would still need a parole-board decision to be released. Offenders given the maximum term of 25 years to life would not be eligible for parole for more than 21 years.

From a penological viewpoint, it would take a number of years to determine how the harsher sentences would affect the brimming California prison system, already the most overcrowded in the nation. There have been estimates that two decades of data might be required to determine whether the harsher sentences would result in a lower rape or crime rate. There were those who expected little or no drop. As early as the 1990s as the three- and two-strikes laws went into effect, there was some indication that they fuel violence. In some states with such strike laws, including California, police have reported that suspects have become more violent in resisting arrest. One Washington state officer has stated it "now looks like" some strike offenders "might try to get away or shoot their way out. Believe me, that's not lost on us. We're thinking about it."

Similarly, rapists might be thinking about it more after their act of sexual violence and then, faced with a helpless victim, may decide that murder has become a necessity. Statisticians probably need a few decades to measure whether rape-murders as distinguished from rapes increase or not.

Orchard, Harry (aka Horsley, Albert E.) (1866–1954) coddled political assassin

When Harry Orchard died in 1954, he was known to much of the media as the "most coddled assassin in U.S. penal history."

The murder of ex-governor Frank Steunenberg of Idaho in 1905 was to result in the most important judicial confrontation between capital and labor in the United States. Had there been a conviction of radical labor leader William D. "Big Bill" Haywood, it most certainly would have altered the history of the U.S. labor movement. Many laborites insisted that the killing was used in a cynical and naked effort to destroy the union movement with fabricated charges.

During his tenure from 1896 to the end of the century, Steunenberg earned the enmity of the union movement for a number of probusiness actions, especially in the bitter labor struggle in the Coeur d'Alene mines. After that, he devoted himself to the lumber business, which would eventually become Boise Cascade.

On December 30, 1905, Steunenberg emerged from his home in Caldwell, Idaho, and as he opened the front gate, his body was shattered by a bomb.

The first man arrested was Harry Orchard (real name, Albert E. Horsley). Orchard confessed to the Steunenberg killing as well as a number of other murders, which would have made him the greatest labor assassin in U.S. history. Orchard went on to implicate three labor leaders in the killing.

Indicted along with Haywood were two other Western Federation of Miners leaders George H. Moyers and George A. Pettibone. Their trial became one that involved the opinions of every American. The defense was handled by the brilliant Clarence Darrow, who eventually destroyed the entire prosecution case, especially after another informer withdrew his confirmation of Orchard's charges, saying that his statements had been inspired by the Pinkerton Detective Agency. Darrow completely discredited Orchard's written confession, which bore a number of inked corrections, many in the hand of the noted Pinkerton operative James McParland; three decades earlier McParland played a key and controversial role in the successful prosecution of the Mollie Maguires, a secret labor society operating in the Pennsylvania coal fields.

Darrow won acquittals for Haywood and Pettibone, and Moyers was discharged, to the unbounded joy of the labor movement.

In the end, only Orchard was convicted; he was sentenced to death, but this was commuted later to life imprisonment. For many years thereafter, McParland appealed for a parole of Orchard, but he never won on that. Perhaps tellingly, even agency head William A. Pinkerton would not go along with the appeals.

This did not mean that Orchard was completely abandoned by others. It was later charged that prosecutor James Hawley and Idaho governor Frank R. Gooding (who had vowed before the trial that the accused trio "will never leave Idaho alive") did much to make Orchard comfortable behind bars. Charles Steunenberg, the victim's brother, stated: "The penitentiary outfitted a room for Orchard and paid for the electricity used. Private parties gave him money with which to buy machinery; the state permitted him to use convict labor for his own enterprise in which he manufactured shoes for prominent people in Idaho and rolled up a cash reserve of $10,000.

In 1940 when Orchard was 73, he was, wrote Darrow biographer Irving Stone, "still fat and sleek, oily eyed and unctuous. He told visitors to the prison chicken farm that he 'just can't bring himself [*sic*] to kill a chicken.' To anyone wanting to clear the historic record of the crime Orchard cried petulantly, 'The trouble with you writers is that you never come here to write about me. You always want to use me to write about somebody else!'"

They did write about Orchard when he died in 1954, still in prison, most likely the most coddled assassin in U.S. penal history.

Oregon boot cruel restraint for prisoners
The Oregon boot was an awesome device that made the Oregon State Prison one of the most feared institutions by criminals in the 19th century. Designed by Warden J.C. Gardner, it was required to be worn by all prisoners during their entire terms. Consisting of a heavy iron band that was locked around the ankle and held in place by a steel ring with a pair of braces that were attached to the heel of the wearer's boot, it weighed a crushing 15 pounds.

It undoubtedly cut down on escape attempts, but unfortunately it could produce permanent deformities if worn for long periods. The warden patented the device in 1866, fully expecting that other prisons would rush to use it. However, in a period when brutality toward prisoners was much in vogue, it nevertheless was judged too sadistic to be used by other wardens. During the next decade, the shackle drew considerable growing criticism and finally was relegated to use only on the most desperate criminals.

Quietly, after that, use of the Oregon boot tapered off and finally was withdrawn even in the state that had given it its name.

Osborne, George O. (1845–1926) "Father of prison reform in the United States"
As warden of the New Jersey State Prison in Trenton for more than 20 years in the later 19th and early 20th centuries, George O. Osborne became the first U.S. penologist to institute massive reforms that would eventually spread nationwide. Although other wardens may have, from time to time, eliminated a particularly brutal practice, it was Osborne who attacked a whole string of dehumanizing practices that were standard in U.S. prisons at the time, such as the ball and chain, shaved heads, striped uniforms, and the so-called dark cells or dungeons. Among his efforts to improve the lot of prison inmates (and thus increase the chances of their return to outside life with less risk to society) was placing more emphasis on religious life, improvements in the parole system, and, above all, establishment of schools with practical courses. Osborne died in retirement in St. Petersburg, Florida, in 1922 at the age of 77.

Osborne, Thomas Mott (1859–1926) prison reformer
Perhaps the most unreconstructed prison reformer of the 20th century, Thomas Mott Osborne throughout his career withstood intrigues, smears, and indictment for his beliefs in improving the penal system. A successful manufacturer, he decided in his fifties to campaign for prison reform. Quoting William Gladstone, he said, "The prison must be an institution where every inmate must have the largest practical amount of individual freedom because it is liberty alone that fits men for liberty." Becoming a member of the New York State Commission on Prison Reform in 1913, Osborne sought to gain an appreciation of what prisoners faced behind bars by spending a week inside Auburn Prison as inmate "Tom Brown." That won him considerable support from convicts, prison guards, and the public at large.

In 1914, Osborne was named warden at Sing Sing and stepped into the cauldron of political influence and intrigue. He set about dismantling the status quo, which galvanized his foes to charge him with a myriad of offenses, from homosexuality to perjury and neglect of duty. Osborne was indicted in what appeared to be an act of political vindictiveness. The case was dismissed, and Osborne returned in triumph to his post. He introduced at Sing Sing the Mutual Welfare League, which was widely imitated in other penal institutions. Under it, prisoners were paid for their work and received improved recreational and job-training services.

Osborne won enormous praise from other penologists, but he continued to draw criticism from some politicians of "coddling criminals," and in 1917 he resigned from his post. However, when Lewis E. Lawes took over as warden, he instituted virtually all of Osborne's ideas.

One of Osborne's most important contributions to the study of criminality was his critical analysis of Richard L. Dugdale's famous and later infamous study of the Juke family in which he sought to prove his theory of hereditary criminality. Osborne's three books, *Within Prison Walls, Society and Prisons,* and *Prisons and Common Sense,* which answered the "coddling" charges, are considered to be classics of prison-reform literature.

outside bankers handlers of convicts' "dirty money"

It is far from uncommon for some convicts to have secret accounts for money they accumulate in prison. This "dirty income" never enters the institution at all. Typically, the scheme is used by convict racketeers who deal in drugs, extortion, or "protection services."

An inmate who has the outside resources to avail himself of such services buys what he needs inside the prison and arranges to have the payment sent to the racketeer's "banker" on the outside. The banker then takes care of various chores: He transfers the money to a bank account belonging to the prisoner, a member of the inmate's family, or another party whom the inmate trusts; the banker also arranges to have a relative withdraw the small monthly sum that the institution permits prisoners to receive from the outside for the purchases of such staples as cigarettes or candy from the prison commissary.

The best thing about the set-up is that the debtor never welshes on arranging payment; he is where the inmate-racketeers can always find him.

One of the more active bankers in such operations was a New Jersey woman who handled the income for three convict-operators of a big-time prison poker game. When a loser could not cover losses, the loser was required to have the debt paid on the outside. The woman was uncovered by a suspicious officer in Leavenworth who figured out that the gamblers had to have an outside banker working for them. When the officer checked prison records, he found that the woman was sending money each month to each of them.

The FBI was requested to look into the matter and discovered that the woman was depositing about $10,000 a month in her checking account even though she had no job or any apparent source of income. It was obvious that the three inmate gamblers were netting probably $120,000 a year through their outside broker, money that would be waiting for them if and when they were released.

overcoat, the prison torture method

In most prisons that used the punishment, it was referred to as the "overcoat" or the "jacket." It was often called the San Quentin overcoat because it was used there more than in any other institution, especially on inmates who were regarded as more "socially dangerous."

The story of the overcoat is best told by Ed Morrell, an ex-convict on whom, it was said, was visited by almost all forms of evil practiced in America's prison. He was later pardoned and became a popular hero and prison reformer in this country and elsewhere; in 1918, he became the only ex-convict called to Congress to advise on inmate labor problems.

The overcoat resembled a tight, full-length straitjacket: a coffin-shaped piece of coarse, heavy canvas with brass eyelets along the sides and two inside pockets for the hands. First, the prisoner would be wrapped in a blanket to avoid leaving too many bruises and also to make the overcoat fit more snugly. Then the garment was fitted around him and laced tightly.

Morrell wrote in his autobiography, *The 25th Man,* of his introduction to the overcoat:

> *Jungle travelers have described the awful agony of a native victim being squeezed to death by a giant boa-constrictor. It is all too terrible for the human mind to contemplate, but even this inconceivable spectacle must pale before the death terrors of the jacket.*
>
> *I had not been in it fifteen minutes when pain began shooting through my fingers, hands and arms, gradually extending to my shoulders. Then over my whole body there was a pricking sensation like that of millions of sharp needles jabbing through the tender flesh. . . . Hour after hour I endured the pain and as the time passed the anguish became more and more unbearable. I slept neither night nor day, and how slowly my torture went on when all was silent in the prison! The hours dragged as if weighted with lead.*
>
> *Now a new horror came. The bodily excretions over which I had no control in the canvas vice ate into my bruised limbs. My fingers, hands, and arms grew numb and dead.*
>
> *Thus I suffered incessantly four days and fourteen hours. . . . Released from its pressure I attempted to gain my feet, but was too weak. My limbs were temporarily paralyzed. After a time, mustering all my strength, I reached a sitting posture and finally managed to drag off my saturated clothes.*
>
> *What a sight I beheld! My hands, arms, and legs were frightfully bruised. My body was shriveled like that of an old man, and a horrible stench came from it.*

Morrell's later exposure of the overcoat—not to mention a number of instances in which its victims were crippled for life—led to its being outlawed in California.

overcrowding tensions cause of prison disorders
Overcrowded prisons are a recipe for trouble, often explosive trouble. The general effect of overcrowding is that it makes life in prison far worse than necessary. Of course, prisons are designed to be crowded so that as many inmates as possible can be contained in the smallest cells and prisoners' minimum requirements can be met with the smallest staff possible. In such an environment, guards and inmates alike learn to cope in a very controlled, structured manner.

What happens is that, eventually, the prison will become overcrowded, with a new imbalance created that defies any ability to cope, the goal that convicts desire. Overcrowded prisons magnify the worst in prison existence. There is more violence, more death, and greater danger of uncontrolled homosexual attacks. Prisoners suffer more medical complaints, both physical and mental. Overcrowding puts more inmates in contact with others, with new dangers of mounting tensions. One study has revealed that inmates in overcrowded facilities become more quick tempered (even though the population as a whole is already apt to react violently in general). It was found that inmates turn more assertive and aggressive, resort to force more often, and could become extremely stressed by minor incidents. In one case in the study, an inmate who did not receive his medication on time stabbed another prisoner several times with a pencil. Had he had one of the more usual contraband weapons that are common in prisons, the result could have well been deadly.

Researchers make the point that inmate hostility cannot be ascribed simply to their "natural tendencies" but is an extreme and intense reaction caused by the overcrowded conditions. A classic case was the findings of a federal court in *Ruiz v. Estelle* in Texas:

> *The present extreme levels of overcrowding at TDC [Texas Department of Corrections] are harmful to inmates in a variety of ways, and the resultant injuries are legion. . . .*
>
> *TDC inmates are routinely subjected to brutality, extortion, and rape at the hands of their cellmates. . . .*
>
> *The overcrowding at TDC exercises a malignant effect on all aspects of inmate life. Personal living space allotted to inmates is severely restricted. Inmates are in the constant presence of others. . . . Crowded two or three to a cell or in closely packed dormitories, inmates sleep with the knowledge that they may be molested or assaulted by their fellows at any time. Their incremental exposure to disease and infection from other inmates in such narrow confinement cannot be avoided. They must urinate and defecate,*

Prisoners in a Marion County Lockup cell sleep on the floor on May 22, 2001, in Indianapolis. At least 19 of Indiana's 92 counties recorded jail populations near or beyond their intended capacities. (AP/Wide World Photos)

unscreened, in the presence of others. Inmates in cells must live and sleep inches away from toilets; many in dormitories face the same situation. There is little respite from these conditions, for the salient fact of existence in TDC prisons is that inmates have wholly inadequate opportunities to escape the overcrowding in the living quarters.

Many personal examples of the impact on a prison inmate when overcrowded conditions force sudden changes in a convict's environment can be cited. Pennsylvania prisoner Victor Hassine is typical of an inmate jarred by sudden changes: After about four years behind bars, he said,

I was fairly well dug into my prison routine, working, obeying, and vegetating. I had a single cell, and for better or worse the prison system was functioning at an adequate level.

Then one day, my cell door opened and another man was shoved inside. My world was suddenly turned upside-down.

My first argument with my new co-tenant was, of course, over who got the top and bottom bunk. Then we fought over lights on or lights off, hygiene habits, toilet-use etiquette, cell cleaning, property storage, and whose friends could visit. Then there was missing property, accusations of thievery, snoring, farting, and smoking. As these arguments raged on every day, new ones would arise to make things worse.

At the time, the prison staff was itself shocked by the sudden burst of overpopulation, and there was no time to plan or in any way screen double-celling. Inmates were simply shoved in with each other on the basis of age or race. An inmate had no chance to screen potential cellmates. "If you didn't voluntarily find someone to move in with you, one would be picked for you at random. This practice immensely compounded the problems associated with double-celling. It was bad enough living with a stranger in such close quarters without having to worry about whether he was a Jeffrey Dahmer."

Clearly, fear and loathing can mark a double-celling situation. Many inmates fear the possibility of one day waking up to a cannibal beside them.

Some double-cellers can make the best of it by reaching compromises with one another on many aspects of their too-close-for-comfort existence. One of the more interesting accommodations was one made between a black-and-white pair of inmates in Statesville who learned how to compromise on various aspects of in-cell activities, especially concerning toilet use and what programs to hear on radio. There was more tolerance on sexual needs as well. One prisoner tolerated his cellmate's habit of waking him up early in the morning by "pulling himself off" so that the bunks shook. The other inmate felt he was more considerate in his same activity because he did so at night when he thought his cellmate was asleep.

As simplistic as it sounds, the most economical way to reduce overcrowding is to remove inmates from the system; the building of more prisons with their inevitable rising support costs does not offer the same benefits. To put it another way, it is to reduce the flow of new prisoners into the system, reserving that for the more serious offenders. Other countries with a less serious prison population problem can do this with relative ease. In Norway, for instance, many convicted offenders simply are put on a waiting list to get into prison as the government places a strong emphasis on avoiding overcrowding. Naturally, the lesser offenders have the longest wait. This obviously will not work in the United States with its far more serious imprisonment problem, but it does put a greater need for placing more inmates in parole situations. Of course, this runs counter to the more popular sentiment of instead "locking them up and throwing the key away" in an era when it is fashionable to reduce or even eliminate parole rather than to expand it. It is difficult to make headway on this point even when it is readily demonstrated that recidivist rates from parolees run to only one-third to one-half the number of offenders who are turned loose after serving a full term. This argument does not satisfy antiparole forces who argue that when a criminal is behind bars, the inmate can commit no crimes on the outside population. The refrain goes: "When he's locked up he is doing no more damage." Critics of this view counter that such an outlook is taking the easy way out and amounts to shooting fish in a barrel. When this antiparole fervor dominates, frequently the courts have to enforce strictures against unconstitutional overcrowding—and in the process, sometimes the wrong offenders can go free.

Critics see an ever-growing system of prisons as constituting a "prison expansion bubble" that may well lead to collapse or at least impairment of the prison system as we know it, and so many embrace this with enthusiasm. More than a half-century ago, a distinguished journalist, John Bartlow Martin, wrote *Break Down the Walls: America's Prisons: Present, Past and Future,* which proposed far-reaching reforms. The book ran counter to the growing support of the get-tougher approach, and after a measure of best-selling support, it was in large measure ignored. Today, however, fissures in the present prison system are starting to appear, and it is possible that U.S. corrections are at the beginning of a pendulum reversal that will, at the very least, spark a new debate on the prison systems (see the Introduction), especially with the growing use of adult prisons to house juvenile offenders.

See also: JUVENILE SUICIDE AND MURDER IN ADULT PRISONS.

P

parole

Of the adults confined in prison, a high percentage will be released on parole before completing all the years in their sentence. Somewhere around 70 percent of inmates are eligible for parole in a given year. Most will not be granted parole in that year, but a significant number, possibly a third of those considered, will be; virtually all, as indicated above, will be released early. (The terms of life without parole for the purpose of this situation are hardly significant.)

Parole is similar to probation in that probation is granted before an offender does time, while parole takes place after some time has been served. Both seek to have offenders serve a sentence in a community setting rather than a prison.

Parole boards meet regularly in prisons to look over a convict's record to judge if the inmate is a good candidate for parole. Prison officials are interviewed, as is the inmate himself, to judge emotional state and attitudes toward society's strictures. Important also is whether the inmate has been into trouble while in prison. This last point is a matter of contention among many inmates who feel that they have frequently been punished for causing disturbances or problems for the prison staff while, for instance, seeking to fend off sexual abuse by other prisoners.

If the parole board grants parole, the parolee signs an agreement that stipulates the conditions of his release. The terms may include the prisoner's pledge not to leave the county of residence, not to use alcohol or drugs, not to drive a car or possess a gun, and not to associate with other criminals. The individual must report to a parole officer, who is charged with enforcing the rules imposed. (A frequent criticism of the system is that parole can become untenable if the parole officer is given too many cases to supervise. An ideal caseload is considered to be 20 or 30 and certainly fewer than 50. But many parole officers complain of loads of 200 to 300 so that they can do no real supervision of their wards, often doing no more than give them a urine test on every visit and simply returning offenders to prison if they fail.

The officer can search a parolee's home without a warrant, and a parole can be suspended if the officer believes that the parolee is breaking the law. That means immediate return to prison.

The critical period for a parolee is the first year of release. Most violations occur shortly after release, and persons with a history of arrests prior to going to prison are more likely to break parole. But poverty is often a factor; the more affluent a parolee is, the less likely is the released prisoner to violate parole. Much depends on a parolee's relations with family and how much help they offer. As much as possible, the system tries to help parolees find daytime jobs with regular hours.

Parole is, in the main, American in origin in that English felons, beginning in the 1650s, were granted early release from their sentences provided they went to America, where they were auctioned off to the highest bidders as indentured servants. In effect this was a parole system.

Our contemporary parole system developed out of the concept of "good-time" laws, which shortened prisoners' sentences for good behavior. This led to the introduction of indeterminate-term sentences (e.g, one to 10 years) with the opportunity for release before completion of the sentence. Under this system, which began about 1870 and still exists, the prisoner was required to adhere to certain rules after release and was subjected to supervision.

Within a half-century, the system of parole was an ingrained part of all U.S. prison systems. Invariably, when concern over crime has risen, attacks on parole increased. Edward R. Hammock, chairman of the New York State Parole Board, once said that the public had a "silly notion" that such a board "releases criminals back into the community willy-nilly. It's not true but we're still getting the blame for the fact that people don't feel safe on the streets and in their parks."

Experts insist that the idea that parolees commit a great number of new crimes is false. In New York State, in 1979, only 3.4 percent were returned to prison for committing new crimes while on parole. Another 8.5 percent were sent back for parole violations. These figures have remained fairly static and compare favorably with the overall figure of 30 percent of all ex-prisoners being sent back to prison within five years of their release. Despite this record, the parole system is under stronger attack now than at any time in the last half-century. There has been an obvious shift in national opinion about the method and purpose of sentencing. Concluding that prisons simply do not rehabilitate, more and more judges, prosecutors, and even penologists now insist that if criminals cannot be reformed, they should be given uniform, predictable jail sentences and kept off the streets until they have paid for their crimes. Reformers disparage this view as being no more than taking easy shots at the system. They point out that if would-be parolees end up doing a complete term, they are simply going to become just like the others in that group and thereafter commit three times as many crimes as offenders not granted parole. Prisons will simply become more crowded and more costly to maintain without much assurance that the public will end up being any safer.

By 1980, the number of inmates in state prisons had doubled in fewer than 10 years. "But we're still scared to go on the subway at night," chairman Hammock noted. Since then the numbers have risen even higher. As a result, in various parts of the country, courts have had to order prison systems to reduce their populations; this appears to be done in a truly willy-nilly method, with massive release of prisoners, some of the really bad going out with the good.

Some states, California as an example, have seen shifts in attitudes, and parole officers seem to be making a more concentrated effort to do their jobs despite pressure from hard-liners. Helpful to the situation there is the fact that many parole officers are in the same unions that represent prison guards, a very potent force in politics in the state. Under that cover, many parole officers are less fearful of risking their careers even if a few mistakes will occur. In the final analysis, despite continuous attacks, the parole system probably will survive because of recognition of the fact that its screening system of released convicts provides a measure of control of ex-prisoners; this would be abolished under a system of fixed jail terms that leaves ex-felons free of any checks that might inhibit their return to crime.

PAROLE VIOLATORS AND LONG-TERM INMATES: GENERALLY A SOURCE OF CONFLICT

On the face of it, it may appear somewhat bewildering that there is frequently considerable friction between long-term prisoners and parole violators who are sent back to prison. The attitude of the long-termers quite possibly may be exaggerated at times, but the general belief is that parole violators are much more likely to be snitches. Generally, a parole violator is returned to prison for a fairly limited period and is frequently targeted by the prison administration as responsive to overtures to become an informer, the carrot being that a new recommendation for parole would be favorably considered.

Some recommendations that have been offered to reduce the conflict are to isolate parole violators from the rest of the prison population as much as possible. Similarly, the wholesale use of parole violators should be recognized as a situation that produces turmoil among prisoners. Unfortunately, in the current age of being tough on criminals, it is the path of least resistance for parole officers to lessen criticisms toward themselves by sending every violator back to prison regardless of the seriousness of the violation. A change in such a practice does not seem to be in the cards, and the prison officials insist they do the best they can under the circumstances and with a bulging population must do anything that seems to alleviate their own problem.

WOMEN: HARDER GOING THAN FOR MEN

In discussions of parole—its problems, its rewards—very little is said of the plight of women on parole, even though the female has harder going than the male. The stigma of a prison record is much worse for a woman than for a man. Society has never really gotten completely over the idea that she is a "fallen woman," beyond redemption. If the charge is made that not enough men are given the opportunity to learn trades that are applicable to the outside world, it is nothing compared to the lack of job training available to most women before release. In the 19th and well into the 20th centuries, women in prison were taught to cook, clean, and wait on tables. On release, they were capable at best to be good domestic servants. Journalist John Bartlow Martin quotes one woman on parole as saying, "You learn no trade in there, your mind gets dull. Laundry, shirt factory, weaving room, sewing room, kitchen—who wants to learn how to wash pots and pans? I was told there would be schools and studies, I went there with the idea of benefit and profit. But I didn't learn anything there. I already knew how to cook and sew and scrub."

Women on parole came back into the world basically fitted only for housework, and very few people wanted to take an ex-convict into their homes. Those who did generally were only looking to pay them less than they would have to pay a maid without a record.

By the 1980s, the main training in many institutions was cosmetology—makeup and hairdressing. This did not prepare women to deal with a diverse job market and suggested that a woman's main job was to look attractive.

Making it tougher is that fewer women's clubs than men's clubs interest themselves in aiding people on parole. Civic groups and churches are also less likely to help women than men.

Some women break parole because they want to get married and to leave the state with a man. They want to stay out late. Women with prison records who marry men without records can end up subjected to endless contumely. However, men and women on parole usually are forbidden to marry ex-convicts or to associate with them. One prison administrator recalls a woman on parole who wanted to marry a man she had met in the county jail while both were awaiting trial. He says, "It's probably better if they've both been in trouble."

Many women in prison correspond, or try to correspond, with men in prison; they marry them after both get out. Martin in *Break Down the Walls* notes, "A woman on parole has said, 'They can forgive a man, but the minute a girl does one thing wrong she never gets a second chance. Her whole life is wasted. Trouble comes along to all of us, we're going along, ordinary people, and one day something happens and everything's changed. The women's clubs!—once a girl is in the institution they're bad, through and through. You're an ordinary man—but something might happen to you tomorrow and you'd be in an institution. Would that change you into a bad person? You'd still be the same—but after you've had several years of everybody reminding you of what you'd done and treating you like dirt under their feet you wouldn't be the same.'"

See also: PROBATION.

Further reading: *Crime and Punishment* by Aryeh Neier; *Encyclopedia of Criminology* edited by Vernon C. Branham and Samuel B. Kutash.

pat searches See WOMEN PRISONERS—PAT SEARCHES BY MALE GUARDS.

pauperism "criminality" by 19th-century standards

In the late 19th century, "pauperism" came to be seen as the flip side of criminality. Paupers were seen to be born with the very traits of those who eventually filled our prisons because of hereditary "feeble-minded" behavior. Without destroying pauperism, it was claimed, there could be no wiping out of criminality. In 1893 Henry M. Boies, a penologist associated with the Pennsylvania Board of Public Charities, the Commission on Lunacy, and the National Prison Association, published *Prisoners and Paupers: A Study of the Abnormal Increase of Criminals, and the Public Burden of Pauperism in the United States, the Causes and Remedies.*

Boies declared that it was "established beyond controversy that criminals and paupers, both, are degenerates; the imperfect, knotty, knurly, worm-eaten, half-rotten fruit of the race." Such pauper-criminals had, Boies expounded, to be handled in three "elementary phases": prevention, reformation, and extinction. He wrote, "Reformatory treatment is confined to those who are enveloped in it. The 'unfit,' the abnormals, the sharks, the devil-fish, and other monsters, ought not to be liberated to destroy, and multiply, but must be confined and secluded until they are exterminated."

Boies's vivid vocabulary, which much later might be regarded by some as seeming to fit or at least precede the theories of the Holocaust, threw him into the eugenics camp, then at its pinnacle of support, that inferiors produced crime.

Of course, paupers had, long before Boies, suffered at society's hands and before and after clogged the prison systems, but Boies seemed to offer scientific cover for the ill treatment of many unfortunates. Boies's views tended to fade away well before the final rejection of the theory of eugenics in the 1920s and 1930s.

"peephole visitations" entertainment for proper folks

It was not uncommon for early American jails and prisons to sell rights for people to visit the prisons. This was done in part to earn money for the jailers, which rankled many inmates. In other cases, it was done to "exclude the wrong type of people."

At Auburn Prison, the showcase institution for the New York system as opposed to the Pennsylvania system, Auburn actually instituted a 25-cent visiting fee for being allowed to survey the prison. In short, the 25-cent fee, extremely high for the 1820s, was intended, as it was described, to keep away a "certain class" who "overthronged the prison" and, indeed, the type of people who stormed the Bastille in France. That class, of course, would describe the inmates and their families. Thus, only the rather well heeled could afford the quarter charge that gave them access to the so-called watchposts, effectively peepholes, which allowed them to secretly spy on the convicts just as the keepers were doing.

Pelliccio, Vincent popular escapee

After serving several months of a 10-year sentence in 1946, Vincent Pelliccio escaped from a prison camp near South Hill, Virginia. Forty-one years later, in 1987, Pelliccio, by then a retired film studio electrician in Los Angeles, was taken into custody when a routine records check turned up his past prison and escape record. An exemplary citizen whose five sons knew nothing of their father's past, Pelliccio became an object of nationwide sympathy, even in an era when no quarter was given to criminals of any sort by an angered public. But the argument was made that if prison was ever able to rehabilitate a criminal, this was such a case. Demand grew that California should not send him back to Virginia to serve out his long-ago sentence. While Pelliccio was being held awaiting an extradition hearing, Virginia had had enough of being on the unpopular side of the issue. Gov. Gerald L. Baliles issued a pardon, and the longtime fugitive with a clean record walked out of a Los Angeles court a free man.

pen pals distant friends and sometime victims of convicts

Although it is a phenomenon few prison authorities understand, prison inmates have relatively little difficulties finding women who will correspond with them and, sometimes, eventually marry them. This is true even, some say especially, for lifers who by definition will never be released. Some psychologists say such a situation offers some women a measure of safety and still allows them to develop close relationships with a man.

Some prisoners are clearly lonely and have little ulterior motives for developing a pen-pal relationship. Just as clearly, many others view the operation as a scam, as a way to get the woman so committed that she will send them money to provide them with little comforts. In many of these cases, the convict insists that he is innocent of the crime for which he was sent to prison and coerces the woman to provide funds for him, allegedly to work on an appeal.

The Internet has opened up new opportunities for prisoners for good reasons or ill to seek out pen pals. A typical example is a website offered by PrisonPenPals.Com for an Arizona inmate named Beau Greene. A picture shows the 32-year-old Greene cradling a fluffy cat and asking for pen pals, describing himself as "bored and lonely with a surplus of time." What Greene failed to mention was that he was convicted in 1996 for killing a 58-year-old man by bashing the man's head against rocks.

No evidence has been offered on Greene's success rate, but the Internet has widened the range of prisoners' appeals, and responses have come to Arizona from Australia, England, and Belgium, among others. Many of these women have shown up in person to visit their Internet pen pals.

Some pen-pal relationships last for many years, and some end up being cut off by the inmate, presumably when the well starts running dry.

"permanent prisoners" state-raised convicts

To many observers, the concept of "permanent prisoners" is one of the most troubling situations in penology. A case that came to the fore in the 1970s involved Bobbie Ferguson, who at the age of 39 had spent all but 16 months of his life in Iowa state institutions. In news interviews, he stated a not-uncommon attitude that he wanted to remain in prison. "I don't know how to live outside," Ferguson said. "My home is inside, and I want to stay there the rest of my life."

He had been born in the Iowa Women's Reformatory, where his mother was being held for a crime that no one remembers. Ferguson said of his mother, "I think her name was Vivian."

In an interview reported by the *New York Times*, he related that he was a ward of the state from the day he was born and had remained one ever since. From a parade of orphanages, he went on to hospitalization as mentally retarded, where he said of the discipline imposed there: "We sat at a table all day with our arms folded. If you stood up, without raising your hand for permission, someone hit you."

Thereafter, reformatories followed for him and, finally, prison.

It may be said that no one knows how many such "permanent prisoners" or "state-raised" convicts are lost in the prison and justice system.

phase programs rewarding compliant inmates

In recent decades it has become common for many prisons to operate with "phase programs." When new inmates enter a facility operating in a phase program, they are at first placed in strict confinement in single-inmate cells. Frequently, prison officials see this as a period of "orientation," but to many it is regarded as an initiation, showing that the inmate will get nothing without a demonstration of proper behavior.

The theory behind phasing is that increased "privileges" is the best way to tame a prisoner. Release from the isolated single-inmate cell permits a prisoner to climb the ladder of more privileges and freedom. He or she may be shifted from one tier level or building to another as he or she continues to improve. Inmates who complete the entire phase may even be rewarded with transfer to a more desirable institution. Some observers have called this a "promised afterlife" with an "escape" from a worse prison to a better one, often to an institution nearer the inmate's old home so that it is easier for family to visit with less financial strain.

Critics claim that phase programs inevitably push out any rehabilitative programs more likely to help an inmate after release. Instead, the prisoner knows to become a more pliant inmate. There is little room for programs aimed at dealing in advance with the inmate's eventual return to society, which is the fate of most prisoners. Some prisoners do become more compliant, but others tend to become more aggressive toward guards and other prisoners. What these prisoners have, say the critics, is plenty of time to grow more angry about privileges that they don't have, and, therefore, they have no incentive to work in hopes of winning a parole or to increase their chances of beating the odds and never going wrong again.

The phase programs, critics say, represent little more than a "containment" strategy aimed at making prison more pleasant for the keepers rather than the kept.

phrenology bumps on the skull and criminality

Today, phrenology is a lost "science," no longer taken seriously, but in the 19th century in the United States, it was as widely followed as in its European birthplace. (It is worth noting that such social thinkers as Karl Marx, always in search of an ever-perfect science, embraced what is now regarded as pseudoscience.)

Phrenology held that most of the functions of the brain were localized in various regions of the brain and that their development was discernible in conformations or bumps of the skull. Naturally many researchers saw the theory as a boon to a study—and dare they hope—even as a cure for criminality.

One of the first in the United States to promote phrenology was Charles Caldwell of Transylvania University in Kentucky in the 1820s. Thereafter, prison visitors of various persuasions charged to penal institutions, especially to study and measure the skulls of executed criminals. Thus, one study indicated that a New Jersey murderer named LeBlanc had massive organs of "destructiveness," "acquisitiveness," and "secretiveness"—seemingly the perfect picture of a criminal and killer. There was also seeming confirmation at the other end of the spectrum when one measured the skull of one Tardy, a pirate, who was found to have very small centers of "conscientiousness" and "veneration."

Of all the U.S. popularizers, George Combe became the most influential and greatly impressed a number of penologists, especially Eliza Farnum when she was matron of Sing Sing prison. She developed an encyclopedic work that utilized the latest phrenological principles. Farnum later took over at Mount Pleasant Prison for women and continued her work with the new "science." In that, she was a child of her era, and, in fact, her applications represented much false science that infected the field of penal activities.

In due course, phrenology would be discredited but only after it caused numerous serious errors in its treatment of offenders, including the "feebleminded" and the insane. Before that fully occurred, Italian physician Cesare Lombroso took the so-called new science of "modern" criminology to another level, once again impressing U.S. penologists for a time.

See also: LOMBROSO, CESARE.

pig laws and black codes Treatment of early black convicts

At the end of the Civil War, southern states were not geared to hold black inmates in their prisons, as the antebellum South only thought it necessary to confine white felons in its penitentiaries. Punishment of blacks was left to the slave owners or, in cases of severe infractions, to execution. In 1865, the defeated states sought to tighten laws that would most readily punish blacks for their predictable conduct (and, it must be noted, with little opposition of occupying forces).

Racist legislation—"pig laws" and special black codes—was passed that meted out exceptionally harsh sentences for offenses most likely to be committed by newly freed but impoverished blacks. Thus, the stealing of a pig by blacks for food became almost as onerous as in feudal Europe for hunting the gentry's reserves. There the penalty was death; in the United States, long prison terms. Of course, there was little interest in confining and feeding such prisoners, and most southern states approved labor-leasing systems that allowed white farmers or factory owners to lease state prisoners for an annual fee.

Essentially, this simply returned black prisoners to slavery and, perhaps, a more deadly form of it because plantation owners and the like had little need to keep their workers alive compared to the more financially prudent pre–Civil War method of keeping "property" relatively healthy. There were more supplies available. As a result, black prisoners' death rates soared.

pillory universal colonial punishment method

In the immediate days of the founding of every new colony in America, it is believed that the very first symbol of authority and law-and-order punishment device introduced was the pillory (even if some colonists had been subject to it in the Old World). Even when there were colonial shifts from one European power such as the Dutch to the English in

New York or the Spanish to the French to the American in New Orleans, there may have been scourges of many elements of the old rule, but one that remained inviolate was the pillory. It was the law-and-order symbol that was considered eternal.

In some new communities, shelter was first built and was immediately followed by the construction of a pillory. The work was assigned to all as a matter of vital civic responsibility.

In many cases, more than one pillory was needed to meet different requirements of punishment. The standard pillory consisted of a wooden frame with boards containing holes through which the head and hands and, sometimes, the legs of an offender could be inserted. In addition to this style, another pillory held only the fingers of one or both hands with the first joints bent.

An offender who was sentenced to the pillory sat on a platform, usually with a sign around his or her neck that read:

My name is _______,
I am a thief [or whatever],
I stole from _______,
Sentenced to _______, days' exposure at the pillory.

Persons in the pillory were often subject to ridicule by other citizens—this often was the real purpose of the punishment. Youngsters took it as sport to throw garbage or rotten fruit and vegetables at the victims. Because there was the chance that the victims might exact retribution later, many of the abusers preferred to operate after dark. There were numerous instances in which women alleged that they had been abused sexually or otherwise after dark. If the woman was considered to be of ill repute and disbelieved, she might have some time added to her sentence.

Although the South was generally believed to be more stern in its punishments in general, the pillory fell into disfavor there first. It was deemed inappropriate to allow blacks to see whites suffering such maltreatment. By and large, the punishment for whites ended by 1840. New Orleans abandoned the practice in 1827 for whites but continued it as punishment for blacks for two more decades.

See also: COLONIAL PUNISHMENT.

The pillory, here pictured above a whipping post, was a commonly used form of criminal punishment.

prerelease problems for prisoners

increased vulnerability

It should have been a godsend for the young prisoner. He had won parole very early in his term. It should have left him elated, but the most striking feeling he had was fear. He did not fear going back to society; he simply was worried if things could still go wrong before he was freed. He had been in prison long enough to have witnessed the problems many inmates about to be set free faced while still behind bars.

Being an inmate about to go free, he faced serious problems. Above all, he had to keep his nose clean, but there were some convicts who now looked upon him as an easy victim. He couldn't really fight back. They could demand tribute from him. Worse yet, they could make sexual demands on him.

Previously, he could fight back, resisting their advances. Now involvement in a fight, he feared, could "queer" (jeopardize) his release. He knew that, and so did those preying on him. Desperately, the young prisoner volunteered to go into protective custody, meaning solitary confinement, often in the "Hole." He felt he had no choice. It is the price paid for being confined with murderers, extortionists, rapists, shakedown artists, and other criminals who reveled in being in an environment where there were so many victims ready for plucking.

In this case, isolation proved to be salvation for the young releasee, and he was able to leave the prison his last few weeks free of fear of being molested.

In a lighter vein, perhaps, was the experiences of an inmate who won lasting fame under the sobriquet of "Hammerhead Fred" who did his time in Pennsylvania's tough Graterford Penitentiary. Hammerhead was slated for release after doing 10 years and celebrated by staging a one-man drunken riot. Graterford was notorious as a prison where homemade hooch was plentiful, although inmates took care to make it less than obvious to the guards. Hammerhead did nothing of the sort. He paraded about with a five-gallon plastic bag of the prison-brewed wine, guzzling and singing and screaming that he was going free. The hooch spilled down his prison clothes, and enraged guards sought to corner him. Hammerhead guzzled away and outraced them for several minutes until his imbibing started to slow him.

The inmates of the entire cell block cheered him on, urging him to keep on running and keep drinking. As one fleet-footed guard closed the gap, a prisoner darted out of his cell and "accidentally" bumped the guard, sending him sprawling, his companions then tumbling over him in a scene mindful of the Keystone Kops.

Hammerhead kept on going, took a long swig, and jumped over the side to the tier below, landing on his rump on a table of that level. Amazingly, Hammerhead did not drop the hooch bag. He took another big gulp and then tossed the bag to inmates who surrounded him, bellowing in joy and drinking from the hooch.

It took guards several moments to battle through the crowd and finally drag Hammerhead from his perch. It was off to the hole for Hammerhead, amid boos and hisses from the inmates for the correction officers.

Hammerhead's rampage did not serve him ill, although it did make "Hammerhead's Run" a celebrated memory among the inmates. Prison officials could do nothing other than keep their villain prisoner locked up one final night in solitary. After that, Hammerhead was free and clear, having completed the last day of his sentence; he had to be released. He was safe from any retribution, having no parole or probation time to do. Hammerhead had won his grand race.

prerelease programs help for prisoners due for release

Prerelease programs to assist inmates who are due for release shortly do vary from state to state and, of course, are complicated as well by the general attitude that convicts should be held as long as possible. Various institutions offer varying amounts of assistance and guidance for convicts who face release. Programs in some institutions appear to be limited to instructions on how to tie a necktie, but others focus on aid in how to interview for a job and then go on to discuss changing social mores and the new etiquette.

These may seem minor considerations, but there is general consensus among professionals that there are severe problems that releasees face when they move from the restrictions imposed within prison to conditions in the outside world. The federal government clearly follows the rules offered under the Prisoner Rehabilitation Act of 1965, and most states since that time have followed up with state mandates of their own.

Today, furloughs are part of many state programs, not that the concept of furloughs is new. Warden Lewis E. Lawes, during his tenure as warden of Sing Sing, frequently allowed prisoners leave for compassionate reasons, often without accompanying supervision, which certainly put his position at risk. No prisoner ever betrayed his trust. Part of the romantic legend around the western outlaw Butch Cassidy stemmed in popular culture from his situation in 1894 when he was slated for transfer to begin a two-year sentence in state prison. He asked to be allowed to leave his jail cell unescorted for the night, saying, "I give you my word I'll be back." Perhaps surprisingly, permission was granted, and, sure enough, Cassidy returned, never revealing whom he visited; he simply turned in his guns and went off to prison.

Furloughs of today hardly have the same dramatic or entertaining factors but have been granted to visit ill or dying relatives or to attend funerals. But they are also allowed, depending on the institution and its attitude on furloughs, to enable a prisoner to secure a job, obtain a driver's license, arrange for housing, and work out affairs with family members. In some states, the inmates meet with future parole officers. Experts approve of all these activities because it moves the prisoners closer to an awareness of what the outside world will be like and will permit them, perhaps for the first time in years, to reach decisions on their life on their own, so uncommon within the closely watched prison routine. In some cases, depending on the place, it allows communities, especially small towns, to have the time and perspective to adjust to the offender as well. All these programs tend to be short ranged and generally last only for a day to, at most, a week or so.

Many jurisdictions also offer work-release setups that allow an inmate to be released from incarceration to attend school or work. Inmates may hold a job in a community or take classes at a vocational school or at a more general educational institution.

A study of work-release programs in North Carolina has found that work releasees later had much lower unemployment rates and higher wages than inmates who were freed without having taken part in any work-release program. The fact that inmates earn enough in work-release to make some support payments to their families greatly enhances their own self-esteem. A psychological study has also shown that work releasees end up with being less hyperactive in their later behavior and less antisocial and amoral. Even when the releasees fail to achieve full acceptance from their families, they acknowledge that such efforts have some benefits still and are helpful in their general attitudes.

There are certain drawbacks to situations in which an inmate has to adjust to an outside environment during the day and then return to his prison at night. In some cases, prisoners may miss out on programs that will have a most beneficial value for them.

One reason that more support might exist for work-release than might normally be expected, given the public attitudes to all convicts at the turn of the 21st century, is the fact that some work releasees actually pay back part of the costs for their imprisonment, that they pay taxes, and in some localities, that they are required to make contributions to victim-restitution funds. This last benefit seems to be popular even with administrators of states with aggressive imprisonment practices as it frees up some cells for other convicts.

Of course, it would be illogical to think that any work-release program is without failures. Some participants commit additional crimes or even escape from supervision. This will happen even with the most careful screening of prerelease inmates, but the clear consensus among professionals, aside from the more rigid punishment-minded foes, is that such programs clearly are a plus and overall do cut postrelease criminal activity.

principle of least eligibility antiprisoners'-rights view

About 1970, the principle of least eligibility came to the fore in prison practices and, in effect, greatly weakened the goal of rehabilitation. Least eligibility holds that because offenders had violated the law, they do not deserve more programs than do ordinary citizens and that they are not entitled to earn college degrees, have exercise equipment, and receive other benefits that ordinary taxpayers do not enjoy and indeed are not able to afford.

Least eligibility was not invented in 1970 but went in and out of vogue several times earlier. Around 1900, there had been a similar reaction to any "luxuries" for prisoners and to the sense of wasting time and money "coddling criminals."

Least-eligibility views lost ground in the next few decades as reports of brutalization of prisoners outraged public opinion, such as the treatment of such prisoners as Ed Morrell (who became probably the most popular ex-prisoner) and Robert Elliott Burns (whose maltreatment was greatly responsible for the end of chain gangs).

The principle of least eligibility returned in 1970, gaining support as it coincided with renewed anticoddling views of the public at large. Probably nothing outraged public opinion as convicts who gained a law degree during their confinement, this being viewed as nothing more than an example of a criminal using the system to gain knowledge and ability to thwart justice, as many viewed criminal defense lawyers in general.

Although quite a few rehabilitation programs have been weakened or even dropped, other public demands about weightlifting programs, television, and the like have been met by most prison officials, who regard these not as benefits for prisoners but for the prison administration itself as they curb aggressive behavior by prisoners. Inmates, because of this, have a different outlet for their frustrations, and this offers administrators control by making these items privileges that can be withdrawn for any misbehavior. It can be pointed out that in many institutions the cost of exercise equipment is paid for out of profits from commissary sales (at generally high prices) or by revenues gained by other prison industries.

Television remains an inviolate right in many prisons, again for the benefit of the prison administration. Hard-liners in a few jurisdictions have forced through statutes forbidding prisons to furnish television sets, but some prisons have made an end run around such prohibitions by rebuilding old sets already in their possession. The federal prison system allows television most consistently in its so-called supermax institutions. As one prisoner put it, "They'll replace a broken TV before a broken toilet."

See also: TELEVISION FOR PRISONERS; SOAP OPERA FANS.

prisoners, older should they be kept confined? Although it is not popular in recent years to be in favor of releasing prisoners before the expiration of their sentences, many if not most prison administrators probably would like to have older inmates removed from their institutions. Like many experts on the outside, wardens and keepers regard the old inmates as less threatening to society, even if they

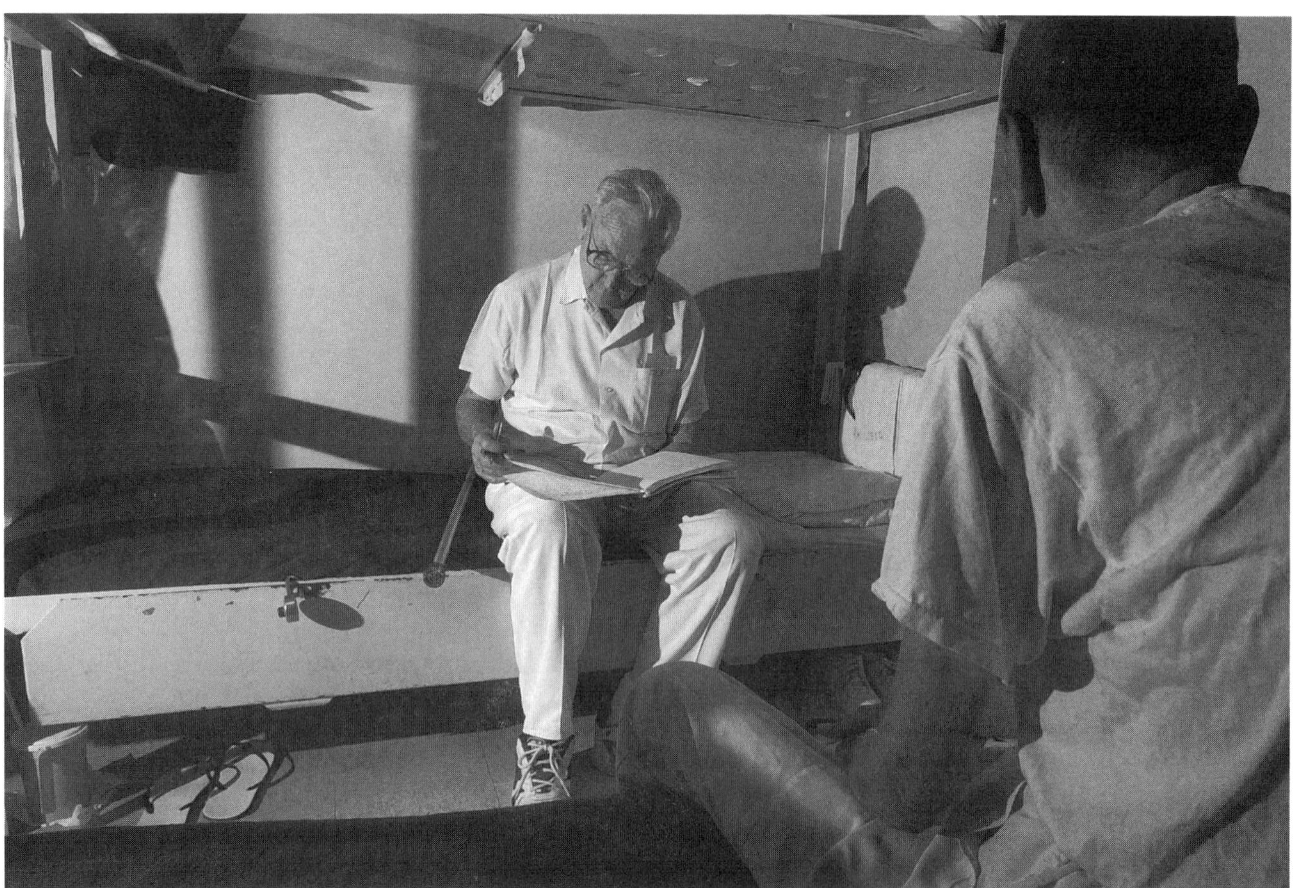

An elderly prison inmate works on his journal while sitting on his bunk at the Hamilton Correctional Facility for the Aged and Infirm in Hamilton, Alabama. Inmates await a slow death behind bars at the prison and are a testament to Alabama's get-tough-on-crime era, when the number of life-without-parole sentences began to rise. (AP/Wide World Photos)

were originally confined for violent crimes. All know that as criminals age they tend away from committing violence. It is generally acknowledged, even by prosecutors, that after the age of 29 or 30, the rate of violence drops by such offenders.

However, we are dealing here with much older prisoners, who some observers fear will eventually become a time bomb for the prison system, taking up room that would be put to much better use to house younger, far more dangerous criminals. As prisoners age, they develop serious health problems that many institutions are incapable of handling.

Paradoxically, they also do actually represent a center of violence within the prison. Just as older persons on the outside represent easy targets, so do aging inmates caught within a sea of violent men. Prison guards—if they are vigilant—must spend an inordinate amount time seeking to protect the aging inmate.

With longer sentences the norm since the 1980s, more older prisoners are taxing the system. As one corrections official states off the record because it will not gain him accolades from the hard-liners among the public or politicians, "That time bomb keeps ticking and will eventually blow. Prison overcrowding will cause more inmates to be released early, and among them inevitably will be many who should not be allowed out. I don't know if that will be the outcome usually. It will be that or finally a realization that the tax coffers will run dry, and even hard-liners will find their tax bills intolerable."

prisonization explanation of inmate violence
There is the standard belief that inmate violence on one another is merely indicative that they are violent people who are prone to go on the attack, often maiming or killing others for any sort of perceived cause. However, a growing psychological opinion holds that such explanations are at best superficial in some cases.

In a June 2001 murder trial in New Jersey, psychology professor Craig Haney of the University of California at Santa Cruz, an expert on prison life, introduced the term *prisonization* to describe what he said produced a mindset among convicts that they must defend themselves to the death or face becoming a victim. It is clearly a code of conduct that is verbalized one way or another among many prison inmates.

Is this prison inmate "paranoia" or prisonization? In an interview at the New Jersey trial site, Dr. Haney said, "Prison—I don't care what prison—they're dangerous places. These guys learn that they have to watch their backs, their fronts, their sides and at the slightest sign of weakness, they're a victim."

Dr. Haney's testimony was instrumental in getting an acquittal in the murder case, one that drew nationwide interest. It was the first time in modern New Jersey penal history—and perhaps anywhere ever in the United States—that one condemned man killed another in the death house.

Black inmate Ambrose Harris was charged with murdering Robert Simon, once a member of a white-supremacist motorcycle gang and a three-time murderer who had bragged of killing a prisoner in a Pennsylvania prison.

The prosecution argued that Harris was guilty of a brutal murder by punching, kicking, and stomping on Simon's face long after the victim had stopped moving to send a message to the 15 other condemned prisoners that he was a tough man.

The prosecution, however, proved unable to counter witness testimony that Simon attacked Harris first, but there was no denying that Harris had ended the attack by jumping off a table onto Simon's shattered head. The two had previously been enemies when they were placed together, contrary to regulations, in a recreation cage. Harris had been in administrative segregation from other prisoners for hitting a guard. The defense latched on to the possibility that the guards may have deliberately broken the rules. Defense attorney Robert F. Gold later said, "You had to look at this from Harris's point of view and his honest and reasonable belief that he was getting set up." The lawyer had produced witnesses who testified that Simon had frequently taunted Harris.

The prosecution kept hammering away on the brutality of the murder and claimed that Harris's attack on Simon had lasted too long to be considered self-defense, and it also sought to belittle the prisonization testimony.

The defense attorney embraced that testimony, declaring, "As Dr. Haney said so eloquently, when you have been confined in prison as long as Mr. Harris had, for as long as Mr. Simon had, when you have an encounter like that, it is a lethal encounter."

The defense arguments clearly convinced the jury that Harris had reason to believe that he had been set up by guards to be attacked by Simon. The jury acquitted Harris of all charges, and it was apparent to courtroom observers that other defenders of prisoners charged with attacks on fellow inmates would in the future make use of the prisonization defense, especially if some malfeasance could be alleged against guards or prison administrators.

prison labor—pay rates

An ad from the Wisconsin Department of Corrections aimed at businesses reads: "Can't Find Workers? A Willing Workforce Waits."

A reason advanced by some business executives for the choice of using prison inmates as part of their workforce is simple hype. As one says, "We can put a Made-in-the-U.S.A. label on our product."

Clearly, the use of prison labor is very attractive for many companies. Here is a short list of states offering prison workers and the products/services involved, as complied by C. Stone Brown in an article "Crime, Capitalism and Black America" in *Z Magazine.*

- California—logos for Lexus automobiles
- Hawaii—packing Spalding golf balls
- Maryland—modular houses; processed hot-dogs
- New Mexico—hotel-chain reservations
- Oregon—designer blue jeans, called "prison blues"
- South Carolina—electronic cables
- Washington—Eddie Bauer garments

Very few observers credit such work as springing from a desire to enhance the lives or futures of prison inmates but rather from a clear attraction

The CMT plant, Convicts Making T-shirts, is one company using inmate labor to produce their products. Located at the R.J. Donovan Correctional Facility in Chula Vista, California, CMT-employed inmates make minimum wage rather than the usual, much lower prison wage. (AP/Wide World Photos)

to lower costs. In fact, critics as well as in-prison groups describe the states as supplying a slavelike workforce.

Courts have ruled that the Fair Labor Standards Act, which mandates the minimum wage for Americans, does not apply to government-employed prison inmates. As a result, Federal UNICOR, which is an independent federal-prison-industries corporation, pays from 23 cents to $1.15 per hour, and up to 50 percent of that is subject to deduction. Private companies are required to pay the minimum wage, but even so, the inmates see little of the money. Deductions are made for room and board, taxes, family support, restitution for crime victims, and savings for release. A Unibase employee working a sewing machine at Soledad makes 45 cents, and a worker doing data entry at Lebanon Correctional in Ohio receives 47 cents, according to labor writer Jane Slaughter in "Captive Labor: Jobs Without Justice" in *The Witness,* November 1998.

The U.S. Department of Justice publication sells the program of using prison labor: "Inmates represent a readily available and dependable source of entry-level labor that is a cost-effective alternative to work forces found in Mexico, the Caribbean Basin, Southeast Asia, and the Pacific Rim countries."

Left unsaid was a number of additional "perks" such as that the convict force received no additional benefits and no vacation time, and that snow, sleet, rain, and the like did not keep the convicts from their appointed chores. The only inconvenience might be the occasional lockdown, keeping all inmates in their cells for security or other reasons. Aside from that, the employers had carte blanche to fire any worker for any reasons, including back talk. Also, when the workload fell, the workers could be dismissed with no need to worry about fighting claims for unemployment compensation. Writer Slaughter, with a touch of the quick needle, commented, "It's easy to imagine a scenario in which a worker loses his job, commits a crime out of desperation, and then ends up working for his former company in jail. But at least he's got the job, not the foreign competition."

prison punishments in early America

Confinement in early America seldom allowed for escapes, but the authorities still proscribed a variety of punishments, usually for what was called "forbidden behavior," especially the "secret vice" or masturbation. In the 1830s Pennsylvania's Eastern Penitentiary physician, William Darrach, denounced this vice as a leading cause of insanity, chronic pleurisy, pulmonary tuberculosis, and suicide.

Among the punishments or "cures" for this and other misconducts, the Eastern staff meted out such penalties as starvation diets, denial of work, the use of forms of straitjackets, "iron gags," shower baths, and the "mad chair."

The iron gag was described by an official investigative committee as "a rough iron instrument resembling the stiff bit of a blind bridle, having an iron palet in the center, about an inch square, and chains at each end to pass around the neck and fasten behind. . . . This instrument was placed in the prisoner's mouth, the iron palet over the tongue, the bit forced back as far as possible, the chains brought round the jaws to the back of the neck; the end of one chain was passed through the ring in the end of the other chain drawn tight to the 'forth link' and fastened with a lock; his hands were then forced into leather gloves in which were iron staples and crossed behind his back; leather straps were passed through the staples, and from thence round the chains of the gag between his neck and the chains; the straps were drawn tight, the hands forced up toward the head, and the pressure consequently acting on the chains which press on the jaws and jugular vein, producing excruciating pain, and a hazardous suffusion of blood to the head."

The shower bath was almost as brutal, consisting of the repeated dumping of cold water from a considerable height onto an exposed prisoner who was under restraint and unable to avoid the stream. An official investigation into the treatment of one Seneca Plumley found: "In the depth of winter, he was tied up against the wall attached to his cell by the wrists, while buckets of extremely cold water were thrown upon him from a height which partly froze on his head and person, and he was shortly discharged as incurably insane." The shower bath was destined to be used in many prisons for many decades to come.

The mad chair had been invented by the "father of American psychiatry," Dr. Benjamin Rush. It was so called because it resembled a large boxlike chair into which a prisoner was strapped and bound so that his body was prevented from resting, with a result of extreme pain. (It probably could be said to banish all interests in masturbation, at that moment at least.)

prison riots and the 1952 "sea change" in inmate behavior

Prison riots have long been a part of prison culture and protest, even though most inmates realize that in the end they cannot win. By 1952–53, a certain sea change was occurring in convict behavior: It became more common for prisoners to turn their vengeance less on their keepers than on the institutions where they were being kept. In October 1952, 300 convicts of Utah's new prison, just two months old, locked up eight guards in cells, turned loose death-row inmates, smashed windows, tore up library books, flooded floors, and ransacked the commissary. Clearly, the acts of the inmates were aimed more at the facility than the keepers.

Similarly and more striking was the riot at the Ohio State Penitentiary on October 31, 1952. During a six-hour period, prisoners wrecked and burned a million dollars' worth of building. They did not take hostages, made no demands, and clearly had no other intent but to destroy their 120-year-old prison.

It cannot be said that in many other riots of this period there was no attempt to exact punishment on guards, but the destruction of state property to such a large extent met with a strong reaction on the outside.

The *Chicago Tribune*, known as a strong opponent of "coddling of prisoners," complained:

> *The idea that convicts are entitled to indulge in larks causing destruction of a couple of million dollars in prison property, as happened at Jackson, Mich., is confined to soft-headed governors and mixed-up sociologists. The convicts have only themselves to blame for being in the penitentiary. They aren't given the right of collective bargaining under the law, nor are they to be regarded indulgently as college boys playing a prank.*
>
> *What the prison needs are honest and tough-minded state administrations, firm wardens, and centrally controlled built-in gas outlets to bring into play if the inmates start breaking things up. It might also be salutary if, at the first sign of disorder, the prison administration announced over the loudspeaker that the convicts would be left to live with any broken furniture or wrecked quarters for which they were responsible, and that the cost of repairing the damage would be paid for in the loss of time off for good behavior.*

It turned out that many experienced wardens considered built-in gas outlets very poor insurance against riots and that depriving prisoners of the good time would only increase, rather than decrease, the cost of keeping them in prison.

Placing the 1952–53 period in a historical perspective shows that the changing nature of at least some prison riots coincided with what became a growing recognition of the prisoners'-rights movement.

prisons

See JAILS AND PRISONS.

private prisons dynamic growth and then crisis

In 1986 the Corrections Corporation of America opened the nation's first modern private state prison in Marion County, Kentucky. It was a 300-bed institution for inmates slated to qualify for parole within three years. The concept quickly caught fire, and the trend exploded.

In point of fact, the growth of private prisons hardly represented a new idea. In the 19th and early 20th centuries, many states had private prisons. Texas leased prisons to private contractors who then leased the inmates out to work in industry and on farms. Most such prisoners were ill treated. Such contractors had little or no interest in "reforming" inmates, and beatings were the common "incentive" for prisoners to meet brutal work standards. As a result many prisoners died within seven years of their imprisonment, a number of escapes followed, and others sought their own escape through another method—committing suicide. Eventually, these privatized earlier prisons and others like them around the country were scrapped under various reforms.

However, the private prisons made a comeback, starting with the Marion facility. There were many factors that contributed to the new private, for-profit prisons. These soaring prison budgets, overcrowding, and the court ordering of "caps" on how many inmates a prison could hold, and a public perception taking away some prisons from the government meant less government control and a downsizing of bureaucracy. The private sector, it was thought by public opinion and many politicians, would be far better building new prisons faster than the government. Many corrections departments opposed such ideas that somehow cheaper meant better. On the other hand, hard-liners insisted on privatization, which became a quick-fix solution for state corrections systems that were swamped with a flood of offenders with no place to house them. But by 1991, many observers, who were held in high regard by corrections people, began to express considerable doubts on the process. In *No Escape* John J. DiIulio Jr., associate professor of politics and public affairs at Princeton University and a consultant to a number of state and local corrections agencies, wrote, "The paramount question in the debate over the privatization of corrections is not whether private firms can succeed where public agencies have ostensibly faltered, but whether the privatization movement can last." He reported some observers believed by then that the movement "is already running out of steam."

It must be said that the observations appeared to be wrong. By 1998, there were 159 private adult prison facilities up and running. However, by then the fissures in the system, said reformers, were widening. In fact, 1998 seemed to have represented the high-water mark for privatization. When private prisons first came into being, it was assumed the corporations investing in them would limit them to small, low-security institutions, and, at first, this was the case. But that changed as the more prisons operated privately, the more profits there were. Some private companies started to run all sorts of prison at all security levels, some with populations of as many as 2,000 inmates. Thus, private prisons appeared in detention centers, reformatories, penitentiaries, and supermax prisons. Then, by the late 1990s, the roof started to collapse on the concept of private prisons. Exposés indicated that they had the same problem of poor administration, insecure institutions, and mistreatment of inmates found in some public facilities.

This became apparent in juvenile facilities, with private ones revealing clear evidence of abuse. A facility in Colorado had to shut down when it was found that it had overused restraints against its 184 inmates, allowing sex between staff and inmates and many other abuses. Conditions culminated with the preventable suicide of a 13-year-old boy. In 1998 South Carolina canceled a contract with Corrections Corporation of America (the largest firm in the business) because of many escapes and charges of excessive force. "Torture by claustrophobia" was documented when as many as 18 boys were packed into a one-inmate prison cell with only cups for toilets. Perhaps the worst case involving a juvenile prison was that involving the Jena, Louisiana, juvenile prison run by the Wackenhut Corrections Corporation, the second-place private-for-profit company in the nation. A New Orleans judge and the Justice Department found that inmates were being physically abused and deprived of adequate food and clothing. The judge became so irate by what was found that he released 11 boys he had sentenced. The Louisiana Department of Public Safety and Corrections took over the prison when a state investigation found that part of a videotape reportedly showing abuse by a guard was mysteriously missing. After a series of lawsuits over conditions at Jena, Wackenhut decided to abandon its contract.

The "selling technique" used by private companies involves not contracting with a prison system that has too many prisoners, but with a town desperate for jobs. This was the case in Youngstown, Ohio, when the CCA contracted directly with the city to build a prison that would provide 400–450 jobs. Youngstown jumped at the offer, and the Northeast Ohio Correctional Center was born, built on land provided by the city for $1.

Unfortunately, from the very beginning, the prison was plagued with problems, stabbings including two fatalities, and escapes. One report stated, "The CCA prison became a chaotic gladiator's pit where nonviolent burglars and crack addicts were haphazardly thrust into cells with seasoned rapists, habitual killers and other high security predators, many shipped in from other states and the District of Columbia." This last activity had not been sanctioned by the city, but the prison's top priority seemed to be to load up the institution quickly, a theory being that an empty cell was a money-losing cell. It was found that the prison operated with low-paid employees who received very poor training, a fact pressed by a number of whistle-blowing employees and ex-employees. A woman guard told of being handed a shotgun and told to patrol the perimeter of the prison. She complained that she had no knowledge of how to use a gun and was simply informed to get out there anyway.

What finally riled up the population was the escape of six prisoners in broad daylight. Four of them were murderers, and the city was held in terror until police finally captured them all.

As a result of the bad publicity surrounding the prison, many reforms were instituted that produced rigorous oversight on the operations of CCA. There was also a remarkable alliance between the city and inmates resulting in a settlement by the company to pay the prisoners for their previous treatment.

Meanwhile, other private prison scandals were erupting elsewhere. In the Brazoria County Detention Center in Angleton, Texas, it was found that guards had made a "training video" of themselves beating and stun-gunning prisoners. There were sequences of dogs being sicced on naked prisoners from Missouri who were shipped there for incarceration. Injured prisoners were dragged face down back to their cells. To prevent the Missouri prisoners from calling home about their plight, the cell block telephones were cut off.

Lawyers later got hold of the video, and it was shown nationally. One of the star performers was a corrections officer who had done six months in federal prison in the past for offenses he had committed while working as a Texas state prison guard. He had no trouble acquiring his present job, although it paid only a puny $8 an hour. After a riot in Tennessee, which housed inmates shipped from Wisconsin, and where a guard was left in a coma, retribution was taken on 15 to 20 inmates by an assault team based outside the prison and brought in by the CCA whenever and wherever needed. At first, CCA and Wisconsin denied the story, but in time the denials wouldn't wash, and state officials and the FBI launched an investigation. Several CCA staffers were fired. Perhaps more significant was the statements by Tennessee officials that the rate of serious injuries in CCA prisons ran as much as 28 percent higher than in state prisons.

Another private prison firm located on New York's Long Island moved to Florida and stayed in business with a change of name after being labeled by federal officials as having caused "the worst disturbance ever in a New Jersey institution." If, as has been charged, many private prisons poorly train their guards, it may also be observed that top brass in such companies may not have sufficient correctional experience. At one firm the CEO's previous experience was investing in and managing hotels. On the company's board was a director of Frederick's of Hollywood.

On the horizon, some criminologists see added problems so that although the private prisons may survive scandal, they will inevitably be forced to adapt to conform to state and federal standards and to accept the authority of local jurisdictions to regulate and inspect them. For now, the prisons use persuasion, low-key or very pointed, to get their way.

The latter seemed to have been used in Youngstown where there were some calls to get rid of CCA. The company was said to have used a lobbying campaign to warn it would simply respond by pulling out the 450 jobs in Youngstown and put them in another prison elsewhere. It was obvious to the political leaders that losing 450 jobs would have been political suicide.

Private prison firms are accused of using lavish junkets to influence the right people. Christian Parenti, in his 1999 book *Lockdown America,* is particularly critical of the cultivating of "paid opinion makers." Notable in his criticism is the Private Prisons Project at the University of Florida, Gainseville, "which receives over $60,000 in grants every year from private jailers. The project's staff of researchers focuses on tutoring journalists and churning out predigested policy briefs which are spoon-fed to state and federal lawmakers. The center's director, Charles W. Thomas, has been quoted literally hundreds of times as a non-partisan expert, despite the fact that he personally owns stock in CCA, Wackenhut," and many other for-profit firms.

The use of junkets and other methods of influence are usual in other businesses, but the private firms face other charges as to the motives behind their practices. Jenni Gainsborough of the ACLU's

National Prison Project finds "a basic philosophical problem when you begin turning over administration of prisons to people who have an interest in keeping people locked up."

By the last couple of years of the century, private prisons were in deep trouble for all the reasons mentioned above, but there was far greater trouble steaming toward them. The growth of prison populations was definitely slowing, but the privatization movement went on blindly. The companies pressed on, interesting desperate communities in the joys of a prison system. Some localities actually built prisons on their own, floating expensive bond issues. Suddenly, some started to find that nobody came to their party. The communities faced bankruptcy, unable to pay off their bonds. The private companies fared little better. CCA built a $106 million giant prison in the sands of the Mojave Desert. The firm was sure that it would win a contract to house California prisoners, but the sudden stall of growth in the state's prison population was coupled with fierce opposition from unionized state prison guards, who were fearful of losing their jobs. (This was true in other states, too, where, for example, protests twice stopped CCA's ambitious plan for complete privatizing of the entire state prison system in Tennessee. The prison-guards' unions have gained considerable clout and have become an important group of voters, including wives and other family relations. In Pennsylvania, Gov. Tom Ridge, a great believer in privatization, faced prison guards marching and shouting "Death to privatization." Ridge killed plans to lease the state's newest lockup to a private company. Private company plans came to grief in other states, including Nebraska, Wisconsin, and Virginia.)

The Mojave prison lay empty, and the impact of this and other oppositions that the company felt elsewhere showed up in CCA's stock. Wall Street had been up until then, enchanted by the future profits to come from privatization, but started to sour as the value of such stocks took a bigger hit than many technology high-flyers would take. CCA's long-term debt soared to $1.09 billion in 1999 from only $127 million just two years earlier, and CCA was losing tons of money. Its stock dropped to $4.50 a share in 1999 from nearly $45 in 1997. In 2000, the stock fell as low as 19 cents.

Now the word on Wall Street was that private prison companies could be facing capital punishment.

Then surprisingly, some said amazingly, a white knight appeared—the U.S. Bureau of Prisons (BOP). Unlike state prisons, the federal system was loaded with new inmates, thanks to strict enforcement of new laws for imprisonment of immigration and drug violators in ever-increasing numbers. The BOP was very interested in the Mojave facility.

What was startling about the turn of events was that the BOP, hardly surprisingly, never cared much for the private prison movement. The general opinion was the BOP had to embrace the arrangement because many legislators and other policymakers believed there would be large cost savings. The BOP had to go along, even though they made it clear that they still doubted that privatization and outsourcing prisons would save taxpayer money. Yet, it set up very high reimbursement for the CCA and other firms slated to run other facilities. The bureau gave CCA, for instance, a guarantee of 95 percent occupancy, with cash paid out if the figure ever fell lower.

Because the BOP agreed with private-prison skeptics that the industry could not handle medium- and high-security inmates, it specified that the Mojave institution could only handle the least-risky inmates, such as criminal aliens. Yet, the BOP agreed to pay CCA $21,880 per inmate, which actually was slightly more than the $21,601 the bureau spends on average for the entire federal system. That includes medium- and high-security inmates who are more dangerous prisoners and need greater security. But the BOP insisted that because the private prisons would have to replicate its own high standards, it had to allow the private sector a premium.

The Wall Street Journal concluded in November 2001 that there could be another explanation for their generosity: "If privatization at the federal level turns out to be an expensive experiment, the chances that Congress and the White House would push for broad-scale outsourcing of federal prisons would diminish. The public system would survive intact, and public employees would keep their jobs."

The BOP strategy was even more inviting to their own system. It had committed itself to only three years of service and avoided financing constructions for criminal aliens. If in the meantime there would be a move to legalize the entry of some who came in illegally, or if the flow of drug offenders eased off, the BOP could walk away from the private prison, leaving the operator "stranded in the desert without a paddle."

There was considerable opinion by observers that the lot of the private prisons might not be a happy one, a possibility at least broached back in 1991 by John DiIulio.

probation

From time to time, attacks on the probation system by hard-line critics claim that it is often administered in too soft-headed a manner, but there has never been nearly the vitriol as there is on parole. The justice system could not exist without all sorts of probationary methods, and probation, rather than imprisonment, is the standard method of punishment used in the United States and even more so in other countries. We have far more people on probation than behind bars. In 1932, the Supreme Court, in considering the revocation of probation, stated that the purpose of the practice is to "provide a period of grace in order to aid the rehabilitation of a penitent offender; to take advantage of an opportunity for reformation which actual service of the suspended sentence might make less probable."

There are those who do regard probation as no more than an ineffectual slap on the wrist, but many find prisons to be expensive, excessive, and unable to make the public truly safer; after all, nonviolent youthful offenders are placed with older, hardened, and violent prisoners who can teach them so much more about crime. The second group also argues that prisons should be for violent offenders who have to be both kept away from society and incapacitated. For virtually all other offenders, they contend, prison should not be the primary form of correction. That opinion is held by Norman Carlson, the former director of the Federal Bureau of Prisons: "Prison space is scarce and you've got to use it judiciously. For nonviolent offenders, there are better alternatives to prison." He is hardly alone in that view: In a 1994 survey, 92 percent of all wardens around the country favor alternatives to incarceration.

The celebrated father of the probation movement was a wealthy Boston businessman named John Augustus, who sought to come to the aid of drunkards. In 1841, he persuaded a judge to release a "common drunkard" to his custody. Augustus took him home, gave him clothes, and found him a job. Weeks later, Augustus returned to court with the man, now totally changed in appearance and manner, and the judge, thoroughly impressed, released the man with a fine of one cent.

For the last 18 years of his life, Augustus won probation for almost 2,000 persons. He soon went far beyond drunkards to include defendants who had been charged with more serious offenses. Augustus's record was amazing and far greater than those achieved by later probation programs. Less than a dozen of his charges took the opportunity to escape, and only a few committed new crimes. Another Bostonian, Father Rufus W. Cook, and a Philadelphian, William J. Mullen, who eventually became a prison agent for the Philadelphia Prison Society, became the leaders of the probation movement.

Today, probation departments generally claim a rehabilitation-success rate of 70 percent or more. The National Probation and Parole Association declares: "Far more effective than deterrence as an objective of sentencing is rehabilitation, the satisfactory adjustment of the offender to law-abiding society. Whether it takes the form of probation—proved to be the most practical approach where circumstances warrant its use—or of commitment and ultimately parole, it is based on the principle that the best way to protect society is to change convicted offenders into law-abiding citizens."

Not all observers, even among liberals, accept in full the rehabilitative value claimed for probation. Aryeh Neier, executive director of the American Civil Liberties Union, states: There is no evidence that probation rehabilitates people any more than if people were simply left alone. Probation is punitive, however, and its principal use should be as an alternative to prison for people who have committed minor crimes and who deserve some punishment."

The reason why prosecutors don't attack probation en masse is that the system is vital to their needs. Granting probation is a prime way to reward police informers. However, it is also used to allow the probationer to work and provide restitution to the victim for his or her loss or injury or to keep the prisoner's family intact and off the charity rolls. Probation is considered an effective way to promote guilty pleas, and most judges agree that it is necessary to provide them with a way to invoke a relatively mild form of punishment for first offenders. Above all, it is vital to any hopes of reducing prison overcrowding. The cost is about one-tenth that of maintaining a person in a penal institution. That fact alone probably ensures the system guarantee of its own continuation.

procreation by inmates controversial ruling

Perhaps one of the most controversial expansions of prisoners' rights at the beginning of the 21st century was the surprise ruling by a federal appeals court that male prison inmates have a constitutional right to procreate. The inmate involved in the ruling was William Gerber, who was serving life without parole in California for making terrorist threats, discharging a firearm, and narcotics offenses. He insisted it was a violation of his constitutional rights not to allow him to ship semen out of prison for the artificial insemination of his 46-year-old wife.

The ruling was made by the United States Court of Appeals for the Ninth Circuit in San Francisco, a court, critics frequently charge, that has a reputation for liberal rulings. The 2-1 decision, affirmed by Myron H. Bright and Stephen Reinhardt, found that modern techniques for procreation without sexual relations raised new legal issues. The majority found that procreation is "not inherently inconsistent with one's status as a prisoner." The dissent by Judge Barry G. Silverman (like the other two jurists appointed by Democratic presidents) ridiculed the ruling as inventing a right to procreate "from prison via FedEx."

The ruling called for a trial court to determine whether there are legitimate prison-management issues that would justify a total ban by correction officials on Gerber's ability to procreate. Not surprisingly, the decision drew severe criticism in many circles, and many lawyers predicted that the opinion would be overturned by the U.S. Supreme Court, especially considering the makeup of that body at the time. Dora Schriro, senior policy fellow at the University of Missouri at St. Louis and a former corrections official, disputed the ruling as ignoring the fact that prison inmates lose certain rights, even if they lose them permanently because of life sentences.

Schriro declared, "Life means life, and some new technology should not affect sentencing and its many ramifications." The president of the Criminal Justice Legal Foundation, a conservative group in Sacramento, insisted that it was bad policy for the courts to make it easier for prisoners to father children.

There was some support voiced for the findings. Eric Balaban, a lawyer for the National Prison Project of the American Civil Liberties Union, insisted that the courts had recognized that prisoners like the one in this case did not lose all their rights. "He wasn't sentenced to be sterilized."

Other observers noted that other courts were "in a box" if their states permitted conjugal visits in the past (an overall growing trend even though many states decline to do so). They pointed out that certainly procreation possibilities abounded in such visitation situations unless the state insisted on having a witness present to make sure all proper birth-control procedures were followed. One lawyer, commenting anonymously, found that this might limit the Supreme Court's determination to interfere in the matter. He also raised the possibility that the prisoner was also "pushing the envelope" to gain support for a contention that his life sentence might not be warranted based on the charges against him.

However, there was no doubt that technology itself was pushing the envelope of prisoners' rights and would do so in future situations as well.

property crime drop and imprisonment
is there a connection?

One of the most usual claims of the value of imprisonment to reduce crime is the drop in property crimes. However, many experts tend to dismiss such claims. They insist there is a more obvious cause for the drop in crimes against property that has nothing to do with the rate of imprisonment. The Campaign for an Effective Crime Policy finds that the drop in property crime is more a matter of possible shifts in the types of victimization over time.

For instance, while the rate of burglaries and theft showed a marked decrease starting in the

1980s, other types of crimes, such as auto theft and drug trafficking, rose—despite the much harsher prison sentences meted out for these offenses. The nonpartisan Effective Crime Policy group, formed by a number of criminal justice officials in 1992, declares: "As criminologist Joan Petersilia has noted, even the most cursory examination of today's inner cities would reveal a shift in street crime for the riskier crime of burglary to the more lucrative crime of drug dealing. Thus, a decline in the NCVS [National Crime Victimization Survey] burglary rate does not necessarily mean that less crime is being committed; rather, it may indicate that offenders are opting to commit different crimes. This raises a serious question about the accuracy of the 'decrease' in crime."

Certainly, in the drug-trafficking ghettos, there is general disdain for offenders who turn to such "dumb"—and far less lucrative capers—as housebreaking and burglaries.

protective custody taking inmates out of harm's way

A must in every prison is the procedure of protective custody whereby inmates who face a threat to their safety can be kept away from other convicts for any number of reasons. A new inmate, very young and fresh looking, frequently is a target of sexual predators; another, suspected of having financial resources on the outside, faces possible shakedowns in the form of "protection" from prison toughs for regular payments; still others may be the object of murder tries for failing to pay gambling debts, welshing on drug deals, or being suspected of being a snitch or informer.

Some such unlucky prisoners may be confined to the "Hole" in solitary confinement, but, normally, they have a wing or a section assigned to them. This does not necessarily guarantee the inmate's safety unless guards are especially vigilant against ploys to penetrate the protective procedures. Sometimes important figures in the general prison population are so desirous of wreaking vengeance on a victim that they hire a "hit man"—of which there are a great many in prisons—to do the job.

In one case in a federal penitentiary, a convicted murderer asked for protective custody, claiming that he owed a large sum of money in gambling debts that he couldn't pay and said that he would be killed as an object lesson to other debtors. Prison officials did not buy the story because the convict was known as a real tough guy who knew how to take care of himself. More likely, it was figured, he was being sent into the protective-custody wing to get someone else, because among other attributes, he had been a reputed hit man for a violent biker gang.

Still, he had to be accepted as a protected inmate. However, prison officials refused to put him in the custody wing, instead sending him to the Hole as an alternate safety measure. The convict became enraged and insisted that he should be put in the regular custody section, that the Hole really represented punishment.

The officials held firm and said that as long as he needed protection, their way was the best. Within a few days, the convict decided that he felt safe enough to return to the general prison population.

A less-confirmable report has it that Mafia boss John Gotti was subject to a murder attempt while he was held in close confinement in Marion Penitentiary in Illinois after his conviction in 1992. How this was possible in Marion is perplexing because he was held in virtual isolation in what can be regarded as the equivalent of protective custody. He generally was confined to a cell for 23 hours a day, the other hour allowed out for exercise and showers and the like, never permitted to speak with or even see another prisoner.

Nevertheless, the rumor was gossiped about by crime reporters, who, however, were unable to gain any confirmation.

psychotic inmates "prison made"

It has been long charged that many prisoners turn psychotic during their confinement, especially those held in "supermax prisons" and those held in security housing units (SHUs) in other high-security institutions. Kept in confinement usually for 23 hours a day with very little human contact for years on end, the mental degeneration that follows is awesome and can be blamed on the architectural, social, and physical violence they face when, certainly in part due to their treatment, they prove incapable of maintaining quiet and following orders. In an interview with writer

Christian Parenti, Dr. Terry Kupers, a leading psychiatrist and one of only a few independent medical experts to have witnessed the operations of SHUs in Indiana, Pennsylvania, and California, stated, "psychotic inmates are—unequivocally—the most disturbed people I've ever seen. They scream and throw feces all over their cells. In a mental hospital you'd never see anything like that! Patients would be sedated or stabilized with drugs. Their psychosis would be interrupted."

The case can be made that the conditions of psychotics in prison is as shocking as anything found by such reformers as Dorothea Dix in the mid-19th century.

Pelican Bay State Prison, the pride of California Corrections as the maximum-security prison and logical successor to Alcatraz as holding the "worst of the worst," has been accused of being the worst of other things as well. In *Lockdown America,* author Parenti reports on a federal-court civil ruling and findings of fact that were "packed with gory, almost unbelievable, details about the routine sadism. . . . It seemed that psychotic prisoners were being beaten, tortured, and left chained in their own excrement for days. In one case a prisoner who had gone mad in solitary confinement was submerged in a vat of boiling water until his skin dissolved." This did not mean there were not better days of "'therapy' for mentally ill prisoners consist[ing] of watching cartoons from inside a phone-booth-sized cage."

While a controversy might rage about television for prison inmates, there did not seem to be any charges of "coddling" in such cases.

"pulling your choke" masturbation

In prison, the phrase *pulling your choke* is used to describe masturbation. Behind bars, masturbation frequently is done openly and a source of pride for many convicts because many others lose the ability to masturbate because of the psychological or physical consequences of incarceration. Therefore, other forms of forced sexual activities are widely-practiced, or prisoner-prostitutes are utilized.

punks sex-possession prisoners

Sex is generally available to prisoners in three forms:

1. Male prostitutes, mainly homosexuals who sell their favors.
2. "Fuck boys," nonhomosexuals who are forced into prostitution by a tough pimp who has a stable of such "stock" that he has forced into the "life" under penalty of severe injury or death. Some prison pimps trade with others to offer fresh talent to the areas in which they operate and who, for a proper offer, will sell one of their possessions to a single inmate who is looking for a mate.
3. Punks, heterosexuals who trade sex with another prisoner for protection. Having accepted a protector, the punk can walk the corridors with immunity because his "sponsor" is a genuine hard-case who generally is feared by other inmates. Punks even exist on death row, as for instance did John LeVasseur, a condemned man facing the death penalty in Virginia's Mecklenburg prison. It can't be said that LeVasseur volunteered for punkdom. He was raped within two weeks of entering death row. Aged 21, LeVasseur could hardly avoid his fate. He was the youngest inmate on death row and at 130 pounds and five feet seven inches, not likely to be able to offer much resistance.

LeVasseur later told a reporter, "One of the inmates said that I had to get it on with him, because if I didn't, then everybody else would think I'm open season. He said we could go through it in three ways: either minimal force; or he could just beat me up, knock me out and do it; or he could beat me up, knock me out and let *everybody* do it. There's no compromise or leaving me alone. Besides my size, I ain't that strong. So I didn't fight. I figured this guy is going to overtake me anyhow, so that's not going to accomplish a damn thing." Actually the victim later reported the rape and several others inflicted on him by the inmate, but he never pressed charges, saying, "I didn't want to die."

It is hardly ever true that the owner and the punk become genuinely interested in one another. The master has little interest in the punk other than for the service he can offer, sexual and otherwise. The punk generally is required to do his owner's laundry and clean his cell. When a master is asked if his punk ever suggests a reversal of the sexual favors, he will generally become incensed. "I'd smack him right through the cell bars," one says.

The masters all regard themselves as heterosexual making do with what is available. Sex is often not the main consideration in prison rape; as in the regular world, having a rape victim is often an expression of power.

The punk does have some rewards, however. He is able to parade through the cell blocks, flaunting his master's protection, so that even tough cons will do nothing to him.

On death row, racial tensions are much less than in the general prison population because all the inmates face eventual execution. Still, there is much competition by black prisoners to own a white punk, again as a symbol of power, although it will be concluded when the first of the two is executed.

R

Ragen, Joseph E. (1896–1971) last of the tough-guy wardens

The description of Joseph E. Ragen, longtime head of Statesville and Joliet penitentiaries, as the last of the tough-guy wardens may be a slight overstatement, but there is little doubt that Hollywood modeled roles of iron disciplinarian prison heads after his image. Ragen ran his twin prisons, some five miles apart, like a king with virtually unchecked power.

He demanded obedience from the inmates as well as from his guards, whom he bossed with paramilitary strictness. After taming Menard Prison in 1933 as much as any such institution could be tamed, Ragen took over at Statesville-Joliet. At the time, politics determined the composition of prison staffs. A Democratic appointee, Ragen fully expected to be fired should there be a change in political control of the state, just as he had dismissed scores of guards when he was given his post. It must be said the majority of his firings were based on performances of the guards.

When a Republican governor took over in 1941, Ragen figured that he was gone and resigned. It was not a popular situation since Ragen was by then regarded as the one man who could put a lid on Joliet. Then in 1942, gangster Roger Touhy escaped with six other convicts, and the governor summoned Ragen back. From that time, Ragen's authority was never challenged again. He was not regarded as an enlightened corrections official and cared little for rehabilitation and far more about security.

Operating in an era devoid of civil-rights revolutions, Ragen did what he did best—enforcing rules, preventing riots and escapes, and reducing prison violence through threats of vigorous crackdowns. Violations of the rules, guards knew, could cost them their jobs. One rule that Ragen enforced was that no guard could be mixed up with inmates or their relatives. He once caught a guard in a hotel with an inmate's wife. Not without a hint of pride, Ragen always noted later, "I didn't get a chance to fire him—he went home, told his wife about it, and shot himself."

Ragen seldom had trouble with critical reporters, simply barring them from his prison to the extent, it was said, that they could not even attend executions as witnesses if they had a black mark against them.

When Ragen retired in 1961 from his twin prisons after 26 years, things changed, and they opened up to public view. Inmates took their complaints to the courts, and the old Ragen discipline broke down. Ragen served as the state's director of public safety for four years and later was a consultant to prisons around the world.

Further reading: *Inside the World's Toughest Prison* by Joseph E. Ragen.

rape as a capital offense generally reserved for black offenders

For a time, the crime of rape was considered in many states very deserving of the death penalty. In many states in the South, it most certainly grew out of the lynch-law justice against blacks who raped white women or committed even the lesser offense of smiling at a white woman.

A personal view on rape as a capital offense has been offered by author William Styron, who reflected on its practice in his home state of Virginia. He notes that the execution of felons has "a long and sturdy tradition" and, in fact, that "no state in the union can claim a greater number of confirmed executions; this is partly due, of course, to Virginia's status as the oldest political jurisdiction in America. But one has always had a sense that in the Old Dominion there exists a particularly strong lust for vengeance."

Styron tells of growing up in the 1930s and 1940s and being "perpetually haunted by news stories, in the paper or on the radio, of condemned men trudging that Last Mile to the electric chair at the state prison in Richmond. Many of them were accused rapists and all of these rapists, without exception, were Negroes. It was not until I'd grown much older, and was able to regard Virginia's use of the death penalty from a critical perspective, that I understood that for more than half a century the state had convicted hundreds of white and black men for rape, but only the black men—fifty-one of them—had been executed. Rape as a cause for the death penalty was eliminated only as recently as 1977."

Critics for the death penalty for rapists had long been opposed by critics who insisted that the presence of the death penalty removed any inhibitions by the perpetrator to finish the job by murdering the victim to lessen the risk of his being identified. In addition, there is now the fact that many men convicted of rape have later been set free with the introduction of DNA findings that eliminated them as the rapist, despite the identification made by the victim and sometimes with concurrence of a male witness who then is found through DNA evidence to be the guilty party.

rape in prison not a sometime thing

Donnie is a youthful offender now doing hard time in an adult facility. He is in his late 20s and faces at least another 20 years behind bars, if he qualifies for his earliest release time. He had had sexual encounters with females during his youth, but that was nothing to compare to his fate behind bars. He has been raped many, many, many times. Rape in prison, he says, is not like it is on the outside. There, a person, male or female, may be raped, but it is a sometime thing. It is different behind bars, Donnie has learned. "Rape here is forever," he says. He has been raped, gang raped, abused, and passed around as a prostitute for his "sponsors" many times. Innocent newcomers, or "fish" as they are referred to in prison jargon, can face the next 30 or 40 years as a regular rape victim, seldom with help from anyone after being "turned out"—this is jargon for a prisoner who finally accepts his fate as a jailhouse whore. In many prisons, rape victims are subjected to what may be considered "benign indifference" by officials—if not something much worse than that.

Eve Powell, now in her 30s, was sentenced to 114 years after she was convicted, at age 13 with four older teenagers, of burglarizing the home of an 85-year-old Miami man who was beaten to death in the process. Sent directly to the maximum security women's prison in Broward County, she was immediately introduced to prison sex and frequently had sex with officers as a teenager. Willingly or not, Eve was a victim of rape, and the officers under regulations faced termination if caught, but this was not much of a worry. Eve herself never gave a thought to turning them in. She was flattered by her forced sex. She called the experiences "affairs" and explained in later years to a reporter, "We're human. We're locked down."

Male rape victims have no choice. Rape is the central reality, if perhaps an invisible one as authorities sometimes do nothing to stop it. By many, it is considered "just desserts" for a criminal past, and no concern is paid to the terrible physical and emotional tortures that thousands of men and women inmates suffer. It is as though rape is simply an unwritten part of an inmate's sentence. Another horror of the wrongfully accused can be testified by inmates now being released after DNA evidence proves them innocent. Understandably, many of these men do not admit directly about the subject although perhaps amazingly some do, bravely, angrily tarring themselves in the public mind in a new way, despite the miscarriages they had endured.

How many prison inmates are subjected to buggery and the like? The literature is sparse compared to reality, and one can pick up a dozen or two books on prisons and find no or only very limited study of the subject. Academic studies are hardly overwhelming in number. A study in a Midwest prison determined that 22 percent of male respondents had admitted to having been raped while behind bars. Even that figure has been judged as being too low because it was based on anonymous self-reporting by the prisoners and thus is probably an underestimation.

Another study regarded by many as offering lowball figures was completed in 1982 at a California state prison; it showed that 14 percent were pressured into having sex against their will. Using such limited estimates, it was still possible to extrapolate that 200,000 inmates are raped each year. Groups like Stop Prisoner Rape would add at least 50 percent to that figure and point out that these estimates hardly measure the rate of terror in prisons and jails and fail to consider inmates who decide to pair off for their protection, nor concern themselves with the higher rates at juvenile facilities.

Youthful offenders sent to adult facilities have been quoted as wondering as they enter how long they will be able to avoid sexual aggression. An estimate can be gleaned from a 1992 issue of the *International Journal of the Sociology of Law* by Robert Dumond, a mental-health clinician with the Massachusetts Department of Corrections. Dumond wrote that the chances of a young prisoner avoiding rape in an adult facility are "almost zero. . . . He'll get raped within the first 24 or 48 hours. That's almost standard."

After that, the die is cast, and the prison grapevine instantly learns that the newcomer is vulnerable. He is then subjected to continual sexual assaults, a nightmare that will go on for years—or until, as sometimes happens, a young prisoner commits suicide. The early rapes may be the work of a single powerful attack or in a gangbang routine, sometimes known as a "blanket party," whereby the attackers throw a blanket over the victim's head so that he cannot identify them to prison authorities, also so that if he turns out to be a tough resister, he won't know where to strike.

The charge has been made that prison authorities are singularly disinterested in rocking the boat concerning prison rape to the extent that, at the very least, it would bog down the prison investigating a myriad of embarrassing cases. This is so despite a 1994 Supreme Court ruling that required penitentiary officials to protect prisoners from sexual predation. One civil-rights attorney asks in a variation of Andrew Jackson's famous dictum, "How many troops does the Supreme Court have?" Denial in such cases, he adds, "lets the system off the hook on lawsuits." Thus, in Massachusetts, officials continued denying an explosive prison rape as part of an exposé in the *Boston Globe* even while the victim was in the hospital undergoing rectal surgery.

According to Christian Parenti who researched many of the cases mentioned here in *Lockdown America,* "Nor is it uncommon for prison officials to 'accidentally' lose crucial evidence and 'forget' to conduct medical exams when rapes are reported." Such a case was reported in the *Indianapolis Star* in 1996, two years after the Supreme Court's ruling.

Terms such as *slaveocracy* and *sex-chattel system* have been used to describe the fate of prison rape victims and the official indifference and, indeed, collusion of correction guards and their superiors. Parenti reports a 1997 case involving a "28-year-old married man used as a prostitute by a prison gang which peddled him from cell to cell in full view of guards. In at least two cases, COs even brought customers to the victim's cell or escorted him down the tier to other cells where customers raped him and then paid the inmate pimps with cigarettes, drugs, and candy."

The inmate eventually contracted HIV, a not-uncommon situation for sex slaves, but this was not considered worthy enough for winning damages in a lawsuit.

Wilbert Rideau, the award-winning and acclaimed dean of prison journalists, cites a young inmate in an Angola, Louisiana, maximum-security prison (often called the South's worst prison), who sheds light on how the administration enforced or did not enforce rape control:

> *Everything and everybody in here worked to keep you a whore—even the prison. If a whore went to the authorities, all they'd do is tell you that since*

you already are a whore, they couldn't do nothing for you, and for you to go back to the dorm and settle down and be a good old lady. Hell, they'd even call the whore's old man up and tell him to take you back down and keep you quiet . . . the most you'd get out of complaining is some marriage counseling, with them talking to you and your old man to iron out your difficulties.

Through the years, there have been a number of prison guards who become so sickened by prison rapes and the attitudes toward them that they finally turn whistle blowers. One Louisiana CO was quoted in the *Los Angeles Daily News:* "There are prison administrators who use inmate gangs to help manage the prison. Sex and human bodies become the coin of the realm. Is inmate 'X' writing letters to the editor of the local newspaper and filing lawsuits? Or perhaps he threw urine or feces on an employee? 'Well, Joe, you and Willie and Hank work him over, but be sure you don't break any bones and send him to the hospital. If you do a good job, I'll see that you get the blondest boy in the next shipment.'"

This situation also allows for a "profit" that keepers can gain, especially from newcomers—the manufacturing of snitches. If the prisoner agrees to turn snitch and will offer some valuable information, he is accorded "protection." How much that guarantee really offers on a 24-hour basis is debatable, and snitching, newcomers learn, can be a life-threatening situation. However, the offer is not extended to all incoming fish. The *Boston Globe* reported that one inmate who sought protection for fear of contracting AIDS was simply told by guards at Shirley State Prison: "Welcome to Shirley. Toughen up, punk."

The threat of prison rape is used to advantage by the entire justice system. Defense lawyers insist that the threat of prison rape is used to cut sentences through plea bargaining by some prosecutors to force inexperienced defendants to enter a guilty plea so that, at least, the defendants will not be sent to a notoriously tough prison. Such prison threats will hardly meet much disapproval by many judges who will regard such threats and pressure as being nothing more than "investigative tools."

At times, some prosecutors can overstep the use of the tactic. The *Seattle Times* reported a case in which a U.S. attorney seeking to extradite three Canadians on fraud charges leaned on them by warning them that if any of the trio resisted extradition, they would be guaranteed a long, hard prison term as "the boyfriend of a very bad man." The comment so incensed the presiding Canadian judge that, for a time, he blocked the extradition that he was obligated to order.

Prisoners are, at times, subjected to the added horrors of staff-on-inmate strong-arm rape, generally involving a guard simply overpowering the inmate. Such incidents, according to prisoner Victor Hassine in his much acclaimed *Life Without Parole,* a book sanctioned by reform-minded commissions of corrections and now required reading in a number of criminal justice courses, do not take place openly in the general population sections but rather in the isolation sections. Generally, Hassine says, guards can win their ways with such prisoners by concentrating on those who have no personal or written contact with family or friends on the outside. Staffers can learn how to pick and choose by having access to personal files. In other cases, inmates can be denied entitlements such as positive parole reports unless the prisoner agrees. In other cases, prisoners are forced into cooperation under threats of infractions of discipline write-ups, real or fancied.

Among female prisoners, the preferred seduction method of guard-rapists is pressure, strong-arm tactics hardly ever needing to be used.

Rapes are hardly uncommon; even on death row, some of the stronger doomed men have "punks" among their numbers and have offered them to others for pay as well. A famous executed man in Virginia, Dennis Stockton, kept a diary and had many excerpts printed in a major state newspaper, leading to the dismissal of many prison personnel. His writing drew attention to cases of bribed guards, marijuana plants, home-brew alcohol, weapons stashes, unlocked doors, and jailhouse sex, including a prison guard's late-night oral servicing through cell bars by a doomed man and his return of the favor later.

As prison administrations do little or nothing to prevent rapes, a reaction has set in on the part of some prisoners to prevent such sexual atrocities, including the opinion of some that rapes are a condition that administrators use for their own advantage. This leads to some revolts and attacks on prison gangs that are used by some institutions to maintain order. These gangs are permitted to operate at will and lessen the power of other groups. One Pennsylvania gang leader operated in such fashion until there was an uprising by inmates in which he and his cohorts were attacked in the prison corridors in a surprise move. The leader barely made it to the protection of guards and had to be transferred out to another prison that same night. The following day several of his gang members were stabbed in separate incidents and many others had to go into self-lockup.

In Angola, inmates led by "Hooks" Wallace organized an opposition to rape attacks on weaker men. They stood in the way of fresh fish and saw to it that frightened newcomers were screened away from marauders and protected until they felt safe to be on their own. In one case, a convict named Ervin Braux died trying to stop a prisoner from being raped. According to the prison grapevine, Wallace and some of his supporters were framed for the murder of a white guard and were confined to solitary, demonstrating, it was claimed, the vital nature of rape to control overcrowded prisoners.

In Walla Walla Penitentiary in Washington, a group headed by Ed Mead organized Men Against Sexism. Composed of gay and bisexual inmates, they became known as "tough fags" and used violence to protect weaker prisoners from rape. There were reports of the tough-fag militancy spreading to other institutions and of the movement gaining recognition on some university campuses.

However, organized resistance is not much more than a sometime thing in a prison atmosphere. Individuals are on their own, usually, to withstand attacks. Inmates come to realize their only hope is strong resistance that will convince marauders to pass them by for easier victims. A New York prisoner recently freed of a wrongful conviction told interviewers that the horrors of prison was an endless struggle. One prisoner who successfully beat off rapists was sent gifts of cigarettes and candy by a known marauder. The would-be victim took the booty and promptly traded it for a metal pipe. When the would-be seducer showed up, his quarry beat him savagely.

recidivism contrary findings on repeaters

A massive study a few decades ago of nearly 88,000 persons arrested in a two-year period showed that at least 82 percent had been arrested previously, 70 percent had been convicted previously, and 46 percent of those convicted had been imprisoned for three months or more. Among those arrested for murder, rape, robbery, or felonious assault, 75 percent had already been convicted of a crime. Other studies in some states have come up with higher figures; in both California and Massachusetts, it was found that 85 percent of male felons imprisoned in California and Massachusetts previously had been in correctional institutions.

But other studies point to a different conclusion. Studies of recidivism among parolees put the repeater rate at about 25 percent. It is true that such a figure may not be reliable in many cases because the figures only represent cases of recidivism known to parole officers, and in many areas parole staffs do not have the human resources needed to assemble complete facts. It is also true that many areas with more supervision tend to report a larger number of crime repeaters. On the other hand, noting that 85 percent of those returned to prison had been convicted before does not exactly mean that 85 percent of all released persons are crime repeaters. Thus, many conclusions about recidivism are subject to dispute.

The fact is that all types of custody—probation, prisons, or parole—have considerable numbers of recidivists. This has been an impetuous factor behind the growing chorus of hard-line demands to "throw the book" at criminals and, especially, to eliminate parole. Serious studies to determine how to compare the recidivist rates among like groups of prisoners are quite difficult to set up. However, one obvious solution to that problem appeared in a landmark decision of the U.S. Supreme Court, which presented a unique opportunity for analyzing the problem—and one that has been largely ignored by the hard-liners' approach. The Court, in *Gideon v. Wainwright,* threw out the convictions of more than 1,000 indigent Florida prisoners on the ground that they had not been represented by lawyers. This presented the Florida Corrections Department a unique opportunity to set up two groups of 110 each of recently released inmates who had just completed their original sentences and 110 inmates who had been abruptly released far short of their original sentences as a result of the *Gideon* decision. Care was taken to match up as much as possible the individual characteristics of the members of the two groups. In the 28 months following their release, 25.4 percent of those who had fulfilled their sentences had committed another crime. During that same period, the prisoners set free by the *Gideon* ruling had a repeat crime rate of only 13.6 percent.

Many who considered long imprisonment as the solution to the recidivism problem have found the "logical conclusion of this research . . . shocking," said Leonard Orland, professor of law at the University of Connecticut. The researchers at the Florida Corrections Department concluded, "Baldly stated, it is that if we, today, turned loose all the inmates of our prisons without regard to the length of their sentences and, with only some exceptions, without regard to their previous offenses, we might *reduce* the recidivism rate over what it would be if we kept every prisoner incarcerated until his sentence expired."

Clearly, studies in the future need to focus on the repeat crime rates under programs of amnesty, pardon, and the like. Some findings developed variables, some perhaps more relevant than others. An Illinois study found that on release, younger, black, and single offenders are more likely to be rearrested than older, white, married offenders. Reformers found nothing unusual in such determinations. They saw nothing unexpected in the fact that younger prisoners doing time are more likely to use prison as a "learning experience" to find ways of more lucrative criminal activities and that the poor young from racially distressed neighborhoods were simply being returned to the areas where their criminal offenses had first flourished. Perhaps more interesting and undoubtedly less known to the public was the fact that most repeat offenses tend to involve property offenses rather than violent crimes.

But the main reason against abandoning probation and parole in the name of fighting recidivism is confirmed by the very fact that doing so has actually failed in the main, that to do so would instantly more than double the needs for more prisons, something that would leave the corrections system in a shambles and face an ever-growing influx of more and more prisoners that would stretch the system even further.

Reformers use the words of a New York City judge who strongly declared that critics of the New York parole system "should consider the fact that we do not measure the success rate of an operating room in a hospital by the number of bodies in the morgue. We measure the success rate by indicating how many individuals, after the operation, are well and able to function and are able to contribute."

By the beginning of the new century, observers noted growing appreciation of a long-disparaged word, *rehabilitation,* and a willingness of a growing number of persons involved in parole and probation to risk hard-liner wrath, convinced that their course was actually the antirecidivism way.

Rector, Ricky Ray (?–1992) brain-damaged executed man

The execution of Ricky Ray Rector in 1992 is often cited as a case in which a clearly brain-damaged African American should not have been executed and was so only for political reasons. Rector was convicted of killing a police officer in Arkansas in 1981, and even the fact that he had had a lobotomy aided his case. At the time, Gov. Bill Clinton was running for president, and not only did he refuse to halt the execution, but actually broke off his campaign at the height of the New Hampshire primary to preside over the lethal-injection execution of Rector.

Critics of the execution, including probably most of Clinton's most ardent supporters, now freely admit that his act was guided in part at least to give him the stamp of a law-and-order candidate.

It is perhaps instructive to consider Rector's thought processes and actions hours before his execution when obviously posturing would have been of little value. According to the *Washington Post,* hours before he died, Rector "carefully put aside the slice of pecan pie that came with his last meal. Rector always liked to eat his dessert right before bedtime, and he apparently expected to return to his cell for his pie after he had received the fatal injection ordered by Arkansas Gov. Bill

Clinton. . . . Just hours before he died, Rector told [his attorney] Rosenzweig: 'I'm going to vote for Clinton in the fall.'"

red shirts unbreakable prison toughs
Most prison inmates see their incarceration as an effort by the authorities to "break" their spirits, and they resist accordingly. Some do so passively, others much more aggressively and defiantly. Those among the latter who demonstrate to other inmates that their spirits cannot be broken become known in prison lingo as "red shirts." Their supreme test comes when they are consigned to the "Hole," or dungeon, and then demonstrate to their own standards the ability to cope with guards on a more equal basis.

The term appears to have originated in the Michigan City State Prison in the 1920s, where determined convicts, in the eyes of themselves and their fellow inmates, effectively countered the boredom, the beatings, and the privations to which they were subjected. Even when forced to sleep naked on bare cement floors in the hole, these rebellious inmates hardened themselves by not eating their daily ration of a half-loaf of bread, instead molding a few of them into a pillow. They suffered strong pangs of hunger during the first three days but after that were said to have achieved an almost pleasant state of euphoria that would numb them and leave them unfazed by any other harsh punishment. Their secret was that they found they were capable of punishing themselves more severely than the establishment could.

The red shirts also used play as a method of countering solitary confinement, utilizing what is now recognized as a children's game, that of Battleship. Two prisoners in separate cells could mark off 100 squares numbered A to J laterally and 1 to 10 horizontally. Each player had five groupings valued from one to five ships, which could be positioned along connecting squares. One of the players would "commence firing" by calling out something like "B-8." If his opponent had a ship located on that square, he would announce it was hit. According to one convict's description of this prison game: "For years the more obtuse guards wondered what was being plotted when they heard men calling, 'B-7' 'Miss.' 'C-8' 'Destroyer sunk.'"

The game of course required the personal honesty of the players, a trait not usually expected among convicted criminals, but prison old-timers insisted that the game was on the square because the convict code regarded the game itself as flouting prison rules that disallowed communication among prisoners and, therefore, a higher reward than winning as such. Some convict-historians insist that the game of Battleship was invented behind bars, but this can probably be disputed. Nevertheless, it was a valuable form of protest in the red-shirt arsenal.

Sometimes red-shirt defiance takes the form of baiting guards into actions they do not wish to take. In a Wisconsin maximum-security prison, some high-risk inmates retaliated against what they regarded as painful and unnecessary cell extractions by covering their cell windows so that guards could not see inside the cell. This forced the guards to "suit up" in body armor, helmets with visors, neck supports, and heavy leather gloves so that they could enter the cell to check on the inmates and remove the coverings. Suiting up is a rigorous job and in this case was compounded by the fact that a total of 26 cell extractions were required in a row. As one inmate later reported triumphantly, "Five hours and 26 'cell extractions' later . . . guards were tired and mad. They put in a lot of work that day." Obviously, the inmates did not expect to win any concessions by their defiance—but defiance was the game as far as they were concerned.

release-from-prison trauma basic problem for ex-offenders
In *Crime and Criminology,* Sue Titus Reid points out that two of the major problems facing ex-convicts upon release are the difficulty of finding jobs and the continued discrimination and harassment. Reid cites this as indicating why some released prisoners are traumatically affected and warns that if the dilemma is not solved, "their chances of returning to the institution on additional charges will be greatly enhanced."

Joanne Page, for years director of the Fortune Society in New York City, an ex-offenders support group, sees a similarity in the reactions of many released persons following their long incarceration and those of soldiers who return home from war.

The ex-convict has learned to cope with imprisonment and with the problems there but is now thrown into an environment of freedom. Many offenders find it hard to trust and are in fear of the unknown. Thus, they react as they did during incarceration. They are jostled in the subway and are tempted to react as they did in prison by fighting back. If someone reaches across them in a washroom to reach a paper towel, they may see this as the first move in an attack on them. Some may see this as a start of a homosexual advance, which they thought they had left behind them in prison. According to experts working with ex-offenders, they see everything in terms of black-and-white with little shades of gray. Even if someone seems to be staring at them (or perhaps deep in thought and not mindful of how or where they are looking), that may be seen as a precursor to some form of aggression on the inside.

For similar reasons, many ex-prisoners have trouble in their relations with a family member or loved one. Often, ex-prisoners have difficulty in their relationships and are incapable of talking the matter out fully. This results at times in a lack of communication and brooding or quite possibly in a violent blowup.

In a job environment, rising tensions can result in a loss of temper or in long periods of absenteeism, endangering their employment, which is often required under terms of their release. Such released persons need deep counseling about their situation and the realization that they must learn to cope with their new environment because the environment will be either oblivious or indifferent to the situation—often with no sense of malice.

Rideau, Wilbert (1942–) award-winning prison journalist

He is recognized as the most accomplished prisoner in the United States today, even though behind bars. Wilbert Rideau has served almost 40 years into the 21st century for the murder of a bank teller and bank robbery. It had taken three trials to convict him in the first place: His first conviction was overturned because of excessive pretrial publicity and the second for improper jury selection, and the third resulted in the death sentence. After 10 years on death row, Rideau was freed of the death-penalty threat when the U.S. Supreme Court for a time halted all executions. Rideau now faced a sentence of natural life.

Since then, Rideau's case has gathered innumerable sympathizers who have cited his clear rehabilitation. Shortly after his release from death row, Rideau took over the editorship of *The Angolite,* the prison's inmate journal, and raised it to a level where it is regarded by many observers as the best prisoner publication in the nation. In 1992 he and Ron Wikberg coedited *Life Sentences: Rage and Survival Behind Bars,* a book that has become required in many criminal-justice courses. The book culls *Angolite* material that is instructive on how what is regarded as a particularly harsh southern state prison operates and its vast differences from a northern prison. The section labeled "The Sexual Jungle" is frequently cited as the most incisive description and explanation of rape behind bars. Other moving sections deal with such subjects as life on death row and prisoners dying from natural causes in prison.

Rideau has acknowledged his crimes and takes full responsibility for them, but he has pointed out frequently that nearly every other Louisiana prisoner in his circumstances received a commutation of sentence. According to Rideau's supporters, he has probably fallen victim to his own acclaim and success in the outside world. Had he not had such a high profile, they said, the governor would probably issue him a pardon, but because he had achieved such fame, governors had to fear that they would be considered soft on crime, not a very good posture in Louisiana. The state's pardon board has consistently sided with Rideau's supporters and recommended that he be set free, but governors have all refused to go along with the board's recommendation, which is almost always otherwise automatic.

As it is, Rideau enjoyed considerable freedom on his activities, moving into broadcasting and filmmaking. His 1998 film, *The Farm,* earned international recognition as a grim study of life inside Angola, was a cowinner of the Grand Prize Award at the Sundance Film Festival, and received an Academy Award nomination for Best Documentary. Rideau's tracing of the fate of a half-dozen inmates—an armed robber, a drug dealer, a rapist, a wife-killer, and two other murderers—proves to be a wrenching experience for both the ordinary filmgoer and the seasoned, even hard-

Wilbert Rideau listens to a question during an interview in the offices of the prison newspaper of Louisiana State Penitentiary in Angola. During his time in prison he has become an award-winning prison magazine editor, lectured extensively, and made an Academy Award–nominated film. (AP/Wide World Photos)

ened professional. It is a grim portrayal of lost hopes and remorse and an inevitable study of a sense of mortality.

In late 2000, Rideau and his supporters gained heart when the U.S. Court of Appeals once more vacated his sentence, saying that the grand jury that indicted him improperly excluded blacks from the grand jury. The court ordered the case sent back to state court. The state appealed, but the U.S. Supreme Court rebuffed the move. In July 2001, prosecutors decided to indict Rideau anew after almost four decades since the original crime and retry him for robbery and murder.

Meanwhile Rideau has not had an easy time with the prison administration in Angola. The current warden, Burl Cain, is often described as rather hostile to Rideau as deserving of being treated by some as a fully rehabilitated citizen and worthy of honor and respect. When the Louisiana Bar Association decided to award Rideau with its

Excellence in Legal Journalism for his film on the death penalty, accepted procedure was to allow Rideau to attend the awards dinner. Earlier, under a previous warden, he was allowed to go to Washington, D.C., with an escort to accept honors at two press conventions.

This warden took a different tack. Without notifying Rideau of his award, he sent his first deputy to the affair and kept the plaque in his office.

See also: *ANGOLITE, THE.*

"right guys" and "shots" good and bad inmates
Any study of prison socialization will soon discover that inmates know how to separate the good from the bad and how to find the grays in between. Generally, convicts divide their fellow inmates into two basic groups. One is the "shots" or "politicians" who have pull of some kind and hold prison positions that allow them to distribute food and exploit other privileges. They use their position to extort money and other services from the mass of the unprivileged. They are hated of course, just as by contrast the "right guys" win much respect. Of them, sociologist Hans Reimer wrote: "They are men who can be always trusted, who do not abuse lesser inmates, who are invariably loyal to their class—the convicts. They are not wanton trouble-makers but they are expected to stand up for their rights as convicts, to get what they can from the prison officials, to never permit an opportunity to pass from which they might secure anything from a better job to freedom."

In various prisons, the terminology may vary slightly, but the meaning is the same. One old timer in Joliet said that inmates tried to judge newcomers to determine if they would act like "men," that is to say, members of the elite among the cons. The newcomers, said the old-timer, had to have principles that they would not sacrifice, such as loyalty to his fellows, while disdaining the rats and finks and sharpies and wolves. Men, according to this credo, would share whatever they had with their friends and "refused to act like an animal in spite of the grinding horror of prison life," and thus such a prisoner "won the respect of his fellows whose respect was worth having."

The prisoners were able to distinguish some exceptions to their rule but one grounded in a strong reality. That was the prison "peddler," a sharp operator whose motto was "anything for money." But he was a man, inmates knew, who might be needed. As one account put it, "Not a man you liked, but a man you might need; not a man to inform on you, but not a man to trust beyond the point where his material interest coincided with your own. He'd get you a comfortable mattress for a price; get you a quart of whisky—for a price; get you a law book—contraband—a box of cigars, extra writing paper, a uniform made to your measure." In summary peddlers could be utilized on the prison version of "let the buyer beware."

See also: "TRUSTY."

right to counsel *Gideon v. Wainwright* decision
It hardly seemed likely that Clarence Earl Gideon, a 51-year-old fragile and stooped convict at Florida State Prison at Raiford, could shake up the prison system so much. He was indigent, was friendless on the outside, and had no one on his correspondence list. Gideon was not a violent man, but he was in and out of police trouble for various violations—and he was in and out of prison. At his latest trial, he was convicted of breaking and entering a poolroom with intent to commit a misdemeanor, which was a felony under Florida law.

He argued that he was entitled to a lawyer at the trial because he had no money, but the judge turned him down, saying under state law an indigent was not entitled to a court-appointed lawyer except in a case that could result in a death sentence. Gideon was vociferous on his claim but was convicted and sentenced to five years. On January 8, 1962, the U.S. Supreme Court received a large envelope from prisoner #003826 in Florida. It contained a request written in pencil for the High Court to hear his case.

Gideon's case was accepted, and he was given an attorney from a leading Washington, D.C., law firm to represent him. The argument was made and won that the right of a poor person to have legal representation in even a noncapital case was established. The Supreme Court held that a person "too poor to hire a lawyer, cannot be assured a fair trial unless counsel is provided for him. . . .

The right of one charged with crime to counsel may not be deemed fundamental and essential to fair trials in some countries, but it is in ours."

The *Gideon v. Wainwright* decision in 1963 caused an earthquake in Florida prisons. As a result, more than 1,000 indigent convictions were thrown out because the defendants had not be accorded a defense lawyer.

If that was to be a problem, at least the Florida Corrections Department used the special situation to do some different research. It set up two groups of 110 recently released inmates, the first 110 being composed of those who had completed their original sentence and the other 110 being composed of inmates who had been abruptly released far short of their original sentences as a result of the *Gideon* decision. Care was exercised to match up the individual characteristics of the members of the two groups as much as possible. In the 28 months following their release, 25.4 percent of those who had fulfilled their sentences had committed another crime. During that same period, the prisoners freed by the *Gideon* ruling showed a repeat rate of only 13.6 percent.

Many who considered long imprisonment as the answer to the recidivism problem have, in the words of Leonard Orland, professor of law at the University of Connecticut, found the "logical conclusion of this research . . . shocking." The researchers at the Florida Corrections Department concluded, "Baldly stated, it is that if we, today, turned loose all the inmates of our prisons without regard to the length of their sentences and, with only some exceptions, without regard to their previous offenses, we might *reduce* the recidivism rate over what it would be, if we kept each prisoner incarcerated until his sentence expired."

These results can be said to have cried out for further studies on repeat crime rates under programs of amnesty and pardon. However, not long after *Gideon,* public opinion hardened to a get-tough-on-criminals stance, and for the last few decades of the century, reform and such findings were hardly what was wanted.

Rikers Island "house of pain"

It was labeled by New York City councilman Peter Vallone "the largest penal colony in the world"; it is one of the most violent as well. New York's Rikers Island is situated in the East River and is only accessible by bridge. It is a massive complex with a fluctuating convict population of about 15,000. There are 10 main buildings, and it holds all sorts of inmates. The jail holds parole violators of both the city and state, sex offenders, sentenced drug addicts, and those facing murder charges or lesser charges. There is one building for women and two for prisoners with special needs.

But the worst spot is the special disciplinary section, where, as the *New York Times* put it, corrections officers battle with violent prisoners for control of what has been called the "house of pain." Tough convicts attack other inmates and corrections officers; guards engage in what has been described as "gruesome" combat with more to be expected in an Amnesty International report on some backwater country. It is often a no-man's land for guards. One horrid incident that typified the violence in the house of pain was the mugging of a guard inside the prison; he was trapped by three inmates at a stairwell. The guard ended up with a broken jaw and rib, and he was robbed of his jewelry including a gold chain. Guards often were regarded as eligible victims.

There are probably at least 1,000 gang members in Rikers, an estimate regarded on the low side. The gang members defiantly wear beads around their necks to show their affiliations. Latin Kings (big in Connecticut) wear black and gold, and the Netas (originally a Puerto Rican gang) white, red, and gold beads. Gang members also routinely use hand signals to communicate with one another in defiance of the rules that the guards are supposed to enforce.

In an effort to maintain control of the house of pain, it was determined that when prisoners were put in the special disciplinary unit, they often faced "greeting beatings" as a portent of the brutality they could later expect. Common were cases of jail supervisors ordering assaults on antagonistic inmates. In the warfare to control the section, prisoners ended up, by one medical count, with 50 cases of broken bones and head injuries, often resulting in damage to internal organs. At least 35 men had busted eardrums, a painful injury that often causes hearing loss.

For a long time, until about 1998, when a crackdown by officials was imposed because of class-action lawsuits, officials insisted that the worst problems were being handled. The court record was replete with guards meting out punishment and laughing about it over beer. One custom was for prisoners to receive head wounds in beatings that occurred while the victim was in handcuffs. Many were "beaten down," as a guard called it, in isolated areas, sometimes for mouthing off. Some had their heads held in toilet bowls while guards flushed the toilets. A class-action lawsuit brought by 15 inmates was settled by the city to avoid greater restrictions on the institution. The city admitted many abuses and admitted that the officers covered them up. Through the years, the city paid $2 million to settle suits, and several corrections officers were convicted of criminal abuse. Depositions by former guards, wardens, and other corrections officials suggested that for years poor training and weak supervision left many guards thinking that they could rough up recalcitrant inmates whenever they wished. Some national prison analysts said that they had never seen a jail where excessive force was so routine. One expert, Vincent N. Nathan, reported that the Rikers punitive unit for many years occupied "the third ring of hell in the field of corrections in the United States."

This was only possible well into the mid-1990s because of a hands-off policy by high-ranking officials. What is more, the cover-ups that occurred were described as being so transparent that they were "almost comical." Beyond the filing of false reports, some guards punched and kicked one another so that they could claim that they had been acting in self-defense. Another trick was to rub carbon paper on their cheeks to create bruises and some who seemed more seriously injured after self-beatings "were all laughing and even stopped and got a six-pack of beer for the ride to the hospital." In one case, after the beating of seven inmates on suspicion that they might be planning a disturbance, a supervisor threw down a jagged shank and told his men to report that the inmate had brandished it.

The most tragic result of the hands-off policy involved a prisoner, Anthony Bryant, in the disciplinary unit who died shortly after he was beaten by guards. A supervisor with a reputation as being overzealous himself was ordered to investigate the case. The supervisor's examination had to be regarded as uniquely superficial because he reported back three days after the inmate's death to say that the dead inmate—Bryant—should be arrested for assaulting the staff.

Eventually, in the later 1990s, the Corrections Department sought to fix problems by setting up a new facility unit where 300 cameras were mounted on the walls. However, the court records show, and department officials admitted, that in the first months of the new building, prisoners were injured in altercations with guards outside camera range. When squads of guards entered cells to extract troublesome prisoners from their cells, they were supposed to record the entire procedure with hand-held video cameras, but they often did not do so. The new commissioner, Bernard Kerik, who later became police commissioner in the Giuliani administration, was credited with taking additional steps to improve matters by changing the jail's leadership to give guards better training in using nonviolent holds and pepper spray to disable uncooperative prisoners. Additional searches were made for weapons and violent criminals were charged with new crimes rather than simply given detention. In recent years, stabbings and slashings among prisoners were said to have declined 80 percent.

By the turn of the century, it could be said that cases of guard-inmate violence had definitely decreased under the Kerik program, but it hardly meant that Rikers did not remain a tinderbox. The Legal Aid attorney who had handled the successful lawsuit on behalf of maltreated inmates still had his doubts that the reforms were that complete. He noted that, after the settlement had been reached, another prisoner's face was lacerated in a fight with guards right after a handheld camera was turned off, and the attorney continued to have doubts that jail cameras were being used properly.

Rikers continued to have a raft of additional woes. The institution came under severe criticism for its attitude toward mentally ill inmates being released. In a sense, it could be understood; there was criticism that Rikers was incapable of dealing with the incredible mix of prisoners that it must handle. In the course of a year as many as 25,000 inmates receive mental-health treatment, many in Rikers. A state supreme court judge ruled that the city was required to arrange for continued care for mentally ill inmates and could not, in the judge's words, simply "drop them in the middle of the night at a subway station with $3 in tokens or a MetroCard fare." While New York State at least supplied inmates with a supply of their medications on release, New York City did not. The Giuliani administration announced an appeal, claiming inmates had no legal right to the kind of prerelease planning required for mental patients under state law.

It was clear that Rikers could still be accused of offering inmates a new kind of pain in what was, in part, a house of torment.

Rockefeller, John D., Jr. (1839–1937) financial supporter of eugenic prisons

One of America's wealthiest men, John D. Rockefeller Jr. was a committed backer of the eugenic movement of crime control whereby criminality often was judged to be an inherited trait, carried through the generations in the "germ plasm." The solution to the eugenicists simply was a matter of preventing "carriers" from "breeding." This could be accomplished by holding criminals with bad "germ plasm" either for life or until they could no longer have children. In some states, sterilization of prisoners was carried out, and "eugenic prisons" established.

Rockefeller carried the idea of eugenic prisons a bit further in New York State by becoming part owner of the women's reformatory at Bedford Hills and paying for research carried out on female mental defects and psychopathy. Even in more recent developments of private prisons, nothing since has approached the ownership of a state penal institution by Rockefeller. By the mid-1920s, the eugenics movement was in decline, and its beliefs concerning "germ plasm" were dismissed as pseudoscience.

See also: DAVIS, KATHARINE BEMENT; EUGENICS.

Further reading: *Prisons in America* by Nicole Hahn Rafter and Debra L. Stanley.

John D. Rockefeller, Jr. (AP/Wide World Photos)

rodeo events in prison

When Sam Lewis took charge of the Arizona Department of Corrections in the mid-1980s, he presented a strong get-tough posture to the system. He cut out a number of programs that appeared to be coddling prisoners. One was to ban the prison rodeo, presumably because it offered prisoners too much fun.

There has been no such reaction at Angola, the grim maximum-security Louisiana State Penitentiary, which has held its rodeo since the mid-1960s. It is regarded as a bizarre spectacle, with murderers, rapists, and armed robbers competing in the annual event during which these lifers, without the chance of parole, have been trampled and gored by bucking bulls and broncos before thousands of cheering fans. The rodeo, billed as "The Wildest Show in the South," lures in the public with promises in the local paper of untrained cons being "thrown every which way." The convicts, who may envision themselves in a gladiatorial spectacle for which they may well receive shattered ribs, punctured lungs, and broken shoulders, wrists, or ribs daily, compete for a handful of dollar prizes and at least a momentary escape from their normal prison existence. (In one case, a rider taking part in a past slapstick event called "Buddy Pick-Up" died of a heart attack.)

A relatively new sporting event at Angola is called Convict Poker. It is played without cards. Four folding chairs are positioned around a bright-red table, and four convicts take up their positions around the table as though to play cards. Then the emcee calls out "Brrrrring on the dealer!" The dealer is a huge black bull that is electric-prodded into the arena. The convicts sit there quietly, hoping to be the last man sitting and thus win a $100 prize. The action can start off relatively subdued as bulls aren't too attracted to stationary targets. The bull may simply circle the men's backs as they sit there palms flat and fingers spread. If after three minutes with more than one contestant still sitting, the person who has moved the very least is declared the winner and gets the prize money.

But some movement is guaranteed as a clown appears to taunt the bull, tossing his own hat at the bull and then posing as a bull pawing the ground with his hands as though ready to charge. Still getting no response, the clown jumps up on the table, shuffling his feet, ready to jump over the convicts' heads if the bull charges. Finally, the bull brushes right up against one of the men's shoulders with a sort of side caress of horn. It is enough to send one man running out of the contest. The bull simply moves a few yards away and does not pursue him. The clown picks up the vacated chair and hurls it into the bull's snout.

Now the bull is offended and slams its horns into one of the convicts, but happily it hits the back of the folding chair instead of the man's kidney. The man goes down, and the bull is ready to spear or stomp. But then the third man panics and darts for the fence. The bull catches a glimpse of him and goes after this new moving target, steadily closing the distance. The third man climbs over the fence with a bare 12 inches to spare. Convict Poker is over to some screams, some applause, some laughter, and some terror. The reactions are predictable and apparently acceptable because the players are all murderers. There is also some disappointment because there had been no real goring.

Still, there was the sentiment, as in the baseball chant, to "wait till next year." Besides, there were other events later in the day, such as bull riding with a renewed chance of resultant genuine mayhem, and although the participating convicts might be unhappy if they were not winners, at least, for a while, they could revel at being an Angola cowboy. Again, wait till next year; the convicts will definitely be there.

Further reading: *God of the Rodeo* by Daniel Bergner.

Rose Man of Sing Sing (1858–1930) murderer
Charles Chapin

In the lore of Sing Sing prison, few inmates enjoyed more notoriety than Charles Chapin, the legendary city editor of the *New York Evening World* for 20 years until he murdered his wife of 35 years in 1918. Viewed by his underlings as tyrannical, he was noted for firing reporters on Christmas Eve. Once, when his staff uncovered a murder that had been labeled an accident, Chapin chortled that it had "been a good day. . . . I've started a man on the way to the electric chair."

Staffers tried to return Chapin's attitudes in kind. Once, when he was too ill to work, a reporter, Irvin S. Cobb, volunteered, "I hope it's nothing trivial."

Chapin's personal life was chaotic. He associated with the superrich well beyond his means. Fifty thousand dollars left him by his great-uncle, Russell Sage, the wealthy financier, evaporated in stock-market losses. His debts piled up, and by 1917, he feared that if he died—he was in poor health—his wife Nellie would be left penniless. He took his wife to Washington on a holiday trip along with a revolver he borrowed from an aide to the New York City police commissioner. He planned to put a gardenia in his buttonhole—he was known to love flowers more than people—attend a musical show, and shoot her and himself to death, but he lost his nerve.

Chapin continued in his strapped financial condition for another year, but in September 1918, he shot his wife to death as she lay asleep. He headed to Central Park, determined to shoot himself, but he ended up in Brooklyn's Prospect Park sitting on a bench reading—true to his newsman background—his press notices after his wife's body was discovered. Then he surrendered, telling police, "This is the first time in five years that I have been happy. The sooner I go to the electric chair, the better."

However, Chapin did not get the chair, ending up with a sentence of 20 years to life. In Sing Sing, he became a most unusual prisoner, becoming editor of the prison newspaper, *The Star of Hope,* later renamed *The Bulletin.* Filling it with the type of spicy items that marked the *World,* he printed lurid confessions of inmates, telling them to keep their tales "heavy on the human interest, tell 'em all about love." Because quite a few convicts had relationships that went far beyond love, there was a reaction in Albany, the state capital. *The Bulletin* was suppressed. It was the last editorial job Chapin held, but he was able to boast that, under him, the circulation of the prison newspaper had soared.

This did not impress Chapin's former reporters, who deluged Warden Lewis E. Lawes with mail diatribes about their former chief. One comment: " . . . I used to think of him as sort of a devil sitting on enthroned power in the *World* office and making Park Row gutters flow red with the blood of ambitious young men. If you enjoy him I hope you keep him long and carefully."

Yet, through the years, Lawes and his wife and, indeed, the inmates of the prison saw a different Chapin. Although he was for a time despondent at the loss of his prison newspaper, Chapin made a new suggestion to the warden and asked that he be allowed to replace the gravel, cinders, and crushed rock on some of the prison grounds with "a little garden." Lawes gave permission but said that there was no money available. Chapin said that was no problem. He wrote to garden magazines, and soon bone meal, fertilizer, rose plants, tulip bulbs, and hundreds of pounds of seed deluged the prison. Chapin grew rose plants and dahlias and the like all around the prison, including the death house, where in 1928 murderers Ruth Snyder and Judd Gray paused in turn to inhale the fragrance of Chapin's roses before passing through the grim doors.

Some of Chapin's old co-workers now visited him in prison and stared in awe at the gardens of the now-famed Rose Man of Sing Sing. Cobb, Arthur Brisbane, and others traveled up the Hudson to marvel at the new Chapin, a man a great many convicts now called Uncle Charlie. Horticulturists visited the prison to view Chapin's amazing work, as did philanthropist Adolph Lewisohn, who later sent a truckload of plants from his own gardens.

However, in 1930, much of Chapin's beloved gardens had to be gutted for installation of a new drainage system. In *20,000 Years in Sing Sing* Lawes wrote: "I think it affected him deeply. He was never the same. He suddenly became the helpless invalid, unable to carry on." Chapin died in December of that year at age 72. His last words to Lawes were: "I want to die. I want to get it over with."

Now Lawes received scores of letters from journalists around the country who had once served under Chapin. After his death, none were critical of him. One wrote, "As an old *Evening World* man who owes whatever success he has attained to the fact that he received his early training under the greatest newspaper general in the world, I send you this word in memory of Charles Chapin."

Rosenberg, Ethel (1915–1953) and Julius (1918–1953) executed atomic spies

Ethel and Julius Rosenberg were charged with passing atomic secrets to the Soviet Union, were convicted of espionage, and were executed in Sing Sing on June 19, 1953. The details of the case are not particularly germane to this work, but the drama of the execution is.

The federal government right up to the end sought to get confessions from the Rosenbergs and for them to identify others. A last-minute appeal was made by Attorney General Herbert Brownell through Rabbi Irving Koslowe, the Jewish chaplain of Sing Sing (who served for 49 years), to carry a message to the doomed pair. Brownell told the rabbi that if the Rosenbergs would give him a name, a stay of execution would be considered. The Rosenbergs refused, and Julius went to the electric chair.

Rabbi Koslowe returned to Ethel, recalling, "I came back and told her her husband was dead. Did she have anything to say to me, a name, to stay the execution? She said, 'No, I have no names to give. I'm innocent,' and she was much more stolid than he. She came right behind me, sat down and was executed."

There has been speculation whether the government ever expected any sort of last-minute confession in exchange for any kind of stay and the possibility of a further reprieve. If it had, observers

Ethel Rosenberg and her husband, Julius, are pictured here as they ride to separate jails in New York City following their convictions as traitors in the nation's first atom spy trial. (AP/Wide World Photos)

said, they would not have sent Julius to his death first rather than his wife.

The case, of course, was Rabbi Koslowe's most important execution. As good a term as any, he was often described as "quaint," being noted for bringing visitors with him to visit prisoners as well as bearing Jewish newspapers, books, foods, and items for holiday rituals. "People ask me," he once told an interviewer, "what I'm doing, bringing matzo ball soup to a bunch of killers. But maybe we can make some change. Maybe we can bring some good in their life. Some of the guards would say I'm crazy, but I do what I can do."

rule of silence declining disciplinary method

The rule of silence, always regarded as one of the harshest forms of discipline ever utilized in U.S. prisons, was first enforced at Auburn Prison in New York in the 1830s and received its most famous use in the 20th century at Alcatraz Prison.

As originally planned, the rule of silence was imposed on inmates when they were let out of their cells by day to work in the shops. They had to maintain silence and march in lockstep with downcast eyes. Violation of these rules resulted in a flogging. But at least prisoners were allowed to talk in the cell blocks.

It was different a century later at Alcatraz, where it was first used in 1934 as a punishment for problem prisoners. The rule of silence was to be so enforced that it was conceivable that a convict could forget the sound of his own voice. Inmates were not permitted to talk in the dining room, in the workshops, or in the cell blocks. The rules proved to be unworkable. Prisoners found a way to talk to each other despite the risks of punishment, which could result in being sent to the "Hole."

What made the rule of silence so ludicrous was that it could be used against the authorities at critical times. During an early escape attempt at Alcatraz, a convict hit a guard over the head with a hammer more than a half-dozen times, and then two others dragged the bleeding, dying guard into a corner where they covered him with some old work clothes. A half-dozen other convicts were present at the time, but none stirred or said a word. They simply obeyed the rule of silence.

From Auburn to Alcatraz, many other U.S. prisons sought to establish silence codes. In due course, all of them were more or less abandoned as unworkable. The elimination of the silence rule in some cases seemed to please both the inmates and their keepers. At the Massachusetts State Prison, officials steadily eased up on their original rules. On the Fourth of July in 1864, Warden Gideon Hayes surprised the prisoners by ending the decades-old practice of silence with a surprise announcement. At first, there was only a stunned silence, but then, as Hayes recounted,

> *The shout that then burst forth from those four hundred throats, the delirium of delight into which they were immediately plunged, at once relieved me from all the fear as to the result. They shook hands, embraced one another, laughed, shouted, danced and cried; one of them caught up my little boy, rushed into the crowd, and I saw no more of him till the bell called them to order. At the first stroke of the bell every voice was hushed; silently and quietly they fell into line in their respective divisions, and save for the flush of excitement and the animated expression which flashed from the eyes of all, giving them more the appearance of the men God created in his own image than I had ever seen in that place before, they, in their usual good order, passed into their cells.*

Joliet State Prison had their happy Fourth 11 years later when Warden R.W. McClaughry allowed the inmates to use the large prison yard for the first time. The warden reported that they "talked, laughed and sang, engaged in athletic sports, and improvised minstrel performances to their hearts' content, while the occasion was enlivened with instrumental music by the Wheaton cornet band."

Of course, such joyfulness was not widespread during this period. Warden E.C. Watkins did get rid of the lockstep, but he ran into fierce resistance to ending the rule of silence by prison contractors, who insisted that allowing men to talk on the job would cause them to fall behind on their quotas.

Still, the rule of silence continued to founder even while it was attempted anew in other localities. In Alcatraz, the rule of silence was eliminated from the no-talking restriction in a number of areas. Still, long periods of silence were enforced, and Alcatraz maintained its premier spot as the hellhole of federal prisons, where enforced monotony drove, it was said, many inmates "stir crazy." Today, the so-called supermax federal and state prisons enforce a sort of code of silence by keeping many prisoners in virtual isolation.

"running the gears" brutal stabbing technique
Stabbings by prison inmates are pretty much determined by the weapon of choice or, at least, its availability. Knives can be fashioned from almost any sort of metal or even tough plastic. More importantly, for the violent-determined inmate, knives allow for brutal stabbing techniques whether or not actual death is the intention. The convict attitude is that for certain offenses where death is intended, there is also a determination that the victim "die hard." If a lesson other than death is the intention, there is still a desire for inducing sufficient suffering. Often, such motivation springs from a determination that the victim has been "disrespecting me."

That calls for "running the gears." In the *Hot House,* author Pete Earley quotes a convicted murderer explaining, "You slam a shank into his chest and then pull up and over and then down and over, just like shifting gears in a car."

Rush, Benjamin (1746–1813) signer of Declaration of Independence and prison reformer

A signer of the Declaration of Independence and the young nation's preeminent physician, Dr. Benjamin Rush was to become known as the "father of American psychiatry" and as an important advocate of rehabilitation as the guiding principle of penology. As such, because of his support for rehabilitation of prisoners, he was regarded to be a most farsighted advocate; however, it must be noted he had some warts as well.

Rush aligned himself with Pennsylvania's Quakers for the complete abolition of the death penalty. The campaign was not entirely successful because four felonies remained subject for capital punishment—murder, rape, arson, and treason. Rush denounced capital punishment as "the natural offspring of monarchial governments" and opted for imprisonment instead because, as he put it, "a prison sometimes supplies the place of a church and out-preaches the preacher in conveying useful instruction to the heart." Unlike the Quakers, however, Rush did not favor forcing convicts to do hard labor because making prisoners work might render labor itself "ignominious."

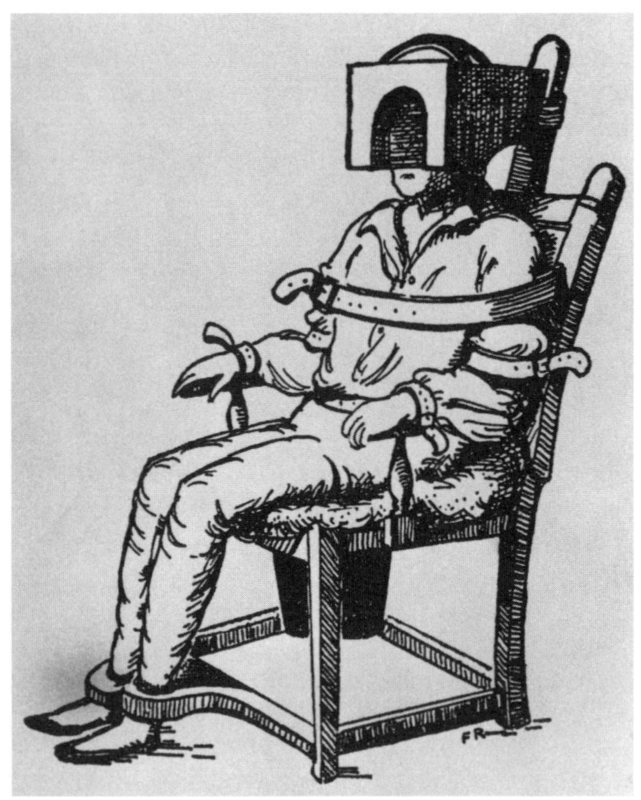

"Tranquilizing" chair used by Benjamin Rush to restrain unmanageable cases (Bettmann/CORBIS)

Benjamin Rush, American patriot and physician (CORBIS)

Rush was outspoken for the principle that criminal punishments be proportionate and not just fit the crime. He felt that the punishment should be invoked "according to the temper of criminals and the progress of their reformation." Rush also declared that the duration of any sentence should be kept from offenders, a tactic that he felt was "of the utmost importance in reforming criminals and preventing crimes as [t]he imagination, when agitated with uncertainty, will seldom fail of connecting the longest duration of punishment, with the smallest crime."

A professor of medicine at the University of Pennsylvania after the Revolution, Rush published the first American work in the field of psychiatry and delved into many subjects. He produced two works on crime and punishment. His *Medical Inquiries* was the first work on medical jurisprudence written in America, and in 1787, he offered

"Enquiry into the Effects of Public Punishments upon Criminals and upon Society." It was first delivered as a speech at the home of Benjamin Franklin. In "Public Punishments," Rush condemned the state's practice of inflicting humiliating public punishment on offenders. Rush held that "crimes should be punished in private, or not punished at all." He said, "the only design of punishment is the reformation of the criminal."

Actually, Rush has come to be regarded by some as a "gadfly," and his version of punishment to be conducted in private was not without warts, especially for "the father of psychiatry." Rush was the inventor of the so-called mad chair, an instrument for punishment that produced exquisite pain. It was a sort of large boxlike chair, into which a prisoner (most often one usually mentally disturbed) was strapped so that his body was prevented from resting. The resultant pain was excruciating. The mad chair was best utilized, as Rush preferred, "in private."

Whatever Rush's excesses, he is for his time still today accepted as one of the most forward-looking figures in penology.

S

San Quentin death row nation's most violent

It has long been the perception that death row is generally the tamest area in any big prison throughout the country. It is a belief that, by the very early years of the 21st century, was in the process of being challenged. The hints of this change probably date back to the 1980s when death-row violence against keepers started to increase and the first mass escape from death row occurred in 1984 at the Mecklenburg Correctional Center in Virginia. In the ensuing years, it became more common for condemned men to struggle on their way to the execution chamber and apparently do more damage to guards in the process than was revealed by authorities.

By 2000, the most violent death row in the Western Hemisphere had become that in San Quentin, with 593 condemned men awaiting their eventual execution. The death row erupted in hostility and violence that was previously unexperienced by California authorities. Death-row inmates had to be classified in two separate groups, the average condemned persons and the much more violent, so-called Grade B individuals, a group of about 85 and growing, who were guilty of unruly behavior and attacks on guards. They had to be separated and housed in a separate death row in a three-story building, the Adjustment Center. In 18 months, the Grade B's attacked guards 67 times, triple the rate for which the group was responsible just a few years previously.

From May 2000 to the following May, 45 Grade B's made assaults or attempted assaults on guards. Guards had their wrists slashed with crude, homemade razors and paper clips fashioned into minispears. Guards were kicked viciously without warning, and they were also "gassed" constantly with stored, fermented feces and urine that were used as bombs thrown in an officer's face.

The more the violence increased, the more officials tried to crack down, and the more tensions increased, leading to campaigns by violent gang leaders. When one death-row inmate in a gang-related motive stabbed another in the visitation center, San Quentin responded by suspending all visiting rights for the condemned for a year. (Later, the prison reversed the ban as it applied to Grade A prisoners. They were permitted to have visitors in a glass-walled cell, completely separated from any other inmates and their guests.)

Further tensions boiled over among Grade B inmates when they lost all outdoor exercise privileges following another attack on a prisoner by a fellow inmate.

The problem faced by the prison is that its death row is antiquated with no remote locking system or Plexiglass doors, putting guards at a serious disadvantage dealing with inmates in in-your-face confrontations. Because of the steady parade of attacks, much of the guard contingent became demoralized; 14 officers requested and

Death Row at San Quentin Prison (Bettmann/CORBIS)

were granted transfers from the Adjustment Center. Four others quit outright. Adjustment Center guards were equipped with riot gear, including helmets with shields, padded vests for protection against stabbings, and a full array of guns and batons. In addition, the staffing of the Adjustment Center was increased so that there would be three officers to escort each inmate to the exercise area.

Staff members tend to see the rise in violence as being caused by rabble-rousers who are gang connected and have brought their mentality and behavior from the streets. Of course, there is little reason for such inmates to do otherwise, one rationale being that the death penalty offers little fear for them. With appeals likely to stretch out an execution for as many as 15 years, some inmates can feel that they would have been more likely to die in gang violence in that span on the outside.

Naturally, this has led to demands that the execution pace be speeded up, something that probably could not be done under California procedures. Before a condemned person can launch an appeal, the inmate must first obtain a lawyer, not an easy procedure, and then an appeal transcript must be worked up. In California such transcripts, which can run up to 10,000 pages, must be certified for accuracy by the trial judge, and each page of the appeal transcript has to be reviewed for errors by all those involved—court reporters, court clerk, and trial attorneys as well as the judge. This alone can add years of delay. In one case, a condemned prisoner was, after seven years, still not eligible to even start a formal appeal because the trial record certification process had not even been completed. While the man was already on death row, he was convicted in another capital case so that his rights of appeal in that case were going to have to lag well behind the first one.

From the time when the death penalty was reinstated in the state in 1978 to mid-1996, only three persons were executed. The buildup of the condemned population in San Quentin had, by the turn of the century, produced enough death-row inmates to populate a small prison within a larger prison, with control being ever harder to maintain. The point is often made that the large prisons in the United States are more and more out of control and being run by the inmates, not so much de facto but by the recognition by prison authorities that their basic ability, and perhaps duty, at most is simply to contain the situation by jumping from one crisis to another to "keep the lid on."

The situation worsens on death row as well, and more and more of the condemned see striking out as no different from the acts for which they had been convicted. Death row simply has become an ever-growing problem of prison with no solution in sight.

See also: "GASSING"; PRISONIZATION.

Screws v. United States previous "hands off" policy of federal courts

Until the 1940s, except in a few cases, the federal judiciary followed a "hands off" or "out-of-sight, out-of-mind" attitude toward the treatment of prisoners. This would change radically in the 1950s and 1960s when the concept of prisoners' rights would flourish to an extent that shocked the get-tough-on-criminals mindset. By the end of the century, there has been some curtailment of the prisoners'-rights concept but certainly not a return to the old hands-off policies, as typified by *Screws v. United States,* a 1945 case that well illustrated the reluctance of the federal courts to side with state convicts.

Sheriff Claude Screws of Baker County, Georgia, took custody of a black man named Robert Hall, hauled him into the courthouse yard, and repeatedly struck him with a blackjack until Hall died. When the state of Georgia refused to bring any murder charges, federal prosecutors sought and obtained conviction under a civil-rights statute from the Reconstruction period. Screws then appealed on what many thought to be a curious position—that he had not sought to deprive Hall of his civil rights but rather merely to kill him. The U.S. Supreme Court strictly interpreted the word *willfully* in the statute and reversed the verdict. Retried under this interpretation, Screws was acquitted and later was elected to state office.

selling goods to convicts a growth industry

Few situations in U.S. prisons have been more criticized by much of the public and politicians than the ability of convicts to buy consumer goods to make their lives more livable—or, from the more harsh proponents' view, more enjoyable. In view of the fact that most people favor keeping amenities to prisoners at a bare minimum, it would appear that suppliers of goods to the convict market have much to worry about. The exact opposite is the case: Business is booming for such suppliers. Against the idea that prisoners should be able to buy very little is the contrary view that tapping into this huge market is beneficial to the nation's economy as a whole and provides honest citizens with jobs and profits.

The result is apparently an entrenched business practice that is impervious to any complaints or scandals. One of the most startling occurrences involved a plot whereby a guard's uniform was smuggled into a prison inside a television set. After a brief stir, business ingenuity came to the fore, and in several states now, only clear-case sets have been permitted.

Clear, indeed, as well applies now to much more than TVs and includes hot pots, shavers, and any number of products that are permitted to be in an inmate's possession, all the way down to clear trash cans. For makers of headphones—a standard requirement in many prisons to reduce bickering about what is being played in sound or music—clear is almost a universal rule. Koss Corporation is a leading supplier of "listening accessories" in the prison market. The ear cups and housing must be clear so that drugs cannot be stashed in them. There are many other safety measures: The headband must be plastic and have no metal springs that would allow a knife to be fashioned; the cord is much more fragile than in the regular market and has to be weak enough that it will snap if it is used as a garrote to attempt to dispatch a guard or a cellmate.

Koss generally offers a life warranty, but it has learned to change that for the prison market where products tend to be very much abused by inmate customers. Clear products now only carry a 90-day warranty.

Prison TVs have proven to be a hit in the civilian market as well, their minimalist translucent casings catching the eyes of many consumers, especially children. The prison versions have a number of no-nos. They can have no antennas, flip-down doors, or remote (it could be converted into a bomb detonator).

Many companies serving the prison market keep their activities hush-hush and take extra precautions. Workers on such products hand in their Exacto blades at the end of their shift. Says one executive: "We can't have something like that accidentally shipped behind bars." In addition, companies are extremely careful about whom they hire for such work, making sure, for instance, that an applicant does not have relatives behind bars.

Any new product is subjected to close scrutiny before it can gain access to the market. As one prison official puts it, "Can this be altered and become a threat to security?" It is recognized that prisoners will look for ways to adapt any items, especially electronic ones, and they can come up with ingenious uses.

See also: TURNER, WILLIE LLOYD.

sentencing of criminals a major bone of contention

The sentencing of offenders remains one of the most trying procedures facing the criminal justice system. Perhaps other aspects—interrogation, arrest, trial, or conviction—of the system are more rife with actual or perceived error or lack of balanced judgment than the sentencing process. Complaints about sentencing almost always play a prominent role in the causes of prison riots.

Despite guidelines, some judges sentence "long" and others "short." In *Crime in America* former attorney general Ramsey Clark offered some recent illustrations of inequality in sentencing, often in different courtrooms in the same courthouse:

Two boys fail to report for military induction—one is sentenced to five years in prison, the other gets probation and never enters a prison. One judge sentences a robber convicted for the third time to one year in prison, while another judge on the same bench gives a first offender ten years. One man far more capable of serious crime than another and convicted of the same offense may get a fine, while the less fortunate and less dangerous person is sentenced to five years in the state penitentiary. One judge, because of his personal values, thinks homosexuality the most heinous of crimes and gives long sentences. Another hates prostitution. A third judge regularly gives juvenile offenders prison terms for first offense car theft, while others turn them over to custody of their parents.

Inevitably involved in the process are diverse judicial temperaments and philosophies as well as varying geographical attitudes. Willard Gayling in *Partial Justice* relates a story often told by Judge Edward Lumbard:

A visitor to a Texas court was amazed to hear the judge imposed a suspended sentence where a man had pleaded guilty to manslaughter. A few minutes later the same judge sentenced a man who pleaded guilty to stealing a horse to life imprisonment. When the judge was asked by the visitor about the disparity between the two sentences, he replied, "Well, down here there is some men that need killin', but there ain't no horses that need stealin'."

Certain crimes draw varying penalties, depending on the economy of the area. Thus in Oregon, Gaylin noted that 18 of 33 Selective Service violators were let off with probation, and none of the others were given prison terms of more than three years. On the other hand, in southern Texas, a defense-oriented state, 16 of 16 received prison terms, 14 of them the maximum allowed—five years.

One of the leading critics of the disparity of prison sentences was James V. Bennett, director of the Federal Bureau of Prisons for 27 years. He cited a lengthy string of unfair sentences. In one case a 32-year-old unemployed man whose wife had just suffered a miscarriage forged a government check. He had no prior criminal record but drew a 15-year sentence. In his memoirs, *I Chose Prison*, Bennett quoted the judge in the case as saying, "This court intends to stop the stealing and forging of government checks." That same year, another judge in the same circuit gave a defendant just 30 days for a like crime.

In an effort to address such inequities, Bennett was instrumental in the establishment in the late 1950s of so-called sentencing institutes, where judges could exchange views on sentencing theories. These were followed by other limited advances. In *Crime and Punishment,* Aryeh Neier, executive director of the American Civil Liberties Union, noted, "'Sentencing councils' are another relatively recent innovation. The councils bring together probation officers and judges in an area to review recommendations for sentences by trial judges before the sentences are imposed. Although the trial judge can reject the views of his colleagues, the discussion tends to circumscribe extreme disparities in sentencing." Unfortunately, Neier added, such programs were only moderately popular in the federal court system and were not used "in most court systems where the great majority of criminals are sentenced."

There was a period in recent decades when indeterminate sentencing was viewed by reformers as the only viable alternative to sentencing inequities. In the 1970s, Ramsey Clark was a leading spokesman for this view. Since that time, however, the idea of sentencing without a fixed term fell into relative disfavor, although it was a way to lift a great burden off many judges. Alan M. Dershowitz, professor at Harvard Law School, later wrote: "The era of the indeterminate sentence . . . is quickly drawing to a close. Reaction is beginning to set in."

Many criminologists tend to agree that indeterminate sentences actually tend to result in longer prison terms than most judges would mete out on their own, and the disparity in sentencing is often increased rather than reduced. An added problem, say such critics, is that such sentences tend to give correctional officials too much control over prisoners' lives and are psychologically dangerous to many prisoners because they can never be sure when they will be released. These factors often are cited as the reason behind many prison riots. Still, it can be said that the complete end of indeterminate sentencing is itself indeterminate.

Recent proposals call for the abolishment of the federal parole system and a reduction in the sentencing latitude given to judges. In 1976, former attorney general Edward H. Levi called for a permanent sentencing guidelines commission. He said, "If a judge decided to impose a sentence inconsistent with the guidelines, he would have to accompany the decision with specific reasons for the except, and the decision would be subject to appellate review."

Of course, even without such a system, appellate review of a sentence is possible, but it proves to be extremely rare. "When it happens," Neier noted, "it is generally because judges have gratuitously offered their reasons for particular sentences and included impermissible considerations, as when a New Jersey judge cited an anti-white poem by LeRoi Jones [Imamu Amiri Baraka] as the reason for giving him an extended prison term." In other cases, judges have refused to give shorter sentences or probation because a defendant insisted on a jury trial. To many observers, it is as though justice often goes awry as soon as society attempts to apply fitting punishment. They say that the idea of "fitting punishment" is a fine one but that it remains a subjective one, often determined by the flow of public opinion.

SENTENCING FOR CRIMES VS. ACTUAL TIME SERVED

According to the Bureau of Justice Statistics, *Truth in Sentencing in State Prisons,* 1999, the following indicates the average maximum sentence length and the time served for selected state-court convictions:

Type of Offense	Average sentence	Average time served
All violent	7 years, 1 month	3 years, 3 months
Homicide	15 years	7 years
Rape	9 years, 8 months	5 years, 1 month
Other sexual assault	6 years, 9 months	3 years, 3 months
Robbery	7 years, 8 months	3 years, 4 months
Negligent manslaughter	8 years, 1 month	3 years, 5 months
Assault	5 years, 1 month	2 years, 4 months
Other	5 years, 7 months	2 years, 5 months

The average time served includes jail credit and prison time. Excluded are life and death sentences.

See also: JUVENILE SUICIDE AND MURDER IN ADULT PRISONS.

ship schools Civil War juvenile detention

During the Civil War, a novel experiment in the north was made to confine juvenile delinquents. Through the years, it had been suggested that young male juveniles would respond positively to the military life. So-called ship schools were set up so that errant youths up to the age of 16 could be subjected to military discipline and training in an environment that precluded any chance of escape. On board ship, the youths were separated into rotating work and study groups. Those on work duty spent their time in, as an account of the day put it, "domestic employments; in repairing sails and rigging; in going through sheet and halyard, brace and clewline, and the technical language of sailors; in short, in becoming practical seamen."

The ship-schools concept survived for only a few years beyond the Civil War, proving to be a public-relations nightmare to the country. There were rumors, incorrect, of the young convicts taking control of the vessels, putting into shore, and staging mass escapes. Many potboiler novels were themed to such fictional happenings. Besides the fear that enveloped many communities at the thought of ship schools near their shores, authorities were faced with real disciplinary problems, heavy operating expenses, and the economic depression that put adult seamen out of work with the end of the great conflict. In this last sense, the ship schools suffered the same fate as many prison rehabilitation work projects, with prisoners taught skills that were not really applicable to outside life.

"shot callers" prison gang leaders

Many riots in prison spring not from a spontaneous cause but are plotted out in advance by various gang leaders who watch for the perfect time when their adherents will have a distinct advantage over the other side. A hotbed for fights and race riots has long been California's Pitchess Detention Center, a Los Angeles County prison. These battles are masterminded by tattooed gang leaders called shot callers.

Like military battles of old, the shot callers have an overview of the situation and issue orders for the start of action at a precise moment when guard supervision might be a bit relaxed or when the other side is feeling relatively safe.

This same shot-caller control was exhibited at Pelican Bay State Penitentiary, California's newest supermaximum prison, known popularly as the state's new Alcatraz, housing as it does the state's most dangerous troublemaker prisoners. The situation can turn volatile, especially when the prison population is divided up in large measure into various ethnic gangs and yet allowed to be integrated in the prison yard. Fights under such situations are inevitable. In a major riot, every member of the southern Mexican gang showed up for the exercise yard, a very unusual event because many inmates opt to pass on the yard at any particular time.

The south Mexicans were at the time warring on the largest black gang, and at a given moment when a shot caller signaled, they pounced on the blacks. In a 30-minute-long battle, during which the shot callers rather than the guards controlled the battleground, numerous stabbings and maimings resulted until guards finally took control under shoot-to-kill orders.

The fact that Pelican Bay lost control of the situation was cited as an indication that even such a high-security prison can lose mastery to the shot callers. Naturally, punishment was exacted for the Pelican Bay riot, but within their own structures, the inmates considered the shot callers and planners the big winners.

shower survival avoiding a murder attempt

A favorite place for prison killers to catch a victim off-guard is in the shower. Because a number of inmates may be in the shower, an inmate always has to be on alert. That involves being properly "unattired" in the shower, which means bare feet rather than wearing leather or plastic thongs. When a victim is fallen upon by one or more assailants when wearing thongs, either in the shower or upon getting out, he will invariably slip on the wet and soapy floor and is helpless to fend off fatal knife "stickings."

Sing Sing See LYNDS, ELAM; "SWING SWING."

"Sissy Shank" prisoner-made knife

Shanks are knives made by prisoners for use to kill or maim other prisoners. The killer type is fashioned from scrap metal of some sort and ground down to a sharp point. Some need several heavy stabbings to achieve killer effect. However, most shanks are not that murderous and aren't really intended to kill. These are so-called sissy shanks. These weapons are made by melting a toothbrush around a razor blade. They are almost valueless for murderous purposes but are very effective when used to slice an opponent's face.

See also: "RUNNING THE GEARS."

"6 percent solution" forerunner of three-strikes-and-out laws

The so-called 6 percent solution may be regarded as the forerunner of various three-, two-, or one-strike laws. It is a decades-old theory developed by Marvin Wolfgang and, say various experts, misinterpreted constantly by officials and politicians to justify the benefits of the theory of incapacitating criminals. The theory of the so-called 6 percent solution was often cited in the 1993 congressional debate on the federal three-strikes-and-out law. In 1994, President Bill Clinton claimed that "most violent crimes are committed by a small percentage of criminals." Some criminologists have insisted that such claims are a misinterpretation of Wolfgang's 6 percent study to hold that imprisoning 6 percent of all criminals would take care of 70 percent of all crime. This would mean that isolating this notorious 6 percent would virtually eliminate all crime.

However, critics point out, Wolfgang had simply studied juveniles—and only juveniles—in one city (those born in Philadelphia between 1945 and 1958). All Wolfgang had done was to indicate that 6 percent of these juveniles were responsible for all boys' crimes within their population grouping. This merely reflected these juveniles and not criminals in general. If it had reflected criminals as a whole, the total would be far greater that 6 percent of all offenders, and there is no way the justice system could handle such a total—it starts to creak badly at a 1 percent rate.

There were a number of other problems with the 6 percent solution. Says Marc Mauer of the Sentencing Project: "The membership of the six percent group of high-rate offenders is not static. New high-rate offenders enter the population each year, and former high-rate offenders reduce their criminal activity because they 'age out' or for other reasons. . . . It is important to remember that studies conducted on a group of boys born in one city forty or fifty years ago are not necessarily relevant to crime patterns today. The wider availability of guns, the spread of the drug trade, and other factors suggest that patterns of crime commission are likely to be very different today."

In *The Tough-On-Crime Myth,* Peter T. Elikann finds the "erroneous uses of statistics" as the methodology of "a small group of proponents of the viewpoint that 'nothing works' except incarceration." The National Rifle Association (NRA), as part of a well-orchestrated, highly financed campaign to divert any blame for crime on guns, and to attribute blame, rather, on the idea that not enough people are incarcerated, came out with a report based on a very skewed statistic. About the same time, former United States Attorney General William Barr came out with a similar report called *The Case for More Incarceration,* based on similar distorted statistics.

The gist of the NRA study was that between 1980 and 1991, a period when there was a 150 percent increase in incarceration, there was a drop of "serious victimization" of 24 percent. This is determined by reviewing the rate of six types of violent crimes along with one specially selected violent crime, in this case, burglary. Burglary had decreased in that period by 39 percent. Elikann finds this to be "a textbook example of manipulating statistics to make a desired point." He points out that if auto theft had been substituted for burglary, it would alter dramatically the results reported by the NRA and Barr. According to the highly acclaimed criminologist, Joan Petersilia, the drop in burglaries did not indicate that fewer crimes were occurring, but rather that criminals were opting for other crimes instead. Street criminals had decided that they wanted less to do with a risky crime such as burglary in favor of more lucrative crimes such as drug dealing.

There are a great number of criminologists who regard Wolfgang's 6 percent solution as well as its later offspring, the various strikes laws, as failures in reducing crime at all, but the premise is still frequently cited.

"sliming" degrading prison warfare
One of the most appalling practices in prison that gives inmates a way to strike back at their keepers is "sliming." A mixture of urine and feces saved by inmates in a plastic cup for use against guards and left to curdle for several hours or days, it makes a potent weapon against guards when tossed in their face, burning their eyes.

Humiliation is the name of the game and is one of the few ways prisoners have to degrade their keepers. Of course, retaliation follows quickly and very severely. Because an inmate knows that he or she faces a sure beating, the prisoner does what he or she can to make matters hard for the guards who storm into the cell. The inmate soaps up his or her entire body and the cell floor as well so that the guards will slip and fall as they move in. Eventually though, the offending inmate is shackled to a bunk and left there for hours on end or is chained to the metal toilet and left incapacitated there for eight hours or so.

The sliming terror of Sing Sing is a character nicknamed by guards and inmates alike, although with different levels of admiration and hatred, as "Mr. Slurpee." In *Newjack: Guarding Sing Sing*, writer Ted Conover, who failed to obtain permission to interview Sing Sing's guards for his project, applied for and was hired for a guard job secretly without revealing his real identity and purpose. He described Mr. Slurpee as one "who would project a spray of urine and feces at officers—from his *mouth*." As one supervisor lectured Conover: "You're the zookeeper now. . . . Go run the zoo."

smoking in prison

Until recent years, the population group with the highest percentage of smokers in the nation was probably prison inmates. Studies indicated that as many as 80 percent of the prison population were addicted to cigarettes. However, this is changing rapidly now as many institutions have either barred cigarette smoking outright or have placed stiff restrictions on their consumption.

This is so despite the feelings of many prison authorities that the elimination of smoking will tend to increase stress and prison violence. Not all prisoners enter prison as smokers but adopt the habit precisely to reduce stress as they try to cope with the realities of an incarcerated life.

By the early 1990s, prison officials found that they had to be cognizant of the general health attitudes concerning the dangers of smoking and secondhand smoke as well. In 1993, in *Helling v. McKinney*, the Supreme Court ruled that inmates had a right not to be subjected to secondhand smoke hazards. As a result, the following year, the Federal Bureau of Prisons put in place a no-smoking policy in all its institutions.

This represented quite a turnaround for the bureau, which, for example, in Alcatraz more than 60 years earlier, had offered a bountiful policy of issuing each prisoner three packs of cigarettes a week, and when that supply was gone, the inmate could obtain all the loose tobacco he wished from free dispensers to roll his own. That policy was intended to cut the bribing power of cigarettes as was the case in other prisons because they were used to pay debts, as in gambling debts and for protection.

With the smoking ban in federal prisons in place by 2000, many state prisons started to follow suit, but they have been subjected to legal actions from both sides of the spectrum. Smoke for some inmates creates a cruel and harmful environment, which violates the Eighth Amendment. However, other prisons have launched action that it was cruel and too punishing to deprive inmates of the right to smoke.

In an effort to find some sort of common ground, some prisons tried to loosen the restrictions by allowing some smoking in specified areas, and in one case at least, a warden sought to counter jittery nerves among his wards by handing out celery sticks, carrots, potato chips, and popcorn. Many prisons have set up programs to help wean prisoners away from the habit. But a worry remains that bans drive up the value of cigarettes as valuable contraband.

Overall, whatever intermediate steps are taken, there is no doubt that the trend to smoke-free prisons will continue, even though there seems to be some whispering campaigns to halt smoking bans by warning that the cost to taxpayers will continue to rise and that lifers, for instance, might end up simply living longer.

"snitch boxes" prison metal detectors
Few Americans can avoid being checked by metal detectors. They may be students entering troubled

schools or persons entering airports, courthouses, or other public buildings. However, the first major use of such devices occurred more than 70 years ago in prisons, where they were and still are used to screen inmates for possible possession of guns, knives, and other weapons. Convicts subjected to such checks referred to them as "mechanical stool pigeons" or "snitch boxes." A prisoner who set off an alarm would find himself descended upon by a number of officers.

Perhaps surprisingly, a number of guards have never thought highly of such detectors, which have been circumvented by resourceful inmates. More importantly, it is impossible to use them very extensively on prison occupants who are frequently on the move and would have to be checked a dozen or more times a day and would lead to huge tie-ups at meal times. As a result, guards have to make judgment calls on who to run through the detectors and who to let go unchallenged. Unfortunately, guards can make wrong decisions and in such cases may be subjected to disciplinarian acts for neglect of duty. Thus, in effect the snitch boxes can at times end up "snitching" on the guards.

More tie-ups can result because the detectors do not always discriminate between dangerous and harmless metal. When Al Capone was serving his sentence in Alcatraz, he was constantly setting off alarms. It developed that Big Al's metal arch supporters were the sources of the false alarms, and exasperated officials finally replaced the supporters with a plastic pair.

Officials faced even more frustration when Capone's mother showed up to see her "good boy" on visiting day. The electric alarms blared away and guards pounced on the old lady in an eager hunt for gun or hacksaw. Nothing.

When Mrs. Capone was sent through the machine again the result was the same. It took a considerable amount of time to finally discover the problem. Mama Capone was wearing an old-fashioned full-length corset with metal ribs. She was then permitted to proceed, but on each later visit, the routine had to be repeated for fear that this time the old lady might be carrying lethal contraband. In the end, prison officials dropped any efforts from checking her further or to dissuade her from wearing such a corset, fearing this would be regarded as very disrespectful by the public.

snitches most-hated prison inmates

It was not so much a prison riot as a bloodbath. On February 2, 1980, inmates of the New Mexico State Penitentiary at Santa Fe ran amok, taking over the prison, and engaged in wholesale slaughter, destroying much of the institution and leaving the state with a repair bill estimated at $60 to $70 million. During the next 36 hours, 33 prisoners were killed most horribly: Some were burned to death with blowtorches, decapitated, hacked to pieces, or castrated. No other riot in the United States produced more deaths of inmates by inmates in history. By contrast not a single guard, several of whom were taken hostage, was killed. Investigators identified the usual causes of riots as being present—rotten food, overcrowding, poor mail and visiting privileges, lax security, and corrupt officials. However, this did not explain the full scope of the tragedy. Most of the 33 dead were identified by other convicts as being snitches or informers, and many were seized in segregated areas in which they had been held for their own protection. The New Mexico facility was known for operating one of the most aggressive campaigns to recruit informers anywhere. Every member of the staff seemingly was involved in the attempts to make prisoners "flip," and it was reported even a minister told an inmate, "My son, God wants you to be a snitch."

Although, of course, the deadly riot could hardly be excused because of snitches, it is a fact that snitches are the most-hated convicts. One psychological explanation offered as a reason is that convicts feel that they have the whole weight of society stacked against them as it is and that they still must cope with betrayal—rightly or wrongly—from within their own ranks. All incoming prisoners are surveyed by other inmates to determine if they are or were snitches. Very often, snitches become so notorious that administrators find that the only solution is to shift them elsewhere. To inmates, this will not cause a snitch to change stripes. It is common prison belief that former snitches immediately have their feet put to the fire by guards, warning them that they must cooperate once again or their informer past will be leaked. Hence the term, "once a snitch, always a snitch."

According to prisoners, newcomers to the prison system are immediately pressured. Young, good-looking prisoners, they say, are slyly warned that they face certain homosexual abuse unless they give guards some reason to protect them. They are promised that one guard will not reveal their informing even to another guard to provide secrecy. In theory, that might work to some extent, convicts admit, but they point out guards work only eight-hour shifts; what happens the remaining 16 hours? To inmates the survival code has only one rule: Never snitch.

It is never difficult to find men in any prison who blame their incarceration on snitches. Or if they are subjected to discipline for prison infractions, the cause has to be snitches. If they are denied parole, some informer has set them up.

The jailhouse snitch, convicts say, is one who will make up any facts the police want to hear. Such a snitch usually can count on either walking himself or being given a short sentence at worst. In Louisiana, in January 2001, two death-row inmates having served 14 years awaiting execution, Albert R. Burrell (who once came within 17 days of execution) and Michael R. Graham Jr., were exonerated for the murder of an elderly couple in 1985. There was no physical evidence linking either to the crime; the two men were convicted largely on the testimony of a jailhouse snitch, Olan Wayne Brantley, who, one law-enforcement official acknowledged, was known as "Lyin' Wayne." Brantley said that both men, while in jail, had confessed to killing the elderly couple.

Later, in court, Brantley admitted that he had spent time in several mental hospitals for manic depression. He also agreed that he had written so many bad checks that he could give no tally of them. Although no witness put them at the scene of the killing and ballistics tests of their guns did not link them to the murders, the pair was convicted on the testimony of Lyin' Wayne. They were sentenced to death. It took until 2000 for a new trial to be ordered. A federal judge ruled that among other things the prosecution failed to mention that Lyin' Wayne won a plea agreement after he agreed to testify against the pair or that the state's witness had previously been found to be mentally incompetent. It was also revealed that the prosecutor in the case had signed an affidavit that he viewed the case against Graham and Burrell as "so weak that the case should never have been brought to a grand jury."

Such reversals reinforce the belief by convicts that false snitch testimony is more important than the word of any defendant or prisoner, until closely examined, which, they say, is seldom done. Thus, as one prisoner stated, "going after snitches is just self-defense."

The fear of snitches is so pervasive that many prisoners have a rule that says never trust a lifer. This is considered even more so in these days of life without parole. Prisoners are fearful of ever taking lifers into escape plans because such men are considered to be most likely to talk. There may be many psychological explanations for this, but to most convicts the reason is plain: Because lifers have no hope for themselves, they seek to get what little rewards they can get from prison authorities, even something as little as a loosening of the visitor or mail restrictions. There had been cases of lifers taking part in an escape plan right up to the breaching of the walls and then stepping out of harm's way until waiting guards seized the plotters.

If the state embraces snitches, very few in prison do, not even the guards—at least when they fear a snitch is being used against them. Guards have their own "blue code," or rule of silence, that insists that no guard ever give any testimony against any other guard accused of misconduct. When any sort of inquiry is undertaken and another guard is summoned to make a statement, other guards at their posts in the prison control center will know it and record the time the interview ran. Short: assumption that the guard denied any knowledge of any misconduct. Long: indications that the guard was doing some snitching. Such a guard might then be subject to much retribution, from middle-of-the-night obscene phone calls to "snitch-graffiti" decorations on the locker or in the message box. If the guard then complained to the prison administration, that would merely confirm that he was a violator of the blue code. Some guards quit their jobs or request transfers elsewhere.

Thus, the war against snitches behind bars is always ongoing and is sure to boil over when snitch activities seem to become even more oppressive. Attempting to justify the New Mexico riot against snitches, one convict cited the growing atmosphere in an aggressive system that offered rewards to inmates who were willing to inform.

The convict cited an atmosphere that led to bitter rage. "Hell," he said, "you can't trust your best friend anymore."

See also: BLUE CODE; NEW MEXICO PRISON RIOT; SNITCH BOXES.

"snitch test" convict method for screening out informers

The "snitch test" is used to pick out likely informers when a new batch of inmates are shipped into a prison. Old-hand prisoners insist they can "smell" out a snitch. Once they find a likely suspect, they try to draw him or her out, using methods as sophisticated as those used on criminals when they are interrogated by detectives.

A typical scenario would involve a new arrival who has either come from another prison or is being returned to prison for a new stretch. The question is was he or she released early previously because he or she had aided The Man by snitching? If the inmate was shipped in from another institution, is it because his or her snitching became so prevalent that he or she couldn't stay any longer without the likelihood of being killed? If the inmate is shipped to a new prison for his or her own protection, the new prison administration knows of his or her past and will immediately put pressure on the inmate to produce once more—or else.

Former snitches have to play it cagey. They can't let on about their past sins. It takes special interrogation to break them down. They are befriended by foxy old-timers who finally reveal to the new inmates that, 15 or 20 or more years ago, they had been put in a position where they had to rat on a fellow prisoner or a cellmate to avoid harsh treatment from guards. The old-timers keep mentioning this over and over again for many days until the suspected snitches come to feel that they have a soulmate who can be regarded as allies.

Finally, new prisoners unburden themselves saying that they once had turned in another prisoner to save themselves from a charge. For a brief time, the newly arrived snitches have a feeling of relief.

The old-timers will nod with a curt smile and stroll away.

Sometimes, the reaction will come quickly. Suddenly, a half-dozen convicts will appear on an old-timer's signal and take it from there. They will beat the confessed snitch so badly that guards will have to take him or her away to be hospitalized and kept under guard until, very often, he or she has to be shipped out to yet another institution. The beating is severe, but almost never is the snitch killed. Tough convicts know the value of such object lessons on other new prisoners: Never snitch.

A new shipment of prisoners comes in, and the brutal cat-and-mouse game continues.

soap-opera fans inmates who are dedicated viewers

Many prisoners become soap-opera groupies to the extent that they have not failed to watch a single episode of their favorite soap opera in years. They become so addicted to their favorite show that they will pass up even their recreation hour rather than miss anything. Some experts say this addiction is caused by the fact that the inmates have more or less lost any connection to their previous family life and that the characters in the show become their new family.

Inmate activists denounce the "soap-opera syndrome," claiming that it makes the inmate a "bunk potato," one who becomes so passive that he or she becomes a "lamb," precisely what the prison administration wants.

There is another form of activist who resists soap operas: the violent white supremacist or Aryan Brotherhood types who are outraged when black actors appear.

solitary confinement See *JORDAN V. FITZHARRIS.*

southern prisons

Throughout U.S. penal history, there has been a great divide between southern prisons and those in other parts of the country. In the 19th century, not all southern prisons kept adequate records, so it was difficult to measure the degree of cruelty involved in the institutions below the Mason Dixon line. But from the *known* death rate, it was at least three times higher than that found in northern prisons. To be sure northern prisons were generally vicious institutions; inmates had very few rights and little sympathy from the guards. Beatings, tortures, neglect, and deliberate murders were quite common.

Still, in the South, there is little doubt that the death rate was far higher than what was admitted. Disappearances were very common in southern work camps: In 1882, a survey showed that 1,100 prisoners had successfully "escaped" from southern prisons in a two-year period; the rate annually among northern inmates was 63. This gave rise to the suspicion that many of the missing 1,100 died of wounds inflicted on them or were victims of foul play that the prisons had need to cover up.

Because after the Civil War an enormous number of the inmates were black, there was great suspicion that little of their welfare was a measure of any importance to their keepers. One Louisiana prison official stated, "Before the Civil War we owned the Negroes. If a man had a good Negro, he could afford to take care of him, if he was sick, get him a doctor. He might even get gold plugs in his teeth. But these convicts, we don't own them. So, one dies, we get another."

Accommodations in many prison camps were extremely brutal and might even have been regarded as a method of torture rather than "normal" living conditions. Many prisoners were housed in steel-reinforced railcars, generally about 18 feet long and about 8 feet high and wide. Some 18 inmates were stuffed into such cars each night. Actually, they were better described as cages, often with tin roofs that became sizzling hot. The convicts often wore shackles at night that bound their legs and waists. The cars had armed guards patrolling in front.

The South relied more on prison farms and camps rather than large, fortresslike prisons to contain convicts. Restraints came in the form of wire fences, chains, guns, dogs, and frequent punishments to restrain them. Also, of course, the chain-gang system was southern grown. As late as 1912, an official of the National Committee on Prison Labor called the status of the southern prisoner as being "the last surviving vestige of the slave system."

Many observers considered the plight of convicts in Florida as just about the worst in the South, with perhaps more fatal beatings, unsanitary facilities, and an almost total lack of even the most simple medical care. In 1891, J.C. Powell, a longtime Florida prison official, wrote *The American Siberia,* which described the prisoners trying to endure in an environment marked by starvation, disease, exposure, and unlimited brutality. He described a prisoner who was left hanging by his thumbs in agony until he finally died. Powell described prisoners' thumbs that were so extended that they were the length of their index fingers; their hands "resembled the paws of certain apes."

Other investigators found equal horrors. In 1912, one reported, "Seven convicts died in this camp in a single year from diseases connected with standing or working in water up to their waists at all seasons of the year and that prisoners were forced to labor even when sick and being flogged or shot to death if they did or could not."

One could explain away the difference between North and South by noting that the southern system was and is more decentralized. There are far fewer walled prisons and many more farms and work camps. In some states, the latter represented 90 percent of the confinement procedures. This lack of major prison facilities can be explained in part by costs. It was very expensive to build and maintain real prisons; it was much cheaper to keep the convicts behind barbed wires in primitive accommodations, working in open areas from dawn till nightfall or even leasing some convicts out to outside contractors, who then bore the responsibility and costs of containing the men. Under such a system, the convict population had to be more unruly because, if as many as 90 percent were in camps or farms, it meant that inmates of all sorts, from first offenders to brutes, were left basically unrestrained. Sample ages were once described by one authority as being age "12 and up." Only "serial escapees" were kept behind prison walls.

Most outside workers engaged in farm or pick-and-shovel work, most for the upkeep of state roads. In the old days—early in the 20th century—prisoners were kept in half of a boxcar that was mounted on iron wheels. The bunks inside, up to five tiers high with only 18 inches between them, held a large number of prisoners. Now more prisoners are kept in double-decker-bunked barracks that contain 100 or more men. The "cages" still exist but more often resemble house trailers, heated and rubber tired. Not that this was or is pleasurable. As one southerner put it, "Even if it's a custom-built, stainless steel cage, it's still a cage, and if you put forty or fifty men into something the size of a house trailer, they won't be very comfortable."

In the 1950s, journalist John Bartlow Martin described the southern central prison as "ordinarily little different from northern prisons except that it is likely to be a little more tolerant about sex, a little more lax about discipline, and a little more brutal about punishment. In one southern prison the inmates eat out of salmon tins, in another they eat off rusty pie tins, in another they drink out of tomato cans. One warden has said, 'What do I care what they eat off of, they oughtn't to be here.'"

The standard rule in southern prisons is that convicts are to work as much as possible to support the system. As far as punishment is concerned, the theory in some facilities is that inmates in prison are there not as punishment but *for* punishment. Whenever some prison work camps run short of enough prisoners for their work gangs, some prisoners claim, they round up vagrants and imprison them to provide an adequate labor supply.

Despite his many criticisms, Martin is not so sure that the southern system is not superior in some ways to the massive lockups in the North, noting, "One may wonder whether a man working in a southern road camp may not suffer less personality damage than a man locked up in a place like Jackson Prison. Moreover, some men who had been imprisoned in both the South and North, clearly prefer the South, with all its discomfort, hard work, and brutality." It should be noted that some men who have proved to be good workers as convicts have been hired by state highway departments after their release, which is more than can be said for help given to ex-convicts in the North.

Clearly, the southern prison system, like the rest of the South has been for a half-century, is now in the throes of change. Martin held out a promise, not yet fully achieved, that "if the South could preserve the best features of its camp and farm system and eliminate the worst, it might well outstrip the North in progressive penology. At least it is not saddled with the enormous institutions that hobble progress in the North."

spears, jailhouse awesome prisoner-killing weapons

Not all prisoner-made weapons are killing weapons; at the least, persistent action is required to turn, for example, a shiv, or a homemade knife, into a deadly weapon. That cannot be said of the jailhouse spear, which is an awesome weapon, one that strikes fear into all in the prison, inmates and guards alike. It is generally fashioned out of scrap-metal blades and a shaft of tightly rolled newspapers.

Naturally such a spear can seldom be concealed for any length of time, and if an inmate is found in possession of one, he or she is certain to go immediately into the "Hole" or similar isolation as it is obvious that the weapon is going to be used soon in a jailhouse hit. Probably the most famous confirmed kill with a spear was the skewering of a San Quentin corrections officer in 1989, which of course triggered a wide crackdown and arrests. More often, it is intended for business hits by convicts who are involved in the prison drug trade, followed by the swift dismantling of the weapon by quick-acting prison gang members in an effort to halt detection.

Speck, Richard (1942–1991) mass murderer and controversial convict

Twice in his criminal career, Richard Speck became a "poster boy" for the tough-on-crime forces. The first was his murder of eight student nurses in Chicago in 1966. Speck, a drifter often high on alcohol and drugs, apparently was in that condition or at least later claimed to have been on July 13 when he found himself in front of a row house serving as a nurses' dormitory for the South Chicago Community Hospital. Forcing his way into an apartment shared by nine student nurses, he committed one of the nation's most heinous mass murders.

Armed with a knife and a pistol, he trapped six nurses present and tied them up. He waited until three more nurses came home and did the same to them. Speck took their money and then led the nurses, one at a time, from the room where he was holding them, strangled five, and stabbed three. He sexually assaulted one of his victims. In the process, Speck lost count, and the ninth nurse, 23-year-old Corazon Amurao, managed to slip under a bed and was not noticed by the kill-crazed assailant. She cowered there for four hours, not knowing what had happened to her roommates or if Speck was still in the apartment. An alarm clock went off at 5 A.M., but the place remained still. After another two hours, the petrified nurse finally crawled out of her hiding place. She found some of the bodies in the next room and rushed screaming to the street.

Speck was able to avoid arrest for several days until he attempted to slash his wrist and was rushed to a hospital, where he was identified as the killer.

His sentence of death in the electric chair was widely approved by the public but was commuted when the Supreme Court outlawed the death penalty in 1972. The outrage that followed in Speck's case made him a "poster boy" of sorts for those who objected to the High Court's decision. Speck was resentenced to eight consecutive terms of 50 to 150 years, meaning that he faced a possible penalty of 1,200 years in prison. By 1976, he was entitled to a parole hearing but was turned down. He was permitted to file again each year, but he never won his release.

Mass murderer Richard Speck enters court in 1967. (Bettmann/CORBIS)

But he was eventually to win his second "poster-boy" distinction. Speck died in prison in 1991, a heart attack described as the reason. A few years later, the public became informed about some of his bizarre activities behind bars. Speck became what was described as a "flaming homosexual," but, more than that, he made a porno videotape of his practices. *The Waco Tribune-Herald* headlined its account: "Richard Speck in Lingerie: They Call This Punishment."

On the tape, Speck was shown taking drugs, engaging in various sex acts with another prisoner, and bragging that he was having a wonderful time in prison with more lovers than he could count. Speck peeled off his prison jumpsuit to show off his blue women's undergarments. Speck looks directly at the camera and says, "If they only knew how much fun I was having here, they would turn me loose."

It was a performance for a so-called poster boy to show what hard-liners insist was behavior totally abhorrent to the general public and showed what convicts can get away with behind bars. Senior editor Rowland Nethaway of the *Times-Herald* commented that "lawmakers and prison officials should make sure that prisons are not turned into Club Med for felons." He added, "Prison becomes a comfortable home and a way of life for many convicts. Once released, they easily return to crime because they do not fear returning to prison. They can shoot baskets, read books, watch color TV, lift weights, renew friendships and eat three nutritious meals a day. . . .

"But taxpayers don't want happy prisoners. Taxpayers don't want prison riots, either. But they do want prisoners to feel punished for their crimes. They want prisoners to regret their crimes each and every day and swear that they will do anything in their power to never return to such a living hell. There's a big difference between cruel and unusual punishment and no punishment."

Richard Speck died in 1991, just short of age 50.

"splitting time" partial jail time

An alternate sentencing method that allows for fewer restrictions and more innovations in dealing with mostly misdemeanants is called splitting time. Originally used in drunk-charge cases, including driving while intoxicated, it has now been broadened to cover many low-weight offenses, including some that might result otherwise in triggering three-strikes-and-out laws if previous felonies are on record. The principle applied is that the offender should have some liberties restricted but without removal from home and family. Often, such a tack is worked in combination with some form of public service with a governmental agency or public service organization. Split timers see duties in nursing homes, boys' clubs, counseling agencies, or other like settings.

Often, the courts extend a form of community supervision, which in addition to a probation officer involves a third-party advocate to help keep the offender on a reliable path. Such advocates can aid the person to find a job, child care, or counseling. Such advocates usually come from offender assistance organizations.

"standing mainline" listening to inmate complaints

For many years now, it has been the practice for wardens in the federal prison system to "stand mainline." Each day at the lunch meal, the warden and his senior staff stand in the inmate dining room while the prisoners are eating. Inmates are permitted to approach the warden or others to voice complaints or make other statements. By doing this out in the open, the inmate is not likely to be viewed by the rest of the convicts as a snitch or informer.

Previously, inmates went to visit officials in pairs so that each could vouch for the others that neither had been informing. Under the mainline system, there was little need for a "corroborating witness." If some prisoners feared that there is some snitching taking place, they could walk up to the spot and hear what is being said.

Some wardens have been unhappy about standing mainline because they feel that it encourages continual whining about minor matters. However, federal officials see an important plus in the practice because the warden and his aides are completely unarmed and could easily be overwhelmed and perhaps killed by the inmates. Thus, standing mainline serves the added benefit for the institution that the warden and others are free of fear, an important image to project.

Stanford University prison experiment mock prison research

In what became a famous, or perhaps infamous, research study, a California professor, Philip Zimbardo, set up a mock prison in an effort to investigate the psychological impact of incarceration. He randomly picked students to play prisoners and others as correctional officers. Video covered the students experiences, which soon presented a frightening picture. The student guards rapidly became more cruel to the "prisoners," who suffered quick psychological deterioration.

Within six days, the experiment had to be called off. A 1990 film, *Quiet Rage: The Stanford Prison Experiment,* covering the experiment and postexperiment interviews on both student prisoners and guards, offered a most disquieting portrait. A remaining dilemma was whether the true conditions in a real prison were actually better or worse.

Stop Prisoner Rape, Inc. organization fighting sexual violence

Stop Prisoner Rape, Inc., a national nonprofit organization organized in 1979, seeks to prevent rape in all its forms in prisons, including sexual slavery, forced prostitution, and harassment. The organization seeks to educate inmates, the public, and correctional professionals by offering training, free literature, an audio tape called "Becoming a Survivor," and legal support as well to survivors. Reaching out to survivors both in prison and out, it aids in class action suits and cooperates with lawyers for survivors who file damage claims against institutions that have failed to protect inmates.

Stroud, Robert Franklin (1887–1963) "Birdman of Alcatraz"

As a 19-year-old pimp who shot a client to death and later in prison killed a guard, Robert F. Stroud

One of the best-known inmates of the Rock, Robert Stroud, or the "Birdman of Alcatraz," was permitted to keep birds in his cell and maintain a laboratory during his prison terms. (Bettmann/CORBIS)

ended up spending the last 54 years of his life behind bars, most of them in solitary confinement. Yet, in the process, he became a brilliant self-taught expert on birds and possibly the best-known example of self-improvement and rehabilitation in the U.S. prison system. He was the subject of a book, a movie, and numerous magazine and newspaper articles about both his accomplishment behind bars and the kind of treatment he received at Alcatraz.

When he was living in Juneau, Alaska, in 1909, Stroud argued over money with a bartender who had enjoyed the favor of one of the younger man's "ladies" and then refused to pay the going tariff. Stroud shot him dead. Stroud drew a 12-year prison sentence, which he served first in McNeil Island Penitentiary on Puget Sound and later at Leavenworth.

Shortly before he was scheduled to complete his term, Stroud had an altercation in the dining hall at Leavenworth with a guard and stabbed him in the chest. There was controversy as to whether the guard had been about to club him or Stroud had stabbed the guard without provocation. Authorities held to the no-provocation view, even though many of the 300 other prisoners insisted that Stroud had acted in self-defense. Also a matter of dispute was whether the guard had died of the stab wounds or as the result of a heart attack.

In any event, Stroud was tried and sentenced to be hanged. After an appeal to President Woodrow Wilson for clemency by Stroud's mother, Wilson at first refused, but at the behest of Mrs. Wilson he relented. While Stroud's sentence was changed to life, the president also stipulated that he spend all his remaining years in solitary confinement.

One day, while in his solitary exercise yard, Stroud happened on an injured sparrow, which he managed to smuggle back into his cell. He studied the sparrow intently, nursed it back to health, and even got the warden to allow him to keep some canaries in his cell. Although Stroud had only had a third-grade education, he devoured all he could find on ornithology and, in time, gained his Birdman nickname for producing two books on bird diseases and establishing a makeshift laboratory. He developed into one of the country's genuine authorities on bird ailments.

As the years passed, campaigns to win his release were launched by thousands of supporters, including veterinarians, bird breeders, and poultry raisers. But Stroud had killed an officer of the federal prison system, and government authorities were committed to keeping him behind bars and in isolation for life. It was obvious that if he, Stroud, had been given his freedom, morale among the prison-guard cadre would have sagged badly, possibly affecting the entire operation of the system.

In 1934, Alcatraz opened as the ultimate cage for supercriminals. It soon housed convicts deemed to be the most troublesome and those considered most likely to attempt an escape. In 1942, Stroud was ordered, on 10-minutes notice, to prepare to leave Leavenworth. He was not permitted to take his laboratory, his birds, or his books. All his equipment was disassembled, crated, and shipped to his brother. Because Stroud seemed unlikely to escape or to lead a riot, his transfer to Alcatraz—ironically known as the isle of the Pelicans—smacked of official sadism, fostered by the clear anger of his guards for his notoriety.

Ironically, Stroud became known as the Birdman of Alcatraz although he never conducted any of his bird studies there because he was confined under conditions that prevented him from carrying out such work.

At Alcatraz, Warden James A. Johnston seems to have done what he could to lighten Stroud's burden, at least permitting him to have books and writing material and to communicate with his publisher. Stroud busied himself on a giant history of the federal prison system. In 1946, Stroud got out of his isolation cell for the first time in 26 years during the famous Alcatraz rebellion when six convicts attempted the most dramatic and bloody escape from the Rock. In the riot that ensued, Stroud was released into the cell block. He took no part in the violence and was, in fact, instrumental in getting the authorities to stop their bombing of the cell block by giving the warden his word that none of the prisoners in the block had guns. Even this deed, along with a new rash of news stories about him, did not help Stroud's plight. He was returned to solitary confinement.

In 1948, a new warden, E. B. Swope, who succeeded Johnston, tightened controls on Stroud so that he no longer could keep in touch with his supporters or write any more business letters.

The Birdman kept on fighting, but he knew that his chances now were nil of his ever winning parole. In 1962, Stroud's story was told in an acclaimed movie starring Burt Lancaster.

Three years earlier in 1959, after a string of illnesses, Stroud had been transferred to the Federal Medical Center at Springfield, Missouri. His isolation, however, had remained as complete as ever. He died in 1963, one year after the motion picture, at the age of 76.

Stroud's giant manuscript, said to have been finished, was confiscated by the U.S. Bureau of Prisons which never permitted it be released, let alone published.

"Sudden In-Custody Death Syndrome"

probing "unexpected" deaths

In 1996, in a commission report published by Santa Clara County, California, a team of specialists explained why jail detainees seemed to die under mysterious circumstances after "tussling" with guards. They came to the conclusion that many might be victims of what was declared to be "Sudden In-Custody Death Syndrome." Besides identifying the syndrome, the report suggested that jail guards and medical people had to become aware of the "risk factors" involved in the syndrome.

At risk were:

- prisoners who had just engaged in a violent struggle.
- those who did not respond to pepper spray or pain-compliance holds.
- those handcuffed while lying in a prone position, especially face down.
- those who were drugged or drunk.
- those overweight.
- those older than 50 years of age.
- those who exhibit a period of silence.

One of the authors of the report stated, "We are increasingly concerned about this issue. In-Custody Death Syndrome is slowly being recognized as a problem with risk factors to be watched for."

Although the report was obviously presented with good intentions, some prisoners'-rights groups found it more stating of the obvious.

A unique publication, *Prison Legal News*, published in the Washington state prison system with a wide network of correspondents in state and federal prisons, printed comments by one of its coeditors, Dan Pens, on the report, hardly noncaustic and certainly mightily satiric:

> *Of course, this "syndrome" is one which has long been recognized by prisoners, who usually refer to it as "Sudden-Torture and Fatal-Beating Syndrome." Risk factors identified by prisoners over the years include: guards who smile and say "It's time you learned a lesson, boy," while swinging batons at your head; guards taking a number and standing in line outside a mop closet in which you are hog-tied, naked on the floor; guards who use racial epithets, and who may also have blood stains and bits of teeth and bone embedded in their jack-boots; and guards who exhibit periods of intense, violent rage.*
>
> *Perhaps a bilateral commission composed of experts from both the corrections community and*

those who have experienced some "corrections" first-hand could further study this mysterious syndrome and develop solutions that would allow prisoners to be tortured without actually dying in the process.

Super Bowl Sunday Chicken Riot taking over a prison

"The cons run the prison." It's a saying one hears a lot, and in many cases, it is true. It is especially true about Graterford State Prison, built in the early 1930s to hold all of Pennsylvania's most violent prisoners. It did not complete that mission, although by the late 1990s, it bulged with more than 3,500 inmates and counting, the state's largest and most violent penal institution. Today, the question can be asked: Who runs the prison? Inmates and staffers give the same answer: The inmates do.

Of Graterford, the *Philadelphia Inquirer* analysis of the institution's history in 1996 depicted a prison taken over from the nominal authorities: "Gangs proliferated, both for predation and protection, and guards, afraid for their own lives, usually looked the other way."

One defining moment for the surrender of Graterford to the inmates probably can be fixed as Super Bowl Sunday 1983. It was then that the Super Bowl Sunday Chicken Riot occurred.

The signs in the prison dining room dictated: "NO FOOD IS TO LEAVE THE DINING ROOM." It was not an order that was generally obeyed. In point of fact, inmates frequently took food with them, but it was no particular problem because guards never searched inmates. The food simply was kept out of sight, and everyone was satisfied.

But this was Super Bowl Sunday, and one inmate simply decided that he no longer wanted to waste time in the mess hall while the game was on. He simply loaded a paper plate full of chicken with the appropriate trimmings and headed for his cell. A guard challenged him and told him to either eat his food in the room or throw it away. The inmate, reflecting the growing power of the inmates in the prison, told the guard he was going back to his cell and enjoy the football game. The guard then grabbed the plate away from the rebellious inmate. It was not a judicious act—not on Super Bowl Sunday, when many, perhaps most, of the inmates had started to celebrate early on an important sports day by getting drunk on contraband hooch, an activity the prison had not been able to stop.

An explosion followed. Dozens of prisoners charged the guard and beat him severely. Dozens more defiantly mobbed the serving tables and loaded up on chicken to head for their cells. But first, every guard present was assaulted and many locked in cells. The riot was now out of control, but unlike other riots, none of the inmates took the opportunity to assault other inmates as well. It was as though the inmates were working on a coherent plan, although they probably were not.

Someone got hold of a guard's radio transmitter and called for reinforcements. Scores of inmates seized sticks and clubs and readied to greet the reinforcements. When about a dozen guards charged in, they were fallen upon, subdued, and tossed into cells. Many of the guards were abused and humiliated, but not seriously injured. Once the convicts were satisfied, they opened the main door to the cell block and let other guards in to tend to their trapped buddies.

As far as the inmates were concerned that was the end of the riot. The inmates were perfectly content back in their cells, gnawing on their chicken, boozing, and watching the game. There was no retribution during the game, until the late count, when a number of rebellious inmates were quietly taken to the "Hole."

But as perhaps the best inmate-expert on conditions in Graterford, Victor Hassine (who is authorized by the Pennsylvania Department of Corrections to participate in telephone conferences with students in college classrooms) declares in *Life Without Parole:*

> *By then it was too late. The point had been made. Inmates had joined together to defeat the guards fair and square. The interests of the inmate population had been advanced and defended, thus ensuring the livelihood of each and every man in the triumphant Kingdom of the Inmates.*
>
> *To this day, Graterford is still the most violent prison in the state system. It now houses over 4,000 men and is home to the most politically active inmate population in Pennsylvania. If you ask any staff member or inmate who runs Grater-*

ford, the answer will always be the same: "The inmates run Graterford."

In succeeding years, it can be said that Graterford went on to more violence and greater scandals, for which Super Bowl Sunday represented perhaps the opening kickoff.

"supermax" prisons return to concept of near total isolation of prisoners
There are many distinctive qualities to the new Administrative Maximum Facility in Florence, Colorado. It is regarded as the premier so-called supermax institution in the nation and the crown jewel of the Federal Bureau of Prisons. Jewel may be regarded as a proper description as far as cost is concerned. The institution holds fewer than 400 prisoners and has almost one prison employee per inmate. Behind the concept of supermax is the desire to modify the behavior of violent prisoners by what can only be entombing them in isolation cells for up to 23 hours a day—a practice instituted in the early 19th century in both the Pennsylvania and the New York (or Auburn) systems.

Supermax is set up to be completely silent (exactly as contemplated by the nation's early prisons). There is an empty fluorescent-lit hallway, and, according to administrators, there are no shouts and screams across cell blocks, or convicts banging on bars, or even the sound of a radio. Movements in the prison are restricted by 1,400 electronically controlled gates and viewed by 168 television monitors.

The budget for supermax runs about $50,000 a year for each prisoner, about two-and-a-half times the approximately $20,000 average cost elsewhere.

Unsurprisingly, supermax is the prison confinement that convicts fear most, conjuring up terror. A good example of this is John Gotti, who was sent to Marion Penitentiary in Illinois in 1992 for life for his Mafia activities. At the time, the Florence institution was not yet completed. Marion was regarded as the most feared prison in the country and was cited as being inhumane by Amnesty International. Marion—like the new supermax in Colorado—operates under a quota system, calling for the transfer of lifers to less harsh institutions after they have served 30 months and demonstrate the ability to be subject to discipline. Under such a set-up, Gotti was eligible for transfer in 1995, but he remained in Marion. It was well known that his lawyers were fearful of making an issue of his situation because there was general suspicion that if they did so, their client would be simply shipped off to the still harsher supermax.

At supermax, the prisoners fall into two basic groups. The smaller group is the so-called bomber wing, in which some of the nation's most notorious offenders or bomber terrorists are held under very close confinement, among them Unabomber Theodore J. Kaczynski and 1993 World Trade Center bombing mastermind Ramzi Ahmed Yousef. They are put in supermax not for behavior problems but because authorities say they would very likely face violence in less-secure prisons. Another consideration is that supermax offers far fewer opportunities for escape.

Of course, supermax is basically set up to take the "worst of the worst" among the 100,000 inmates in the federal prison population. In supermax about 35 percent have committed murder in prison, 85 have committed assaults in prison, and 41 percent have made escape attempts. After doing three years in supermax, prisoners who are not transferred elsewhere are offered the chance to spend more time out of their cells. However, among them, it has been said that there is such a strong hatred for supermax that many refuse. One inmate told a *New York Times* reporter: "Prolonged isolation is the worst punishment you can put on a human being. The common denominator among prisoners is rage, pent-up range, frustration." Many prisoners stay in their cells and refuse to come out for recreation. They turn jumpy and become enraged when having to deal with people.

Yes, there is the occasional prisoner who adapts well to supermax—or in prisoner parlance, they can "beat the system." One is Charles Harrelson, the hit-man father of actor Woody Harrelson, doing two consecutive life sentences for murdering a federal judge in the 1970s. His son has been trying for years to get him a new trial. The elder Harrelson has managed to make supermax attuned to his interests to some extent. He notes that his previous prison did not have a shower in the room but did have a lot of noise. He told the *Times*, "Peace and quiet is paramount for people like me

Supermax U.S. penitentiary, Marion, Illinois (Federal Bureau of Prisons)

who like to write. But for people who can't read and write it must be pure hell. They designed this place for sensory deprivation. It's an Orwellian experience."

The Florence supermax authorities insist that they have found "no evidence to show that people are deteriorating." Inmates' lawyers find their experiences different. One who represents the leader of a New York gang, the Latin Kings, says his client "has retreated into himself; that is where the destruction of his personality is taking place. He has deteriorated to the extent that he prefers to stay in his cell. He takes no recreation."

Many experts agree that the real determination on how much psychological damage is caused probably has to be judged for a longer span of years. It has been noted that by the time Alcatraz was closed in 1963, it was estimated that as many as 60 percent of the prisoners were "stir crazy," or insane, and despite its awesome reputation, Alcatraz had eliminated many of its truly restrictive measures, so that today supermax can be regarded as far more fearful than the long-shuttered prison by the bay. Some critics note that the possibility of release to a less restrictive prison is itself a recognition that the prison is not very conducive to prisoner well-being.

Also, in late 2000, the supermax was hit by scandal involving alleged brutality by some prison guards who supposedly belonged to a renegade group called the Cowboys and who were said to have choked handcuffed inmates (until their eyes bulged), mixed waste into inmate food, and threatened other guards. According to the allegations, a guard who criticized the abuses was told that his colleagues that might not help if he were attacked by an inmate. Group beatings were justified for such minor offenses as kicking a door. Under a federal indictment, five alleged Cowboys and two others faced trial and, if convicted, would face up to 10 years in prison and fines of up to $250,000.

Critics saw the charges as a logical outgrowth of the concept of the prison holding the "worst of the worst." Slogans like this, they have complained, give a green light to brutal acts against inmates who deserve no better.

It has been charged, too, that supermax and many other imitators in various state institutions produce brutal results because they concentrate on the fact that concentrating problem and violent inmates in one institution leads to a resultant drop in prison violence elsewhere, a specific claim made by supermax.

Unfortunately, the fact remains that most prisoners held in various supermaxes eventually leave the prison system under their finite sentences. Their condition in many cases leave them "grossly disorganized and psychotic," according to Dr. Stuart Grassian, a Harvard psychiatrist who has studied the effects in a number of supermax institutions. Convicts were found to be "smearing themselves with feces, mumbling and screaming incoherently all day and all night, some even descending to the horror of eating parts of their own bodies."

Pragmatic observers might allow such harsh practices if, as one journalist has stated, the victims never are loosed into civil life. But most of them will be. Most prisoners receiving supermax treatment in various institutions are released. The question arises: In what shape? Dr. Grassian sees the practice as "kind of like kicking and beating a dog and keeping it in a cage until it gets crazy and vicious and wild as it can possibly get and then one day you take it out into the middle of streets of San Francisco or Boston and you open the cage and you run away."

Some find the results predictable. In an article in *The Celling of America,* federal prisoner and supermax inmate Ray Luc Levasseur said in 1996 that "a prisoner released from the isolation and brutality of California's notorious control unit at Pelican Bay killed a cop before he got home and unpacked his bag. Apparently, someone forgot to explain the finer points of deterrence to him. The response of the state representative from the district including Pelican Bay was illuminating. He introduced legislation mandating that released Pelican Bay prisoners be transported directly to their destination, so that when the bodies drop it will be in some other bailiwick, and not stain the Department of Corrections."

If that sentiment reflects too much of a convict's eye view, there is the further observance of Dr. Grassian to his wild-dog release allusion: "That's no favor to the community."

See also: "COWBOYS, THE"; MARION PENITENTIARY.

sweatboxes prison torture
A standard prison torture exacted for decades in U.S. prisons was that of the sweatbox. In southern jurisdictions, the sweatbox was a narrow enclosure that was not unlike the accommodations offered many work-camp prisoners, narrow spaces of cagelike sleeping quarters in which a large number of chained inmates were confined during sleeping hours. With tin roofs that allowed in and retained sun heat, they could be said to make prisoners eager to get out in the predawn to escape the discomfort by working instead. The sweatbox was one for punishment of recalcitrant prisoners with little space for just one inhabitant and virtually no ventilation because the sides of the box were closed. Men could simply lie there and roast in the grueling heat, enough in some cases to cause death or, little better, madness.

An added "virtue" of the sweatbox is that plunges of temperatures during the night would turn conditions in the box severely colder so that it became a "cool box" until the morning heat returned. Men released after many days in the sweatbox frequently could not stand for hours. This led to some temperance of the length of punishment because such a victim could not immediately be put to productive labors. Sweatboxes in various forms were used against colonial or Tory offenders, against Indians who would not be "civilized," and blacks both before and after the Civil War. In the Reconstruction era, chain gangs enforced by Union troops also included sweatboxes and could be used against freedmen offenders for such offenses as "using abusive language towards a white man."

It was the chilling details about the particular sweatbox used in the Georgia penal system as described by Robert Elliott Burns in his book and the film *I Am a Fugitive from a Chain Gang* that genuinely shocked the United States. The sweatbox in this case was a barrel with iron staves on top.

In some areas where sweatboxes could not be utilized year round, the problem was solved by providing for inside versions that could be positioned near a heat outlet. In the 1950s, a unique form of a sweatbox was utilized. The cells in the "Hole" contained a curved, inner-steel door, and inmates could be fastened in them between it and the regular cell door; they were left there so closely confined that they could not even move. After a stint in such confinement, the regular portion of the Hole cell must have been regarded as on the luxurious side.

"Swing Swing" the rise and decline of Sing Sing
Perhaps the best-known U.S. prison is New York's Sing Sing. Although its story could be told in a long book, for this work it is best told through various individuals who left their mark on U.S. penology and who should be studied in terms of their own works because they represent the mores and manners of a particular time. There was, of course, Elam Lynds, the man who built Sing Sing on the backs of hundreds of suffering convicts and today is generally regarded as the worst warden in U.S. penology; such beacons of enlightened wardens as Thomas Mott Osborne and Lewis E. Lawes deserve study as do famous or infamous inmates who for one reason or another gained national or international attention.

Aside from certain periods of acclaim, Sing Sing itself did not enjoy too much approval. Back in the 19th century, the town of Sing Sing was so outraged by the methods that were used in the prison and was so disparaged by outsiders that it abandoned its name for that of the Indian word *Ossining*.

After Lawes retired in 1940, it appeared that his imprint on Sing Sing was so great that his reforms would never die, but, slowly, they withered on the vine despite the efforts of some administrators to

The roofless original Sing Sing prison cell block sits in the middle of the present-day maximum security prison in Ossining, New York. (AP/Wide World Photos)

live by them. Improvements were not carried on in the prison, and by the early 1980s, the institution had long been marginalized by the pressing need for new prisons. State money poured in elsewhere, and Sing Sing was on its own. It gained an enhanced reputation as being loose and wild. Guards and their superiors were charged with corruption and being paid to smuggle marijuana and hard drugs. There were takeovers of cell blocks by prisoners and a major hostage crisis. The ability of the prison to hold its inmates came into question. An example of this was the escape of three inmates, two of them murderers. They used smoke bombs as a cover and then went through a window in the school building down to railroad tracks below, using wire cutters and a 30-foot rope made of shoelaces.

Then public attitudes toward the grim prison became even worse when in 1988 news stories broke about such things headlined in the press as "Sing Sing Sexcapades." The *New York Daily News* bannered a report called "SWING SWING" that read:

> *Sex, drugs and gambling have been rampant in Sing Sing prison over the last two years under the protection of a clique of rogue correction officers, according to guards and a former prison official.*
>
> *The sexual escapades in the maximum-security prison allegedly include trysts between male inmates and female guards—including two suspected of prostitution—in the prison chapel, projection room and a cell.*
>
> *Guards who tried to crack down on inmate drug use were subject to death threats—purportedly by corrupt officers, according to one guard.*

It was revealed that random urine tests indicated that 21 percent of the prison's inmates were on drugs. This compared with a statewide prison average of 6 percent.

At the time, tottering Sing Sing was well more than a century and a half old. By contrast, the federal prison of Alcatraz lasted a mere three decades. The town of Ossining renewed demands that Sing Sing should be shut down. What was particularly galling to town officials was the fact that the town could collect no taxes on 55 acres of prime riverfront land.

In 2000, a book, *Newjack: Guarding Sing Sing,* offered a condemnation and was hailed by critics for offering an incisive and indelible look "at the dark life of the penal system." The author, Ted Conover, had sought to follow a "newjack," or rookie guard, through his training and early career in Sing Sing but was refused permission. Instead, he secretly applied for and acquired such a post for himself.

Despite the book's revelations, Sing Sing still stands, required in a state where prison space is too valuable to be lost, despite descriptions of it as little more than metal junk, or as the *Chicago Tribune* called it, leading proof today of the view that "It is hard to know if there has ever been an institution that cost more and achieved less than a prison."

T

television for prisoners a contradictory battle
When, in the 1970s, prison inmates and their supporters started to campaign for television, correctional officials took a hard-nosed opposition to the idea. Then, as a few television permissions were granted, a strange reversal of positions occurred. Prison officials couldn't get enough televisions for their inmates, and militant prisoners started to campaign for the removal of the sets that they had demanded. They now saw television as nothing more than a pacification program to keep convicts docile. There was a three-way fight involving the inmates, the vast majority of whom want TV, the keepers who want them to have it, and the militants who don't want them to have it. The public, fired up by get-tough proponents and many elements of the media that were often described as "conservatives," were involved in the melee as well, in effect siding with the prison militants—often described as "radicals" or "Marxists"—against what the latter group especially refers to as "the boob tube."

Although there have been some victories or, at least, partial victories by the get-tough elements so that televisions were pulled or their use restricted in some fashion, the clear winners remain prison officials. For the best way to measure the scope of that triumph, one has only to look at the actions by the Federal Bureau of Prisons. To calls for withdrawal of television rights from inmates, the bureau has maintained what probably can be best described as "benign indifference."

U.S. officials and many state corrections authorities who follow their lead, or perhaps the cover that they offer, have held to that line. One federal prisoner notes caustically that authorities "will fix a broken TV before they'll fix a broken toilet."

Prison keepers have frustrated the get-tough-and-no-television forces in many cases. In Massachusetts, former federal prosecutor William Weld was elected governor as a hard-line Republican, vowed to "get tough on crime," and had pledged in his campaign to rid the state's prisons of television sets. He was incapable of keeping the promise. Under pressure from hard-liners in Florida, the Department of Corrections (DOC) was ordered to stop allowing prisoners to own TV sets privately, which would have effectively eliminated television in most facilities. The DOC simply sidestepped the law by interpreting it to mean that it could not expend funds on new sets, and it continued to repair and refurbish older TVs. Corrections officials had predicted that strict enforcement of the rules would lead to more violence in prisons. In other jurisdictions, courts have ruled that prisons were required to sell TVs in their commissaries (in one state the rule was the sets had to be limited in price to $140 and be equipped with earplugs or earphones).

The fact is that television is a boon for prison authorities, turning many prisoners into "bunk potatoes." Inmates hooked on television are docile and are no problem to control. One prison sought to keep it that way by showing five full-length movies each day. There are inmates totally addicted to soap operas. There are prisoners, many lifers, who have not missed a day of *All My Children* in 15 or 20 years, ignoring yard time or other vital activities in favor of keeping up with the doings of soap character Erica Kane and the others, whom they regard as family.

The drumbeat against television for prisoners continues in the mainstream press. Concerning the Jefferson City Correctional Center in Missouri, *Reader's Digest* once complained in an article about some prisons being "resorts" and said that inmates there "run their own around-the-clock, closed circuit TV studio. Four channels routinely broadcast movies containing sex, horror and violence." In a reply by prison activist Jon Marc Taylor in *Prison Life,* which perhaps surprisingly made it into the mainstream press as well, the response came that "JeffTown"—the name of the system—is completely funded by profits from items purchased in the commissary and is watched on prisoner-bought TVs. The claim was made that the movies matched the R, PG, and G-rated films available from Blockbuster.

Taylor notes, "In addition to funding the cable system and using fees, JeffTown weekly rebroadcasts over a hundred hours of educational, PBS, and religious programs, another key point omitted from the article. Periodically, the superintendent uses the system to talk directly to the 2,000-man population and on one occasion credited JeffTown's service with helping calm the institution after a major disturbance, thereby avoiding further costly trouble." JeffTown produces programs made available around the country on such matters as substance abuse/recovery stories. It also makes available to other state agencies production facilities when they cannot afford the $10,000 fee that outside companies would charge.

Taylor also adds, "The final interesting twist is that no one, from the superintendent on down to the video technicians, was ever contacted by anyone from *Reader's Digest.*"

The point to be made is that television is a vital aid to prisons, and most administrations are simply impervious to charges of "coddling." They do not seek to coddle prisoners but to make them, for better or worse, pacified or what may be called "contented cons."

Similarly, the prison militants go nowhere with characterizing inmates as saying, "Look, you all can do anything you want to us, so long as you let us watch TV." Nor are their warnings that nothing makes the public's blood boil as much as the thought of convicted killers and violent criminals sitting around watching TV. Militant Adrian Lomax, writing in *Prison Legal News,* declared, "Many people are even moved to support capital punishment because they so loathe the notion of convicted murderers watching TV in prison."

Nothing works. Administrations and prisoners hold on to those sets. When Timothy McVeigh was executed in 2001 for the devastating bombing of the federal building in Oklahoma in 1995 at the federal penitentiary at Terre Haute, Indiana, it was said that corrections people were on alert for possible violent protests by inmates. It turned out to be a relative nonevent. One inmate said that it would have been different if the preparations and carrying out of the execution interfered with television programming. "There will be trouble if we don't get to watch the NBA basketball playoffs."

Television remains alive and well behind bars.

tent cities "price-is-right prisons"

In Arizona, there has been a steady growth of incarceration of prisoners in tent cities, which opponents disparage as "price-is-right prisons." There are rows and rows of army tents set up on the outskirts of Phoenix that appear to be a military compound. It does not accommodate members of the armed services, but rather prisoners, and this tent city is not overseen by an army commander, but rather by an Arizona sheriff named Joe Arpaio, who has gained a folk hero status within the "get-tough-on-prisoners" movement.

Arpaio is head law enforcer of Maricopa County and as a sheriff is the holder of a very powerful position in Arizona. Arpaio, say some reformers, is pretty much a law unto himself. Legendary for his hard-line approach to incarceration, Arpaio has erected tent cities to house inmates doing a year or less time. Temperatures at times in tent cities in Arizona can hit 120 degrees, but Arpaio dismisses any objection to the living conditions. "Our men and women went to Saudi Arabia [as part of Desert Storm] and lived in tents, and they didn't even commit a crime. Why would someone complain about putting convicted prisoners in tents?"

Conditions in the tent cities can be described as "frill-less" and there is no basketball, no weights, no coffee, no cigarettes, and no television, but there are dogs with cameras strapped to their backs patrolling the perimeter of the tents, which house 20 inmates each. Besides being tough-on-convicts, it can be said to be easy on the government budgets. Bologna is a favorite item on the menu because it is just about the cheapest meat obtainable.

The sheriff makes no bones about inmates working in the community chained together and some wear striped prison uniforms, long discarded at many institutions. "That's the way it should be," Arpaio says.

"People are fed up with crime, and they want somebody to do something about it instead of talking about it.

His uncompromising comments have won him wide popularity in the state, and some supporters are boosting him for the governorship. He has written a book, *The Toughest Sheriff in America,* which just might make a campaign biography.

Needless to say, prison reformers have little good to say about him and his tent cities. They point out that his charges are low-term prisoners, which makes penal enforcement somewhat akin to shooting fish in a barrel. Many prisoners are young, and their "warehousing," critics say, will only cause them to become more antisocial and be a worse problem when they are freed. They argue that amenities are not only proper but a must to keep prisoners from causing trouble. A representative of the American Civil Liberties Union declares: "Things like sports, that's just simple common sense. Most people in prison are of a young age and full of energy. They are going to find some way of releasing it." The spokesman added without amenities as an outlet, "prison become[s] very difficult to manage, and it becomes very dangerous for the staff that works in there."

Not long ago 400 inmates at the tent cities rioted, setting fires and holding 11 guards hostage until they got a meeting with the sheriff to discuss conditions at his prison.

The sign at the entrance to Tent City at the St. Lucie County Jail in Fort Pierce, Florida, welcomes weekend prisoners who will stay in U.S. Army surplus tents. The tents are used to alleviate jail overcrowding. (AP/Wide World Photos)

Thayendanega (Two-Sticks-of-Wood-Bound-Together) (1742–1807) Mohawk critic of U.S. penal systems

Thayendanega (Two-Sticks-of-Wood-Bound-Together), the Mohawk leader also known as Joseph Brant, was perhaps the most eloquent Indian spokesman to denounce the U.S. penal system, among which the Indians had traditionally been among the most ill treated. Thayendanega-Brant had been educated in Connecticut and then attended Dartmouth College, where he translated the Bible into Mohawk. Brant sided with the British during the American Revolution and, according to American sources, had taken part in massacres of American civilians.

In a remarkable letter sent to Thomas Eddy, who got to know Brant during his philanthropic activities, the Indian leader dismissed the claims that Indians were less civilized than whites. The communication was a damning indictment of white prisons, in which, for another century or more, Indian prisoners were subjected to terrible mistreatment.

Brant wrote:

> *In the government you call civilized, the happiness of the people is constantly sacrificed to the splendor of empire. . . . [A]mong us we have* no *prisons. We have no pompous parade of courts; we have no written laws, and yet judges are as highly revered among us as they are among you, and their decisions as much regarded. Property, to say the least, is well guarded, and crimes are as impartially punished. We have among us, no splendid villains above the control of our laws. Daring wickedness is here never suffered to triumph over helpless innocence; the estates of widows and orphans are never devoured by enterprising sharpers. In a word, we have no robbery under the colour of law. . . . The palaces and prisons among you form a most dreadful contrast. . . . Go to one of your prisons;—here description utterly fails. Kill them, if you please—kill them, too, by torture; but let the torture last no longer than a day. Those you call savages, relent; the most furious of our tormentors exhausts his rage in a few hours, and dispatches the unhappy victim with a sudden stroke. Perhaps it is eligible that incorrigible offenders should sometimes be cut off—Let it be done in a way that is not degrading to human nature; let such unhappy men have an opportunity, by the fortitude of their death, of making an atonement, in some measure, for the crimes they have committed during their lives. . . . And will you ever again call the Indian nation cruel? Liberty, to a rational creature, as much exceeds property, as the light of the sun does that of the most twinkling star. . . . I had rather die by the most severe tortures ever inflicted on this continent, than languish in one of your prisons for a single year.*

Thomas, Clarence (1948–) Supreme Court justice

It was a case that prisoner's-rights advocates expected to win, and they did, but the result left them with much trepidation. It came in the dissent written by Supreme Court Justice Clarence Thomas.

The case was *Hudson v. McMillian,* in which a prisoner at the Louisiana State Penitentiary at Angola was viciously and brutally beaten by prison guards while he was handcuffed and chained. One guard held him, while two others, 200-pounders, kicked and punched him. The inmate ended up with bruises, facial swelling, and cracking of his dental plate. The Supreme Court had to decide whether or not the guards used excessive force beyond what was necessary to maintain discipline. It turned out that one of the guards did suggest to the other two "not to have too much fun."

Hudson argued that the beating violated the Eighth Amendment's protection from cruel and unusual punishment. The High Court's majority agreed, stating, "[W]e hold that whenever prison officials stand accused of using excessive physical force in violation of the Cruel and Unusual Punishments Clause, the core judicial inquiry is . . . whether force was applied in a good-faith effort to maintain or restore discipline, or maliciously and sadistically use force to cause harm, contemporary standards of decency always are violated. This is true whether or not significant injury is evident. Otherwise the Eighth Amendment would permit any physical punishment no matter how diabolic or inhuman, inflicting less than some arbitrary quantity of injury."

While the decision did set a standard for determining when prison physical punishments violate the Eighth Amendment, prisoners'-right advocates were not totally happy, given the dissent of Justice Clarence Thomas, which raised the possibility that the findings might not last. Justice Thomas argued that "primary responsibility for preventing and punishing such conduct rests not with the Federal

U.S. Supreme Court Justice Clarence Thomas (AP/Wide World Photos)

Constitution but with the laws and regulations of the various States."

Thomas also stated opposition to "the pervasive view that the Federal Constitution must address all ills in our society. . . . The Eighth Amendment is not, and should not be turned into, a National Code of Prison Regulation."

To advocates of the prisoners'-rights movement, this was a throwback to the old hands-off doctrine, during which time the courts were loath to intervene for the rights of prisoners for almost any reason.

What some observers really feared, observed Nicole Hahn Rafter and Debra L. Stanley in *Prisons in America,* was that "If Thomas's view prevails in the long run, prisoners would no longer fall under the protections of the U.S. Constitution."

Thomaston, Maine, state prison determinedly dark and comfortless

Before the Auburn and Pennsylvania prison systems came into being post-1816, the concept of *penitentiaries* and the theories behind them were little known throughout other U.S. prisons. The term *penitentiary,* under the Pennsylvania system, indicated that prisoners were to be kept in total isolation from other offenders and thus free of, as one writer put it, "earthly corruption, contamination, or infection." This would under such a system allow the prisoners to repent and be reformed, that is, the term *penitentiary.*

Early American prisons did not necessarily see their responsibility in that light. The key was punishment. In 1815, Massachusetts's Charlestown Prison was ordered by its directors that discipline "should be as severe as the laws of humanity by any means tolerate."

Undoubtedly, the institution most determined to test such limits was Thomaston State Prison in Maine. It had been founded by a physician, Dr. Daniel Rose, who insisted that prisons should be as dark and comfortless as possible. He set up underground cells that could only be accessed through a 2-feet-square hole. As Scott Christianson noted in *With Liberty for Some:* "Convicts were planted like so many potatoes."

"toilet training" prison survival tactic

It is sometimes referred to as "toilet training" or "leg in, leg out." Whatever the terminology, it is vital for new prisoners to learn the life-saving tactic quickly. An inmate must be alert for an attack at all times. Killers know that the best time to catch an inmate off guard is when he or she is sitting on the toilet in his or her cell. Attackers break in suddenly and do their deadly work quickly unless a potential victim knows how to fight back.

The most important survival tack is for an inmate to sit on the toilet with one leg completely free of clothes. Thus, he or she at least can jump up and defend himself. If, however, both legs are in clothes, the inmate will trip when hit in a surprise attack and, helpless on the floor, make an even easier target for a deadly knife onslaught.

Tombs New York City's prison

New York City's original prison, the Tombs, was a violent place, housing violent offenders and indeed having a violent birth. The need for a large prison was the idea of city officials following the business collapse of 1807–08. The poor became more violent and threatened major riots and revolt. The building of a large prison, it was decided, would provide work for the poor and for many tradespeople who were facing ruin.

The prison was to be built on a huge marshland in lower Manhattan, and the draining and filling of the swamp would take years to complete, which was deemed quite acceptable because it kept idle hands away from lawbreaking. When the landfill was complete, work on construction finally began on a huge area for the Criminal Courts Building and the Tombs Prison. Completed in 1838, the Tombs bore the name of the Halls of Justice, but became better known as the Tombs because its design was copied from that of an ancient mausoleum, which John L. Stevens had illustrated in *Stevens' Travels,* a book he wrote after an extensive tour of Egypt.

Almost from the beginning, the Tombs was rocked by scandal. The popular observance was that a mausoleum was intended to keep intruders out, but this one failed to keep insiders from leaving. Escapes through bribery and corruption were said to be common.

From the beginning the Tombs was subject to calls for prison reform. Inmates were kept in conditions that were denounced as "harsh and bleak and cold and damp." It was said that anyone confined there for an extended period of time faced a likely death sentence. Repeated calls for its closing because of uninhabitability reached an unrelieved crescendo by 1850.

However, the first major scandal erupted not over the ill treatment of the many but rather the tender treatment of the few, especially in the case of John C. Colt, a young playboy member of a millionaire merchant family and brother of Samuel Colt, inventor of the Colt revolver and the Colt repeating rifle. At 22, in 1841, John was tall, slim, and handsome with curly blond hair and steel-gray eyes. He was the darling of society and fancied himself a writer, numbering among his friends Edgar Allan Poe, Washington Irving, George Palmer Putnam, Lewis Clark, and John Howard Payne, author of *Home Sweet Home.*

Despite his literary bent, young Colt had a fast, uncertain temper, and in a violent argument, he killed Samuel Adams, a printer whom he had hired to produce his book. Colt was tried and sentenced to hang. There were many whispers that Colt would never be executed, that his family was too powerful.

The concept of his apparent invulnerability gained popular support when it was disclosed that he received fine treatment behind bars, which provided him with a very happy life for a condemned man, far different from other residents of Murderer's Row. He had flowers on his table and a pet canary. A young reporter for the *Tribune,* Charles Dana, informed readers: "In a patent extension chair he lolls smoking an aromatic Havana. . . . He has on an elegant dressing-gown, faced with cherrycolored silk, and his feet are encased in delicately worked slippers. His food was not cooked in the Tombs, but brought in from a hotel. It consists of a variety of dishes—quail on toast, game patés, reed birds, fowl, vegetables, coffee, cognac. Then it is back again to his easy chair with book and cigar."

The public outcry about such a situation proved nothing compared with the bizarre events that occurred on November 18, 1842, when Colt was scheduled to be hanged. The authorities made a concession to Colt's grand station by granting permission for him to marry his fiancée, Caroline Henshaw, that very morning. Newspaper announcements of the combined nuptials–gallows ceremony brought out thrill seekers by the thousands to Centre (later Center) Street at dawn. Because of the throngs, Miss Henshaw's carriage had to go to a side-street entrance at about 11:30. While the actual wedding ceremony was going on, carpenters assembling the gallows in the courtyard obliged by suspending the hammering, a fact relayed to the crowd outside. Then there was word, "They're married!" More news followed as it occurred. "The guests have left. . . . There are silk curtains across the cell door. . . . They've ordered champagne. . . . They're testing the gallows!"

A little after 1 P.M., the bride was informed that it was time for her to leave, and she did so "smiling bravely." Later, there would be considerable speculation that Caroline slipped her groom a large dagger with which he could stab himself in the heart and so escape the noose. At 3:30 P.M., the Rev. Henry Anton, who had officiated at the wedding, was advised to offer his final service to the condemned man.

At that very moment, the tinder-dry wooden cupola atop the Hall of Justice mysteriously caught fire. Within three minutes, smoke poured into the interior of the building. Panic ensued and most of the guards fled the building, while trapped prisoners banged on their bars, begging to be released. Apparently some of the remaining keepers did so. In the confusion, the Reverend Anton rushed to Sheriff Monmouth Hart and shouted, "Mr. Colt is dead! He has a dagger in his heart!"

Instead of racing to the cell, Sheriff Hart went off looking for the doctor who was there to pronounce Colt dead after the hanging. At 7 P.M., a hurriedly convened coroner's jury officially declared Colt to be dead by suicide. It was a remarkable hearing with no official identification of Colt being made. The family had declined to view the body because of the reported distortion of Colt's features. Not even Reverend Anton was called to testify. The body was released and buried the same night. Afterward, the young Widow Colt disappeared from the city, never to be seen there again.

At first, newspaper conjecture concentrated on the source of the death weapon. Under suspicion was every member of the wedding party, and most especially the now-missing bride. Only when authorities finally conceded that a number of prisoners had escaped during the fire did it suddenly occur that Colt could have escaped in the confusion—if there was a body to take his place. The theory developed that another prisoner could have been "recruited" for that role. It appeared useless to dig up Colt's body because his family would now say it was he while families of the escaped prisoner could be expected to identify him as their kin, thus calling off any future search for him. Needless to say, Tombs officials wound up with a very black eye. The *New York Herald* commented, "We have no doubt that Governor Seward will order an investigation at once into this most unheard of, most unparalleled tragedy." No investigation was held, although the newly appointed chief of police, George Walling, indicated considerable credence to the possibility of a substitute corpse.

So, too, did Colt's writer friends, men noted for a delight in dark conspiracies. In the late 1840s, Poe received an unsigned manuscript written, he insisted, in the unmistakable hand of John Colt. He rushed to the offices of *The Knickerbocker* to show it to editor Lewis Clark, only to find that the latter had also received a copy. Both decided this was Colt's way of informing them that he was still alive and still trying to establish a literary career. Then, in 1852, a close friend of Colt, Samuel Everett, returned from a visit to California and informed others in the sympathetic Colt circle that he met John Colt while horseback riding in the Santa Clara Valley. Everett told his happy listeners that Colt was living in a magnificent hacienda with his wife, Caroline.

There have been many in later years who have derided the substitute-corpse tale and Everett's account as apocryphal, insisting that the so-called conspiracy was just an effort to keep a good story going. Poe, especially, was noted for making up facts from whole cloth. On the other hand, the true believers found the very idea of Colt committing suicide at the precise time that a mysterious fire would break out, allowing a number of prisoners to escape, staggering to the imagination, and, they added, there remained the mystery why Mrs. Colt disappeared from New York City after her husband's death.

These conspiracy believers joined in a general condemnation of the Tombs administrations with the first cries made for closing down the prison as uninhabitable, saying all should be fired for running a prison that was more like a sieve.

The sieve charge would dog the Tombs for the rest of its days. There were so many escapes, the public believed, that they could not be ascribed to mere incompetence. With every escape, the belief grew that payoffs to keepers, high and low, were involved. A typical case was Jack Mahaney, a thief and great escape artist. He became a poster boy for the *National Police Gazette,* which reveled in his exploits. Mahaney had a record of numerous escapes: Twice he escaped from the Tombs, twice from Sing Sing, and several times from a number of prisons, as well as leaping from speeding trains and escaping without injury. The public accepted him as a great escaper, but so bad was the reputation of the Tombs that the suspicions wouldn't die down that he used an old time-honored method of breaking out—simple bribery.

The Tombs never escaped charges of very suspicious escapes and terrible maltreatment of minor prisoners. Finally, in 1902, it was shut down and replaced by a new Tombs. Tombs II could not be said to have fared any better in public opinion. Escapes were so many that some newspapers wondered if New York City was capable of holding dangerous criminals. Finally, the second Tombs was closed by a federal justice who ruled that it, like its predecessor, was uninhabitable.

"tough fags" new movement by gay and bisexual prisoners

There has been, in recent years, the growth of a new but forceful prison group in some correctional facilities to deal with the problems of prison rape. The lead group has been one forged by Ed Mead at Walla Walla Penitentiary in Washington who organized Men Against Sexism. It has been described as being composed of gay and bisexual inmates known as "tough fags" and has used violence to protect weaker inmates from rape. The tough fags will physically punish sexual predators, whom many inmates in any number of facilities say are given carte blanche by prison authorities in the name of a more "quiet" prison. The net result as tough-fag militancy spreads is that at least some institutions will have to do more to prevent sexual harassment of prisoners.

Further reading: "Concrete mama: prison profiles from Walla Walla," presentation by Ed Mead and Bo Brown at Critical Resistance, Beyond the Prison Industrial Complex Conference, September 23–25, 1998, University of California, Berkeley.

tower guards feared and hated prison guards

It is wrong to assume that there is constant open hostility between most guards and prisoners, but there are exceptions. One can find the guards whom prison inmates genuinely hate. They are in the gun towers.

To hear the inmates, conflicts or attacks against guards are the result of guards enforcing what the prisoners regard as petty rules. In *Life Without Parole*—a generally acclaimed book written with the permission and support of a Pennsylvania commissioner of corrections—by prisoner Victor Hassine, the author, a law school graduate, said he was surprised when he entered prison to find that many guards and inmates go out of their way to establish good relationships with each other.

Hassine writes, "Inmates befriended guards in the hope that they would get such benefits as an extra phone call, special shower time, or the overlooking of some minor infraction. In turn guards befriended inmates because they wanted to get information or just to keep the peace and make it through another day without getting hurt. . . . Thus, an unwritten agreement has been established between inmates and guards: inmates get what they want by being friendly and nonaggressive, while guards ensure their own safety by not strictly enforcing the rules. For the most part, inmates manipulate the guards' desire for safety, and the guards exploit the inmates' need for autonomy."

Such arrangements are acceptable to inmates and most guards, but that can change in altered circumstances. Graterford Penitentiary, the state's largest maximum-security prison, started to go into chaos in the mid-1980s when discipline broke down and the guards could no longer control the situation. Because of overcrowding there was a great need to offer guards considerable overtime. Any guard who wanted to make extra money could get the extra duty.

According to Hassine, "This phenomenon had the immediate impact of introducing many exhausted, irritable guards into the work force, often on shifts with which they were not familiar." Guards from different duties in the prison, says Hassine, were strangers "to the unique inmate hierarchy of his newly assigned unit" and were unable "to conform to longstanding customs and practices. . . . In every prison there is a percentage of guards who are so rigid and unpopular with inmates, or so incompetent, that they are given work assignments that keep them away from contact with prisoners, such as tower duty or the late-night shift. Any prison administrator of intelligence knows that these kinds of guards can jeopardize the tenuous order and operation of a prison. With the advent of unlimited overtime, however, these guards have found their way into the prison mainstream."

Thus, it is hardly surprising that tower guards are bitterly resented by inmates when they are brought "in the inmates' faces" in new situations. In most prisons, tower guards are regarded as "shoot-to-killers." There obviously is a case to be made for such a situation from the prison's perspective: It may be wholesome to have tower guards who are always considered to be feared. But when tower guards are put in close contact with prisoners, there is seething anger, distrust, and hatred. In a prison with control problems, the mix can be deadly.

transfers of prisoners

Prison administrators have learned the virtue of transferring prisoners between institutions as a method of isolating inmates who are regarded as troublemakers. Some inmates establish themselves as leaders of other prisoners by their violent acts, and prisons use a sort of interstate compact as a common method to defang persistent violence by transferring such troublemakers. They are transferred to prisons or jails in other states. Of particular value is a new out-of-state facility where such a prisoner will need a year or two to build up a following with political preachments that could cause trouble for the new state institution. Such a prisoner is put on the transfer shuttle again to another state or back to the original state.

Particular beneficiaries of such a system are prisoners who have to be shifted out of a prison because of their reputation as informers. In the new prison, with the aid of the administration, they are permitted to claim the reputation of being troublemakers at their original institution. But there have been some expressions of thought that such transferees are put in a position of "owing us one," meaning that they could be ordered to keep on snitching.

transportation England's shipping of criminals to America

It is somewhat questionable to claim that the American colonies were for the most part a refuge for persons fleeing political or religious persecution. By 1650 most British emigrants to colonial America went as prisoners of one sort or another; in short, they were the dregs of English jails that were so overcrowded at the time that the colonies could be viewed by the Mother Country as a convenient dumping ground, with many businessmen involved in profits that could be derived from the traffic. Many such arrivees had been murderers. The economic basis for shipping major criminals was simply need. There was a typical case of a man who was convicted of manslaughter and condemned to hang, winning a reprieve "because he was a carpenter and the plantation needed carpenters." Many others "volunteered" for transportation to escape execution, imprisonment, or starvation in English jails.

After 1650 the transportation of criminals escalated. During the last four decades of the 17th century, almost 5,000 convicts were shipped to America. In the following century, the rate soared. From 1732 to 1776, an estimated 50,000 to 100,000 English convicts were sent to the American colonies. (England saw no incentive to provide any exact count.) From 1745 to 1775, almost 9,000 convicts were known to have landed in one port, Annapolis, Maryland. What upset the local citizenry particularly was that in one shipment of 26, five were convicted murderers.

In Virginia, the populace fought back by inspecting incoming female prisoners, and if they had become pregnant en route they were shipped back to England on the ground that it was necessary to stamp out promiscuity in the colony. Of course, this hardly prevented the English authorities from simply reshipping the women to another colony, and there was considerable evidence that this was done, the women sometimes never even leaving an English dock.

Other protests took the form of pamphlets that traced the criminal deeds of new arrivals. One example was Thomas Lutherland, a convicted felon who was sent to New Jersey as a bound servant. Within days of his arrival, he was convicted of stealing and punished. That did little to convince him to become upright, and a short time later, he murdered a boat trader and hid the victim's goods in his home.

Such protests did not impress Parliament, and that body turned a deaf ear to an official resolution by the Virginia House of Burgesses that declared, "The peace of this colony be too much hazarded and endangered by the great number of felons and other desperate villains sent hither from several prisons in England."

It cannot be said that prisoners sent found much sympathy from the colonists. In 1756, Elizabeth Sprigs, who had been sent to Maryland, wrote to her father about her life as a servant in the New World. She was forced to work day and night and was often tied up and whipped. Her diet was limited to corn and salt.

The more logical way to stop the transportation system would have been for colonists to refuse to take bonded criminals, but there was considerable profit for those who did, especially if they held the costs of upkeep low—and, of course, traders made fortunes. One convict trader wrote his partner across the ocean that their business "if properly managed will in a few years make us very genteel fortunes." Others appear to have been accorded the kind judgment of history. Gen. James Edward Oglethorpe, often called a "prison reformer," who organized the new colony of Georgia to be peopled by released prisoners, was deputy governor of the Royal African Company. In the 1730s, some 10,000 prisoners were turned over to Oglethorpe and Micajah Perry, who was both a leading colonial agent for servants and convicts and a secretary to the company. One of the company's ships, *The Eagle,* served the company as a slave ship and thus was eminently qualified for the transporting of prisoners.

The monetary rewards for shippers of transported prisoners can be gleaned by the records of Jonathan Forward, a London merchant with excellent buyers in Maryland. He received a subsidy of three pounds for every Newgate felon and five pounds for every convict he took from the provinces. Forward readily afforded the requirements put on him to bear all transportation costs, including jail fees.

The fruits of the transport system were most valuable to England for the reduction of its prison population and the costs involved, but actually as well from the "good will" by the so-called prerogative of mercy that countered the view that it engaged in the blind severity of justice. Indeed, a study of the period 1607 and 1616 indicated the average of executions annually was 140, but from 1749 to 1799, the figure had dropped to 33. It was one might say the pleasurable aspects of transportation. The drop occurred even though, with the passage of the so-called Bloody Code, the number of punishments rose astonishingly to a total of 50 and included such capital crimes as damaging trees, poaching fish, stealing a silver spoon, and appearing disguised in a game preserve. Sentences of death were many, but so were reprieves, and the lucrative transportation system prospered all the more.

In the 18th century, the transportation trade continued to grow, and it continued right up to the American Revolution. In England, the transportation method hardly skipped a beat, and the convict flow shifted to Australia. Ironically, the flow of thugs from England went on virtually unabated. Now, many Europeans were fleeing to America to start a new life, but included in them were large numbers of offenders looking to escape arrest in England and Ireland. These newcomers flooded into the larger American cities but, instead of finding jobs, they discovered only privation and slums generally the equal of those they had fled. These occupants of the crowded slums banded together and, by the 1820s, formed the first criminal gangs; transportation and its immediate aftermath deserve much of the credit for the beginnings of organized crime in America.

transportation of criminals from America

Although the American colonies were greatly angered by the transportation of criminals and other jailed offenders by England to their shores, it must be noted the colonies and later the states themselves engaged in the same sort of practice and for the same motivations. It was one thing for a black slave or a white indentured servant to commit crimes and face the death sentence but another matter for penalty to be meted out—to the financial detriment of the person bearing title to them. Would it not be better, more sober individuals observed, for these offenders to be transported for cash to reimburse the rightful owner as well as the government for keeping them confined until such arrangements could be made.

George Washington, a third-generation slaveholder, engaged in the reverse-transportation policy. Whenever he had to deal with a troublesome slave, he had the slave shipped off to the West Indies.

Benjamin Franklin, having been the victim of a burglary perpetrated by a transported English felon, offered a unique form of "transport out." Calling the unloading of felons on the colonies "an insult and contempt, the cruellest that ever one people offered to another," he suggested a sort of counterattack, whereby some of the plentiful American rattlesnakes be crated off and transported to Britain. It would be proper he said that they be distributed in St. James's Park and other haunts of the gentry, "but particularly in the gardens of the prime ministers, the lords of trade, and members of Parliament, for to them we are most particularly obliged."

In the notorious uprisings of slave revolutionaries like Denmark Vesey and Nat Turner, for which a great number of offenders were executed, many others were subject to transportation.

Virginia was the most proficient at transporting offenders outside the United States. Between 1800 and 1850, the state transported more than 600 slave criminals. Slaves were generally only held in the penitentiary until they were executed or sold outside the country. Reimbursement costs rose for the state so that Virginia in 1820 paid slightly more than $512 a head for 25 Negroes and had a rather difficult time recovering the costs from foreign buyers who drove very hard bargains.

The governor was empowered to commute any death sentence on condition that the condemned be deported—with sufficient recompense.

In 1857, Gov. Henry A. Wise reported, "I examined the record of the case of Dolly, a slave, the property of B.S. Crouch, who was condemned to be hung by the county court of Henrico, for burning a dwelling house; and because of the insufficiency of the testimony against her, and of the recommendation to mercy by the justices of the peace who composed the court, I commuted the capital punishment, and ordered the prisoner to sale and transportation beyond the limits of the United States." It was a decision that Mr. Crouch probably found more equitable.

Of course, transportation of the slaves was turned over to slave ships, even if the traffic in slaves had become forbidden. Once a slave trader took charge of the commodity, the state simply took no further interest in the matter.

In some states, the law became that when any slave finished his prison term he or she could be sold at auction and transported. The clear intent of these laws was to control free blacks because, as Gov. William Smith of Virginia put it, their freedom adversely affected the value of our slaves.

On the West Coast, California was plagued by independent transport into the country from Australia, which presumably had enough of many of the convicts shipped there after England was unable to use the United States after the Revolution. After the most notorious of the criminal imports of a number of who then had to be imprisoned in Australian penal colonies and seemed incorrigible, they were granted "tickets of leave." They eventually washed up on California shores in 1849. These felons were far worse than most American badmen and soon dominated crime in San Francisco. After a rash of murders in the hundreds during the next few years, quite logically, Californians did not take kindly to these surreptitious transports and started to solve the problem in true western style—with the vigilante noose. Scores of these imports, now known as the "Sydney Ducks," were strung up. They, in turn, fought back with more violence, but eventually the Ducks were defeated as one top leader after another went to the noose, and they had to flee voluntarily on vessels back to Australia while others hopped on steamers up the Sacramento River, a satisfactory distance from San Francisco.

Trenton Prison riots

New Jersey's Trenton Prison, built in 1836, was almost from the beginning regarded as a prison "hellhole," a reputation that persisted well into its second century. In the 19th century, "stretching" was one of the more common punishment-tortures. In 1878, Jacob Snook died of the torture. The ensuing investigation by a special committee uncovered an additional horror practiced on epileptics: Alcohol was poured on them, and they were then set on fire to determine possible faking.

The worst episode of the 20th century occurred in the early 1950s. Late Saturday night, March 29, 1952, 52 inmates in 5-Wing, the disciplinary section, revolted. These most violent inmates included prison wolves, passive homosexuals, and the most unstable men in the institution. Some had been segregated for a long time. They claimed that they were enraged because a sick man in the wing had not gotten medical treatment. They smashed toilets and other fixtures but took no hostages and surrendered a few at a time during the next two days.

The warden had suspected that trouble was brewing for a long time, and he felt 5-Wing was part of a general revolt plan. He picked out men who were suspected of being the chief plotters and transferred them to the nearby State Prison Farm at Rahway. On April 15, Trenton erupted again. Sixty-nine inmates in the printshop grabbed four guards and civilian printers as hostages, wrecked the shop, and demanded that an outside agency investigate the prison and the parole system. While negotiations were going on, Rahway also blew. The Trenton plotters shipped there were being held in segregation, and rumors spread that they were "being worked over." On April 17, about 300 inmates seized a dormitory and nine guards as hostages, wrecked the place, and started negotiations as well. Meanwhile, the Trenton uprising ended when Trenton officials agreed to an investigation by the Osborne Association, an organization specializing in prison reform. Back at Rahway, prisoners were demanding a new parole board and an end to brutality. They wrote their grievances on bedsheets when food and water ran out and they were forced to drink from a rusty radiator and a fire hose. They finally surrendered.

The official investigation that followed recognized some basic facts: One-quarter of all cells were nightmares; cell doors were solid, with thresholds so high that inmates had to crouch and step up at the same time; the only ventilation and light came from a narrow slit in the wall; many such cells held three or four men, and there was recognition that men so caged would do the only thing they could, seek to destroy their cages.

The investigators stated:

> *It is incontestable that one of the major basic causes of the riots was the fact that the inmate population of Trenton Prison included, in addition to the "ordinary" prisoners who constitute a majority of the population, insane and near-insane, metal defectives, unstable psychopaths, some of them highly assaultive, prisoners convicted as sexual psychopaths, passive homosexuals, aggressive "wolves" with long records of fights and stabbings, escape artists, agitators and "incorrigibles" of all ages. The presence of these men in the prison played a large part in creating the explosive situation which was bound to blow up eventually, and it was men of these types in the segregation section who started the riot that set off the whole series. . . . If the Trenton prisoners who belong in institutions under medical or psychiatric auspices were removed, the prison would still have more than its share of serious problem cases. The removal of those who need*

psychiatric supervision, however, would relieve the prison greatly and would correct a situation now indefensible.

Much of this was known earlier after the riots of 1952 when the population was cut, with changes in the parole laws. The state hired some new guards and raised guard pay. A career warden was appointed, in place of the old system in which wardens were determined by the amount of political strength a would-be warden could gather. A new segregation block was started, and money was allocated for athletic equipment and clothing. The practice of making inmates pay guard salaries during evening yard time was instituted. The budget for prisoners' food was raised 14 cents per day, and plans were laid for a food survey as to the choice of meals. Some disciplinary rules were changed and inmates were permitted a longer yard period. The prison was painted (by the prisoners naturally). Even more important, corrections officials, the governor, the Budget Commission, the legislature, and the prison itself started to cooperate. However, Trenton itself, which should have been abandoned decades earlier, was not replaced by a new prison. It was said there was not enough money to do that.

"trusty" prisoner with authority to manage other inmates

Contrary to public opinion and some Hollywood treatments, the life of a "trusty" is one rife with controversy and, in some cases, considerable brutality and violence.

The Arkansas correctional system had long been regarded as one of the worst uses of trusties. When a reform-minded warden, Tom Murton, entered the system in the 1960s, he found the Tucker farm system essentially under the control of armed trusties and the prisoner population divided roughly in three groups: "rank men," "do-pops," and trusties. The rank men, by far the largest group, were kept in the least desirable barracks and received meager servings of such food as head stew and pig's knuckle soup and wore inferior clothing (and no underwear).

The do-pops, so called because among their main duties was to scrape before staffers and pop open doors for their superiors, fared only slightly better. Trusties by contrast had far better food and decent clothing and many other benefits. Trusties were armed to guard other prisoners but were trained and encouraged to shoot. Any trusty who killed an escaping prisoner could expect early parole. As Scott Christianson noted in *With Liberty for Some,* "Some likened them to kapos in Nazi concentration camps."

The situation was not dissimilar at Angola Prison in Louisiana, except that Angola suffered from most severe financial shortages. In 1917, the security staff was shaved from 150 to 11 with convict guards taking over the main duties, armed with shotguns and rifles and, later, submachine guns. As late as the 1960s (before life without parole came into vogue), Angola's warden offered six months' reduction in sentence for shooting of any escaping prisoner. What was most difficult to ascertain, of course, was how convict-guards defined *escaping* when offered such incentives.

One thing was certain: Trusties themselves were hardly likely to attempt to escape. If they were caught, they would inevitably be returned to rank in the general population where they might be subject to vengeance for their own past behavior. (Penal institutions were not always successful in picking likely trusties. In New York's Auburn Prison, a highly organized escape plot was hatched with a key role played by a trusty, who threw acid in a guard's face and grabbed his keys so that arms could be distributed from the prison arsenal. Before the violence ended, the principal keeper and eight inmates were dead, and many other prisoners and employees were injured.)

Where the trusties themselves were armed by authorities, taking away those weapons was no easy task. When Tom Murton came into office, his trusties heard that he planned to take away their weapons. Some of them then promptly planned to strike, a move that could force Murton to close down Tucker. He met with the trusties and told them he normally would take over an institution and would simply declare how the institution would be run. He added, "But this is ridiculous in a situation like this because you guys have the guns and the keys and you're running things so there's no way I can take over."

"The men laughed and we were off to a good start."

There was probably a good deal of "soft soapery" here because Murton had laid out a two-year plan to eliminate the trusty system. He also had determined that no trusty could be put back in ranks where he could be subject to reprisals.

Murton never accomplished his aim because, within two years, he was forced out of his post by the governor and the state corrections system for allegedly holding up the state to ridicule as he uncovered gross mismanagement and clear evidence of murder.

Today, the trusty system is continually being weakened with a return to the position that the late Warden Lewis E. Lawes of Sing Sing said he would not permit any prisoners to have—power over others. There have, through the years, been contentions made that trusty positions had been attained through bribery and other undue influences.

tuberculosis prison disease with a dangerous aftermath for the public

At the turn of the century, much attention was paid in the United States to the rampaging effects of tuberculosis during incarceration. But what was being viewed with alarm was not the perils of the infectious disease in U.S. prisons but rather that in Russia, where the death rate for TB reached a level in Europe that had not been equaled for decades.

Of course, the mortal dangers of tuberculosis should have been cited about conditions in U.S. prisons as well, which, even though not at a par with the ravages in Russia, was frightening to public health officials, not only for the spread of the infection at such a high rate behind bars, but because released prisoners were bringing the disease back into outside life.

At one time, before the disease was brought under control in the early 20th century, tuberculosis resulted in up to 25 percent of deaths annually in this country. Then in the 1980s, the disease started to make a comeback, and in prisons it rose at the most alarming rates. A study for the Centers of Disease Control and the National Institute of Justice in 1992–93 found that prison inmates suffered the disease at a rate 13 times higher than the general population, and women were infected more than men. Compared to the outside world, the conditions for nurturing tuberculosis were classic. The highly infectious disease could be spread by coughing, spitting, sneezing, and even by little noticed expectoration during normal conversation. Because people live and work in very close proximity in prisons where ventilation is poor at best, and most especially in punishment areas, prisons became a fertile ground for the resurgence of the disease. Not only the prisoners were affected: The survey revealed that 43 prison employees had tuberculosis, and another 600 or so more were infected with TB.

In 1991, a TB outbreak in New York State facilities took the lives of 36 prisoners and one corrections officer. (In another instance, a prison guard picked up TB on the job and transmitted it to his baby child at home.) In 1994, state and federal prisons found as many as 69,000 inmates tested positive for TB.

To outside society, the real dangers to the public are the release of short-term prisoners after their sentences. Tuberculosis is curable, but the treatment is difficult and requires prolonged medication and isolation of the infected person. Isolation serves two purposes: stopping carriers from infecting others and preventing reinfection of the carriers while they are receiving recovery treatment.

The problem that arises in the penal system is that short-term prisoners can contract TB and then return to the community before they have received full treatment. This gives rise to yet another problem: The penal system is not, and probably cannot be, responsive to such public health dilemmas. As a result, inmates are released as carriers, to ride planes, trains, buses, and other means of mass transportation with the awesome ability to spread the disease. Also, many prisoners return to their home communities, which often are crowded and depressed and very susceptible to picking up the disease. As has been shown in the treatment of AIDS, it is very difficult to supervise released prisoners to take the best possible medicines. The very fact that some patients thus fail to complete a long-term antibiotic treatment (often for another 10 or 12 months) has led to the growth of stronger strains of TB.

Courts have okayed the rights of correctional institutions to require testing and treatment and isolation of TB victims within the prison, but a court ruling of that sort is not always the end of the matter. Some prisoners object for religious reasons to having needles inserted under their skin. Other convicts object to the restrictions on their movements, which traditionally have been a general punishment for bad behavior, and other losses of privileges. In some cases, violence increases and riots result.

Treatment for TB has to include better air circulation, for which many prisons were not built. Some prisoners see campaigns to eliminate any use of air conditioning as not opposing "coddling" of prisoners but rather killing them. Relief from prison overcrowding becomes of paramount importance and, the prisoners insist, the jamming in of two, three, or four inmates in a cell intended for one represents, on top of all else, a matter of life or death.

Tucker, Karla Faye (1959–1998) executed murderer

Without a doubt, the most controversial execution under Texas Gov. George W. Bush involved Karla Faye Tucker. In 1983, Tucker spent 72 hours drinking tequila and shooting up Dilaudid, methadone, heroin, and speed along with handfuls of tranquilizers. Then she killed. She struck a man 20 times with a pickax and then left it imbedded in a sleeping young woman. At her trial, she said she had had an orgasm with every strike of the ax.

Tucker was sentenced to death and then seemed to undergo a death-row conversion to Christianity. She married the prison chaplain and was acknowledged to be a model prisoner. She garnered many Evangelical Christians who regarded her conversion as clear proof of the transforming power of God, and religious leaders such as Pat Robertson, Sister Helen Prejean, and Pope John Paul II called on Governor Bush to grant clemency. Tucker appeared on a number of talk shows, pleading for her life and recognition of her heartfelt reformation.

Bush did not relent, despite his own well-known religious awakening in helping him swear off alcohol and right the course of his own life. On February 3, 1998, Tucker was executed.

Later, after the execution, Bush was portrayed in a *Talk* magazine interview as mocking the woman's appearance with Larry King in which she asked the governor to spare her. The magazine reported that Bush had imitated her in a whimpering voice. After the article appeared, Bush campaign aides insisted that the magazine reporter had misread his comments, but the magazine stood by the article.

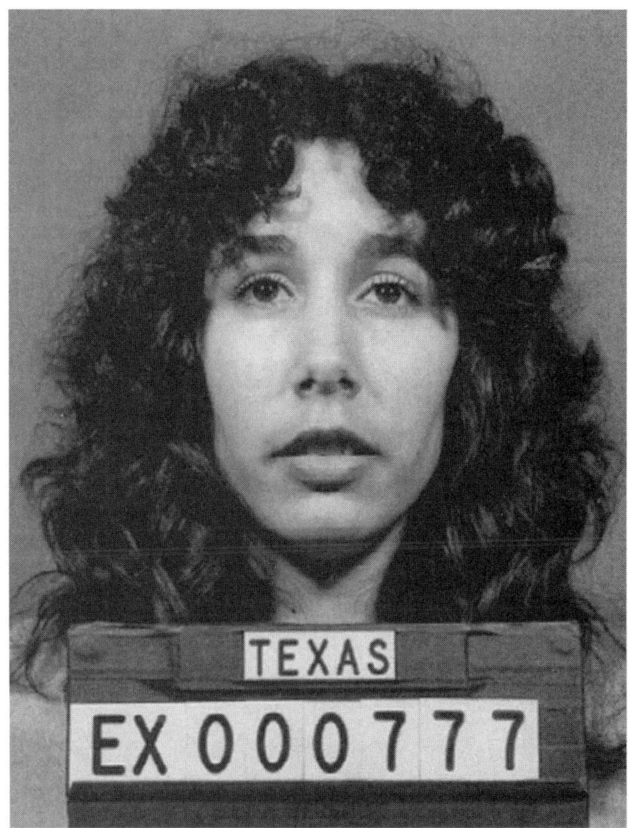

After losing an appeal before the U.S. Supreme Court, Karla Faye Tucker became the first woman executed in Texas since 1863. Tucker was convicted of a 1983 killing of a Houston man with a pickax. (AP/Wide World Photos)

Tucker telephone electrical torture method in Arkansas

The Arkansas prison system was subject to much criticism in the 1960s, especially at its Cummings and Tucker prison farms. A number of charges of tortures and other malpractices were made and often only partially verified, mainly because the new superintendent at Tucker, Tom Murton, was fired by Gov. Winthrop Rockefeller, as his investigation began to hit paydirt. What was definitely verified at the time, however, was the utilization of the so-called Tucker telephone. The device was simply composed of an old telephone, a heavy-duty battery, and some wiring. A prisoner was stripped. One end of the wire was attached to his wrist or ankle, and the other end to his penis. The resulting electric shocks would be excruciating, and the pain stopped only when the convict fell screaming into unconsciousness.

When the use of the Tucker telephone became known, the media cited the fact that the only other official authority in the world that was known to use a similar instrument of torture was SAVAK, the Iranian secret police, under the Shah.

See also: MURTON, TOM.

Turner, Willie Lloyd (1945–1995) "The Genius of Death Row"

No condemned man caused a U.S. prison more embarrassment than did 49-year-old Willie Lloyd Turner, who consistently during his stay on death row humiliated the state of Virginia. When he was executed after 15 years of fighting his death penalty with what can only be described as brilliant trickery, Willie Turner outraged his executioners with one final frustrating ploy that humiliated the state even more in about as monumental a joke as ever could be played by someone on the very edge of death. *The New Yorker* published a long profile, "The Genius of Death Row," which posthumously solidified his reputation.

Turner was a brutal murderer, but that played no role in anyone's mind on death row, where very different standards apply. When Turner arrived on death row, he had already a long record of violence behind him and a steady ability to escape. He learned the first lessons of his craft in reform school, and within three days of his first incarceration, he took off. Having quickly learned the art of picking a lock, he grabbed his street clothes, which he stuffed into plastic bags that he used for flotation across a swampy river outside the institution. Unfortunately, he was soon captured, pretty much the story of his criminal life thereafter; escaping was easy for Turner, but staying out was another matter. In the end, plotting an escape was a game, and not going through with it was an end game. Of course, Turner may not have realized this, and certainly his keepers did not think it was so. His final "plan," however, did prove the point in truly bizarre fashion.

Turner really came to his calling when he was finally clamped in death row for the last 15 years of his life. In theory, there was no escape from death row, especially apparently from Mecklenburg Correctional Center, about 100 miles from Richmond, built to be "escape proof," but Turner was in on a planned massive breakout and was originally involved in the caper. His input had been vital, and he was the armorer who could offer homemade weapons for the caper. It was to turn out to be the only successful mass escape from a death row in modern U.S. penology. In the end, only six men went and became known, nationwide and indeed worldwide, as the Mecklenburg Six. Some of the others had cold feet; a couple of them thought that they had a better chance with appeals (which they did not, the Virginia court system being the Virginia court system). Then there was Willie Turner, who did not go, a development that rattled the escapers who viewed him as a vital player. He told a few the reasons why, in the end, he had not joined in—mainly that he was sure that the plot was imperfect and that they would be shot down at the final wall. Actually, Turner was a vain individual, and he was insulted when some wrinkles he wanted included were ruled out by the others. That was for Turner enough to say the hell with it, and in a way he proved right: All were caught in relatively short order, the final two in 19 days.

The escapees received harsh treatment back in captivity, but Turner himself was watched even more than the others. The keepers knew that he was a most dangerous man who could really do a successful breakout, both before and after the exploits of the Mecklenburg Six.

For the very first time during his adult incarcerations, Turner busied himself in producing prison weapons and ways to hide them, revealing a handicraft ability that was enhanced by private confinement where he could develop his capabilities by constant attention to detail, the sign of a true scientific researcher. Prisoners would try to steal cutlery that they sharpened into knives, but Turner knew better. He stuck to plastic utensils, which he heated, molded together, and produced weapons just as sturdy as metal. He also learned how to hide them in almost plain sight. He could add molding to a table that looked like part of the original design and conceal the weapon underneath part of it.

He was a wizard with keys and could duplicate them without even getting the original in his hand. He could watch a guard day after day, using the key on his cell door and remember the cut of the key and, by trial and error, manage to duplicate it with a file that he developed as well.

Turner was in time transferred from one prison to another because his keepers were fearful of losing him. Actually, he managed to use his mechanical prowess to get himself out of prison once in more acceptable fashion. Unable to read and write, Turner early on studied the subjects in prison. He had learned during his youth the tragedy of not being literate. Taken with a young girl, he sought to send her a Valentine's card. Being illiterate, he mistakenly sent a Father's Day card instead. Young Turner probably never lived down that embarrassment until he learned to read and write behind bars.

This was during a phase when Turner was on his way to possible rehabilitation. He enrolled in a prison's vocational school and learned barbering. He did so well that his record showed he had shown great "personal growth" and "exceptional work in the barbering field." He became the prison barber and was accorded access to potentially deadly weapons of his trade. Needless to say, he studied them, but he did not use them for any nefarious purpose. Later, Turner's record was updated with a commendation for "outstanding work he is doing toward his own rehabilitation." Eventually, he was paroled.

On the outside, however, he was not acclaimed for his accomplishments in prison and soon fell back to drinking and to crime. He eventually murdered a jeweler and faced a possible death sentence. Held in the county jail for his trial and sentence, Turner ingeniously used a thin piece of plastic to make an impression of the cell-block door lock and then fashioned a pick that would open it. In the meantime, in the middle of the night, he slipped out of his cell while everyone was sleeping and worked on a couple of bars on the window of the jailhouse itself, covering the work on the window bars with homemade paste until that chore was completed. Then one night, he pulled out the bars and walked. Unfortunately, Turner's freedom lasted only a few hours

Willie Lloyd Turner (AP/Wide World Photos)

at his great-aunt's house across the state line in North Carolina. Police grabbed him in the middle of the night, sleeping on a couch.

Turner was sentenced to death and once again in prison he went back to his escape and weapons workings.

As he produced more weapons, Turner became obsessed with finding enough "hidey-holes" for them. He made shanks from the metal around his cell door and filled in the gaps with a paste made of coffee creamer and water, which hardened like cement. Turner hid his shanks in the hollow pipe connecting his table to the floor. He effectively covered the hole. Turner trusted no one, realizing that other prisoners might rat on him to win favors for themselves, so he decided he needed several hidey-holes. Then, if anyone snitched on him and shakedown guards came to his cell to search, they found only one stash and assumed that there were no more.

Sometimes, guards kept searching, and Turner would reveal some additional stashes in the hope that others would still be left. There was a hacksaw blade, several shanks, a couple of fake guns made of plastic and wood, and a 3-feet-long Samurai-type sword. Turner had cut slits in his metal toilet to slip in several of these items.

Most embarrassing of all were the keys—all sorts of keys. As Turner was led away from his cell in his underwear to do some hard time, he bragged that he could have let loose half of the inmates of M-Building. It turned out not to have been an empty boast; his keys opened several cells and hall doors. Maintenance people were brought in to block up holes with heavy steel, and locksmiths did wholesale changes of cell- and hall-door locks.

A year later, Turner was back at it. There were more keys, shanks, a sword, and more weapons. He had made a hole in the ceiling with a replaceable cell bar and planted them there. Turner revealed them all, apparently no longer intent on breaking out—his execution time was nearing after years of legal delays and postponement—and he seemed more interested in showing officials what dolts he considered them to be.

Yet, as death approached, he kept boasting that he might not be the only one to die, that he might take out the men of the death watch before it happened.

That did not happen. By that time, Willie Turner was tired of all the games. He wanted to die, but he would not be content to go without the most astonishing revenge caper, one that surpassed all his other deeds.

Before he went to the death house, Turner told his lawyer to take his electric typewriter after he was dead and look at it carefully. Turner cryptically hinted there would be a surprise for him—and prison authorities. When the attorney got back to his motel that May evening in 1995 in the company of his wife and two news reporters, he decided to open the casing of the typewriter. He found tucked in a cut-out hiding case that appeared to be part of the typewriter construction a .32-caliber Smith & Wesson revolver. It was loaded and there was also a plastic bag of extra bullets. There was also a handwritten note in the typewriter. It was one word, "Smile."

The discovery scandalized the state's Department of Corrections and an angry law-and-order governor, George Allen, ordered a full investigation by the state police. More than 20 special agents worked on the case for two and a half months and questioned more than 100 persons, inmates, guards, visitors, and others and found nothing beyond the fact that way back in 1954, it had been bought by a North Carolina man who was long dead. After that there was nothing. It was a very unsatisfactory conclusion to a matter considered by many as humiliating as the mass escape from death row by the Mecklenburg Six.

Willie Turner could have chosen to go out in a blaze of gunfire, but he apparently was much happier to exact his devastating measure of revenge.

By Turner's measure, his life probably had been a success. Oddly, he probably could have achieved other roads to success in his life on the outside. Even on death row, he had invented a barbering device he called De-Ending Shears for the purpose of removing split ends of hair. Under prison rules, he could not have a ruler or a drawing compass, so he surreptitiously made his own and submitted the drawings and descriptions of his device to the U.S. Patent Office. He was granted U.S. Patent No. 4,428,119.

It was obvious Turner knew that he was "the greatest" and could have made it in prison or outside if he had ever really tried. He had had the potential to make it anywhere.

See also: MECKLENBURG SIX.

Further reading: *Dead Run* by Joe Jackson and William F. Burke Jr.; *The New Yorker,* pp. 64–70, December 4, 1995.

Tyson, Mike (1966–) celebrity prisoner

When former heavyweight champion Mike Tyson was sent to prison in Indiana for a six-year term, there was concern voiced about his safety, that state's system often cited as one with a terrible record. Many cons felt he was likely to have it rough from inmates who wanted to gain a "rep."

Boxer Mike Tyson on his way to prison in 1992 to begin serving a sentence of six years for rape and deviant conduct (AP/Wide World Photos)

One commented, "There are guys who'll run extortion on him. Tyson may be vicious, but we have guys in here who are barbaric. . . . A left jab ain't going to get it. It would be flesh against steel."

Apparently, Tyson had the right answer. In three years before he won parole, Tyson was involved in only a couple of minor disciplinary matters.

victim-offender mediation programs

newer restitution methods

In place of standard restitution programs that are part of the punishment in criminal cases and are imposed by the judge, there has been a growth of victim-offender mediation programs since the late 20th century. Such methods, experts agree, would have wider acceptance except for the fact that some resistance is offered because of the majority popular public opinion that crimes should be punished by imprisonment—period.

Despite such attitudes, these newer mediation programs for victims and offenders are considered to be quite successful. Such programs let victims meet face to face with their attackers or other offenders in the presence of a trained mediator so that they can negotiate a settlement of their claims. A study in Minnesota by the Citizens Council on Crime and Justice and the University of Minnesota estimated that there were about 100 programs in existence by the 1990s. Surveying programs in five localities—St. Paul, San Francisco, Minneapolis, Austin, and Albuquerque—showed that 87 percent of the offenders and 79 percent of the victims who participated in the programs were satisfied with the process. Equally important, restitution in full was paid in such cases, compared to 58 percent in which the courts set the amount without any mediation.

Generally as well, the victims felt that they now suffered a much lower level of personal anxiety and fear.

visiting prisoners

Probably the worst punishment possible for many inmates is the loss of visiting rights by their families. Although Hollywood offers a typical visiting scene showing inmates separated from their visitors by plexiglass or some other material so that no physical contact is possible, such is seldom so. That is only the case involving some convicts doing long terms largely in maximum-security situations. Usually, visitations take place in a much more open environment, with a mingling of inmates and various visitors. It is simply impossible for the average institution to provide enough space and equipment for more sealed-off methods.

As a result, various illegal activities occur, the most troublesome, of course, being the smuggling of drugs. These may occur in the act of kissing with a visitor passing the contraband to the inmate's mouth. Usually this is in the form of a condom that the prisoner swallows and retrieves later in his cell. In some cases, children in the visiting party then repeat the same process with the prisoner, which to them represents a sort of game.

All prisons have to maintain a certain number of sealed-off compartments as well, and they are used at the request of either the visitor or the inmate. The former may request such a setup because he or she fears the visitor will exhibit great anger toward them. A more common reason occurs in the case of a wife informing the inmate that she wants a divorce and sometimes adds that she intends to remarry. A particularly messy situation can take place when a girlfriend of the prisoner shows up at the same time when the spouse is visiting. Guards have to escort one of the females from the prison before the other leaves.

There is often the matter of blatant sex taking place in the visiting sections. A few years ago a high political figure doing time in Washington, D.C., was visited by a prostitute who performed various sexual acts on him more or less in view of other visitors and guards. Guards have to be on alert for cases of "stand-up sex" that in Sing Sing can take place in a separate play area for small children.

Particularly disturbing to some guards is the fact that some female visitors are extremely good looking, and they cannot understand why such women stick with prisoners who will not go free for many years or even decades. One such woman recently was having a second baby born in her relationship with her imprisoned spouse. In some cases, such wives married the inmate when they met for the first time during visiting hours, frequently occurring among female visitors joining a friend visiting another prisoner. After a couple is married, they are, in Sing Sing, generally admitted into the Family Reunion Program, which at times permits conjugal visits. In some prisons, inmates have access to the Internet, and a woman who had had a crush on an inmate long before he was sent away for murder was able to continue contact with him; when he was paroled after 17 years, she divorced her husband, father of her children, to marry the ex-convict.

There can be many explanations for such relationships, the most common being that such women come from deprived areas or backgrounds and incarceration of men is essentially a way of life to which they accommodate.

Generally, guards are bewildered by the number of women who maintain a romantic relationship with men who may not ever be set free.

In *Newjack*, author Ted Conover retells a situation told in the film *Birdman of Alcatraz*. The Birdman, Robert Stroud, was transferred to Alcatraz and was visited by a woman from the Midwest whom he had met by mail while in Leavenworth. The woman was married, but she showed up one day in Alcatraz to visit Stroud. Puzzled, Stroud wanted to know why in heaven she had come so far to visit him. Her answer: "Because you're the only life I have."

voting rights of ex-felons

Thirty-seven states at recent count restore voting rights to felons who have served their time. Some states, however, insist released prisoners also complete a waiting period before their rights are extended. In 2001, backing for such voting rights for ex-felons in Virginia was pushed by Richmond's Catholic diocese, and the Virginia Conference asked the general assembly to make it easier for felons to regain their voting rights. Virginia, at the time, required a case-by-case approval by the governor.

In various clemency decisions, some felons are required to accept certain strictures that in some fashion curtailed some or all their political rights, not so much on voting but rather on running for some sort of office. In a one-of-a-kind stipulation, socialist Eugene Debs, who had run for the presidency in 1920 even while in federal prison in Atlanta for making an antiwar speech in 1918, garnered an amazing 919,000 votes. He was pardoned by President Warren G. Harding in 1921. Harding made a stipulation that Debs would never again run for the presidency (probably a must for Harding to pacify his more conservative supporters). It was something Debs could not disagree on because his health had been sapped by his imprisonment; he died five years later.

Jimmy Hoffa, the former Teamster labor boss, went to prison in 1967 for misappropriating $1.7 million in Teamster pension funds and had done 58 months when the balance of his eight-year sentence was commuted by President Richard Nixon in 1971. There was a provision in Nixon's action that required Hoffa to stay out of union politics. Nevertheless, by 1975, Hoffa was engaged in a struggle to retake control of the union from his former protégé, Frank Fitzsimmons. Hoffa was challenging the legal stipulation on the ground that his eight-year sentence would have expired.

The government took no serious action in the matter because a short time later, Hoffa was removed from all union activities by the underworld, and he disappeared permanently.

It is generally accepted today that the run-of-the-mill felon should be granted voting rights, partly on the basis that voting would become a part of the key ingredient of his or her rehabilitation.

Warren, Earl advocate of prison reform
Although Earl Warren is best remembered for his tenure as chief justice of the Supreme Court, where he was described as producing the liberal "Warren Court," mostly known for its decisions on such issues as schools and a woman's right to an abortion, another important batch of decisions had to do with criminal-justice reform, something Warren had advocated starting in 1942 when he became governor of California. Warren immediately ordered an investigation of the state prison system, which was in due course reorganized to emphasize prisoner rehabilitation, utilizing the principle of indeterminate sentencing, which meant that inmates could be held until they appeared to be rehabilitated. Thus, it was hardly surprising that on the High Court, he was a guiding force that expanded the rights of racial minorities, minors, the poor, criminal defendants, and prisoners. Eventually, the legacy of the Warren Court spread to cover the treatment of prisoners to a considerable extent, something most courts up until that time had declined to do, often being guided by popular sentiments.

Former U.S. Chief Justice Earl Warren (AP/Wide World Photos)

"water boys" inmate hustlers
It is one of the most desirable, even if menial, inmate jobs to have in prison—that of being a "water boy." Water is one of the most priceless

commodities behind bars, and a water boy wheeling his cart from cell to cell can do a brisk business selling extra pails of hot water to convicts. Before the 1971 Attica prison rebellion, inmates were allowed to shower only once a week, and they received two quarts of water a day with which to wash themselves, shave, clean their cells, and launder personal clothing (only prison-issue clothing could go to the prison laundry once a week). Just prior to the Attica violence, Commissioner of Corrections Russell B. Oswald visited the institution to hear the inmates' complaints, but as one prisoner said later, "He didn't so much as make one concession, such as giving a man soap . . . or an extra shower." Another prisoner, alluding to the water situation, explained, "It is very expensive to live in prison." Water boys would say the same thing, that they need the extra income to meet their other personal expenses.

water cures of prisoners

One of the punishments of choice by prison administrators in the 19th century, which survived in some institutions in the following century, were various water punishments or tortures. One favorite used by keepers was shackling a naked prisoner to a wall and turning a high-pressure water hose on his back. The man was literally plastered to the wall. The treatment was extremely painful but had the "virtue" of leaving no mark.

Another tactic, one that sometimes resulted in death, intended or not, was fastening a prisoner's neck in an iron yoke and pouring a steady stream of frigid water on his head. It was said that a number of prisoners died of such "cures," while others were driven insane.

"weak sisters" nonguards in prisons

On the staff of the typical prison, guards represent the largest pool of employees, probably about half of the normal total, but they are seldom among the best-paid staffers. A listing of staff members at Leavenworth Penitentiary indicates that slightly more than 50 percent are guards, while there are hospital workers, maintenance men, ministers, psychologists, secretaries, food stewards, teachers, counselors, administrators, and supervisors. Because many of these qualify for better-paid jobs on the outside, they have to be compensated at a higher rate.

Of course, the guards—and their superiors—hold the basic power inside the prison, and, effectively, their actions govern how the inmates are treated. There is no doubt, as Pete Earley states in *The Hot House,* that "the hostility between convicts and guards is palpable and enduring."

It is also true that guards, with or without the disparity on pay scales with other employees, tend to regard all other prison employees as "weak sisters," most especially those in positions that require them to deal with helping inmates.

weight-lifting controversy convicts pumping iron

Although prisoners have been lifting weights in some prisons for many decades, the controversy about convicts pumping iron only erupted in the 1990s, when many proponents of a get-tough policy for inmates raised a number of objections that met with approval by considerable parts of the public. Several states banned weightlifting as among various concerns that it made inmates more dangerous when they were set free and it represented a waste of public moneys for what was regarded as coddling for criminals. Perhaps surprisingly, considering the "great press" corrections officials could garner by going along with a ban, most jurisdictions have tended to ignore the controversy.

The fact is that weightlifting by inmates is highly popular with prison guards as a way for prisoners to work off excess energies that might otherwise make them more dangerous. An additional factor was that among the main "customers" for weightlifting were the guards themselves, some of whom insisted it made them sharper in carrying out their duties and reducing their stress.

Wardens basically like weightlifting because it is very cheap, consisting largely of iron weights that don't have to be replaced very often and because, frequently, weight rooms are financed by the inmates themselves. In some states, the costs for equipment are paid for out of the profits brought in by the sale of goods to inmates from the prison commissary, at what are usually inflated prices.

Additionally, weightlifting is a privilege that can be used as a discipline measure and can be withdrawn for misbehavior on an inmate's part.

Generally, regulations require that prisoners take at least one hour of exercise a day. Strenuous exercise reduces muscle deterioration, boosts the immune system, and cuts the risk of cardiovascular disease. If such activities are needed by the general population, they are all the more necessary in a sedentary environment, which is what prisons offer, coupled with food that is often high in fat and cholesterol. Without exercise, the medical burdens on prison budgets would be enormous. By and large, prison weight facilities are not flush with state-of-the-art exercise equipment, although some recent additions made in prisons under some court or legal supervision are cited by critics as more common than they are. Of course, the public sees weight rooms in prisons as representing something for which the average person on the outside would have to pay, which can produce considerable anger, even though the outside gym or health club is on a far different level.

The most caustic attack on the critics comes, of course, from inmates who see the attacks on weight rooms as nothing more than, writes Paul Wright, coeditor of *Prison Legal News,* seeking "to take away what modest privileges prisoners have and replace them with idleness. This has historically led to violence and the level of overcrowding in prisons today will only exacerbate the level of conflict."

Using a jargon reflective of many inmate publications, Wright says, "The political cover is that weight-lifting is a public safety hazard because 'criminals are bulking up.' Anyone familiar with weightlifting or exercise knows this is a crock. First off, when was the last time someone was attacked by a weight-lifting ex-con? Secondly, however much bulk someone puts on (many weight lifters train for tone and not bulk) is quickly lost if the person doesn't continue working out. Most released prisoners quickly lose any bulk they gained when locked-up, as weight lifting, for whatever reason, is not a part of their outside lifestyle."

Even in those prisons where weight rooms are not available, some inmates cope by buying some heavy cans of commissary food and using them as weights for in-cell activities. Others, like Mafia boss John Gotti, restricted to his maximum-security cell up to 23 hours a day, compensated by doing 1,000 push-ups daily.

Perhaps the most ironic aspect to opposition to weightlifting and other exercises by convicts is that, frequently, such critics are effusive about the tough treatment prisoners receive in boot camps as compared to prisons. The three most basic activities there are calisthenics, calisthenics, and calisthenics.

Welfare Island prison scandal

There have always been prison scandals that showed favored prisoners receiving favored treatment and indeed exercising a considerable control of operations. Nowhere, however, were conditions as bad as in New York City's Welfare Island Penitentiary, where the favored inmates were doing as they wished, up to and including committing murder with immunity in the warden's office.

In 1932, two convict mobs in the prison vied for control of the lucrative narcotics business. One was headed by George Holsoe, better known as Horseshoes, and the other by the Italian mobsters under Joie Rao. It was decided to settle the dispute in a conference that, on corrupt Welfare Island, logically was to be held in the office of Warden Joseph A. McCann. The Rao forces showed up with concealed knives, which were made to order in the prison's machine shop. When it was clear that there would be no resolution to the dispute, knives flashed, and Horseshoes lay bleeding to death all over the warden's rug.

Word spread quickly throughout the institution, and the rival mobsters ran amok, doing battle. It took 200 policemen, fireboats circling offshore, and police aircraft flying overhead to quell the disturbance. The incident drew front-page coverage, grand juries were convened, and tons of witnesses called. The result: The Horseshoes murder stayed unsolved, and the prison administration went back to running Welfare Island as it had in the past. It remained no secret that Welfare Island, built more than a century previously, was one of the most corrupt in the nation, and it apparently had not occurred to any city administration to do something about it. Wardens apparently saw nothing wrong with—and perhaps found somewhat rewarding—the fact that the mobs ran four very lucrative rackets: the drug trafficking, the sale of stolen food, the sale of inmates' clothing, and the sale of privileges. Prisoners who had money could buy food, drugs, and other amenities and could even shorten a sentence for a mere $100 per month. (Rao did not have the slightest interest in such an arrangement for himself. He knew a gold mine when he saw one.)

That changed in 1934 when reform Mayor Fiorello H. La Guardia ordered his newly appointed corrections commission, Austin H. MacCormick, to clean up Welfare Island. Like many other prisons, many of the inmates received too little food and almost no heat in winter, while Rao and Ed Cleary, Horseshoes's successor, came to an accommodation. In theory, Welfare Island was a tough prison, but actually it was a "country club for the chosen few gangsters." The kingpins reigned in grand style. Rao and about 30 of his top boys resided in cells with doors that could be lifted off their hinges. This convenience meant they didn't have to wait for a guard to open the door if they felt like going for a stroll—or perhaps engage in some necessary mayhem against others.

Commissioner MacCormick learned of this and a lot more on January 24, 1934, when he ordered Warden McCann to his downtown office on a ruse that he had some appointments to make. When the warden arrived, he was shoved into a car, one of a convoy of vehicles carrying 30 policemen and 25 keepers from other institutions over to Welfare Island for a raid that was dubbed Operation Shakedown. MacCormick simply wanted the warden where he could watch him and not sabotage the investigation.

Operation Shakedown shocked New York and the rest of the country. The raiders did not find Rao in his nominal cell residence but in the hospital building, where he had claimed an entire floor for his own use. No sick persons were to apply. In fact, Rao was being shaved by his personal barber. Other residents on the floor were Rao henchmen. Some who were not part of the Rao entourage could stay there as well for a mere $75 a week, which included all the luxuries with the best food cooked by the best chefs available. Rao personally insisted on his meals being served on the finest china, the meals including shrimp, lobster, chicken, nuts, and fruit, and the like prepared by his private chef.

Rao had a wardrobe of a dozen suits, and because he very often did not deign to stay on the island for dinner, he would dress up and sojourn to his favorite restaurant in Manhattan. Rao had his own garden on the grounds, complete with a private guard, where trespassers, guards, or convicts could not tread. Rao also kept a milch goat—which naturally required a private shepherd, whose duties included keeping the goat out of the flower garden.

Rao also was a pigeon enthusiast of sorts, in the style of a nobleman with his falcons. This provided Rao with the method of importing narcotics for his rackets—something the prison administration apparently never suspected.

If Rao lived in princely manner, his Irish mob ally, Ed Cleary, was not far behind. He also had headquarters but in the Dormitory Hospital in another building. Cleary sported the title of "day nurse," which apparently allowed him to keep a stiletto stuck in the wall over his bed. Cleary had a pet police dog that he kept chained by his bed. He named the dog Screw Hater, with no complaint from the guards.

Rao, Cleary, and about 80 others were rounded up by the raiders and locked in a special wing. When it was apparent that Operation Shakedown was determined to break the power of the so-called "top cons," the rest of the prisoners broke out in cheers. They applauded as the raiders stormed the cells, filling the corridors with contraband, lead pipes, knives, meat cleavers, surgeon's scalpels, electric grills, huge portions of uncooked meat, canned goods, razors, decks of heroin, and cans of home brew. There were even poker chips made to order in the prison machine shop. There were also a number of walking sticks, indicating some of the kingly inmates had a certain aristocratic air about them.

On the other hand, the bulk of the cells were bare, the "convict politicians" keeping everything, including food to which the inmates were entitled. As a result, most of the inmates readily told their stories.

One said, "All the food was available from the mob. The prices were steep, but it made life here better than in any other prison—if you could pay the price. The mob controls the distribution of the meat, so most of us guys ate nothing but meatless stew."

Those who could afford meat had it delivered directly to their cells; a regular delivery entitled an inmate to have a little electric stove to whip up his own steak and onions. Owning the stove was gratis, but each month such an inmate received an "electric bill" for being allowed to cut in on a hot wire running through the cells. There was an extra charge if the inmate wanted his own radio. Payments were collected by the cell-block bagman.

The prison guards were often the most demeaned of all because they had to take orders from important cons. Aware that this was not a good situation, Rao ordered life made more bearable for the guards by providing them with a supply of 250 pounds of boneless beef daily for the keepers' mess, working out to 5 pounds per day per guard. Rao wanted the keepers to eat well, but he had one demand: The guards had to be careful not to spoil the leftovers, which reverted to being mob property. Then, for a preferment charge of $2 a week, some of the prisoners deprived of sufficient food in the prisoners' mess hall could take over a guard's chair and partake of the remaining portions of steak dinners and other top-flight meals.

More scandals came to light. The mob even ran a special lingerie and accessory set-up to service the institution's homosexual population, and they ran a racket involving the buying out of one's sentence at $100 for each month.

In the aftermath of Operation Shakedown, Warden McCann, his deputy, and the prison doctor were relieved of their duties. MacCormick saw, however, that there was no chance to revitalize Welfare Island, which for 1,700 inmates was basically uninhabitable for correctional use. In 1935, with a new penitentiary on Rikers Island ready for full occupancy, the Welfare Island facility was demolished, ending a blot on the correctional system. After serving in his post for six years, MacCormick took over as research director of the Osborne Association, a national organization dedicated to correctional reform.

See also: OSBORNE, THOMAS MOTT.

Whitman, John Lorin (1862–1926)

"The Boy Guard"

Known affectionately as the Boy Guard, John Lorin Whitman accomplished the near impossible feat of being respected by both prisoners and the public in an era when punishment rather than "coddling" was frequently considered to be the proper approach in penology.

Whitman became a jailer at the Cook County Jail in Chicago, Illinois in 1890 when he was about 28 years old. Slender in build and very youthful in appearance, he was regarded by inmates as a mere boy, and although they were criminals themselves, they were much celebrated in the press for being very affectionate and protective toward him and going out of their way to cause no trouble when he was on duty. Whitman returned this behavior by exhibiting a humane and compassionate attitude toward the prisoners that few other guards could understand. Whitman's success with inmates was, however, not lost on his superiors, and he won a promotion to head jailer. In his new position of authority, Whitman instituted a number of reforms in the running of the institution.

In 1907, he was made superintendent of the House of Correction in Chicago, where he again was noted for the kinder, more gentle treatment of prisoners. As a result, the House of Correction had far fewer inmate problems than other penal institutions. Right up to his death in 1926 at the age of 64, he was still known to his prisoners as the Boy Guard.

"Willie Hortonization" of criminal justice policy

stirring antifurlough opinion

During the 1988 presidential race, Vice President George Bush hammered away at an incident in which a convicted murderer in Massachusetts, one Willie Horton, was released on furlough and committed a horrific home invasion and rape. Most Americans were rightfully upset by this particularly heinous act. Bush's opponent, Massachusetts governor Michael Dukakis, found himself tarred—some political observers described Bush commercials on the issue as brilliantly effective—and incapable of giving a cogent response. He failed to respond that virtually every state in the union, as well as the federal government under Reagan and Bush, had a work furlough program. Of course, thousands of inmates were furloughed from time to time with the practice generally regarded as a positive one, and most jurisdictions used furloughs as part of a carrot-and-stick approach to curbing excesses among their prisoners.

Murderer and rapist William Horton Jr. Under the Massachusetts furlough program, Horton was released from prison although he was serving a life sentence. In 1987, during his 10th furlough, Horton fled to Maryland, raped a woman, and assaulted her fiancé. (AP/Wide World Photos)

However, the Horton incident, which was one among a handful of others including some far more violent and tragic, became so politicized that the public had only this one situation as a reference point for prison furloughs. As a result, most furloughs skidded to a stop. As Peter T. Elikann asked in *The Tough-On-Crime Myth,* "Could any politician in that year have stepped forward as 'profurlough'?"

Thereafter, said critics, crime initiatives came under new attack in the Willie Hortonization of the justice system. After Horton, any stand on anything that could indicate a real or fancied "soft on crime" position was sure to trigger problems. Critics said it was impossible to debate any issue without politically suicidal results. There was a proposal made to make murder a federal offense. South Carolina senator Ernest Hollings agreed with two Supreme Court justices when they complained that the federal courts would be overwhelmed if dozens of gun charges became federal offenses, but he warned that trying to oppose making such murders a federal crime would guarantee that your opponent will accuse you of favoring murder. He added, "That's the kind of childish nonsense that goes on up here."

As the get-tough fervor grew, a popular political strategy was to comb through the record of every federal judge that a particular senator had confirmed. It did not matter if the judge had been confirmed by a large majority, as long as one case could be found that the judge opposed some capital charge case. That would become a case of being "soft on crime." Then a move could be made to nail the senator on that. Elikann points out, "For example, graphic ads depicting the horrible details of a murder were used against California Senator Dianne Feinstein, because she had voted with the majority to confirm a federal judge in Florida, who later refused to order the execution of the man who committed that terrible murder." Calling the tie to Feinstein as being in support of a murderer, Elikann said it "was tenuous at best."

"But it was characteristic of the evolution that exploiting politicians now use in 'tough-on-crime' political advertising. Political pollster Frank Luntz said, 'Posing with cops—that's way behind the curve.'"

While some may see it as somewhat of an overstatement, there are those who say that Horton has had nearly as great an impact on the justice system and imprisonment of alleged offenders as Miranda.

What is certain is that Willie Horton in later years of case verdicts and decisions was not dead.

Wines, Enoch Cobb (1806–1879) agitator for prison reform

Few men in the 19th century did more to recruit supporters for prison reform in the United States than Enoch Cobb Wines. Born in 1806, Dr. Wines started out as a teacher and eventually became a professor of classical languages. His whole life changed when he became secretary of the New York Prison Association in 1862, and from then until his death in 1879 he devoted himself entirely to the reform of the penal system.

In previous decades, there had been many individuals and local organizations concerned with prisons from a humanitarian viewpoint. Most of these were basically religious and confined their activities mainly to visiting inmates and helping them when they got out. In early years, prisoners were not allowed to be visited by relatives and friends but just by state officials and quasi-official visiting societies. The latters' purpose was not to remake the prison system but to mitigate the miseries inflicted on inmates.

In New York, Wines and another prominent reformer, Dr. Theodore Dwight, declared war on the conditions in the state's aging prisons, demanding that they concentrate less on being profit-making industrial institutions and instead seeking to make reformation of prisoners their prime focus, most especially as concerned younger offenders. In their 1867 detailed *Report on the Prisons and Reformatories of the United States and Canada,* they concluded that no state sought to reform prisoners and instead turned out releasees often far worse than when they went in.

In 1870, under call of Wines, reformers and organizations from around the nation congregated in Cincinnati, Ohio, to form the first national prison organization, which soon became the American Prison Association and is now the official organization of penology. It issued what was, at the time, an extraordinary and progressive "Declaration of Principles," defining the purpose of imprisonment as reformation, not the infliction of vindictive suffering.

Among other calls were for the abolition of flat-time sentences and their replacement by indeterminate sentences linked to parole. An offender would draw an unfixed term, and his or her release would require proper behavior and progress toward reformation. The Cincinnati Declaration sought the abolition of the silent system and methods to improve an inmate's self-respect. Such goals were not achieved more than in part to the present day, as were many other suggested reforms, such as training for guards, nonpolitical appointment of guards and wardens, uniform prison statistics, smaller prisons, improved prison designs, and the classification of inmates with proper segregation in various institutions.

Enthusiastic support for the declaration was offered by the meeting's host, Gov. Rutherford B. Hayes, later president of the United States, who said, "It may seem to be in advance of the present day, but it is, as we believe, but anticipating an event not far distant, to suggest that sentences for crime, instead of being for a definite period, especially in cases of repeated convictions, will, under proper restrictions, be made to depend on the reformation and established good character of the convict."

While the aims of the Cincinnati declaration had not been fully achieved during the next century, much of their programs remain in effect in many jurisdictions to greater or lesser extent, even during the last three decades of the 20th century when the guiding principles became "lock-em-up-and-throw-away-the-key." By the start of the new century, some reformers seemed to detect a growing desire by major portions of the population back toward reformation as the proper role for the prison system.

After Cincinnati, Enoch Wines continued his unceasing activities for the cause, even traveling abroad and helping launch an international congress on the subject before he died in 1879. Wines's son, Frederick Howard Wines, picked up the prison-reform mantel after his father's death and became in turn a leading reformer. Indeed, it could be argued that he was no less a force than his pioneer father.

See also: WINES, FREDERICK HOWARD.

Wines, Frederick Howard (1838–1912) prison reformer and opponent of criminal anthropology

The son of pioneer prison reformer Enoch Cobb Wines, Frederick Howard Wines proved to be an outstanding successor in his father's work. Indeed, he fought many battles against the so-called scientific researchers who sought to categorize persons by their physical appearances as criminal types. He also vigorously sought to force states to separate the mentally ill from criminal elements behind bars. In much of this, he proved successful.

Graduating from Princeton with a seminary degree, he became a pastor in Illinois. In 1869 with the establishment of the Illinois State Board of Public Charities, he became its secretary, a post he held for three decades. In that position, he was able to develop penal practices in line with his father's main tenets. He organized a national conference on charities and corrections and served as a delegate to the International Penitentiary Congress in Stockholm, carrying on the international efforts of the elder Wines in the final years of his life.

A major effort of his activities was seeking to curb the use of prisons as a social laboratory with convicts as human guinea pigs. This work greatly aided the development of the promotion of eugenics and criminal anthropology, which Wines regarded as improperly studied. In 1898, he announced, "I do not believe in inherited crime any more than I believe in the imaginary criminal type." As for the study of criminal anthropology and eugenics in prisons, he declared: "It needs no apparatus for minute measurements, with rules, scales, calipers, and goniometers—no chemical analysis of blood, tissues, and excretions—no careful experiments to test the degree of nervous susceptibility of different sensory organs—no specially devised physical test—to enable a common man, familiar with criminals through his relation to them as an office of the police or of a court or prison, to describe their most obvious and striking characteristics."

Wines disparaged the current positive notions of the so-called criminal brain. He noted the wide list of physiological peculiarities that were attributed to criminals, including "disordered nervous action, insensibility to pain, quick and easy recovery from wounds, defective taste and smell, strength and restlessness of the eye, mobility of the face and hands, left-handedness, excessive temperature, perverted secretions, abnormal sexual appetites, precocity and so forth." Wines noted the contradictions between the works of various researchers. Some found that criminals suffered from defective hearing, but others reported that their hearing was acute. Criminals were often color-blind or, on the other hand, never seemed to have that problem. There were those medical reporters who found criminals did not blush.

Wines's chief criticism of criminal anthropologists was their questionable methodology, which did not include control studies to compare those behind bars and those in free society who were not accused of crimes. Where researchers started to check the claims the Lombrosians advanced, the results proved startling. Research by Dr. Charles Goring, a leading prison physician, failed to support the claims of the criminal anthropologists. Goring studied some 3,000 convicts, all of them recidivists and certainly most likely to represent the criminal type. Goring found no difference between these prisoners and various outside control groups, including one group of Oxford undergraduates. Goring said, "The preliminary conclusion reached by our inquiry is that this anthropological monster has no existence in fact. The physical and mental constitution of both criminal and law-abiding persons, of the same age, stature, class, and intelligence are identical."

Wines died the year before the Goring study was finished, nor did he live to hear labor leader Eugene Debs's evaluation after his prison term: "I have heard people refer to the 'criminal countenance.' I never saw one. Any man or woman looks like a criminal behind bars."

Wines died in 1912, and perhaps his most profound book, *Punishment and Reformation,* was published posthumously in 1919 and was regarded a standard work for many years.

women on death row not an overly endangered species

Few executions draw as much public attention as that of women. Protests against the execution of a female usually engender more activities than that of a condemned man. The 1998 execution of Karla Faye Tucker, a pickax murderer of two, drew considerable protests from even some considered among the most staunch supporters of the death penalty in general. Many on the religious right argued for a commutation of her sentence because they agreed with her claim that she had "found God."

When Tucker suffered death by lethal injection in Texas, she, whatever other matters that made her a cause célèbre, represented an unusual striking exception concerning the death penalty and women. Americans don't like to execute women, even in an era known for being hard on criminals. In fact, since the death penalty was restored by the U.S. Supreme Court in 1976, only three women have been executed, and this historically represents a marked slowdown from the past. From the time of the first execution in the early 1600s through 1900, about 1,000 women were put to death, compared to about 20,000 men. This represents both legal executions and lynchings. As far as executions under government order, slightly more than 500 women were put to death, compared to about 11,000 men, or around the 5 percent mark. This included 27 women charged with witchcraft.

The 1-in-20 ratio dropped dramatically during the 20th century as the number of executed women was only 0.5 percent that of men. Before the death penalty was halted temporarily in 1972, only 37 women died of a total of almost 7,500. And after the restoration of capital punishment, more than 500 men died compared to three women.

The first of the new-era women to die was Margie Velma Barfield, who paid for the murder of her fiancé, Stuart Taylor. He drank beer that was supplied by her and that was laced with ant poison, and he died three days later. It turned out there had been a number of previous deaths of people associated with Barfield, but because she already faced the death penalty, no further proceedings were necessary on them. As Barfield's death approached, she was subjected to considerable public sympathy. A guard told her it was virtually certain that she would get a commutation, but Barfield seemed to be more sanguine about what she would face under North Carolina law, saying that southern states had to be more circumspect about executing a lot of blacks first, now that capital punishment had been restored, and would go after a white first, "and what could be better than a white woman." It turned out that she was slightly wrong. A white man went first and Barfield second.

The third condemned woman was Judias Buenoano, who died a few weeks after Tucker and was the first Florida woman executed since 1848. Buenoano gained the nickname of "The Black Widow," and among her crimes was poisoning a husband and one lover; when arsenic failed to do in another lover, she blew him up as he sat behind the wheel of his car. Her family

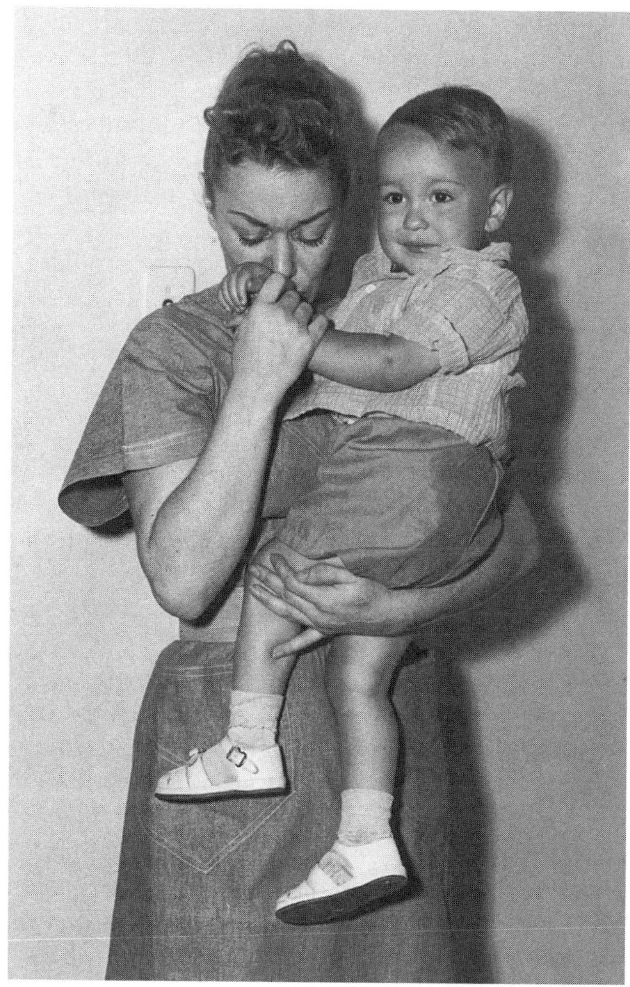

Barbara Graham with her 19-month-old son
(Author's collection)

members claimed that she was a born-again Christian, but her appeals for mercy went unheeded, probably as much for another of her murders, that of her crippled son, who was paralyzed below the knees and wore 15 pounds of leg braces. She shoved him out of a canoe so that he drowned; then she sat around drinking a beer as rescue workers searched for the boy. Buenoano collected $108,000 in life insurance before her conviction.

Although the three women could be found to have committed heinous crimes, it probably could not be claimed that they were no worse than many others, some of whom were not given the death penalty. Often cited by critics that the law is too soft on women murderers is the case of Susan Smith, who was convicted of driving her car into a lake so that her two young children, locked inside, drowned. Contrary to expectations, Smith escaped with only a life sentence.

Conservative critics particularly object to the light treatment afforded women murderers. "There's a tendency to believe in female innocence," says Cathy Young, a researcher for the Cato Institute and vice president of the conservative Women's Freedom Network. She insists that female offenders are historically treated more leniently than males who have committed similar crimes, saying, "Feminists haven't paid attention when gender bias goes in the other direction."

Statistics show that women account for 1 in 8, or 13 percent, of murder arrests with 1 in 53, or 1.9 percent, of death sentences imposed at the trial level. About 1 in 79, or 1.3 percent, are at recent count on death row, and again the execution rate since 1977 is less than 0.6 percent.

At a recent count there were 48 women awaiting execution, but with the past as a guide, not many of these will be carried out without achieving a cause célèbre status. It may be argued that there remains a bias against executing women that actually leads, in time and through appeals, to a "shrinkage" of female capital punishment and that this represents an immutable development in U.S. culture during the past 100 years. The question asked by some social observers is if this is merely the forerunner of an erosion, albeit at a very slow process, even in a period of high popularity for executions in general for all.

Despite the obsession by much of the U.S. public with female executions, there are no collections dealing with the weighty matters of their last meals and final words, understandable given the lack of any great number of female victims. Probably the most memorable of this sort would have to be the final words of murderer Barbara Graham, portrayal of whom in the film *I Want to Live* earned Susan Hayward an Academy Award. At the end, Graham reverted from her "sob sister" portrayal of herself and asked for a blindfold, saying bitterly, "I don't want to have to see people."

Moments before the lethal gas was released, a guard leaned down and whispered in her ear, "If you take a deep breath, it won't be so bad." Graham chose her reply very carefully and said, "Oh, yeah, how the hell would you know?"

women prisoners—pat searches by male guards

One of the major grievances made by female prison inmates is being subjected to pat searches by male guards, primarily searching for contraband. Most forward-looking prisons today seek to prevent that from happening, but in the 1990s the most explosive case of this sort occurred at the Washington Corrections Center for Women in Gig Harbor. In 1993, women prisoners claimed their constitutional rights were violated because they were forced to random, nonemergency, clothed-body pat-searches by male guards.

The prison sought to justify the policy, which was launched in 1989 for two reasons. It insisted that it was too burdensome to conduct random searches using only female guards because they had no occasion to interrupt their lunch breaks when the order was given. The prison also asserted that the new superintendent, Eldon Vail, was in the right because he felt he could better control contraband through random searches.

The Ninth Circuit Court decided against the state as follows:

> *Before mid-1989, routine, suspicionless searches of inmates were performed only at fixed checkpoints by female guards. Male guards were permitted to search inmates only in emergency situations. Vail decided to change the policy . . . [d]espite warnings from psychologists on his staff that the cross-gender clothed body searches could cause severe emotional distress in some inmates. . . . According to the prison training material, a . . . guard must '[p]ush inward and upward when searching the crotch and upper thighs of the inmates.' All seams in the leg and crotch are to be 'squeez[ed] and knead[ed].' Using the back of the hand, the guard is also to search the breast area in a sweeping motion, so that the breasts will be 'flattened.' At a minimum, each response and movement* [sic] *officer was expected to perform ten random searches per shift during the two daytime shifts.*
>
> *Several inmates were searched by male guards on the first (and only) day of implementation. One, who had a long history of sexual abuse by men, . . . suffered severe distress: she had to have her fingers pried loose from bars she had grabbed during the search, and she vomited after returning to her cell block.*

The Ninth Circuit found it unnecessary to rule that the search policy violated the women's Fourth Amendment right to be free of unreasonable searches, stating that the Eighth Amendment sufficed, declaring, "We conclude that the Eighth Amendment prohibition against the unnecessary and wanton infliction of pain forbids these searches under the circumstances of this case."

The court noted that women who had suffered previous sexual or physical abuse could react differently than men to cross-gender pat-searches. The court found the prison's "security is not dependent upon cross-gender clothed body searches" and that Superintendent Vail was urging "in effect, that is proper to inflict serious psychological pain on the inmates because otherwise it may be necessary to interrupt the lunch periods of female guards."

What the decision determined was that there were significant differences between male and female inmates owing to their personal histories and treatment needs.

During the period when the state was deciding whether or not to appeal the ruling to the U.S. Supreme Court, some inmates alleged that one guard commented on a possible resumption of the practice of cross-gender pat-searches, "I can't wait."

It turned out he would allegedly have to wait because Governor Mike Lowry prevented the appeal from going forward.

women prisoners—sexual abuse

Exposure of a prostitution ring at the Indiana State Prison the mid-1800s led to the eventual founding of the Indiana Reformatory Institution for Women in 1873, the first completely independent women's prison with an entirely female staff. In addition to the practice of offering women prisoners to outside men for sexual services at the state prison, investigators, including Quaker prison reformers Charles and Rhoda M. Coffin, discovered that officials and guards allowed women prisoners to have sexual contacts with male prisoners. In addition, proof was found that male guards made it a habit at times to whip women inmates fearsomely into have sex with them.

The Coffins launched a long effort for completely separate institutions for women prisoners, and the exposure of conditions at the state prison created such a firestorm reaction among the public that the movement became irresistible.

One thing that was not accomplished was the end of sexual abuse of women prisoners, a condition that persists to the present. In August 2000, Amnesty International U.S.A. announced that it planned to ask its members around the world to call for an inquiry into allegations of abuse at Connecticut's only prison for women. A spokesman for the group reported that not only were guards doing pat-down searches of female inmates (a practice found to be in violation of the Eighth Amendment by the federal courts), but guards also saw to it that they were present when inmates were ordered to undress or shower. A Corrections Department spokeswoman, Christina Polce, said that the agency was not aware of any recent claims of sexual abuse at York but would investigate. Much of the reason for charges of sexual abuse traced back to the Washington State Corrections Center for Women, which was the subject of court challenges for its pat-down policies toward women prisoners. There had been a number of earlier scandals there as well, such as one in which a female inmate won more than $1 million from the state for a suit she filed after being made pregnant by a guard.

In a more recent case, a guard was assigned to watch over a hospitalized unconscious female inmate. Discovered to have instead taken liberties with her, he was fired. Another guard retired rather than explain why he had been sending money and gifts to four female inmates.

Although there is often a claim made that victimized females frequently initiate such activities, Human Rights Watch Women's Rights Project in a 1996 study documented how a female prisoner is utterly trapped and sexually abused because there is no escape from the abuser. By and large, Human Rights Watch noted, and even if there are investigatory procedures, which is not always the case, they often do not work, so corrections employees simply continue with more of the same, regarding themselves certain to get away with it. According to the Human Rights Watch, the extent of abuse is not known to many people, and little is done about it by those who do know.

A state that in recent years came under much suspicion about similar sexual misconduct and corruption is South Carolina. In January 2001, a state grand jury was delving into charges of various sex scandals. The matter came to public attention the previous August when Susan Smith, doing life for the highly publicized drowning of her young sons in 1994, told authorities she had had sex with two prison supervisors. The supervisors were arrested, and a further investigation came up with charges against 14 other prison workers in connection with sexual misconduct and possession of contraband.

For a considerable time, opponents of Gov. Jim Hodges had been calling for him to dismiss William D. Catoe, the state prisons director. Hodges ignored the calls until January 2001 when a new and embarrassing scandal broke. Two prison guards were accused of allowing inmates to have sex at the Governor's Mansion in Columbia. The inmates, two men and two women, were among 44 minimum-security prisoners working at the governor's residence as maids, cooks, groundskeepers, and butlers. The two guards who supervised them were charged with allowing the sexual activities and planning an abortion for one of the women who had become pregnant. The sexual liaisons took place in both the private and the official residence of the governor.

It proved to be the last straw for the governor, who fired Director Catoe, a prison system employee for 30 years. Governor Hodges said, all but sputtering in anger at a news conference, "The sanctity of my home has been violated. I'm simply outraged. I can't express to you how I feel, when your family is in a home, and you find out that things have occurred while you're away, in your residence."

He added, "We've got to get competence back in the Department of Corrections, but the first and most important thing to me is to get those folks out of my house. Get them out!"

women's prisons

A common misconception is that female offenders are treated more lightly than male offenders. The raw figures may seem to confirm this. For instance, the numbers of women in prison runs, in recent years, between 6 and 7 percent compared to the number of men. Also, women tend to serve lesser sentences than men. The median maximum sentence (half above and half below) for men in prison is 120 months while it is 60 months for women. Overall, women in prison receive sentences on average 48 months shorter than do men (excluding death sentences and life). Of course the basic difference arises because of the types of crimes in which the sexes engage. Women are far more likely to go to prison for drug and property offenses, which usually carry shorter sentences than do violent crimes.

Within their month of activity before the offenses for which they were convicted, women are more likely to have used heroin, cocaine, crack, LSD, or PCP. Offenders are twice as likely to have used a major illegal drug daily before their latest offense. More than half of women say that they committed their crimes while under the influence of drugs or alcohol; about a quarter of imprisoned women say they committed their specific crime for money to buy drugs.

There are many other causes for women to turn to crime, including such common ones as the breakup of families, poverty, increased drug use, affiliation with gangs, and lack of jobs. Many women are caught in welfare cheating, being single mothers faced with the problem of putting food on the table for themselves and their children. All of the above can lead to dependence on drugs, and twice as many women as men admit to using a major drug daily.

The fact is that the way of life of women involved in crime is far too overlooked in most studies of criminality, and as a result, much less is done to deal with the problems or, generally, to fund adequate prisons and treatment of convicted women. The situation is such that, in some respects, it has not changed in hundreds of years. There had long been a traditional belief that women are, as stated by Nicole Hahn Rafter and Debra L. Stanley in *Prisons in America,* "more childish in nature than men [which] has historically led to harsher sentences. In the late nineteenth century, as a result of the reformatory movement, women could be sent to state prisons for out-of-wedlock sexual activity and minor public-order violations that were overlooked in the case of men." Rafter and Stanley also point out that women could be held for long periods and that women convicted of the usual run of crimes such as burglary could receive longer sentences than men who were convicted of the same offense. The thinking was that because women were weaker, they needed more "help." The result was that what was regarded as female-specific care resulted in unequal and harsher treatment.

In the 1970s and 1980s, even though get-tough rules were spreading dramatically, feminist lawyers pushed arguments for equal treatment and convinced courts to strike down some laws that subjected women to harsher treatment. Corrections departments were also forced to develop more job-training programs, in place of the usual mix offered by many states for classes on to how to clean, cook, and serve food; this left women capable only to do domestic work, which was frequently not an option because families did not want ex-jailbirds in their homes. Some states went so far as to acknowledge that women inmates had different needs than men. Women generally are victimized by sexual or physical abuse more so than men prior to their confinement. In prison, many women suffer from special stress because of their responsibility both before and after their confinement. Some programs now allow special extra visits to mothers by their children.

But the fact remains women offenders enter prison far more likely than men to be addicted to drugs, to suffer from mental illnesses, and to have more employment records on the outside. In a get-tough era, there is little public opposition to drug counseling and instructions on parenting and personal improvement for inmates. But perhaps even more than with men, there is strong opposition to tennis courts and bowling alleys, which produce cries of "country club atmosphere" and niceties being provided at taxpayer expense. Reformers tend to claim that providing women with certain activities that are commonly enjoyed by middle-class Americans motivates some women coming from poverty, broken homes, and their own broken families and can have a positive effect.

However, even though some states would like to do more, they are limited by what is called the "numbers problem." In 19th-century penitentiaries, officials tended to overlook the few female inmates in favor of dealing with male prisoners. Additionally, most prison guards did not know how to deal with special female problems such as pregnancy. Even when women are housed in separate facilities, the numbers problems persist. Most corrections departments seek to deal with funding the male institutions first, and only the "leavings" go to female prisons. The fact that women's prisons tend to be smaller is dictated by the smaller number of inmates that make the support system—the prisons themselves, the need for their own wardens, doctors, engineers, and the like—eat up a far greater portion of the budget.

Jean Harris, convicted slayer of "Scarsdale Diet" author Dr. Herman Tarnower (Author's collection)

Some say reductions in supervision become, therefore, a more serious problem as corners are cut, especially on the very programs that could do the most good for women inmates.

At the same time, women's prisons have many of the similar situations found in male facilities. One is obviously sex. Homosexual relationships thrive of course, although seldom with anywhere near the same incidence of forcible rape. Almost all sexual relationships are more or less consensual in nature although obviously one partner is in a way induced to be cooperative in an often exploitive situation. Most relationships are not truly lesbian in nature but are recognized as a temporary accommodation in a substitute universe. With such attitudes, it is not unusual for other inmates to help out in an affair. In a cottage environment, lovers may be in different cottages, and other inmates are obliged to let them make out. A "pinner" or lookout is often obliged to keep the guards unaware of forbidden activities. The pinner sometimes scouts out safe trysting areas and, either alone or with other pinners, seeks to keep the spot available for unhindered lovemaking, if necessary giving misleading facts to guards who happen too close.

There are those affairs, of course, that are limited to sexual gratification and with "straying" by one or both of the partners, but there are others that are regarded by all as sincere relationships with complete trust and affection by both, again within the realm of the confinement periods. Frequently, however, the wife or "weaker" partner may be devastated as the stronger partner nears her release time. A few months before the end of the relationship, the stronger or "male" partner will start "cleaning herself up." She will start to drop her so-called male attributes because she now knows she must reassert her own femininity as she is faced with returning to the outside world. Some "wives" feel betrayed when they are dropped somewhat sooner than expected.

If that is a reality in sexual situations in prison, it is probably nothing compared to what has become a major torment of women prisoners—sexual abuse by male guards. This was a problem in 19th-century "coed" prisons, especially in the Indiana Penitentiary where women were impressed into prostitution rings, servicing supervisory personnel and male inmates who could pay for the services. That particular revelation led to the establishment of the first separate prison for women. That has not solved the problem because in many cases, women in separate prisons still tend to be guarded by male guards. In 1996 Human Rights Watch released a report entitled *All Too Familiar: Sexual Abuse in U.S. State Prisons*. The organization had no trouble at all filling out a 347-page report detailing sexual abuse in the form of vaginal, anal, and oral rape and other forms of sexual assault. In addition, *All Too Familiar* reported on male officers taking time during mandatory pat-frisks or room searches to grope the vaginal or anal areas as well as to watch women undress in showers, bathrooms, or sleeping quarters. Other harassments take the form of verbal degradation. It is a situation in which terrified women are trapped with little chance of escape. Some institutions, not a majority, have in place investigative procedures, but they often do not work. Women inmates frequently complain that the guards simply deny such activities and charge women with "trying to make a case or a lawsuit." Between a corrections employee and a female inmate, the charges seldom go the woman's way. As Rafter and Stanley point out, under the circumstances, "correctional employees continue to engage in abuse because they believe that they can get away with it. Few people outside prison walls are aware of the problem, and those who do know about it do little to address it."

There are a few "showcase" women's reformatories, but they too have been squeezed in recent get-tough attitudes. Early in the administration of prison hard-line Gov. John Rowland of Connecticut, reformers say, perhaps the most progressive female warden, Carol Dunn, was forced out of her post by the simple expedient of transferring her to another prison with a pay cut of $12,000. Since that time, the state was put under attack by Amnesty International for alleged abuses of female prisoners.

Overall, it cannot be said that women inmates in prisons around the country enjoyed anything close to enlightened treatment.

WOMEN'S PRISONS—THE "NUMBERS GAME" SHORTCHANGING FEMALE INSTITUTIONS

Advocates of better and more fruitful treatment for women prisoners insist that this is extremely difficult because of the so-called numbers game, reflecting a bias on the part of the corrections authorities, which results in shortchanging female institutions.

This was hardly an unusual situation throughout U.S. penal history. Because there were so many more male prisoners than female, officials concentrated on the early penitentiaries as institutions of confinement for male prisoners and tended to make short shrift of the treatment of female prisoners. In a sense, this overlooking of the problem of female inmates was understandable because there were relatively few of them. Additionally, prison officials did not want to deal with the problem because there were often so many unusual matters that had to be dealt with, typically, the problem of pregnancy.

Later, when women in many states were removed to separate reformatories, it became even easier for corrections leaders to put the matter even further out of mind. The guiding principle seemed to be "How little can we spend on them?" Funding of male prisons remained a top priority; funding for female institutions received what one official referred to as the "leavings."

This is part of the numbers game against which women's groups rail. Female institutions are trapped by the economies of scale. Per capita costs soar in female prisons, because they tend to be smaller. When a prison population is larger, say with 1,000 inmates, it costs much less to feed and clothe and provide other services on a per capita basis than in a female institution, where the numbers are always much smaller. All institutions require a warden and a hierarchy of support, such as maintenance people. Male institutions have a number of hard-labor activities that can be handled cheaply by the inmate population. Female institutions lack enough of a workforce or the capabilities to do the same work—shoveling coal, for example. As a result, the cost per capita goes up and corrections officials try to make it up by cutting corners on almost everything.

To this day, there are many states that lack separate institutions for female prisoners and simply dump them into their general institutions. That practice, most penologists agree, works to the detriment of female inmates and subjects them to generally a higher level of abuse.

But that is all the numbers game.

wooden gun escapes generally untrue lore

Probably not a single American in 1934 did not know about one of the most electrifying jail escapes in U.S. history. Public enemy John Dillinger carved a fake gun out of wood and used it to break out of the "escape-proof" jail at Crown Point, Indiana! It was astonishing, exciting, and downright "romantic."

It also never really happened, but the tale caught the imagination of an awestruck public and has remained ever since a striking case of folklore that never let the facts catch up with the truth.

The newspapers of the era generally blindly accepted the fake-gun story, which sold a lot of papers, but Dillinger actually used a *real* gun. According to the first reports of the startling escape, Dillinger used a knife to whittle a wooden gun out of the top of a washboard, colored it with shoe polish, and used it to escape. But how did America's number one criminal get hold of a knife in jail? Well, let's make that a razor blade.

The second version was as silly as the first. The true facts behind his escape were known to his lawyer, an incredible rogue named Louis Piquett, who met with a prominent Indiana judge on the grounds of the Century of Progress in Chicago and handed over an envelope containing several thousand dollars. In return, the judge arranged to have a gun smuggled into the jail. Dillinger used the gun to capture and lock up several guards. He then moved on to the warden's office, where he grabbed two machine guns.

Dillinger gave one of the weapons to a black prisoner, 35-year-old Herbert Youngblood, and the pair proceeded to lock up several more officers. They then snatched the car of a woman sheriff, Mrs. Lillian Holley, from the institution's parking lot and made their escape, taking two hostages with them. Dillinger later released the hostages, giving one of them, an auto mechanic, $4 for his troubles. He also bragged that the had used a wooden gun to trigger his plot.

Naturally, the claim made headlines (and Dillinger probably realized that it gave him, in the eyes of the public, a sympathetic or even heroic quality). Sometime later, however, a secret investigation conducted by the Hargrave Secret Service of Chicago, on orders of Gov. Paul V. McNutt, uncovered the real story. McNutt and Indiana attorney general Philip Lutz Jr. decided not to make the information public because they most properly didn't want Dillinger to know that certain informants whom he might trust in the future had talked to private detectives. By the time Dillinger was killed, the judge too had died, and the findings about the gun were not made public for many years.

By then, Dillinger was basking in the glory of the wooden-gun tale and sought to perpetuate it. He sent a letter to his sister, telling her not to worry about him and that he was "having a lot of fun." He debunked some theories that he must have had a real gun, saying:

> *Thats just a lot of hooey to cover up because they don't like to admit that I locked eight Deputys and a dozen trustys up with my wooden gun before I got my hands on the two machine guns. I showed everyone the wooden gun after I got a hold of the machine guns and you should have seen thire* [sic] *faces. Ha! Ha! Ha! Pulling that off was worth ten years of my life. Ha! Ha!*

Obviously, Dillinger's intention was to cover up the fact that he had had a real gun smuggled in to him; probably he was required to embrace the wooden hoax as part of the deal. It also massaged Dillinger's ego.

After their escape, Dillinger and Youngblood separated. Thirteen days later, on March 16, 1934, Youngblood was mortally wounded in a gun battle with lawmen in Port Huron, Michigan. Dillinger was to live a while longer, and the tale of the wooden-gun exploit would ride into accepted fact.

Fabrications of wooden-gun escapes were common grist for dime novelists of the 19th century, but one of the few genuine—and authenticated—wooden-gun capers was pulled by Ben Cravens, a storied Cherokee Strip outlaw, who was sent to the Kansas State Penitentiary in 1897 under a 20-year sentence. Within a very short time, Cravens pulled his wooden-gun escape after being assigned to coal-mine work. This provided cover for him to fashion his wooden weapon, which he then covered with tin foil from cigarette packages. In the ill light of the mine shaft, Cravens pulled his "gun" on a guard, who surrendered his own weapon. Cravens forced the guard to hoist him to the top of the shaft. Cravens shot the guard dead and made good his escape.

Cravens's career was "prettified" in dime outlaw literature into a more cunning and heroic sort, and Dillinger, known for a studied interest in such works, probably was familiar with Cravens and could at least concoct a plot about a wooden gun, even if he never made one.

Nevertheless, Dillinger's fake exploit did inspire two of his most loyal gang members, Harry Pierpont and Charles Makley, who attempted a death-house escape from the Ohio State Prison a few months after Dillinger was shot and killed in a FBI trap. The pair used pistols carved out of soap to overpower one guard and were smashing though a door exiting the death house when other guards opened fire on them. Makley was killed and Pierpont was wounded, but he recovered sufficiently to die in the electric chair a month later.

See also: YOUNGBLOOD, HERBERT.

work for condemned prisoners Arizona's controversial plan

In July 1995, Arizona governor Fife Symington announced plans to implement a program in which the state's 119 death-row prisoners would be put to work breaking rocks and digging holes. Perhaps because a work program limited to just breaking rocks and digging holes might not stand federal legal tests, the program was altered on November 22, 1995, in the memo distributed to death-row inmates. Relating to an order issued by then Department of Corrections (DOC) head Sam Lewis, it read in part:

> *Arizona Revised Statute 31–151 gives the Director of Corrections authority to require that each able bodied prisoner in the department engage in hard labor for not less than forty hours per week. . . . Be advised that the statutes* do not *exempt you, because of your Death Sentence, from performing work or hard labor, nor is it unconstitutional. The program is an opportunity for you to improve status while on Death Row. Even though hard work may be considered punishment, it does provide you with a means to earn some money and you are able to perform an assignment that is beneficial to the inmate population as a whole, while working in the garden growing vegetables.*
>
> *Inmates refusing to turn out for work assignments shall be forcibly removed from their cells and taken to the work site, secured accordingly [chained to a post], and then be subjected to the disciplinary process.*

An inflamed public debate followed. A longtime prisoners'-rights activist, former judge and organizer for the prisoners'-rights group Middle Ground

An armed horseback corrections officer checks on the progress of a group of death-row inmates working in a vegetable garden at Arizona State Prison in Florence, Arizona. (AP/Wide World Photos)

in Arizona, Donna Hamm, declared that the program would be sure to be challenged in court and could spark "a physical protest in the form of riot or disturbance. . . . I'm just astounded they would open themselves, their staff, not to mention the public, to that type of risk, all for the sake of [the governor's] self-aggrandizement. It's just an insane idea."

The governor's press secretary offered the reasoning for the forced-labor program for death-row inmates: "The food they grow, the taxpayers don't have to pay for. Before, these guys were costing us lots of money because they were sitting idly in their cells."

Next weighing in were Dan Pens and Paul Wright, coeditors of *Prison Legal News:* "Not surprisingly, this reasoning is complete bunk: On December 7, 1995, the first work crew of 23 death-row prisoners was put to work weeding and hoeing a 19-acre field within the State Prison Complex in Florence. The 23 prisoners were supervised by nine armed guards on horseback. The prisoners are paid 10 cents an hour. The total pay for 23 prisoners for eight hours is then $18.40. Assuming that the cost for the guards is $11 per hour (not to mention the cost for boarding and feeding the horses), the total pay for nine guards for eight hours is $792. Mike Arra, the Arizona DOC spokesman, said that the vegetables raised on the 19-acre plot would supplement food purchased by the DOC to feed prisoners. Considering the labor cost for the death-row vegetable patch averages $800 a day, those are some mighty expensive vegetables."

The death-row work gangs (which also involved chain-gang restrictions) proved to be as troublesome as predicted, with fights breaking out between the condemned men, a hardly unusual behavior pattern for violent men generally kept in isolation from one another in separate cells.

It is possibly only of parenthetical note that DOC head chief Sam Lewis resigned in December 1995 and that Gov. Fife Symington was convicted in federal court on multiple fraud charges in September 1997 and resigned as governor shortly thereafter. More relevant to the matter of work for death-row inmates is that the idea made little headway elsewhere, probably for the dollar-and-cents analysis made by *Prison Legal News*.

World War II and prison inmates unexpected patriotism

Although to some observers this may seem unusual, it can be said that prison inmates are fairly reflective of the general population on the popularity or unpopularity of certain wars. Often, inmates seem supportive of war efforts (although it is probably true to a certain extent that some prisoners hope to win their freedom in exchange for military service). However, when public opinion about the feasibility of a war leads to divided stands, prisoners overall will have the same sympathies, so, for example, prison support for the Vietnam War tended to be on the subdued side.

By contrast, World War II was by far the most popular war behind bars. Prisoners supported the war effort by giving an astounding amount of blood to the Red Cross. Although there had been a divided feeling as to whether or not prisoners should be involved in industries and thus appear to be taking jobs away from free citizens, these objections dropped away at this time. It was estimated that 98 percent of all inmates were engaged in war work. In some respects, Illinois enjoyed an enviable record, with prison officials proudly proclaiming the work of "our boys."

They made mattresses for the armed services, model planes for pilot training, naval assault boats, engines, shoes, uniforms, bunks, bomb fins, rubber nets, flags, and ration books. They made Army Ordnance Department fuse gauges for shells and many other items. Inmates tended to follow war news avidly and purchased war bonds. Perhaps the most laudable action by prisoners was volunteering for medical research projects and functioning as human guinea pigs. The notorious thrill murderer Nathan Leopold took part in programs that produced effective toxic drugs for treatment of malaria. Leopold did not win his freedom for this work but was released some 11 years later for a series of "good works" among other activities.

See also: LEOPOLD AND LOEB.

Youngblood, Herbert (1899–1934) partner with Dillinger in alleged "wooden-gun" escape

When, in March 1934, John Dillinger staged his so-called wooden-gun escape (which was and is a long-enduring myth) using his weapon (actually a real one) to get the drop on guards at the supposedly escape-proof Crown Point, Indiana, jail, he then gained access to the weapon supplies and grabbed two machine guns. He offered other prisoners in the lockup to join in the breakout, but only one accepted: Herbert Youngblood, a 35-year-old black inmate being held on a murder charge.

The pair left the jail with two hostages in tow and made good their escape. In time, they dumped the two hostages and continued on their way. Then Dillinger told Youngblood to hide down between the seats because a white man and a black man traveling together were sure to attract attention. Soon, it was obvious that the pair had to separate, but Youngblood's brief encounter with Dillinger made a huge impact on him.

Youngblood lived only 13 more days. On March 16, Youngblood was trapped by three deputy sheriffs in a tobacco store in Port Huron, Michigan. The escapee shot one of the officers to death and wounded the other two, but was hit himself by six bullets. Before he died, he said under questioning that he had been with Dillinger the previous day.

Herbert Youngblood, the murderer who escaped with John Dillinger from the Lake County Jail in Crown Point, Indiana, in March 1934 (Bettmann/CORBIS)

It was a lie. But it triggered a manhunt in the surrounding area, and reports started to come in that the most-wanted fugitive had crossed the St. Clair River into Canada in the company of two other men. At the time, Dillinger was actually in hiding with his girlfriend, Billie Frechette, in apartment 303 of the Lincoln Court Apartments in the exclusive Hill section of St. Paul, Minnesota, a town that at the time was notorious as one where fugitives seldom were caught.

Undoubtedly, Youngblood misled the police because he owed Dillinger a favor. It was another example of the intense loyalty Dillinger inspired in others—until he was at last betrayed by a woman.

Youngstown privately-run prison scandal

"They don't care about the corrections officers, and they don't care about the inmates. . . . Everything there is about money." The statement was made by a former guard at the Northeast Ohio Correctional Center at Youngstown, Ohio, to the *Cleveland Plain Dealer* as a burgeoning scandal exploded. The privately owned prison is frequently cited by critics of the new privatized prisons as an example of the very worst of the type.

From the very time it was opened by the Corrections Corporation of America (CCA, largest firm in the business) in July 1997, there was trouble. Although the argument was frequently made that privatized prisons could provide more efficient, less costly, and much safer conditions for inmates, such boasts were not apparent at Youngstown. With various concessions made by political leaders, such as the company being given the land for $1, Youngstown was built supposedly free of cost for the Ohio community and would provide 400–450 jobs. It was an offer not likely to be refused.

Yet, within the first few months of operations, there were stabbings of 20 inmates, including two fatalities. There were quick charges that the 1,700-inmate facility was poorly constructed, understaffed, and quickly jammed with medium- and maximum-security convicts, even though only the former were to be housed there. As one account put it, "the CCA prison became a chaotic gladiator's pit where nonviolent burglars and crack addicts were haphazardly thrust into cells with seasoned rapists, habitual killers and other high security predators, many shipped in from other states and the District of Columbia." Despite numerous complaints by inmates and some guards as well, the authorities did nothing about it for months. When state inspectors finally showed up, news accounts reported that they were turned away at the gate.

Much of public opinion against the facility finally turned when six inmates, four of them murderers, escaped by cutting open a chain-link fence, crossing an electric barrier, cutting through yards of razor-wire obstructions, and running. It all occurred in the middle of the afternoon.

Fear gripped Youngstown. For almost a week, manhunters of all sorts—dog teams, tactical squads, and helicopters—pressed the search over a widening area. Finally, all the escapees, many seriously wounded by the razor wire, were caught individually, the last being found in the yard of a grandmother of three, living on the outskirts of the city.

Now the criticism of the prison came in torrents. It turned out that the guards were paid $1,300 a year less as starting pay than in other prisons, that two-thirds had never worked in corrections before, and that their training was inadequate. A corrections officer told of being handed a shotgun and ordered to patrol the perimeter of the prison; when she explained that she did not know how to shoot it, she was simply told to get out there anyway. It was said that CCA passed on firearms training because state certification cost as much as $3,000 a person. Another guard said the company had guards take food from inmates to increase profits. "They gave us a rundown saying two slices of bread per inmate costs this much. If you can cut corners here, it would mean a possible raise for us."

There were many criticisms made from all sides, and in the end, there was a most unusual alliance achieved by the city of Youngstown and the inmates who had complained about safety and prison conditions as they joined together in a common lawsuit. Civil lawsuits charged that prison medical records were unaccounted for and that 200 chronically ill inmates were left untreated; that regulations were violated when tear gas was used inside; that tactical teams dragged, stripped, and shackled prisoners; and that during cell searches, inmates were forced to kneel naked and were shocked with stun guns if they moved.

Improvements did follow. Hundreds of potentially dangerous inmates were transferred, and the CCA agreed to pay inmates $1.7 million, enforce numerous rigorous standards, and pay for a city employee to monitor the prison. Youngstown mayor George Mckelvey expressed satisfaction with the changes but said, "They surely gave us reason not to trust them. We know we have to monitor everything they do."

There were some calls for getting rid of CCA in Youngstown or imposing further restrictions on their operations. The company countered with "soft" TV commercials intoning: "CCA. Quietly going about the business of public safety." More important, it was said the company used a lobbying campaign to warn lawmakers that the company could simply respond by taking its 450 jobs to another state. Just as the firm's original offer to create 450 jobs could not be refused, its later "counteroffer" could not be accepted either.

See also: PRIVATE PRISONS.

Yuma Penitentiary Old West hellhole prison

No prison in the Old West was more feared and hated by criminals than the Arizona territorial prison at Yuma. Built in 1876 on the east bank of the Colorado River, where it is joined by the Gila

Cell blocks at historic territorial prison in Yuma, Arizona (Mark E. Gibson/CORBIS)

River, the prison was not one concerned with such trivialities as the rehabilitation of prisoners. The byword was restraint—restraint of the convicts from escaping, rioting, or creating any kind of a problem. The cell doors were a latticework of iron with many of the 9-feet-square cubicles exposed to the direct rays of the desert sun. Prisoners were permitted to work and exercise during the daytime, but at night they were chained to the stone floors of their cells from dusk to dawn.

Besides brutality, graft was common at Yuma, and, in fact, a prisoner might not only win favored treatment, but those who had the financial resources might even have later bought themselves a position as a guard after completing a term of imprisonment.

Happily, Yuma was abandoned as a prison in 1909, and its crumbling remains later were turned into a museum. In a sense, the penitentiary had at least one claim to fame: Because of the vile treatment of inmates, there were so many attempted or successful escapes that Yuma became the first prison in the country to be equipped with Gatling guns.

Z

zero disrespect Aryan Brotherhood nontolerance for any disparagement

When the Aryan Brotherhood (AB) became a powerful force in San Quentin about 1970, it immediately seized the mantle of a prison gang that tolerated no "disrespect" in any form by any other prisoner or gang. Thus, even a casual comment that in any way was less than admiring about the AB called for fast and brutal retaliation. The byword was that the AB allowed "zero disrespect" from other inmates. Even what could be considered merely a hard look could result in a stabbing. As time passed, zero disrespect was picked up by a number of other ethnic gangs in many prisons around the country. The term *being dissed* became in the outside culture a call to war by street gangs against both rivals and police as well.

By contrast, within prison walls, "love and respect" is demanded by gang members and most certainly toward their leaders. Thus, when an important leader ends up in the "Hole," his followers look for a way to pay him homage in a most practical manner. One way is for another gang member or perhaps a wanna-be to get sent to the Hole for some infraction. He will often come bearing a gift in the form of a package of marijuana in his rectum.

BIBLIOGRAPHY

Abbott, Jack Henry. *In the Belly of the Beast: Letters from Prison.* New York: Vintage Books, 1991.

Abu-Jamal, Mumia. *Death Blossoms: Reflections from a Prisoner of Conscience.* Farmington, Pa.: The Plough Publishing House, 1997.

Bergner, Daniel. *God of the Rodeo: The Search for Hope, Faith, and a Six-Second Ride in Louisiana's Angola Prison.* New York: Crown, 1998.

Branham, Vernon C., and Kutash, Samuel B. (eds.). *Encyclopedia of Criminology.* New York: Philosophical Library, 1949.

Brockway, Zebulon R. *Fifty Years of Prison Service.* Montclair, N.J.: Patterson Smith, 1969 (orig. pub. 1912).

Burton-Rose, Daniel (ed.). *The Celling of America.* Monroe, Me.: Common Courage Press, 1998.

Christianson, Scott. *With Liberty for Some: 500 Years of Imprisonment in America.* Boston: Northeastern University Press, 1998.

Cleaver, Eldridge. *Soul on Ice.* New York: Dell, 1968.

Conover, Ted. *Newjack: Guarding Sing Sing.* New York: Vintage Books, 2001.

DiCanio, Margaret. *Encyclopedia of Violence.* New York: Facts On File, 1993.

DiIulio, John J., Jr., *No Escape: The Future of American Corrections.* New York: Basic Books, 1993.

———. Governing Prisons: *A Comparative Study of Correctional Management.* New York: The Free Press, 1987.

Earley, Pete. *The Hot House: Life Inside Leavenworth Prison.* New York: Bantam, 1992.

Elikann, Peter T. *The-Tough-On-Crime Myth.* New York: Insight Books, 1996.

Emrich, Duncan. *It's an Old Wild West Custom.* New York: The Vanguard Press, Inc. 1949.

Frost, Richard H. *The Mooney Case.* Stanford, Calif.: Stanford University Press, 1968.

Giallombardo, Rose. *Society of Women: A Study of a Women's Prison.* New York: John Wiley & Sons, Inc., 1966.

Godwin, John. *Alcatraz 1868–1963.* New York: Doubleday & Company, 1963.

Grapes, Bryan J. (ed.). *Prisons.* San Diego, Calif.: Greenhaven Press, 2000.

Hassine, Victor. *Life Without Parole: Living in Prison Today.* 2d ed. Los Angeles: Roxbury Publishing Co., 1996.

Hecht, Ben. *A Child of the Century.* New York: Simon & Schuster, 1954.

Hjelmeland, Andy. *Prisons: Inside the Big House.* Minneapolis: Lerner Publications Company, 1996.

Jackson, George. *Soledad Brother.* New York: Coward-McCann, 1970.

Jackson, Joe, and Burke, William F., Jr. *Dead Run.* New York: Times Books, 1999.

Johnson, Robert. *Hard Time: Understanding and Reforming the Prison.* Belmont, Calif.: Wadsworth, 1996.

Johnston, James A. *Alcatraz Island Prison.* New York: Charles Scribner's Sons, 1949.

Kauffman, Kelsey. *Prison Officers and Their World.* Cambridge, Mass.: Harvard University Press, 1988.

Lawes, Warden Lewis Edward. *Twenty Thousand Years in Sing Sing.* New York: R. Long and R. R. Smith, Inc., 1932.

Liberatore, Paul. *The Road to Hell.* New York: Atlantic Monthly Press, 1996.

McLoughlin, Denis. *Wild and Wooly.* Garden City, N.Y.: Doubleday & Company, Inc., 1975.

Martin, John Bartlow. *Break Down the Walls.* New York: Ballatine Books, 1954.

Morrell, Ed. *The Twenty-fifth Man.* Montclair, N.J.: New Era Publishing Co., 1924.

Morris, Norval, and Rothman, David J. (eds.). *The Oxford History of the Prison: The Practice of Punishment in Western Society.* New York: Oxford University Press, 1995.

Murray, George. *The Legacy of Al Capone.* New York: G.P. Putnam's Sons, 1975.

Neier, Aryeh. *Crime and Punishment; a Radical Solution.* New York: Stein and Day, 1976.

Oliver, Marilyn Tower. *Prisons: Today's Debate.* Springfield, N.J.: Enslow Publishers, 1997.

Osborne, Thomas Mott. *Within Prison Walls.* New York: D. Appleton, 1914.

Parenti, Christian. *Lockdown America: Police and Prisons in the Age of Crisis.* New York: Verso, 1999.

Peterson, Virgil. *Barbarians in Our Midst.* Boston: Little, Brown, 1936.

———. *The Mob.* Ottawa, Ill.: Green Hill Publishers, Inc., 1983.

Rafter, Nicole Hahn. *Creating Born Criminals.* Urbana: University of Illinois Press, 1997.

Rafter, Nicole Hahn, and Stanley, Debra L. *Prisons in America.* Santa Barbara, Calif.: ABC-CLIO, Inc., 1999.

Ragen, Joseph E. *Inside the World's Toughest Prison.* Springfield, Ill.: C. C. Thomas, 1962.

Reid, Sue Titus. *Crime and Criminology.* Fort Worth: Holt, Rinehart and Winston, Inc., 1988.

Rideau, Wilbert, and Wikberg, Ron. *Life Sentences: Rage and Survival Behind Bars.* New York: Random House, 1992.

Rierden, Andi. *The Farm.* Amherst: University of Massachusetts Press, 1997.

Teresa, Vincent, with Renner, Thomas C. *My Life in the Mafia.* Garden City, N.Y.: Doubleday & Company, 1973.

Toland, John. *The Dillinger Days.* New York: Random House, 1963.

Wicker, Tom. *A Time to Die: The Attica Prison Revolt.* New York: Quadrangle/New York Times Book Co., 1975.

Note

All the books above and others mentioned with specific entries in the text were extremely helpful to the author. However, special note should be made of some works of import from which readers could gain greater insight in the subject by specific full reading of them.

A personal favorite is Earley's *The Hot House,* which I have read and reread constantly over the past decade when writing anything on crime, far and beyond the prison system. It is a work that etches the criminal mind with insight. Another prison study is Conover's *Newjack,* which views Sing Sing through the prism of the guards rather than the inmates. Hassine and Rideau and Wikberg capture the savagery of imprisonment (with Rideau's success in his efforts having clearly blocked his chances of clemency or the like that has almost always been granted to others for similar offenses). Rafter and Stanley offer a fine handbook on the subject, and Christianson is a penetrating study of five centuries of justice and injustice in the U.S. system. A valuable work from a clear and often necessary perspective of outrage is Parenti, which collates an amazing set of many notorious practices. Perhaps the best from the outrage front comes from Burton-Rose et al. In *The Celling of America,* written by inmates in various prisons, perhaps controversial at times but always told with biting and telling observations. Finally, Jackson and Burke's *Dead Run* captures the full terror of a system that insists on its right to put people to death and the extraordinary lengths that the victims will use to resist.

Index

Numbers in **boldface** indicate main entries; *f* indicates an illustration.

C

H

N

T